T0289290

364 DAYS OF
DEVOTION

ANDREW C. SCHROER

NORTHWESTERN PUBLISHING HOUSE
Milwaukee, Wisconsin

TO MY WIFE, CLARIZA; MY DAUGHTER, ISABEL; AND MY SON, ANDY.
AFTER JESUS, THEY ARE WHAT I AM MOST THANKFUL FOR.

Cover Photos: iStockphoto, Lightstock
Design Team: Pamela Clemons, Diane Cook

All Scripture quotations, unless otherwise indicated, are taken from the Holy Bible, New International Version®, NIV®. Copyright © 1973, 1978, 1984, 2011 by Biblica, Inc.™ Used by permission of Zondervan. All rights reserved worldwide. www.zondervan.com.

The "NIV" and "New International Version" are trademarks registered in the United States Patent and Trademark Office by Biblica, Inc.™

Scripture quotations marked EHV are from the Holy Bible, Evangelical Heritage Version® (EHV®) © 2019 Wartburg Project, Inc. All rights reserved. Used by permission.

Scripture quotations marked ESV are from the ESV® Bible (The Holy Bible, English Standard Version®). Copyright © 2001 by Crossway, a publishing ministry of Good News Publishers. Used by permission. All rights reserved.

All hymns, unless otherwise indicated, are from *Christian Worship: A Lutheran Hymnal* © 1993 by Northwestern Publishing House.

Northwestern Publishing House
N16W23379 Stone Ridge Dr., Waukesha, WI 53188-1108
www.nph.net
© 2021 Northwestern Publishing House
Published 2021
Printed in the United States of America
ISBN 978-0-8100-3143-2
ISBN 978-0-8100-3144-9 (e-book)

23 24 25 26 27 28 29 30   10 9 8 7 6 5 4 3 2

TABLE OF CONTENTS

PREFACE

In 2015, I published my first book, *364 Days of Thanksgiving*. Honestly, it was more a journal than a book. In it, readers were encouraged to write down one thing every day for which they were thankful. There was only one catch: they could never repeat an entry. They had to thank God for a different blessing each day.

The name, *364 Days of Thanksgiving*, came from a quote by the British author Charles Dickens. According to Dickens, we are somewhat backward here in America. Instead of having just one Thanksgiving Day each year and spending the rest of the year griping and complaining, we should have 364 days of Thanksgiving. "Use that one day just for complaining and griping," he said. "Use the other 364 days to thank God each day for the blessings he has showered upon you."

Instead of spending that last day griping and complaining, however, I encouraged readers to review the 364 entries in their journal. Through that simple exercise, eyes have been opened. Lives have been changed. People have grown in their love and appreciation for God's many and varied gifts.

To aid readers in their thanksgiving journeys, I included 26 devotions to help them think of things for which they normally wouldn't consider giving thanks.

The one regret people expressed to me about the book was that it did not contain a devotion to correspond with every day of the journal. The thought of writing 364 devotions seemed overwhelming to me at the time. I thought it would take forever.

It turns out it only took eight years.

For the past eight years, I have written a weekly syndicated devotional column for eight different newspapers here in Texas, and for the past four years I have also served as a contributing editor for the national Christian magazine *Forward in Christ*. During that time, I have composed nearly 400 devotions.

I have edited those devotions and included the majority in this book.

Because the devotions were written for the newspaper and magazine, they often reference current events from the time in which they were written. They have been adjusted to fit the context of this book, but you may notice me speaking at times about events from the past as if they were current events.

Included with each devotion is an opportunity for readers to once again write one thing for which they are thankful.

I personally am thankful for all those who helped make this book possible, especially for my friend Christy Bagasao who once again was invaluable in the editing process.

Most important, I thank my God for his amazing grace that saved a wretch like me.

Pastor Andrew Schroer
June 2020

HOW TO USE THIS BOOK

The difficulty in writing a yearlong devotional is that people won't always begin reading it on January 1st. Also, depending on the year, holidays fall on different calendar days. To have devotions specific for those times of year fall in the right place is nearly impossible.

In order to overcome those difficulties, the majority of devotions in this book are applicable any time of year. At the end of the book, however, I have included a section of devotions written for specific holidays and times of the year. On holidays and during certain seasons, I encourage you to skip to those devotions and then return to where you left off in the general devotions.

The devotions written for specific holidays can and will be applicable at other times of the year as well. It won't hurt you to read those at any time.

God's truths are true every day.

Included with each devotion is a place to write down one thing for which you are thankful that day. I encourage you to make the most of this unique opportunity to see and appreciate all the blessings God has given you.

There is one catch. Please do not repeat a blessing. Challenge yourself. Look around. See God's many and varied gifts to you and write down a different blessing each day.

The final devotion will then encourage you to take the time to read through all of the blessings God showered on you throughout the year.

Before you begin this journey of devotion, understand that this book is a spiritual exercise. It gives you the chance to feed your faith with God's Word and exercise your faith with thanksgiving. Just like with diet and exercise for our bodies, we begin with lofty goals, but too often give up after only a few days.

Experts say it takes three to six weeks to form a good habit, so make these devotions a consistent part of your daily routine. Set aside a specific part of each day as your devotional time with God. For many people, ideal opportunities are when they first wake up, when they go to bed at night, or at meal times. Do what works best for you.

May God bless you as you grow in your devotion and thanksgiving to him!

DAY 1
COUNT YOUR BLESSINGS

**Because of the LORD's great love we are not consumed,
for his compassions never fail. They are new every
morning; great is your faithfulness.**

LAMENTATIONS 3:22,23

◆

"Count your blessings." That phrase is used so often in our world today that it has become cliché. But do you know where it comes from?

It originates from an old Jewish tradition. According to Jewish law, a faithful Jew will speak one hundred blessings every day. In other words, he or she will thank and praise God out loud for one hundred different blessings every day.

**SEE HOW GOOD
GOD HAS BEEN TO YOU.**

Orthodox Jews count their blessings to make sure they have said all one hundred. Imagine trying to come up with one hundred things every day for which to thank God. That must be hard to do.

Actually, it's not.

As the prophet Jeremiah reminds us in the passage above, God's mercies are new every morning. Every day God showers us with blessings—both old and new. The problem is that we don't always notice them. We don't always count them. We don't always say, "Thank you."

We take God's blessings for granted so often. We don't even notice the blessing of air conditioning until it breaks down in the middle of summer. We don't recognize the gift of speaking until we lose our voices. We don't appreciate the ability to walk until we are sitting in a wheelchair in the nursing home.

That's why it is important to count your blessings.

See how good God has been to you. You have a home and food, clothes and cars. You have clean air to breathe and fresh water to drink. You have air conditioners, smartphones, computers, and indoor plumbing.

Even more important, you are forgiven. You have a home in heaven waiting for you because of Jesus. God even forgives you for all the times you failed to see his goodness, for all the times you blindly took his blessings for granted.

1

God has given us so many blessings that we can't even count them all, but that doesn't mean we shouldn't try. This book is a tool to help you do that. After every daily devotion in this book, there is a space to write down one thing for which you are thankful. Make a habit of writing one thing down every day. There is only one catch: you can never repeat. It has to be a different blessing every day.

Can you come up with a different blessing every day for a whole year? That's the challenge. You don't need to come up with one hundred a day, just one. As your list grows and this book fills, see if it doesn't change how you look at your life. See if it doesn't change how you look at your God.

Count your blessings every day of your life.

Today I am thankful for/that _____

_____

*Heavenly Father, open my eyes and my heart
to see and appreciate all the blessings
you have showered on me. Amen.*

———————◆———————

DAY 2
J. J. S. D. G.

**So whether you eat or drink or whatever you do,
do it all for the glory of God.**

1 CORINTHIANS 10:31

◆

Johann Sebastian Bach (1685–1750) is considered one of the greatest composers of all time. Together with Beethoven and Brahms, Bach forms part of the big "Three Bs" of classical music. Christians still sing his hymns. Choirs still perform his cantatas. Orchestras still play his concertos.

Bach was a deeply spiritual man. He composed the majority of his music to be performed in church. His goal was to praise God and proclaim his love to the world.

Overwhelmed by the import of his work, Bach would often scribble two mysterious letters at the top of each score of music he composed:

J. J.

Short for the Latin *Jesu Juva,* it simply means "Jesus, help." For all his talent and ability, Bach realized that he could accomplish nothing without the help of his God and Savior.

Jesu Juva. Jesus, help. What a wonderful reminder for us as we begin each task of our daily lives! Without our Savior's help, we can do nothing. Without his help, it would all come to ruin. Because of our sinfulness—because of our selfishness and pride—we mess everything up.

Only with God's help and the forgiveness, which Jesus won for us on the cross, are we able to do anything of value in God's eyes. With his help, though, we—like Bach—can compose great works of art.

Sure, you may never compose a famous symphony or hymn, but a child raised in his Word is music to God's ears. A life lived in humble service to God is a work of art.

GOD GETS ALL THE CREDIT.

Your opus to God may be your faithful love to your wife or your diligence at your job. It may simply be your off-key singing of his hymns at church. With Jesus' help, *Jesu Juva,* such simple songs of praise are wondrous symphonies to God's ears.

Every time J. S. Bach finished one of his masterpieces, he scratched three more letters at the end of his manuscript:

S. D. G.

Short for *Soli Deo Gloria,* it means "To God alone be the glory." Bach understood that everything he accomplished in his life wasn't because of him. It was God working through him. Bach composed his music to thank God for his love and forgiveness. God gets all the credit.

As you begin each task of your life, whether it be a massive project at work or school or one of life's simple, mundane duties, don't forget to scratch your "J. J." at the top. Ask your Savior for his help and blessing. Remember that without him, all our efforts come to nothing.

Then when you've finished, be sure to add your "S. D. G." God gets all the credit. Everything we are and everything we accomplish is because of his power and love.

Today I am thankful for/that _____

_____

Jesus, help me, for without your help I can do
nothing. I thank you for everything I have
and everything I have accomplished.
To you alone be the glory. Amen.

───────────◆───────────

DAY 3
JUST AS I AM

In him and through faith in him we may approach
God with freedom and confidence.

EPHESIANS 3:12

◆

Charlotte Elliott was born in Clapham, England, in 1789. In her younger years, Charlotte was a writer and artist, but by age 30 her health began to fail. For the next 50 years, she would live in pain and illness. Because of her constant sickness, she frequently became frustrated and despondent. She would often say, "If God loved me, why would he do this to me?"

One day, a Swiss minister came to the Elliott house for dinner. During the meal, Charlotte, as she was prone to do, burst into a temper tantrum and stormed out of the room, much to the embarrassment of her family.

The minister followed her into the next room and quietly told her that she felt such anger because she had nothing to cling to. Her only hope, he told her, was to turn to the Lord.

But she didn't know how she could do that. "How could I, such an angry and bitter person, turn to God?" she asked.

"You can go to God," the minister told her, "just as you are."

4

Charlotte Elliott never forgot that pastor's advice and years later she penned what would become one of the most famous hymns of all time. She wrote: "Just as I am, without one plea But that thy blood was shed for me And that thou bidd'st me come to thee, O Lamb of God, I come, I come" (CW 397:1).

For those of us who struggle with self-esteem, who look at ourselves in the mirror and don't like what we see, who feel like nobody who really knows us could love us, there were no more comforting words ever spoken.

God accepts me. God loves me. God receives me just as I am.

It is important, however, that we understand what that means. God accepts you just as you are, but that doesn't mean you are acceptable just as you are.

Acceptance doesn't mean God sees the good in everybody. It doesn't mean you are good enough just the way you are. You are a sinner. You are a liar. You are stubborn. You hold grudges. You worry. You doubt. You have dark and dirty sins no one else knows about. You are not good enough just as you are. You are not acceptable by God's standards.

GOD ACCEPTS YOU BECAUSE OF JESUS.

Yet he still accepts you because he made you acceptable in his eyes. God rejected his Son, Jesus—punished him for your dirty sins—so that he could accept you. You have been washed clean in the blood of Jesus and the waters of Holy Baptism.

God accepts you because of Jesus. He accepts you because of his love. His love and acceptance make you special. You are a dearly loved child of God. You are perfect in God's eyes—not because you are perfect, but because you are washed in Jesus' blood.

It doesn't matter who you are or what you have done, you can go to God . . . just as you are.

Today I am thankful for/that _____

"Just as I am, thou wilt receive, wilt welcome, pardon, cleanse, relieve; because thy promise I believe, O Lamb of God, I come, I come." Amen.
(CW 397:5)

DAY 4
THE CHAIR

Pray continually.

1 THESSALONIANS 5:17

◆

A young pastor moved to a new church. Soon after arriving, he received a phone call from one of his new members. She introduced herself and told the pastor that her father was bedridden and couldn't attend church. She asked if the pastor would be willing to visit him, pray with him, and give him Holy Communion. The pastor said that he would be delighted.

The next day the pastor went to the member's home where the young woman greeted him at the door. After some small talk, she told the pastor that her father's room was the second door on the right and that he could go see him if he liked.

The pastor walked to the room and knocked on the door. "Come in," a voice told him. The pastor opened the door and there he saw an elderly man lying on a bed. A chair sat alongside, facing the bed.

The man gave an exuberant, "Hello!" The young pastor replied with a smile, "Hello! I see you're expecting me."

"No, who are you?" the elderly man replied.

"I'm your new pastor. I saw the chair sitting there and I just assumed you were expecting me."

"Oh, the chair," the elderly man responded. "Pastor, can you please close the door?"

Curious, the pastor closed the door.

TALK TO JESUS LIKE YOU'RE TALKING TO ME RIGHT NOW.

"Please sit down, pastor," the man continued. "For years I didn't really understand what prayer was. I would go to church and we would pray. The pastor would always tell us to pray. I would say 'grace' at mealtimes. But I really didn't understand what prayer was until a buddy of mine told me, 'You know what you need to do, John? Put a chair in front of you and imagine Jesus sitting there. Remember he is there even though we can't see him. Then just talk to Jesus like you're talking to me right now. That's what prayer really is.'

6

"I tried it, pastor," the elderly man continued, "and I liked it so much that I do it for at least an hour every day.

"But," he added, "I have to be careful, because if my daughter catches me talking to an empty chair, she is going to send me to the old folks' home."

The pastor smiled and encouraged him to continue praying in that way. They had a devotion and the pastor went home.

About two weeks later, the pastor received another phone call. It was the daughter. She was in tears. Her father had just passed away. She explained to the pastor how she had gone to the store that morning and when she came back, she found him dead.

"But something strange happened, pastor," the young woman added. "It seems that in the moments right before he died, my father got up from his bed, sat on the floor and laid his head on the chair next to his bed."

Today I am thankful for/that _____

_____

Heavenly Father, thank you for the wonderful privilege of being able to talk to you every day in prayer. Thank you for always listening. Amen.

———————◆———————

DAY 5
A DROP IN THE BUCKET

**I consider that our present sufferings are not
worth comparing with the glory
that will be revealed in us.**

ROMANS 8:18

◆

After Hurricane Harvey hit our community in 2017, there was a phrase I heard repeated again and again: "This is just a drop in the bucket."

What we endured in Edna, Texas, because of Hurricane Harvey was difficult and frustrating. Our yards were a mess. Our roofs leaked. Trees and limbs wreaked havoc. Many residents were without electricity for weeks.

And don't even get me started on the mosquitoes.

But what we went through was just a drop in the bucket compared to what Houston, Rockport, and other places suffered. They had it much worse.

When we suffer pain and loss, it helps to keep things in perspective. It's good for us to remember those who have it worse than us. Comparatively speaking, our pains and problems are often just a drop in the bucket.

A pastor told me that even the flooding in Houston was just a drop in the bucket compared to another flood. That flood occurred thousands of years ago. The whole world was destroyed. Only eight people on the planet survived.

GOD POINTS US TO HEAVEN.

Compared to the biblical flood, Houston was just a drop in the bucket.

Such perspective can be helpful when we are facing the storms of life, but that's not the perspective God gives us in his Word. To help us keep a proper perspective, God doesn't point us to those who have it worse than us.

God points us to heaven.

The apostle Paul wrote to the Romans, "I consider that our present sufferings are not worth comparing with the glory that will be revealed in us." Because Jesus lived and died as our Savior—because God forgives all the junk and garbage of our lives—we have a home waiting for us in the glory of heaven.

When we get to heaven, even the worst pains and problems of this world will seem like an insignificant mosquito bite.

Right now it hurts. Right now it's hard, but when we get to heaven the joy will overshadow the sorrow.

Paul compares our struggles to pregnancy. For nine months, the mother-to-be suffers nausea, discomfort, and sleeplessness. The labor is painful and traumatic, but when the nurse lays her baby on her chest, all of that becomes a distant memory.

She is left with pure joy.

Keep that perspective. Yes, it is helpful to remember that no matter how bad your situation, there are others who have it worse. Even more important is to remember that no matter how bad it gets here on earth, the happiness and joy of heaven will overshadow it all.

This is just a drop in the bucket.

Today I am thankful for/that _____

_____

Lord, as I suffer the pains and problems of my life, help me to keep it all in perspective. Keep my eyes focused on the joy of heaven which is coming. Amen.

DAY 6
TRUE PEACE

"Peace I leave with you; my peace I give you. I do not
give to you as the world gives. Do not let your hearts be
troubled and do not be afraid."

JOHN 14:27

◆

The story is told of two rival painters who were always trying to outdo one another. One day they decided to have a contest to see who was the better artist. The rules of the competition were simple: They would each create a painting that represented the idea of peace.

The first artist painted a beautiful mountain scene with a lake in the middle. The lake was as clear as crystal and as blue as the sky. No wind or movement interrupted its tranquility. For the first artist, that is what peace looked like.

The second artist painted a very different scene. He painted a violent waterfall. The sky was dark and ominous. The wind blew across the canvas. Alongside the waterfall stood a dead grey tree. A branch from the tree reached out in front of the waterfall. There on that branch of the dead grey tree, in front of the violent waterfall in the middle of the storm, quietly sat a small bird unaffected by the chaos which surrounded it. The bird was at peace.

On the night before he died, Jesus promised his disciples and us, "Peace I leave with you; my peace I give you. I do not give to you as the world gives. Do not let your hearts be troubled and do not be afraid."

OUR ROAD TO HEAVEN WILL PASS THROUGH MANY HARDSHIPS.

Jesus promises us peace. But what kind of peace? God doesn't promise us the peace of the first painting. He doesn't promise us a life of tranquility here on earth, free of problems and pains. He doesn't promise us that all our hurts here on earth will suddenly disappear if we merely believe or pray hard enough. God doesn't promise us that kind of peace.

In fact, he tells us, "We must go through many hardships to enter the kingdom of God" (Acts 14:22). Our road to heaven will pass through many hardships. On our road to heaven, we will pass through cancer and heart attacks, heartbreaks and hurt. We will see the greyness of death in the faces of people we love. We will face our own mortality. The peace God promises isn't the absence of pain and problems here on earth. Rather, it is the peace painted by the second artist, a peace in the middle of the storm.

The peace the world cannot give is the peace of knowing that, because of Jesus, God forgives you and loves you even though you have said and done terrible things in your life. The peace the world cannot give is the peace of knowing that, because of Jesus, the tranquility of heaven is waiting for us where "'there will be no more death' or mourning or crying or pain" (Revelation 21:4). The peace the world cannot give is the peace of knowing that our God will be with us, give us strength, and carry us through every hardship and heartbreak we face.

Don't expect that God will take away your problems here on earth if you just have enough faith or pray hard enough. That's not the peace God promises. Rather, find in our God—in his Word and sacraments—the true peace he promises: a peace in the middle of the storm.

Today I am thankful for/that _____

_____

Lord, as I face the struggles and pains of this world, point me to your promises where I can find the peace the world cannot give. Amen.

DAY 7
SPLANCHNIZOMAI

When [Jesus] saw the crowds, he had compassion on them, because they were harassed and helpless, like sheep without a shepherd.

MATTHEW 9:36

◆

Splanchnizomai. That is my all-time favorite Greek word. It just rolls off the tongue. Try it. Say it out loud. *Splanchnizomai.*

Splanchnizomai is found 12 times in the Bible. Every time it describes what Jesus or God the Father was feeling. *Splanchnizomai* literally means "to have your intestines moved."

I'm not kidding. Look it up.

When Jesus saw people hurting, lonely, or lost, the Bible tells us his intestines were moved. Most translations simply read, "Jesus had compassion on them," but that's not actually what it says. It literally says, "His intestines were moved for them."

When we talk about our feelings today, we talk about our hearts. If your feelings are hurt, your heart breaks. If you're in love, your heart swells. If you are full of joy, your heart bursts.

In Jesus' day, they felt things a little deeper. If you think about it, it makes sense. Sometimes when we see something heartbreaking—people starving in Africa, a mother mourning her dead child, terrorists torturing and killing helpless victims—we don't actually feel it in our hearts.

We feel it deep down in the pit of our stomachs.

When Jesus saw people hurting, when he saw them lost and confused, he felt it deep down in the pit of his stomach. When God the Father saw his lost son return in Jesus' parable, he felt it deep down in the pit of his stomach.

HIS HEART ACHES FOR YOU.

When God sees you hurting, lonely, or afraid, he feels it deep down in the pit of his stomach. God's love for you is boundless. His heart aches for you.

When he saw humankind fall into the dark depths of sin, it broke his heart. When he thought of you spending an eternity in the torture of hell, he felt it deep down in the pit of his stomach. So, he came to this world. He became one of us. He suffered our punishment and died our death.

That is how deeply your God loves you.

Sometimes it feels like God doesn't care. Sometimes it seems like he is angry with us. We hurt. We struggle. We fall and he doesn't pick us up right away. He doesn't immediately take away our sorrows or pains.

Don't think that means he doesn't care. When you hurt, he feels it deep down in the bottom of his stomach. He loves you. He doesn't want you to suffer, but he also knows that sometimes you need to struggle. Sometimes you need to hurt for a while to learn or to grow, or because in his love he has plans for you that you can't see or understand at this moment.

When you are hurting, remember the most awesome of all Greek words: *splanchnizomai*. God knows your pain. He loves you more deeply than you will ever fully understand. One day he will deliver you. Meanwhile, he will be by your side to give you the courage and strength you need.

How do I know? *Splanchnizomai.* God loves you so much he feels it deep down in the pit of his stomach.

Today I am thankful for/that _____

_____

Dear Jesus, thank you for loving me so deeply and for forgiving me so freely. Help me to love others as you have loved me. Amen.

DAY 8
A TEAM EFFORT

I planted the seed, Apollos watered it, but God has been making it grow. . . . For we are co-workers in God's service.

1 CORINTHIANS 3:6,9

Years ago, all six of my siblings and I got together with our families for a week at a lake. We stayed in a big house with a tiny dock.

Every day, my children and their cousins fished off the dock in three feet of water. The water was so clear they could see the tiny bluegills swimming around the baited hooks.

One afternoon, the children were on the dock when suddenly one yelled, "It's a monster!" A 21-inch, 5-pound bass was swimming among the tiny baitfish. The fathers sprang into action. We started dropping lures into the water as the children followed Moby Dick in the water.

Then Uncle Tom had an idea. His nine-year-old daughter Grace quickly caught a small bluegill with her pink bobbered pole. Uncle Tom put it on a hook and, with the help of the children, dropped it in front of the giant bass. The bass sucked the bait into his massive mouth and the battle began. Uncle Tom slowly worked the fish to the dock as I nervously maneuvered the net.

After five chaotic minutes, the children cheered as the trophy fish was brought on shore. "It was a team effort," Uncle Tom announced with a smile.

Jesus' first disciples were from families of fishermen. One day, Jesus stood on the shore and invited them to go fishing with him. "Come, follow me," Jesus told them, "and I will send you out to fish for people" (Mark 1:17). Jesus was inviting them to be his messengers, making disciples of all nations.

Jesus has also invited you to go fishing. He has called you to be his messenger—to tell others of his love and forgiveness. Sometimes fishing is a team effort.

SOMETIMES FISHING IS A TEAM EFFORT.

Many years ago when I lived in Mexico, we held worship services on the patio of a butcher shop. The owner and most of his family were members of the church. His nephew Chago was not. He would usually stay upstairs as we worshiped.

A month before I left Mexico, Chago suffered a kidney infection which required surgery. I went to visit Chago in the hospital. I prayed with him. I told him about God's love and the forgiveness Jesus won for him on the cross. He didn't seem too interested in what I was saying.

After I left, though, one of the Mexican pastors followed up with Chago. The pastor continued to share the good news of God's love with him. His family continued to encourage him to go to church. Two years later, Chago joined the church.

Three years later, Chago went to heaven.

Sometimes fishing is a team effort. You may tell someone about Jesus. You may share the good news of God's love and forgiveness, but you may not see any results. That doesn't mean God isn't working through your message. To use the apostle Paul's metaphor, you have planted a seed. Someone else may water it and see it grow.

So don't give up. Go fishing. Talk about Jesus and his love with everyone you can. Though you may not always see the results, you may be a part of a bigger team God is using to help that person see his love.

Sometimes fishing is a team effort.

Today I am thankful for/that _____

_____

Dear Jesus, help me to never give up as
I go fishing for you. Amen.

DAY 9
DADDY, I DON'T WANT TO DIE

**In peace I will lie down and sleep, for you alone,
LORD, make me dwell in safety.**

PSALM 4:8

◆

I will never forget that moment. My daughter was six years old. I tucked her into bed. Then we prayed as we do every night:

Now I lay me down to sleep, I pray the Lord my soul to keep;
If I should die before I wake, I pray the Lord my soul to take.

My daughter began to cry. We had said the prayer hundreds of times before, but this time the words hit home. "But, Daddy, I don't want to die," she said as tears rolled down her cheeks.

At that point in her life, my daughter had limited experience dealing with death. She had been to a couple of funerals. She heard about death in her Sunday school lessons at church. Though we try to shield our children from violence and adult topics on TV, she knew what death looked like.

That night, however, for the first time in her young life, my daughter faced her own mortality. For the first time in her life, she realized she was going to die.

So we talked. I told her how all of us one day are going to die. That didn't help. Suddenly the slow stream of tears became a roaring river. "Daddy, I don't want you and Mommy to die!"

Few people want to die. Whether you want to or not, though, you are going to die. Death is part of this life. Unless Jesus comes first, you will attend many funerals in your life, the last of which will be your own.

> **JESUS CONQUERED SIN, DEATH, AND HELL FOR US.**

Death is scary because deep down we all know it means we will face God's judgment. We deserve death. We deserve hell. But Jesus conquered sin, death, and hell for us.

His words of comfort to a mourning Martha also comfort us. He said, "I am the resurrection and the life. The one who believes in me will live, even though they die; and whoever lives by believing in me will never die" (John 11:25,26).

For us who believe, death is simply the door to heaven. One day we will close our eyes in death and open them to life in heaven. There we will bask in God's presence. There we will be together with all our loved ones who died in Christ. There we will never attend another funeral again.

On that night years ago, I sat on my daughter's bed holding her as she cried. We talked about the pain of death and the sorrow of missing our loved ones, but then we talked about heaven. I reminded her how we would be together forever in heaven because of Jesus. I told her that death wasn't a bad thing because heaven is so much better than this world. The tears slowed and her breathing steadied.

Soon she fell asleep.

Whether you are six years old or sixty years old, death can be a scary subject. God's promises of forgiveness and heaven, however, allow us to close our eyes and rest in peace. I find great comfort in knowing that my daughter can now say with confidence: "If I die before I wake, I know the Lord my soul will take."

Today I am thankful for/that _____

_____

Almighty God, help me to close my eyes every night with the confidence and peace of heaven. Amen.

DAY 10
FAITH IS HARD

**Now faith is confidence in what we hope for and
assurance about what we do not see.**

HEBREWS 11:1

◆

A man was walking down a narrow path along a steep cliff. He tripped and fell over the side. As he fell, he grabbed onto a small branch sticking out of the side of the cliff.

Hanging on for his life, he cried out: "Is anyone up there?"

"I am here," a voice replied.

"Who's there?" the man asked.

"It's me . . . God," the voice answered.

"Lord, help me!" the man squealed.

"Do you trust me?" God asked.

"I trust you completely," the man said resolutely.

"Good," God said, "then let go of the branch."

"What?"

"I said, 'Let go of the branch.'"

"Is there anyone else up there?"

Faith is hard. We hear God's voice in the distance telling us to let go. He will catch us, but that's hard. It's hard to trust completely when we can't see or understand why.

Faith is hard when the credit card bills pile up. Faith is hard when the doctor tells you that it's cancer. Faith is hard as you watch your child die. We ask ourselves, "If God loves me, why is he doing this to me?"

We think, "It would be so much easier if we could just see." If only we could see what God's people of the Old Testament saw. They saw the ten powerful plagues in Egypt. They saw God divide the Red Sea. They saw the glory of God descend on Mount Sinai.

Or what about Jesus' disciples? They saw Jesus in the flesh. They saw him walk on water. They saw him feed thousands of people with a couple loaves of bread and a few small fish. They saw him raise the dead. If only we could see what the people of Israel saw, if only we could see what the disciples saw, it would be much easier to trust. Then faith wouldn't be so hard.

Or would it? Despite all the wonders they saw, the people of Israel constantly complained. They persistently rebelled and continuously rejected. For all the miracles the disciples witnessed, they still ran away the night Jesus was arrested. They still cowered in fear behind locked doors on that first Easter evening.

SEEING ISN'T BELIEVING. BELIEVING IS SEEING.

Seeing didn't help the Israelites. It didn't help Jesus' disciples, and it wouldn't help us because seeing isn't believing. Believing is seeing.

If you are looking for visible evidence or scientific proof, I cannot give it to you. There is no pill which will make believing easier. Faith by definition is believing in something we cannot see.

If it were left up to us, faith would be too hard. We wouldn't be able to let go. We wouldn't trust God. But God sends us his Holy Spirit to help us trust. As we hear God's promises and see all the examples in the Bible of God keeping his promises, the Holy Spirit works in us the faith to trust that what God says is true.

If God kept his promises to Adam and Eve, Abraham, Isaac, and Jacob—if he kept his promise to send his Son to live and die as our Savior—we can trust that he will keep the rest of his promises.

Do you find yourself doubting? Do you find yourself worrying? Do you find yourself struggling? We all do at times. At those times, say the prayer a hurting father once prayed to Jesus, "I do believe; help me overcome my unbelief!" (Mark 9:24).

When you struggle with doubt, go back to God's promises. Go back to God's Word. See how God always does what he says he'll do.

And then let go of the branch.

Today I am thankful for/that _____

_____

Lord, I do believe. Help me overcome my unbelief. Amen.

DAY 11
THE MARATHON OF LIFE

**"Be faithful, even to the point of death, and I will give
you life as your victor's crown."**

REVELATION 2:10

◆

A few years ago, I ran a marathon—26.2 miles. It was the hardest thing
I have ever done. The last couple of miles were pure agony. I actually
cried from the pain. The only thing that kept me going was the thought
of how good it would feel to cross the finish line and be with my family
waiting there.

In many ways, life is like a marathon. Just like a marathon, the last part is
often the hardest. In my years as a pastor, I have had the privilege of serving
elderly people in our congregation and our area nursing homes.

We often don't realize how hard those last miles are.

When I was a boy, there was a man who lived on my newspaper route—
good ole Mr. Kutz. He was a member of our church, lived to be 104 years
old, and was still chopping firewood when he was 90. At his 100th birthday
party, Mr. Kutz pulled my dad, his pastor, aside and told him, "Pastor,
being 100 is not all it's cracked up to be."

Getting older is not all it's cracked up to be. Our bodies break down. Our
knees ache. Our backs hurt. Our feet swell. Our eyesight and hearing fade.
It gets harder to remember things. Soon we end up in wheelchairs and
nursing homes. We lose our independence. We can no longer drive. People
start to treat us differently.

The longer we live, the more funerals we have to attend. The longer we live,
the more goodbyes we have to say—to our parents, our spouses, our
brothers and sisters, our childhood friends. Getting older is not all it's
cracked up to be. The last miles of life's marathon are often the hardest.

Just like my marathon, what can help us keep going is to remember how
good it will feel to cross the finish line. You see, no matter how hard the
marathon is, no matter how many times you stumble and fall, you will
eventually win the race.

You will win, because Jesus won the victory for you. You could never win
life's marathon on your own. You have stumbled and fallen too many times.

You have stumbled into sin. You have stumbled over your anger, over your drinking, over your gossiping. You don't deserve to win. You don't deserve the prize to heaven.

Yet the victory is yours because Jesus suffered the punishment of all your anger, your drinking, your gossip—your sins—in your place. With his death and resurrection, he won the victory for you. You don't have to win the race. You just have to finish. The Lord's promise is: whoever finishes the race in faith, whoever dies believing in Jesus, the victory of heaven is yours. Your loved ones who died in Christ will be waiting for you at the finish line.

KEEP YOUR EYES FOCUSED ON THE FINISH LINE.

Once you cross that finish line, there will be no more aches and pains, no more wheelchairs or nursing homes, no more sin or sorrow. The victory celebration of heaven will last forever.

The last few miles of the marathon are often the hardest. Getting older is not all it's cracked up to be, so keep your eyes focused on the finish line. Think about how good it will feel to cross that line and to see your loved ones there. At the finish line, all your pains will disappear. I know it hurts, but don't give up now.

I'll see you at the finish line!

Today I am thankful for/that _____

_____

Lord, thank you for getting me this far in my life.
Please give me the strength and help
I need to finish the race. Amen.

DAY 12
RUSSIAN ROULETTE WITH YOUR SOUL

"Do not put the Lord your God to the test."

LUKE 4:12

◆

Nobody is quite sure of the origin of the term. *Russian* refers to its supposed country of origin; *roulette* refers to the spinning of the gun's chamber and the gamble the person is making.

Russian roulette is a foolish and dangerous game. Throughout the decades, countless people have been maimed or killed by playing it. Yet some still play it today. Some play it because they have a death wish; others because it makes them look tough. Still others think it makes them cool.

In the end, Russian roulette is the epitome of stupidity.

Yet you and I often play Russian roulette with the Holy Spirit. It goes something like this: God promises to always forgive us when we repent of our sins. No matter how far we fall, no matter how badly we mess up, Jesus died for that sin and God will forgive it.

That's what he tells himself as he buys the case of beer at the gas station on the way home from work. That's what he tells himself as he sits behind his computer in a dark room after everybody has gone to bed. That's what she tells herself as she sits alone in her car with the guy from work who seems to understand her so much better than her husband.

"God will forgive me. He'll always take me back. Nobody's perfect."

We let ourselves fall. We tell ourselves it's a one-off. We can always ask for forgiveness tomorrow.

That is the lie of the devil. *That* is playing Russian roulette with the Holy Spirit.

Yes, God has and will always forgive you because of Jesus, but are you really sorry if you plan on doing it and then asking God for forgiveness afterward? Once sin gets a foothold in your heart, it doesn't want to let go. We become slaves to addictions. We become ensnared in our passions. We get desensitized to sin and soon aren't even sorry any more.

The biggest problem with playing Russian roulette with the Holy Spirit is that you could die. At what point when we knowingly sin are we turning away from God into unbelief? At what point are we risking our souls and our eternal salvation? I can't look into a person's heart, nor do I presume to know the mind of God, but if you play Russian roulette with the Holy Spirit and die, what will happen to you?

As I said before, Russian roulette is the epitome of stupidity.

Our God is an extremely patient God, but his patience is not absolute. There comes a point when God says, "Enough is enough." Our God of mercy and grace is also a God of justice who punishes those who willfully reject him.

Consider the teenagers who think they have a lifetime to turn to God. Right now they are busy with school and friends. They want to live life and have fun. They want to do their own thing. One day they will settle down. One day they'll get back to church. One day they will get back to God.

What they don't know is if God will say what he said in Jesus' parable: "You fool! This very night your life will be demanded from you" (Luke 12:20).

DON'T PLAY GAMES WITH GOD'S GRACE.

Don't play games with God's grace. He loves you. He forgives you. He is extremely patient and will take you back no matter how far you've fallen—no matter how badly you've messed up.

But his patience does have an end. Sin has a way of trapping us in addiction and pulling us away from God. One day you will die, and you don't know what day that will be. So cling to God's grace every day. Don't listen to the lies of the devil. Fight against the temptation to play games with sin. The stakes are too high.

You are gambling your soul.

Today I am thankful for/that _____

_____

Merciful God, forgive me for the times I have played games with your grace. Help me to live every day for you who lived and died for me. Amen.

DAY 13
THE SON OF GOD

**For God so loved the world that he gave his one and
only Son, that whoever believes in him shall not perish
but have eternal life.**

JOHN 3:16

◆

In 2014, the movie *Son of God* hit theaters. Soon afterward, a member of
my church asked me what that meant.

"I've always wondered, pastor," she said, "what does it mean that Jesus is
the *Son of God*?"

Good question. Jesus is God's Son, but that doesn't mean God the Father
got married and together they had a son. Yes, Jesus was born here on earth
to the virgin Mary, but he has always existed. Just like God the Father and
God the Holy Spirit, God the Son is eternal (John 1:1-14; Revelation 1:17).
Jesus is completely God in every way (Colossians 2:9). Our simple human
minds cannot fully understand that.

God is three distinct persons—Father, Son, and Holy Spirit—yet only
one God.

When God reveals himself as a Father and Son, however, he is not referring
to time, but to a relationship. God the Father loves his Son and is proud of
him (Matthew 3:17). Jesus, the Son, loves his Father and obeyed him by
coming to this world to be our Savior. By using the human terms "Father"
and "Son," God gives us a glimpse into the relationship between those two
persons of the Trinity.

By calling himself "Father" and "Son," God gives us a glimpse into his great
love for us.

I once heard the story of a pastor who one Sunday after church announced
that a special guest wanted to say a few words to the congregation. Slowly
an elderly man made his way to the front of the church.

"Many years ago," the old man began, "I took my ten-year-old son and his
friend out in my sailboat for a day on the water. A terrible storm came up
and capsized the boat. I was able to grab on to the boat, but the boys were
quickly being pulled out to sea. I was able to reach a life preserver, but had
only a split second to decide which boy to throw it to."

The congregation held its collective breath as the old man paused to catch his. Finally, he lifted up his head and said, "I threw it to my son's friend."

He paused again. His voice trembled, "You see, I knew my son believed in Jesus. I knew where he would go if he died. I also knew my son's friend didn't go to church. I couldn't take the chance. I threw him the life preserver."

THE FATHER LET HIS SON DIE TO RESCUE YOU. THERE IS NO GREATER LOVE.

By that point, there wasn't a dry eye in the church. The pastor slowly walked up behind the old man and put his arm around him. He looked out at the congregation and said, "That's a true story. I know, because I was the boy he saved."

Could you do that? Would you do that? Sacrifice your own child to save someone else's? As a parent, I can't imagine making that sacrifice.

The point of calling Jesus "the Son of God" is to help us understand the height, breadth, and width of God's love for us. God loved you so much that he made that awesome and awful sacrifice. The Father let his Son die to rescue you.

There is no greater love.

Today I am thankful for/that _____

_____

Thank you, Lord, for your great love that led you to sacrifice so much for me. Amen.

DAY 14
COMMITTED

**As the time approached for him to be taken up to
heaven, Jesus resolutely set out for Jerusalem.**

LUKE 9:51

◆

Do you know the difference between being involved and being committed? It's the difference between bacon and eggs. Yeah, that's right—bacon and eggs.

BE COMMITTED. You see, in bacon and eggs, the chicken is involved, but the pig's life is committed.

I live in rural Texas. Fourteen thousand people live in our entire county, and we have 50 churches. We must be a very Christian community, right?

A few years ago, a fellow pastor from our area shared with me a study that showed that 85% of our county is *not* in church on any given weekend. Eighty-five percent!

How committed are any of us really, even those of us who go to church regularly? Sure we put in our hour a week, but is that what it means to be a Christian—to park our posteriors in the pew for an hour each week?

To understand what it means to be committed, we need to look at Jesus. In his great love, Jesus, the King and Creator of all things, left behind the cushy comfort of heaven to be born in a manure-smelling barn. God became a helpless baby. On that night, God felt hunger and pain for the first time. On that night, God cried.

God lived a humble life of poverty and pain here on earth. Then, when he was 33 years old, he marched straight into Jerusalem, knowing what was waiting for him. Think about that. If you knew thugs were waiting outside your front door with baseball bats to pound you, would you go out that door? No way. You would sneak out the back. You would call the cops.

Jesus walked into Jerusalem knowing the pain, horror, and hell he was about to suffer, yet he willingly suffered it all. He suffered God's punishment for our lack of commitment. He suffered God's punishment for our lack of love. He suffered God's punishment in our place for all the bad things we do. Then he died our death.

That is commitment.

Because of Jesus' commitment to us, we are forgiven. God will not punish us for our half-hearted service because he already punished Jesus in our place. Even now, God is still committed 100% to you and your salvation. He is working everything in your life to lead you to heaven.

When we see such love, such sacrifice, such commitment, it changes us. God gave everything for me. What can I give for him? An hour a week? Two hours a week? How about my whole week? How about my whole life?

Don't just be involved. Be committed.

Today I am thankful for/that _____

_____

Dear Jesus, thank you for being committed to me and my salvation. Forgive me for all the times my service to you has been only half-hearted. Help me to be committed. Amen.

DAY 15
A REALLY DARK PLACE

Yea, though I walk through the valley of the shadow of death, I will fear no evil.

PSALM 23:4 KJV

◆

It is an oft-repeated scene in my ministry: I'm standing next to the bed of a person who is breathing their last here on earth. I pull out my Bible and begin reading.

"The LORD is my Shepherd, I shall not want."

As I read the well-known, comforting words of Psalm 23, some people smile; others cry. Some do both. Hurting family members and friends hang on every beautiful and profound word.

But then I read, "Yea, though I walk through the valley of the shadow of death, I will fear no evil." At that point, I often hear an audible gasp or whimper as they react to such poignant words.

Their loved one is passing through that dark valley of death.

The truth is, however, that is not exactly what Psalm 23 is saying, or at least not in the way people often think. When people hear the phrase "the valley of the shadow of death," they think David is talking about passing through the dark valley of death.

In the original Hebrew, the word often translated as "the shadow of death" seems to mean "deep darkness." In other words, even when we walk through the valleys of deep darkness, we don't need to be afraid. Dark valleys in David's day were dangerous. A modern paraphrase might be, "Even when I walk through a dark alleyway in the bad part of Houston at two o'clock in the morning, I will fear no evil."

The valley of the shadow of death includes all the dark and scary times in our lives. We've all experienced such dark places—when we are hurting, afraid, and confused. When we find ourselves in those really dark places, we don't need to be afraid. Our Good Shepherd is with us. He will protect, guide, and comfort us.

YOUR GOOD SHEPHERD WILL NEVER LEAVE YOUR SIDE.

No matter where you go, no matter how scared you are, no matter how dark of a place you find yourself in, your Good Shepherd will never leave your side. You don't have to be afraid. He will protect you. He will make it all work out for your good.

And, no matter what, he will lead you to heaven.

Sometimes the really dark place is death. In fact, death is the darkest and scariest valley through which we must pass. Even as we walk through the dark valley of death, however, we don't need to be afraid. Our Good Shepherd is with us the whole way.

Because of Jesus, your Good Shepherd, death is not the end. Death is not darkness. Death is not something to be feared.

Because Jesus, your Good Shepherd, gave his life to rescue his sheep— because he won for you forgiveness and a home in heaven—death for you is simply a door. When you go through that door, you will see the table he has prepared for you in the banquet hall of heaven where your cup overflows. Through faith in Jesus, you will live in the house of the Lord forever.

Psalm 23 isn't meant to be read only at a person's deathbed or funeral. It reminds us of God's providence, protection, and presence every day of our lives. It points us to the luxurious banquet of heaven waiting for us.

It comforts us and takes away our fears, especially when we are in a really dark place.

Today I am thankful for/that _____

_____

Dear Good Shepherd, thank you for always being with me, even in my darkest times. Take away my fears and help me to trust you. Amen.

DAY 16
IT'S NOT EASY BEING GREEN

Dear friends, I urge you, as foreigners and exiles, to abstain from sinful desires, which wage war against your soul.

1 PETER 2:11

As a socially awkward boy growing up in the '70s and '80s, I related to one character on TV more than any other: Kermit the Frog. I remember watching him sitting on a log in the middle of a swamp, playing his banjo and singing, "It's not easy being green."

I can remember thinking to myself, "This guy gets me."

It's not easy being green. It's not easy being different. We all, to some degree, want to fit in. We all want to be normal.

But is being normal such a good thing? I have a rather eccentric friend who likes to say, "Being normal is overrated."

Just look at what is normal in our world today. Over 40% of marriages in our country end in divorce. Divorce has become normal. About 71% of teenagers have had sexual relations by the time they are nineteen. Premarital sex is normal. Every year, there are hundreds of millions of searches for pornography on the internet. Pornography has become normal.

Abortion is legal in our country. Recreational marijuana use is becoming the norm in many states. Gay marriage is not only permitted, it is celebrated. In a sinful world, sin is normal.

In that sense, we were all born normal. We are just like the other 7.2 billion people in this world. We are selfish. We lose our tempers. We struggle in our marriages and with our children. We are just like everybody else, yet as Christians we are different.

We are different because God took us, who were dirty slaves to sin, and adopted us as his children through Holy Baptism and his Word. He washed us clean of all our sins in Jesus' blood. We are different because we are forgiven. We are different because we are God's adopted children. We are different because we are going to heaven.

WE AREN'T "NORMAL." WE ARE DIFFERENT.

As Christians, we are just passing through this world. Heaven is our home. That truth changes how we live and how we act here on earth. We aren't like the rest of the world. We aren't "normal." We are different.

I used to live in Mexico. When I first moved there, I stuck out like a sore thumb. I dressed like a gringo. I spoke like a gringo. I acted like a gringo. But as I spent more time down there, I started talking more like a Mexican. I started dressing more like a Mexican. I started acting more like a Mexican. They call that cultural acclimation. The more time you spend with a group of people, the more you start talking and acting like them.

How often don't we become culturally acclimated to our sinful world? You get a new job in the oil fields. The other guys like to cuss, drink, and go to the strip club. How long before you start sounding and acting like them? At school, you start going to parties where kids are drinking or smoking pot. You tell yourself, "I can go without it affecting me. I won't do it." Then, before you know it, you become culturally acclimated.

You are different. God has washed you clean of your sins. You have been adopted as his son or daughter. You are going to heaven. So come out of the closet. Stand up and say, "I am not ashamed to be a Christian."

I know it's not easy being green. It's not easy being different. A part of us still loves the sins from which God has freed us. A part of us wants to fit in and be like everybody else. But you aren't like everybody else. You are different. You are a forgiven child of God. Don't let yourself become culturally acclimated to this sinful world.

Dare to be different.

Today I am thankful for/that _____

_____

Dear Lord, thank you for making me different.
Help me not be ashamed to be who you
made me to be. Amen.

DAY 17
BE STILL

"Be still, and know that I am God."

PSALM 46:10

◆

That's one of my all-time favorite verses of the Bible. I've always felt like God was speaking directly to me when he said it. It has brought me great comfort and peace during tumultuous times in my life.

But now it turns out God may not even be speaking to me in that verse.

In Psalm 46, the writer reminds us we don't have to be afraid even if the whole world collapses around us. We have a refuge where we can hide—a mighty fortress whose great walls will protect us.

That mighty fortress is our God.

He will be with us, the writer promises. Though nations and kingdoms rise up against him and us, he will break their bows and shatter their spears. He will make wars cease to the ends of the earth.

And then in verse 10, God himself speaks. "Be still, and know that I am God."

When I worry, my stomach turns in knots. I get anxious. I can't sit still. I can't sleep.

But God tells me to be still—to take a deep breath and remember that he is God. He's got this. He's in control. He is my refuge. He is a mighty fortress.

He is God.

It turns out, though, God may not actually be speaking those words to me. A fellow pastor recently pointed out to me that if you look at the verses right before verse 10, it's talking about God dealing with those who rage and fight against him—how he destroys their weapons of mass destruction and brings an end to their conflicts.

Then God says, "Be still, and know that I am God." In that context, it seems like God is speaking to those who wage war against him and us. It seems like he is saying, "Be still! Knock it off! I'm God. I'm in charge here."

In that sense, verse 10 would be analogous to when Jesus was on the Sea of Galilee with his disciples in a terrible storm. As the waters roared and foamed, Jesus rebuked the storm. "Quiet!" he said. "Be still!" And the storm stopped immediately (Mark 4:39).

GOD IS WITH US. HE IS IN CONTROL.

If you have a chance today, read through Psalm 46 in its entirety. We honestly can't say with certainty to whom God is speaking in verse 10. In the end, though, it doesn't matter. The point is still the same.

We don't have to worry. We don't have to fret. We don't have to be afraid. God is with us. He is in control.

The forces which rage against us cannot win. The Coronavirus cannot win. Terrorists cannot win. Jesus wins. God's got you. Even if they take our lives here on earth, we have forever waiting for us in the happiness of heaven because of Jesus. You cannot lose. You never need to be afraid.

At this moment, it feels like the world is falling apart around us. A pandemic surrounds us. The economy is collapsing. Our country is divided. It's scary.

Take a deep breath. You've got this. Better yet, God's got this. He's got you.

So be still, and know that he is God.

Today I am thankful for/that _____

_____

Dear Lord, help me to remember who you are and what you have done for me. Open my eyes to see that you are with me at this very moment. Help me to be still and to trust that you've got this. Amen.

DAY 18
ANYONE CAN PLANT A SEED

**"The kingdom of heaven is like a mustard seed. . . .
Though it is the smallest of all seeds, yet
when it grows, it is the largest of garden
plants and becomes a tree."**

MATTHEW 13:31,32

◆

Have you ever heard of Edward Kimball? Probably not. You might have heard of Dwight L. Moody, though. Dwight L. Moody was a famous Christian itinerant preacher from the late 1800s. He started the Moody Institute in Chicago and preached the gospel to hundreds of thousands of people in his lifetime.

Edward Kimball, on the other hand, was a simple Sunday school teacher at Mount Vernon Church in Boston, Massachusetts. In his autobiography, however, Dwight Moody credits Edward Kimball's Sunday school class with bringing him to faith in Jesus.

But the story doesn't end there.

Dwight Moody came to have a profound influence on another Christian preacher named J. Wilbur Chapman. Chapman in turn greatly influenced the faith of a former professional baseball player named Billy Sunday.

You might have heard of Billy Sunday. At the beginning of the 20th century, he was the most famous Christian preacher in the United States. In fact, many historians say that, after Charles Lindbergh, he was the most famous person in America at the time. Billy Sunday's preaching is credited with over one million conversions in his lifetime.

In 1924, Billy Sunday helped establish a Christian organization in Charlotte, North Carolina, which later became known as the Charlotte Businessmen's Club (CBMC). In 1934, the CBMC invited a Baptist preacher named Mordecai Ham to lead their revival. A curious 17-year-old kid attended one of those revivals and came to believe in Jesus.

You might have heard of him. His name was Billy Graham. He is credited with preaching the gospel to more people than any other person in the history of the world—all of which can be traced back to a seed planted by an unknown Sunday school teacher named Edward Kimball.

Jesus once compared the gospel—the good news of his love—with a mustard seed. A mustard seed was the tiniest seed found in Palestine at the time, but it grew into one of the largest plants. In the same way, the good news of Jesus and how he saved us can have very humble beginnings, but can grow and spread and accomplish great things.

The first people to plant that seed were Jesus' 12 disciples, a group of poor, uneducated fishermen and social outcasts. Yet through them the New Testament was written and the good news of God's love spread to the known world.

In 1517, a poor German monk named Martin Luther nailed a piece of paper to a church door. It listed concerns he had with the Christian church of his day and the corruption found within it. The good news about Jesus and the forgiveness he won was no longer being preached.

Just about every non-Catholic Christian church in the world can trace its roots back to that moment. Even Roman Catholics owe a debt of gratitude to Martin Luther. Because of him, the Bible was translated so they can now read the good news of God's love in their native tongues and worship in their own languages.

The tiny seed of the gospel changes hearts and lives. It spreads like a spark on a dry prairie. The amazing thing is that anyone can plant that seed.

Anyone can light that spark.

Even if you never become a great preacher like Dwight L. Moody or Billy Sunday or Billy Graham, even if you never change the world like Peter or Paul or Martin Luther, you can be an Edward Kimball. You can tell others of Jesus' love, because anyone can plant a seed.

Today I am thankful for/that _____

_____

Holy Spirit, thank you for planting the seed
of faith in my heart. Use me to share the
seed of the gospel with others. Amen.

DAY 19

AN UNFINISHED MASTERPIECE

**[I am] confident of this, that he who began a good work
in you will carry it on to completion until
the day of Christ Jesus.**

PHILIPPIANS 1:6

The history of art and literature is littered with unfinished masterpieces—works of art which, for one reason or another, were left incomplete. For example, the picture of George Washington which adorns our dollar bill was taken from a portrait painted by an artist named Gilbert Stuart, but the actual portrait was never finished. Three-quarters of the canvas remain a sea of white. Gilbert only completed Washington's face.

The composer Wolfgang Amadeus Mozart ironically never finished his funeral dirge *Requiem,* because he died while composing it.

The author Charles Dickens famously released his books in weekly or monthly segments in the newspaper—they were called serial publications. The problem is he died halfway through the writing of his final novel *The Mystery of Edwin Drood*. We will forever have to wonder what actually happened to Edwin Drood.

Our world has long been fascinated by the unfinished masterpieces of great artists. What would their works have looked or sounded like and how would they have ended had the artists been able to finish them?

I was thinking about unfinished masterpieces this last week as I conducted the funeral of a good friend from my church. The text for her funeral sermon was Philippians 1:6.

My friend's life was a masterpiece—a masterpiece of God's grace. God began "a good work" in her on the day her parents took her to be baptized. In her baptism, he planted a seed in her heart—the seed of faith. Through his Word and sacraments, he watered and cared for that faith. God's hand moved time and space so that she could know Jesus and what he did to save her.

Now she is enjoying the heaven Jesus won for her when he painted his blood on the canvas of the cross for all her sins. Her time here on earth and her life forever in heaven are truly a masterpiece of God's grace.

Yet her masterpiece remains unfinished.

HER MASTERPIECE WON'T BE FINISHED UNTIL JUDGMENT DAY.

Yes, she is in heaven. Yes, she is happy and celebrating and enjoying perfection. But according to Paul, her masterpiece won't be complete "until the day of Christ Jesus."

Her masterpiece won't be finished until judgment day.

When we die, our bodies and souls separate. Our bodies return to dust. Our souls go before God for judgment. The souls of those who believe in Jesus in this life will enjoy the forgiveness and heaven he won for them. The souls of those who do not believe will receive the punishment in hell that we all deserve.

But on the Last Day, Jesus will physically raise all the dead and glorify the bodies of all believers. Our souls and our bodies will be reunited. We will then live together, body and soul, in the new heaven and new earth forever.

One day, my friend's soul will be reunited with her body. Then she will run and jump and make cinnamon rolls again. Then the work which began on the day of her baptism will be complete. Then she will be complete. God's masterpiece will finally be finished.

For now, she is with God. She is happy and perfect and safe. One day I will see her again, because God is a prolific artist. He has many other masterpieces, including my life and yours.

They just aren't finished yet.

Today I am thankful for/that _____

_____

Lord, thank you for the good work you began in me so many years ago. Help me to trust that you will bring it to completion one day. Amen.

DAY 20
OXYGEN MASKS

Fathers, do not exasperate your children; instead, bring them up in the training and instruction of the Lord.

EPHESIANS 6:4

On April 17, 2018, Southwest flight 1380 was en route from New York to Dallas when it was forced to make an emergency landing in Philadelphia. At 30,000 feet, one of the engines blew, sending shrapnel into the plane, breaking a window, and damaging the fuselage.

One passenger died and seven others were injured.

I remember watching it on the news. It was only later that I learned I knew one of the passengers from Flight 1380. A fellow pastor and his wife were flying to San Antonio for a pastor's retreat. He shared on Facebook the panic-filled moments as the oxygen masks fell, passengers screamed, and everyone braced for impact.

By God's good grace, my friend and his wife walked away uninjured. Their harrowing experience got me thinking about the oxygen masks on the airplane. As the cabin depressurized and smoke billowed through the broken window, those oxygen masks became invaluable.

I wonder if everybody on the plane followed the flight attendant's preflight instructions about those masks. If you've ever flown, you've heard the preflight speech: "If the cabin loses pressure, please put on your own oxygen mask first before helping other passengers who may need assistance."

The first time I heard that, I thought it was selfish. You should help other people first and worry about yourself later. But then I understood. If you pass out from lack of oxygen, you can't help anybody.

As Christian parents and grandparents, God has given us the responsibility to raise up our children in the training and instruction of the Lord. God wants us to help them breathe deeply the pure oxygen of his Word. But the truth is we won't be able to help them if we don't have our own masks on first.

Only when we see in God's Word our own sinfulness and the amazing forgiveness Jesus won for us will we be properly motivated to share that good news with others. Only as we grow in his Word will we have the courage, words, and understanding we need to help others see his love.

God has given us parents the difficult task of guiding our children through the treacherous maze of this sinful world. The only way we will be able to lovingly help them traverse the trials to come is if we first have our own masks firmly in place. Through his Word, God will help us engage our children in the important conversations and answer their tough questions.

So put your oxygen mask on. Go to church every Sunday. Go to Sunday school. Read your Bible at home. Breathe deeply from the pure oxygen of God's Word.

Then help your children and grandchildren put on their masks. Take them to church. Talk about the pastor's sermon with them on the way home. Pray with them every day. Have a devotion with them at bedtime.

They may not always want to. They may complain that it is boring. But imagine if you were on Flight 1380. If your children whined or complained that they didn't want to wear the oxygen mask, would you allow them to keep it off?

YOUR KIDS NEED THE OXYGEN MASK OF GOD'S WORD.

Of course not. They need that oxygen. Their life depends on it.

Your kids need the oxygen mask of God's Word. They need church. They need

Sunday school. They need you to firmly and lovingly help them keep their oxygen masks on. There is nothing more important you could ever do for your children.

Their souls depend on it.

Today I am thankful for/that _____

_____

Almighty Lord, open my eyes to the great responsibility you have given me toward the children in my life. Use me and others so that they may see your great love and trust in you as their God and Savior. Amen.

DAY 21
INFLUENCE

Fathers, do not exasperate your children; instead, bring them up in the training and instruction of the Lord.

EPHESIANS 6:4

In 1874, Richard Dugdale, a member of the executive committee of the Prison Association of New York, made a routine visit to the jails in upstate New York. In one jail, he noticed six inmates with the same last name.

He investigated further and discovered they were all blood relatives. Curious, he undertook an in-depth study of 13 county jails from upstate New York, as well as court and poorhouse records.

In 1877, Dugdale published his findings. He traced an abnormally large number of inmates back to one man named "Max," a frontiersman of Dutch descent who was born somewhere between 1720 and 1740. Dugdale gave him the pseudonym "Max Juke." According to Dugdale, Max Juke was an uneducated drunkard, an idle and wild man.

Of the 1,200 descendants of Max Juke whom Dugdale studied, he found 140 were convicted criminals, 280 at some point were destitute, over half of all the women were considered harlots, 50 were paid prostitutes, 18 ran brothels, 7 were convicted murderers, and 67 died of syphilis.

In recent years, some scholars have compared the Juke family to that of Jonathan Edwards. Jonathan Edwards was a prominent and well-educated preacher from the 1700s. He was married to a godly woman named Sarah Pierpont, the daughter of James Pierpont, the founder of Yale University. Together, Jonathan and Sarah Edwards raised 11 children.

In 1900, A. E. Winship conducted a study of their descendants. Of the 729 descendants, Winship found nearly no lawbreakers. Instead he found 100 lawyers, 30 judges, 13 college presidents, over 100 college professors, 60 physicians, over 100 pastors and missionaries, 75 army or naval officers, three U.S. Congressmen, and one U.S. Vice-President.

Such studies show the tremendous influence parents have on their children and future generations. Consciously and subconsciously we all pass on values and habits—both good and bad—to our children. We often don't even realize how much of who we are is because of who we saw our parents be.

As Christians, we should recognize and thank God for the faith and values our parents passed on to us. May God help us to pass them on to the next generation. But we also need to humbly recognize the sins and foibles we have learned and assumed from our parents.

Though it's hard, with God's help and forgiveness, you can stop the cycle in your family—the cycle of alcoholism, the cycle of abuse, the cycle of anger or divorce. Pray about it. Talk about it openly with your children. Find strength in God's Word and support in his church.

NEVER FORGET HOW YOU ACT AROUND YOUR CHILDREN.

Never forget that how you act around your children today will not only shape who they are, but also affect generations to come.

Take a moment today to ask yourself these questions: What godly values and habits did my parents pass on to me? What negative traits and sins have I inherited? What lessons are my children learning by watching me?

Today I am thankful for/that _____

_____

Heavenly Father, help me to be an example of faith and faithful services to the generations who come after me. Amen.

DAY 22
HOME

"My Father's house has many rooms; if that were not so, would I have told you that I am going there to prepare a place for you?"

JOHN 14:2

Where are you from? That seems like such a simple question.

For some of us, though, it's not quite so simple. You see, I've moved quite a bit in my life. I was born in Toledo, Ohio. I spent half of my childhood in the city of Saginaw, Michigan, and the other half in a tiny town called Stevensville, Michigan. Since then, I've lived in Watertown, Wisconsin; Mequon, Wisconsin; Milwaukee, Wisconsin; Monterrey, Mexico; Mexico City, Mexico; Miami, Florida; and now Edna, Texas.

So how should I answer that question? Where am I from? Usually I say I'm from Michigan because that's where I spent most of my childhood. That's what I've always considered home. Realistically, though, I could now say I'm from Edna, Texas, because I've lived here longer than any other place in my entire life.

Where are you from? What do you consider your home?

On the night before he died, Jesus told his disciples, "My Father's house has many rooms . . . I am going there to prepare a place for you." I recently read that verse to the residents at our local nursing home. Then I thought about it. That verse probably doesn't sound so appealing to them. The nursing home has many rooms as well.

When you hear Jesus speak about the "rooms" of heaven, don't picture the small two-person rooms at your local nursing home or even your bedroom or living room or kitchen. That's not what Jesus was talking about.

The King James Version of the Bible translated it this way, "In my Father's house are many mansions." Now we're getting somewhere.

Don't think small and simple. Picture big and luxurious. Honestly, though, the word Jesus used doesn't literally mean "mansion" either. It means "a permanent dwelling place"—a permanent residence. It means "home."

"My Father's house has many *homes*. . . . I am going there to prepare a place for you." Right now, Jesus is preparing a home in heaven just for you—a room, an apartment, a house, a mansion—with your name on the mailbox.

It's a fact. You can be sure you are going to heaven—not because you are such a good person or because you go to church every Sunday, but because Jesus left his home in heaven to be born in Bethlehem, to be raised in Nazareth, to live in Capernaum, and to die on Calvary.

You can be sure you're going to heaven because it doesn't depend on you. Jesus suffered God's anger for your sins in your place. He died your death and suffered your hell. He said, "It is finished!" It is all taken care of. You are forever forgiven because he took your place.

ALL WHO BELIEVE IN JESUS . . . HAVE A HOME WAITING FOR THEM IN HEAVEN.

All who believe in Jesus as their Savior from sin have a home waiting for them in heaven, prepared specifically for them by Jesus, with their name on the mailbox.

That truth gives us a confidence and a peace the world cannot understand. In the end, what do I have to worry about? I'm going to heaven.

When you struggle with the pains and frustrations of this world, just remember that your current address is not your permanent address. You aren't home yet. Because of Jesus, your home is waiting for you in the happiness of heaven.

Your name is already on the mailbox.

Today I am thankful for/that _____

_____

Dear Jesus, thank you for winning and preparing for me a home in heaven. As I struggle with the pains and problems of this sinful world, turn my eyes and heart to my eternal home. Amen.

---◆---

DAY 23
SAYING GRACE

Rejoice always, pray continually, give thanks in all circumstances.

1 THESSALONIANS 5:16-18

◆

It's a scene often repeated in Christian homes. Due to soccer practice, ballet rehearsal, and a meeting at work, supper is late. The family finally sits down together. Everybody is starving. Kids and Dad start piling food on their plates.

Mom walks into the room just as Dad lifts his fork to his mouth. She immediately lunges toward him in what looks like a slow-motion scene from an action movie.

"Noooooo!" She grabs his arm. "We haven't prayed yet!"

Or maybe you sit down with your family for dinner and Mom suddenly asks, "Wait a minute. Did we already pray?" The kids look at each other dazed and confused.

"I don't remember," Dad replies, scratching his head. "I think so. Maybe we should pray again just to make sure."

Then there is the whole dilemma of snacks and light meals. Do you pray for a bowl of soup? Does a salad count as a meal? Do nachos and popcorn at the movie theater warrant a prayer? What if it's a hotdog?

For centuries, Christians have said grace. They have given thanks. They have asked God's blessing on the food they are about to eat.

But sometimes we forget. We often say the words without thinking about what we are saying (and then can't remember if we even prayed or not). For some, "Thou shalt pray before thy meal" becomes the Eleventh Commandment. If you don't pray before you eat, you are in danger of the fires of hell.

Maybe it's time we re-evaluate the whole matter of praying before we eat.

First of all, we have to admit that nowhere in the Bible does God command us to pray before a meal. He doesn't. Lightning will not strike you down if you do not pray before you eat.

MEALTIME PRESENTS A WONDERFUL OPPORTUNITY TO PRAY.

God does, however, tell us to pray continually and to give thanks in all circumstances. Mealtime presents a wonderful opportunity to pray. It gives parents the opportunity to teach their children to say "thank you" to the Giver of all good gifts. It keeps us in the habit of praying together as families.

Sadly, many Christians have fallen out of the practice of praying at mealtime. Many families don't even sit down together to eat anymore. The TV is on. The kids are eating in the living room. Everybody is on their phones.

You don't have to pray before you eat, but it is a wonderful way to begin each meal. It's good for you. It's good for your children. It brings joy to God's heart to hear your prayers.

Allow me, however, a few friendly tips to help you and your family avoid the pitfalls of mealtime prayers.

First of all, mix it up. Every so often, instead of praying the same memorized prayer before the meal, have one member of the family say a prayer in his or her own words. Sometimes the simplest prayers are the best.

Occasionally, go around the table and have each person in the family say one thing for which they are thankful. A brief pause and reminder before you pray to think about what you are saying can help everyone focus. Of course, turning off the TV and putting phones away is also a good habit.

In the end, though, you are free. There is no Eleventh Commandment. You are not going to hell if you take a bite of your hotdog without first saying a prayer.

But it is so good for you to talk to God in prayer. He loves to hear from you. We have much for which to give him thanks.

So pray continually. Give thanks in all circumstances—even at mealtime.

Today I am thankful for/that _____

_____

Oh give thanks to the Lord, for he is good.
His mercy endures forever. Amen.

DAY 24
GOD'S NOT DEAD

Jesus called out with a loud voice, "Father, into your hands I commit my spirit." When he had said this, he breathed his last.

LUKE 23:46

◆

"God is dead."

That is what college freshman Josh Wheaton refused to write down on a piece of paper in the 2014 movie *God's Not Dead*. The movie is the story of Wheaton's struggle to stand firm in his faith as he faced a failing grade and taunts from his atheist professor.

The statement "God is dead" did not originate with the movie. It was made famous by a German philosopher named Friedrich Nietzsche. Nietzsche, however, didn't believe God had died. Rather, he believed the idea of God had died. Nietzsche never really believed God existed. He insisted man invented God to fill his need to explain life and its meaning.

With the rise of the theory of evolution and the increasing secularization of Europe, Nietzsche boldly declared God to be dead. Society—the world—no longer needed the crutch of faith.

As Christians, we stand with Josh Wheaton and refuse to affirm such a lie. God is not dead.

There was a time, though, when that statement was true. God did die.

It is hard for us to wrap our minds around such a thought. God is eternal. He has no beginning or end. God cannot die, yet God died.

Our simple human minds cannot fully understand how. Doctors of science, philosophy, and theology cannot explain it. The Bible nevertheless clearly proclaims it.

God became a man. That man died. Therefore, God died. Though we cannot fully explain or understand it, we cling to that truth.

The almighty, eternal God who fills all things became a human being in time and space in order to take your place. He became a man in order to die the death you deserve for all the mistakes of your youth, for the dark and dirty secrets hidden in the closets of your life, for every bad word and ugly thought you have ever had. You deserve to suffer the death of hell, but God loved you so much he came to take your place.

On a dark hill two thousand years ago, God died. On that day, the sun stopped shining, the earth shook, and God breathed no more.

Yet God is not dead.

On the third day, Jesus' spirit once again entered his body. Air once again entered his lungs. His heart began to beat. God would not stay dead. Death could never win.

That is what we celebrate every year during Holy Week. We stare in awestruck gratitude watching our God die on the cross in our place. Then we peek with giddy joy into the empty tomb. God is not dead! He is alive and he promises us that because he lives, we too will live (John 14:19).

"NIETZSCHE IS DEAD—GOD."

Can I prove any of this? No. It is a truth we accept by faith. I am reminded, however, of a T-shirt a friend of mine had in college. On the front it said, "God is dead—Nietzsche." On the back it said, "Nietzsche is dead—God."

Nietzsche died, and when he did, he stood before the almighty God whose existence he denied in life.

You will die one day. I will die one day. Then we will see with our physical eyes what we can only see now by faith. Then we will enjoy the life our God won for us with his death. Until then, there will be those who doubt—those who refuse to believe. Through faith, however, we know and believe the truth.

God is not dead.

Today I am thankful for/that _____

---

*Dear Jesus, in our world today, we are made to
feel foolish for our faith. Help me to trust every
day that you are real, that you did die
and rise again for my sins. Amen.*

◆

DAY 25
REPETITION

**These commandments that I give you today are to be on
your hearts. Impress them on your children. Talk about
them when you sit at home and when you walk along
the road, when you lie down and when you get up.**

DEUTERONOMY 6:6,7

◆

For over 15 years, I have taught a weekly Bible study at our local nursing home in Edna, Texas. I'll be honest. Teaching a Bible class at a nursing home isn't always easy. Interruptions and distractions are a constant problem. Some of the residents suffer from Alzheimer's or dementia. It's hard to keep some of them awake for the entire class (though, honestly, I have that problem at church as well).

One of the fun things, however, about going to the nursing home is that my jokes never get old. The same joke which makes my wife roll her eyes because she has heard it a thousand times, makes them laugh every time.

But jokes aren't the only things I repeat at the nursing home. I also find myself repeating the same Bible truths and stories over and over again. I talk about our sins—the mistakes and regrets of our lives, our anger and drinking, our lies and laziness. I talk about our Savior—how he suffered the punishment of our sins on the cross, how he won for us the gift of heaven. I talk about heaven a lot—how beautiful it will be, how good we will feel, how happy we will be. Over and over again, they hear the same truths: sin, Savior, heaven.

One of the complaints I often hear as a pastor is that we are always repeating the same things—how we are sinners and how Jesus saved us. The young people and children of our congregation complain that we make them memorize Bible verses and hymns, saying and singing them over and over again. It honestly gets a little repetitive.

REPETITION IS A GOOD THING.

But repetition is a good thing. There's an old Latin proverb which says, "*Repetitio mater studiorum est.*" Literally, "Repetition is the mother of learning." We need to hear the basic truths of the Bible over and over again because we too easily forget. We need to hear the basic truths of the Bible over and over again because they are vitally important.

A little over 10 years ago, a wonderful woman named Hazel went to my first Bible study at the nursing home. For eight years, she rarely missed a class. She heard me repeat the same jokes again and again. She heard me repeat the same Bible truths over and over.

Towards the end, Hazel became extremely confused and disoriented. She could no longer remember names or faces. But I could still read to her Psalm 23 or John 3:16 or sing "Amazing Grace" or "Jesus Loves Me," and she would be right there with me. She never forgot those Bible verses and songs because she had heard them repeated often during her life.

Two years ago, I went to see Hazel in her room. She could no longer speak. Her mind was mostly gone. She barely opened her eyes. But then I sang to her "Amazing Grace" and "Jesus, Loves Me"—those songs she had heard repeatedly since she was a child. Her eyes grew moist. She smiled. Hazel entered heaven four days later.

Repetition is a good thing. Oh, did I already say that?

Today I am thankful for/that _____

_____

Lord, help me to never tire of the oft-repeated
truths of your Word. Keep them always
in my heart and mind. Amen.

DAY 26
SLEEP TIGHT

**In peace I will lie down and sleep, for you alone,
Lord, make me dwell in safety.**

PSALM 4:8

◆

According to recent studies, anywhere from 40 to 60 million Americans suffer from insomnia. They can't sleep.

How about you? Do you struggle to fall asleep? Do you wake up in the middle of the night unable to go back to sleep?

The causes of insomnia are many. Some are physical. Drinking too much caffeine, using your computer, or watching TV before going to bed can keep you up. Some illnesses affect our ability to sleep. Even our age affects our sleep patterns.

Many of the people I know who have trouble sleeping tell me it's because they have a hard time turning off their minds. The problems of today and the challenges of tomorrow roll around in their heads and keep them from drifting to sleep.

For others, it's guilt. Regret over ugly words said yesterday or a mistake made years ago creeps into their thoughts as they lie in the quiet of the night.

Fear is another sleep killer. For some reason, as we lie in our beds, our minds often drift to our own mortality. Many people are afraid to close their eyes at night for fear they won't open them again.

Do you have a hard time turning your mind off at night? God can help. His promises to help us deal with many of the worries and fears which keep us awake at night.

Do guilt and regret tie your stomach in knots? No matter how many hours you stay awake fretting over what you said and did, you can't go back and change it. You can, however, find comfort in God's forgiveness. No matter how badly you messed up, Jesus already suffered your punishment on the cross. God's forgiveness knows no end. God has let it go. You can too.

Because of the forgiveness Jesus won for us, God promises us a home with him forever in heaven. Death is not the end. It is merely a door through which we pass on our way to the happiness of heaven.

When I was a boy, my parents taught me to pray every night: "Now I lay me down to sleep; I pray the Lord my soul to keep. If I should die before I wake, I pray the Lord my soul to take." What a comfort! If I don't open my eyes again here on earth, because of Jesus I can be sure I will open them to the glories of heaven.

YOU DON'T HAVE TO WORRY ABOUT TOMORROW.

And, if Jesus suffered our hell in our place, if he won for us a home in heaven when we die, then we can also be sure he will make everything else in our lives work for our good (Romans 8:28-32). You don't have to worry about tomorrow. God is in control.

Do you have a hard time turning off your mind at night? As you lie in bed, take your regrets, fears, and worries to God in prayer. Remember his promises of forgiveness and heaven. Remember his presence and protection in your life. If nothing else, open your Bible and read for a while from the book of Psalms.

May God grant you peaceful sleep.

Today I am thankful for/that _____

_____

Lord, take my fears and worries. Help me to
Trust in you and sleep in peace. Amen.

DAY 27
LET'S TALK ABOUT HELL

"Then he will say to those on his left, 'Depart from me, you who are cursed, into the eternal fire prepared for the devil and his angels.'"

MATTHEW 25:41

49

I don't know how it happened. Somehow I just slowly stopped talking about it. I mean, I would refer to it briefly in passing in my articles and blog. I would mention it by name in my sermons, but I didn't really talk about it anymore.

Then the other night, one of the children in my catechism class asked me, "Pastor, what is hell like?" As I answered her question, reality rear-ended me like a Mack truck. I couldn't remember the last time I had talked about what hell is like.

A number of years ago, Gallup surveyed Americans about their belief in the afterlife. The survey showed that 81% of Americans believe in the existence of heaven. Surprisingly, 70% said they believed in the existence of hell. Ever the optimists, 77% of Americans rated their chances of going to heaven as "good" or "excellent," while less than one-half of 1% believed they would end up in hell.

Though most people in our country believe in the reality of hell, few believe there is actually a possibility they could end up there.

What is hell like? Jesus described hell as a place of "weeping and gnashing of teeth" where "the worm does not die and the fire is not quenched." Hell is a prison originally prepared for the devil and his demons.

The punishment of hell is complete separation from God and his love—being locked out of his presence forever. One of the horrific ironies of hell is that those condemned to its dungeons will be able to see the heaven they are missing. They will be watching through a window from the outside looking in.

Hell is horror. Hell is suffering. Imagine the worst pain you have ever felt in your life. Now multiply that by 10,000 and think about it never ending. That is hell. Hell is real and you deserve to go there. So do I. The punishment of just one sin is the perpetual pain of hell.

Only when we feel the flames of hell nipping at our feet can we truly appreciate what Jesus did for us. He rescued us. Like a heroic fireman, he came to our home and pulled us from the flames. In fact, he gave his life to do so. On the cross, Jesus suffered our punishment—that complete separation from God and his love we deserve for every one of the millions of sins we commit in our lives.

Because he took our punishment, we have been rescued from the flames. With his death on the cross, Jesus won the gift of heaven for all people. That gift becomes ours personally through faith. Whoever believes in Jesus as their Savior receives the gift of heaven. Whoever does not believe in Jesus, though, will be condemned to the death penalty of hell.

Of the over seven billion people who populate our planet today, 2.2 billion profess to believe in Jesus. That means five billion people in our world today don't believe in Jesus. According to the Bible, what is going to happen to them?

IT IS LOVE TO TALK ABOUT HELL.

Nobody likes to talk about that. It's not politically correct. It's a buzzkill. It's depressing. But it is love to talk about hell. It is love to warn people of the hell they deserve and assure them of the heaven Jesus won for them. Only when the flames of hell are singeing the soles of our feet, can we truly appreciate what Jesus did to save us.

So let's talk about hell.

Today I am thankful for/that _____

_____

Lord, thank you for saving me from the horrors of hell which I deserve. Help me to always remember and appreciate what you sacrificed and suffered for me. Amen.

———————◆———————

DAY 28
CASTING CARES

Cast all your anxiety on him because he cares for you.

1 PETER 5:7

◆

Peter's words are simple enough to understand. When you are worried, when you are afraid, when you are stressed, turn it over to God. He loves you. Let him take care of it.

We do that as Christians, don't we? We go to church. We hear God's promises. We return home encouraged. We decide we aren't going to worry any more. We aren't going to stress. God is in control. He loves me. He forgives me. I'm going to heaven.

But then on Monday morning, the credit card bill comes. How did we get so far into debt? How are we going to pay for this? What are we going to do?

You go to the doctor on Tuesday. He says that he has to run more tests, but it looks like cancer. Why God? Why are you doing this to me?

On Wednesday, your boss tells you that this year the company is going to have to lay people off. What else can go wrong?

It's fitting that Peter tells us to "cast" our anxiety on God. Whenever I hear that verse, it makes me think of fishing. In fishing, when you cast, you throw the lure away from you into the water.

After you cast, though, you always reel it back in.

How often don't we do that as Christians? We walk out of church on Sunday renewed and refreshed, relying on God. We cast all our cares on him. But then come Monday's problems, Tuesday's troubles, Wednesday's worries, and we reel the anxiety back in.

A young lady from my congregation recently wrote on Facebook, "FROG (Fully Rely on God). That's what I'm going to do from now on." A friend quickly and wisely responded, "Just wish it was as easy to do as it is to say."

FIND IN GOD'S PROMISES THE PEACE YOU NEED.

So how do we do it? How do we trust God on Tuesday with the same confidence we feel walking out of church on Sunday? Just think about what happened in church that gave you such peace and confidence.

Simply put, in our worship, we have a conversation with God. We talk to him in prayer. We cast on him all our worries and cares. We then hear him speak to us in his Word and sacraments. Then we walk out of his presence feeling refreshed and renewed.

Do you find yourself reeling your worries back in during the week? That's because you need to converse with God during the week as well. Talk to him in prayer. Cast your cares on him. And then turn to the promises of his Word. Open up your Bibles. Read Romans chapter 8, Psalm 23, Psalm 46, or any of the other hundreds of comforting passages of Scripture. Find in God's promises the peace you need.

As frail human beings, we will always struggle to fully rely on God. We all at times forget to let go and let God take care of our troubles, and we reel our worries back in. When we do that, we must go back and have a conversation with our Savior God.

Cast all your cares on him. He cares for you.

Today I am thankful for/that _____

_____

*Heavenly Father, you know my worries and fears.
You know the struggles I am having. Help me
to leave them all in your loving and
powerful hands. Help me to trust
that you care for me. Amen.*

DAY 29
THE SOPHOMORE SYNDROME

**If you think you are standing firm, be careful that you
don't fall!**

1 CORINTHIANS 10:12

When I was in my second year of high school, my father would often remind me of what it meant to be a sophomore. The word *sophomore* comes from the Greek language and literally means, "wise fool."

The idea is that as a sophomore you have one year of studies under your belt. You have some knowledge, but you still have a lot to learn.

You are a wise fool.

What gets many sophomores—and teenagers in general—in trouble is they think they know more than they do. They are on their way to adulthood and are growing more aware of the world around them. They are becoming free thinkers, but they still lack experience, maturity, and knowledge. The older we get the more we realize how much we really don't know.

In that sense, all Christians are sophomores.

The apostle Paul once wrote a letter to his young protégé, Timothy, and reminded him: "From infancy you have known the Holy Scriptures, which are able to make you wise for salvation through faith in Christ Jesus" (2 Timothy 3:15).

If you know and believe in Jesus as your Savior, you are truly wise.

As Christians, though, we need to be aware of the Sophomore Syndrome. We have some knowledge. We have some wisdom. Yet we still have a lot to learn. We are wise fools.

One of the devil's big tricks is to tempt us to be overconfident in our faith. He whispers in our ears, "You went to Sunday school as a kid. You've gone to church over the years. You know what the Bible says. You don't need to go to church anymore. You don't need to read your Bible or go to Sunday school. You know what you need to know."

The problem is we easily forget how easily we forget. If you don't use it, you lose it. The longer we get away from God's Word, the more we lose. Even if you are able to remember everything you learned as a child, there is still a lot that you don't know.

Take me, for example. My father is a pastor. I went to a Christian elementary and middle school. I went to Sunday school every Sunday. I attended Catechism classes. I went to a Christian high school, college, and seminary. I have been a pastor for over 20 years, and I am still learning new things from God's Word.

Don't become complacent in your faith. Be careful of thinking you know more than you do. Remember Paul's warning to the Christians in the city of Corinth: "If you think you are standing firm, be careful that you don't fall!"

WE ARE ALL SOPHOMORES. WE STILL HAVE A LOT TO LEARN.

We are all sophomores. We still have a lot to learn. We won't graduate until the day God hands us our diploma at the gates of heaven.

For now, we are wise fools.

Today I am thankful for/that _____

_____

Lord, thank you for the wisdom and knowledge you have given me, especially about you. Help me to humbly recognize how much I still need to learn and grow. Amen.

DAY 30
AN ENDLESS WINTER

**"We must go through many hardships to
enter the kingdom of God."**

ACTS 14:22

❖

"There is no way that this winter is ever going to end."

That is a line from one of my favorite movies, *Groundhog Day,* starring Bill Murray. In the movie, Bill Murray's character is forced to relive the same cold winter day, Groundhog Day, over and over again. He feels trapped, like the day is never going to end. It leads him to despair.

I thought of that movie last week as I watched The Weather Channel. You see, while I now reside in Texas, I'm from Michigan. I'll be honest. I don't miss the snow or cold. I don't miss scraping off my car or shoveling the sidewalk. I remember when February came around each year, I would look out the window and think, "Is this winter ever going to end?"

Sometimes in our lives it feels like our own personal winters are never going to end. The non-stop arguing with your husband, the other kids at school making fun of you, the pain of sickness or the worry of debt—when we have problems in our lives, it feels like we are stuck in a snowdrift spinning our wheels. It feels like it will never end.

Two thousand years ago, a group of Christian churches was having problems. They were being persecuted for their faith. They were being ridiculed, beaten up, and even thrown into prison. They were in the middle of a dark and cold winter which seemed like it would never end.

So the apostle Paul went to visit them. He encouraged them with these words: "We must go through many hardships to enter the kingdom of God." That doesn't sound very encouraging, does it? Basically, Paul was saying, "You're going to suffer."

The encouraging word in that verse is the word "through." We are going *through* the hardships. In other words, they will end one day. The ancient Persian proverb is right: "This too shall pass."

Just look back on your life. God has gotten you through every storm and hardship so far. How will he not also get you through this one? The winter is going to end . . . but it may be a while. Your pains or problems may last for months or even years, but God will eventually get you through.

WINTER IS GOING TO END . . . BUT IT MAY BE A WHILE.

They will end—if not here on earth, then when you get to heaven. Remember, we are going through these trials on our way to heaven. You can be sure of that because Jesus, your Savior, came and suffered the winter of God's discontent in your place.

For all your doubts and worry, for all your complaining about your lot in life, for all your failings and sins, Jesus died. You will never have to suffer the endless hardship of hell because Jesus suffered it in your place. You are forgiven. You are on your way to heaven.

Know that you will have hardships along the way. God promises you, though, that his hardships serve a purpose. He promises they are for your good. He promises they will one day end.

Today is Groundhog Day. As I write these words, we still don't know if Punxsutawney Phil will see his shadow or not. We don't know how much longer this winter will last, but be sure that it will end, just like your trials and fears will one day end. God will get you through them on your way to heaven.

Today I am thankful for/that _____

_____

Lord, give me peace and patience as I wait for this winter in my life to end. Amen.

DAY 31
SALAD BAR CHRISTIANITY

**If anyone takes words away from this scroll of
prophecy, God will take away from that person
any share in the tree of life and in the Holy
City, which are described in this scroll.**

REVELATION 22:19

◆

I remember the first salad bar I went to when I was a kid. Back then it was
a relatively new concept. People could pick and choose what they wanted.
No more having to take the tomatoes off or ask for extra dressing.

You get to decide.

Today, salad bars and buffets are seemingly everywhere. People love them.
You are in control—you choose what you want to eat.

The same mentality is more and more popular in Christian churches today.
I call it "Salad Bar Christianity."

Salad Bar Christianity is a relatively new innovation. As science and
invention bloomed in the 18th and 19th centuries, so did man's image of
himself. Scientists began to say, "God is unnecessary." Philosophers began
to say, "God is dead." Theologians began to say, "The Bible isn't completely
true." *Humanism*—the idea that humankind can achieve whatever it puts
its mind to—became the dominant way of thinking.

It was the Tower of Babel revisited. Humans in their pride no longer
needed God.

Soon, many Christians were being taught that the Bible was an ancient
book full of myths and legends. Sure, truths about God could be gleaned
from its pages, but first we had to cut out all the myths and legends.

As the 19th century turned into the 20th, the optimism of *humanism* turned
into the skepticism of *modernism* which turned into the relativism
of *postmodernism*. That sure is a lot of *-isms*, but what it means is simply
that our world stopped believing in absolute truth. As Pilate skeptically
asked Jesus on the first Good Friday, "What is truth?" (John 18:38). For
our world, absolute truth doesn't exist, or at least no one can claim to
know it.

Now each person chooses for themselves what is true. To criticize or judge another person's philosophy or choice is considered intolerant. Every opinion is equally valid.

That way of thinking has led to Salad Bar Christianity. Many Christians today treat the Bible like a buffet. They pick and choose what they want to believe from the Bible. They look for churches that teach what they want to believe. They tell God, "This is what I want you to tell me."

The problem with Salad Bar Christianity is it means you believe in a God who can't even get his own story straight. What kind of God would we have if his book of revelation to us is full of errors and outdated ideas?

Even more importantly, Salad Bar Christianity makes you god. That's its appeal. God is no longer telling you what you should believe. You are telling him what you want to believe. You are the boss. You decide.

THE BIBLE ISN'T A BUFFET.

Is the Bible always easy to understand or accept? No. As sinful human beings, we don't always like what it says. Our modern world definitely doesn't like what it says. But the Bible isn't a buffet. It's not our word. It's God's Word.

We have no right to change it.

Today I am thankful for/that _____

_____

Eternal Lord, your Word is completely true. Help me to hold tight to its teachings all the days of my life. Amen.

DAY 32
SUFFERING IN SILENCE

**"If your brother or sister sins, go and point out their
fault, just between the two of you. If they listen
to you, you have won them over."**

MATTHEW 18:15

◆

A friend on Facebook recently suggested a blog by a young woman who is about to get married for the second time. In her blog, she speaks of the lessons she learned from her first marriage.

"I didn't speak my mind about how I truly felt. I shoved it down, in an effort to be pleasing and perfect. . . . Anger, resentment and self-loathing had taken center stage in our marriage." After seven years of keeping it all in, the blogger found herself in the hospital with a bleeding ulcer.

As a pastor, I have dealt with numerous people who have struggled in relationships because they allow others to hurt them. They suffer in silence until the resentment and anger eat away their health, their relationships, and their lives.

Are you a compulsive people-pleaser? Do you put up with bad behavior? Do you suffer in silence?

Sadly, the advice our friends give us is to give that person a taste of their own medicine. You can't let people walk all over you. You have to look out for yourself. The advice professional counselors often give is to express your anger. You have to let steam out of the kettle before it blows.

The problem with such advice is that it is based on selfishness. It doesn't really deal with the anger. In fact, oftentimes it gives way to the anger.

When someone slaps you on the cheek, what does Jesus tell you to do? Turn so they can strike the other one as well (Matthew 5:39). Jesus speaks of loving our enemies and praying for those who do us wrong (Matthew 5:44). The apostle Paul urges us to overcome evil with good (Romans 12:21).

But won't that lead to the problems the young woman mentioned in her blog? Won't that enable the other person to continue in their bad behavior? Won't that eventually give me a bleeding ulcer?

Patiently showing love and forgiveness doesn't mean suffering in silence. It is not love to allow someone to treat you poorly.

Yes, God wants you to forgive the person, but he also wants you to speak the truth in love (Ephesians 4:15). When your husband cusses at you or calls you unrepeatable names, it doesn't help him for you to suffer in silence. God wants you to speak up—not in anger, but in love. He wants you to patiently help him to be the man God wants him to be.

Such love is patient but firm. Such love doesn't enable the person to continue in bad behavior. Such love may eventually lead you to leave in order to help the person see how hurtful their behavior is. The motivation, however, is always love and not anger.

But then how do we get rid of the anger? How do we keep the resentment from building up inside us?

The only way is by forgiving just as God forgives you in Jesus.

Stop looking at what the other person has done to you. Look at yourself and all the ugly things you have done in your life. God forgives you because of Jesus. You can forgive your husband. You can forgive your wife. I know it's hard. It takes prayer and the strength God gives in his Word, but you can forgive.

LOVE DOES NOT SUFFER IN SILENCE. LOVE SPEAKS.

Forgiving, however, doesn't mean allowing them to continue in their bad behavior. Love does not suffer in silence. Love speaks.

Today I am thankful for/that _____

_____

Merciful God, give me the mercy to forgive those who do me wrong. Give me the courage to speak up and try to help them. Amen.

DAY 33
COMPLICATED

**I do not do the good I want to do, but the evil I do not
want to do—this I keep on doing. . . . Who will
rescue me from this body that is subject to
death? Thanks be to God, who delivers
me through Jesus Christ our Lord.**

ROMANS 7:19,24,25

◆

When my daughter was nine years old, I took her to see Disney's reimagining of *Sleeping Beauty*, called *Maleficent*, starring Angelina Jolie.

In the original film/version/story, Maleficent was the evil witch who placed a curse on the newborn Princess Aurora. According to the curse, young Aurora would prick her finger on a spinning wheel before her 16th birthday, casting her into a death-like sleep. The only thing which could wake her from her slumber was "true love's kiss." In *Sleeping Beauty*, Maleficent is pure evil. She is finally defeated by Prince Phillip, who awakens the sleeping princess with a kiss.

The modern reimagining gives us the backstory of the wicked witch. We follow her on her journey from good fairy to wicked witch. We are allowed to see her struggle with love, hurt, and hate. In the remake, Maleficent is not pure evil.

She is complicated.

**CHRISTIANS ARE
COMPLICATED.** Christians are complicated. We like to categorize people into simple Disney categories: good guys and bad guys. Your friends and family are the good guys. Your ex-husband, your unfair boss, and that child molester who just moved into town are the bad guys. People are either good or evil.

Sadly, the truth is much more complicated. According to the Bible, all people are born sinful (Psalm 51:5). We all have done evil things in our lives (Romans 3:23). We have lied and hurt and cheated. By nature, we are the bad guys.

That's why Jesus came. He is the only true hero of our story. Jesus is not complicated. He is pure love. In his love, he gave his life to save us from the fiery punishment our evil deeds deserve.

He then sent his Holy Spirit into our hearts through Baptism and his Word. He gave us faith. He took us hurting and hating villains and made us children of God.

If God is the King of the universe and you are his child, then you are a prince or a princess. Because of Jesus, you are the good guy. Because of Jesus, you are going to heaven.

But, as I said before, Christians are complicated. Though we have faith in our hearts—though we love God and want to serve him—we are not yet perfect. We still have a part of us that is selfish and angry. We have an inner struggle between good and evil. Sometimes the evil wins out. We fall. We fail. We act like the bad guy.

That doesn't mean, however, that we are pure evil. We are forgiven. We are still princes and princesses. We are at the same time sinners and saints. We are complicated.

So what about your ex-husband? What about your unfair boss? What about that child molester? Are they pure evil? We can't look into their hearts. They may be pure evil or they may simply be sinful believers who struggle with weakness and sin.

So instead of labeling people as "good" or "bad," remember that people are complicated. Try to look at them through Jesus' eyes. What does he see? He sees souls loved by him—sinners in desperate need of his forgiveness. Forgive as he has forgiven you. Remember, when Jesus looks at you, he doesn't see pure evil.

He knows you're complicated.

Today I am thankful for/that _____

_____

Almighty God, thank you for not treating me as I deserve. Thank you for your unconditional forgiveness in Jesus. Thank you for also understanding how complicated I am. Help me in my struggle against sin, as I try to be who you made me to be. Amen.

DAY 34
FAITH WE WILL FIND HOPE

**By faith even Sarah, who was past childbearing age,
was enabled to bear children because she considered
him faithful who had made the promise.**

HEBREWS 11:11

◆

I have a confession to make from my college days. It's rather embarrassing, but here goes: Every day after lunch, a large group of us guys would gather in the commons of our dorm to watch *Days of Our Lives*.

That's right—the soap opera. It's not something I'm proud of, but I was young and foolish.

I remember one storyline in particular that lasted a couple of weeks. A number of characters from the show went on a ski weekend in the mountains. There was an avalanche. A woman named Hope was lost. They searched and searched, but could not find her. Her husband, Bo, was beside himself, but then his friend John Black stood up to address the group. "We have to have faith we will find Hope," he said.

For many in our world today, that is their definition of faith. Faith is positive thinking. Faith is grasping, hoping, convincing yourself that things will work out the way you want them to.

Smiling preachers on TV tell you to think positively. God is all-powerful. He can do the impossible. They quote the apostle Paul who said, "I can do all this through him who gives me strength" (Philippians 4:13). You can achieve your dreams—you can accomplish anything—if you have enough faith.

They're right when they say God is all-powerful. He can do the impossible. Paul did say, "I can do all this through him who gives me strength." That doesn't mean, however, that Paul thought faith was simply positive thinking.

Paul wrote those words to a church in the Greek city of Philippi. He was in prison at the time and didn't know if they would set him free or execute him. Yet over and over again in the letter, he encourages us to rejoice. Paul was a positive thinker, but not in the same way some preachers use that term today.

If you have a chance over the next few days, read Paul's short letter to the Philippians. Paul didn't believe he could accomplish anything he put his mind to. Paul believed that God could accomplish everything he promised. You see, faith isn't trusting that things will work out the way you want them to. Faith means trusting in God's promises.

Paul trusted that God would use his imprisonment for his good and for the good of others. Paul knew that, even if his captors killed him, he had a home in heaven waiting for him because of Jesus.

HE PROMISES YOU A LIFE FREE OF SUFFERING IN HEAVEN.

God doesn't promise you a life free of suffering here on earth. He promises you a life free of suffering in heaven. What he promises here on earth is that he will be with us and make all things, even the pains and problems, work for our good. Faith trusts those promises.

At the end of his letter, Paul told the Philippians, "I have learned the secret to being content in any and every situation." Paul could be happy whether things worked out the way he wanted them to or not. What was the secret? "I can do all things through him who gives me strength." Paul could be happy. He could be content. He could handle anything and everything that came his way with the strength God gives in his promises.

Faith isn't simply positive thinking. Faith doesn't mean that if you just believe hard enough things will work out the way you want them to. Faith means trusting God's promises. That faith gives true hope.

Today I am thankful for/that _____

_____

*Holy Spirit, give me the faith to trust
your promises. Amen.*

DAY 35
POTUS

Let everyone be subject to the governing authorities,
for there is no authority except that
which God has established.

ROMANS 13:1

◆

When I was a kid, I wanted to be president of the United States. In school, we learned about George Washington and the cherry tree. We learned about Honest Abe and Old Hickory. Presidents were patriots. Ronald Reagan was my hero.

But as I got older something happened. I learned that not all presidents were heroes. I read about President Nixon and Watergate. I found out about President Kennedy and Marilyn Monroe. I watched as the Monica Lewinsky scandal unraveled live on TV.

Today, like many Americans, I am somewhat jaded when it comes to our political system. I have heard the promises and seen the corruption. I have watched the chasm between red states and blue states grow into a canyon.

Suffice it to say, I no longer want to be president of the United States.

The world of politics today often appears to be all about sound bites and talking points, Fox News and CNN, pundits and politicians screaming at the top of their lungs. Sincere passion too often turns to pride and prejudice. Our world has lost the ability to respectfully disagree.

Sadly, many Christians fall into that category.

The apostle Paul lived during the time of the Roman Emperor Nero. Emperor Nero was a scumbag. He murdered his own mother and poisoned his stepbrother Britannicus. He purportedly played his fiddle while the city of Rome burned, and then he blamed the Christians. Nero is the first Roman emperor to begin a statewide persecution of Christians. Peter and Paul were supposedly martyred in Rome during his rule.

It was during Nero's reign of terror that Paul wrote a letter to the Christians in the city of Rome. Even as they lived under the control of a tyrannical and corrupt government, Paul told them, "Let everyone be subject to the governing authorities, for there is no authority except that which God has established."

Nero was emperor because God had given him that position of power. Did God condone Nero's wickedness? By no means. Yet, he used it as a part of his plan of love for his people. Paul's point was that whether a government is good or not, God wants us to honor and obey it out of love and respect for him.

When we respect the authority figures he has placed over us, we are respecting God.

AS CHRISTIANS, WE RESPECTFULLY DISAGREE.

Does that mean you have to agree with everything the president of the United States says and does? Of course not. But as Christians, we respectfully disagree. We do not deride or defame our president. We don't call him a jerk or other crasser expletives.

We don't even call them Obama or Trump or Biden. We call them President Obama, President Trump, and President Biden. We pray for the president. We ask God to bless him and us through him. When he acts in a way that is contrary to God's will and Word, we ask God to forgive him. We speak up. We let him and the world know we disagree, but we do so respectfully.

By honoring him, we honor our God who placed him over us. By respecting our president, we respect our Creator God who has given us everything we have and made us everything we are. By obeying our government, we are living for our Savior who lived and died for us.

God bless our president and God bless America.

Today I am thankful for/that _____

_____

Almighty God, you are the King of kings and Lord of lords. Please bless and guide the leaders you have placed over us. Help them to govern wisely and according to your will. Amen.

DAY 36
HOMECOMING

**"My Father's house has many rooms; if that were not
so, would I have told you that I am going
there to prepare a place for you?"**

JOHN 14:2

This week we celebrate homecoming in the town where I live. This year is extra-special for our family because our oldest is now in high school. This will be her first homecoming—her first time marching in the band in front of such a large crowd, her first homecoming game, her first homecoming dance.

Homecoming is always fun. Excitement fills the air. You get to see people you haven't seen in years. You get to come home.

When you come home, however, it's never quite the same. The author James Agee was right: "You can never go home again." You can't go back to the way it was before. My parents, for example, no longer live in the same home I grew up in. When I go home, it doesn't quite feel like home.

Home changes here on earth. Our houses grow old. The roofs leak. The plumbing goes bad. Even the home which we call our body wears out. You can't go back. There is no permanent home here on earth.

And that's okay because we aren't really home yet.

God has prepared a home for you in the happiness of heaven. Our homecoming in heaven will be fun. Excitement will fill the air. You will get to see people you haven't seen in years. You will be free from all the fumbles and foibles of this world. Your home in heaven will never wear out. Everything will always be new and perfect.

There will be no more death or mourning or crying or pain.

You can be sure you have a home waiting for you because Jesus paid for it with his blood on the cross. He died so that when you die you won't be dead. He promises that he has gone to the mansions of heaven to prepare a place especially for you. There is a mansion in heaven waiting for you with your name on the mailbox.

But sometimes homecoming comes at unexpected times. One of our neighboring towns this year did something strange. They celebrated homecoming on their very first home game. I had never seen that. It caught a lot of people by surprise. Homecoming is usually not that early.

For some Christians in this world, homecoming comes early. Sometimes God chooses to take people to heaven sooner than we expected—sooner than we would have wanted. We struggle with that at times. We wonder why God would take them so soon, so young.

IT'S FUN TO ENJOY THE JOURNEY, BUT THIS ISN'T HOME.

What we forget is that we are just passing through this world. God's goal—our goal—is that we get to go home one day. Sure, God gives us many good things here on earth. It's fun to enjoy the journey, but this isn't home.

I love my hometown, but it's nothing compared to heaven. If God chooses to take someone home to heaven sooner, why would we want to keep them here? It's hard for us, but they get to celebrate their homecoming.

Besides, God promises us that one day we will see them again. One day, we will hug them again. One day, we will celebrate with them.

That day will be our homecoming.

Today I am thankful for/that _____

_____

Heavenly Father, help me to never forget that I am but a stranger here. Heaven is my home. Give me patience and peace as I wait to celebrate my homecoming. Amen.

DAY 37
FAITHFUL

If we are faithless, he remains faithful,
for he cannot disown himself.

2 TIMOTHY 2:13

◆

On July 8, 2010, the NBA's biggest star, LeBron James, went on national television and uttered the fateful words, "I'm taking my talents to Miami." James was leaving his hometown Cleveland Cavaliers to play for the Miami Heat. It was a public relations nightmare.

Instantly James became *persona non grata* in his hometown. Fans burned LeBron James jerseys. The owner of the Cavaliers, Dan Gilbert, wrote a scathing public letter calling LeBron's actions a "cowardly betrayal" and a "shameful display of selfishness."

Then a few days later, LeBron once again went on national television with his new teammates and promised, "not one, not two, not three . . . not seven" championships to Miami. Four years later, LeBron and his Miami Heat teammates had played in the last four NBA championships, winning two.

On July 11, 2014, James announced in a much more subdued manner, "I'm coming home." He returned to once again play for the Cleveland Cavaliers. Fans in Cleveland erupted with joy. Clevelanders flocked once again to buy LeBron James jerseys. Dan Gilbert wrote on Twitter: "Welcome home @kingjames. I am excited for the fans and people of Cleveland and Ohio."

Fans in Miami responded by desecrating a LeBron James billboard.

HUMAN BEINGS ARE FICKLE CREATURES. . . . GOD IS DIFFERENT.

Human beings are fickle creatures. We flip-flop. We are undependable. We change our minds like teenagers falling in and out of love. One moment you can't wait for the cool weather of winter; the next you are complaining about the cold. One year you vote for a politician; the next you vote against him. One day you are deeply in love; the next you are divorced.

Our God is different. Another James (not LeBron) once wrote that our God doesn't "change like the shifting shadows" (James 1:17). The apostle

69

Paul reminds us, "If we are faithless, he remains faithful, for he cannot disown himself."

Theologians call that God's "immutability." Our God never changes. As we are tossed about in the sea of this ever-changing world, God's immutability is our anchor.

God never changes. That means his love for you never changes. God will not wake up one morning and say, "I don't love you anymore."

Because he never changes, God will always do what he promises to do. God promised the first people, Adam and Eve, that he would send a descendant of Eve who would crush Satan's power. Thousands of years later, Jesus defeated the devil with his death on the cross. God kept his promise. He can't help it. If he says he will do something, it always gets done.

What does God promise to do for you? He promises to forgive you (1 John 1:8,9). He promises to be with you (Matthew 28:20). He promises you will live forever in heaven (John 11:25,26). You can be sure he will do those things because he never changes. You can be sure because his love for you never changes.

In 2018, LeBron James once again left Cleveland—this time taking his talents to the Los Angeles Lakers. Will that be his last stop? Will the fans in Cleveland turn on him again? I don't know.

What I do know is that our God is not a fickle fan. He will still love you next year, ten years from now, and forever. He is immutable. He never changes. That is our comfort. That is our anchor in this ever-changing world.

Today I am thankful for/that _____

_____

Dear Lord, in an ever-changing world, thank you for never changing. Thank you for always loving me and always keeping your promises. Amen.

DAY 38
NOT-SO-RANDOM ACTS OF KINDNESS

**"Let your light shine before others, that they may see
your good deeds and glorify your Father in heaven."**

MATTHEW 5:16

A few months ago, a woman from my church went to the local Sonic Drive-In. She had been working hard outside with her daughter all day. She was a tad disheveled and extremely tired. She didn't even notice she was crying. Her fatigue and the burden of her problems had brought about an unexpected flow of tears.

When she came to the spot to give her order, the teenage girl who took her order asked her, "Excuse me, ma'am," she asked. "Have you been crying?" Surprised, my member quickly responded, "No." The young lady, however, was not fooled. When the young woman brought out the order, my member's arm was sticking out the open truck window. The young lady began to lovingly pat her hand. She stayed with her for a couple of minutes encouraging and consoling her.

That simple, random act of kindness affected my member deeply. She still gets emotional when she speaks of it. She has not seen the young lady since and doesn't remember her name. Nevertheless, she will never forget her simple act of kindness.

Nearly every Tuesday morning, I teach a Bible class at the nursing home in Edna. Every so often I will walk down the hall and one of the residents will yell, "Help me! Help me!" Her mind is nearly gone. She is lost and confused. When I can, I kneel down and speak with her. I touch her arm and then I start singing "Jesus Loves Me" and "Amazing Grace." The fear and panic in her eyes are briefly replaced with peace and joy.

GOD USES US TO HELP AND COMFORT OTHER PEOPLE.

I once heard another pastor comment that we are Jesus' hands and feet here on earth. Random acts of kindness carried out by Christians are not so random. God is using them. God uses us to help and comfort other people. We are his lights, shining the love of Christ for others to see.

It's not hard to perform a not-so-random act of kindness, but it does mean keeping your eyes open. It does mean taking a deep breath and diving into unknown situations. It means stepping up and stepping in and saying, "Excuse me. Are you okay? Can I help you?" It means a smile and a touch. It means a prayer and the simple words of God's love.

Two thousand years ago, a man carried out a not-so-random act of kindness. He stepped in and stepped up. He took a deep breath and then breathed his last for you and for me. Jesus accomplished the greatest act of kindness ever committed. He suffered your punishment in your place. He died so that you could live with him forever in heaven.

Now he calls you to pass on his kindness to the world—to be his hands and feet. Could you stop at the nursing home one day on your way home from work? Could you quietly pay for the groceries of the person behind you? Could you mow your elderly neighbor's yard?

Open your eyes. Opportunities abound. Take a deep breath. Step up, step in, and let your light shine.

Today I am thankful for/that _____

_____

Dear God, open my eyes to see the opportunities you give me every day to do not-so-random acts of kindness for those around me. Amen.

DAY 39
IGNORANCE IS NOT BLISS

Brothers and sisters, we do not want you to be uninformed about those who sleep in death, so that you do not grieve like the rest of mankind who have no hope.

1 THESSALONIANS 4:13 NIV 1984

72

One of the many wonderful advantages to having a Mexican wife is the food she makes. I love Mexican food and I'm usually up to trying just about anything. For example, I remember the first time I tried menudo.

No, I'm not talking about the Puerto Rican boy band from the 1980s. Menudo is a Mexican soup. From the first time I tried it, I loved it. Only later did I find out what it's made of.

Menudo is tripe soup. It's made out of the lining of a cow's stomach.

From that moment on, I decided if the food was good I didn't want to know what was in it. Ignorance is bliss.

We say that all the time, don't we? "Ignorance is bliss." And sometimes that's true. As long as the food is good, I am happy to eat it in blissful ignorance.

When it comes to death, however, ignorance is definitely not bliss. Have you ever been to a funeral with people who do not know or believe what the Bible says? Have you ever seen a mother clinging desperately to her daughter's casket, screaming inconsolably? I have. I've watched as they pried her hands from the cold casket. When it comes to death, ignorance is not bliss.

The Christians in the Greek city of Thessalonica were confused about death. The apostle Paul was only with them a short time. He had taught them Jesus was coming back at the end of the world to take them to be with him in heaven. That was good news! But then Grandpa Joe died. Then Aunt Kathy died. "Oh, no!" they thought. "What's going to happen to those who die before the end of the world? They won't be here when Jesus comes."

They got so upset that Paul wrote them a letter. "Brothers and sisters," he told them, "we do not want you to be uninformed about those who sleep in death, so that you do not grieve like the rest of mankind who have no hope." You'll notice that Paul didn't tell them not to grieve. Death hurts. We are going to miss our loved ones who die. It's okay to cry. It's okay to grieve.

But we don't grieve like the rest of humankind who have no hope. We don't grieve like that mother clinging to her daughter's casket, because we know. We know Jesus died and rose again.

We know Jesus died on the cross to save us. We know he died on the cross for our sins. But what does that mean? How did Jesus' death save you? How did a guy being nailed to a cross take away your sins?

It's because the wages of sin—the punishment sin deserves—is death, and not just physical death: Sin deserves the death of hell. While he was on the cross, Jesus suffered the death of hell—complete and total separation from God's love—the punishment we deserve for our sins. Jesus died our death. He suffered our hell.

You can be sure you are going to heaven when you die because Jesus died your death in your place. You can be sure you are going to heaven because Jesus rose again. The tomb could not hold him. Death had no power over him, and he promises that now all those who believe in him will live even though they die (John 11:25,26).

KNOWING CHANGES EVERYTHING.

Because of God's great love, because of Jesus' life, death and resurrection, you have a home waiting for you in the happiness of heaven when you die. You know that. Knowing changes everything. Knowing is bliss.

Today I am thankful for/that _____

_____

Risen Savior, knowing that you conquered death for me and all who believe changes everything. Thank you for the peace and comfort knowing gives. Amen.

DAY 40
A MIGHTY FORTRESS IS OUR GOD

God is our refuge and strength, an
ever-present help in trouble.

PSALM 46:1

His name is Wismond Exantus. You might have heard of him. On January 12, 2010, Wismond Exantus was shopping at a local fruit and vegetable store near his home in Port-au-Prince, Haiti. Without warning, the world came crashing in around him. A magnitude 7.0 earthquake leveled the city in which he lived and the building in which he was standing.

In the blink of an eye, Exantus dove under a nearby desk. There he found safety and protection as the two-story building crashed on top of him.

He stayed in that small space until they dug him out 11 days later. He stayed alive by consuming soda, beer, and cookies which he found within arm's reach. Wismond Exantus survived because he found a hiding place, a refuge where he could be protected as the world fell apart around him.

OUR SAVIOR GOD OFFERS US A HIDING PLACE, A REFUGE.

Our Savior God offers us a hiding place, a refuge, a place where we can be protected when our world falls apart around us. Psalm 46 tells us, "God is our refuge and strength, an ever-present help in trouble. Therefore we will not fear, though the earth give way and the mountains fall into the heart of the sea, though its waters roar and foam and the mountains quake with their surging" (verses 1-3).

Martin Luther loved Psalm 46. The world's most powerful men wanted him dead. The fanatical armies of the Islamic Turks were at the gates of Europe, ready to conquer the world for their god Allah. Luther was surrounded by constant pressures, problems, and poverty.

Yet Luther found a refuge, a fortress where he felt safe. His God would protect him, provide for him, and, most important, give him a home in heaven. His enemies could rage against him, the world could fall apart around him, but his God would make it all work out for his good. No matter what happened to him or around him, Luther was sure he had a home waiting for him in the joys of heaven because of Jesus.

Luther was so confident of that truth that he wrote a hymn based on Psalm 46, which has become one of the most famous hymns of all time. It is called "A Mighty Fortress Is Our God."

> *A mighty fortress is our God, a trusty shield and weapon;*
> *He helps us free from ev'ry need that has us now o'ertaken.*
> *The old evil foe now means deadly woe;*
> *Deep guile and great might are his dread arms in fight;*
> *On earth is not his equal. (CW 201:1)*

When you find yourself in the middle of one of life's storms and feel your world crumbling around you, turn to Psalm 46. Read again the comforting words of "A Mighty Fortress is our God." Turn to God's Word and find peace in the middle of the storm. As the earth quakes and the world crumbles, you have a refuge.

The Lord Almighty is with us; the God of Jacob is our fortress.

Today I am thankful for/that _____

_____

Heavenly Father, help me to be still and trust
that you will protect me. Amen.

————————◆————————

DAY 41
FAN THE FLAME

Fan into flame the gift of God, which is in you.

2 TIMOTHY 1:6

◆

My wife is from Monterrey, Mexico. I remember the first time her family invited me over to her grandparents' house for a *carne asada* (a barbecue). My wife's brother was in charge of the grilling. He poured the charcoal into the grill, lit the coals, and walked into the house.

He returned a minute later with a hair dryer. I watched, wondering what he was going to do next. He plugged the hair dryer into a long orange extension cord and proceeded to blow hot air on the coals.

What happened next was impressive. Within seconds, the coals were ablaze. Within a couple of minutes, they were white hot, ready to grill. Contrary to popular opinion, wind doesn't blow out fire. It feeds it.

I knew that before my brother-in-law pulled out his hair dryer. When I grilled, though, I would usually blow on the coals until my head got dizzy or fan them in futility with a towel. Now I simply pull out my wife's blow dryer. She's not too happy about it, but it sure makes grilling a whole lot faster.

Wind doesn't blow out fire. It feeds it. The apostle Paul understood that. As he sat in chains waiting to be executed, he wrote a letter to his protégé, young Pastor Timothy. He encouraged Timothy to "fan into flame" the gift of faith God had given him.

Faith is a fire burning in our hearts, but that fire needs to be fed. Fire needs oxygen to survive. Did you know that in Hebrew and Greek, the original languages of the Bible, the word for "spirit" also means "wind"?

The Holy Spirit is literally the Holy Wind.

When the Holy Spirit descended on Jesus' disciples on the day of Pentecost, they heard the sound of a violent wind blow through the house as tongues of fire came to rest on each of them. The Holy Spirit, the Holy Wind, blew into their hearts and fanned the flame of faith. With their hearts still burning, they went out and began to preach the good news of God's love without fear.

On the day of your baptism or as you heard the good news about Jesus for the first time, the Holy Spirit lit that fire of faith in you. He now feeds that flame with his Word and sacraments.

When you hear the good news of how God forgives you for hurting your wife or for that stupid thing you said to your sister—when you hear the good news of how God is with you, of the heaven that is waiting for you, of all that God does for you and through you—it feeds the flame burning in your heart.

But like my former grilling methods, we often don't fan the flame as well as we could. We go to church sporadically. We skip Sunday school. We rarely read our Bibles at home. The flame in our hearts becomes weak. We aren't on fire for God.

FEED THE FLAME OF FAITH IN YOUR HEART.

Don't just settle for a slight breeze. Pull out your hair dryer. Make the most of every opportunity to go to church. Go to Sunday school. Dust off your Bibles at home. Feed the flame of faith in your heart. Be on fire for your Savior God.

Today I am thankful for/that _____

Holy Spirit, through your Word and sacraments fan into flame the fire of faith in my heart. Set me on fire to live for and serve you. Amen.

DAY 42
PRACTICALLY PERFECT

"Be perfect, therefore, as your heavenly
Father is perfect."

MATTHEW 5:48

◆

Have you ever seen the movie *Mary Poppins*? Early in the movie, when Mary Poppins first met young Michael and Jane, she pulled out a magical tape measure to see how they measured up. According to the tape measure, Michael was "extremely stubborn and suspicious" and Jane was "rather inclined to giggle and not put things away." But then the children asked if they could measure Mary Poppins.

Their new nanny stood tall as the children stretched out the tape measure. When they finished, Mary Poppins looked at the line for her height and said, "Just as I thought: Mary Poppins, practically perfect in every way."

If you were able to use Mary Poppins' magical tape measure, how would you measure up? Would it point out some glaring weaknesses in your life or would it say you are practically perfect in every way?

In his Sermon on the Mount, Jesus stretched out his tape measure to show us exactly how we measure up. "Be perfect," he tells us, "as your heavenly Father is perfect." That is the standard God uses to measure us: perfection.

Have you ever felt like that wasn't fair? Sometimes to our minds God can seem like a cranky, unrealistic teacher who refuses to be satisfied with anything less than 100%. I mean, what's so bad about getting 95%? That's still an A, right? That's practically perfect, isn't it? Why does God demand complete perfection?

God demands perfection because that is what God created man to be. He created us to be perfect. Only that which is perfect can stand before him. Our perfect God can't and shouldn't settle for anything less.

GOOD ENOUGH ISN'T GOOD ENOUGH FOR GOD.

As human beings, though, we're happy to settle. Every day we find ways to lower our standards. We say, "Sure, I may be having sex before marriage, but only with someone I love." We say, "Yeah, I may lose my temper sometimes, but that doesn't make me a bad guy." We say, "Nobody's perfect. Good enough is good enough." But good enough isn't good enough for God. Practically perfect isn't perfect enough for God. Only that which is completely perfect can stand in his presence.

But we haven't achieved perfection, have we? We don't measure up. We don't even come close. Thankfully, God in his love sent Jesus to be our substitute. Jesus wasn't practically perfect in every way. He was completely perfect in every way. He took our place and then he allowed God the Father to punish him for all our imperfections.

Because of Jesus, you don't have to be perfect to go to heaven. You are forgiven. Forgiveness, however, doesn't mean God lowers his standards. God still wants and expects complete perfection.

So thank God for the forgiveness and heaven he gives by setting perfection as your goal. When you fall short, know that God has and will always forgive you. Just don't use that forgiveness as an excuse to lower your standards.

Today I am thankful for/that _____

_____

Merciful God, forgive me for failing to be the person you want me to be. Thank you for your forgiveness in Christ, but help me to never use your forgiveness as an excuse to lower my expectations of myself. Amen.

DAY 43
SOCIAL MEDIA 101 FOR CHRISTIANS

A gentle answer turns away wrath,
but a harsh word stirs up anger.

PROVERBS 15:1

◆

My Facebook feed is constantly on fire. With every election, every political move by the president, and every major social issue, people post their opinions on Facebook. Sadly, the posts and discussions often and quickly turn angry and ugly.

Because social media has evolved so quickly, few have taken the time to evaluate how they use the megaphone they have been given. Below are ten simple encouragements for Christians to think about as they use this powerful tool God has given us:

HELP ME TO SPEAK THE TRUTH IN LOVE.

1. Being right is not enough. God wants us to speak the truth in love. Rudeness, name calling, and sarcasm are not loving or effective ways to communicate with others.

2. Not everything people share on social media is true. God does not want us spreading rumors, lies, or even half-truths. If you cannot verify that it is true, you should not share it.

3. Whenever you write a response on Facebook, in a text, or in an email about something which irks you, frustrates you, or in any way bothers you, wait five minutes before you hit send. Walk away, calm down, say a prayer, reread what you wrote, and then decide whether you really want to send it or not. This may seem tedious and unnecessary, but you will save yourself a lot of heartache if you do.

4. Public posts and threads are no place for private discussions. Even private messages and texts are no place for emotionally charged communication. The other person cannot see your body language or hear the tone of your voice. If you are frustrated or have a tense relationship with another person, give them a call. Talk to them face to face.

5. When you send or post something, even on a private message or text, it is no longer under your control. It can become public at any time by the accidental hitting of a button, hackers, or another person's vindictiveness. Remember, once something is on the internet, it never really goes away.

6. Sexting and sending racy pictures of yourself to someone other than your spouse is always a sin. Sexting and sending racy pictures of yourself to your spouse is at best unwise (see number 5).

7. Don't go fishing for compliments. Pride and vanity are always trying to sneak into our hearts. Be honest with yourself about why you are posting selfies or talking about your accomplishments.

8. Nowhere in the Bible or in the U.S. Constitution are your minor-age children guaranteed the right to privacy. You need to know what is on your kid's phone, tablet, and computer. If you do not, you are being an irresponsible parent.

9. Arguing or debating with someone publicly on social media rarely changes anyone's mind. It usually just makes people dig in their heels. Don't get sucked into arguments. Just because you have a thought or opinion doesn't mean you need to post it publicly for all to see.

10. Understand that sharing political articles, advocating for a certain politician, or sharing a meme that says, "Share if you love Jesus" are not effective ways to help people see the heaven and forgiveness Jesus won for them on the cross. Such posts are just adding to the white noise.

The best way to let your faith shine on social media is by sharing the good things God has done for you personally, by asking for and offering prayers for others, and by encouraging people with God's gospel promises.

With great power comes great responsibility. Think about what you post on social media. Pray about it. May God's grace shine through it.

Today I am thankful for/that _____

_____

Lord, give me a forgiving and kind heart which takes people's words and actions in the kindest possible way. Help me to speak the truth in love, especially on social media. Amen.

DAY 44
WORTH THE WAIT

**Wait for the LORD; be strong and take heart
and wait for the LORD.**

PSALM 27:14

◆

I am not a patient man. I hate waiting in line. Traffic jams fluster me. Sitting in the waiting room at the doctor's office is torturous for me.

Some things, however, are worth the wait. When I visited Disney years ago, I waited in line over an hour to ride on the Tower of Terror. It was well worth the wait. I once waited an hour and a half to be seated at a fancy restaurant. I still dream about the steak I ate that night. It was worth the wait.

I had to wait 23 years to meet my wife. She was definitely worth the wait.

But waiting is hard.

I recently visited an elderly friend who is struggling with chronic pain. I shared with her God's promise in Psalm 50: "Call on me in the day of trouble; I will deliver you, and you will honor me" (verse 15).

**SOMETIMES GOD'S
TIME IS NOT OUR TIME.**

I pointed out to her that God invites, "Call upon me in the day of trouble," but he doesn't promise, "I will deliver you that very day." Sometimes God makes us wait. Sometimes God wants to teach us patience. Sometimes God's time is not our time.

"But it's hard to wait," my friend told me in tears.

God promises to deliver you from all your pains and problems, if not here on earth, then when you get to heaven. God will deliver you from pains in your body. He will free you from your cancer, your arthritis, and your chronic back pain.

God will deliver you from the pains in your heart. He will heal your emotional scars. He will take away your fears. He will free you from your sorrow and stress.

God will deliver you from every one of your problems, but he never promises to do it today. King David encourages us, "Wait for the Lord; be strong and take heart and wait for the Lord."

Wait for the Lord. He is coming. In fact, he is here. He is working right now in your heart and life. He has a plan for you and a purpose for your pain. I know it's hard, but be patient.

Wait for the Lord because he always keeps his promises. He promised Adam and Eve he would send a Savior from sin. Over four thousand years later Jesus was born. God kept his promise to send a Savior. He keeps all his promises, so wait for the Lord.

Wait for the Lord because what he is coming to give you is better than any adrenaline inducing roller coaster, better than the juiciest steak, better than even the love of your soulmate. Jesus is coming to take you to the joy and perfection of heaven. There he will free you from every grief and frustration. There you will be reunited with loved ones you haven't seen in a long time. There you will bask in his glory forever.

So be patient. Wait for the Lord. He is well worth the wait.

Today I am thankful for/that _____

_____

Blessed Lord, give me patience as I wait for your deliverance. Amen.

DAY 45
STAR WARS MORALITY

"The grass withers and the flowers fall, but the word of our God endures forever."

ISAIAH 40:8

"Stretch out with your feelings. . . . Let go of your conscious self and act on instinct." That was the encouragement wise old Obi-Wan Kenobi gave to young Luke Skywalker in the movie *Star Wars*.

"Let your feelings be your guide. Do what feels right." That is the mantra of our world today. How do you know what is the right job, right spouse, right church for you? Search your heart. Let your feelings be your guide. Do what feels right.

From early on, our children are taught in our public schools and on television to search their hearts to find truth. They are told to follow their hearts no matter what anyone else says. But is that such a good idea?

My feelings change from day to day. Some days I feel happy. Some days I feel sad. Some days I feel like eating pizza. Some days I feel like eating hamburgers. Some days I don't feel like making any decisions at all. We are fickle humans; our feelings are always changing. Even worse, because we are sinful humans, our feelings are stained with selfishness and doubt.

A woman once came to me in tears. "I don't *feel* God's presence in my heart anymore," she said. "God has left me. I am going to hell." I asked her if she knew Jesus died for her sins. She said, "Yes." I asked her if she was sorry for her sins and trusted that God had forgiven her because of Jesus' sacrifice. Again, she replied, "Yes." "Then you are saved," I told her, "no matter what you *feel*."

OUR FEELINGS CAN BETRAY US. . . . FAITH IS NOT A FEELING.

Our feelings can betray us. Sometimes we truly feel the overwhelming joy of salvation and the warming presence of our God. Some days, however, God feels far off. He seems to hide his face. All we feel is the cold, dark stare of the world around us. Thankfully, the roller coaster ride of our emotions does not change the fact that Jesus died for us, that God is with us, and that we have heaven.

Faith is the knowledge and trust in Jesus as our Savior. Faith is not a feeling. At times faith produces the feelings of sorrow, regret, joy, and satisfaction. As a sinful human being, though, I cannot always trust my feelings.

In the end, just because we feel something is right, doesn't make it right. What feels right for a teenage boy in the back seat of his car with his girlfriend isn't what is right in God's eyes. What feels right when you are in the middle of an argument with your husband isn't necessarily what is right in God's eyes. Too many people today make important decisions such as what church to attend or how to live their lives based on how they feel in their hearts.

Don't base your faith and life on the quicksand of feelings. Rather, base them on the rock of God's never-changing Word. Base them on the absolute truth revealed by a God who doesn't change like shifting shadows.

Our world today is always changing. Fads and fashion are outdated with the blink of an eye. Politicians flip-flop with every opinion poll. Our economy seems to go from boom to bust every other week. Our feelings jerk us around like a roller coaster.

In such an ever-changing environment, what a comfort to stand on the never-changing, absolute truth of the Bible.

Today I am thankful for/that _____

_____

Lord, your Word is the anchor in my life, without which I would be lost. Help me to hold fast to its Truth every day. Amen.

DAY 46
A LIFE LIKE MR. PANZA'S

My times are in your hands.

PSALM 31:15

◆

Mr. Panza is 97 years old. His parents met when his father fought in World War I. A farmer from Le Mans, France, offered his farm to the Americans to set up their operations. There the farmer's daughter met and fell in love with Mr. Panza's father, a strapping young Italian-American G.I.

After the war, they married and moved to his home in Chicago. From the beginning, Mr. Panza's mother struggled with life in the United States, especially the rough streets of Chicago. She begged her husband to allow them to move back to France. She was miserable.

Soon after arriving in Chicago, they had a son together. When she became pregnant again, however, Mr. Panza's mother decided she couldn't take it anymore. She would have an abortion, leave her husband, and return to France.

The abortion procedure failed. The baby refused to die. By that point, she couldn't bring herself to try another abortion.

That was 97 years ago.

My friend, Mr. Panza, was a failed abortion. Soon after his birth, his mother took the boys to vacation in France, but then informed her husband she would not return.

After a difficult custody battle, Mr. Panza's father returned to Chicago with the two boys. They lost touch with their mother and would not find her again until they were adults. It was only before she died that she finally confessed to her son her failed attempt to abort him. She begged him to forgive her.

Mr. Panza did.

God has blessed Mr. Panza with a full and abundant life. His father remarried, this time to a Mexican-American woman. He was raised speaking Italian, Spanish, and French. He himself fought in World War II on the Pacific Front, helping to liberate New Guinea from the Japanese. For years, he owned and operated a small factory in California which made jackets for Sears and J.C. Penney. He married, had two sons of his own, and now has numerous grandchildren and great-grandchildren.

None of them would be here today if the abortion hadn't failed. Even today, it is impossible to speak with Mr. Panza without being moved by his infectious kindness and *joie de vivre*. His life has touched hundreds, if not thousands, of people.

Since the United States Supreme Court legalized abortion with its Roe v. Wade decision in 1973, an estimated 60 million babies have been aborted in the United States. To put that into perspective, that is ten times the amount of people killed in the Holocaust.

EVERY LIFE, EVERY SOUL, EVERY PERSON . . . IS IMPORTANT TO GOD.

Sixty million babies. Sixty million souls. Sixty million lives unlived.

Though one can understand a woman's desire to have autonomy over her own body, what about the baby's right to live, to breathe, to survive? Just because a pregnancy is unwanted or unplanned does not mean the baby's life is any less precious or important. Every life, every soul, every person on this planet is important to God.

If you are hurting like Mr. Panza's mother, if you are struggling with an unwanted pregnancy, understand there are other options. Yes, it is more difficult in the moment to have the baby and then give him or her up for adoption, but you are saving a life. You are saving yourself the burden of a lifetime of guilt and regret. You are allowing a life to be lived.

A life like Mr. Panza's.

Today I am thankful for/that _____

_____

Dear Lord, thank you for the life you have given me. Use me to help others see and value the sanctity of life. Amen.

DAY 47
NO SMALL THING

"Who dares despise the day of small things?"

ZECHARIAH 4:10

There are times in our lives when God lovingly pops the balloon of our pride. God did that for me a while back. I was feeling pretty good about myself. The weekly devotion I write was being published in three newspapers and my blog received nearly a thousand views a week. My Facebook page was nearing 500 likes. Over 100 people were following me on Twitter.

I was feeling pretty good until I looked up some other Christian writers and bloggers online. Many had thousands of likes on Facebook and tens of thousands of followers on Twitter. Thousands of people read their writing every single day.

Compared to them, I was small potatoes. I had a little article I wrote for three small newspapers and a blog which reached maybe a couple hundred people. I was the pastor of a small church in a small town in rural Texas. I was small potatoes.

Do you ever feel like small potatoes? You watch Joel Osteen on TV and see the 15,000 people who fill his arena-sized church. Then you go to your church on Sunday and see 26 people parked in the pews. You hear the beautiful singers in your church choir and feel embarrassed by your creaky little voice croaking out the hymns. When we see the amazing things God accomplishes through other people, we can easily begin to feel like our efforts are small potatoes.

In the year 539 B.C., thousands of Jews returned to their homeland after seventy years of exile in Babylon. One of the first things they did was try to rebuild the temple in Jerusalem. The project stalled, however, as many realized they were never going to be able to build a temple as beautiful and glorious as the one King Solomon had built. Their temple would be small potatoes in comparison.

It wasn't small potatoes to God, though.

Speaking through the prophet Zechariah, he asked them, "Who dares despise the day of small things?" When it comes to God and our service to him, there are no small things.

What God does for you is no small thing. God became a man. That man suffered the hellish fury our sins deserve. Because he did that, God forgives you every minute of every hour of every day. That is no small thing.

He provides everything you need for body and life—clothing and food, shoes and drink, house and home, family and friends. Everything that happens to you and around you is a part of his master plan of love. Every moment of your life has purpose and meaning. That is no small thing.

WHAT GOD DOES FOR YOU IS NO SMALL THING. . . . NEITHER IS YOUR SERVICE TO GOD.

Neither is your service to God. When you baptize your children and bring them to church, the angel choirs of heaven break into song. The quiet prayers you say at night powerfully affect the course of your life and the lives of others. When you lovingly cook for your family, clean the toilets at church, and toil away at a tedious job—whenever you faithfully live and work for God and others—God smiles and the angels sing. Your service to God is never a small thing.

God has blessed me personally with the opportunity to share the good news of his love and forgiveness with the handful of people who attend my church and read my writing. Even if nobody else reads this devotion, you have. Through it God has reminded you of the great things he does for you and through you.

That's no small thing.

Today I am thankful for/that _____

_____

Merciful God, forgive me for the times I have felt like small potatoes. Help me to see the great and amazing things you have accomplished in me and through me. Amen.

DAY 48
YOU DON'T NEED TO KNOW

"For my thoughts are not your thoughts, neither are your ways my ways," declares the LORD.

ISAIAH 55:8

A friend of mine works in the oil fields. He told me that his company has a book in which they can find the answer to any and every question they might have about how to do their job. They call it the "Red Book."

A while back, his sister gave him a Bible as a gift. The Bible also had a red cover. He carried it around in the front seat of his truck. The other day, his crew ran into an issue that they couldn't figure out. A coworker said, "Let's check what the Red Book says." So my buddy went to his truck and grabbed his Bible.

His coworker didn't notice as my friend handed him the Bible. When he looked down, though, he rolled his eyes. "That's the book which has all the answers," my friend told him.

As Christians, we like to say that, don't we? The Bible has all the answers.

89

But is that true?

If we are honest, we have to say no. The Bible doesn't tell you how to fix an oil pump. The Bible doesn't tell you which career you should choose or whom you should marry. In fact, as we read the Bible we find ourselves asking even more questions.

Why did God put the forbidden fruit in the Garden of Eden if he knew Adam and Eve would eat from it? Why do some people never get a chance to hear the gospel? What happens to a baby who dies before he or she is born?

Silence. The Bible doesn't tell us. If you are looking for the answers to all of life's questions, you won't find them in the Bible.

In the 1996 movie *The Rock,* Nicolas Cage plays an FBI agent sent to fight U.S. Marines turned terrorists who had taken over Alcatraz prison. At one point, Cage's character asks too many questions and his boss tells him, "That's on a need-to-know basis and you don't need to know."

God often says the same thing to us. If he doesn't tell you something in the Bible, that's because you don't need to know. Where exactly was the Garden of Eden? You don't need to know. What did Jesus look like? You don't need to know. When will the end of the world be? You don't need to know.

The Bible doesn't tell us everything we *want* to know. It tells us everything we *need* to know. The Bible tells us how sin came into the world and how God sent his Son to save us from our sins. The Bible confronts us with the bad things we do and then shows us exactly how Jesus won forgiveness for us by suffering our punishment in our place. The Bible tells us what we need to know to believe in Jesus and serve him here on earth.

GOD WANTS YOU TO TRUST HIM.

That's what we need to know. If the Bible is silent on a matter, that means you don't need to know. God wants you to trust him.

If you have questions about God, by all means open your Bible. Many of life's questions are answered there. The most important questions are answered there. As for the rest of your questions, that's on a need-to-know basis and you don't need to know.

Today I am thankful for/that _____

_____

Holy Spirit, thank you for revealing to me in the Bible all I need to know for my salvation. Help me to accept and trust when you don't reveal to me everything I want to know. Amen.

DAY 49
BOOTSTRAPS

**It is by grace you have been saved, through faith—and
this is not from yourselves, it is the gift of God—
not by works, so that no one can boast.**

EPHESIANS 2:8,9

◆

I am a Yankee living in the great state of Texas. Amazingly, it took me almost 12 years of living here before I finally got my first pair of cowboy boots.

Now I understand firsthand what it means to "pull yourself up by your bootstraps." People use that expression today to describe rags-to-riches stories—the stories of self-made men and women who pull themselves up from poverty to success through their own hard work and gumption.

Originally, however, the expression didn't mean that. When it was first used in the 1800s, the phrase "pull yourself up by your bootstraps" meant something that was ridiculously impossible to do. If you think about it, it is ridiculously impossible to pull yourself up by your bootstraps.

Try it sometime. It is physically impossible to do.

No one can pull themselves up by their bootstraps. If you look closely at the rags-to-riches stories in our world today, none of them did it by themselves. They had help along the way. Somebody lent them a hand. Somebody encouraged them. Somebody gave them a chance.

And even if nobody helped them out, they still didn't succeed by themselves. Who gave them their mind, body, and ability to work? Who gave them the opportunity to live and work in this country? Who gave them parents, teachers, and mentors to guide them?

Nobody can pull themselves up by their bootstraps. That's never more true than when it comes to our salvation.

As a pastor, I often ask people this question: "Imagine you were to die tonight and you found yourself standing at the gates to heaven. God is there and he asks you, 'Why should I let you into heaven?' What would you say?"

Here are the answers I hear most often: "Because I try to live a good life." "Because I am a Christian." "Because I go to church." "Because I haven't killed anybody." There's a problem with all those answers.

The word "I."

THERE'S A PROBLEM WITH ALL THOSE ANSWERS. THE WORD "I."

The reason you are going to heaven has nothing to do with you and what you do.

If you want to go to heaven by what you do, God tells you exactly how in the Bible. He says, "Be holy, as the Lord your God is holy." He says, "Be perfect, as your heavenly Father is perfect."

But you're not perfect. Neither am I. We are far from it.

The only reason we can go to heaven is because God so loved the world that he gave his one and only Son. The only reason you can go to heaven is because Jesus loved you so much he took your place, suffered your punishment, and died your death.

He did it all for you.

You can't even say, "I'm going to heaven because I found God or because I chose Jesus as my Savior."

You didn't find God. He found you. You didn't choose Jesus. He chose you. The reason you and I believe in Jesus is because the Holy Spirit came to us through his Word and sacraments and gave us faith. The only thing we are capable of doing on our own is rejecting him.

Ask yourself that simple question: Why am I going to heaven? If there is an "I" in your answer, there's a problem. You can't do it. That's like trying to pull yourself up by your bootstraps.

Today I am thankful for/that _____

_____

Lord, thank you for all you have done for me, especially for the forgiveness Jesus won for me on the cross. Everything I have and everything I am is because of you. Amen.

DAY 50
I AM BAPTIZED

Baptism . . . saves you also—not the removal of
dirt from the body but the pledge of a clear
conscience toward God. It saves you by
the resurrection of Jesus Christ.

1 PETER 3:21

◆

I was baptized on September 1, 1973, when I was just four days old.

Do you remember when you were baptized? Some of you, like me, were baptized as babies; others when you were 12 or 13 years old; still others as adults. If you are a Christian, most likely at some point you were baptized.

Did you know, that's actually not the right way to say it? As Christians, we don't say, "I was baptized." We say, "I am baptized."

Your baptism isn't merely a fleeting moment from your infancy. Baptism isn't just something that happened you in the distant past. Your baptism defines you. It is who you are. You are baptized.

The word *baptize* literally means "to wash." At your baptism you were washed clean, not of dirt from your body but of sin from your soul.

In Baptism, we are forced to see ourselves for who we really are. We are dirty, rotten sinners. We are covered from head to toe in the filthy, stinky manure of our sins. No offense, but you are gross. Your mind is stained with dirty thoughts. Your mouth wreaks from the angry and hurtful words which come out of it. Your drunkenness, your arrogance, your jealousy, your pettiness, your selfishness all stain your souls.

No matter how hard we try, we can't get rid of that stain ourselves. In Shakespeare's tragedy, *Macbeth,* Lady Macbeth is tormented by guilt after convincing her husband to kill the king of Scotland and take his throne.

At night she sleepwalks and in her nightmares she tries desperately to wash the blood off her hands. "Out, out damned spot," she cries. But she can't wash the stain from her hands. That's us. That's who we are. We are dirty, stained sinners.

Baptism makes us face that truth. We need to be washed because dirty sinners aren't allowed into heaven. Dirty sinners deserve hell. That's the beauty of Baptism. In Baptism, our God washes us clean.

YOUR BAPTISM DEFINES WHO YOU ARE. . . . THAT IS WHO YOU ARE.

He doesn't just wash you clean of the sins you have at the time of your baptism. You weren't baptized. You are baptized. You live in the promise of your baptism. You are defined by it. You are washed clean of all your sins.

How does Baptism wash us of our sins? In Baptism, the Holy Spirit gives and strengthens the gift of faith (Acts 2:38). Through faith in Jesus, all your sins are washed away forever. Jesus suffered the punishment in your place. His blood is the bleach which washes you clean. That is the promise of your baptism. As long as you continue to believe in Jesus, your baptism continues to define you. You are a baptized—washed—child of God.

So live like it.

When I was a little boy, every Saturday evening my mom would give us a bath so we would be clean for church on Sunday morning. I still remember a few times in the summer when I would go outside and get dirty after my bath. My mom would not be happy. "I just got you clean. Why are you getting dirty all over again?"

You are baptized. God has washed you clean. Why would you want to go and roll around in the filth and manure all over again? Your baptism defines who you are. It should affect what you do and how you live every day of your life. Through the faith given in Baptism, you are washed clean of the stain of sin. You are a forgiven child of God. That is who you are. Now live like it.

Today I am thankful for/that _____

_____

Holy Spirit, thank you for the gift of my baptism.
Keep me in the saving faith and help me to
live in your baptismal grace all the
days of my life. Amen.

DAY 51
RIP KOBE

"Blessed are the dead who die in the Lord
from now on."

REVELATION 14:13

◆

When I got home from church on January 6, 2020, I sat down and turned on my phone. Facebook was blowing up. Kobe Bryant, one of the greatest basketball players of all time, was dead. Bryant, 41, and his daughter Gianna, 13, together with seven other people, were killed in a helicopter crash on their way to his daughter's basketball game near Los Angeles.

Beginning Sunday afternoon and into the night, Kobe's death dominated the news cycle and social media. Tens of thousands of people posted the same simple phrase on Facebook, Twitter, and Instagram.

RIP Kobe.

That's what we write or say when somebody dies, right? RIP. Rest in Peace.

Originally from the Latin *Requiescat in pace,* the initials "RIP" have been used on tombstones for centuries. The phrase is a prayer or wish that the soul of the person may now rest in peace after death.

The phrase flows from a fear that they may not rest in peace. Many cultures believe that tormented souls remain here on earth if they have unfinished business or have committed wrongs which do not allow them to rest in peace.

Some Christians believe that after death souls must go through a time of suffering and purification to pay for their sins before they can enter the rest and glory of heaven. In fact, many Christians pray for the souls of the dead, asking God to spare them from suffering and to allow their souls to finally rest in peace.

The truth, however, is that, as the writer to the Hebrews tells us, "people are destined to die once, and after that to face judgment" (Hebrews 9:27). When a person dies, the soul and body separate and the soul goes before God for judgment. Though we all deserve God's punishment for our failings in this life, those who die believing in Jesus are forgiven and given the gift of heaven. Those who do not believe in him, however, are condemned to an eternity in the torment of hell (Mark 16:16).

God's judgment is final. There is no changing places (Luke 16:26). When a person has died, no prayer or wish or request on our part can change their eternal situation. By then it is too late.

Though I understand the love, respect, and sorrow expressed when people say or write RIP, there are better ways in which we as Christians can express our condolences.

Some experts believe the phrase RIP can be traced back to another Latin phrase found in the catacombs of early Christians: *Dormit in pace*, literally, "He/she sleeps in peace." Instead of a wish or prayer, it is a statement of fact.

ALL THOSE WHO DIE IN CHRIST REST IN THE PEACE.

Those who die in Christ are now resting from the pains and problems of this world in the glory and happiness of heaven.

I did not know Kobe Bryant personally. Though he experienced embarrassingly public moral failings, he also was a professing Christian. Raised in the Catholic Church, Kobe continued to attend church as an adult and especially turned to God after scandal rocked his career.

Kobe took his daughters to church. There they heard about God's love and about their Savior Jesus who lived and died for them. I cannot look into his heart, but there is nothing to make me doubt his faith in Jesus.

That's why I don't have to wish or pray that Kobe Bryant rest in peace. It wouldn't change anything even if I did. What I can do is pray for his family and all who are sad in this hour. What I can do is share with them a simple truth.

All those who die in Christ rest in the peace and happiness of heaven.

Today I am thankful for/that _____

Heavenly Father, comfort all who feel the loss and pain caused by the death of a loved one. Give them and me the joy of knowing that those who die in Christ rest in peace. Amen.

DAY 52
IF GOD IS FOR US

If God is for us, who can be against us?

ROMANS 8:31

❖

I still don't know how it happened, but I am now officially a soccer coach. Don't get me wrong. I love the game of soccer. I have played it recreationally for years. I've never, however, played organized soccer.

One moment I was signing my son up to play and the next I found myself coach of the Edna Rebels U-9 soccer team.

Though I often feel overwhelmed and under-equipped for the task, we have had a lot of fun this season and have even managed to win a couple of games. Some teams in our league, however, are way out of our league.

During a recent game, which we eventually lost 8–2, one of my eight-year-olds walked up to me on the sideline and blurted out, "God is against us!"

Trying to be both coach and pastor, I told him, "No, God loves us. We just need to play better defense."

How often do we feel like that exasperated eight-year-old? Everybody at school seems to hate you and make fun of you. Your aging mother's needs and anger seem to be more than you can bear. You're sick. Your brother is in the hospital. Your husband lost his job. You feel beaten down, overwhelmed, and underequipped.

Sometimes it feels like God is against us.

But he's not. God is on our side. He is the God who joined our team—who became a human being just like us—to live and die as our Savior. He is the God who loves us unconditionally and whose forgiveness is unbounded. He is the God who conquered sin and death so that you could live victoriously with him forever in heaven.

As the apostle Paul said, "If God is for us, who can be against us?" The answer: Nobody. With God on our side, we can't lose.

But wait a minute. The Edna Rebels still lost that game 8–2. In fact, we lost a bunch of games this season. My brother still has cancer. My job is still demanding. My problems haven't suddenly disappeared. It doesn't seem like God is for us.

That's when we need to remember that God uses the defeats and problems to teach us, to help us grow, and to lead us to trust in him more. I can honestly say the Edna Rebels U-9 soccer team has improved much more because of our losses than because of our victories.

GOD LOVES US SO MUCH, HE LETS US LOSE.

God loves us so much, he lets us lose. He loves us so much, he allows us to suffer, to struggle, to face obstacles so that we can grow in our faith and draw closer to him.

I know it's hard to see and understand. We won't fully comprehend until we cross the finish line of heaven. There we will receive the victor's crown—the trophy—Jesus won for us.

Meanwhile we will have some games we lose 8–2. That doesn't mean God is against us. It just means we need to play better defense.

Today I am thankful for/that _____

_____

Lord, you know when I feel overwhelmed and exasperated. At times it seems like you aren't there or that you have forgotten about me. Help me to trust that you are on my side and that with you I cannot lose. Amen.

DAY 53
ASK NOT WHAT YOUR CHURCH CAN DO FOR YOU

"The Son of Man did not come to be served, but to serve, and to give his life as a ransom for many."

MATTHEW 20:28

◆

On a sunny but brisk January afternoon in 1961, 43-year-old John F. Kennedy stood on the eastern portico of the United States Capitol in Washington, D.C.

The newly elected president had just been sworn into office by Chief Justice Earl Warren. He stood before a nation energized by his youth and entranced by his charisma.

In the concluding remarks of his inaugural address, President Kennedy spoke words which have echoed down to our day: "And so my fellow Americans: Ask not what your country can do for you—ask what you can do for your country."

Recently I read an interesting little book by the author Thom S. Rainer called *I Am a Church Member.* The book proposes that much of the decline in Christian churches today can be traced back to a basic misunderstanding of what it means to be a member of a Christian church.

Many people today look for churches that will give them what they need or want. For them, being a member of a church is like joining a country club. You pay your dues and then you enjoy the privileges. The church serves you. The choir sings to you. The pastor preaches to you and your needs.

If the church isn't meeting your needs, if the music isn't inspiring enough for you, if the pastor doesn't give you what you are looking for, then you hunt for another church which will. But is that what it means to be a member of a church?

When the Bible talks about joining together with other Christians as a church, it usually doesn't talk about what you get out of it, but rather what you give. The writer to the Hebrews encourages us, "Let us consider how we may spur one another on toward love and good deeds" (Hebrews 10:24).

As Christians, we follow the example of our Savior "who did not come to be served, but to serve." When we truly grasp God's grace—when we see and appreciate his sacrifice and love and forgiveness—then we will willingly want to serve him and others with thankful hearts.

My fellow Christians: ask not what your church can do for you—ask what you can do for your church.

Don't go to church only to get, but also to give—to serve your Savior God and others out of love and thanks for all that God has given you. Being a member of a church means more than just parking your posterior in the pew on Sunday. Don't just go to church. Be the church. Participate. Serve. Give.

DON'T JUST GO TO CHURCH. BE THE CHURCH.

The amazing thing is that as you serve the church and others, you too will be blessed. There is no "I" in team, but there is a "u" in church. As you serve God and others in church, as you participate in worship, as you hear God's Word and receive his Sacrament, you too will be encouraged. You will be strengthened. You will be blessed. As you give, God promises you will also receive. Being a member of a church means serving and being served.

Remember that this Sunday as you go to church. I am not here only for me. I am here first and foremost to thank my Savior God for all his blessings, and I am here to encourage and serve my fellow believers.

The amazing thing is I will be blessed as I do.

Today I am thankful for/that _____

_____

Lord of the church, thank you for the blessings I receive from being a member of my congregation. Help me to always see my membership as an opportunity to serve you and others. Amen.

DAY 54
THE QUILT OF YOUR LIFE

We know that in all things God works for the good of
those who love him.

ROMANS 8:28

❖

My grandmother was a master quilter. In her lifetime she made dozens of quilts, each one a work of art. Quilts don't start off as works of art, though. Quilts are made from scraps of cloth. Old shirts and dresses, curtains and even jeans are cut into small pieces and sewn together in different patterns.

As a boy, I remember watching my grandmother sew the odd, mismatched scraps together into small squares. I remember thinking to myself, "That isn't going to look good. Those little squares are ugly."

But then patterns began to emerge. By the time she was finished, each quilt had become an amazing mosaic masterpiece.

I think of my grandmother's quilts every time I read the story of Ruth in the Bible.

Ruth and her mother-in-law Naomi had been through a lot. Naomi had suffered a severe famine. She was forced to move to a foreign land hundreds of miles from her home in Bethlehem. There she lost her husband and buried her two sons. She returned to Bethlehem years later poor and bitter with a young foreign daughter-in-law clinging to her skirt.

There in Bethlehem, young Ruth was forced to glean grain to survive. By law, harvesters could not pick up any grain that fell to the ground as they were harvesting. They were to leave it for the poor. Every day, Ruth went out and gathered the leftover grain so she and her mother-in-law could eat.

"HERE'S THE REST OF THE STORY." Ruth ended up gleaning in the field of a man named Boaz, a distant cousin of her dead husband. To make a long story short, Boaz and Ruth fell in love. They were married and Boaz took care of Ruth and Naomi the rest of their lives.

Even if that was the end of the story, it is a wonderful example of how God makes all things work together for the good of his children. But, as Paul Harvey used to say, "Here's the rest of the story."

Ruth and Boaz ended up having a son named Obed, who had a son named Jesse, who had a son named David. Do you remember hearing about a David from Bethlehem in the Bible? Yep. That's right. Ruth was King David's great-grandmother.

Even more importantly, one thousand years later another descendant of Ruth was born in Bethlehem. His name was Jesus. God worked all the events of Naomi and Ruth's lives in order to bring about the birth of our Savior from sin.

When Naomi and Ruth lost their husbands and suffered near-starvation, do you think they knew it was so that Ruth would marry Boaz and have a great-grandson who would become king? Could they see that the Savior of the world would be born because of it?

No. At the time, they could only see the ugly, mismatched scraps of their lives. They couldn't see how God would sew it all together into a beautiful work of art.

The same is true in our lives. We face sickness and heartache. We watch people we love suffer and die. Oftentimes we look at our lives and think, "God, you're messing this up. Why are you doing this to me?" The problem is that we can't see what God sees. We only see a small part of the quilt.

Your life is a beautiful work of art sewn together by a master quilter. So trust him. Even though sometimes it seems like he is messing everything up, he has a plan and a purpose. His plans brought Jesus into the world to live and die for your sins. His plans end up with you in heaven.

Though right now you can only see pieces and scraps, one day you will see the beautiful quilt that God has made of your life.

Today I am thankful for/that _____

_____

Heavenly Father, forgive me for complaining and feeling sorry for myself during hard times. Help me to trust your plans for me and my life. Amen.

DAY 55
THE WAITING TIME OF DAY

We believe that Jesus died and rose again, and so we
believe that God will bring with Jesus those who have
fallen asleep in him.

1 THESSALONIANS 4:14

◆

As I prepared for a funeral recently, the daughter of the deceased handed
me an old yellow newspaper clipping. It was a poem. Her grandmother
had laminated it after her husband's death. Though we did an exhaustive
search, we couldn't find the original author. This is what it said:

> The waiting time of the day for me is just like it was before.
> It's the time of day when I listen and wait for the sound of you at the door.
> It's the time of day when I make-believe that soon you'll be home with me.
> Then my world will be lovely and bright again, the way it used to be.
> I'll think of your smile and hear your voice as plainly as if you were here.
> And all the sorrow and grief I've known will magically disappear.
> Please God, let me go on pretending, for this is the only way
> I can bear the silence around me at the waiting time of day.

If you've ever experienced the death of a loved one, you know that feeling.
At times it seems like a dream. They didn't really die. They are going to walk
through the door at any moment. They are going to call you on the phone.
You can practically see them. You can hear their voice.

Certain times and certain days are more difficult. For the poet, it was the time
she used to wait for her husband to come home from work—the waiting
time of day.

Being a Christian—knowing what we know and believing what we believe—
does not take away the pain of loss. The deeper the bonds of love, family, and
friendship, the more our hearts ache when we no longer can be with them.

Though our faith doesn't make the pain of loss magically disappear, it does
guard us from despair. It gives us true hope and comfort.

"We believe," the apostle Paul wrote, "that Jesus died and rose again, and so
we believe that God will bring with Jesus those who have fallen asleep in him."

Jesus died. He suffered the punishment of every one of our failings and
fallings. He gives forgiveness free of charge to all those who believe in him.
His death paid our ticket to heaven.

Jesus rose again. He conquered death. He promises that because he lives, all those who believe in him will also live. Those who fall asleep in Jesus—that is, those who die believing in him—will live forever with him.

All those who die in Christ will one day be reunited.

One day.

WE WAIT WITH HOPE. WE WAIT WITH CERTAINTY.

For now, though, we wait. As we wait, our hearts ache. As we wait, we cry. As we wait, we struggle to adapt to life without them.

But we wait with hope. We wait with certainty. We wait knowing that one day they won't be the ones walking through the door.

We will.

One day we will walk through the door of heaven into a room full of hugs. We will be reunited, never to be separated again, all because of a God who suffered in our place the separation of death we deserve.

Because of Jesus, one day we will see them again. That truth is what gets us through the waiting time of day.

Today I am thankful for/that _____

_____

Lord, give me peace and patience as I wait to
see my loved ones again. Amen.

DAY 56
A FOCAL POINT

**I resolved to know nothing while I was with you
except Jesus Christ and him crucified.**

1 CORINTHIANS 2:2

◆

If you ever visit the city of Ystad, Sweden, I have heard that it is well worth your time to stop at St. Mary's Lutheran Church. The church in and of itself is not particularly beautiful. The architecture is nothing extraordinary. But when you go inside, there is a life-size and life-like crucifix hanging in the back of the church. It even has real human hair mangled beneath the crown of thorns.

How did this unusual crucifix come to find itself in a Swedish Lutheran church? It seems that in the early 1700s, the King of Sweden paid an unexpected visit to the church. When the pastor saw the king in attendance, he was overwhelmed. He ignored the text for that Sunday, and replaced it with a long and glorious tribute to the king.

Soon afterward the church received the crucifix from the king. With it came the following instructions: "Hang this within the church so that whoever stands in the pulpit will be reminded of his proper subject."

Since that time, every pastor who has stood in that pulpit of St. Mary's Lutheran Church in Ystad, Sweden, has been forced to look at Jesus Christ crucified as he preaches his sermons.

In our churches today, we can become so distracted by toilets breaking down, ladies' socials, and bake sales that we lose focus of why we are here. In our world, we can become so distracted by our jobs, homes, iPhones, and high-definition televisions that we lose focus of what is really important. In our lives, we can easily start to focus on ourselves, on all the good things we do, on how we try to be good people, so that we forget the real reason we are going to heaven.

**JESUS CHRIST CRUCIFIED. . . .
THAT IS OUR FOCAL POINT.**

Like the preacher in Ystad, Sweden, we all need a focal point to remind us what is really important. That focal point is Jesus Christ crucified. As a church, we exist because of Jesus Christ crucified. We exist to share the good news about Jesus Christ crucified with everyone we can. That is our focal point.

This world is passing away. Life here on earth is short. We need to be ready for what comes next. How do we get ready? Through faith in Jesus Christ crucified.

I am not going to heaven because of what *I* do. The price of heaven is perfection and I am definitely not perfect. I haven't earned heaven. Jesus earned it for me with his perfect life of love and horrific death on the cross. I am also not going to heaven because I went out and found God. I didn't find Jesus. He found me. The only reason I am going to heaven is because of Jesus Christ crucified.

Everyone needs a focal point. May God help us to keep Jesus Christ crucified as the focal point of our lives and churches.

Today I am thankful for/that _____

_____

*Dear Jesus, please help me to always keep my
eyes firmly fixed on you and what you
did to save me. Amen.*

DAY 57
SOMETHING TO GET EXCITED ABOUT

Then a great and powerful wind tore the mountains
apart and shattered the rocks before the Lord, but
the Lord was not in the wind. After the wind there
was an earthquake, but the Lord was not in the
earthquake. After the earthquake came a fire, but
the Lord was not in the fire. And after the fire
came a gentle whisper. . . . Then a voice said
to him, "What are you doing here, Elijah?"

1 KINGS 19:11-13

The story is told about a woman who one day walked into a Baskin Robbins in her hometown to buy an ice cream cone. As she turned around to put her change in her purse, she came face to face with her favorite actor, Paul Newman, who happened to be in town filming a movie. Overwhelmed with emotion and unable to speak, she sheepishly shuffled out the ice cream parlor door.

When she got outside, however, she realized she didn't have her ice cream cone. Embarrassed, she walked back into the store where once again she came face to face with her screen idol. Paul Newman looked at her with a smile.

"Are you looking for your ice cream cone?" he asked. She quietly nodded yes.

"Look down," he said, as he pointed at her purse. Sure enough, her purse was dripping with wet, sticky ice cream. In her excitement, she had put the ice cream cone in her purse.

When was the last time you got that excited about meeting God at church?

When we worship, we come face to face with our God and Savior. We lay our prayers and offerings at his feet. We sit before him and hear him speak to us in his Word and sacraments. In worship we meet our Maker.

WHY DO WE OFTEN CONSIDER OUR TIME WITH GOD BORING?

So why don't we get more excited about worship? Why do we often consider our time with God boring and mundane?

Because we fail to see his face.

Though we meet God in worship, he seems distant. His glory is hidden behind the cross, his body and blood behind the bread and wine. His voice whispers to us in the distant readings of his Word. He stands behind and speaks through weak, sinful, and sometimes dull preachers.

Oftentimes worship bores us—or at least doesn't excite us—because it fails to meet our foolishly high expectations. We want a mountaintop experience. We want to see the fire of Mount Sinai and the glory of the Mount of Transfiguration. We want to feel the earth quake and hear angels sing. When the music and the preacher fail to meet our grandiose expectations, we feel like worship failed. We fail to see God's face.

Do you want to get excited about worship? Don't go shopping around for a church with mountaintop music and a fiery preacher. Simply remember that God doesn't usually come through earthquakes and fire, but through the gentle whisper of his Word.

Hear God's voice speak to you as the pastor quietly assures you your sins are forgiven. See God's face hidden behind the small wafer of bread and sip of wine. Know that the angel choirs of heaven are singing backup for you.

Every Sunday in Word and sacrament, we come face to face with our Savior God who died our death and suffered the hell we deserve.

That's something to get excited about.

Today I am thankful for/that _____

_____

Heavenly Father, help me to see your face and hear your voice every time I hear your Word or receive your sacraments. Amen.

DAY 58
HUNGRY?

Through the law we become conscious of our sin.

ROMANS 3:20

◆

I ate a burrito once. It was the best burrito I have ever eaten.

My wife and I had missed breakfast. We were flying that day from her home in Mexico to our home in Miami. About halfway into the flight, we were both starving. That's when the flight attendant served lunch. She gave us burritos. They were amazing. My wife and I still talk about them.

I wonder, though, if part of the reason they tasted so good was because we were so hungry.

As a pastor, I sometimes hear people ask, "Why do you have to talk about our sins so much in church? Why can't you be more positive?"

Good question. Why talk about the bad stuff we do? Why point out those ugly things you said to your husband or those images you stared at on your computer or the case of beer you drank on Friday night? Why talk about our lies and gossip and pride?

First of all, that's the only way we will ever be able to change. You can't fix a problem until you admit you have one.

There is another reason, though. When we stop looking at our sins, we start thinking we aren't so bad. We start thinking we are good people who deserve heaven.

If you are a good person who deserves heaven, why would you need a Savior? Seriously. If you can make it to heaven on your own, why would you need Jesus?

Only when we look honestly at our sins—when we see all the hurtful and ugly things we have thought, said, and done—do we realize we are in trouble. Only then do we realize that on our own we are lost and condemned creatures, stumbling down the road to hell.

That truth makes us hungry—hungry for help, hungry for God's love, hungry for forgiveness. Then when we hear the pastor announce that God forgives all our sins because of Jesus, that truth tastes oh-so-sweet. Then when we approach the altar to receive Jesus' body and blood in the Sacrament, we appreciate the feast of forgiveness God is offering to us.

AT CHURCH, OUR GOD OFFERS US A BUFFET OF THE FINEST FOODS.

Every Sunday at church, our God offers us a buffet of the finest foods: his promises of forgiveness and heaven, protection and providence. That smorgasbord of God's love tastes all the more delicious when we realize how hungry we are, how sinful we are, how lost we are without him.

So don't complain when your pastor talks about sin in church. He does so to make you hungry. He shows you your sins so that you can appreciate and savor the feast of forgiveness your Savior offers in his Word and sacraments.

Today I am thankful for/that _____

_____

Almighty God, help me every day to see how terrible my sins are so that I can appreciate even more your amazing grace that forgives me. Amen.

DAY 59
THANK GOD MY BROTHER HAS BRAIN CANCER

Not only so, but we also glory in our sufferings,
because we know that suffering produces
perseverance; perseverance, character;
and character, hope.

ROMANS 5:3,4

◆

There are many things for which I thank God—for my home and my children, for the air I breathe and the food I eat, for God's protection and forgiveness, for the heaven he gives.

Oh, and I also thank God my brother has brain cancer.

A number of years ago my brother Adam had a seizure. The doctors found tumors in his brain. He had cancer. Surgery was out of the question. The tumors were too deep.

So far the doctors have been able to keep my brother's cancer under control and he has lived a relatively normal life. He has a beautiful wife, a precocious daughter, and two rambunctious boys. We don't know, however, how long doctors will be able to control his cancer. We don't know what will happen in the future.

So how can I thank God my brother has brain cancer?

I can for the same reason you can thank God your marriage is on the rocks and your son is flunking out of college. I can for the same reason you can thank God you lost your job and your grandfather died.

I know. All of this sounds a bit crazy and even a tad offensive. Why would we thank God for tragedies in our lives?

At one of the darkest moments in Israel's history, at a time when most of his people had given up hope, God told the prophet Jeremiah to write them a letter. "I know the plans I have for you," God said in the letter, "plans to prosper you and not to harm you, plans to give you hope and a future" (Jeremiah 29:11).

God has plans for you and his plans are for your good. The problem is that God's plans are not always our plans. You may not understand fully why God is doing what he is doing. It may hurt.

When you visit the dentist, it often hurts as he fixes your tooth. Though it hurts, he is not harming you. He is helping you. You may not always feel like thanking him because of the pain, but you can thank him because you know he is doing it for your good.

God works in the same way. Your pains and problems are actually blessings in disguise.

If you have a hard time understanding that, read the stories of Ruth or Job or Esther in the Bible. God used suffering in each of their lives to bring about wonderful blessings.

God uses our trials and troubles to teach us lessons and bring us closer to him. He uses them to bring about future blessings we cannot see or comprehend at the time.

What makes this especially hard is that God never promises to let you see or understand why he is doing what he is doing. I don't know exactly why my brother Adam has cancer. I don't know exactly what good will come from this.

I can be sure, though, that good will come from it. I can be sure, because God promises that it will. I can be sure, because God's plans end with Adam and his family (and me) together in heaven.

GOD'S PLANS END WITH YOU IN HEAVEN AS WELL.

God's plans end with you in heaven as well. That's why you can thank God your car broke down. That's why you can thank God your pet goldfish died. That's why you can thank God for your insufferable boss.

Is it easy? Of course not. You may struggle to see and accept God's plans when you are in the middle of the storm. It's hard to thank God when you are hurting. Your heart may ache and tears may roll down your cheeks as you mouth the words "Thank you, God." It isn't easy when God lets us hurt here on earth, but never forget it is all for our good.

And that is why I can, with tears in my eyes, thank God my brother has brain cancer.

Today I am thankful for/that _____

_____

Lord, thank you for the struggles and pains in my life, because I know that in some way you are using them for my good. Amen.

DAY 60
A MATTER OF DEGREES

I do not do the good I want to do, but the evil I do not
want to do—this I keep on doing. . . . Who will rescue
me from this body that is subject to death? Thanks
be to God, who delivers me through
Jesus Christ our Lord!

ROMANS 7:19,24,25

❧

I hear it more frequently every day. A young man overcomes addiction and begins a new life. "He turned his life around *360 degrees*." A woman changes her mind. "She made a *360-degree* turn."

Do you see what's wrong with those statements? It's an innocent mistake. A circle is exactly 360 degrees. To go half-way around is 180 degrees, so to get turned around is to turn exactly 180 degrees. "He turned his life around 180 degrees" is the correct figure of speech. If you go 360 degrees, you end up where you began.

God turned me around 180 degrees. I was born an unbeliever. I was born on the road to hell. I was born unable to see God or love him.

When the Holy Spirit put faith in my heart through water and the Word, God picked me up and turned me around. I am no longer on the road to hell; I am on my way to heaven. I now believe. I can see God through the eyes of faith. I love him and trust him.

That is what the word *convert* means. God converted me. He turned me around 180 degrees. As the hymn writer once wrote, "Amazing grace—how sweet the sound—that saved a wretch like me! I once was lost, but now am found; was blind, but now I see" (CW 379:1).

Now I see. I get it. I understand what he did to save me. I trust that because Jesus suffered my punishment in my place, I am forgiven. I am on my way to heaven.

Because of that God-given faith, I now want to live for God. I struggle daily to turn away from my pet sins.

Faith in God means turning away from those sins 180 degrees. Sometimes though, I don't turn completely away. "Ninety degrees is good enough," I tell myself. "Just this once," the devil whispers in my ear. "Nobody is perfect," our world chimes in.

"What's so bad about looking at the *Sports Illustrated* swimsuit edition? At least I'm not looking at porn." "What's so bad about drinking a little too much? I only do it on weekends, and besides I never get behind the wheel."

My friends, sin is a slippery slope. Once we start giving in, we soon end up where we began. We make a 360-degree turn.

WE FAIL TO MAKE THAT 180-DEGREE TURN.

We've all been there. Even though we believe, even though we love God, we slip. We fall. We fail to make that 180-degree turn. If you have a chance sometime today, read Romans 7:14-25. Read how the apostle Paul struggled with sin even after God had turned him around.

Paul found comfort, however, in Jesus. He found comfort in the forgiveness Jesus won for him. No matter how many times we mess up—no matter how many times we slip—God always forgives us because of Jesus.

Just don't use that forgiveness as an excuse to keep on sinning. God saved you from sin. He picked you up off the road to hell and put you on the road to heaven. Show him how thankful you are. Show him how much you love him by turning from sin 180 degrees.

Today I am thankful for/that _____

_____

Merciful God, thank you for your amazing grace that forgives me. Help me to now turn away from sin and live for you. Amen.

DAY 61
FOR SUCH A TIME AS THIS

**"Who knows but that you have come to your
royal position for such a time as this?"**

ESTHER 4:14

❖

Esther was a young Jewish orphan living in ancient Persia. When she was a teenager, King Xerxes, ruler of the mighty Persian Empire, grew angry with his wife, Queen Vashti, and deposed her.

A search was made for a replacement. The most beautiful maidens in the empire were brought before the king. He chose Esther.

Esther's is truly a Cinderella story. Seemingly overnight, she went from poor orphan to queen of the most powerful empire in the world.

Soon, however, one of the king's top advisors convinced the emperor to exterminate the Jews of the empire. Esther found herself caught between a rock and a hard place. If she went to her husband and asked for mercy for the Jews, she could lose everything. If she said nothing, her people—her own flesh and blood—would be wiped from the face of the earth.

As she struggled with her moral dilemma, her cousin Mordecai sent her a message: "Who knows but that you have come to your royal position for such a time as this?"

For such a time as this.

Esther's life was not a series of coincidences and happenstance. It wasn't by chance that her family was carried off into exile. It wasn't a twist of fate that her parents died when she was young. It wasn't a stroke of luck that she was chosen to be queen of an empire.

God's hand powerfully and lovingly maneuvered the events of Esther's life in order to protect his people from annihilation. If he hadn't saved his people through Esther, they would never have returned to Israel. If he hadn't saved his people through Esther, our Savior Jesus would never have been born.

Sometimes it feels like we are victims of fate. When tragedy strikes and the world seems out of control, we can begin to feel like life is meaningless. We look around and can see no purpose to our existence.

Have you ever felt like your life is one big accident? Have you ever felt like you have no purpose?

Every year at Christmas, I make a point to watch Frank Capra's classic, *It's a Wonderful Life*. The movie's main character, George Bailey, felt that his life was meaningless. He thought the world would have been better off if he had never existed.

So God sent the angel Clarence to show George what the world would have been like if he had never been born. George was allowed to see all the lives that he had touched and helped and saved. His life had tremendous purpose and value.

So does yours. God has you here for such a time as this. He has worked the events of your life to bring you to this point. He has placed people in your life whom you can help and encourage—to whom you can show God's love in Jesus.

YOUR LIFE IS NOT A SERIES OF COINCIDENCES AND HAPPENSTANCE.

Your life is not a series of coincidences and happenstance. It is no coincidence you have the family you have. It is no coincidence you work with the people you do. It is no coincidence you live in the town you do next door to the people you do. It is for such a time as this.

You may at times struggle to understand God's purpose for your life, but never doubt that there is a purpose. God has placed you here at this time to serve him, to help those around you, to be a beacon shining the light of his love to the world.

You are here for such a time as this.

Today I am thankful for/that _____

Heavenly Father, as I struggle with difficult circumstances in my life, help me to trust that you have a good purpose for them. Use me to help others see your love. Amen.

DAY 62
PRIORITIES

"Seek first his kingdom and his righteousness, and all
these things will be given to you as well."

MATTHEW 6:33

❖

The story is told of two young men living every football fan's dream. They won tickets to the Super Bowl. Wanting to make the most of this once-in-a-lifetime opportunity, they arrived at the game early and excitedly found their seats. They then watched as the rest of the stadium filled up around them.

As kick-off approached, the young men noticed that a seat in front of them remained empty. The game began, yet no one came. The first quarter came and went. The young men couldn't believe it. How could a person not use their ticket to the Super Bowl?

By halftime, they couldn't take it anymore. They finally broke down and asked the other people in the row if they knew whose seat it was.

"Yes," said the woman sitting next to the empty seat. "It was my husband's, but he passed away."

"I'm so sorry," replied one of the young men "But I'm surprised a family member or friend didn't want to use the ticket."

"I am too," the woman replied with a shrug, "but they all said that they would rather attend the funeral."

We all have to make choices of how we use our time. We all have important things we need to do with the 24 hours we are given each day and the seven days we are given each week. In fact, we have so many important things to do we can't do it all. We have to make choices.

THE CHOICES WE MAKE SHOW WHAT OUR PRIORITIES ARE.

The choices we make show what our priorities are. Do you know what your top priorities are? If you're not sure, just look at how you spend your time and money. That will show you what is most important to you.

God wants to be the most important thing in your life. God deserves to be the most important thing in your life. He is our Creator. He is our

Savior and Friend. Everything we have and everything we are is because of him.

A wise old pastor once told me that priorities are like a button-down shirt. If the first button isn't buttoned right, all the other buttons will be crooked. But if you get the first button right, all the other buttons fall into place.

Get your top priority right, and all the other buttons will fall into place. Give God the first part of your time and money, and he will make sure you have enough for everything else. Take time every week to go to church. Take time every day to pray and study his Word, and everything else will fall into place. Don't give God what is left over. Set aside for him first.

In the Old Testament, God's people weren't giving to him first, so God challenged them. "Test me in this," he said, "and see if I will not throw open the floodgates of heaven and pour out so much blessing that there will not be room enough to store it" (Malachi 3:10).

Test God. Give him your time and money first and see if he won't make sure that you have enough for everything else.

Today I am thankful for/that _____

_____

Merciful Lord, forgive me my poor priorities. Help me to always keep you first in my life. Amen.

117

DAY 63
NOT ANY WORSE

Christ Jesus came into the world to save sinners—
of whom I am the worst.

1 TIMOTHY 1:15

❖

Over the last couple of weeks, the topics of homosexuality and gay marriage have dominated news cycles and Facebook threads. Up to this point, I have been hesitant to wade into the dark and dangerous waters of this topic, but I have heard something stated again and again during the discussion which I think we as Christians need to consider more carefully.

"Homosexuality is no worse than any other sin."

Of course, that statement is true. Sin is sin.

Sadly some Christians believe—or at least give the impression—that homosexuality is worse than other sins. They are shocked and outraged by gay marriage, but barely blink an eye when a heterosexual couple moves in together before marriage. They are disgusted by homosexuality, but laugh off their own stubbornness, pride, and gossip.

Many proponents of homosexuality and gay marriage are quick to point out the double standard and what they consider to be hypocrisy.

In the debates and discussions, we are often reminded that homosexuality is no worse than any other sin. In other words, we shouldn't act so shocked or outraged.

Yet, the Bible calls homosexuality "detestable," "degrading," "shameful," "unnatural," and "indecent" (Leviticus 18:22; Romans 1:24-27). When God speaks of homosexuality, he does so in outrage and disgust.

Our problem isn't that we overstate the wickedness of homosexuality. Our problem is that we often understate the wickedness of other sins.

"Homosexuality is no worse than any other sin." As Christians, we shouldn't respond to that statement by treating homosexuality as any less wrong. We should respond by showing the same shock and outrage for other sins, including our own.

In God's eyes, a boyfriend and girlfriend sleeping together before marriage is detestable and degrading. The little white lies you tell your boss or your wife are wicked and evil and deserve the horrors of hell.

Every dirty thought is shameful. Every ugly word disgusts God. Every sin is evil. The sin of homosexuality should disturb and sadden me, but so should my own gossip and pride and selfishness.

Sadly, we often shrug off our own sins as no big deal.

SADLY, WE OFTEN SHRUG OFF OUR OWN SINS AS NO BIG DEAL.

"Nobody's perfect," we say.

"At least I'm not as bad as Joe Schmoe over there," we think.

Yet God utterly detests my sins. They are dirty and disgusting and deserving of hell. The apostle Paul understood how deplorable his sin was. The greatest missionary the world has ever known confessed, "Christ Jesus came into the world to save sinners—of whom I am the worst."

That is the truth we boldly confess as Christians. That is how we avoid the accusation of double standards and hypocrisy. We preach the law in all its condemning power. We don't speak of homosexuality as if it were any less evil. We just make sure we treat our own sins with the same outrage and shame.

Then we cling to our Savior Jesus who came to save detestable, shameful, deplorable sinners like you and me.

Today I am thankful for/that _____

_____

Lord, have mercy on me, a sinner. Amen.

───────◆───────

DAY 64
BEING ARNOLD HORSHACK

And I said, "Here am I. Send me!"

ISAIAH 6:8

◆

Long before he starred in *Pulp Fiction,* even before he appeared in *Grease* and *Saturday Night Fever,* John Travolta was Vinnie Barbarino on the TV show *Welcome Back, Kotter.*

As a child of the late '70s, I remember watching Vinnie Barbarino and the rest of the Sweathogs sit in Mr. Kotter's class at James Buchanan High School in Brooklyn, New York. Vinnie Barbarino, however, was not my favorite Sweathog. That honor belonged to Arnold Horshack.

Arnold Horshack was the smartest and neediest of all the Sweathogs. I can still see him raising his hand in Mr. Kotter's class, begging Mr. Kotter to call on him, his arm nearly coming out of its socket, pleading in his Brooklyn accent, "Ooh, ooh, ooh, Mr. Kotta, Mr. Kotta."

As a kid, I thought Arnold Horshack was hilarious.

The prophet Isaiah lived during a time of spiritual apathy in Israel. God's people had for the most part rejected him. Many followed idols. Few still worshiped God faithfully in the temple. Even those who did gather at the temple often only went through the motions of religion without true faith in God in their hearts.

It was during such a time of spiritual laziness that God called Isaiah to be his prophet. He gave Isaiah a vision of heaven. In the vision, Isaiah saw the Lord on his throne in the temple. His glory filled the room. Smoke was everywhere. Fiery angels flew all around him proclaiming his holiness.

Isaiah was terrified. He knew nothing sinful can stand in the presence of our holy God. He knew he deserved God's punishment. He knew he deserved hell.

So God sent one of the fiery angels with a live coal from the altar to touch Isaiah's lips. "See, this has touched your lips; your guilt is taken away and your sin atoned for," the angel told him.

God forgave Isaiah through the sacrifice of the altar. Isaiah could stand in God's presence without fear. He was forgiven.

Then God himself spoke from his throne. "Whom shall I send?" he asked.

"Who will go for us?"

That's when the prophet Isaiah turned into Arnold Horshack.

He raised his hand. He jumped up and down. "Oooh, ooh, ooh, God," he said. "Here am I! Send me! Send me!"

Do you get that excited when God calls you to service? Do you jump up and down when you get asked to serve on a committee at church or to help clean the bathrooms? When God asks, "Who will go out and tell other people about me and my love?" does your arm come out of its socket hoping he calls on you? Or do you hide behind the person in the pew in front of you?

Sadly, like many in ancient Israel, our service to God is often only half-hearted. We think that parking our posteriors in the pew on Sunday morning is all it means to be a Christian. God, however, wants our whole lives. He wants joyful and willing service—service which we often fail to give or at best give grudgingly.

Thankfully, God has taken a live coal from the altar and touched our lips. He forgives our spiritual apathy through Jesus' sacrifice on the altar of the cross. God is not going to punish you. You are not going to the hell you deserve. You are forever forgiven in Christ.

Now knowing that—seeing God's forgiveness and all the good he gives you—raise your hand. Get excited about serving your God even when the job isn't so fun. Remember, it is a privilege. You get to serve your God who so faithfully and lovingly serves you.

WHEN GOD CALLS, BE ARNOLD HORSHACK.

When God calls, be Arnold Horshack.

Today I am thankful for/that _____

_____

Almighty God, here am I. Send me.
Send me! Amen.

DAY 65
IT IS WELL WITH MY SOUL

I have learned the secret of being content in any and
every situation, whether well fed or hungry, whether
living in plenty or in want. I can do all this through him
who gives me strength.

PHILIPPIANS 4:12,13

◆

Horatio Spafford was a wealthy real estate lawyer from Chicago who lived
in the late 19th century. A Christian man, Spafford often marveled at how
God had blessed him with wealth, a beautiful wife, four young daughters
and an infant son. But all that changed in a blink of the eye. In the winter
of 1871, scarlet fever took the life of his infant son. A few months later,
the Great Chicago Fire swept across his home city, wiping out his real
estate holdings.

In 1873, he decided to move his family to England to make a fresh start.
He bought six tickets on a French luxury liner. The day before they were
to set sail, he was told that he would need to attend to some business in
Chicago before leaving for England, so he sent his family ahead of him.

Four days into the voyage, a terrible fog descended on the North Atlantic.
Another ship broadsided the luxury liner. It sank in only 12 minutes. Two
hundred and twenty-six people died, including Horatio Spafford's four
daughters. An hour later, his wife was pulled from the icy water, barely
alive. Days later she arrived in England and cabled her husband with two
simple words: "Saved alone."

Spafford quickly boarded a ship to join his wife in England. Three days into
the journey, the captain informed Spafford that they were passing over the
place where his daughters had died. As Spafford looked out over the icy
sea, a hurricane of emotion came over him. He went to his room and wrote
a poem to God, a poem which was later put to music.

"When peace, like a river, attendeth my way," Spafford wrote, "when
sorrows like sea billows roll—whatever my lot, thou has taught me to say:
It is well, it is well with my soul" (*Let All the People Praise You*, p. 154).

Horatio Spafford was hurting. He was filled with unimaginable sorrow over
the loss of his five children. He was filled with regret. Yet he found peace.

In the middle of unimaginable sorrow, he was able to say, "It is well with my soul."

How could he say that? He tells us.

"My sin—oh the joy of this glorious thought—my sin, not in part, but the whole, is nailed to the cross, and I bear it no more: Praise the Lord, praise the Lord, O my soul!" (*Let All the People Praise You*, p. 154).

Every Good Friday at our church, we give people a nail as they enter the church. After the service, we ask them to place their nail in the cross at the front of church as they quietly file out. That nail represents their sin and guilt. We leave that nail at the cross because it was there that sin and guilt were paid for. We don't have to carry guilt around with us. We are forgiven.

But that is not the only reason Horatio Spafford could say, "It is well with my soul." He ends his beautiful hymn with the words, "And, Lord, haste the day when my faith shall be sight, the clouds be rolled back as a scroll; the trump shall resound and the Lord shall descend; even so, it is well with my soul" (*Let All the People Praise You*, p. 154).

WE CAN'T ALWAYS SEE OR UNDERSTAND WHY GOD DOES WHAT HE DOES IN OUR LIVES.

Right now, we can't always see or understand why God does what he does in our lives. Horatio Spafford couldn't understand why God would take all his children. But he trusted in God his Savior. He looked through the eyes of faith and saw that God had a good reason. He also looked forward to the day when he would be able to see with his physical eyes—see God face to face, see his children again, see the heaven that was waiting for him.

In the midst of unspeakable heartache, Horatio Spafford could say, "It is well with my soul," because by faith he trusted that God had forgiven him, heaven was waiting for him, he would see his children again, and God would make everything work out in the end.

Knowing that, we too can sing with confidence, "It is well; it is well with my soul."

Today I am thankful for/that _____

_____

In good times and bad, O Lord, help me to be able to say, "It is well with my soul." Amen.

DAY 66
MY BUCKET LIST

For to me, to live is Christ and to die is gain.

PHILIPPIANS 1:21

◆

Do you have a bucket list? You know. A list of things you want to do before you "kick the bucket."

For years I have kept a mental bucket list:

- Run a marathon. Check. (Although technically I walked a part of it and cried like a little child.)

- Write and publish a book. Check. (This is actually my second book. My first book, *364 Days of Thanksgiving,* is still available—shameless plug.)

- Jump out of an airplane. (My wife says I can do that after I turn 80 . . . only 34 more years to wait.)

I have a few other items on my bucket list, both big and small, which I would like to do before I die. What is on your bucket list? What do you want to do before you die?

Simeon had one item on his bucket list. He was waiting for the "consolation of Israel" (Luke 2:25). God had promised he would see the Messiah, the coming Savior, before he died.

When Baby Jesus was just eight days old, his parents took him to the temple. Moved by the Holy Spirit, Simeon also went for a walk in the temple courts. When he saw Mary and Joseph and Baby Jesus, he took the child in his arms and said, "Sovereign Lord, as you have promised, you may now dismiss your servant in peace. For my eyes have seen your salvation, which you have prepared in the sight of all nations: a light for revelation to the Gentiles, and the glory of your people Israel" (Luke 2:29-32).

In other words, Simeon was saying, "I can die in peace right now because I have seen my Savior." Simeon may have had other things he wanted to do here on earth, but none of them really mattered. If God wanted to take him that day, that very moment, that was just fine with Simeon.

What a contrast to how many in our world today look at death! As he watched his father slowly die, the poet Dylan Thomas wrote: "Do not go gentle into that good night, . . . Rage, rage against the dying of the light."

Few people want to die. They want to live long lives. They want to do many things before they die, so they fight and rage and run away from death.

Many years ago, I sat in my eighth-grade confirmation class. My pastor (who coincidentally was also my father) asked us, "What would you like to do before you die?"

The class gave a number of answers: "Get my driver's license." "Have my first kiss." "Get married."

I'll never forget what my father said next. "All those things are good," he told us, "but none compare with how great heaven will be."

Your first kiss, getting married, jumping out of an airplane—none come close to the glory and happiness and fun of heaven.

Like Simeon, our eyes have seen our salvation. Our God has allowed us to see our Savior Jesus through his Word. Through that same Word, he gives us glimpses of the glory of heaven. Seeing that—knowing that—helps us say with Simeon, "I can die in peace right now."

WE DON'T CONTROL WHEN WE WILL DIE.

Is it wrong to have a bucket list? No. Is it wrong to want to live more years here on earth? Of course not. But we do so understanding we don't control when we will die. We do so trusting that heaven is far better than anything we could ever experience here on earth.

Today I am thankful for/that _____

_____

Almighty God, thank you for the life you have given me here on earth and even more importantly for the life Jesus won for me in heaven. Help me to be able to say every day, "I can die in peace right now." Amen.

DAY 67
THE DAY THE DEVIL WENT TO CHURCH

Be alert and of sober mind. Your enemy the devil
prowls around like a roaring lion looking
for someone to devour.

1 PETER 5:8

❖

Jesus was just beginning his ministry here on earth. He was in the fishing town of Capernaum on the northwest shore of the Sea of Galilee. He had just called four fishermen—Andrew and Peter, James and John—to be his first disciples.

The next Sabbath, they went together to the synagogue—to church. The custom in those days was that if a visiting rabbi was in town, he would be asked to teach. So during one of the seven Scripture readings, Jesus was handed a scroll. He was asked to read and comment on it. As he did, the people were amazed because he taught with such authority.

Just then, however, a demon-possessed man cried out, "What do you want with us, Jesus of Nazareth? Have you come to destroy us? I know who you are—the Holy One of God!"

Immediately Jesus scowled. "Be quiet!" he said sternly. "Come out of him!" The man shook violently. The spirit came out of him with a blood curdling shriek. The people sat stunned.

Every time I read that story, one detail jumps off the page. The devil went to church that day in Capernaum.

Sometimes we can think the sacred walls of our church will keep the devil and his demons out. But no. The devil goes to church every Sunday.

If you ever have a chance, read C. S. Lewis' short little book, *The Screwtape Letters*. It's the fictional story about one demon instructing another demon how to tempt us. The sections about how to tempt us in church are particularly interesting.

During church, get them to think about what they have to do later that day. If they realize what you are doing, get them thinking, "I should be paying attention," because if they are thinking, "I should be paying attention," they still aren't paying attention.

Puff them up with pride by getting them to look at the people in church who are "worse" than they are. Point out all the failings of the preacher and how boring he is. Get them thinking about anything other than God speaking to them in his Word and sacraments.

The greatest trick the devil ever pulled was to convince the world he didn't exist. When we forget the devil goes to church, we leave ourselves open to his tricks and temptations.

Take the Lord's Prayer for example. I firmly believe that more people sin while praying the Lord's Prayer than doing just about any other activity on the planet. Think about it. How often do people pray the Lord's Prayer? Yet how often do we actually think about what we are saying?

When I am watching TV at home, sometimes my wife will try to talk to me. In my guyhood, I often nod and respond without really listening to her or thinking about what I am saying. Let's just say she doesn't like that very much.

How do you think God feels? During worship, we are conversing with the King of the universe who fills all things—our Savior who suffered our hell in our place so we could live with him in heaven.

THE DEVIL GOES TO CHURCH EVERY SUNDAY.

Yet often we aren't thinking about what we are saying. We are thinking that pizza would be good for lunch or how that woman's skirt is too short for church or how those parents should control their child. And the devil smiles.

Remember that the next time you go to church. Watch out. Be on your guard. Pay attention. Never forget that the devil goes to church.

Today I am thankful for/that _____

Heavenly Father, help me to stay alert to the devil's attacks, even at church. Amen.

DAY 68
THERE, BUT FOR THE GRACE OF GOD

"Let any one of you who is without sin be the first
to throw a stone at her."

JOHN 8:7

◆

Brian Williams messed up. America's most trusted news anchor told a lie. In 2013, he told David Letterman that a helicopter on which he was traveling in the Iraq War had been shot down. He later repeated the lie on the *Nightly News* in 2015. When confronted with the truth, he then apologized, but still did not tell the whole truth.

In 2015, Williams was suspended without pay for six months. His reputation was forever tarnished. One popular marketing poll showed that within one week, he dropped from the 23rd most trusted man in America to the 835th.

Many were saddened by Williams' sudden and dramatic fall. Others joked and taunted. As we watch famous people crash and burn from personal failures and mistakes, we easily find ourselves shaking our heads. How could they be so stupid? How could a person sink so low?

Dr. Dwight Moody was a famous preacher who lived a little over 150 years ago. He was also the founder of the Moody Institute, a Christian college in Chicago. One day as Dr. Moody was walking home from classes with one of his students, they came upon a drunk passed out in a pool of his own vomit on the sidewalk.

Wanting to impress his professor, the student asked Dr. Moody, "How could anyone stoop so low?" Dr. Moody looked at the drunk and then at his student. "There, but for the grace of God, go I," Moody replied.

That could easily have been him. That could easily have been you. So often we fail to realize we are two or three bad choices away from losing our happy families, our happy jobs—our happy lives.

Most times, you can come back from one bad choice and not lose everything. If Brian Williams had just admitted his lie right away and fully apologized, he probably wouldn't have lost everything, but then he lied again and then again.

Before we shake our heads in disgust, though, we need to listen carefully to the apostle Paul's warning: "If you think you are standing firm, be careful that you don't fall!" (1 Corinthians 10:12).

You let one drink become ten. Then you get in your car. Now a person is dead and you are going to prison.

It was just harmless flirtation. Then one day you offer to give her a ride home after work. Then you go in just to talk for a while. Now you have lost your wife and children. Everybody hates you.

When you see the famous and not-so-famous fall, remember that could be you. We are all just two or three bad choices away from losing everything.

Also remember that even if you did lose everything, it is never too late. As long as we have air in our lungs and blood flowing through our veins, it is not too late to repent.

God's grace is amazing. His forgiveness knows no bounds. You never have to lose everything. Whether you make one or one million bad choices, God will always take you back. He will always forgive you because Jesus suffered your punishment in your place on the cross.

NO MATTER HOW LOW YOU SINK, GOD'S GRACE FOR YOU KNOWS NO LIMITS.

So if you mess up, admit it. Don't let one bad choice lead to another and then another. But also trust that no matter how hard you fall, no matter how low you sink, God's grace for you knows no limits. Turn to him and find full and free forgiveness.

Today I am thankful for/that _____

_____

Lord, give me the humility to see that I am no better than those who fall into sin. Give me the wisdom and strength I need to make good choices in my life. Amen.

DAY 69
COME HERE!

Let us draw near to God with a sincere heart and with
the full assurance that faith brings, having our hearts
sprinkled to cleanse us from a guilty conscience
and having our bodies washed with pure water.

HEBREWS 10:22

◆

When Bill Cosby was in the news for being charged for unseemly crimes, it got me thinking back to a more innocent time when the name Cosby was synonymous with family.

I remember watching the very first episode of *The Cosby Show* with my mom and six brothers and sisters. We laughed hysterically as Mr. Huxtable used Monopoly money to teach Theo a lesson about "regular people."

Then he walked into the hallway where his two daughters were banging on the bathroom door in towels with shampoo in their hair. "Come here," Mr. Huxtable said sternly. The girls didn't move. "Come heeeere," he insisted. "Here. Come heeeere." The girls stood frozen. "Come heeeere!"

It's funny because it's true. If you are a parent, you probably have lived that scene. You tell your kids, "Come here," and they don't come. They hear the tone of your voice. They see the stern look. They know they are in trouble. So they freeze. They don't want to come any closer.

When the people of Israel arrived at Mount Sinai, they watched in horror and amazement as God's glory descended upon the mountain in smoke and fire, in lightning and thunder, in earthquakes and trumpet blasts.

From the billowing smoke and blazing fire God called to Moses. Would you have gone?

Seeing God's glory can be scary. It can be scary because it's the glory of a holy God—a God who hates sin and always punishes it. It can be scary because it shows the awesome power of our holy God who can squash each of us as if we were a tiny bug.

If you were Moses, would you have gone up that mountain? He did. God said, "Come here," and Moses went. Moses wasn't afraid. Moses didn't look at God as an angry parent who was going to punish him. He saw him as his loving Father and Friend.

Moses had heard God's promises and had seen God's grace. He trusted in the Savior who was to come. Though Moses had sinned against God, God had forgiven him. God was inviting Moses to come and bask in his glory.

Often when we have done something bad or are living in a way God doesn't want, we try to run away from God. We stay away from church. We stop praying. We don't want to face God. We don't want to see his glory or witness his holiness.

Yet God never stops inviting. He calls to us through his Word, "Come here." He calls not as a frowning Father prepared to punish, but as a loving Daddy with his arms wide open. He invites us to come to church and hear how he has and will always forgive us. He invites us to come and hear how Jesus suffered God's holy anger in our place. He invites us to come and hear about the heaven which he won for us.

BECAUSE OF JESUS, YOU DON'T HAVE TO BE AFRAID.

One day you will look up and see God's glory. You will hear God's voice say to you, "Come here!" Because of Jesus, you don't have to be afraid. Because of Jesus, one day you will go up the mountain and bask in God's glory forever.

Today I am thankful for/that _____

_____

Heavenly Father, I come to you just as I am, without fear. Help me to trust in the forgiveness Jesus won for me and to turn to you every day. Amen.

DAY 70
THE MAN WITH THE PLAN

The plans of the LORD stand firm forever, the purposes
of his heart through all generations.

PSALM 33:11

◆

It was Super Bowl Sunday 1983. I don't remember who won the game. I don't even remember who played. All I remember is the show which came on afterward. For a nine-year-old boy, it was the greatest show ever.

There were helicopters and rocket launchers and a really cool black van. Howling Mad Murdock was hilarious. Face was cool. B. A. Baracus was awesome. Colonel Smith was the man with the plan.

The A-Team quickly became my favorite show. In every episode, the team found themselves in seemingly impossible situations. Colonel Smith, however, would always come up with a plan. Cut to a montage of the team creating weapons and tripped-out vehicles as the theme music played loudly in the background.

Every episode ended with Colonel Smith biting down on his cigar and saying with a smile, "I love it when a plan comes together."

Just like Colonel Smith, God always has a plan. When God called Jeremiah to be his prophet, he told him, "Before I formed you in the womb I knew you, before you were born I set you apart; I appointed you as a prophet to the nations" (Jeremiah 1:5). God had plans for Jeremiah.

God has plans for you. In fact, he had plans for you before you were even born. He chose you from eternity to be his child. He planned who your parents would be. He planned whom you would marry. He planned how many children you would have.

The fact that you are reading this devotion right now is a part of God's plan.

The problem is that God's plans are not always our plans. We often don't understand God's plans. How can God plan and control all things, yet give us choice?

We aren't helpless, hapless victims of fate. You are free to choose whom you will marry. You are free to choose what you will study in college and which job you will take. In the end, though, it is all a part of God's plans.

We can't understand that. God's plans exist in a place we cannot see. Oftentimes our lives appear to be a chaotic mishmash of unrelated events, but God assures us that he has a plan and that his plans are for our good.

God's plans for you and for your life on earth end with you in heaven. From the very beginning, God knew the bad things you were going to do. He knew how you would mess everything up, so he planned a way to pay for your sins. He worked all of history to bring a Savior into the world. Pharaohs and kings and Caesars wittingly and unwittingly formed part of that plan.

Then, when the time was just right, God sent his Son into the world. At times it seemed like God's plans were falling apart, but it was all a part of God's plans.

On the cross, Jesus suffered your punishment in your place, just as God had planned. You believe in him right now because God planned and placed people in your life who shared with you the good news of his love. There is no such thing as chance. There is no fate. There is no luck.

TRUST THAT GOD'S PLAN FOR YOUR LIFE ON EARTH ENDS WITH YOU IN HEAVEN.

It's all a part of God's plan of love for you. Trust that plan even when you can't see or understand it. Trust that God's plan for your life on earth ends with you in heaven. Trust that one day, as you stand before him, God will smile and say, "I love it when a plan comes together."

Today I am thankful for/that _____

_____

Eternal Lord, thank you for working all of time and history for my salvation. Help me to trust your plans for my life. Amen.

DAY 71
THAT NEW CAR SMELL

He who was seated on the throne said,
"I am making everything new!"

REVELATION 21:5

◆

Have you ever bought a new car? When I was growing up, my family always bought used vehicles. A few years ago, my wife and I bought our first *new* car—a van. That was fun. It had that new car smell. It was shiny and clean. We drove out of the dealership with big smiles on our faces, vowing to keep it shiny and clean.

Suffice it to say, our van no longer has that new car smell. It has dents and dings and scratches. Our kids have spilled every liquid known to humankind on the interior.

New cars don't stay new very long. Nothing in this world does. Our clothes wear out. Our socks get holes in them. Our lawn mowers break down.

Our bodies get old. Though I can't seem to get anyone to feel sorry for me, I am now feeling my age. My body doesn't quite respond the way it used to. It has its dings and dents and scratches. It definitely doesn't have that new car smell.

If you have a chance today, read Revelation chapter 21. There God gave the apostle John a glimpse of the glory of heaven. There God will make everything new, including our bodies.

Do you ever watch those shows on *The History Channel* about people who find and restore antiques? They take rusty, dirty pieces of junk and make them look brand new. That is what will happen to us. When Jesus comes at the end of the world, he will raise our bodies and make them new and perfect and glorious. Never again will we hurt. Never again will we get sick. Never again will we grow old.

Oh, and God will be there. I know. That's not new. He's here with us right now, but in heaven it will be new because we will be able to see him. We will be able to talk to him face to face. We will see his glory in its fullness. There we will be reunited with our loved ones who have died in Christ. There our broken and strained relationships from here on earth will be given a new beginning.

How can I be sure? Because God told John, "It is done" (Revelation 21:6). Jesus said something similar as he hung from the cross: "It is finished" (John 19:30).

Perfection is the price of heaven. Jesus came and paid that price by living a perfect life in your place. Then, with his death on the cross, he paid the debt for your millions of sins. He suffered God's punishment for your jealousy and pride, for those ugly words you said and ugly things you thought. On that cross, Jesus paid the price. It is finished. It is done. It is paid for.

God's promise to every sinner, including you and me, is the promise of heaven. As we struggle with relationships gone bad, as we deal with cancer and pain and death, as our cars and homes and bodies grow old, the promise of heaven gives us peace and confidence.

[IN HEAVEN], NOTHING EVER WEARS OUT OR GROWS OLD.

Trust God's promise. Because of Jesus, one day God will take you home to heaven. There you will live where nothing ever wears out or grows old.

There you will smell that new car smell forever.

Today I am thankful for/that _____

_____

Heavenly Father, as I struggle with
a world in which everything gets
old and wears out—including
me—help me to look forward
with joy to the day when
everything will
be new. Amen.

DAY 72
FORGIVENESS ISN'T JUST FOR FAIRY TALES

Be kind and compassionate to one another, forgiving
each other, just as in Christ God forgave you.

EPHESIANS 4:32

❖

I was surrounded by a sea of blue and pink. Tiny three-foot princesses excitedly pranced around me. That's what dads do, isn't it? They wait patiently in line so their daughters can see *Cinderella*.

For the most part, the latest adaptation of the Disney classic followed the traditional story line: an orphan girl left to live with her spoiled stepsisters and embittered stepmother.

A courageous prince. Friendly mice. A fairy godmother.

As with many of Disney's modern adaptations, the creators of *Cinderella* tried to help us see how the wicked stepmother could become so cruel. Tragedy had traumatized her. She was bitter and afraid. In the end, though, no amount of trauma could excuse her selfishness and cruelty.

The most poignant moment in the movie came at the end as Cinderella said goodbye to her wicked stepmother. Her scheming had been discovered, her dark heart exposed for all to see.

As Cinderella and her prince turned to leave, Cinderella looked up at her former taskmaster and quietly whispered the most powerful words in the English language: "I forgive you."

A dramatic silence followed as those potent words echoed in our ears. How could anybody be so merciful? Words cannot describe the pain, hurt, and shame the stepmother had caused Cinderella. This had to be a fairy tale, because no one in the real world could be so gracious and forgiving.

FORGIVING IS THE MOST DIFFICULT THING OUR GOD ASKS US TO DO.

I truly believe forgiving is the most difficult thing our God asks us to do. Your husband of 20 years cheated on you. Your best friend lied to you. Your child disappointed you. Your parent abused you. How can you forgive? How can you let go of all the hurt and anger?

As the soldiers tied his hands to the posts, as they raised the hammer and drove the nails deep into his flesh, pinning him to the wood, as his enemies watched in morbid pleasure, Jesus spoke words of forgiveness. "Father, forgive them" (Luke 23:34).

This was no fairy tale. God himself was paying the price of their wickedness. God's forgiveness isn't that he simply lets go of the pain. It isn't that he somehow forgets or doesn't care about our sins. God forgives you because Jesus suffered your punishment as your substitute. God isn't going to punish you because he punished Jesus in your place. God turned his anger for your sins onto Jesus.

Every day, even now that you believe in him, you do terrible things to your God. You hurt him with your lies, your gossip, your anger, your laziness, and your pride. Yet every day he speaks those powerful words, "I forgive you."

If God can forgive you the millions of sins you have committed against him—if he has let go of his anger forever because of Jesus—you can forgive your wicked stepmother or your cheating husband or your lying friend. Forgiveness isn't saying that what they did is okay. Forgiveness is saying, "You hurt me, but I will let go of the anger—I will forgive you—because God has forgiven me."

It's hard to do, but it's not impossible. With God's help and by his grace, you too can say and mean those powerful words.

Forgiveness isn't just for fairy tales.

Today I am thankful for/that _____

_____

Lord, help me to forgive those who have hurt me as you have forgiven me. Amen.

DAY 73
WHY?

We know that in all things God works for the good
of those who love him.

ROMANS 8:28

◆

A while back I read an amusing article by pediatrician and best-selling author Dr. Alan Greene entitled, "Why Children Ask Why."

If you are the parent of a toddler, you've endured the seemingly never-ending barrage of questions: Why is the sky blue? Why do I have to go to bed? Why are boys and girls different? Why do people wear underwear? Why can't I lick the dog's face?

As Dr. Greene points out, "Sometimes their insistent questions seem like the drip, drip, drip of ancient water torture." Little children desperately want to know why.

And so do we.

A few years ago, our tiny Texas town was rocked as five children—ages 5 to 16—died in a house fire. Only Mom, Dad, and their four-year-old brother managed to escape the inferno.

As I stood on the street corner with the distraught family that morning—as I walked among the tear-filled community at the candlelight vigil that night—one word echoed over and over again: Why?

Why did those sweet children have to die? Why would a God of love do such a thing? Why? Why? Why?

My children are often disappointed when I try to answer their *why* questions. I don't always answer them as fully or clearly as they would like. In the end, I frequently find myself telling them, "Because I said so."

They don't like that answer very much.

Oftentimes, we get frustrated when we hear God's answer to our *why* questions. Why did I lose my job? Why did my mom get cancer? Why did those children have to die?

To our *why* questions, God answers: "It's for your good" (Romans 8:28) or "I have a plan" (Jeremiah 29:11) or simply "Because I said so" (2 Corinthians 12:9).

HE SIMPLY ASKS US TO TRUST HIM. BUT THAT'S HARD TO DO.

God doesn't tell us exactly why he does what he does. He simply asks us to trust him. But that's hard to do.

If you are struggling with the problems in your life, if you find yourself asking *why*, if you are not happy with God's answer, it may help to look at the answer to another *why* question.

As Jesus hung on the cross, suffering excruciating physical pain and felt the fists of God's fury for all the sins of all people of all time, he cried out in agony, "My God, my God, why have you forsaken me?" (Matthew 27:46). God the Father had abandoned God the Son.

But why?

God the Father forsook his Son because he loved you and me. God died so you and I could live with him forever in heaven. That is God's plan and purpose for our lives—to get us through this sinful world of suffering to our perfect home of happiness in heaven.

Is that not what God did for those five children? Why he did it at this time and in that way, I cannot tell you. Right now, I really don't know what good will come out of this for their family and friends. This side of heaven, we may never fully understand.

Yet you can be sure that all those who believe in Jesus will be reunited one day to live forever in the happiness of heaven. That is God's answer. That is God's plan. That is why he does what he does.

Today I am thankful for/that _____

_____

*Lord, help me to trust your plans of love,
even when I don't understand
why you are doing what
you are doing. Amen.*

DAY 74
A CHRISTIAN RESPONSE TO PANDEMIC

In his hand is the life of every creature and
the breath of all mankind.

JOB 12:10

◆

They were running out of hand sanitizer when I went to the grocery store this evening. That's just one of many little signs that people are beginning to worry. As I write this, the media has now confirmed a second death from the Coronavirus here in the United States. Experts agree that containment of the virus is no longer an option.

People are beginning to panic.

But not everybody. Some aren't worried. They don't think it's a big deal. They think people are overreacting and that the virus isn't as dangerous or deadly as some are portraying it.

Most people simply don't know how to react or what to think. Social media is full of funny memes about the outbreak. News articles about the virus—some trustworthy, others not so reliable—are overtaking my Facebook feed.

How should we react as Christians living in the United States? I claim no degrees in virology or medicine, but from what I can glean from reliable sources, the coronavirus will most definitely spread throughout the world.

So far, the mortality rate for the Coronavirus—that is, the percentage of deaths per cases reported—is roughly 0.2%. The mortality rate of the flu is just under 0.1% this season here in the United States. In other words, the Coronavirus is more deadly than the flu, but not much. What we often forget is that 30,000–50,000 Americans die annually from the flu.

If the experts are correct, tens of thousands of people in this country and hundreds of thousands of people around the world are going to die from the Coronavirus—and we are still months away from a vaccine.

This is serious.

Yet we shouldn't panic. The world has learned a lot over the years about the spread of such viruses. Scientists have already made great strides toward a vaccine. Just like with the flu, the overwhelming majority of healthy adults seem to be surviving the virus just fine.

Most importantly, though, we don't need to panic because God is still in control.

His promises are still true. He will be with us every moment of every day (Matthew 28:20). He will make all things—even catching the Coronavirus—work for our eternal good (Romans 8:28). No matter what happens to us here on earth, we have a home waiting for us in the perfection and happiness of heaven because of Jesus (John 3:16).

So how should we react as Christians living in this country? We should be concerned. We should be wise. We should be cautious. But we need not worry.

GOD'S GOT YOU.

Worry doesn't help, and panic makes everything worse. Besides, God's got you.

So be smart in the upcoming weeks and months. Take the necessary precautions. Buy some hand sanitizer.

But then trust. God is still in control.

Today I am thankful for/that _____

_____

Lord, when I face pandemic and pain,
hurricanes and heartaches, give me
the courage not to panic. Help me to
trust that you are in control. Amen.

DAY 75
LET'S GO FISHING

"Come follow me," Jesus said, "and I will send
you out to fish for people."

MATTHEW 4:19

◆

My father is from the great state of Minnesota, the Land of 10,000 Lakes. Years ago, he told me the story of a fisherman from Minnesota who was extremely well-prepared for fishing. He knew everything there was to know about fishing. He had everything you need to be a good fisherman: the poles, the bait, the nets. He even had one of those hats (you know, the ones with all the lures sticking out).

But this fisherman had a problem. You see, for all his preparation, he never caught fish. Not one. Not ever. Can you guess why? The answer is easy.

He never went fishing. He never got into the boat. He never left the dock. Therefore, he never caught a fish.

When Jesus was 30 years old, he went walking along the shore of the Sea of Galilee where he came upon two sets of brothers: Peter and Andrew, and James and John. They were fishermen. As they stood in their boats preparing their nets, Jesus called them. "Come, follow me," Jesus said, "and I will send you out to fish for people" (Mark 1:17).

So they followed Jesus for three years—three years of ups and downs, three years of learning. Jesus taught them. They saw his miracles. They heard his promises. For three years, Jesus trained them. These guys were extremely well-prepared for fishing.

Then Jesus sent them out to go fishing.

God has prepared you in much the same way. Through his Word and the waters of Holy Baptism, he has called you to follow him. He has trained you with that same Word as you've gone to church and Sunday school, read your Bible, and grown in your faith. He gives you all the tools you need to be a good fisherman: his Word and sacraments.

Fishing in Jesus' day wasn't complicated. They didn't use poles, hooks, and bait. They didn't have a different color lure for every fish and season. They simply threw nets into the water and pulled.

Being a fisher of men isn't complicated. We just throw out a net. We tell people the truth about their sin and its consequences. We then tell them about Jesus and how he suffered the consequences of their sins in their place.

You don't have to bait people. You don't have to hook them. Simply tell them about Jesus and his love. God has trained you and given you all the tools you need to be a good fisherman.

You are extremely well-prepared for fishing.

You aren't going to catch a thing, however, if you don't get off the dock. Jesus has called each of us to go fishing. We all have friends, family members, neighbors, and coworkers who either don't believe in Jesus or have gotten away from God's Word and church.

How can they know about Jesus unless somebody tells them? And if they don't know—if they don't believe—what will happen to them when they die? The Bible is clear. "Whoever believes and is baptized will be saved, but whoever does not believe will be condemned" (Mark 16:16).

YOU ARE EXTREMELY WELL-PREPARED FOR FISHING.

Fishing isn't always easy. Some people won't listen. Some may even get mad, but this is important. Souls are in danger. People are dying. Your Savior is calling and his call has urgency.

So talk about your faith. Talk about your Savior with everyone you can. Don't be left standing on the dock. Let's go fishing.

Today I am thankful for/that _____

_____

Dear God, thank you for sending people into my life who shared with me the good news of what Jesus did to save me. Give me courage and wisdom so I too can share that good news with others. Amen.

DAY 76
THEY ALWAYS COME BACK

Count yourselves dead to sin but alive
to God in Christ Jesus.

ROMANS 6:11

❖

Over the years, movie aficionados have compiled lists of tips for characters to survive horror movies. Following are some common horror movie survival rules:

- Never say, "I'll be right back," because you won't ever come back.
- Never say, "Who's there?" because you really don't want to know.
- Never say, "I think we're finally safe," because you aren't.

And whatever you do, never, under any circumstances, assume the killer is dead. One bullet will not finish them off. Cut off their head and kick it at least 10 feet from the body. Then burn the remains and scatter the ashes in at least five different cities—unless, of course, you have the ability to rocket them into outer space.

Because if there is one thing horror movies have taught us, it is that the killers never stay dead. They keep coming back over and over again, sequel after sequel.

Each one of us has a monster—an evil, psycho murderer—living inside of us. No, you aren't the title character in an upcoming horror film. You are a sinner.

The Bible calls the monster our "flesh." Theologians call it our "Old Adam." You and I were born under the control of a selfish psycho hiding in our hearts. In fact, that monster is who we are at birth. Sure we may look cute and cuddly, but sin and selfishness fill our hearts (Psalm 51:5).

Then God steps in. Through his Word and the waters of Holy Baptism, the Holy Spirit works faith in our hearts—faith which trusts in God's promises and wants to live for him. A new man or woman is born who loves God and clings to the forgiveness Jesus won for us on the cross.

On that day, the battle begins. A war wages within the heart of every Christian. Sadly, we don't always consider the monster in us to be the

144

enemy. A part of us wants to be angry. A part of us enjoys those dirty sins. A part of us doesn't think sin is very dangerous.

Yet every time we give in to our selfish desires and yearnings, the weaker we become. We grow numb to the guilt and shame. The monster tears away pieces of our heart until the new man or woman is no more.

Yes, Jesus died for our sins. Yes, God forgives us no matter how badly or how often we mess up, but sin is dangerous. When we give in to the selfish monster in our hearts, it grows more powerful and more dangerous.

HELP ME TO FIGHT THE GOOD FIGHT. That's why we need to feed our new man or woman every day with God's Word. That's why we need to kill that monster by daily repenting of our anger, lust, and pride. We need to do so daily because the monster always comes back. Just when we think we finally have him defeated— when we think we are safe and secure in our faith—the monster once again rears his ugly head.

The early reformer Martin Luther once explained what our baptisms should mean for our daily lives. This is what he said: "Baptism means that the sinful nature in us should be drowned by daily sorrow and repentance, and that all its evil deeds and desires be put to death. It also means that a new person should daily arise to live before God in righteousness and purity forever."

This side of heaven, you will never be completely free of that monster in your heart. Don't be like the naïve teenagers of a horror movie who say, "I think we're safe now." Be on your guard. Every day cut off the monster's head with the sword of God's Word. Drown him with daily sorrow and repentance. Be constantly on guard because the monster always comes back.

Today I am thankful for/that _____

_____

Heavenly Father, help me to fight the good fight against my sinful nature every day. Amen.

DAY 77
TEARFUL GOODBYES

"He will wipe every tear from their eyes."

REVELATION 21:4

◆

My wife and I both live hundreds of miles from our nearest relatives. That means when we visit our respective families, everybody gets excited. When we arrive, everybody smiles. Everybody laughs. We chatter and talk and catch up. Visiting our families means happy hugs when we arrive. It also means tearful goodbyes when we leave.

The last day of vacation for us is always the hardest. As we give our goodbye hugs, we can't help but think how long it will be until we see each other again. Tears flow. Hearts ache.

It's hard to say "goodbye" to those we love. If you have ever had to stand next to your father's bed in a crowded hospital room—if you have ever had to hold a friend's hand as she breathes her last—you know how hard goodbyes are. Tears flow. Hearts ache.

Our loving God has good news for our hurting hearts. The apostle Paul wrote to the Christians in the Greek city of Thessalonica, "Brothers and sisters, we do not want you to be uninformed about those who sleep in death, so that you do not grieve like the rest of mankind, who have no hope. For we believe that Jesus died and rose again, and so we believe that God will bring with Jesus those who have fallen asleep in him" (1 Thessalonians 4:13-14).

You'll notice Paul doesn't say we shouldn't grieve. Saying "goodbye" hurts. Our hearts will ache. Tears will flow. But we don't grieve like the rest of men who have no hope.

We know that because Jesus suffered the punishment on the cross of all the bad things we do—because he defeated death with his resounding resurrection—we have hope. We have the sure and certain hope that all who believe in Jesus will live with him forever in heaven. We have the sure and certain hope that *we* will live forever in heaven.

That means we will see our loved ones again. Though right now we are separated by a great distance, we will be reunited one day. On that day, we will share happy hugs and warm embraces. Tears of sorrow will turn to tears of joy. Heaven is a giant family reunion.

In his Word, our God reveals to us many of the wonderful aspects of the happiness of heaven. He tells us we will see him face to face. He tells us we will be perfect. He tells us we will be free of all pains and problems.

As we say goodbye to our family and friends here on earth—as we tearfully stand next to the casket or in front of the tombstone—may we never forget one other comforting characteristic of heaven.

IN HEAVEN THERE WILL BE NO MORE TEARFUL GOODBYES.

In heaven there will be no more tearful goodbyes.

Today I am thankful for/that _____

_____

Lord, as I struggle with tearful goodbyes here on earth, give me the comfort of the resurrection and the family reunion of heaven. Amen.

DAY 78
WHAT'S IN A NAME?

"Salvation is found in no one else, for there is no other name under heaven given to mankind by which we must be saved."

ACTS 4:12

"What's in a name?" young Juliet asked as she perched aloft her famous balcony. Her one true love, Romeo, was a Montague, the arch-enemy of her family, the Capulets. If he had any other name, they could be together.

Because "What's in a name? A rose by any other name would smell as sweet." In other words, a rose doesn't stop being a rose even if you call it by another name.

My name is Andrew. It comes from a Greek word. It means "manly." Most people chuckle when I tell them that. My name doesn't describe me. If I changed my name, it wouldn't change who I am.

Many in our world would say the same about God. They claim that all the religions of the world are basically the same. All religions lead to the same place. We worship the same God; we just use different names for him.

That sounds so good—so loving, so tolerant. The problem is that it isn't true.

Do you know what the name *Jesus* means? It literally means "He saves." Jesus is our Savior.

Imagine your house is on fire. You're trapped in your bedroom—no way out. A firefighter bursts in and carries you out. He's a hero. He saved you from the fire. Now imagine if that firefighter died while rescuing you. You would never forget his sacrifice.

Jesus is our Savior. He swooped down and rescued us from the fires of hell. He died to save us. He suffered the pain, the punishment, the hell we deserve. You see, the fire is of our own making. You aren't some innocent victim. You are the arsonist. You are the liar, the cheat, the one who deserves to burn in hell forever for all the shameful and hurtful things you do.

Yet Jesus saved you. He rescued you from the fire. He died so that you might live. What's in a name? Jesus' name says it all. He is our Savior.

Now compare his name with that of the gods of other religions. For example, the god of Islam is called Allah, a name which simply means "god." They call him loving, but he will only love you if you fight your *jihad* against his enemies. If you die in your fight for him, you will enjoy paradise with virgins who will pleasure you forever. Does that sound like the same God of the Bible by a different name?

Or how about Shiva, one of the chief gods of Hinduism? The name Shiva means "The Auspicious One," but he is more often called "The Destroyer." Shiva is a paradox. He is considered the source of both good and evil. Does that sound like the God of the Bible by a different name?

My favorite, though, is the Aztec god, Huitzilopochtli. His name means, "Left-handed blue hummingbird." He is the god of war who demands human sacrifice in order to protect you from your enemies. Does that sound like the God of the Bible by a different name?

I cannot prove to you that my God is the true God. I cannot prove that the gods of other religions are false. I can't force you to believe what I believe. But to say that all religions are basically the same or that they are the same god by a different name is ludicrous.

In the end, all other religions of the world tell you what *you* have to do to win their god's love or to earn paradise. Christianity is the only religion in the world whose God gives heaven and forgiveness freely. Christianity is the only religion in which God's love doesn't depend on you or what you do.

JESUS' NAME SAYS IT ALL.

So what's in a name? Jesus' name says it all.

Today I am thankful for/that _____

_____

Dear Jesus, you are the one and only true God. Help me to trust in you and to share your name with everyone I can. Amen.

DAY 79
THE GOOD OL' DAYS

"Forget the former things; do not dwell on the past. See, I am doing a new thing!"

ISAIAH 43:18,19

Anniversaries are fun. This Sunday, my church celebrates its 50th anniversary. Over the last few months in anticipation of the big day, former pastors have visited and preached for us, our ladies published a cookbook, and we wrote a history of our congregation. Two weeks ago, we celebrated a "Retro Sunday" in which we dressed and worshiped just as the original members would have in 1965.

At times like these, we can't help but be a bit nostalgic. Our thoughts wander back to a simpler, more innocent time. As the years pass, I see our society becoming more and more obsessed with sex. I see prejudice and politics tearing our country apart. I see Christians slowly drifting from God and church. The older I get, the more I yearn for the good ol' days.

But were the good ol' days really that good?

Every generation at some point suffers from what I call "The Good Ol' Days Syndrome." As the years pass, the world of our younger years is transformed in our minds into a time of innocence—a time when people treated each other with more respect, when the world wasn't as cynical or cold, when people were more Christian and moral.

Now, I am not denying that the morals of our society in many areas of life continue to decline. Jesus said it would be that way. The world will continually become more evil as we wait for judgment day. The love of most will grow cold.

But is our generation really that much worse than the last?

Yes, we live in an oversexualized society. Then again, 50 years ago we were in the middle of the sexual revolution of the sixties. Our country was bitterly divided politically by the war in Vietnam. The racial divide in our country was violent and virulent. Women were often mistreated and demeaned.

Wise old King Solomon once said, "There is nothing new under the sun" (Ecclesiastes 1:9). The epidemic of sin has infested humanity since Adam and Eve. Though the outward symptoms and manifestations of that disease change with time, the root cause remains the same. People were just as selfish and lustful and full of bitterness and envy 50 years ago as they are today.

Thankfully, the truth of God's Word remains the same with every passing generation. God's promise of forgiveness has no expiration date. Just as God guided and protected our forefathers, he promises to be by our side and get us through every struggle and fear in our present world.

Though it's fun to look back and remember the good ol' days, and it's important to see God's grace which has brought us to this day, as Christians we don't yearn for the good ol' days. As we remember the past, we need to be careful not to get stuck in it.

Rather, let's look around and say, "God, what can I do to thank and serve you today." Let's look ahead to the happiness and heaven which Jesus won for us. The good ol' days are nothing compared to the good "new" days which are to come.

Today I am thankful for/that _____

_____

Lord, thank you for the blessings of the good ol' days, but help me now to keep my eyes focused on the good new days to come. Amen.

DAY 80
THE SKY IS FALLING

"What will be the sign of your coming and
of the end of the age?"

MATTHEW 24:3

In the fairy tale *Chicken Little,* an acorn falls on Chicken Little's head. He tells his friends, "The sky is falling!" Mass hysteria ensues as the animals stare fearfully at the sky thinking it's the end of the world.

I don't want to cause mass hysteria, but . . . the sky is falling.

On Saturday, April 25, 2015, an earthquake measuring 7.8 on the Richter scale shook Nepal. The death toll measured nearly 9,000 lives, while over 22,000 people were injured.

On that same day in Baltimore, Maryland, crowds began to gather to protest the death of Freddie Gray, a 25-year-old resident of Baltimore, who died from injuries purportedly suffered at the hands of the police.

The protests soon turned violent. The rioting raged for three days. Thousands of police and National Guardsmen were brought in. Millions of dollars' worth of property was destroyed. Police and civilians alike were injured. Chaos reigned.

Right now, wars rage around the world. Christians are being massacred by ISIS and Boko Haram. People are leaving Christian churches in droves. Sins like homosexuality are not only being tolerated by our society; they are being celebrated.

The sky is falling.

During the last week of his life, Jesus' disciples asked him, "What will be the sign of your coming and of the end of the age?"

Jesus gave them many: "You will hear of wars and rumors of wars. . . . There will be famines and earthquakes in various places. . . . You will be handed over to be persecuted and put to death. . . . Many will turn away from the faith. . . . Many false prophets will appear. . . . Because of the increase in wickedness, the love of most will grow cold" (Matthew 24:6,7,9-12). All of those signs are happening right now. The end of the world is coming.

When we as Christians say that, however, people roll their eyes. They look at us as if we were Chicken Little shouting, "The sky is falling!" They look at us as if we were that crazy guy in Times Square wearing poster boards and yelling, "The end is near!"

But the end *is* near. This is not paranoid hysteria. The world is really coming to an end. Jesus is coming to judge all people and to destroy this world with fire. The signs he gave so that we would be ready are happening right now. In fact, they have been happening to some degree since the day Jesus ascended into heaven.

HELP ME TO STAY READY EVERY DAY.

You see, Jesus wants us to continually be ready—to be on high alert at all times—because he could come back at any moment. When we see earthquakes and riots, wars and apostasy, it should remind us that this world is coming to an end. It should remind us to be ready.

If you believe in Jesus, you are ready. When Jesus comes to judge on the Last Day, he will declare all believers to be innocent because he already suffered our punishment in our place. Whoever believes in him will be saved. Whoever does not believe in him, though, will be condemned forever to the death sentence of hell.

When you see earthquakes, riots, and terrorist attacks on CNN, it should sadden you, but it shouldn't shock you. Jesus said such things would happen. They are a reminder to be ready. The end is near.

Today I am thankful for/that _____

_____

Almighty God, as I see all around me the signs of your coming, help me to stay ready every day. Amen.

DAY 81
DECISION ANXIETY DISORDER

For to me, to live is Christ and to die is gain. If I am to go on living in the body, this will mean fruitful labor for me. Yet what shall I choose? I do not know! I am torn between the two.

PHILIPPIANS 1:21-23

I believe both my children suffer from a mental illness. After careful research, I have not found it listed in any major medical journal, so I am going to name it myself. I call it "Decision Anxiety Disorder."

Grandpa comes for a visit. He takes my son to the store to buy him a toy. My son finds two toys he really likes and grandpa tells him he can pick whichever one he wants. The next hour is spent in agony and tears as my son cannot decide.

If Grandpa had simply bought him one of the toys, my son would have been elated. Tasked with the decision, however, both my son and daughter fall to pieces. They agonize. They stress. They suffer because deep down they fear they will make the wrong decision. They worry that they will later regret their choice.

Do you know anyone who suffers from Decision Anxiety Disorder? I am thinking about starting a support group.

The apostle Paul at one point suffered from a form of Decision Anxiety Disorder. At the time, he was imprisoned in the city of Rome. He didn't know what was going to happen to him—whether the authorities were going to kill him or let him go.

And he didn't know which he would choose if he were given the choice.

In his letter to the Philippians, Paul told them he was having a hard time deciding. If they killed him, he would get to go to heaven and be with Jesus. He would be free from all the thorns and prison cells of this world. Death would be better by far. Yet if they let him go, he would be able to share the good news of God's love with more people. More people could be saved.

Paul didn't know which to choose. "For to me, to live is Christ," he wrote, "and to die is gain."

PAUL DIDN'T KNOW WHICH TO CHOOSE. . . . FEW PEOPLE THINK THAT WAY TODAY.

Few people think that way today—that to die is gain. But it is. When we die, we can be sure we are going to heaven because Jesus paid it all. He suffered our punishment in our place. He promises that all those who believe in him will live forever in heaven.

And that is gain.

I mean, I love living in Edna, Texas, but it is not heaven on earth. No place, no experience, no joy here on earth can compare to the happiness of heaven.

It may sound crazy, but for a Christian it is better to die than to live here on earth.

Yet, for us, to live is Christ. If we are still here, that means we have the opportunity to live for our Savior who lived and died for us. If we are still here, it means God has jobs for us to do and blessings to shower upon us.

It's actually a tough choice. Which would you choose?

In the end, Paul didn't need to stress about that decision. You also don't need to worry about which to choose, because it's not your choice.

It is not your decision whether you live or die.

Your heavenly Father has made that decision for you. If you are still here on earth, it is because God still has life for you to live, things for you to do, blessings for you to receive. When he decides—when the time is just right—he will take you to be with him in the happiness and perfection of heaven.

So don't worry about it. Don't stress about dying. Don't give up on living when life gets hard. If you're still here, God has plans for you. When you die, you get to go to heaven.

Either way, you win.

Today I am thankful for/that _____

_____

Eternal Lord, help me to live every day for you,
knowing that my life has purpose. Help me to
live every day free from the fear of death,
knowing that to die is gain. Amen.

DAY 82
TO TELL THE TRUTH

They received the message with great eagerness and
examined the Scriptures every day to see if
what Paul said was true.

ACTS 17:11

◆

"Welcome to our church. We are a Bible-based church. Here we teach what the Bible says. Here we teach the truth."

Most churches you visit will tell you that. Yet they are all different. They all teach and believe different things. So which one is telling the truth?

Many in our world would say it's impossible to know. They say the Bible can be understood in many ways. "Everybody has his or her own interpretation of the Bible."

The thing is that the Bible isn't vague. It says what it says. Sure, there are parts of the Bible which are more obscure and difficult to understand. Thankfully those passages are made clear and explained by other sections of Scripture. The Bible interprets itself. It says what it says.

The reason different churches teach different things is because as sinful human beings we try to make the Bible say what we want it to say. We add to it. We subtract from it. We twist it.

Some churches add to what the Bible says. "It is a sin to drink alcohol," they say. "It is a sin to dance." "It is a sin to use contraceptives." Where does the Bible say that? It doesn't.

Some cut out parts of the Bible. I call that Salad Bar Christianity. They pick and choose what parts they want to believe as if the Bible were a buffet. What the Bible says about human sexuality, for example, offends their societal sensibilities, so they claim that part doesn't apply today.

Finally, others twist the Bible to make it say what they want it to say. The Bible is a big book. You can pull verses out of their context and, with a little elbow grease, you can cut, paste, and twist God's Word to say just about anything.

Then how can you know who is telling the truth? In Acts chapter 17, the apostle Paul left the Greek city of Thessalonica and traveled to the nearby city of Berea. Luke tells us that "the Bereans were of more noble character than the Thessalonians." Why? Because "they received the message with great eagerness and examined the Scriptures every day to see if what Paul said was true."

In other words, the Bereans didn't trust the apostle Paul. Every time he preached to them, they went back and checked in their Bibles to see if what he was saying was true. Therein lies the answer. If you want to know who is telling the truth about God's Word, open your Bibles and see!

Don't trust me. I'm a sinful human being. I make mistakes. Just because something in one of these articles sounds good or interesting or funny doesn't mean it's true. Open up your Bibles. See for yourself.

God has given you a monumental responsibility. It takes work to study, read, and chew on God's Word. It's much easier to just go to church and trust the preacher. It's much easier to shop for a church that tells you what you want to hear, but that's not what God wants.

BE A BEREAN.   Be a Berean. Be of noble character. Don't just blindly accept what you are taught. Open up your Bibles and read it for yourself.

Today I am thankful for/that _____

Lord, thank you for faithful churches and preachers who teach your Word in truth and purity. Give me the wisdom to always go back to your Word to find the truth. Amen.

DAY 83
WHAT HAPPENS IN VEGAS

**For your ways are in full view of the Lord,
and he examines all your paths.**

PROVERBS 5:21

In January of 2003, the city of Las Vegas launched a controversial new advertising campaign. The risqué ads included the tagline, "What happens here, stays here." The ads became a cultural phenomenon. They inspired Hollywood blockbusters like *What Happens in Vegas* and *The Hangover.*

The basic gist of the campaign is that you can visit Las Vegas, do crazy things you would never otherwise do, and then return home like it never happened. Las Vegas would never tell.

If you do it in Las Vegas, somehow it's okay. Somehow it's like it didn't really happen.

The whole campaign is based on an old adage used by businessmen: "What happens on the road, stays on the road." The same mentality dominates annual parties like Mardi Gras and spring break. People young and old find themselves far from home. They do things they would never otherwise do because somehow it's okay at Mardi Gras or spring break.

Even Christians fall into such thinking. God isn't invited when we go to Las Vegas. God isn't invited on the road trip for spring break.

We just won't think about him while we're there. When we get home, we'll get back to church and life like nothing ever happened. Las Vegas will never tell what we did.

Do you have times and places in your life where God isn't invited? When you are on the road for business, do you watch movies in your hotel room you wouldn't watch with your wife? Do you go with the guys to bars and strip clubs because what happens on the road stays on the road? When you go camping for the weekend, do you bring a cooler overflowing with beer and come home with it empty, because that's what you do when you go camping?

When you go with your girlfriends to Las Vegas for a bachelorette party or to Cancun for spring break, do you hook up with a guy for a one-night fling, knowing you will never see him again?

WHETHER YOU INVITE HIM OR NOT, GOD IS THERE.

We all have times and places in our lives where God is not invited. Whether you invite him or not, God is there. God is in Las Vegas. God is in your hotel room. God is watching you on spring break.

God knows what you did and it's not okay. What happens in Vegas saddens and angers him. What you did on spring break disappoints him. What you did deserves hell.

It's not that God is a party pooper who doesn't want us to have any fun. The "fun" offered in Las Vegas and spring break and Mardi Gras—the "fun" you have on the road with your friends—can cause lasting damage and shame to your life. Las Vegas has ruined many a marriage. Spring break has forever scarred young lives. One weekend of that kind of "fun" can cause a lifetime of pain.

Thankfully, our loving and patient God forgives us. On the cross, Jesus suffered the horrific punishment for your drunkenness and sexual sins. He promises full and free forgiveness for all your foolish "fun." All of the bad things you've done were forever nailed to the cross.

Never forget, though, that wherever you go, God is there—even in Las Vegas. So don't go anywhere without inviting him.

If you do, though—if you mess up and foolishly fall into the snare of drunkenness and sexual sins—take it to your Savior in prayer. Ask him to forgive you. Trust that what happened in Vegas now stays forever at the cross.

Today I am thankful for/that _____

_____

Merciful God, forgive me for the sins I've
committed when I've been away from
home. Help me to remember that you
are always watching. Amen.

DAY 84
FORGETFUL

"Can a mother forget the baby at her breast and have
no compassion on the child she has borne? Though
she may forget, I will not forget you! See, I have
engraved you on the palms of my hands."

ISAIAH 49:15,16

They say two things happen to you as you get older. One is that you start forgetting things.

I can't seem to remember the other thing.

I don't know if it is age or busyness or both, but I'm starting to forget things. I sometimes walk into my office and forget what I was going to get. My wife sends me to the store and I inevitably forget something. I forget names. I forget appointments. I would forget my head if it wasn't attached to my body.

To help me remember, I've started to write things down. The problem is I often forget where I put the piece of paper or calendar on which I wrote down what I needed to remember. For a while I tried writing reminders on my hand. That way, every time I looked down at my hand I would remember. The problem is that my hands would get sweaty and the ink would rub off. Besides, people look at you funny when you have a bunch of writing on your hand.

There was a time when God's people of the Old Testament felt like God had forgotten about them. They felt like he didn't care about them anymore.

Have you ever felt like that?

Your life is falling apart. You lose your job. Your husband dies. Your doctor tells you your unborn baby will never be born. Where is God? Doesn't he care? Has he forgotten about me?

Listen to how God answered his people of the Old Testament: "See, I have engraved you on the palms of my hands."

NO MATTER WHAT HAPPENS, MY GOD WILL NEVER FORGET ABOUT ME.

God can't and won't ever forget about you. You are tattooed on his hands. You are important to him. He knows you perfectly. He thinks about you constantly. You are and will always be his dear child.

Sometimes it feels like God has forgotten about us because he allows pain and problems in our lives. Sometimes it feels like God has forgotten about us because we pray to him and nothing seems to happen.

God promises us in his Word that he does hear our prayers. He promises to answer them for our good, but in his own time and in his own way. Just because God doesn't do what you want doesn't mean he's forgotten about you. It may not be the right time. He may have different plans for you.

That doesn't mean he doesn't care. He cared for you so much it hurt. He cared for you so much he suffered your pain and punishment on the cross. That's right—when he died on the cross, God remembered you before you were even born. He did it all for you.

As I get older, I am probably going to get even more forgetful. There may come a point in my life that I don't remember anybody's name, including my own. Thankfully I can know that, no matter what happens, my God will never forget about me.

Today I am thankful for/that _____

_____

*Heavenly Father, help me to never forget
your promises and to trust that you
will never forget me. Amen.*

DAY 85
BLIND SPOTS

If you think you are standing firm,
be careful that you don't fall!
1 CORINTHIANS 10:12

✦

One of the things I love about living in the state of Texas is the 75 mph speed limit. When I'm in a hurry, I can simply get on the highway and go. The problem with higher speed limits, however, is they reduce your margin for error while driving.

A while back I was cruising down the highway about to change lanes when my wife screamed. I jerked the car back just in time to miss a small roadster that was hiding in my blind spot.

Blind spots are dangerous.

King David loved God. He trusted God. He served God faithfully. Trusting in God's promises, David slew a giant and grew a kingdom. David, however, had a blind spot. Living in the fast lane, he didn't even see the temptation coming. He grew careless in his faith.

A little peek turned into a peep show. After a while, he wanted more. He was king, after all. It didn't matter that she was married. It didn't matter that he was married. Then came the car wreck—the pregnancy, the lies, the murder.

As I said before, blind spots are dangerous.

We all have spiritual blind spots. We all have weaknesses and sins we don't see or we refuse to see. Left unchecked, those blind spots lead to car wrecks in our lives.

A Christian husband goes to church every Sunday. He loves his wife and family. He doesn't, however, see anything wrong with checking out the secretary at work whenever he has the chance. "It's just harmless flirting," he tells himself. Then comes the car wreck.

A Christian pastor is thriving in his new church. The congregation is growing and everybody loves his sermons. Because things are going so well, he doesn't even hear himself as he barks at those who disagree with him or see the looks of hurt and anger on their faces. He convinces himself it is okay because he is right. He is the pastor.

Soon the goodwill of the congregation turns to resentment. The church divides between those who support the pastor and those who feel he needs to leave. People stop going to church. Some never come back. His blind spot leads to a twenty-car pileup.

SO WHAT CAN YOU DO ABOUT YOUR BLIND SPOTS?

So what can you do about your blind spots? First admit you have them. As Christians, we often overestimate our own spiritual maturity. The apostle Paul warns, "If you think you are standing firm, be careful that you don't fall!"

Second, pray about it. Jesus said, "Watch and pray so that you will not fall into temptation" (Matthew 26:41). Ask God often to help you honestly see your weak spots.

One of the greatest gifts God gives to help us see our blind spots is mature Christian friends and family. A true friend is one who will tell you the truth about yourself even when you don't want to hear it.

Finally, nothing helps us see more clearly than the light of God's Word. God's Word not only helps us see ourselves and our blind spots more clearly, it also gives us the strength we need to avoid the inevitable fender benders they cause.

If in your pride and weakness, however, you get in a wreck, do what David did. Confess your sins to your God whose mercies never end. No matter how badly you mess things up, no matter how hard you crash and burn, God will always take you back. Because of Jesus, he will always forgive you.

All that could be avoided, however, if we would just check our blind spots.

Today I am thankful for/that _____

_____

Holy Spirit, open my eyes to see where I am spiritually weak. Give me the humility, wisdom, and strength I need to overcome my blind spots. Amen.

DAY 86
BE THAT GUY

Be on your guard; stand firm in the faith; be
courageous; be strong. Do everything in love.

1 CORINTHIANS 16:13,14

❧

"He's such a guy," she says rolling her eyes. All her friends nod knowingly
as they sip their coffee.

His eyes follow every pair of yoga pants that walks by. He always leaves his
socks on the floor and the toilet seat up. He refuses to ask for directions.
His favorite place to be on the weekends isn't home with you, but at deer
camp with the other guys.

He's such a guy.

Somehow in our world today, being a guy has become a bad thing. Sadly,
our weaknesses as "guys" have come to define us. In fact, at times it seems
like our world is raising a generation of boys to avoid being "guys." That
worries me.

I feel I need to say something now which may surprise you: Men and
women are different. I know. Shocking, right? God made us different. That
one extra chromosome changes everything.

Men tend to be more aggressive and physically stronger. Women tend to
be more accommodating and nurturing. Women tend to be more in touch
with their feelings. Men tend to be visually stimulated. Women tend to be
more physically affectionate.

And those are just a few examples of the myriad of differences.

Now obviously those are generalizations. Not every man or woman falls
neatly into those categories. Yet most men and women demonstrate some,
if not all, of those tendencies. It has a lot to do with the levels of testosterone
and estrogen a person has. Men tend to have much higher levels of
testosterone, and women, much higher levels of estrogen.

In the end, God made men and women different. If you don't agree with
that, there is no point in continuing to read this article.

Because men tend to naturally be bigger, more aggressive, and less in touch
with their feelings, the temptation for them is to be incommunicative, rude,

or even violent. Because they tend to be visually stimulated, yoga pants and porn tend to be a greater enticement for them than for a woman.

That, by no means, excuses such behavior. It is sin. Christian men can and should fight against the sinful tendencies of their natural instincts. But those temptations don't and shouldn't define what a man is.

Being a guy can be a good thing. A good guy works hard and provides for his family without complaint. A good guy protects his family at all costs. A good guy teaches his sons to be strong and his daughters that they are worthy of love and respect. A good guy brings his family to church and shows them what it means to lead and serve.

STAND UP AND BE THE GUY GOD MADE YOU TO BE.

My encouragement to all the fathers and men out there is to be that guy. Stand up and be strong. Lead your families. Teach your boys to be men.

And when you fail to be the guy God wants you to be, be a man and admit it. Tell your wife you're sorry. Tell your God you're sorry with the confidence that he has already forgiven you because of Jesus.

Then stand up and be the guy God made you to be.

Today I am thankful for/that _____

_____

*Lord, help me and the men in my life to be
the men you have made us to be. Amen.*

DAY 87
SHHH!

The LORD came and stood there, calling as at the other
times, "Samuel! Samuel!" Then Samuel said,
"Speak, for your servant is listening."

1 SAMUEL 3:10

◆

In the olden days before refrigerators, people used what were called "ice houses" to preserve their food. Ice houses had thick walls, no windows, and a tightly fitted door. In the winter, when streams and lakes were frozen over, large blocks of ice were cut out and transported to the ice houses where they were covered with sawdust. Often the ice would last well into the summer.

The story is told of a man who lost a valuable watch while working in an ice house. He searched long and hard, but could not find it. His fellow workers helped him carefully dig through the wet sawdust looking for the watch, but to no avail. Later that day, however, a small boy, who had heard about the lost watch, slipped into the ice house while everyone else was out to lunch. A few minutes later he emerged with the watch.

Amazed, the men asked him how he found it. "I closed the door," the boy replied, "laid down in the sawdust, and kept very quiet. Soon I heard the watch ticking."

We live in a stereo surround sound world. Noise is everywhere. In fact, scientists hypothesize that if time travel were possible, one of the things that would shock us the most about the past would be the silence. They say that if you could travel back in time a thousand years, the silence would be almost deafening. Think about it: a world without cell phones, TVs, radios, airplanes, cars, refrigerators—all that noise which surrounds us, gone.

With all that noise, it's hard to hear. It's hard to hear God's voice speaking to us. God doesn't usually yell. He doesn't usually communicate in thunder bolts or burning bushes.

God speaks to us in the gentle whisper of his Word. He speaks to us as we sit quietly in church hearing his Word read to us. He whispers into our ears as we sit quietly in our homes reading our Bibles.

Often the question is not whether God is speaking to us, but whether we take the time to sit quietly and listen. So turn off the TV. Silence your cell phone. Put your child's gaming console away. Sit together as a family listening to God speak to you through his Word.

Through the gentle whisper of his Word, God will convict you and comfort you. Through the gentle whisper of his Word, he will teach you and guide you and give you hope.

DON'T WAIT FOR GOD TO YELL.

Don't wait for God to yell. Don't expect him to speak to you in thunder or in dreams or with visions of angels. God is speaking to you right now. Can you hear him? Turn down the volume, open up your Bible, and hear him speak.

Today I am thankful for/that _____

_____

Speak, Lord, for your servant
is listening. Amen.

DAY 88
PERSPECTIVE

"The harvest is plentiful, but the workers are few.
Ask the Lord of the harvest, therefore, to send
out workers into his harvest field."

LUKE 10:2

◆

At the turn of the last century, two competing shoe companies in the United States looked to expand their business. Both heard about a developing country in Africa that was opening its doors to foreign companies and investors.

Hoping to gain an advantage on its competitor, each company sent a sales representative to scout the possibility of opening new markets. The first sales rep got off the boat and began walking around the small coastal community. After a couple of hours, he hurriedly made his way to the telegraph office.

"Halt production. Possibility of opening new market in Africa slim to nil. Nobody here wears shoes."

NOBODY HERE WEARS SHOES. The other sales rep soon disembarked from his ship and made his way through the same coastal village. After a short time, he too ran to the telegraph office.

"Build more factories. Send as many shoes as you can. Nobody here wears shoes!"

Many Christians right now are disenchanted and disappointed by the Supreme Court decision legalizing gay marriage. Over the last few decades, the values of our society have deteriorated. The atheist movement in our country is growing stronger and louder. A recent survey conducted by the Pew Research Group shows that currently 70% of Americans claim to be Christian. That's down from 78% just eight years ago.

Such news should sadden us. God hates sin. The sins of our society anger him. Yet God also loves sinners and wants people to turn to him in repentance and trust in Jesus as their Savior. What is happening in our society should sadden and concern us.

But we don't need to wring our hands and throw up our arms in defeat. Jesus himself said that many would turn away from the faith. He said that the love of most would grow cold, but that doesn't change what we do as Christians.

When we see large numbers of people who don't believe or who have turned away from what God says in his Word, we don't say, "Well, I guess we need to close the doors of our churches. There is nothing we can do. Nobody here wears shoes."

No. We say, "Let's get to work. God is giving us new opportunities to share his message of sin and forgiveness—the message of Jesus and his love—because nobody here wears shoes."

When Jesus saw the crowds of lost and hurting souls before him, he told his disciples, "The harvest is plentiful, but the workers are few. Ask the Lord of the harvest, therefore, to send out workers into his harvest field." Then Jesus sent his disciples to get to work.

You may be saddened by the state of our country and our world today. I know I am, but I am also excited by the challenge. This just means more opportunities to share and show our Savior's love.

So when you see our society turning further and further away from God and his Word, don't give up. Get to work. Opportunities abound.

Nobody here wears shoes.

Today I am thankful for/that _____

_____

Lord of the harvest, please send out more workers into your harvest field. Use me to share your love of salvation with everyone I can. Amen.

DAY 89
THANK YOU, GOD

Call on me in the day of trouble; I will deliver you, and you will honor me.

PSALM 50:15

Mr. Rogers-mania is upon us. In November of 2019, the Tom Hanks biopic about Mr. Rogers debuted to gushing reviews and a media frenzy. Having grown up with Mr. Rogers, I honestly can't wait to see the movie.

Called *A Beautiful Day in the Neighborhood,* it is loosely based on the story of journalist Tom Junod, who in 1998 was assigned the task of writing an article about Mr. Rogers for an upcoming "Heroes Issue" of *Esquire* magazine.

Junod entered the project cynically while struggling with issues in his personal life. He came away from the experience changed forever by his encounter with Mr. Rogers.

With all the attention the movie is garnering, I decided to find the original article and read it before seeing the movie. Two quick searches on Google led me straight to the piece, entitled, "Can You Say . . . Hero?" What struck me personally as I read Junod's words is how Mr. Rogers really wasn't playing a character on TV.

That is how Fred Rogers acted and spoke in real life.

What touched me about Junod's article were the themes interwoven throughout. He spoke often of Mr. Rogers' fascination with the Greek word for "grace" and marveled at this mysterious concept which the author himself struggled to understand.

The article itself begins and ends with the topic of prayer. Junod tells the story of his childhood friend—a stuffed animal named "Old Rabbit." One night, as a child, he accidentally threw his beloved friend out the car window.

That was the night he learned how to pray.

"He would grow up to become a great prayer," Junod wrote about himself years later, "but only intermittently, only fitfully, praying only when fear and desperation drove him to it. The night he threw Old Rabbit into the darkness was the night that set the pattern, the night that taught him how to pray. He prayed for Old Rabbit's safe return, and when, hours later, his mother and father came home with the filthy, precious strip of rabbity roadkill, he learned not only that prayers are sometimes answered but also the kind of severe effort they entail, the kind of endless frantic summoning."

In his encounter with Mr. Rogers, however, Junod learned one of the great secrets to peace and happiness here on earth. He had spent most of his life intermittently turning to God in times of trouble and despair. But in the end, as he sat with Mr. Rogers, he heard the words which were markedly missing from his prayer life.

"Thank you, God," Mr. Rogers said.

God wants us—he urges us—to turn to him in times of trouble. No problem is too big. No worry is too small. He will always listen and always answer in the way that is best for us.

TALK TO GOD EVERY SINGLE DAY.

Generally speaking, we do that pretty well. In times of desperation and pain, we turn to God for help. The secret to true happiness, however, is to talk to God every single day. The secret is to look around and recognize all that he has given us. The secret is to dig deeply into his Word and understand his amazing grace which forgives us because of Jesus and gives us much more than we could ever earn or deserve.

The secret is to see God's goodness in our lives and say every day with Mr. Rogers, "Thank you, God."

Today I am thankful for/that _____

Thank you, God, for always listening and
helping in times of trouble. Thank you
for your love and forgiveness.
Thank you for my life. Amen.

◆

DAY 90
SNARKY SELLS

Instead, speaking the truth in love, we will grow to
become in every respect the mature body of him who is
the head, that is, Christ.

EPHESIANS 4:15

◆

snarky [snär′kē] adj.

sarcastic, impertinent, or irreverent in tone or manner

Do you know anyone who is snarky? If there was a picture of snarky in the dictionary, it would probably be of the comedian David Spade. When I was in college, he was the king of snarky. Every character he played on *Saturday Night Live* and in the movies was sarcastic, impertinent, and irreverent. To be snarky is to be bitingly sarcastic, almost to the point of being mean.

Our world today loves snarkiness. (Yes, that is a word.)

Snarkiness is funny—at least when it's not directed at you. Snarky sells. Just look at all the cable news shows in which every other word coming out of the host's mouth drips with venomous sarcasm. If you agree with their politics, you find them amusing and witty. If you disagree with them, you find them bitter and unbearable.

Snarkiness has that effect on people.

Snarkiness seldom convinces anyone of anything. If a person disagrees with you, a snarky remark will probably not help them see your side of the issue. The people who enjoy your snarky remarks already agree with you and want to zing those who disagree.

Why am I bringing this up? On the internet and in the media, I increasingly hear and read Christians being snarky about hot button issues—homosexuality, gender issues, and the like. Blog posts and comments get shared through Facebook and Twitter. In the impersonal world of the internet, sarcasm and mean-spiritedness reign.

Is it wise for Christians to be snarky when speaking out on important issues? If our goal is to be a loving witness to the world, it is not enough to be right. As my father used to always tell us when we were kids, "It's not what you said. It's how you said it."

The apostle Paul encouraged us to build each other up by "speaking the truth in love." There is a time and a place for zingers and sarcastic retorts. While witnessing to the world is not one of those times. A loving discussion among Christians about doctrinal differences is also not one of those times.

What is the purpose of a snarky remark but to mock the person with whom you disagree? Is that love? Does that help the other person see what you are saying?

SNARKY SELLS. . . . BUT THAT ISN'T OUR PURPOSE AS CHRISTIANS.

The problem is that snarky sells. If you have a platform and are witty enough, you can rile up the troops with sarcasm. Your blog posts will go viral. Your supporters will smile and nod in agreement.

But that isn't our purpose as Christians. We aren't out to make those who disagree with us look like fools. Jesus did not call us to help other Christians feel superior. He called us to share the truth of his Word boldly and in love.

Remember that the next time you think about sharing a snarky Christian blog post on Facebook. Remember that as you share your comments or get involved in doctrinal discussion online. It's not enough to be right. Speak the truth in love.

Today I am thankful for/that _____

_____

Merciful God, forgive me the many times I have not spoken your truth in love. Amen.

DAY 91
THAT WHICH SHALL NOT BE NAMED

You will be enriched in every way so that you can be
generous on every occasion, and through us your
generosity will result in thanksgiving to God.

2 CORINTHIANS 9:11

◆

In the Harry Potter novels and movies, one word brought terror to all who
heard it. It was a name—Voldemort. People feared even mentioning the
name of the evil wizard lest he suddenly appear. They called him, "He who
shall not be named."

When anyone did say his name aloud, women would gasp. Children
would cry. Grown men would cower.

This Sunday in church, I spoke of that which shall not be named. I
preached a sermon about stewardship. I was excited about the text and the
sermon. We got to sit back and admire all that God generously showers
upon us—closets full of clothes, refrigerators full of food, cars, trucks,
high-definition televisions, and cell phones.

Even more important, he gives us his Word and churches where we can
hear it preached. He forgives us and gives us heaven because of Jesus. God
has been overwhelmingly generous to us. So we talked about how we, as
Christians, respond by being overwhelmingly generous ourselves.

In encouraging generosity, I mentioned that which shall not be named
in church.

I talked about money.

Now, to their credit nobody gasped. Children didn't cry. Nobody ran
away in fear, but I did hear a comment after church: "We had visitors this
Sunday. I hope they weren't offended." This wasn't the first time. In the
past, I have heard the whispers and murmurs when the topic of money
comes up in church.

Why does the word *money* elicit negativity when mentioned in church? First
of all, that's all some preachers and churches talk about. Many people in our
world today are turned off by churches and religion in general because they
think churches are just out to get their money. The concern my members had

about the visitors in church was a valid one. They could have easily thought we were one of those churches that only talks about money.

Some churches don't talk about money all the time, but when they do, they hit people over the head with it. They motivate people by fear. "If you don't give 10%, then you aren't a truly committed Christian." They motivate by selfishness. "If you want God to bless you, then you need to give to him first"—as if our offerings were an investment on Wall Street.

The reason money is what shall not be named in church isn't just because some churches abuse it. It's also because deep down we don't want to hear it. All of us by nature are selfish; we don't want to let go of our money. If I give—if I'm generous—I won't have as much for me.

WE NEED TO TALK ABOUT MONEY IN CHURCH, . . . BECAUSE GOD TALKS ABOUT MONEY IN HIS WORD.

That's why we need to talk about money in church—not all the time, but often. We need to talk about it because we need to be confronted by our own materialism. We need to see our sin and also our Savior who died that we might live. We need to talk about money because God talks about money in his Word.

So let's do so, but let's do so understanding the abuses that affect people's perception of God and the church. Let's do so guided by God's Word. Let's do so always pointing our people to God's generosity and the riches of heaven which are waiting for us.

Let's talk about that which shall not be named in church.

Today I am thankful for/that _____

_____

Lord, forgive me for the times I have selfishly clung to my money and possessions. Help me to respond to your overwhelming generosity by being overwhelmingly generous in every aspect of my life. Amen.

DAY 92
WE NEED JESUS

But as for me, I am poor and needy; may the Lord
think of me. You are my help and my deliverer;
you are my God, do not delay.

PSALM 40:17

❖

My family loves to binge-watch old episodes of the TV show *Psych*. The family-friendly comedy is the story of two lifelong friends, Shawn and Gus, who decide to open a fake psychic detective agency.

In one episode, Gus is being tempted to cheat on his girlfriend by a sultry older woman. After one of her brazen attempts, Gus looks at her and deadpans: "You need Jesus."

I recently sat in on a meeting of the ethics board of our local newspaper. The discussion was dominated by the killing of George Floyd in Minnesota by police officer Derek Chauvin on May 25, 2020, as well as the subsequent protests and riots. The question was asked, "How could the newspaper responsibly report this national story and its implications on our local community?"

We went around the room talking about what could be done in our community to heal the hurt, to right the wrongs, and to bring our divided society together.

A former college president spoke about the importance of education in the process. A local law enforcement official spoke about how law enforcement agencies need to better recognize police officers who have become jaded after years of service. He talked about the benefits of citizens going on ride-alongs with local police. The newspaper staff talked about conducting town hall meetings and running a series of articles from the point of view of different segments of our community offering suggested solutions to the problem.

As they brainstormed, I heard Gus' voice in my head.

"They need Jesus."

We all do. The ills of our society today are the result of a heart problem. They are a spiritual problem. They are a sin problem. The roots of racism are pride and hate. The hearts of the protesters are overflowing with

174

vengeful rage. The vitriol on social media is fueled by pharisaical feelings of superiority and stubborn refusal to listen to other people.

Education helps. Shining light on injustice helps. People standing up and speaking out helps. But what our world needs most—what our hearts need most—is Jesus.

Jesus is the cure for our heart disease. God so loved you, he sent his one and only Son to suffer the punishment for your pride and anger and racism. Jesus died for your delusions of superiority and your lack of listening. Jesus is the answer. In him, you are forgiven for even the ugliest and darkest attitudes hiding in the recesses of your heart.

But God didn't so love only you. God so loves the world. God so loves George Floyd. God so loves Officer Derek Chauvin. God so loves Donald Trump and Joe Biden. God so loves every police officer in our country—both good and bad. God so loves every person on this planet.

What they need is to know him. What they need is to know the forgiveness he has won for them. What they need is the love he works in our hearts even for our enemies.

With Jesus' help, the racists can learn to love, the protesters can let go of their anger, and we can all grow in the grace of speaking the truth in love.

ONLY ONE SOLUTION GETS TO THE HEART OF THE ISSUE.

May God help us as we continue to look for ways to heal the divides in our society. In the end, though, only one solution gets to the heart of the issue.

We need Jesus.

Today I am thankful for/that _____

Dear Jesus, we need you. Forgive us. Heal our hearts. Help our nation. Amen.

DAY 93
RUNNING ON EMPTY

**Like newborn babies, crave pure spiritual milk, so that
by it you may grow up in your salvation.**

1 PETER 2:2

◆

I have a friend who is a pastor. He's a good guy, but he has a problem. I don't know if there's a name for it, but I'm convinced it's a psychological disorder. You see, like Kramer on *Seinfeld,* my pastor friend feels a pathological need to see how far he can drive after the gas gauge reads empty.

He doesn't just wait until the warning light comes on. He doesn't just wait until the needle points directly at E. He waits until the needle is well below the E. He wants to see how far he can really go. And when he gets there, he takes a picture of the gas gauge and posts it on Facebook.

Like I said, he has a problem. Sometimes I picture him driving down the road with a crazed look on his face, singing the old Jackson Browne song "Runnin' on Empty."

Do you ever feel like you're running on empty? You're tired. Maybe you don't sleep well at night. You're frazzled, dealing with stress from your job or your marriage or your kids. You're depressed because everything seems to be going wrong in your life. You're on the edge. You feel like giving up.

That's how the prophet Elijah felt.

Elijah felt alone and afraid. Most of God's people had rejected the true God to follow the false god Baal. Wicked King Ahab and wicked Queen Jezebel were out to kill him. Elijah felt forced to flee. He ran for days until he came to the mountain of God, Mount Sinai, several hundred miles away.

There God came to Elijah in a gentle whisper. "What are you doing here, Elijah?" God asked.

"I have been very zealous for the Lord God Almighty," Elijah replied. "The Israelites have rejected your covenant, torn down your altars, and put your prophets to death with the sword. I am the only one left, and now they are trying to kill me too" (1 Kings 19:10).

They say that when you stick your nose in limburger cheese, the whole world stinks. That was Elijah's problem. He was tired and worn out. In his mind, all was lost. He was all alone. He was the only believer left.

Elijah felt sorry for himself.

So God came to him in a gentle whisper to remind him of the truth. Elijah wasn't all alone. God had reserved 7,000 true believers who hadn't bowed down to Baal. He was going to send another prophet named Elisha to help him. He would get rid of wicked King Ahab and wicked Queen Jezebel. God was in control. Everything would be okay.

YOU'RE PROBABLY RUNNING ON EMPTY. YOU NEED TO REFUEL.

Refueled by God's promises, Elijah got back to work.

Are you tired, stressed, and frazzled? Have you dug yourself into a pit of self-pity? That means you're probably running on empty. You need to refuel.

You need to hear the gentle whisper of God's promises. As we quietly sit and hear his Word, he reminds us that we are not alone. He reminds us that he is in control and will work all things for our good.

He whispers to us words of forgiveness. Because Jesus died your death, you don't have to carry around the guilt and regret that keep you up at night. You are completely forgiven forever—even for the sin of feeling sorry for yourself. You are going to live forever in the happiness of heaven where there is no more stress or worry. God is going to be with you. He will get you through this. It's going to be okay.

When you're running on empty, open up your Bible and listen carefully to the gentle whisper of God's promises. That's how God refuels you.

Today I am thankful for/that _____

_____

Holy Spirit, thank you for refueling my faith with your wonderful promises. Amen.

DAY 94
A PARENT'S PRAYER

Train up a child in the way he should go; even when he
is old he will not depart from it.

PROVERBS 22:6 ESV

❖

We were on our annual college trek. My parents were dropping me off for my sophomore year. At a gas station, my dad got out to pump gas. My mom quickly turned and looked at me.

"I know you and your sister do things you shouldn't when you're away at school," my mom said as she nervously checked to see if my dad could hear.

My heart skipped a beat. What did she know? I quickly scanned my memory bank to try to pinpoint which specific event she could be referencing. Meanwhile, I did my best to keep a poker face.

"I know you do things you shouldn't," my mom repeated. "I just wanted you to know that every night I pray that God would keep you both safe until you grow up and learn."

Amazingly, miraculously, graciously God did.

Twenty some years later, I am now a father. In a few years, I will be driving my children to college. This morning, I simply have to drive my daughter to junior high school for the first time.

The world she is entering terrifies me. When our children are little, we can shelter them. We have a certain amount of control over their environment and behavior. As they grow older, though, our control and influence diminishes.

Today, as I drop my daughter at middle school for the first time, that diminishing begins. Puberty and peer pressure will soon become torrential forces beating against her heart and mind.

As I sit here this morning, contemplating this new stage in her life, I find comfort in the first verse my daughter memorized when she entered Sunday school seven years ago. "Train a child in the way he should go," wise old King Solomon once wrote, "and when he is old he will not turn from it."

I cannot force my daughter to believe in Jesus her Savior. In the end, her faith is hers, not mine. I can, however, train her. I can show her God's love and guidance.

Still, as I take my daughter to school today, I worry. I worry if I have done that well enough. I know I definitely have not done it perfectly.

Today I cling to God's forgiveness and I pray.

I pray because I know that my daughter will make mistakes—as I did, as my sisters and brothers did, as my parents did. I pray because I trust in God's full and free forgiveness.

I pray that God would give my daughter Christian friends who will influence her. I pray that God will help me to continue to guide and comfort and correct her.

I pray that whatever poor choices she makes—whatever hurts and heartbreaks she must suffer because of them—God keeps her safe. I pray that he does not give up on her. I pray that he keeps her close to him all her days.

IN THE END, THAT'S THE ONLY THING THAT MATTERS.

I pray that she never forgets—that she never stops trusting in Jesus her Savior. In the end, that's the only thing that matters.

I want my daughter in heaven with me. So today I pray, "God, please keep her soul safe and close to you."

Today I am thankful for/that _____

_____

Lord, watch over my children. Keep them close to you. Guide them, keep them safe and help them to always trust in you. Amen.

DAY 95
SPITTING IN THE WIND

"Meaningless! Meaningless!" says the Teacher. "Utterly
meaningless! Everything is meaningless."

ECCLESIASTES 1:2

◆

When I was in college, I studied German under the aptly named Professor Daniel Deutschlander. Whenever something silly or strange happened in class, Professor Deutschlander would tell us with a smirk, "I am going to include that in my autobiography, *Spitting in the Wind*."

I often feel like that should be the title of my life's story as well.

Sometimes it seems like I am spitting in the wind. Sometimes I ask myself what good any of this really does. As a pastor, I share with people what God wants them to do and then watch them do the exact opposite. I share with them the endless forgiveness Jesus won for them and then see them take that forgiveness for granted.

I look out and see our world spiraling deeper and deeper into depravity. I see myself falling into the same old stupid sins again and again. Life in this world often feels empty and meaningless.

Have you ever felt that way? Have you ever felt like what you do doesn't really matter—like it doesn't serve any real purpose? Do you ever find yourself just going through the motions of life?

Wise old King Solomon could relate.

Solomon wrote the book of Ecclesiastes toward the end of a life lived extravagantly. God blessed Solomon with great wisdom and intelligence. He enjoyed wealth and fame beyond our wildest imagination. He tasted just about every earthly pleasure, including having a harem of 700 wives and 300 concubines.

And what was Solomon's conclusion after a life lived big? "Meaningless, meaningless!" he wrote. "Utterly meaningless! Everything is meaningless" (Ecclesiastes 1:2). Throughout Ecclesiastes, Solomon describes his great wisdom, his wealth, and the largess of his life. In the end it was all meaningless to him.

The Hebrew word we translate as "meaningless" literally means "breath." It is something that is here today and gone tomorrow. The old King James Version of the Bible calls it "vanity."

All of our great efforts, all our goals, all our hard work is meaningless. It doesn't last. It is here today and gone tomorrow. It is vanity—a "chasing after the wind," Solomon tells us.

It's like spitting in the wind.

Life under the sun, life lived in this world, is utterly meaningless . . . without God.

At the end of his book, after teaching us the utter vanity of wealth and fame and life lived under the sun, wise old King Solomon encourages us to remember our Creator and to fear God.

That is the answer. That is where meaning is found—not under the sun, but beyond it. Life is meaningless without God. It is like spitting into the wind.

Life with God, however, has purpose and meaning. We know and trust that Jesus came to save us from all our stupid sins. We know that he will one day free us from this meaningless, fleeting, and vain world. Knowing this changes how we look at and live our lives.

Sure my life may seem at times monotonous. I may not see my efforts produce any fruit, but God promises that a life lived in service to him is never in vain. He has plans and purposes for us. He works through sinners like you and me to bring about his will for the world. He uses us and our lives to share his message of salvation with others.

NO LIFE LIVED FOR GOD IS EVER MEANINGLESS.

You may not always be able to see it. You may not always understand God's plans for you. You may feel like you are just spitting in the wind, but your life has purpose.

No life lived for God is ever meaningless.

Today I am thankful for/that _____

Dear Lord, thank you for giving meaning and purpose to my life. Amen.

DAY 96
DEAR DAD

Because you are his sons, God sent the Spirit of
his Son into our hearts, the Spirit who
calls out, "*Abba*, Father."

GALATIANS 4:6

◆

My children are growing up in a bilingual home. One of the more curious results of hearing both English and Spanish since they were babies is what they now call my wife and me.

My children call my wife, who is from Mexico, "Mommy." They call their gringo father Papá. In fact, my children do what many Mexican children do. They shorten it. They call me *Apá*.

I love it when my children call me *Apá*—even when my six-year-old says it over and over and over again. To hear my children call out to me in love and trust warms my heart in ways words cannot express.

This last week I was thinking about that as I posted a paraphrase of the Lord's Prayer on my blog. In my paraphrase, "Our Father who art in heaven" became "Dear Dad."

A number of people commented how they didn't like that. They felt it was disrespectful.

One of the themes throughout Jesus' teachings is his insistence that we pray to God as our Father. Our God loves us. He promises to protect us and give us everything which is for our good. He promises to always listen and answer us for our good. We can pray to him with confidence.

When I speak to my dear father, though, I never call him Father. I call him Dad. In no way is that term ever lacking in respect. For some people, the word *father* in English seems too formal or distant.

I'm not saying you have to call God Dad or Papa, but you can. In fact, I have good friends from the Dominican Republic where most people call God, *Papi Dios*—literally, "Daddy God."

You may not feel comfortable referring to God in such a way, but it is not wrong to do so. That is the heart of what Jesus is teaching us. The all-powerful King and Lord of the universe who fills all things in every way is my dad. I can talk to him about anything, as a dear child talks to his dear father.

Some Christians, however, struggle with the image of God as our Father because of the relationship they had with their own dads. You may have had a horrible father. You may be frightened of him. You may have been the victim of abuse. For you, it may be a struggle to see or understand the joy and wonder of calling God our Father, our Dad, our *Apá*.

If your father is not what he is supposed to be—if you feel like you can't talk to him—God invites you to find in him what your father never was. He will be the dad you need. He forgives all your sins because of Jesus. He is not a frowning father who is angry or disappointed in you. He is your loving and proud dad who wants to hold you in his arms and bless you.

TO TALK TO GOD WITH TERMS OF ENDEARMENT DOES NOT SHOW LACK OF RESPECT.

To talk to God with terms of endearment does not show lack of respect; it shows loving confidence. It does not diminish his majestic sovereignty; it highlights his amazing grace. What a wonderful, astounding, sublime privilege it is to be able to call the Lord and creator of all things "My Dad."

Or, as my kids would say, "My *Apá*."

Today I am thankful for/that _____

_____

Almighty and Holy God, thank you for the wonderful joy and privilege of being able to call you my dad. Amen.

DAY 97
THE PURPOSE OF SEX

Marriage should be honored by all, and the marriage
bed kept pure, for God will judge the adulterer
and all the sexually immoral.

HEBREWS 13:4

◆

The young bride slowly unties the ribbon and opens the box. Her new husband holds his breath, hoping he picked out the right one. She squeals with joy as she pulls out the beautiful diamond bracelet.

She hugs her new husband and then giddily tapes the bracelet to the bottom of her shoe. She runs out to the yard and stomps around in the mud.

Her new husband watches hurt and incredulous.

Let's try that again.

The new wife unties the ribbon and opens the box. This time she quietly thanks her husband for the gift, puts it in a drawer, and never pulls it out again.

Once again the new husband's heart is hurt.

Let's try this one more time.

The young bride unties the ribbon and opens the box. This time she hugs her husband and puts the bracelet on her wrist. She uses it every chance she gets. Every time she wears it she looks at her husband with a knowing smile. His heart swells knowing how much his gift has meant to her.

Our gracious God has given a gift to marriage—the gift of sex. He made men and women to be sexual beings and blessed sexual relations inside of marriage. He said, "That is why a man leaves his father and mother and is united to his wife, and they become *one flesh*" (Genesis 2:24, emphasis added).

When the gift of sex is used outside of marriage, however, it is like taking God's beautiful gift, taping it to the bottom of our shoes and stomping around in the mud. When young men and women have sex before marriage, when couples introduce pornography into their marriages, when our world twists sex into any one of its many perversions, they are taking God's gift, taping it to the bottom of their shoes, and stomping around with it in the mud.

How do you think that makes God feel?

Many Christians, however, swing the pendulum to the other extreme. They treat sex as something dirty, even within marriage. They say that sex should only be used for childbearing. They imply it is wrong to enjoy it. They take God's gift and put it in a drawer.

How do you think that makes God feel?

HELP ALL OF US TO LEAD PURE AND DECENT LIVES.

God has given you a beautiful diamond bracelet. He wants you to use and enjoy his gift—but to use and enjoy it in the way he designed it to be used. The gift of sex is designed for the intimacy of marriage. It needs the commitment of marriage. It is reserved for husband and wife.

I know it's hard to wait for marriage, but it is always worth it. You will save yourself a host of hurt and heartache if you just wait. In this world, we are bombarded with temptations to use our sexuality in ways for which God has not designed it, but that is like taking his beautiful gift and stomping around with it in the mud.

Watch out for the other extreme, though. When used in marriage, sex isn't dirty. In fact, when you use it, when you enjoy it, when you share it with your spouse, you make God's heart swell with joy.

Treat God's gift of sex as the precious gift it is. Use it the way he designed it to be used.

Today I am thankful for/that _____

_____

Heavenly Father, help all of us to lead pure and decent lives in word and action, and help husbands and wives to love and honor one another. Amen.

DAY 98
JESUS CAN HAVE ME

Therefore, I urge you, brothers and sisters, in view
of God's mercy, to offer your bodies as a living
sacrifice, holy and pleasing to God—this
is your true and proper worship.

ROMANS 12:1

◆

In years gone by when poor young boys made money selling newspapers on street corners, a ten-year-old stood on a corner in New York City on an icy Sunday morning in early December, trying to sell the Sunday edition.

Traffic was slow. Few people walked by. He didn't sell one paper.

On the opposite corner stood an old brick church. Tired of the cold, the boy crossed into the church to warm himself. He sat down on the back pew just as the preacher began his sermon.

The pastor preached an inspiring sermon about the poor widow who gave her last two coins as an offering to God. He spoke of Jesus who gave his all for us. Jesus gave his life so we could be forgiven. He died so we could live with God forever in heaven.

"Jesus gave his all for you. What will you give back to him?" The preacher asked.

With that, the offering plate was passed. As the usher approached the boy in the back pew, he asked the usher to please place the plate on the floor. All eyes in the church quickly turned to the boy in the back.

"Pastor," the boy said in a loud voice echoing through the church. "I don't have any money to give. I didn't sell one newspaper today." The boy then stepped into the offering plate. "But Jesus can have me," he said.

GOD TALKS ABOUT MONEY OFTEN IN THE BIBLE.

It's never fun for me to talk about offerings at church. People don't like talking about money. They don't like talking about it because they think that's all churches and pastors really want—their money. They don't like talking about money because in our sinful selfishness, we want to keep it for ourselves.

186

God talks about money often in the Bible. God talks about our offerings. He wants us to give according to what he has given us.

What God really wants, though, isn't our money. What he wants is our hearts. What he wants is us. What he wants is for us to stand in the offering plate and say, "Jesus can have me."

A part of us loves to hear that because we nod and say, "See. God doesn't want or need my money. It's okay if I don't give very much or even anything in my offerings."

On the contrary, giving yourself to God means giving your offerings. It means giving to God first. It means giving to God your best. It means giving as he has given to you.

And God has given you money and many material blessings.

But he also has given you time. He has given you talents and abilities. God wants all of you in that offering plate.

Everything we have and everything we are is because of God's amazing grace and generosity, so give back to him. Set aside a part of every paycheck for him. Set aside Sunday mornings for him and his worship. Use the talents he has given you to serve him in his church and to serve others every day out in the world.

Let Jesus have you.

(But please don't step into the offering plate this Sunday morning. I don't want pastors calling me to complain about broken offering plates.)

Today I am thankful for/that _____

_____

Jesus, you can have me. Amen.

DAY 99
FIRST THINGS FIRST

[Let us not give] up meeting together, as some are in
the habit of doing, but encouraging one another—
and all the more as you see the Day approaching.

HEBREWS 10:25

❖

"First things first."

I can't tell you how many times that phrase has been spoken in our home. When my kids come home from school, the first thing they want to do is get on their electronics and video games.

"Do you have any homework for tomorrow?"

"Yes, but can't I do it later, Dad?"

"No. First things first."

When they are finished with their homework, they again make a beeline for their electronics.

"Are your rooms clean?"

"No, but can't we do it later, Dad?"

"No. First things first."

The truth is, when my children leave their homework and chores until later, suddenly it is nine o'clock and they are still up, stressed, and rushing to get everything done.

When you leave the important things until the end, you often run out of time to do them, or at least do them well.

GOD IN HIS WORD TALKS A LOT ABOUT DOING FIRST THINGS FIRST.

God in his Word talks a lot about doing first things first. In the Old Testament, he commanded his people to give their "firstfruits" as offerings. The first thing farmers were to do when they harvested their crops was to set aside a part of the harvest as an offering to God. They were to give to God their first and their best.

That's one of the reasons we as Christians traditionally worship on Sunday morning, on the first day of the week. We are putting first things first. We

188

give God the first couple of hours of our week, trusting he will give us time to get everything done.

Sometimes, though, we don't do first things first. We get busy. We tell ourselves we will get to church when things slow down in our lives. We tell ourselves that even though we don't go to church on Sunday, we will take some time during the week to talk to God in prayer and read a little from our Bibles. But then the week slips past us and we haven't spent that time with God.

Don't put it off. Keep first things first. Set aside Sunday mornings for God. Make them sacred for you and your family, and see if God won't bless you with enough time to get everything else done during the week. In the same way, every morning before you get busy with your day, take some devotional time with God in prayer and Bible study.

Give to God first, remembering that he gave you his first and his best. He gave you his only Son to live and die so that you could be forgiven for all the times you have relegated God to being second or third or 967th in your life. God gave you his first and best so you could enjoy the firstfruits of heaven.

Thank him. Trust him. Give to God first. Start every week at church. Start every day with prayer.

Keep first things first.

Today I am thankful for/that _____

_____

Forgive me, Lord, for not always keeping you first in my life. Thank you for giving your all for me. Help me in love to give you my first and best. Amen.

DAY 100
THE LITTLE MAN LIVING INSIDE MY HEAD

"The Pharisee stood by himself and prayed: 'God,
I thank you that I am not like other people—
robbers, evildoers, adulterers—or even like
this tax collector. I fast twice a week
and give a tenth of all I get.'"

LUKE 18:10-12

◆

Years ago, I took my 10-year-old daughter to see the Disney/Pixar animated movie, *Inside Out*. The film takes the viewer inside the head of an 11-year-old girl named Riley Andersen. Riley's emotions—joy, anger, disgust, fear, and sadness—are personified by little people living in the control center of her brain.

The movie shows the emotional turmoil of Riley dealing with the trauma of moving far away from her friends and former life. Our movie date was a poignant moment for both my preteen daughter and me. The film captured brilliantly the emotional rollercoaster going on inside a young person's head.

It also got me thinking about the little men living inside my own head. I too have a number of emotions rustling around inside of me. In fact, I also have another little man living inside my head and heart.

He is a Pharisee.

The Pharisees were a group of Jewish leaders who taught the people God's Word. They were highly respected by the people. They practiced what they preached by living outwardly pious lives.

By Jesus' day, however, the Pharisees' zeal to obey God's law was no longer motivated by love and thankfulness to God but by sinful pride. They thought they were better than everyone else. They thought their good living was earning for them God's love and favor.

The Pharisees, therefore, hated Jesus because he told them they were just as sinful as everyone else. He told them they too needed a Savior. He called them "white-washed tombs"—sparkling clean on the outside, dead on the inside.

Suffice it to say, the Pharisees led the charge to have Jesus killed.

I have a little Pharisee living in my head and heart. He rears his ugly head as I watch and read about the public moral failings of politicians, celebrities, and even other clergy. He puffs out his chest as I hear, "Nice sermon, pastor!" or "I love your articles!" He whispers in my head, "God is really lucky to have you on his team."

The little Pharisee who resides in my head and heart is blinded by pride and arrogance. He doesn't want to see the truth.

The truth is I am a despicable sinner who has dark and dirty sins which other people often cannot see. The truth is I was born stained by sin and have rolled around in it like a pig in manure ever since.

The little Pharisee living in my head hates to hear that. He tries to keep me from humbly accepting who I am and what I deserve. Thankfully, he is not the only one who has taken residence in my head and heart.

Through the waters of Holy Baptism and the promises of God's Word, the Holy Spirit now lives in me. Though I still have that little Pharisee inside my head, the Holy Spirit helps me see the truth about who I really am and also about who my Savior is.

Though I am a dirty and despicable sinner, my God and Savior loves me. He lived the perfect life I haven't. He died my death. Everything I am and everything I have is because of him.

FIGHT AGAINST THAT LITTLE PHARISEE LIVING INSIDE YOUR HEAD.

I have a little Pharisee living inside my head. So do you. Don't listen to his lies. Don't think you're better than other people. Don't think God loves you because you're so good or because you do so much for him. Listen to the voice of the Holy Spirit speaking through God's Word. Hear him remind you of your sin and your Savior Jesus.

Fight against that little Pharisee living inside your head.

Today I am thankful for/that _____

_____

Lord, help me in my daily battle with the sinful pride and selfishness which live in my heart and my head. Amen.

191

DAY 101
TIME TO THINK

Everyone should be quick to listen, slow to speak
and slow to become angry.

JAMES 1:19

◆

My mom texted me the other day. For most people in our world today, such a statement is neither shocking nor extraordinary. Millions of mothers text their children every day.

I, however, was taken aback. My parents have never been at the vanguard of technology. In fact, I still remember when my father was dragged kicking and screaming into the world of email 20 years ago.

"It allows people to respond too quickly," was his complaint.

My father made a rule for himself. If he received an emotionally charged e-mail, he would write a response but not send it for 24 hours. Oftentimes he would later change what he wrote or simply not send it.

"They can wait," he told me as I rolled my eyes.

I recently read an article by Alan Jacobs, a professor at Wheaton College, about the demands of social media. In the article he referenced the old Jack Benny radio show.

Jack Benny was infamous for his stinginess. One of his classic routines featured him being robbed by a mugger. In the skit, the mugger pulls out a gun. "Your money or your life," he demands.

Jack Benny stands frozen in silence.

"I said, 'Your money or your life,'" the mugger growls impatiently.

"I'm thinking it over," Jack Benny whines, as the audience roars with laughter.

Professor Jacobs equates the internet to the mugger. But instead of demanding money, it demands our attention and reaction . . . and it wants them right now. "I'm thinking it over" is not an acceptable answer.

Our world wants, expects, and demands an instantaneous response. If someone texts you and you take too long to respond, you get an immediate "Are you still there?"

Our responses, as a result, are often unmeasured, emotional, or uninformed. I have counseled numerous couples whose problems and arguments have escalated through the heated exchange of text messages.

Once words are said, once a post is shared, once you hit send, the damage is done. A wise man once told me that words are like toothpaste. Once it's out of the tube, you can't put it back in.

So what's the answer? Should we never text? Should we never tweet? Should we never post or respond on Facebook? I don't think that's the answer. Social media is a part of the world in which we live. It can be a wonderful tool to share and communicate.

In the end, however, my father was right. Wisdom says wait. Jesus' half-brother, James, put it this way: "Everyone should be quick to listen, slow to speak, and slow to become angry."

If you are texting with someone and the conversation turns emotional or confrontational, type your response, but then wait five minutes, half an hour, or even an hour to hit send. Better yet, wait until you can speak with the person face to face.

IT WON'T HURT TO WAIT A DAY OR TWO.

If you have something controversial or provocative you feel you need to share on Facebook or Twitter, make sure you have all the facts first. It won't hurt to wait a day or two. After some time thinking about it, you may decide it's not even worth sharing.

As we seek to speak the truth in love, it's okay to say, "I'm thinking it over." They can wait.

Today I am thankful for/that _____

_____

Holy Spirit, give me patience and wisdom
that I may speak the truth in love
as I use all of our modern forms
of communication. Amen.

DAY 102
A STRANGER IN A STRANGE LAND

All these people were still living by faith when they
died. They did not receive the things promised;
they only saw them and welcomed them from
a distance, admitting that they were
foreigners and strangers on earth.

HEBREWS 11:13

◆

My wife is from Monterrey, Mexico. Though I feel at home with her family and comfortable speaking Spanish, when I visit Monterrey, I am surrounded by reminders that I am not from there.

I look out the window and see mountains in every direction. People drive more "freely" in Mexico. They act differently. The food, the air, the houses are all different. As I go about the city, people suddenly stare when they realize I am a foreigner.

That must have been how it felt for Abraham when he arrived in the land of Canaan. He was a long way from the place of his birth, a city called Ur in what is today Iraq. The people of Canaan spoke and acted differently. They had different customs and different gods. It was obvious Abraham was a foreigner. It was obvious he was different.

In chapter 11 of his book, the writer of Hebrews compares our situation as Christians here on earth to that of Abraham. Here on earth we are strangers living in a strange land. As Christians, we speak a different language than our world. We act differently. It's obvious we aren't from here just as it is quite obvious I am not from Mexico.

When I stay in Mexico for longer stretches of time, though, something strange happens. I start blending in. I start talking like they talk, driving like they drive, acting like they act. I stop feeling and acting like a foreigner.

How often does that happen to us as Christians? We surround ourselves with people who cuss and swear, and suddenly we begin to speak their language. We begin to feel at home with the violence, sex, and drinking which surround us. We begin to live as if this were our home.

That's what happened to Abraham's nephew Lot and his family. They began to blend in with the people of Sodom and Gomorrah. They made themselves at home in this sinful world. The problem is that, like the people of Sodom and Gomorrah, all the citizens of this world are destined for destruction.

AT TIMES IT'S UNCOMFORTABLE BEING DIFFERENT.

Though we as Christians live in this world, we are not of it. We are but strangers here. Heaven is our home.

At times it's uncomfortable being different. We speak a different language than our world. The citizens of this world look at us as strange. They look at us as foolish and intolerant for calling sin "sin." It's hard being different. We feel pressure to act more like this world—to hide the fact that we aren't from here.

Don't. You are a citizen of heaven. You have been washed in the blood of Jesus and forgiven of your sins. Why would you want to wallow once again in filth? You are different. Act like it. Don't be ashamed of it.

You are a stranger living in a strange land.

Today I am thankful for/that _____

_____

Dear Lord, help me to always remember that I am but a stranger here. Heaven is my home. Amen.

DAY 103
GEORGE BUSH AND ELLEN DEGENERES

"Love your enemies and pray for those
who persecute you."

MATTHEW 5:44

The juxtaposition made for good television. On October 6, 2019, comedian Ellen DeGeneres and her wife, Portia, were invited to sit in Jerry Jones' luxury box to watch the Dallas Cowboys play the Green Bay Packers. The irony was that former President George W. Bush and his wife, Laura, were also invited to sit in the same box.

There sat openly gay, liberal-leaning, Hollywood darling Ellen DeGeneres (and her wife) next to staunchly conservative, Republican President George W. Bush, who—during his presidency—openly opposed gay marriage.

Often during the game, the cameras found them smiling and laughing—enjoying the game and each other's company.

Social media blew up. Twitter melted.

Many followers of Ellen DeGeneres were especially offended. They lashed out. How could Ellen fraternize with someone with whom she markedly disagreed on so many major moral issues? How could she and her wife sit next to a conservative Christian president who openly opposes gay marriage?

Ellen responded to the criticisms the next day on her television program.

"Here's the thing," she told her massive television audience, "I'm friends with George Bush. In fact, I'm friends with a lot of people who don't share the same beliefs that I have. . . . Just because I don't agree with someone on everything does not mean I'm not going to be friends with them. When I say to be kind to one another, I don't mean only the people that think the same that you do; I mean be kind to everyone."

That last part sounded almost like a paraphrasing of Jesus himself.

President Bush responded in kind. "President and Mrs. Bush really enjoyed being with Ellen and Portia and appreciated Ellen's comments about respecting one another. They respect her," said President Bush's spokesperson, Freddy Ford.

Our country is openly divided politically and morally. The debates and divide in our country are deep and significant. We shouldn't gloss over the issues and, as Christians, we need to speak out about what the Bible says concerning hot button topics like human sexuality and abortion.

But as the apostle Paul says, we should speak the truth "in love" (Ephesians 4:15).

God wants us to love those who disagree with us. He wants us to love those who don't believe in him. He wants us to love those who attack us and his church.

In fact, he even wants us to love those who cheer for the Dallas Cowboys and the Green Bay Packers.

One of the best ways to help people see God and his love is by being kind and patient—by being someone's friend first and listening to them before we speak.

WE CAN AND SHOULD BEFRIEND EVEN THOSE WHO DISAGREE WITH US.

As Christians we need to stand firm in the truth of God's Word, but we can do so lovingly and with respect. We can and should befriend even those who disagree with us. We can and should sincerely love them as God has loved us.

Here are some strange words I never thought I would write or say aloud:

We should all be a little more like George Bush and Ellen DeGeneres.

Today I am thankful for/that _____

_____

Heavenly Father, give me courage to stand up and speak the truth of your Word to a world which doesn't want to hear it, but also help me to do so with love and respect. Help me to follow your example and love everybody, even those who disagree with me or treat me badly. Amen.

DAY 104
THE G.O.A.T.

Christ Jesus: Who, being in very nature God, . . . made himself nothing.

PHILIPPIANS 2:5-7

As I write this devotion, football is in full swing. The playoffs have begun in baseball. The hockey season has just started and basketball is right around the corner. This is a fun time of year if you are a sports fan.

No matter what sport you follow, one topic in sports generates more controversy than just about any other.

Who is the G.O.A.T.—the "Greatest of All Time"?

In basketball, it's easy. Most people would agree that Michael Jordan is the greatest basketball player of all time. In other sports that question isn't as easy to answer.

Is Tiger Woods a better golfer than Jack Nicklaus? He has more tour victories, but Jack has more majors. Roger Federer has won more major tournaments than any other male tennis player in history, but how can he be the G.O.A.T. when Rafael Nadal has a winning record against him?

Is Tom Brady really better than Peyton Manning or Dan Marino just because he played on better teams and won more championships? How do you honestly compare athletes from different eras?

The discussion of who is the G.O.A.T. in any particular sport at any particular position is always going to be subjective. Sports fans rarely agree.

There is one person, however, about whom there can and should be no debate. Jesus is the G.O.A.T. He is God himself. He is perfect and powerful. He is the King and Lord of the universe.

But being the G.O.A.T., Jesus didn't pound his chest like Muhammad Ali, shouting, "I am the greatest!" He didn't feel the need to try to convince people he was the G.O.A.T. In fact, he did the exact opposite.

Paul tells us that, "being in very nature God, . . . he made himself nothing by taking the very nature of a servant, being made in human likeness. And being found in appearance as a man, he humbled himself by becoming obedient to death—even death on a cross" (Philippians 2:6-8).

One of the things which makes Jesus the greatest of all time is that he gave it all up—he humbled himself to take our place and die our death on the cross. In doing so, he won for us the gift of forgiveness and the victory of heaven.

You and I, on our own, are a last-place team. We have failed miserably to live up to the perfection God wants and expects of us. We are the Washington Generals. We are the Bad News Bears. We are the 1973 Houston Oilers. We are terrible.

THE GREATEST OF ALL TIME IS ON OUR SIDE.

But the G.O.A.T. loved us so much, he came to this earth to be on our team. With his life, death, and resurrection, he won the victory for us. The greatest of all time is on our side. And as the apostle Paul asks, if he's on our side, "Who can be against us?" (Romans 8:31).

So go ahead and argue about who is the greatest quarterback (Tom Brady) or greatest pitcher (Nolan Ryan) or greatest hitter (Babe Ruth) of all time. Feel free to disagree with me about my picks (though I am right, by the way).

But also understand there is no discussion, no doubt, no room for argument about who the true G.O.A.T. is. Be thankful because he willingly chose to be on your team.

And with Jesus on your team, you can't lose.

Today I am thankful for/that _____

_____

Lord Jesus, thank you for giving up everything to win for me a home in heaven. You are truly the greatest of all time. Help me to trust that because you are on my team, I cannot lose. Amen.

DAY 105
PRICELESS

"What God has joined together, let no one separate."

MARK 10:9

In 1998, the auction house Christie's of New York sold a painting for $21,850. It was purportedly the work of an unknown German artist from the 19th century who was copying the style of the Italian Renaissance. The painting was of a noblewoman from Milan. It has since been dubbed *La Bella Principessa*.

In 2007, the painting was sold for roughly the same amount. In 2011 experts did a multi-spectral digital scan of the portrait and found a fingerprint in the upper right hand corner. The fingerprint was compared to another painting. Experts now believe the work to be much older than originally thought and painted by a guy you might have heard of: Leonardo DaVinci.

A painting that sold in 2007 for roughly $20,000 is now worth $160,000,000—all because it bears the fingerprint of its creator.

Our world today values marriage. It does. Thousands of books have been written about it. Oprah and Dr. Phil tell their eager audiences how to have a happier one. Our world today values marriage roughly like it values a $20,000 painting.

It is important—it is valuable—but not priceless.

If it doesn't work out, you can always get a divorce. That's what nearly half of all marriages in our country do. If marriage isn't your cup of tea or if it's too much of a commitment, just live together.

Our world values marriage like a $20,000 painting because it views you as the artist. You picked your mate. You decided to get married. For our world, marriage is a man-made masterpiece.

If you are the maker of your marriage, then it follows that you are the one to decide what your marriage should be and even how long it should last.

Jesus, however, tells us that we are not the painters of our own marriages. God is. "What God has joined together," Jesus said, "let no one separate."

What God has joined together—God's thumbprint is on your marriage. He is its Creator. He is the one who brought you and your spouse together. It doesn't matter if you got married before a minister, a justice of the peace, or an Elvis Presley impersonator. You spoke your vows in the presence of the one and only true God.

TREASURE IT AS THE PRICELESS MASTERPIECE IT IS. Your marriage is God's masterpiece. It is a $160,000,000 painting. It is priceless. It is sacred. That means that God is the one who defines it. He is the one to tell us what marriage is supposed to be and how long it should last.

That also means we should treat our marriages as priceless works of art. For a Christian, the vows of marriage are sacred. Divorce isn't an option. We made a promise to God and to each other, not just to live together till death do us part, but to love one another as Christ loved us.

So treasure your marriage as you would a $160,000,000 painting.

And if you haven't—if you haven't taken care of your marriage like you should, if you let it flounder or crumble—cling to your Savior Jesus who won for you something even more valuable than a $160,000,000 painting. He won for you the gift of forgiveness. He painted his blood on the canvas of the cross for all the times we have treated marriage as some cheap dime-store knockoff. You are forgiven forever because of Jesus.

Now seeing the beautiful brushstrokes of his forgiveness and knowing that marriage bears his thumbprint, let's treasure it as the priceless masterpiece it is.

Today I am thankful for/that _____

_____

Heavenly Father, thank you for the gifts of marriage and family. Help me to treasure the gift of marriage and the family you have given me. Amen.

DAY 106
GROAN

We know that the whole creation has been groaning as in the pains of childbirth right up to the present time.

ROMANS 8:22

❖

I find myself groaning more than I used to. When I get out of bed in the morning, I make that old man sound. When I sit down after jogging, I moan. When I lift heavy objects, I grunt like Monica Seles.

It's not just the aches and pains that make me groan. When problems arise at church, when my wife is angry with me, when my children frustrate me, I groan.

I groan when I'm tired. I groan when I'm sad. I groan because it hurts.

In the book of Romans, the apostle Paul tells me that I'm not the only one groaning. The whole world—every man, woman, and child; every living creature; all of nature—feels the aches and pains caused by sin.

As we hurt, Paul encourages us to take it to the Lord in prayer. Sometimes, though, I don't know what to say to God. Sometimes I just hurt. I'm just sad. I don't really understand what I'm feeling. Sometimes I don't even know what I should be asking God.

When we are at our weakest and don't even know what to pray, "the Spirit himself intercedes for us through wordless groans" (Romans 8:26).

When I am hurting and don't know why—when I don't know what I want or what's best—the Holy Spirit groans for me. I can just open up my arms to God and groan. I can say, "God this stinks. This hurts. I don't know what to do."

We can say that because he does know what to do. He knows what we are feeling. He knows what is best for us and will always do it. God understands groans.

That doesn't mean, however, that my groans will magically disappear. Prayer is not a pill which immediately takes away all pain. God promises that he will deliver us from all our pains and problems eventually, but often we have to wait like a woman in labor.

Prayer is not a happy pill. For that matter, neither is the gospel. Simply hearing and believing God's promises won't suddenly take away all your pain. That's what our world wants. Our world thinks it has the right to be happy all the time. That's why so many people pop pills or run to the bottle or jump in bed to find relief from their groaning.

PRAYER IS NOT A HAPPY PILL.

God doesn't promise to take away our groaning here on earth. God's promises don't always relieve the pain. Rather, they give us the strength to bear the pain. They give us the sure hope that, like a woman in labor, our pain is only temporary.

By faith we know that Jesus won for us a home in heaven. There we will be free from all the pains and problems of this world. For now, though, we groan in eager expectation, knowing that our relief is coming.

So turn to him in prayer, even if all you can do is groan. He will hear you. He will come to you through the promises of his Word to give you the strength to stand despite the pain.

He will give you the sure hope of a home where you will never groan again.

Today I am thankful for/that _____

_____

Lord, you know my pains and hurts. I often don't even know what to ask for or say to you. Thank you for always knowing exactly what I am feeling and need. Amen.

DAY 107
JESÚS

"You are to give him the name Jesus, because he will save his people from their sins."

MATTHEW 1:21

◆

I collected baseball cards as a boy. Actually, I still do. When I was a boy, though, there was a wonderful man named Mr. Pape who went to our church. Mr. Pape was a baseball card dealer. On weekends he would sell cards at baseball card shows. Sometimes he'd even let me tag along.

I remember one evening I spent at Mr. Pape's house. We were looking at cards and watching a Chicago Cubs game on TV when a batter stepped up. His name flashed on the screen: *Ivan de Jesús.*

"Look, Mr. Pape," I said in surprise. "His name is Jesus." Mr. Pape smiled and patiently explained to me that in Spanish-speaking countries, boys are often named Jesus.

To our American ears that sounds strange. Few American mothers would ever think of naming their children Jesus. Jesus is God's name. Jesus is our Savior. Besides, he would probably get made fun of at school.

That's why it may come as a shock to many American moms that they have named their boys after Jesus without even knowing it. In fact, his is one of the 50 most popular boy names given today.

Confused?

You see, Jesus' name wasn't really Jesus. I mean it was, but nobody would have ever called him that. The name Jesus is the Greek version of his name. In the Aramaic language, the language of Israel at the time, his name was *Yeshua*. That's what his family and friends would have called him.

In English, *Yeshua* is the name Joshua. Jesus and Joshua are the same name. They both mean, "The LORD saves." Jesus, *Yeshua,* Joshua—is our Savior.

We call Jesus our Savior so often, though, that the significance of the name can easily be lost. Jesus saved us. He rescued us. He rescued us from the fires and horrors of hell. He rescued us from an eternity of pain we deserve for all our stupid, hurtful, thoughtless deeds.

He rescued us like the firefighter who sweeps into our house and carries us out of the flames. We call such firefighters heroes. We would feel forever indebted to a firefighter who died saving us.

How much more Jesus? He didn't just die for us. He suffered our hell. He suffered our punishment in our place. That is how he saved us. God is never going to punish us because he punished *Yeshua* in our place.

In the 1997 blockbuster *Titanic,* the heroine of the movie, Rose, recounted how the hero of the story, Jack, gave his life to save her. "He saved me in every way a person can be saved," she said with grateful tears in her eyes.

That's not actually true. Jesus saved us in every way a person can be saved. He saved us from sin. He saved us from death. He saved us from the devil. He saved us from hell.

THAT NAME IS OUR HOPE, OUR PRIDE, OUR JOY.

His name says it all. Jesus, *Yeshua,* Joshua—the LORD saves. That name is our hope, our pride, our joy. Whether you feel comfortable giving your child that name or not, cling to it. Speak it with grateful tears in your eyes.

It truly is the name above all names.

Today I am thankful for/that _____

---

*O Dearest Jesus, thank you for saving me in
every way a person can be saved. Amen.*

DAY 108
IN A FUNK

"So do not fear, for I am with you; do not be dismayed,
for I am your God. I will strengthen you and help
you; I will uphold you with my
righteous right hand."

ISAIAH 41:10

◆

I've been in a funk the last couple of days. That happens to me every so often. Usually I live life at a hundred miles an hour. I have always been energetic. I'm like Tigger on steroids.

Every so often, though, I get into a funk. I hit the wall. I can't seem to get myself motivated and moving. I become irritable and melancholic. Sometimes it's a little funk that lasts only a few hours. Sometimes it's a *George Clinton and the P-Funk All-Stars* funk—a deep funk which lasts for days.

I know I have ministry to do, sermons to write, people to call and comfort, but I struggle to get myself to do it. All I want to do is stare blankly at the TV or computer. I have to force myself to do the job God has called me to do.

Thankfully, God always snaps me out of it. The sun comes out. I go for a run. A switch is flipped and I'm back to Tigger on steroids.

Do you ever get into a funk? For you it may be depression. Maybe you're frustrated with your life. Maybe you're just tired. You're in a funk.

Sometimes those funky feelings last a short time. Sometimes they last a few days. Sometimes they feel like they are never going to end.

Thank God the truth doesn't depend on how we feel.

Our feelings can fool us. When we're down, we feel like the world is crashing in around us. At times we feel like all is lost—like there is no hope, no help, no way things will ever be okay.

That's when we need to be reminded of God's never-changing truth. Many years ago, I was counseling a woman who suffered from a chemical imbalance which drove her into deep depression and melancholy. A wise older pastor encouraged me to have her list God's attributes, his characteristics.

"He is wise, powerful, and eternal," she told me. "He never changes. He is always with me."

"And how does he feel about you?" I asked.

"He loves me," she said, trying to force a smile.

"In fact, he loved you so much, he suffered the punishment of hell in your place," I added. "So if the all-powerful, all-knowing, eternal God who is everywhere loves you more than you can ever imagine, if he forgives you and gives you heaven, if he is with you wherever you go, what do you have to worry about? What do you have to feel so bad about?"

"I guess nothing," she said sheepishly.

That truth didn't make the bad feelings suddenly disappear, but they did help her to start feeling better. She knew the truth even if she didn't feel it. She learned to recognize when her feelings were lying to her.

Don't trust your feelings. You may feel like everything is bad, all is lost, there is no hope. At times like that, you need to say what an old seminary professor used to tell us: "To hell with your feelings."

YOU MAY NOT FEEL IT, BUT YOU CAN KNOW IT.

Remember, know, and trust the truth God promises in his Word. You may not feel it, but you can know it.

And knowing makes all the difference.

Today I am thankful for/that _____

_____

Merciful God, when I fall into funks in my life, reach down your hand with your loving promises and pull me out. Amen.

DAY 109
BURDENED

"Come to me, all you who are weary and burdened, and
I will give you rest."

MATTHEW 11:28

❖

I have a friend who is a hiker. I too appreciate a good hike; that is, I enjoy a leisurely walk in the woods. My friend, however, is a true hiker. He hikes miles through mountainous terrain, carrying backpacks that weigh 60-70 pounds each.

A while back, my friend was preparing for an epic two-week trek through the mountains. In order to train his body, he filled his backpack with large rocks. Every evening after work, he grabbed the backpack and went walking miles through his neighborhood and city streets. I once tried to put the backpack on. It almost tipped me over.

WE ALL HAVE ROCKS IN OUR BACKPACKS.

We all have rocks in our backpacks. Your marriage is crumbling. Your job is in danger. Your mother is dying. You are stressed. You are tired.

If you are carrying a backpack full of rocks right now, Jesus has an invitation for you. "Come to me, all you who are weary and burdened," Jesus says, "and I will give you rest. Take my yoke upon you and learn from me, for I am gentle and humble in heart, and you will find rest for your souls. For my yoke is easy and my burden is light" (Matthew 11:28-30).

Do you know what a yoke is? It's not the yellow part of an egg. A yoke is the wooden frame they used to put over the shoulders of horses or oxen so they could pull the plow.

Yokes were heavy. Yokes were burdensome. Yokes were like backpacks full of rocks.

Your Savior is offering you a trade. "Give me your burdens, your yoke, your backpack full of rocks," he says. "I'll carry it for you and you can carry my yoke."

That then begs the question: What is Jesus' yoke? He tells us that his yoke is easy and his burden is light. But what is his yoke?

Jesus' yoke is his promises.

Promises like, "I am with you always, to the very end of the age" (Matthew 28:20). Promises like, "I know the plans I have for you, . . . plans to prosper you and not to harm you, plans to give you hope and a future" (Jeremiah 29:11). Promises like the promise Jesus made to the thief on the cross.

He was a thief. He was a louse. As he hung from his cross, he knew he would never have a chance to make amends for his sins. Yet what did Jesus promise him? "Today you will be with me in paradise" (Luke 23:43).

How was that possible? It was possible because Jesus was suffering the punishment for all his sins right there on the cross. God punished Jesus instead of punishing the thief. God punished Jesus instead of punishing me. God punished Jesus instead of punishing you.

Jesus paid it all. You are free from sin and guilt. You are going to heaven.

Last week, I had the privilege of preaching at the funeral of a longtime member. When she first joined our congregation many years ago, she was carrying a backpack full of rocks called guilt. She often told me that, when she finally understood the full and free forgiveness Jesus won for her, it was like a huge weight was lifted off her shoulders.

Jesus' promises tend to do that.

Today I am thankful for/that _____

_____

Jesus, you know the pains and struggles I have. You know the worries which weigh heavily on my heart. Please take them, Lord, and give me the comfort and peace of your promises. Amen.

DAY 110
UNANSWERED PRAYERS

"Call on me in the day of trouble; I will deliver you,
and you will honor me."

PSALM 50:15

❖

I saw it again just last week. A Christian friend wrote on her Facebook page: "Here's proof that God answers prayers."

She then went on to explain how she had prayed for someone and God helped the person that very day. As Christians, we've all had similar experiences. We ask God for something and he gives it to us. God answers our prayers.

But what about all the times God doesn't give me what I ask for? Why aren't those prayers answered?

In 1990, the singer Garth Brooks released what would become one of his greatest hits. It was a song about an experience he had years earlier at a hometown football game. He and his wife ran into his old high school flame.

As he introduced them, his mind couldn't help but think of the way things used to be. He remembered how every night in high school he prayed that God would keep them together forever. But as they talked, Garth Brooks looked at his wife and thought, "Sometimes I thank God for unanswered prayers."

Garth Brooks realized God had something better for him. He thanked God for unanswered prayers.

Though I applaud the sentiment and love the song, Garth Brooks is not theologically correct. It's not that God didn't answer his prayer.

God said no.

THE PRAYER OF A BELIEVER WILL NEVER GO UNANSWERED.

The prayer of a believer will never go unanswered. God will always answer the prayers of his children, but sometimes the answer is no.

God at times says no to our prayers because what we ask for isn't what is best for us. If you don't get what you ask for in prayer, God may be saying, "I have something even better for you." Where God closes a door, he often opens a window.

Just ask Garth Brooks.

When you don't get what you pray for, though, God may not be saying no. He may be saying wait. In the Psalms, God tells us, "Call on me in the day of trouble; I will deliver you, and you will honor me."

God wants us to call on him the very day we experience trouble. He promises to always say yes when we pray to be delivered from our pains and problems. Yet, if you look closely, he doesn't promise to deliver us that same day.

In his wisdom and love, God at times does not take away our pain and struggles immediately because he has a purpose we don't always understand. He has lessons of faith and patience to teach us. We may even have to endure a problem for years, but God will eventually deliver us—if not here on earth, then when we get to heaven.

There are no unanswered prayers. When God doesn't give you what you ask, he may be saying no or he may be saying wait. But he is answering you. He does care. He is listening.

Even when the answer is no.

Today I am thankful for/that _____

_____

Heavenly Father, thank you for always hearing my prayers and answering them for my good. Thank you for giving me many of the things I ask for. Help me to accept when you tell me no. Amen.

DAY 111
THAT'S DEBATABLE

Always be prepared to give an answer to everyone who
asks you to give the reason for the hope that you have.

1 PETER 3:15

❖

Many years ago, I sat in one of my seminary classes listening to two
classmates feverishly debate a question presented by our professor.

One of my classmates—we'll call him Bob—was one of the smartest and
most well-spoken men in our class. He had charisma and a powerful
presence. The other classmate—we'll call him Jack—was a middle-of-
the-road student. He was an extremely nice guy, but he was in over his
head with Bob.

Bob destroyed Jack in their debate. The problem was that Jack was right.

Perplexed, I walked up to the professor after class and asked, "What just
happened? Bob seems to have won the discussion, but he was wrong."

My professor smiled at me, rubbed his nose, and said, "Andy, a guy like
Bob will always win a debate with a guy like Jack, but that doesn't mean
he's right."

With the rise of social media, religious discussions and debates have
become commonplace. What was once reserved for seminary classrooms,
church sanctuaries, and conference halls, is now being played out every
day on Facebook, Instagram, and Twitter.

Atheists are debating Christians. Members of distinct denominations
are discussing doctrinal differences. The debates oftentimes become deep
and intense. Some use emotional ploys; others share snarky memes; still
others make profound arguments which go above the average person's head.

**YOU CAN'T
ARGUE ANYONE
INTO BELIEVING.**
As Christians, such debates and discussions present us
with a number of dilemmas. The apostle Peter encourages
us, "Always be prepared to give an answer to everyone
who asks you to give the reason for the hope that you
have." God wants us to speak. He wants us to answer
those who question or challenge what the Bible says.

On the other hand, we recognize that we can't argue anyone
into believing. Our job as Christians is to simply share the truth of God's

Word. We are witnesses. We cannot and will not convince anyone of anything. That is the Holy Spirit's job.

You can't debate someone into believing. In fact, arguments are usually counterproductive. When you get into a debate with someone, both sides usually stop listening. They dig their heels in and try only to prove their point. Besides, just because someone wins a debate or argument doesn't mean they are right.

The truth of God's Word is not debatable. The truth doesn't depend on convincing arguments. A well-prepared orator can win a debate, yet be completely wrong.

So the question is this: As Christians, do we engage in online debates? Do we enter the fray? I would say, yes, but be careful. Be prepared. Listen carefully. Make sure what you say is based firmly on God's Word. Humbly admit when you are wrong or don't know. Speak the truth in love.

And remember you can't argue someone into believing. After a while discussions and debates on social media become repetitive. They devolve into name calling and sarcastic remarks. Once you've clearly shared what God says, let the Holy Spirit work. It's okay to not have the last word.

Our goal isn't to win the debate. That's pride. Winning doesn't make you right. May our goal as Christians be simply to speak the truth in love as clearly as we can.

Today I am thankful for/that _____

_____

Holy Spirit, give me wisdom and humility as I lovingly witness to the truth of your Word. Amen.

DAY 112
WHAT WOULD YOU HAVE DONE?

"Be faithful, even to the point of death, and I will
give you life as your victor's crown."

REVELATION 2:10

❖

I have played the various scenarios over and over again in my head. We do that, don't we? When we hear about tragic events like the mass shooting which occurred at Umpqua Community College in Roseburg, Oregon, on October 1, 2015, we imagine what we would have done had we been there.

Would I have run and hid? Or would I have responded like Chris Mintz, the U.S. Army veteran, who rushed into the building and tried to block the shooter from moving into Classroom 15 where he eventually killed nine people? Chris was shot three times while standing and another four while on the floor. By God's power and grace he survived.

What would I have done had I been in Classroom 15? Witnesses report that the shooter, Christopher Harper-Mercer, asked his victims if they were Christians. According to initial reports, if the person said he or she was a Christian, Harper-Mercer would shoot the person in the head. If the person didn't respond or said he or she wasn't, the person was shot in the leg.

I recently heard someone remark, "The bravest person in the world is the second person who said she was a Christian."

What would I have done? I like to think I would have said without fear or equivocation, "I am a Christian." But I don't know. Would my thoughts have turned to my wife and children? In the end, would it have been a denial of faith to lie to this mad man?

What would you have done?

Whatever your answer, I think we can all agree that those who died have given the world a wonderful witness of the courage Christ gives. Their faith was severely tested and it passed the test.

Honestly, I think many, if not most, Christians would have passed that test. Though it is impossible to say for sure until you are in that situation, I think, with the help of the Holy Spirit, I would not deny my Savior.

A number of years ago, my father fell on the ice and banged his head. His brain began to bleed, but he didn't realize it. When the bleed was finally discovered, the doctors told him if it had gone undetected any longer, he would have died.

"IT'S THE LITTLE TESTS WITH WHICH WE STRUGGLE."

As he dealt with his life-threatening injuries, my father told me he was at peace. He knew the heaven Jesus won for him. But then he poignantly pointed out something I had never really thought about. "As Christians," he told me, "we usually do pretty well with the big tests. It's the little tests with which we struggle."

As Christians, we often face the big trials of death and sickness with courage, but then worry and fret over credit card bills.

God's profound promises of forgiveness, heaven, providence, and his presence in our lives give us the courage to face the bullets of a madman. Those same promises give us the peace and courage to face marital stress, a demeaning boss, or financial downturns.

As you wonder what you would do if you had been in Classroom 15, take a moment to consider what you do as you face the more mundane tests God places in your life every day.

Then turn to the promises of his Word. They will give you the peace and courage you need to face whatever tests God may send.

Today I am thankful for/that _____

_____

Merciful Lord, give me strength and courage as I face every challenge to my faith—both big and small. Amen.

DAY 113
SIX DEGREES OF YOU

"The kingdom of heaven is like a mustard seed, which
a man took and planted in his field. Though it is
the smallest of all seeds, yet when it grows, it
is the largest of garden plants and becomes
a tree, so that the birds come and
perch in its branches."

MATTHEW 13:31,32

◆

In 1994, three students from Albright College in Reading, Pennsylvania, invented a new game. One evening during a heavy snowstorm, Craig Fass, Brian Turtle, and Mike Ginelli watched the movie *Footloose* starring Kevin Bacon. When the movie was over, they put in another video, *The Air Up There,* which also happened to feature Kevin Bacon.

They began to speculate about how many movies Kevin Bacon had appeared in and how many actors had worked with him. That snowy evening in Reading, Pennsylvania, the game *Six Degrees of Kevin Bacon* was born.

The game is simple. A random actor is named and the players need to try to connect that actor with Kevin Bacon through other actors and the roles they played in movies. The person with the fewest degrees of separation wins.

For example: Elvis Presley. Elvis Presley starred in the movie *Change of Heart* in 1969 with Ed Asner. Ed Asner starred in the movie *JFK* with Kevin Bacon in 1991. Elvis Presley can be connected to Kevin Bacon in just two degrees. The premise of the game is that Kevin Bacon can be connected to every actor in Hollywood by less than six degrees of separation.

I was thinking about the game *Six Degrees of Kevin Bacon* this afternoon as I sat with some ladies from our congregation. They asked me about a young lady whom they saw in church on Sunday. It took me a moment to explain who she was and how she ended up in our church.

You see, a little over a year ago, we had a work day at church. A man from our church named Bobby was outside trimming trees and hauling branches. Matthew, a ten-year-old from the neighborhood, rolled up on his bike and asked if he could help.

Bobby told him, "Sure!" and put him to work. When they were finished, Bobby told Matthew that if he wanted, he could come to church and Sunday school the next day. Sure enough, Matthew showed up for Sunday school. The next week, he brought his grandma, Karen. She enjoyed it and brought her other grandchildren the next Sunday. Karen, Matthew, and the other grandchildren are now members of our congregation.

The young woman who came to church last Sunday was Matthew's aunt from California whom Karen had invited. If you're counting, that's four degrees from Bobby.

On Sunday mornings, as I look out over our church, I see degrees of separation. One person came to our church through this person and that person through another person and so on and so forth.

That's how the Christian faith works. It is shared from parent to child, friend to friend, neighbor to neighbor. You are a believer because another person took you by the hand and led you to your Savior.

YOU ARE CONNECTED TO A LONG CHAIN OF BELIEVERS.

You are connected to a long chain of believers which can be traced back to the apostles and Jesus, to the prophets and Abraham, all the way back to Adam and Eve.

Sometimes we think it a small thing when we invite someone to church or teach our children to pray. The lives you touch and the seeds you plant as you tell others of God's great love may be the beginning of a chain reaction, fanning out many degrees of separation from you.

Be Kevin Bacon. Make those connections. Keep that chain going. Share Jesus to the nth degree.

Today I am thankful for/that _____

_____

Almighty God, give me the courage to keep the chain of faith going by sharing Jesus with everyone I can. Amen.

DAY 114
STILL FLYING

Then I saw another angel flying in midair, and he had
the eternal gospel to proclaim to those who live on the
earth—to every nation, tribe, language and people.

REVELATION 14:6

◆

On September 13, 1814, a young American lawyer named Francis Scott
Key helplessly watched from Chesapeake Bay as the British bombarded
Fort McHenry in their attempt to take the city of Baltimore.

Late into the night, Key keenly watched the flag flying over the fort as the
bombs burst in the air. All night long, the artillery kept coming. Key
assumed that by sunrise the flag would no longer be flying, the fort would
be destroyed, and the city would be taken.

At the break of dawn, he went up on deck to see what had happened. To
his amazement, the flag—the Star-Spangled Banner—was still waving over
Fort McHenry.

Moved by the sight, he immediately sat down and wrote a poem which was
later put to music:

"O say can you see, by the dawn's early light,
What so proudly we hail'd at the twilight's last gleaming,
Whose broad stripes and bright stars through the perilous fight
O'er the ramparts we watch'd were so gallantly streaming?
And the rocket's red glare, the bombs bursting in air,
Gave proof through the night that our flag was still there.
O say does that star-spangled banner yet wave
O'er the land of the free and the home of the brave?"

In the book of Revelation, the apostle John saw frightening visions of a
dragon and two beasts waging war against God's people. The dragon, John
tells us, is the devil himself. The first beast represents political powers,
governments, and other powerful people who try to suppress and silence
God's Word. The other beast represents false teachers who rise up within
the church. They look holy and good on the outside, but they ultimately
lead people away from Jesus and the truth.

One of the main points of the book of Revelation is that such things will happen in our world. The devil and God's enemies will fight against his church. They will try to destroy it. They will try to silence the gospel.

But then in Revelation chapter 14, we see an angel—a messenger sent by God—flying through the air proclaiming the eternal gospel. The picture is the same as that of the flag flying over Fort McHenry. God's enemies will try to silence the good news about Jesus, but they cannot win.

Throughout history, governments like the Communist regimes of China, Russia, and Cuba have tried to keep people from hearing about Jesus. Islamic fundamentalists have killed Christians and burned churches. In our own society, a growing segment of the population is actively trying to mute us as Christians.

In the end, they cannot win. In Revelation chapter 14, John was really saying, "O say, can you see the angel still flying in the air proclaiming the eternal gospel?" The word *angel* means "messenger." God will always make sure there are angels—messengers—proclaiming the good news of his love, the good news of sins forgiven and heaven won.

God cannot be silenced.

GOD CANNOT BE SILENCED. The question is this: Can you? God has called each of us to be his angels—messengers who share the good news of what Jesus did to save us. Unfortunately, oftentimes we let embarrassment and fear silence us.

Don't. Tell everyone you can about what Jesus has done for you. And when you see on the news Christians being beheaded in Syria or hear the voices in our own society mocking us or our God, don't worry. They can't win. God can't be silenced.

The flag of the gospel will continue to fly.

Today I am thankful for/that _____

_____

Almighty God, help me to trust that your enemies cannot win. You cannot be silenced. May they never silence me. Amen.

DAY 115
AMAZING

"Look at the nations and watch—and be utterly
amazed. For I am going to do something in
your days that you would not believe,
even if you were told."

HABAKKUK 1:5

◆

A while back, Subaru ran a funny commercial. In it, a dad takes his son to see the giant redwoods of California. As they look up at one of the towering trees, the boy shrugs his shoulders and says, "I thought it'd be bigger."

Next we find them standing on the edge of the Grand Canyon gazing over its majestic beauty. The father looks down at his son. Once again his shoulders shrug. The father can't believe it.

What will it take to impress this kid?

Finally they drive through the wide open country where buffalo are roaming free. A bison walks right up to the car window and stares at the boy. The boy's eyes become as wide as saucers. The father smiles contently. He finally was able to amaze his not-so-easily impressed son.

It takes a lot to amaze us today. I guess that's why many churches go to great lengths to wow us with entertaining music, light shows, dynamic preachers, and giant-screen TVs. People today want to be wowed.

During Jesus' ministry here on earth, that was often a problem. People flocked to see Jesus because they wanted to see a miracle. They wanted to see signs and wonders. Sadly, however, few actually listened to what he said.

We especially see that the last week of Jesus' life. As Christ entered Jerusalem, the crowds went crazy, hoping to catch a glimpse of a powerful prophet performing an amazing miracle.

That's why so many showed up five days later to angrily shout, "Crucify him! Crucify him!" To them Jesus was a fraud—a cheap magician who had tricked them. Why? Because they didn't really listen—they didn't want to listen—to what Jesus was teaching.

219

WE WANT TO BE WOWED. BUT THAT'S NOT WHAT WORSHIP IS ALL ABOUT.

Often we too can go to church wanting to be amazed. We complain if the preacher is boring. We get frustrated if the music is bland or the worship old-fashioned. We want to be wowed.

But that's not what worship is all about. That's not why Jesus came. He came in the form of a poor, plain carpenter. His glory was mostly hidden behind his humility and cross. If you go to church looking to be wowed by power and emotion and a laser show, eventually you are going to become disillusioned like those people in Pontius Pilate's court.

Do you want to be truly amazed when you worship? You just need to listen carefully to the amazing message. Every Sunday in worship, you get to hear how you have messed everything up, yet God loves you anyway. You get to hear how Jesus came and suffered your punishment in your place. Every Sunday you get to have an intimate conversation with God himself. You get to walk up to his altar and physically be united with him in Holy Communion. You get to see and touch the body and blood which died so you could live. You get to reach out your finger and touch the very hand of God.

Remember that this Sunday when you go to church. Remember that the next time you approach his altar to receive the Sacrament of Holy Communion. Remember that every time you feel tempted to shrug your shoulders, unimpressed with worship. Your amazing God loved you with such amazing grace that he came to this earth to live and die for you. He comes and shares that amazing truth with you as you hear his Word and taste his Supper. He allows you the privilege of entering his presence to praise and thank him for all he has done for you. Every Sunday, you get to have an intimate conversation with God himself.

That's simply amazing.

Today I am thankful for/that _____

_____

Dear God, help me to never cease to be amazed at your goodness and grace. Amen.

DAY 116
ABIDE WITH ME

Abide with us: for it is toward evening.

LUKE 24:29 KJV

◆

Henry Francis Lyte (1793–1847) was an Anglican priest who faithfully served for 23 years as a parish pastor in the small fishing village of Brixham in Devonshire, England. Though suffering from ill-health most of his life, Lyte worked tirelessly in his parish, tutored local children, and wrote poetry.

In 1844, Lyte contracted tuberculosis. His already frail health quickly declined to the point where he was no longer able to carry out his pastoral duties. Against the urgings of his family, he preached one last sermon on September 4, 1847. Later that afternoon, he took a short walk on the beach and then retired to his study.

About an hour later, he emerged with a poem based on the words the Emmaus disciples spoke to Jesus on the first Easter: "Abide with us, for it is toward evening" (KJV). Lyte understood that the day of his life was drawing to a close. He made the words of the Emmaus disciples his own:

Abide with me; fast falls the eventide.
The darkness deepens; Lord, with me abide.
When other helpers fail and comforts flee,
Help of the helpless, oh, abide with me! (CW 588:1)

"Abide with Me" was Henry Lyte's prayer. As he faced the coming darkness of death, he asked God to be with him. Lyte's prayer for God's presence was not a desperate plea of a man afraid to die. "Abide with Me" is a prayer of confidence.

Lyte prayed with the confidence that God would come, not "in terrors as the King of kings, but kind and good with healing in [his] wings." Lyte was confident that his Savior—"the friend of sinners"—would abide with him.

Lyte prayed with confidence because he could look back on his life and see how God had been with him, even when in his youth he had been "rebellious and perverse." Throughout his life, God had been his "guide and stay." "Through cloud and sunshine" God had been with him. Lyte prayed with confidence because he knew God would be with him the rest of the way.

A number of years ago, I was watching a hospital drama on TV. A doctor informed a patient she was dying. In tears she wailed, "I don't want to die alone."

"We all die alone," responded the doctor solemnly.

NO ONE HERE ON EARTH CAN WALK THROUGH DEATH'S DOOR WITH US. BUT GOD CAN.

In one sense, the doctor was right. Though surrounded by friends and family, we all die alone. No one here on earth can walk through death's door with us.

But God can.

Soon after preaching his last sermon, Henry Lyte traveled to the city of Nice, now a part of the French Riviera, hoping that the warmer climate would help him recover. Only a few days after arriving, though, on November 20, 1847, God called Lyte home to heaven. A fellow clergyman, who was with Lyte in the hours before he died, reported his last words to be, "Peace! Joy!"

Henry Lyte did not die alone.

Today I am thankful for/that _____

_____

"Hold thou thy cross before my closing eyes;
Shine through the gloom and point me
to the skies. Heav'n's morning breaks,
and earth's vain shadows flee;
In life, in death, O Lord,
abide with me!" Amen.
(CW 588:7)

DAY 117
LIFE'S LITTLE DAY

Time is short.

1 CORINTHIANS 7:29

◆

There was once a high school senior who had just taken his SATs. He was stressed and worried as he waited for the results. Would he get a good score? Would the college he applied for accept him? His stress and worry got so bad that one night God appeared to him in a dream.

"Don't worry," God told him. "You passed your SATs with flying colors and your favorite college will accept you."

"Thank you, Lord!" the young man said with a sigh. "That is a relief—but God, since I have you here, can I ask you a question?"

"Of course, my son," God replied.

"If you are all-powerful, why don't you just end all sin and suffering in the world right now?"

God looked down at him and said with a smile, "I will answer that question for you when you get to heaven."

"God, I don't know if I can wait that long," the young man replied.

"What?" God asked, "You can't wait until next Tuesday?"

Do you think that young man would have been so stressed about his SATs and college if he had known he was going to die on Tuesday? What would you do today if God told you that you were going to die next Tuesday? Would you still get up and go to work, mow the lawn, and wash the dishes? Would you live differently today if you knew it was your last day here on earth?

We all have what the poet Alexander Andersen called "life's little day." We have 70, 80, 90 years here on earth, some even less. The apostle Paul puts it this way: "Time is short."

ARE YOU READY? YOU ARE IF YOU BELIEVE IN JESUS.

Time is short. Young people sometimes think, "I'll get back to God and church later, when I have a family, after I've had some fun." Later may never come. You could die next Tuesday.

Are you ready? You are if you believe in Jesus.

223

Jesus, God himself, came to this earth to live in your place the perfect life you have failed to live. He came to suffer on the cross the punishment—the hell—that all our lies, anger, drunkenness, pride, and gossip deserve. Because of Jesus, God forgives you. Because of Jesus, God gives you heaven as a free gift. All those who believe in Jesus will live even though they die. That's God's promise. Believe it.

You could die next Tuesday. I'm not saying that to scare you. I'm saying it so that you never forget what is important, so that you make the most of every day, so that you know and trust in Jesus today. Time is short. Life's little day is drawing to a close.

Live every day as if it were your last.

Today I am thankful for/that _____

_____

Dear Lord, thank you for the time you have given. Help me to make the most of every day you give me here on earth with the confidence that I have eternity waiting for me in heaven because of Jesus. Amen.

DAY 118
BACK TO THE FUTURE

You also must be ready, because the Son of Man will come at an hour when you do not expect him.

MATTHEW 24:44

October 21, 2015. That was the date Doc Brown took Marty McFly to a future replete with hoverboards, flying cars, and *Jaws 19*. Amazingly, some of the elements of 2015 were quite accurate (the video chatting on large screen televisions) and others not so much (Where's my flying car?).

The biggest disappointment ironically occurred in real life on October 21, 2015. The New York Mets beat the Chicago Cubs, ending the Cubs improbable postseason run. In *Back to the Future II,* a giant marquee announces the Cubs winning the World Series for the first time in over 100 years.

Amazingly, the movie was only one year off. The Cubs finally won the World Series in 2016.

Predicting the future is a risky proposition. Many have tried. All have failed. Sure, some are able to guess with uncanny success. Some psychics, no doubt aided by demonic divulgences, have foretold certain events in detail while failing miserably on others.

Why do all fortune tellers eventually fail to be 100% accurate? Because no one, not even the devil and his demons, can see the future. Demons can see things we cannot see and go places we cannot go. They can make more informed guesses than we, but in the end they cannot see what will happen.

Only God knows, only God sees, only God controls the future.

And God strictly forbids any attempt on our part to try to foresee the future (Deuteronomy 18:9-13). Jesus clearly warns that no one will know the day of his return at the end of the world. While he was here on earth, even he set aside that knowledge. Jesus is coming like a thief in the night (Matthew 24:42-44). Only God knows.

Yet throughout history, faithful Christians have tried to decipher the date. If you have a chance, check out Wikipedia's list of all the failed attempts to predict the end of the world. Famous Christians like Hillary of Poitiers, Martin of Tours, Hippolytus, Jonathan Edwards, John Wesley, and many more have failed miserably at prognosticating the end.

Many have had to face the shame of their errors because they predicted the end within their own lifetime. One of my seminary professors once quipped, "If you are going to predict the end of the world, make sure you pick a date long after you're dead." Why? Because otherwise you will look the fool.

Just think of all the Chicken Littles who cried that the sky was falling at the turn of the millennium in 2000 and at the end of the Mayan calendar in 2012. The world did not end because no one knows when Jesus will come.

But why do so many people try to predict the end of the world? Why do so many scour the Bible looking for hidden codes and messages so they can know exactly when the world will end? Because, like Adam and Eve, we

IN OUR SINFUL PRIDE, WE WANT TO KNOW AND SEE WHAT ONLY GOD CAN SEE.

want to be God. In our sinful pride, we want to know and see what only God can see.

God wants us to humbly trust him. He wants us to see the signs he has given—wars and rumors of wars, famines and earthquakes—so that we are constantly ready for Jesus' coming. You are ready if you believe in him. You are washed of your sins in his blood. When Jesus comes, he is coming to take all those who believe in him to heaven. That's the promise of the one who does see the future.

Jesus is coming. He could come at any time. He could come tomorrow or in another thousand years. We don't know, just like we don't know when the Cubs will win another World Series.

So be ready.

Today I am thankful for/that _____

_____

Heavenly Father, thank you for preparing me for Jesus' coming through faith. Help me to stay alert and always be ready. Amen.

DAY 119
GRACE

If by grace, then it cannot be based on works; if it were, grace would no longer be grace.

ROMANS 11:6

◆

The year was 1997. I sat down with my buddies to watch Super Bowl XXXI. It was the first year the FOX network broadcast the Super Bowl. The game featured the Green Bay Packers versus the New England Patriots.

In the pregame, FOX put together a video segment in which Reggie White, Green Bay's Hall of Fame defensive end, sang "Amazing Grace" while FOX juxtaposed footage of ballet dancers floating gracefully across a stage, football players making graceful catches, and Reggie White making bone-crunching hits.

When our world hears the word *grace,* that's what comes to mind. Ballet dancers floating across a stage. A wide receiver flying past a defender. A quarterback remaining calm under extraordinary pressure.

For FOX Sports, it seemed natural to have Reggie White, the "Minister of Defense," sing "Amazing Grace" as those images flowed across the screen.

Sadly, that is not the grace of which the hymn speaks.

When the Bible uses the word *grace,* it refers not to fluidity of motion, but to God's amazing love. "For it is by grace you have been saved," the apostle Paul tells us (Ephesians 2:8). We are saved—we are going to heaven—because of God's love.

If you are married, why do you love your spouse? I love my wife because she is a beautiful person on the inside and out. I love her because she puts up with me. I love her because of her wonderful faith. I love her because of who she is and all the wonderful things she does.

Why does God love you? It is definitely not because of who you are and what you do. In fact, he loves you in spite of who you are and what you do. He loves you despite your lies and anger and lust. He loves you even though every day you do things he hates. God doesn't love you because you are loveable or sweet.

GOD'S LOVE IS NOT DEPENDENT ON YOU.

God doesn't love you because of who you are, but because of who he is. God loves you because God is love (1 John 4:16). He can't help it. God's love is not dependent on you.

No matter what you do, no matter how badly you mess up, no matter how far you fall, no matter how ugly your sin, it can't make God love you any less.

In the same way, no matter what you do, no matter how many good deeds you do, no matter how many lives you help and how much money you give, it can't make God love you any more than he already does.

God's love doesn't depend on who you are and what you do. He loves you with his perfect, astounding, surprising, marvelous, amazing grace.

And in his amazing grace, he sacrificed his Son for you. In his amazing grace, Jesus suffered your hell in your place. In his amazing grace, God forgives you every sin and gives you a home in heaven.

You don't deserve any of it. I don't deserve any of it. Everything I have and everything I am is because of God's amazing grace—his love I don't deserve.

Today I am thankful for/that _____

_____

Gracious Lord, thank you for your amazing grace that saved a wretch like me. Amen.

DAY 120
PSEUDO-EXPERTISE SYNDROME

When pride comes, then comes disgrace, but with humility comes wisdom.

PROVERBS 11:2

My Facebook feed was flooded. As we continued to deal with the COVID-19 pandemic, everybody was up in arms about whether or not we should wear masks.

For some, it was a question of love. They wore masks to protect others, especially those most at risk from COVID-19. They believed the government and businesses should require the use of masks.

Others refused to wear them. They didn't believe masks really protected anyone from anything. They saw the requirement of wearing masks to be an infringement on their freedom—the first step toward tyranny.

Many of us found ourselves somewhere in the middle. We wondered about the CDC's sudden shift a couple of months into the pandemic. Early on they said masks would not help. Then they told us to wear masks. Did masks really help?

At the time, it was difficult to know what to do.

The discussion about masks was a microcosm of a larger debate dividing our country. Since the very beginning of the pandemic, people inevitably found themselves somewhere on a spectrum between panic and denial.

One extreme was afraid it was the end of the world as we knew it. They felt we needed to take drastic measures to save our planet and protect human life. They considered those who refused to take such measures to be evil and selfish.

The other extreme believed the world was overreacting and driven by fear. COVID-19 was no worse than the flu. People should just use common sense and they'd be fine. At this end of the spectrum, conspiracy theories abounded. The government was purposefully and systematically using the pandemic as a red herring to take away our freedoms. Democrats were pushing extreme social distancing to tank the economy and win the election in November. China released the virus on purpose to weaken the United States.

Is there some truth to such theories?

There could be. Even now it's hard to say. I am not privy to what happens behind locked doors and in high-level conference rooms. I am not a doctor, virologist, or epidemiologist.

You are most likely not either.

The rise of social media in our society has created another pandemic, what I call "Pseudo-Expertise Syndrome." We watch our favorite news channel and read what our friends share on Facebook. We google the topic on our phones. Suddenly, we think we grasp the complexities of epidemiology or constitutional law or international trade.

Ironically, our expert opinions nearly always coincide with our long-held political leanings. Almost to a person, you could tell which political party someone belonged to by their opinions about COVID-19.

PRACTICE ONE OF THE MOST CHRISTIAN OF VIRTUES: HUMILITY.

As a pastor, I encourage you to put into practice one of the most Christian of virtues: humility. Humbly accept you may not have all the facts. Recognize the complexity of these issues. Intelligent people can and do disagree on the wisest and most loving way to respond to our current pandemic.

Think twice about what you post and share on social media. Speak the truth in love. Humbly admit you are not an expert. Remember we are in the middle of another pandemic. The virus of Pseudo-Expertise Syndrome is extremely contagious.

And wearing a mask most definitely won't help stop its spread.

Today I am thankful for/that _____

_____

Holy Spirit, give me the wisdom to humbly admit what I do not know. Amen.

DAY 121
PUTTING THE FUN IN FUNERAL

"I am the resurrection and the life. The one who believes in me will live, even though they die; and whoever lives by believing in me will never die."

JOHN 11:25,26

◆

"They want to put the fun in funeral," a friend told me the other day.

We were talking about how more and more people are trying to make funerals light and cheery affairs—a celebration of the person's life. "They want to put the fun in funeral."

Her statement caught me off guard.

"What?"

"That's what they said when Bill Cosby's son died," she explained.

In 1997, Ennis Cosby was tragically killed by an armed robber. It was reported that at the small family funeral, his parents and sisters took turns telling humorous anecdotes and finding comfort in each other's laughter. Bill Cosby supposedly quipped afterward, "We wanted to put the fun in funeral."

Humor can help heal. Remembering a loved one, especially the good and happy times, helps us cope as we hurt. There is a place for smiles and laughter, even at funerals.

But should our goal be to make funerals fun? Is the purpose of a funeral simply to cherish the happy memories and push away the bad?

My job as a Christian pastor is not to put the fun in funeral, but rather to fill it with joy. In Christian funerals, we remember the person. We talk about his or her life. We may even laugh or smile as we do. But we remember the whole person.

Nowadays it is almost sacrilege to speak ill of the dead. When people die, they are sainted. They could do no wrong; at least we don't speak of it. That would just bring everyone down. It would cause more hurt and pain.

At a Christian funeral, however, we remind family and friends that, though their loved one was kind and giving, loving and generous, he or she wasn't perfect. Sometimes we even speak openly and honestly about specific struggles, because the joy of a Christian funeral is not found in a few carefully selected memories or humorous anecdotes.

The joy of a Christian funeral is found in Jesus. The point of a Christian funeral is not to fondly remember our loved ones, but to joyfully remember Jesus. Your grandmother was not perfect, but Jesus died for her. Your father struggled with his temper, but he was forgiven. With his death and resurrection, Jesus conquered sin, death, and the devil.

At a Christian funeral, we celebrate Jesus' promise: "I am the resurrection and the life. The one who believes in me will live, even though they die; and whoever lives by believing in me will never die." A Christian funeral isn't the celebration of the life our loved one lived but of the life that person is now living in heaven because of Jesus.

At a Christian funeral, our God describes for us the heaven our loved one is now enjoying. At a Christian funeral, he promises us that we will see that person again, all because of Jesus.

FUNERALS ARE RARELY FUN, BUT THEY CAN BE FILLED WITH JOY.

Funerals are rarely fun, but they can be filled with joy, even as the tears roll down our cheeks. That joy, however, is not found in jokes or fond memories.

It is found in Jesus.

Today I am thankful for/that _____

_____

Merciful God, as I feel the sting and hurt of loved ones who have died, fill my heart with the joy of the resurrection and of a reunion with them in heaven. Amen.

DAY 122
DOXOLOGY

Let everything that has breath praise the LORD.

PSALM 150:6

◆

doxology [dox-sol-*uh*-jee] n. *(from the Greek, literally "a word of praise")* a hymn or form of words containing an ascription of praise to God.

Thomas Ken (1637–1711) was orphaned when he was nine years old. He was raised by his stepsister Ann and her husband, author Izaak Walton. Walton coincidentally gained a fair share of fame for his book, *The Compleat Angler,* considered today a classic work about fishing.

When he was 15 years old, Ken entered Winchester College and later studied at Oxford. He was ordained as a priest in the Anglican Church in 1662. After serving at a handful of parishes, he returned to his alma mater, Winchester College, to serve as chaplain.

There, Ken sought to improve the devotional life of his students. He composed three hymns—one to be sung when the student awoke, one before going to bed, and one if the student had a difficult time sleeping. Each hymn ended with the same verse, a doxology. Two of the hymns: "Awake, My Soul, and with the Sun" and "All Praise to Thee, My God, This Night" became popular hymns of the day and are still sung today.

But neither became as famous as the last verse. It became a hymn unto itself. Today most churches simply refer to it as "The Common Doxology."

Praise God, from whom all blessings flow;
Praise him, all creatures here below;
Praise him above, ye heav'nly host;
Praise Father, Son, and Holy Ghost! (CW 334)

"The Common Doxology" is a simple word of praise. Its message isn't complex or profound. It merely praises God because he is the source of every good thing.

YOU CAN'T BE THANKFUL WITHOUT HAVING SOMEONE TO THANK.

Every year come Thanksgiving, we hear a lot about being thankful. On TV, on the news, at work, people talk about being thankful, but rarely do you hear them say *to whom* they are thankful.

You can't be thankful without having someone to thank.

232

Thomas Ken recognized from whom all blessings flow.

But that's not the end of his story. Due to his ability as a chaplain and preacher, Ken was appointed by King Charles II to be chaplain to Charles' sister Mary and her new husband, William of Orange. He lasted less than a year in her court because he insisted that a relative of William keep a promise of marriage made to an English noblewoman.

Ken returned to England and continued to serve in King Charles' court, until he was asked to move because his home was to be used for the king's official mistress, Nell Gwynne. Thomas Ken refused the king.

Later, when Charles' brother, James II, ruled as England's last Catholic king, Ken was imprisoned in the Tower of London for refusing to sign James' Declaration of Indulgence. When William and Mary succeeded in removing James from the throne, Ken once again found himself in deep water because he would not support what they did. Even though he disagreed with King James, Ken had sworn an oath of allegiance to the king and would not break an oath he had made before God.

Throughout his life, Ken boldly stood up for what he thought was right. He not only talked the talk of faith; he walked the walk.

It's easy to thank and praise God with our words and songs in church. God wants more. He wants lives lived in fearless service.

Thomas Ken's life was his greatest doxology.

Today I am thankful for/that _____

_____

"We praise you, O God, our Redeemer, Creator!
In grateful devotion our tribute we bring: We
lay it before you; we kneel and adore you;
We bless your holy name; glad praises
we sing." Amen. (CW 609:1)

DAY 123
JESUS WINS

"Hallelujah! For our Lord God Almighty reigns."

REVELATION 19:6

❖

There was once a janitor who worked for a church. In his free time, he loved to read the Bible. One day the pastor walked by as the janitor was reading his Bible during his lunch break.

"What are you reading?" the pastor asked.

"The book of Revelation," the janitor replied.

"Don't you think that's a little complicated for you?" the pastor asked condescendingly.

"No," the janitor replied. "Actually, Revelation is easy to understand."

"Is that right?" the pastor responded with a smirk. "Well, then, what is Revelation about?"

"Jesus wins," the janitor replied.

Jesus wins. That is the point of the book of Revelation. That is the point of the Bible.

The problem is that sometimes it doesn't seem that way. Sometimes it feels like chaos reigns, like the devil is winning. Just look at what happened in Paris in 2015—the havoc and destruction the devil led people to cause following the lies of Islam. Look at our own country. Our society supports gay marriage. Our government has legalized the murder of babies. Look at our lives—family problems, disease, divorce, death. So often it doesn't seem like Jesus wins.

Just imagine how the disciples must have felt on that dark Friday so many years ago when Jesus died. He was defeated. It was all a lie. He was a fraud.

JESUS WINS AND YOU ARE ON HIS TEAM. THEREFORE YOU WIN.

But death couldn't defeat him. What did Jesus do just two days later? He rose from the dead. He vanquished sin. He conquered death. He defeated the devil and then Jesus descended into hell—not to suffer, but to prove that he reigns even over hell.

Jesus wins and you are on his team. Therefore you win.

234

That's pretty amazing because you are a loser. I know. That sounds harsh. I am a loser too. I am a loser because I lose battles against temptation every day. I am a loser because I lose my temper with my wife and children. I am a loser because I lust. I am a loser because I lie.

But Jesus purchased and won me from all sin, death, and the power of the devil, not with gold or silver, but with his holy precious blood and innocent suffering and death. I am a winner because Jesus died my death and suffered my defeat. I am a winner because he conquered death with his resurrection. Jesus wins and therefore I win.

Jesus wins and therefore our enemies cannot. Sure they can cause us to struggle and stumble here on this earth, but they can't win. They can't stop the gospel. They can't stop Jesus. They can't take away our eternal victory in heaven.

In the book of Revelation, John is given a glimpse of heaven after judgment day—after the defeat of all God's enemies. As the smoke rises from the ashes, the voices of the saved in heaven roar: "Hallelujah! For our Lord God Almighty reigns."

We live in an unstable world where terrorism and tyranny are a constant threat. In the end, though, we need not worry. We don't have to be afraid. No matter what happens, they cannot win. Our Lord God Almighty reigns. Jesus wins.

Today I am thankful for/that _____

_____

Thank you, God, for giving us the victory through our Lord Jesus Christ. Amen.

DAY 124
CAN I GET AN AMEN?

The twenty-four elders and the four living creatures fell
down and worshiped God, who was seated on the
throne. And they cried: "Amen. Hallelujah!"

REVELATION 19:4

❖

Amen. At some point or another, every Christian has said that word. Honestly, though, some Christians say it a lot more than others. In some Christian churches, parishioners periodically shout out their *amens* in approval.

"Amen, brother, preach it!"

My church is a bit more subdued. I think I have gotten two *amens* in 12 years (though that may be more a reflection on my preaching).

Don't get me wrong. We do say amen at our church. At the end of every prayer, each blessing, and even some hymns we say and sing it.

Have you ever wondered why we say amen?

Amen is a Hebrew word which means "confirmed" or, more simply, "true."

In the Old Testament, when the priest offered prayers for the people in the temple, they would respond in one voice, "Amen." "Confirmed." "True." "What the priest said, God, that's my prayer too."

Jesus loved the word *amen*. Every time we find Jesus saying in the Bible, "I tell you the truth," what he literally said was, "Amen. Amen. I tell you." Amen is a word of emphasis—of certainty. Like Martin Luther, Jesus was saying, "This is most certainly true."

Many hymns and blessings in the Bible end with the word *amen*. Amen is an exclamation point. This is true! It is a fact!

That's why we say amen at the end of our prayers in church. You are saying, "God, what the pastor just said, that's my prayer too." You are saying, "This is most certainly true!"

And that's why I can also understand those who shout it out during a sermon. They are saying, "That's true. I agree." Personally I don't feel comfortable doing it. I worry that such displays can become distracting. Like anything else spoken in church, it can become ritualistic. It can take away from the dignity of worship.

In the end, though, when God's children give their amen to his Word, they are confessing their faith. They are telling the world, "This is true." They are letting their light shine.

To amen or not to amen is definitely a matter of Christian freedom.

But did you know we will all say amen in heaven?

In Revelation chapter 19, God gave the apostle John a glimpse of the glory of heaven. There he heard a thundering roar of voices praising God for his justice and grace. The choir of believers and angels responded, "Amen, Hallelujah!" Literally, "This is true. Praise the Lord!"

In heaven we will see God's promises confirmed. We will see Jesus. We will see his glory. We will see the victory he won for us and we will say, "Amen! It is all true!"

YOU DON'T HAVE TO WAIT UNTIL HEAVEN TO SAY AMEN.

But you don't have to wait until heaven to say amen. You can say it even now because God's promises are true. You are forgiven. You are going to heaven because of Jesus. It's true!

Can I get an amen?

Today I am thankful for/that _____

_____

Almighty God, as I hear your Word proclaimed,
help me to trust that it is true and to live
with the confidence that one day I will
say with the saints in heaven, "Amen.
Hallelujah!" Amen.

DAY 125
NO PRICE TOO HIGH

You are not your own; you were bought at a price.
Therefore honor God with your bodies.

1 CORINTHIANS 6:19,20

◆

The story is told of a wealthy business magnate from the United States who lived during the turn of the 20th century. His wife went traveling in Europe and sent him a telegram which read, "Have found wonderful bracelet. Price is $75,000. May I buy it?"

Immediately her husband sent her a telegraph in response: "No. STOP. Price too high. STOP." The telegraph operator, however, forgot to put the first stop in the telegraph. The message his wife received simply read:

"No price too high."

To her husband's chagrin, the wife returned from Europe with the $75,000 bracelet, but all the more enamored with her husband for whom no price was too high to make her happy.

In Luke chapter 14, Jesus teaches us about the cost of following him. The heaven he won for us is a free gift. Forgiveness is a free gift. Following Jesus costs us nothing.

Yet it could cost you everything.

FOLLOWING JESUS MEANS BEING WILLING TO GIVE UP EVERYTHING TO FOLLOW HIM.

Following Jesus means that he is the most important thing in your life. Following Jesus means being willing to give up everything to follow him. Following Jesus means sacrifice and commitment.

Sometimes the price just seems too high. You could lose your job if you don't cut the corners your boss wants you to. You could lose your boyfriend if you keep refusing to have sex with him. Being humble and generous may mean sacrificing some of the pleasures of life.

Following Jesus often involves sacrifice. Doing what is right has a cost.

When you struggle with the cost of following Jesus, when the sacrifices seem unbearable, when it seems the price is just too high, remember the price Jesus paid for you.

No price was too high.

Jesus sacrificed everything. He gave up the glories of heaven and came to this sin-stinking world. He suffered humiliation and abuse. He gave his very life—suffering the agony of hell we deserve—to pay for our ticket to heaven.

And his sacrifice wasn't accidental like the wealthy husband from our story. Jesus came to this earth knowing exactly what it was going to cost him. He loved us so much, no price was too high.

May we forever be so enamored with our Savior for whom no price was too high that we are willing to give up everything for him.

If you have a chance today, read what Jesus had to say about the cost of following him in Luke 14:25-33. Pray about it. Think about what he sacrificed—what he paid—to save you. Then, when he calls you to pay a high price for following him, answer gladly:

"No price too high."

Today I am thankful for/that _____

_____

Dear Jesus, you gave up everything that was good and suffered what is evil to pay the price for all my sins. Help me to give my all for you. Amen.

DAY 126
THE ONLY THING WE HAVE TO FEAR

"Do not be afraid of those who kill the body but cannot
kill the soul. Rather, be afraid of the One who can
destroy both body and soul in hell."

MATTHEW 10:28

❖

During some of the darkest days in our nation's history, President Franklin Roosevelt declared, "The only thing we have to fear is fear itself."

The date was March 4, 1933, FDR's first inauguration. The country was still reeling from the Great Depression. Roosevelt's full quote was this, "Let me assert my firm belief that the only thing we have to fear is . . . fear itself—nameless, unreasoning, unjustified terror which paralyzes needed efforts to convert retreat into advance."

Fear paralyzes us. It leads us to crawl deep into our shells. It keeps us from moving forward. It keeps us from living.

Terrorism literally causes terror. It feeds our greatest fears—an unseen enemy attacking where we are weakest: on planes, at work, at sporting events, at community centers.

Terrorism works. We would be lying if we said otherwise. Terrorism instills terror. It causes us to look over our shoulders, to shut down our airports, to distrust our neighbors. It keeps us from living.

So how do we keep fear from paralyzing us? How do we live when "we walk in danger all the way" as the hymn writer says?

We ask God for courage. Courage is not the absence of fear. Courage is facing our fears. Courage is standing firm even when we are afraid. Courage is trusting God's promises.

The people of Israel were not facing an unseen enemy. They could see their enemy just across the Jordan River. They could see the mighty warriors, the great armies, the fortified cities waiting for them on the other side.

Moses told them, "Be strong and courageous. . . . The LORD himself goes before you and will be with you; he will never leave you nor forsake you. Do not be afraid; do not be discouraged" (Deuteronomy 31:7,8).

We can be courageous; we can live our lives—we can board airplanes and go to sporting events—because our God promises to be by our side the entire way. Are there dangers lurking around the corner? Yes. Could terrorists attack at any time? You bet.

But our God promises to be with us and to make all things work for our eternal good. He promises to deliver us from evil—even if evil men attack and kill us.

Jesus himself said, "Do not be afraid of those who kill the body but cannot kill the soul. Rather, be afraid of the One who can destroy both body and soul in hell."

. . . IS GOD HIMSELF. In other words, the only thing we have to fear . . . is God himself.

Terrorists can kill your body, but they cannot touch your soul. Hell is terrifying. God is the one who sends souls to hell. He is the one who punishes sinners. Therefore, God is the only thing you would ever need to be afraid of.

Yet you don't have to be afraid of God because he loved you so much he suffered the wrath of his own punishment in your place. Jesus faced his fears and courageously suffered the terror of the cross you deserve. You are forgiven. You don't have to be afraid of hell. You don't have to be afraid of God, and, therefore, you don't have to be afraid of anything.

They can't win. Even if you have to suffer, God will be with you and make it work for your good. Even if they kill you, you have a home in the glory of heaven waiting for you because of Jesus.

So take a deep breath. Face your fears. Be courageous.

Today I am thankful for/that _____

_____

Almighty God, take away our fears and help us to trust in you and the heaven you have won for us. Amen.

DAY 127
NOW AND NOT YET

Wait for the LORD; be strong and take heart
and wait for the LORD.

PSALM 27:14

◆

"Now is it my birthday, Daddy?"

Just about every day for the three weeks before my daughter's fifth birthday, she asked me that question: "Now is it my birthday, Daddy?"

"No, not yet."

"Now is it my birthday, Daddy?"

"No, not yet."

Then finally the day came. "Now is it my birthday, Daddy?"

"Yes, it is! Happy Birthday!" I said as she squealed with excitement.

Now and *not yet*. As we live our Christian lives here on earth, it is important for us to understand the difference between the *nows* and *not yets* of God.

The Bible speaks of what we have right now as Christians. Because Jesus suffered our punishment 2,000 years ago, we have forgiveness right now. God forgives you the errors of your youth which still haunt you today. He forgives you that night two weeks ago when you drank more than you should. He forgives you those ugly words you said to your wife this morning. Right now, at this very moment, the warm, comforting blanket of forgiveness covers you completely.

Right now, you have heaven. No, you aren't in heaven yet. You can't see heaven yet, but heaven is already yours through faith in Jesus. It belongs to you right now. The apostle Paul wrote: "Now is the time of God's favor, now is the day of salvation" (2 Corinthians 6:2).

God also promises to be with us right now and to the very end of the age (Matthew 28:20). He promises to make all things which happen right now work for our eternal good (Romans 8:28). That is our *now* as Christians.

But our *now* also includes other things. Our *now* includes conflicts in the Middle East, polarizing politics in our own country, and violence seemingly everywhere. Our *now* includes diabetes, divorce, and depression. Our *now* includes guilt, regret, and heartache. Our *now* includes watching people we love suffer and die.

As we look at the problems and pains of our *now*, the apostle Paul reminds us, "our present sufferings are not worth comparing with the glory that will be revealed in us" (Romans 8:18).

One day we will be free from all the hurt and heartache of this world. One day we will see with our physical eyes that which we can only see now through the eyes of faith. One day we will experience the heaven which belongs to us right now. One day we will have all those things, but not yet. For now we must wait.

Like a four-year-old waiting for her birthday, though, we often struggle with the wait. We get impatient with God when he doesn't free us from our pains right now. We get frustrated as the problems of right now pile upon our shoulders. We question God why he doesn't give us what we want right now.

Yet God lovingly tells us to wait. So often, his answer to our prayers is simply "Not yet." Now we must wait with the patience and confidence he gives us in his Word and promises. As we wait, however, we have the opportunity to live for him who gives us every good *now* and every perfect *not yet*.

WE WAIT IN EAGER EXPECTATION.

Right now we wait in eager expectation. We wait knowing that one day we will open our eyes and squeal in excitement. One day we will be free. One day we will see God face to face. One day we will be reunited with our loved ones who died in Christ. That will happen one day—just not yet.

Today I am thankful for/that _____

_____

Lord, thank you for all the good you have given me now. Please give me patience to wait for my not yets. Amen.

DAY 128
WINNING THE LOTTERY

**My God will meet all your needs according to
the riches of his glory in Christ Jesus.**

PHILIPPIANS 4:19

◆

In October of 2018, our country caught lottery fever. That month, the Powerball jackpot reached $1.5 billion. To put that in perspective, that is larger than the gross national product of 20 different countries. That is 160 times greater than the average NFL player will earn in his *entire* career.

Millions of people bought lottery tickets before last Wednesday night's drawing, dreaming of becoming rich. What would you do if you won $1.5 billion? What would you do if you became rich?

There is a problem with that question, of course. You are already rich.

Did you know that, according to the website The Global Rich List, if you earn $50,000 a year you are in the top 0.31% of the world? You are richer than 7.38 billion of the world's 7.4 billion people.

If you earn just $11,700 a year—the poverty line in the United States—you are still richer than 6.8 billion people in the world. In other words, the poorest people of the United States are richer than 84% of the world.

Yet the devil convinces us that we are poor—or at least that we're not rich. I mean, look at Bill Gates and Mark Zuckerberg. They are rich. We are not.

Rich and poor are actually relative terms. What happens easily is that we look at all the people who have more than us—bigger homes, nicer cars, fancier toys—and we think we are poor by comparison.

We fail to look south of the border. We fail to look across the ocean and around the world at the billions of people who have less than us. By any and every standard, we as Americans are more materially wealthy than just about every person who ever lived in the history of humankind.

The secret to happiness isn't getting what you want, it's recognizing what you've got. Winning the lottery won't make you happy; recognizing and appreciating what God has given you will.

Because the truth is, even if you weren't born in the United States, even if you lived in a grass hut in Africa or in the rubble of war-torn Syria, you would still be rich. You are a child of God, forgiven through faith in Jesus. You have a mansion waiting for you in heaven with your name on the mailbox. The all-powerful King of the universe is your Father and friend.

THERE IS NO SUCH THING AS A POOR CHRISTIAN.

There is no such thing as a poor Christian.

So instead of dreaming about winning $1.5 billion and wondering what you would do if you struck it rich, look around. Try to make a list of everything you own. It would take you days. Look at your family, friends, and church. Look at all the garbage God has forgiven in your life and the heaven that is waiting for you.

You don't have to dream about being rich. You already are.

Today I am thankful for/that _____

_____

*Lord, open my eyes to see how rich
I really am. Amen.*

DAY 129
DIRTY WATER

I warn everyone who hears the words of the prophecy
of this scroll: If anyone adds anything to them, God
will add to that person the plagues described in
this scroll. And if anyone takes words away from
this scroll of prophecy, God will take away from
that person any share in the tree of life and in the
Holy City, which are described in this scroll.

REVELATION 22:18,19

245

In April of 2014, the city of Flint, Michigan, in order to cut costs, began drawing its drinking water from the Flint River instead of Lake Huron.

They failed, however, to treat the corrosive waters of the Flint River with the proper chemicals. As a result, lead leached from pipes and fixtures into the drinking water. Though many residents complained about the water, the local, state, and federal governments waited months to respond. On January 5, 2016, the governor of Michigan finally declared a state of emergency in Flint.

Clean-up and treatment efforts took years. Experts still don't know what long-term effects the lead poisoning will have on the residents and especially the children of Flint.

Dirty water is dangerous. It can damage vital organs. It can make you sick or even kill you.

God has given us the pure unadulterated living water of his Word. The promises of his Word refresh us, comfort us, and give us life.

As sinful human beings, though, we tend to muddy the water. We pollute it by interjecting our own opinions, biases, and traditions. We treat God's Word as if it were a salad bar, picking and choosing what we want to believe. We twist his words to fit our own preconceived ideas.

The waters become contaminated and souls become sick.

Jesus often warned against the dangers of false teachings which spread like leaven. He compared false teachers to wolves in sheep's clothing. In other words, dirty water is dangerous.

Despite our Savior's warnings, however, I am noticing a trend in our world today. Many Christians are knowingly drinking polluted water. They are attending churches they know aren't teaching God's Word in its truth and purity.

They go because that's where their spouse attends. They go because it's a lot closer than their old church. They go because it has programs for their kids, a more charismatic pastor, or more convenient service times.

"Don't worry, pastor," they tell me. "I know what the Bible says and what I believe. It won't affect me." "At least they're hearing God's Word," their parents tell me. "Dirty water is better than no water at all."

And there is some truth to that. If I were dying of thirst—if I had to go three days without anything to drink—and you put a glass of water from Flint, Michigan, in front of me, I am sure I would drink it. Dirty water is better than no water at all.

For a person dying of spiritual thirst, who doesn't know Jesus or the forgiveness he won for them, the gospel, even when muddied by false teaching, can save the soul.

PROLONGED EXPOSURE TO DIRTY WATER IS DANGEROUS.

But if you have the choice between drinking clean water or polluted water, why would you ever pick the polluted water? Prolonged exposure to dirty water is dangerous. It affects our faith. It hurts our souls. In fact, it can be deadly.

Take Jesus' warnings seriously. Don't drink polluted water for the sake of convenience. Expect your church and pastor to be doctrinally pure. If you don't know what that is, open your Bible. Read it daily. Study. Learn.

Drink deeply from the pure, unadulterated spring of God's Word.

Today I am thankful for/that _____

_____

Lord, keep us steadfast in your Word. Amen.

DAY 130
WHAT DOES THIS MEAN?

Now the Berean Jews were of more noble character
than those in Thessalonica, for they received the
message with great eagerness and examined
the Scriptures every day to see if what
Paul said was true.

ACTS 17:11

It's a Lutheran thing.

Just ask anyone who grew up in the Lutheran church that question: "What does this mean?" Like one of Pavlov's dogs, he or she will automatically respond, "We should fear and love God . . ."

It's in our DNA.

If you didn't grow up Lutheran, allow me to explain. Nearly 500 years ago in 1529, the German theology professor and pastor Martin Luther wrote a book called *The Small Catechism*. The book was meant to be a primer to help parents teach their children the basic truths of the Bible.

In his Catechism, Luther included sections on the Ten Commandments, the apostle's Creed, the Lord's Prayer, Baptism, and Communion, among other things. After every Commandment, article of the Creed and petition of the Lord's Prayer, Martin Luther pointedly asked, "What does this mean?"

He then wrote a simple summary which children could memorize. The meaning of each Commandment begins with the words, "We should fear and love God . . ."

What does this mean? Martin Luther didn't ask that question and write those simple meanings in order to impose his will on God's people. He wasn't saying, "You can't understand this without my explaining it to you."

WHY DO THE WORDS OF WORSHIP SO OFTEN BECOME ROTE AND BORING TO US?

To the contrary, Luther simply wanted to emphasize the importance of asking the question. Why do the words of worship so often become rote and boring to us? Why do the words of Scripture so often seem distant and detached from our lives today? Because we fail to ask that simple question, "What does this mean?"

What you say and do in church on Sunday morning has meaning for your everyday life. The Bible is not simply a book meant to entertain our thoughts as we read it. God wants us to read, learn, and inwardly digest it. He wants us to meditate on it day and night and to ask, "What does this mean for me and my life?"

God commands, "You shall have no other gods." What does this mean? "We should fear, love, and trust in God above all things."

The Bible tells us that Jesus died on the cross for us. What does this mean? It means "he has redeemed me, a lost and condemned creature, purchased and won me from all sin, death, and the power of the devil, not with gold or silver, but with his holy precious blood and innocent suffering and death."

God invites me to pray, "Our Father, who art in heaven." What does this mean? "By these words God would tenderly encourage us to believe that he is our true Father and that we are his true children, so that we may ask him confidently with all assurance, as dear children ask their dear father."

248

Whether you're Lutheran or Catholic, Presbyterian or Pentecostal, Baptist or non-denominational, never stop asking that question. As you quietly read your Bible at home, as you sing and say the words of worship on Sunday morning, as you read Bible stories to your children, take a moment to ask yourself, "What does this mean?"

Because God is speaking to you. His words have meaning for this life and the next. In his words, you will find help, hope, and forgiveness.

Know what I mean?

Today I am thankful for/that _____

_____

*Almighty God, help me to read, learn,
and inwardly digest your Word so that
I can believe it and live it every
day of my life. Amen.*

DAY 131
SAFE

**He will command his angels concerning you to guard
you in all your ways; they will lift you up in
their hands, so that you will not strike
your foot against a stone.**

PSALM 91:11,12

On November 30, 2015, Timothy Martin, a former Navy SEAL, died from gunshot wounds suffered during an altercation near his home in Tampa, Florida. Before becoming a Navy SEAL, Timothy considered becoming a pastor. His brother did, in fact, become a minister. I know that because he was the pastor at my father's church in Michigan.

Coincidentally, I also went to school with Martin's pastor from Tampa, Florida. In fact, I ran into him this last week at a conference. As we spoke, he told me about the funeral. The church was full. The family entered behind the casket, followed by dozens of current and former Navy SEALS.

The family sat down in the front, but there was no room for the SEALS. So they fanned out and lined up along the walls on the sides and back of the church. With their hands crossed behind their backs and chests sticking out, they stood at solemn attention during the entire service.

"IT WAS THE SAFEST I HAVE EVER FELT IN CHURCH."

It must have been both awe-inspiring and intimidating at the same time.

"It was the safest I have ever felt in church," my pastor friend said with a smile.

I can only imagine.

The more I thought about it, though, I realized I should feel that safe all the time. You see, I too have highly trained special ops commandos who line the walls of my church and home.

They are called angels. In our modern imaginations, we picture angels as sweet and delicate. The Bible, however, describes them as God's armies, his legions of highly trained soldiers sent to protect his children.

Because we can't see them, we forget they are there. We worry about our own children when they leave home. We tremble as we lie alone in a hospital bed. We lie awake at night filled with fear.

We don't have to be afraid. We are safe. The hallways of our homes are lined with Special Forces. They walk alongside our children. They ride next to us in our minivans and SUVs. The all-powerful God has sent them to protect us.

But then where were God's commandos when Timothy Martin was shot? Why didn't they keep him safe?

A few years ago, *Capital One* credit cards ran a series of ads featuring people getting in accidents because their guardian angels were either lazy or distracted. Is that what happens when we get hurt? Do God's angels at times drop their guard? Do they leave us or forget about us for a while?

No. Where were God's angels the night Timothy Martin got shot? They were there by his side. They could have stopped the bullets, but they didn't. God had other plans and purposes for Timothy.

When we get hurt, when people die, it isn't because God's angels aren't doing their job. It's because God orders them to stand down. He allows such things to test us, to try us, to bring about his good purposes.

God's angels were standing at Timothy Martin's side when the bullets pierced his chest. They were with him in the ambulance. They carried him home from the hospital to heaven. You see, Timothy Martin is safe. He is in heaven with his Savior surrounded by legions of angels.

Are you afraid? Do you worry about your children who are away at school or deployed in the armed forces? Don't. They are safe. So are you. Navy SEALS line the walls of your home and never leave your children's sides.

Yes. They could get injured. They could even die. But that will only happen if God knows it is for their good. Because of Jesus, nothing can truly hurt them, not even death. Nothing can truly harm you.

God's Special Forces surround us. We are safe.

Today I am thankful for/that _____

_____

Almighty God, thank you for sending your holy angels to guard us in all our ways. Amen.

DAY 132
THE MOST MISUSED VERSE OF THE BIBLE EVER

I can do all this through him who gives me strength.

PHILIPPIANS 4:13

◆

"I think I can. I think I can. I think I can."

The little engine that could, did. He believed in himself, and he made it up the hill. That's the power of positive thinking. If you put your mind to it, you can achieve anything.

That's also the mantra with which our children are inundated every day. They are taught it in school. They read it in books. They see it on the Disney Channel.

They also hear it in church.

"I can do all this through him who gives me strength," they are told. You've got the all-powerful God behind you. You can do anything you put your mind to. God wants you to succeed. Just dream it and you can do it.

The only problem is that's not what Philippians 4:13 is saying. If you look at the context, the apostle Paul is talking about how he was able to be content—at peace—in any and every situation. He could do it—he could handle anything that came his way—through his God who gave him strength.

Philippians 4:13 isn't talking about the power God gives us to achieve whatever we dream. It's talking about the strength and peace God gives us to deal with the disappointment when we don't.

FOR MANY, . . . FAITH IS BELIEVING THAT YOUR DREAMS WILL COME TRUE.

For many in our world today, faith is believing that good things will happen. Faith is believing that your dreams will come true.

For a Christian, faith is trust in God's promises. God doesn't promise that if you dream it you can do it. God doesn't promise that if we just work hard enough we can achieve anything.

What he promises us is forgiveness. He promises us a home in heaven because of Jesus. He promises that he will be with us every moment of every day. He promises that he will make all things in our lives, even the struggles and pain, work for our eternal good.

Those promises are the way God gives us strength even as we face the disappointments of this world. Those promises give us peace and contentment no matter what happens in our lives.

What, then, should we tell our children? Should we tell them not to dream?

Tell them that if they really want something, they should pray to God and ask him for it. Tell them to dream big, to think positively, to work hard. With God's help, they can achieve many things which may seem impossible to them.

But also tell them that God doesn't always give us everything we want. He doesn't always let us live our dreams here on earth. What he does do is give us the peace to accept whatever he chooses to give us in his grace. He promises that whatever he gives us is for our good.

Tell your children to think positively and aim for the stars. Then also tell them God will give them the strength to deal with it if they don't make it there.

Today I am thankful for/that _____

_____

Lord, thank you for the strength you give. Help me to trust that you will do everything you have promised me. Amen.

---◆---

DAY 133
VOCATION, VOCATION, VOCATION

Nevertheless, each person should live as a believer in whatever situation the Lord has assigned to them, just as God has called them.

1 CORINTHIANS 7:17

◆

"Location, location, location." That was the answer which the late British tycoon, Lord Harold Samuel, gave when asked, "What are the three most important factors in successful real estate?" In our world today, "location, location, location" has become the mantra of real estate agents around the globe.

Location is key.

Similarly, when it comes to understanding how God wants us to serve him here on earth, there are three important factors to remember: vocation, vocation, vocation.

When most people hear the term *vocation*, they think of their job—their career. But your career is actually only a part of your vocation. The term *vocation* literally means "calling." God has called you to be and do many things. Your job is only a part of that calling.

First and foremost, God has called you to be his child through the waters of Holy Baptism and the promises of his Word. You have been washed of your sins. Through faith in Jesus, you are a son or daughter of the King of the universe. You are an heir of heaven.

That is what God has called you to be.

In loving thankfulness for that heavenly calling, God has also called you to serve him and others here on earth. If he has you here, that means he has things for you to do. Your life has purpose.

My vocation, for example, includes being a husband and father, a son and brother. My vocation includes being a pastor and writer. My vocation includes teaching Spanish to little children in our community and visiting the elderly in our area nursing homes. My vocation is taking my daughter to ballet lessons and playing Wii Bowling with my son.

What is your vocation? Why does God have you here on earth? If you struggle to answer that question, ask yourself three simple questions: Where am I? Who is with me? What abilities has God given me?

Those three factors help define your vocation. I live in a small town called Edna in the great state of Texas. The people around me are my wife and children, the members of my church, my friends and neighbors, and my community. God has given me the ability to preach, teach, and write. He has given me the gift to speak and teach Spanish. He has given me a deep love and concern for the elderly.

EVERY PERSON'S VOCATION IS DIFFERENT. What people has God placed in your life? What gifts and talents has he given you? What opportunities to serve? Every person's vocation is different. You don't have to do what I do. God has made you different. He has placed you in a different location with different people and different opportunities to serve.

Understand, though, that your vocation changes with every stage of life. It changes as your children grow, as you transition jobs, as the people in your life come and go. Your vocation today isn't the same as it was when you were 12 years old. In the same way, your vocation will be quite different when you are 80 years old.

Yet one thing remains a constant. Your Savior is calling you. He has adopted you as his child and washed you of all your sins. One day he will call you home to heaven. Right now, however, he has things for you to do. The key to understanding what those things are can be found in three simple words.

Vocation, vocation, vocation.

Today I am thankful for/that _____

_____

*O Heavenly Father, thank you for making me
who I am. Help me to be the person you have
made me to be and to live the vocation
to which you have called me. Amen.*

DAY 134
FUHGEDDABOUDIT

**"For I will forgive their wickedness and will
remember their sins no more."**

JEREMIAH 31:34

◆

I guess it's a guy thing. I could watch *The Godfather* parts one and two a thousand times and it would never get old (not so much part three). The same is true for *Goodfellas*, as well as numerous other mob-themed movies.

My wife just rolls her eyes.

The other night I was watching *Donnie Brasco* starring Al Pacino and Johnny Depp (for the 20th time). In the movie, Johnny Depp plays undercover FBI agent Joseph Pistone, who is befriended by a wise guy named Lefty Ruggiero, played by Al Pacino.

At one point, Depp tries to explain to his fellow FBI agents the meaning of the phrase "Fuhgeddaboudit."

Fuhgeddaboudit means more than just "forget about it." Among wise guys, *fuhgeddaboudit* was a catch-all phrase which meant many different things depending on your tone and context.

You agree with someone that Raquel Welch is beautiful . . . *fuhgeddaboudit*. You disagree with someone that a Lincoln is better than a Cadillac . . . *fuhgeddaboudit*. The veal you ate was the most incredible food you've ever tasted . . . *fuhgeddaboudit*. Somebody just insulted your mother . . . *fuhgeddaboudit*.

As I listened to Johnny Depp explain the phrase *fuhgeddaboudit*, I thought about something God says concerning our sins. In Jeremiah chapter 31, he tells us, "For I will forgive their wickedness and will remember their sins no more."

That lie you told your wife yesterday . . . *fuhgeddaboudit*. That angry text you sent your boyfriend last week . . . *fuhgeddaboudit*. That dumb night which still haunts you from your sophomore year in college . . . *fuhgeddaboudit*.

FORGIVENESS DOESN'T MEAN THAT GOD FORGETS ABOUT IT.

Now, to be clear, forgiveness doesn't mean that God forgets about it. It's not that our sins have simply slipped his mind. Our God doesn't forget. He chooses to remember them no more. There's a difference.

God chooses to forgive. He chooses to never again look at our sins. He separates them from us as far as the east is from the west.

Forgiveness, however, does not mean that God is saying to us, "Fuhgeddaboudit" in the sense that our sins are no big deal or that he doesn't care about them.

Every sin is a big deal. Every sin, from the smallest lie to the darkest depravity, deserves God's eternal anger in hell.

On a dark Friday we call "good," God chose to direct his anger for our sins onto his Son. From that moment on, he could choose to remember our sins no more because they were forever paid for.

Remember that when you fail and fall. Remember that as you lie awake at night haunted by guilt. Remember that as you stare at the cross on Good Friday. Because of what Jesus did there, God remembers your sins no more.

Fuhgeddaboudit.

Today I am thankful for/that _____

_____

Lord, have mercy on me, a sinner. Amen.

DAY 135
DEALING WITH DOUBT

"Stop doubting and believe."

JOHN 20:27

◆

I have a confession to make. Sometimes I lie awake at night wondering if all this is true. Is God really there? Is the Bible really true? What if Christianity is just some great hoax—the world's worst April Fools' Day joke—made up by a few fanatical followers of a dead prophet?

If this isn't true, if the Bible is myths and fables, if Jesus isn't God, then my whole life has been a waste. As a pastor, my life is dedicated to teaching the Bible and telling people about Jesus. If it's a lie, then I am an idiot and my whole life has been for nothing.

Do you ever have doubts? Do you ever lie awake at night wondering if all this is really true? What about all the other religions of the world? How do we know our God is the true God? Or maybe you have faced problems and pains or stood at the grave of a child and wondered, "If there really is a God, how could this happen?"

If you've ever doubted, you are not alone. Every Christian at one point or another has had misgivings. Even one of Jesus' disciples doubted. In fact, history has dubbed him "Doubting Thomas."

Do you remember the story of Doubting Thomas? On the first Easter Sunday, Jesus appeared to his disciples, proving that he had risen. They saw him. They touched him. He even ate some food to prove he wasn't a ghost.

The only problem was Thomas wasn't there. The next morning, the other disciples went to tell him, "We have seen the Lord!"

"Yeah, right," Thomas replied. "I'll believe it when I see it!"

The next Sunday, the disciples were once again gathered together. This time Thomas was with them. Suddenly Jesus appeared. He showed Thomas the nail wounds in his hands and the spear wound in his side. Finally, Thomas believed.

"Because you have seen me you have believed," Jesus told him. "Blessed are those who have not seen and yet have believed."

But that's not fair. Sure, Jesus calls us "blessed" because we have not seen him and yet have believed; still, it's not fair. Thomas got to see Jesus. Just think how much easier it would be to believe if we could just see what the people in the Bible saw.

Actually, it wouldn't be. Tens of thousands of people saw Jesus. They saw him feed the hungry, heal the sick and raise the dead. Yet how many actually believed? Only a small handful.

THE TRUTH IS, SEEING ISN'T BELIEVING.

The truth is, seeing isn't believing. Even if I had physical proof—even if I had videotape of Jesus doing miracles and raising people from the dead—that wouldn't help. Many would still doubt. They would call it a hoax. They would try to prove it was a fake, because seeing isn't believing.

Faith is hard. I can't prove any of this to you. The only way we can believe is by the power of the Holy Spirit. As we read and hear God's promises, the Holy Spirit quietly convinces us that it is true.

Do you struggle with doubt? Do you wonder at times if all this is true? Are you afraid deep down it might not be? Go to church. Open your Bible. Take Holy Communion. Go back to God's promises. That's how the Holy Spirit convinces us. That's how he strengthens our faith. That's how he helps us deal with our doubts.

Today I am thankful for/that _____

_____

Lord I believe. Help me in my unbelief. Amen.

DAY 136
THE ULTIMATE PREPPER

"So you also must be ready, because the Son of Man will come at an hour when you do not expect him."

MATTHEW 24:44

"You're the ultimate prepper."

Those words made me tilt my head and smile. I was at a children's birthday party with a good friend. He is a prepper.

Do you know what a prepper is? Popularized by reality shows like *Doomsday Preppers,* preppers are people who feel the need to be prepared for unknown future disasters. Are you prepared for a hurricane or flood? Do you have spare food, water, batteries, a generator?

Preppers take that kind of preparation to another level. Preppers prepare not only for hurricanes, but also for the fall of the world's economy, a violent overthrow of our government, major climatic shifts, zombie apocalypses, and the end of the world.

Preppers usually have hidden arsenals of weapons, food, and fuel. They know how to purify their own water and grow their own vegetables. They have getaway vehicles and safe houses. Preppers try to be prepared for any and every major catastrophe that might come their way.

As I said, my buddy is a prepper. While I spoke with him at the party, he introduced me to a group of his friends. They were talking about knives and guns. I asked them, "Are you guys preppers, too?" They all nodded and smiled. Then one asked me, "How about you?"

"No, I'm a pastor."

"You're the ultimate prepper," he told me with a wink.

Christians are preppers. No, most of us don't have stockpiles of food or weapons hidden in secret compartments under our homes. Most of us don't know how to purify water with a sock or grow organic vegetables from a garbage pile, but we are preppers.

In fact, we are doomsday preppers. When the end of the world comes, weapons and survival training won't do you any good. The end of the world is not going to be a major climatic shift which leaves humankind struggling to survive. The end of the world is not going to be a meteor which wipes out most of the world's population. The end of the world is going to be the end of the world.

In the blink of an eye, Jesus will come. Everyone will see him. People won't be running around wondering what is happening. Everyone will know immediately. God will gather all people together and raise the dead.

Then will be opened the books in which is written everything we have ever thought, said, and done. Just one sin, one mistake, one poor choice, means a guilty verdict and an eternity in the prison of hell. For many, the Last Day will be doomsday. It will catch them unprepared.

As Christians, however, we are prepared. We are prepared not because we are better than other people—not because we don't have any sins. We are prepared because Jesus loved us so much that he suffered our punishment in our place. We are prepared because God has justified us (literally "declared us innocent") through faith in Jesus. We are forgiven. When Jesus comes at the end of the world, he is coming to take us to heaven. All who believe in him are prepared.

CHRISTIANS ARE THE ULTIMATE DOOMSDAY PREPPERS.

Christians are the ultimate doomsday preppers. In fact, God now sends you and me to help prepare others. You don't have to know about weapons or survival techniques to prepare someone for the end of the world. You just have to know about Jesus and his love. So share what you know and help others be prepared.

Be the ultimate prepper.

Today I am thankful for/that _____

_____

Dear Jesus, you have prepared me for your coming again by washing me of my sins and giving me faith. Help me to stay ready. Use me to prepare others. Amen.

DAY 137
THE LAMB

"Worthy is the Lamb, who was slain, to receive power
and wealth and wisdom and strength and
honor and glory and praise!"
REVELATION 5:12

Lambs are cute and cuddly, right? When you go to a petting zoo, everyone wants to pet the lambs. When our little children dress up as lambs for the

Christmas program at church, everyone says, "Awww." When they sing, "I am Jesus Little Lamb," we take videos of it on our phones and post it on Facebook. Why? Because lambs are cute and cuddly.

Soon after Jesus' baptism, he was walking near the Jordan River. Suddenly John the Baptist pointed to him and shouted, "Look, the Lamb of God, who takes away the sin of the world" (John 1:29). But why would John call Jesus "the Lamb"?

It wasn't because he was cute and cuddly.

Lambs were at the heart of the Old Testament worship. Every day the sound of bleating lambs and the smell of burning flesh filled the temple. The temple was no petting zoo. It was a bloody place. Every morning and every evening, dozens, sometimes hundreds, of lambs were killed, drained of their blood, and burned on the great altar.

Lambs weren't pets. They were sacrifices.

The punishment of sin is death. But instead of demanding the blood of his people—instead of demanding their death—God provided for them a substitute. A lamb would die in their place.

A little lamb, however, couldn't really pay for their sins. The blood of an animal couldn't wash them clean. The sacrificial lambs of the Old Testament pointed ahead to the Messiah, the coming Savior, the Lamb of God who would take away the sin of the world.

The highest festival in ancient Israel, the Passover, also involved a lamb. The blood of the lamb, painted on the doorposts of their homes, saved the Israelites from slavery and death in Egypt.

It's no coincidence that Jesus died on the day of the Passover. The blood of the Lamb saved God's people from their slavery to sin and death in hell. The Lamb was sacrificed on the altar of the cross as our substitute. He took our place.

And God accepted his payment for sin. God is not going to punish you for your impatience and anger. He is not going to punish you for your lack of love in your marriage. He is not going to punish you for your dark, dirty secrets. The Lamb was punished in your place.

THE CROSS WAS NO PETTING ZOO. The cross was no petting zoo. There the Lamb bled and cried and died for you. There he paid the price for your forgiveness. And because he did, one day you and I will see the Lamb sitting on his throne in heaven.

When we get there, we aren't going to say, "Awww, what a cute little lamb." Together with all the angels and saints of heaven, we are going to sing, "Worthy is the Lamb who was slain to receive power and wealth and wisdom and strength and honor and glory and praise."

Today I am thankful for/that _____

_____

Lamb of God, you sacrificed everything for me.
Give me a heart which never stops praising
and thanking you. Amen.

DAY 138
AS WE COME AND GO

The LORD will watch over your coming and
going both now and forevermore.

PSALM 121:8

◆

I am overflowing with excitement. As I write these words, we are making our final preparations to celebrate our first public worship services as a church in over two months.

People here in Texas are slowly beginning to come and go. Soon most of the country will be coming and going a bit more freely. People are going back to work. Our children will go back to school. You can finally get a haircut.

The truth is, however, that COVID-19 has not suddenly disappeared.

People are still getting sick. The virus is still spreading. The death toll continues to rise.

Not a few people are concerned about everybody coming and going again, which got me thinking about a verse from the Psalms. King David once wrote, "The LORD will watch over your coming and going both now and forevermore."

As Christians, we can come and go with confidence. The all-powerful Lord of the universe promises to be by our side every step of the way. He promises to protect and provide. He promises to watch over us every moment of every day.

Now, that doesn't mean we won't get sick or suffer pains or difficulties. God promises to protect us from everything which can truly harm us. Sometimes what is best for us is to go through times of trials. Through them God helps us grow stronger and closer to him.

In the end, not even death can truly harm us. Because Jesus lived, died, and rose again as our Savior, our final going will be to heaven. God truly will watch over our coming and going both now and *forevermore*.

But please understand that one of the ways in which God watches over us is by giving us common sense and wisdom. God gives us doctors and scientists to teach us and guide us. He places the government over us to protect us. Part of the way God watches over us is by giving us the means to protect ourselves.

For example, even though we trust that God is watching over us, we still wear our seat belts in the car. We still take the medications our doctors prescribe. We still lock our doors at night. Oftentimes it is through such things that God protects and provides for us.

For that reason, as we begin to gather again at our churches, we should take the proper precautions. We should listen to the doctors and governing authorities. We should continue to socially distance ourselves, wash our hands, and wear masks as long as the experts recommend it. Through such precautions, God is protecting us and others.

NOTHING CAN TRULY HARM YOU.

But as you come and go over the next few days, weeks, and months, do so without fear. The all-powerful King of creation is watching over you every step of the way. He will make everything in your life work out for your good. Then one day as you go from this life, he will take you by the hand and lead you to the home Jesus won for you. Nothing can truly harm you.

You can come and go with confidence.

Today I am thankful for/that _____

_____

Almighty God, give me the courage to come and go with confidence. Give me the wisdom to take the proper precautions. Amen.

DAY 139
IT'S NOT JUST THE CAPITAL OF RHODE ISLAND

My God will meet all your needs according to
the riches of his glory in Christ Jesus.

PHILIPPIANS 4:19

◆

In December of 1630, Roger Williams, a Puritan pastor from England, boarded a ship called the *Lyon* and sailed to the New World. He and his wife Mary hoped to find peace from the persecution they had suffered as Puritans. They settled in the Massachusetts Colony and began serving a Puritan congregation in the town of Salem.

Williams, however, was soon expelled from the congregation due to his radical views.

Roger Williams believed that church and state should be completely separate—that the government shouldn't get involved with or regulate churches. To our modern sensibilities, such an idea is far from radical. In fact, it's one of the founding principles of our country, in large part due to Roger Williams.

In the 17th century, however, the separation of church and state was considered fanatical and subversive.

So Williams looked for a place where his family could live and believe what they wanted without government interference. He took a boat to a tiny island called Rhode Island, which at the time was inhabited almost entirely by Native Americans. There Williams founded his own settlement, which he called Providence. That's also the name he gave his first child born on Rhode Island.

Do you know what the word *providence* means? Just take the "-nce" off the end. *Providence* means "to provide." Roger Williams was so thankful God had provided him and others a refuge where they could believe and worship as they wished that he called the place Providence.

IT'S WHAT GOD DOES FOR YOU AND ME EVERY DAY.

But Providence isn't just the capital of Rhode Island.

It's what God does for you and me every day. Just look around at all that you have—homes, cars, phones, beds, clothes, and TVs. We have so much food we periodically have to clean out our refrigerators because it goes bad. We have so much stuff that our biggest frustration with our homes is that the closets are too small.

Yet at times we have the gall to consider ourselves poor, or at least not rich. We look at the "rich" people down the road. We don't have what they have, so we must be poor. We fail to see that the poorest of us are richer than 90% of the world.

God promises to provide everything we need for our bodies and lives. Yet he provides us with much more. Try to make a list of everything you have. Just look at all the good things God has provided for you.

"But wait a minute," you may be thinking. "God didn't provide this. I did. I worked my rear end off to pay for all this stuff." Yes, but who gave you the opportunity to work? Who gave you the ability to work? Who gave you your body and mind?

Everything we have is because God in his love has provided it for us. In fact, he has provided us with the things we need the most—forgiveness and heaven. You and I have fallen and failed many times. We have thought, said, and done so many bad things in our lives that the only thing we deserve is God's anger and punishment in hell.

But in his great love God provided a Savior, Jesus, who suffered our punishment in our place. Through Jesus, God provides the forgiveness we desperately need. Through faith in Jesus, he provides you a home forever in the riches and happiness of heaven.

Look at all that God has done for you. Recognize what he has provided for you. Thank him every day.

Because Providence isn't just the capital of Rhode Island.

Today I am thankful for/that _____

Lord of heaven and earth, thank you for your amazing providence. Open my eyes every day to see your goodness and move my heart to appreciate all you have done for me. Amen.

DAY 140
DRUNKEN COWBOYS

Do your best to present yourself to God as one
approved, a worker who does not need to be ashamed
and who correctly handles the word of truth.

2 TIMOTHY 2:15

◆

Human nature is like a drunken cowboy riding a horse. He climbs into the
saddle, but because he is inebriated he can't sit up straight. After just a few
hundred yards, he falls off the left side of his horse.

Stubbornly he picks himself up and gets back on his horse. He tells himself,
"I better lean to the right this time so I don't fall off again." A few hundred
yards later, he slides off the other side.

As human beings, the pendulum of our emotions and attitudes seldom
stays in the middle of the road. As individuals and as a society we tend to
fall into extremes.

That truth can be seen, for example, in how we deal with the two most
basic teachings of the Bible: the law and the gospel. Most parts of the Bible
fall into one of those two categories.

The law is God's commands. The law tells us, "Do this and don't do that."
The law shows us the punishment we deserve for our disobedience.

The gospel is God's promises. The gospel is the good news about how Jesus
suffered our punishment in our place—how God freely forgives and gives
us heaven.

The law demands; the gospel gives. The law declares us guilty; the gospel declares us innocent. The law shows us our sins; the gospel shows
us our Savior.

Both are true. Both are inspired by God. Each plays a role in our faith and
salvation. The law is a mirror which shows us the parts of ourselves we
don't like to see—all our dirty and ugly failings. The law shows us the hell
we deserve and our utter helplessness to save ourselves.

The gospel shows how God loved us so much he gave up everything to
save us. The gospel offers and gives faith and forgiveness. The gospel
empowers and motivates us to thank God with our lives. The law then

guides us, showing us how we can thank God by lovingly serving him and others.

WE TEND TO SLIP OFF THE SADDLE.

Like a drunken cowboy, however, we tend to slip off the saddle. We fall into the ditch of legalism. We make God's love and the gift of heaven dependent on what we do. "Yes, Jesus died for your sins, but you still have to earn it by obeying God . . . by being a good person . . . by going to church."

The gospel contains no ifs or buts. It makes no demands. It only gives.

But we have to be careful not to fall off the other side of the horse. Yes, heaven is God's free gift. You can't commit a sin God won't forgive, but forgiveness is not a license to sin. Watch out. The devil loves to whisper in our ears, "It's no big deal. Nobody's perfect. God will forgive you anyway."

God hates sin. He wants us to strive for perfection—to serve him faithfully with our lives. But we don't live good lives in order to earn heaven. We live good lives to thank God for the heaven he gives.

Never forget we each have a drunken cowboy living in our hearts who has a hard time staying on his saddle. Sometimes we fall into the ditch of pride and legalism, thinking God's love and gift of heaven depend on what we do. Other times we fall off the other side into the ditch of cheap grace, treating forgiveness as a license to sin.

Properly understanding the relationship between God's law and gospel is the single greatest skill a Christian can learn.

It will help you stay in the saddle.

Today I am thankful for/that _____

_____

Holy Spirit, give me wisdom to properly
understand and live the relationship
between your law and
your gospel. Amen.

DAY 141
WHEN THE EARTH SHAKES

God is our refuge and strength, an ever-present help
in trouble. Therefore we will not fear, though the
earth give way and the mountains fall
into the heart of the sea.

PSALM 46:1,2

❖

It's official. My family will probably never vacation in California. For years, my wife has been trying to convince me that California could fall into the ocean at any moment.

I am starting to believe her.

In a one-week period in June of 2019, over one thousand earthquakes shook Southern California, including two large quakes, measuring 6.4 and 7.1 on the Richter scale. The damage was estimated to be in the millions. The governor of California called it a "wake-up call." People wonder if the "big one" is coming.

My wife is convinced it is.

In California, it's earthquakes. In Texas, it's hurricanes and tornadoes. Just like in California, we who live in Texas honestly don't know if and when the "big one" is coming.

So how should we react when the earth shakes and the buildings rattle? First of all, don't panic. Many people live their lives paralyzed by the fear of "What if?" Yes, the big one could come. If history has taught us anything, it is almost inevitable.

Yet we don't need to be afraid even when "the earth gives way or the mountains fall into the heart of the sea," because "God is our refuge and strength, an ever-present help in trouble."

We don't need to lock ourselves in our homes or look over our shoulders every second fretting about the possible dangers all around. We can be still and know that God is in control. Whatever happens to us is a part of his loving will for our lives—even if it means being caught in the middle of the big one.

You don't need to be afraid, because you have a home waiting for you in heaven through faith in Jesus. Death cannot even harm you. You are baptized children of God. Your God is bigger than the big one.

WE DON'T NEED TO BE AFRAID . . . BUT WE SHOULD BE READY.

We don't need to be afraid when the earth shakes and the buildings rattle, but we should be ready. When Jesus' disciples asked him when the end of the world would be, Jesus gave them signs they should watch out for—signs which would remind them that the end was coming. Among those signs were "famines and earthquakes in various places" (Matthew 24:7).

When the earth shakes and the buildings rattle, it should remind us that the "Big One" is coming. Jesus could come back at any time. This world is waxing old as a garment. It is wearing out. Every earthquake is a reminder to be ready.

You are ready if you believe in Jesus. When Jesus comes back, he will take all those who believe in him to live with him forever in paradise. But if you aren't ready—if you don't believe in Jesus when he comes—the Big One will be horrifying. Hell is real. God's punishment for all the bad things we do is real. Only through faith in Jesus can we stand when the Big One comes.

So when you hear about earthquakes, tornados, and hurricanes—when the earth shakes and the buildings rattle—don't be afraid. Don't let fear paralyze you. Just be ready.

The Big One is coming.

Today I am thankful for/that _____

_____

Dear Jesus, as I witness natural disasters on television and in the world around me, take away my fears. Help me to trust that you are my refuge and strength. Use such disasters to remind me to be ready at any time for your coming again. Amen.

DAY 142
THE VICTOR'S CROWN

"Be faithful, even to the point of death, and I will give
you life as your victor's crown."

REVELATION 2:10

In August of 490 B.C., the Greeks defeated the Persians at the Battle of
Marathon. A messenger named Philippides was sent to the city of Athens
to inform the anxious magistrates of the victory. According to legend,
Philippides ran the entire way without stopping—26.2 miles. When he
arrived in Athens, he burst into the assembly and shouted, "Rejoice; we
have won"—and then he fell dead.

When the first modern Olympics were held in Greece in 1896, the
marathon was the final, crowning event. It followed Philippides' original
route from Marathon to Athens. The winner was a Greek water carrier
named Spyros Louis who ran the race in 2 hours and 58 minutes. He didn't
drop dead at the end; rather, a crown was placed on his head.

In ancient times, that was the prize for winning a race—the victor's
crown. A leafy or flowery wreath was placed on your head marking you
as the winner.

The Christians in the ancient city of Smyrna didn't feel like winners.
They were poor. They were persecuted. They were hurting. So Jesus sent
them a message in the book of Revelation. He told them they would still
have to suffer for a while longer, but he gave them this encouragement:
"Be faithful, even to the point of death, and I will give you life as your
victor's crown."

Today when we hear the word *crown*, we think of royalty. We think of
the golden jewel-encrusted crowns of kings and queens. But that's
not what Jesus was talking about here. He was talking about the victor's crown.

A number of years ago, I ran a marathon. It was probably the most painful thing I've ever done. The last few miles, I had to alternate between
running and walking. I remember actually crying from the agony, but I
finished . . . in 1,372nd place.

Life is like a marathon. It has its hills and valleys. It has its moments when it hurts so badly that you feel like giving up. But Jesus encourages us to be faithful even to the point of death. Finish the race in faith and he will give you the victor's crown of life in heaven.

You see, you don't have to win the race. You can't win the race. You can't earn the victor's crown. To win means perfection. It means not one false step, not one dirty thought, not one angry word.

YOU CAN'T EARN THE VICTOR'S CROWN. JESUS EARNED IT FOR YOU.

You can't earn heaven. You can't earn the victor's crown.

Jesus earned it for you. He earned it, not by running 26.2 miles, but by walking less than one mile. That doesn't sound so bad until you remember that he was dehydrated. He was bleeding profusely. His back was shredded like cheese. He wore a different kind of crown, one that perforated his skull. He carried a large piece of lumber on his shoulders most of the way. Even more importantly, he carried your sins and imperfections.

He suffered your defeat in your place. But Jesus didn't lose. He pulled off the greatest comeback ever recorded. He rose victorious. Jesus wins.

And he promises his victor's crown to all those who believe in him. You don't have to win the marathon. You just have to finish in faith.

So don't give up. Don't stop or stray from the path. Keep trusting in Jesus. I know it's hard, but he will get you over every hill and through every valley. He will pick up when you fall. He will get you to the finish line.

He will give you the victor's crown, even if you finish in 1,372nd place.

Today I am thankful for/that _____

_____

Merciful God and Lord, thank you for winning for me the victory over sin, death, and the devil. Help me to be faithful to you, even to the point of death. Amen.

DAY 143
BLESS YOU

"The LORD bless you and keep you; the LORD make his
face shine on you and be gracious to you; the LORD
turn his face toward you and give you peace."

NUMBERS 6:24-26

❖

Gesundheit. When a person sneezes, sometimes we say that fun-to-spell word, don't we? *Gesundheit* is the German word for "health." That makes sense. When someone sneezes, they may be coming down with something, so we wish them good health.

Sometimes, however, when a person sneezes, we say "God bless you." Why do we do that?

No one can say for sure how the custom began, but numerous theories have been suggested. For example, in ancient times, it was thought that when you sneezed you were expelling an evil spirit. People would say "God bless you," meaning good for you that the evil spirit is now gone. Others believed that sickness was caused by evil spirits. If a person sneezed, you said "God bless you" to ward off the demon.

Whatever the reason, today we say those words simply to be polite.

As the Children of Israel sat at the foot of Mount Sinai—as they prepared to set out for the Promised Land—God told Aaron, the high priest, to bless them. Every time God's people gathered together, Aaron was to tell them, "The LORD bless you and keep you; the LORD make his face shine upon you and be gracious to you; the LORD turn his face toward you and give you peace."

HE WASN'T JUST BEING POLITE.

Every time God's people gathered together, Aaron was to tell them, "God bless you." But he wasn't just being polite. God told Aaron that through his blessing, he would put his name on his people.

The Lord has put his name on you. You belong to him. At your baptism he marked you. You could say that he branded you like a calf in a way. He said, "You belong to me. My name is on you."

And because you belong to him, he will keep you. He will protect you. He will provide all you'll ever need here on earth.

He will be gracious to you. Grace is God's undeserved love. Grace is God giving you what you haven't earned or deserved. You see, we don't deserve God's face to shine on us. We don't deserve to have his face look on us with favor. We deserve to see his face burn with anger. We deserve to have him turn his face away from us because of all the dumb and dirty things we do.

Yet because God turned his face away from Jesus—because his anger burned against Jesus instead of us—we are forgiven.

You can be sure that God will always bless you because his blessings don't depend on you or how good you are. God will be gracious to you. He will forgive you and give you a home forever in heaven because of Jesus.

And he will give you peace. Because Jesus suffered God's anger over your sins, you can now have peace with God. He isn't an angry judge who will punish you. He is your loving Father who blesses you. And that peace with God gives us a peace of heart and mind the world cannot understand.

For nearly 3,500 years, believers have heard Aaron's blessing spoken over them as they gather together for worship. When your pastor or priest speaks those words to you, he isn't just being polite. Your Savior God is putting his name on you. He is promising to protect and provide for you. He is promising to forgive you and give you a home in heaven. He is promising you a peace the world cannot give.

That's nothing to sneeze at.

Today I am thankful for/that _____

_____

Heavenly Father, thank you for every blessing you have showered on me. Please continue to make your face shine on me and give me peace. Amen.

DAY 144
QUID PRO QUO

It is by grace you have been saved, through faith—and
this not from yourselves, it is the gift of God—
not by works, so that no one can boast.

EPHESIANS 2:8,9

◆

One of the things I enjoy most in this world is to get my back scratched. I
think most people can relate. It's in our DNA. When we ask our spouses to
scratch our backs, however, what do we often hear?

"I'll scratch your back, if you scratch mine."

That's the way our world works, right? Quid pro quo. Tit for tat. You do
this for me and I'll do that for you.

Our economy is based on that philosophy. "If you work for me, I'll pay you
for services rendered." "If you pay the price on the tag, I will give you this
product." You scratch my back, I'll scratch yours.

Sadly many people—even many Christians—think God works quid pro
quo. You scratch God's back, he'll scratch yours.

So they bargain with him in prayer. "Dear God, if you heal my mom from
her cancer, I promise I will be in church every Sunday for a year." "Dear
God, if you let me get this job, I promise I will give you 10% of what I
make in my offerings." "Dear God, if you just give us a baby, I promise
to bring him to Sunday school every week."

We think that somehow God will love us more, he will give us more, or
he will forgive us more if we just do more for him. We think that heaven
is something we earn by our good lives and good living. You have to do
your part. You scratch God's back, he'll scratch yours.

God, however, does not work quid pro quo.

You cannot earn God's love and you don't need to. In his amazing grace,
God loves the unlovable. In his amazing grace, he sent his Son to suffer
our punishment and win for us a heaven we don't deserve.

We don't scratch Jesus' back. In fact, because of us, his back was shredded by a scourge. Thorns were pressed into his head. Nails were driven

through his hands and feet. Honestly, the only thing we have ever earned or deserved with our lives is God's anger and punishment.

But because of Jesus he forgives us and gives us a home in heaven we don't deserve. Because of Jesus God gives us good things every day. You don't deserve your house. You haven't earned your TVs and iPhones and Instant Pots. You don't have what you have because you're a good Christian or because you have gone to church your whole life.

Everything we have and everything we are is a gift of God's grace.

But wait a minute. Doesn't God promise to give us good things if we obey him? Yes. He promises to bless a cheerful giver, to give long life to obedient children, to give good things to those who obey him.

Isn't that tit for tat? Isn't that quid pro quo?

When God promises his blessing to those who obey him, he isn't saying, "You are earning my blessing with your obedience." He is saying, "You can obey me without fear, even when it's hard, with the confidence that I will bless you if you do."

GOD DOES NOT WORK QUID PRO QUO.

But you aren't earning those blessings. You aren't making a business transaction with God. The key to an abundant life is not your obedience. God doesn't work that way. His gifts are free—unearned, undeserved, unmerited.

God does not work quid pro quo.

Today I am thankful for/that _____

_____

Merciful God, everything I have and everything I am is because of you. Thank you for not giving me what I deserve and for giving me what I have not earned. Amen.

DAY 145
GIVE THE ANGELS SOMETHING TO CELEBRATE

"In the same way, I tell you, there is rejoicing
in the presence of the angels of God over
one sinner who repents."

LUKE 15:10

◆

Do you remember where you were on September 11, 2001, when you heard about the terrorist attacks in New York? When I turned on the TV that day, one plane had already crashed. I was watching less than five minutes when I saw the second plane slam into the other tower. I was watching as both buildings fell to the ground.

Almost immediately after they collapsed, the search began. Thousands of rescue workers and volunteers worked day and night digging through the rubble, desperately trying to find survivors. When they found somebody alive, people lined the way as the person was carried out. Everyone would cheer. They would cry. It was national news. The whole country celebrated the few survivors who were pulled out of the wreckage alive.

In Luke chapter 15, Jesus tells us that is how the angels celebrate—that is how they cry for joy—when just one person repents and comes to believe in Jesus. That is how the angels celebrated and cried tears of joy the day you first believed in Jesus.

There was a party in heaven.

THERE WAS A PARTY IN HEAVEN. If you have a chance today, read Luke chapter 15. It's all about how God desperately wants to seek and to save those who are lost. At one point or another, we all have been lost. We all tend to wander like sheep. We all have gotten away from God or church. We all have fallen into sin or addiction.

But God desperately chases after us. He sends people and events into our lives to remind us how much we need him and the forgiveness Jesus won for us. Just think about all the people God has sent into your life who brought you to church, who lovingly and firmly reminded you of God's presence and importance in your life, or who helped bring you back to him.

That's how God seeks the lost—through people, through Christians like you and me. God usually doesn't appear to people in visions or dreams to call them to repent or to follow him. He sends us like rescue workers to dig through the rubble of this world, desperately trying to find and help people buried in sin and the wreckage of their lives.

Inviting someone to church isn't merely a sentiment. Talking to people about God and his love isn't just something nice we should do for them. Raising our children to know Jesus isn't something we only do on our good parenting days. Their lives—their eternal souls—are at stake.

Yet so often we don't say anything because it might be uncomfortable. They might not want to hear it, and we don't want to offend anyone. We forget how urgent and important this message is. Jesus himself tells us clearly, "Whoever believes and is baptized will be saved, but whoever does not believe will be condemned" (Mark 16:16).

People are dying. They are buried in the wreckage of their lives. God sent people into your life to pull you out of the rubble. Now he is sending you. My prayer is that God's desperate desire to find and save lost souls spills into our hearts so that we get to work telling, inviting, and sharing God's love with everyone we can.

Let's give the angels something to cheer about.

Today I am thankful for/that _____

_____

Dear Good Shepherd, give me the same love and deep desire to save that you feel for all people. Amen.

DAY 146
ANYTHING FOR MY KIDS

**Fathers, do not exasperate your children; instead, bring
them up in the training and instruction of the Lord.**

EPHESIANS 6:4

❖

Friday Night Lights is once again upon us here in Texas. Football is in full
swing. For me as a parent, home games are awesome. Our high school is a
three-minute drive from my house. If I want to, I can walk to the stadium
to watch my daughter march in the band.

Away games, however, are a different story. Every year the road trips seem
to get longer. Many of the games are two or three hours away. I love my
daughter dearly, but that's just too far for me.

Many parents are much more committed than I. They follow the team to
every game, rain or shine, no matter how far away it is. A couple Fridays
ago, a friend posted a picture on Facebook from a game almost three hours
away. Someone commented how great it was that she made the trip.

"Anything for my kids," she replied.

That got me thinking. In our world today, we sacrifice a lot for our kids.
We want them to succeed. We want them to have every opportunity.

So we drive them to practices. We wait in the car. We pay for private
lessons. We sacrifice our weekends. We spend thousands of dollars on gas,
hotels, team snacks, fundraisers, and uniforms.

Anything for our kids.

The problem is sometimes we forget what is most important for them. We
move heaven and earth so they don't miss a practice or game. Yet it's too
hard to get them up on Sunday morning for church or we can't go to
Sunday services because their select team plays out of town on weekends.

**CHILDREN'S SPORTS
HAVE BECOME OUR
NATION'S NEWEST RELIGION.**

We take the time in the evenings and on
Saturday mornings to go out in the backyard
with them to practice pitching or dribbling or
shooting. But we don't take the time to pray
with them, to read Bible stories with them, or
to have conversations about God with them.

Honestly, children's sports have become our nation's newest religion. It used to be that Sunday mornings and Wednesday nights were sacred. People would feel guilty if they didn't take their kids to church. Now they feel guilty if they miss a practice or a game.

Today's coaches and organizations routinely schedule activities on Sunday mornings and Wednesday nights. Parents are forced to choose.

Many are choosing sports.

"We are doing it for our kids," we tell ourselves. We want them to succeed. We want them to have every opportunity to feel the joy and elation of winning and success. Anything for our kids, right?

We get distracted. We lose sight of the inevitable. We forget that our children are going to die one day.

There is nothing more important you can do for your kids than to help them see and understand what Jesus did to save them. There is nothing more important you can do for your children than to take them to church and Sunday school every week.

Many parents today would love for their kids to get a scholarship to play sports in college. Many would be ecstatic if their kids got accepted into Harvard. That's why they do what they do.

I want my children in heaven.

That means I will take the time every day to pray with them. That means I will talk with them regularly about Jesus and the forgiveness he won for them on the cross. That means I will do everything in my power— come rain or shine—to make sure they are in church and Sunday school every week.

I mean, anything for our kids, right?

Today I am thankful for/that _____

_____

Merciful Lord, help me and all parents to remember what is most important for our children. Give us the wisdom and faithfulness to teach them about you and your love. Amen.

DAY 147
THE ALPHA AND THE OMEGA

"I am the Alpha and the Omega, the First and the Last,
the Beginning and the End."

REVELATION 22:13

◆

The Bible uses many colorful names for Jesus: the Good Shepherd, the Bread of Life, the Light of the World, the Messiah or Christ (both of which mean "the Anointed or Chosen One"), Emanuel (which means "God with us"), and even the name Jesus (which means "Savior").

Every one of Jesus' names describes him in some way. They tell us who is. They tell us what he came to do. Of all of the names the Bible gives for Jesus, however, one of the most obscure is the one found in the book of Revelation.

Jesus is "the Alpha and the Omega."

Most Americans know those words. We talk about *alpha dogs* and *omega-3* vitamins, but few people actually know what those words mean.

Alpha and omega are the first and last letters of the Greek alphabet. In other words, Jesus is the A and the Z, the First and the Last, the Beginning and the End.

EVERYTHING STARTED WITH JESUS AND EVERYTHING WILL END WITH HIM.

But what does that mean? First of all, it tells us that Jesus has always existed. He was there in the beginning. In fact, "through him all things were made" (John 1:3). It also means he will be there in the end; he is coming to judge the living and the dead.

Everything started with Jesus and everything will end with him. He is the Alpha and the Omega. Jesus isn't simply a great teacher or prophet. He is God. He is the creator and judge of all things. For that alone, he deserves all glory, honor, and praise.

But it's what he did between the beginning and the end of time that truly deserves our everlasting gratitude and praise. The eternal creator and judge loved us so much he humbled himself to become one of us. The one who is the Beginning and the End planted himself in the middle of time and space. He suffered the unspeakable horrors we deserve for all of the lousy and hurtful things we think, say, and do. He died so that we might live.

Our sins should be the end of us, but through faith in Jesus we have a new beginning. Death will not be our end. Even when this world ends, we will not.

When Jesus comes to end this present world, he will give us a life without end in a new heaven and a new earth. Because of the Alpha and the Omega, our story has no end.

Today I am thankful for/that _____

_____

Dear Jesus, you are the Alpha and the Omega, the Beginning and the End. Thank you for giving me a life in heaven which will have no end. Amen.

DAY 148
SELECTIVE FOCUS

"Martha, Martha," the Lord answered, "you are
worried and upset about many things, but few
things are needed—or indeed only one. Mary
has chosen what is better, and it will not
be taken away from her."

LUKE 10:41,42

Do me a favor. I'd like to try a little experiment. Raise your index finger and hold it about a foot in front of your face. Now focus closely on that finger. Do you notice how everything else becomes somewhat blurry or distorted?

Now keep your finger there, but focus on something else in the room. Your finger should then become blurry and distorted. You may even see two fingers.

That's called "selective focus." When we focus our vision on certain objects, everything in the periphery becomes blurred or distorted.

In Luke chapter 10, we read the story of two sisters, Mary and Martha. They were good friends of Jesus who lived in the tiny village of Bethany just outside of Jerusalem.

KEEP YOUR FOCUS ON THE ONE THING NEEDFUL.

One day Jesus came for a visit. Martha busily tried to get everything ready, preparing the food, cleaning the house, making sure everything was just right. But while she rushed to get everything done, her sister Mary lounged leisurely in the living room talking to Jesus.

As you might imagine, this frustrated Martha. "Lord, don't you care that my sister has left me to do the work by myself?" she blurted out to Jesus. "Tell her to help me!"

"Martha, Martha," Jesus replied, "you are worried and upset about many things, but few things are needed—or indeed only one. Mary has chosen what is better and it will not be taken away from her."

Was it wrong that Martha wanted to give Jesus a good dinner or have the house clean for him? Of course not. In fact, that was a good thing. Jesus wasn't saying that what Martha was doing was bad. What Mary was doing, however, was infinitely more important.

Mary was sitting at Jesus' feet listening to him speak to her. According to Jesus, the most important thing we can do with our time—the one thing we need the most—is to listen to him speak to us.

And he does that through his Word, the Bible.

In his Word, he reminds us of what is really important. He reminds us of our own mortality. You are going to die one day, and when you do, you will have to face God the Judge. You will have to face the consequences of all your poor choices and failures.

But God also tells us in his Word what Jesus did to save us from our sins and win heaven for us. God's Word shows us the way to heaven through faith in Jesus. God's Word gives us the peace and strength we need to face the storms and struggles of this life. God's Word guides us and helps us make good choices in our lives.

Raise your index finger again. Taking time to listen to God's Word by regularly going to church and reading our Bibles is the one thing we need most.

Sadly, like Martha, we often shift our focus from the one thing needful to all the other things going on in our lives. They aren't necessarily bad things; many are good and important blessings. But they demand so much of our time that we forget what the most important thing is. We forget that one day we are going to die.

There is nothing more important you can do in your life than sit regularly at Jesus' feet and learn from him. So go to church every week. Read your Bible every day.

Keep your focus on the one thing needful.

Today I am thankful for/that _____

Heavenly Father, in my busy life, as I try to do all the things I feel I need to get done, help me to never forget or neglect the one thing needful. Amen.

DAY 149
AMAZING GRACE

Christ Jesus came into the world to save sinners—of whom I am the worst.

1 TIMOTHY 1:15

◆

Have you ever heard of John Newton? John Newton was born in London, England, on July 24, 1725. His father was a sailor, his mother a Christian. Mrs. Newton died from tuberculosis when John was only seven years old. By age 11, he was sailing with his father. Eventually, he became a merchant marine and later enlisted in the English Navy.

Raised among sailors, Newton grew up to be a scoundrel. He deserted the Navy, but was caught and court-martialed. After his release, Newton found work aboard slave ships, transporting slaves to the New World to work in cotton and tobacco fields. In time, he became the captain of his own ship.

During his travels to and from Africa, Newton came into contact with Christian missionaries. Through their message, John Newton the slave trader eventually became John Newton the Christian.

John Newton the Christian eventually became John Newton the pastor.

John Newton the pastor eventually became John Newton the hymn writer who wrote arguably the most famous hymn of all time.

He wrote, "Amazing grace—how sweet the sound—That saved a wretch like me! I once was lost but now am found, Was blind but now I see" (CW 379:1). Grace is God's undeserved love. Grace is God loving the unlovable. Grace is God even loving wretches like John Newton. Grace is God loving wretches like you and me.

"But wait a minute, pastor," you may be thinking. "I never kidnapped people and sold them into slavery. I'm not a scoundrel like John Newton." You're right. You're not a slave trader.

GOD LOVED THE UNLOVABLE. HE LOVED *YOU*.

You are a liar. You are a disobedient child and unfair parent. You are an imperfect wife and an unfaithful husband. You are an underachieving student and a lazy worker. You are a wretch, just like me and just like John Newton.

Yet God loved the unlovable. He loved *you*. In fact, he loved you so much that he left behind the glory and joy and perfection of heaven to be born in a manure-smelling barn. God loved you so much that he suffered beatings, whippings, people spitting in his face. God loved you so much that he suffered your hell in your place, and because he did, you are forgiven. Because of God's amazing grace, you will live forever in a heaven you don't deserve.

Amazing grace—how sweet the sound! Never stop singing that sweet-sounding song. Never stop sharing that sweet-sounding truth with everyone you can. Never forget what your God has done for wretches like you and me.

Because of God's amazing grace, one day you will sing that sweet-sounding song with the angel choirs of heaven.

When we've been there ten thousand years, Bright shining as the sun,
We've no less days to sing God's praise Than when we'd first begun.
(CW 379:4)

Today I am thankful for/that _____

*Gracious God, thank you for loving
a wretch like me. Amen.*

DAY 150
DON'T TAKE A PARACHUTE INTO YOUR MARRIAGE

"What God has joined together, let no one separate."

MARK 10:9

In one of the early scenes of the movie *Indiana Jones and the Temple of Doom*, Indiana Jones wakes up in an airplane which is quickly losing fuel. The pilots have already parachuted out of the plane. Then Indiana's young sidekick, Short Round, gives him the bad news:

"No more parachutes!"

When there are no parachutes, you can't bail. You have to try to fly the plane.

One of the reasons so many marriages fail in our world today is because couples take parachutes with them into their marriage. They get married thinking, "Well, if this doesn't work, we can always get divorced."

YOU CAN MAKE IT WORK.

Divorce is a parachute. It allows you to bail. When things get rough—when you are frustrated or tired or unhappy—you can simply call it quits.

Don't take a parachute with you into your marriage. When a Christian gets married, he or she should enter that marriage with the mindset that divorce is not an option.

When there are no parachutes, you have to try to fly the plane. When divorce isn't an option, you are forced to find a way to make it work.

To be clear, God doesn't want us living unhappily ever after. He doesn't want us staying in unloving marriages, but he doesn't want us getting divorced either. There is another option.

You can make it work. You can get counseling. You can forgive and keep trying.

In marriage, you have made a vow—a sacred promise—to God and to each other to love one another until death do you part. The Bible does give valid reasons for divorce: abandonment and adultery. In such cases a Christian is not sinning by getting a divorce. Otherwise, divorce always involves sin because it means breaking a sacred promise. Though it seems easier to bail when things get hard, it really isn't. You won't have fewer struggles after divorce—only different ones. It's always worth staying and trying to fly the plane. Even the worst marriages can be healed. Even the most difficult relationships have blessings and a purpose.

Just because your marriage is hard doesn't mean it should end. God has a plan and purpose for you and your marriage. Remember Jesus' words, "What God has joined together, let no one separate." If you are married—even if it is hard, even if you feel like it is a mistake—it was God who brought you together.

Trust him. Trust his love for you. Stay. Put in the work. Forgive as God has forgiven you. Love as God has loved you. Don't wait until your marriage is in shambles before you seek help. Don't let it get so bad that you can't take it anymore. Once you start having problems, seek advice. Get counseling. Go back to church.

Do what you have to do in order to make your marriage work. If you are planning on getting married soon, talk with your future spouse about not taking parachutes into your marriage.

When you don't have a parachute, the only other option is to keep trying to fly the plane.

Today I am thankful for/that _____

_____

Blessed Savior, help me and others to be faithful to the sacred promises we have made in our marriages. Amen.

DAY 151
ALONE

Turn to me and be gracious to me,
for I am lonely and afflicted.

PSALM 25:16

❖

I am feeling lonely right now. My wife and kids are visiting Grandpa and Grandma for a week. During the day it's not so bad. I stay busy. The nights are what kill me. The silence. The empty house. The vacant beds.

I miss my family.

Are you lonely? Do you go to bed in an empty house? Maybe you're single or widowed. Maybe you struggle to make friends. You feel alone.

At this point I could do what many Christians often do. I could give you a quick platitude about how God is with you and send you on your way. Yet you already know that. You talk with God in prayer. You hear him speak to you in his Word. Even so, the echoing emptiness of your home still haunts your heart.

God made us to be social beings. People need people. The poet John Donne once wrote, "No man is an island entire of itself." Even the most antisocial among us need some human interaction.

THE TRUTH IS WE ARE NOT ALONE.

The truth is we are not alone. After creating Adam, God said, "It is not good for the man to be alone." From the man's rib God formed a woman, and since that time human beings have had other human beings. Though we feel lonely, God never leaves us alone.

You have people—family, neighbors, fellow Christians—whom God has placed in your life. They may not be the people you want. You may want to find a husband or wife to share your home and bed. You may want your dead spouse back. You may want a different family or other friends who understand you better.

You may not always like the people God has placed in your life. You may only have one or two people with whom you can talk, but you are not alone.

Have you ever noticed how you can be in a room full of people and still feel lonely? We crave certain relationships. We want to be loved and accepted. Sometimes, though, the people God places in our lives don't fulfill those yearnings, and that's hard for us to accept.

So what should you do when you feel lonely? First of all, keep talking to God in prayer and hearing him speak to you in his Word. That conversation is what changes our perspective and gives us the strength to face the dark, lonely nights.

In his Word, God opens our eyes to see the heaven Jesus won for us where we will never again feel lonely, where we will be reunited with our loved ones who died in Christ, where we will finally see and converse with God face to face.

God's Word also helps us to see and accept the people God has placed in our lives. Don't listen to the devil's lie that you are alone. Call your mom. Go out your front door. Say "hi" to your neighbor. Go to church.

Maybe that's the best advice of all. God has given you a family in Christ. Even if you struggle to talk to the people sitting around you in the pew, they are your God-given family. They may not always understand you, but many, if not all of them, love you.

Look around. Though you feel lonely, you are actually not alone.

Today I am thankful for/that _____

_____

Lord, when I feel alone, help me to see your presence in my life, all the people you have given me to love, and all those who love me. Amen.

DAY 152
EVERYBODY'S A CRITIC

[Let us not give] up meeting together, as some are in
the habit of doing, but encouraging one another—
and all the more as you see the Day approaching.

HEBREWS 10:25

❖

Growing up, I never knew their names. I would watch them every week on the Muppet Show, mocking Fozzie the Bear incessantly. But it wasn't just Fozzie. From their perch in the balcony, they made fun of every act, every celebrity guest, and every performance.

They were cantankerous. They were snide. They were funny.

Thanks to the wonders of Wikipedia, I now know their names: Statler and Waldorf.

We all know a Statler or Waldorf, right? They have an opinion about everything. They tell you what is wrong with every show and commercial on TV. They tell you what they think about every restaurant and every waitress. They are the armchair quarterbacks, the backseat drivers, the know-it-alls of our lives.

Honestly, though, we all have a little Statler and Waldorf inside of us.

In fact, that is one of the more subtle temptations of the devil in church. At one point or another, our worship on Sunday morning becomes less a conversation with our Savior God and more "At the Movies with Siskel and Ebert."

We don't even notice it happening. Instead of meditating on the words we are saying and singing, we suddenly find ourselves critiquing the sermon, the music, and the preacher. As we drive home from church, our conversations with the family become more a rating of the pastor's performance that Sunday instead of a discussion about the message which was preached.

We tell ourselves that our concern is genuine. We just want the church to grow. We just want to have good preaching and inspiring music.

The truth is it's hard to see a critical heart when you look in the mirror.

But listen to yourself when you talk about your church and pastor. What thoughts go through your mind as you worship on Sunday? Are you humbly listening and taking to heart the message, or are you wondering why they can't pick more singable hymns or why the preacher can't make his sermons more interesting?

As Christian brothers and sisters, constructive criticism and brotherly admonition have their place, but we have sadly come to expect our worship services to be high-quality Broadway productions. We expect our preachers to be as interesting as our favorite TED Talk and as funny as *Whose Line is it Anyway?*

> **THE PASTOR BETTER BE FUNNY AND HIP. . . . IF NOT, WE SHOP AROUND FOR A BETTER SHOW.**

Many people today flock to churches where the preaching is two thumbs up and the music is at least four out of five stars. The truth of God's Word being proclaimed and the faithfulness of the preacher become irrelevant. The pastor better be funny and hip. If not, we complain. If not, we shop around to find a better show.

Watch out. The devil wants to sneak into your heart and turn you into Statler and Waldorf. He wants to turn your thoughts away from God's life-giving Word to judgmental critiques of our pastors, our churches, and our fellow Christians.

The amazing truth is that God's Word proclaimed by the most boring preachers and the blandest music still feeds, saves, and encourages. Listen humbly to the message and think about the words you are singing. That's how God works. That's how God saves.

Be a positive, encouraging factor in your church. If your pastor or music isn't up to our world's standards, don't leave. Help. Support. Encourage the conversations in your church to be about the message and not the messenger.

In our world today, everybody's a critic. Be different. Be an encourager.

Today I am thankful for/that _____

_____

Almighty God, thank you for my church and my pastor. Help me to speak the truth in love and to be a positive, encouraging person to all those around me. Amen.

DAY 153
COMPOUND INTEREST

Let perseverance finish its work so that you may be
mature and complete, not lacking anything.

JAMES 1:4

❖

Recently a friend shared with me an article from our local newspaper; it was written by a financial planner named Dave Sather. The article extolled the virtues of compound interest.

You see, saving for retirement is more than simply knowing what stocks or mutual funds to invest in. Saving for retirement is about time and consistency. If you begin early and regularly put money aside, even if it isn't very much, the compound interest will make the money grow exponentially.

As he says, "If you merely say, 'I want to be a millionaire tomorrow,' the odds are heavily against you. However, if you save a modest amount of money every paycheck for 30 years, the power of compounding will allow you . . . monumental payoffs."

In his article Sather proposes that the same principle is true in other areas of life—health, exercise, education. Success and achievement rarely come quickly or overnight. They are the result of dedication and discipline. They are the result of small investments made daily—20 minutes of cardio or 30 minutes of reading a day. The compounded product is always exponential.

Exercise every day for a week and you will see modest results. Exercise daily over a lifetime and you can add years to your life.

The reason I mention Sather's excellent article is because the principle is also true for our spiritual life. Many people run to church when they are struggling or hurting. They want to find peace and guidance. They want God to change the circumstances in their lives or to give them the strength to make the changes.

GOD WORKS THROUGH TIME AND CONSISTENCY.

So they pray and go to church, but soon they are disappointed. They don't feel like it makes any difference. They don't see any change. They quickly give up on God.

They give up because, like the 20-year-old who spends half his paycheck on lottery tickets, they

291

want to get results right away. They don't understand that God works through time and consistency.

When you go to church looking for your life to be changed in 60 minutes, when you look for hurricanes of emotion and exponential growth, you are misunderstanding how the Holy Spirit works.

Yes, God can work wonders. His Word is powerful and changes hearts. At times one service, one sermon, can change your life.

But usually God works more slowly on our hearts. The Holy Spirit usually doesn't blow us over with hurricane-force winds, but rather speaks to us in the gentle whisper of his Word. His Word isn't a flood which suddenly overtakes us, but rather a slow drip which reshapes our hearts over time like the subtle erosion of slowly running waters.

If you want to change your life, if you want the strength and peace God gives, if you want to see exponential growth in your faith and spiritual life, the key isn't jumping around between churches trying to find the one which will blow you away and change your life forever in one worship service.

The key is consistency. The key is time. The key is quietly dedicating a portion of every week—of every day—to hearing God speak to you through the gentle whisper of his Word. It may not be as exciting or overwhelming as we think we need, but it will change your life forever.

Today I am thankful for/that _____

_____

Holy Spirit, give me patience and perseverance as I grow in my faith and strive to live for you. Help me to faithfully study your Word my whole life. Amen.

DAY 154
PEACE, MAN!

When the perishable has been clothed with the imperishable, and the mortal with immortality, then the saying that is written will come true: "Death has been swallowed up in victory."

1 CORINTHIANS 15:54

◆

A man with a long ponytail, a tie-dyed T-shirt, and a glossed-over look in his eyes raises two fingers and tells you, "Peace, man." He is the stereotypical "hippie."

The peace sign, however, did not originate with hippies in the 1960s.

The peace sign dates back to the days during and directly after World War II. During the war, in order to encourage each other and the Allied troops, people would often raise two fingers in the form of a "V" and say, "V is for victory!"

On May 7, 1945, the Nazis officially surrendered. A spotlight shone the letter "V" in the night sky over Paris. Church bells rang. Millions celebrated.

The celebrations in the United States, however, were more subdued. We were still at war with Japan. But on August 15, 1945, Japan officially surrendered, ending a war that killed millions of people.

The Allies had won. With the victory came peace. From that time on, two fingers in the form of a "V" became a universal symbol for peace.

We don't see much peace in our world today. Wars still rage. Terrorists continue to threaten us. Our country is divided politically. Families and marriages are in crisis. Millions of people suffer from depression. Sickness, cancer, and death are always lurking around the corner.

WE HAVE PEACE BECAUSE THE VICTORY IS WON.

But in the midst of all the chaos of this world, we have peace.

We have peace because the victory is won. With his death on the cross, Jesus won the victory over sin. He suffered the punishment of sin in our place. With his glorious resurrection, Jesus won the victory over death. Because he lives, we too will live forever. As the apostle Paul proclaimed, "Death has been swallowed up in victory."

293

With that victory comes peace. Because Jesus suffered sin in our place, we don't have to be afraid of God. He will never punish those who believe in him. God the just Judge has become God our dear Dad. We have peace with God. With the victory comes peace.

The guilt we carry for mistakes we've made—the regret we feel for things we have said and done—can weigh on us like a backpack full of bricks. But the forgiveness Jesus won frees us from guilt and regret. With the victory comes peace.

Unless the world ends first, you are going to die. I am going to die. But because of Jesus' Easter victory, we aren't really going to die. We are going to live forever in heaven, so we don't have to be afraid of death. We don't have to despair when a loved one dies, because we will see them again. We will not die but live. With the victory comes peace.

The victory is won. You are free from sin, free from guilt, free from death. So chill out. Be cool.

Peace, man!

Today I am thankful for/that _____

_____

Dear Jesus, thank you for giving us the peace the world cannot give. Amen.

---◆---

DAY 155
GET BUSY LIVING

For to me, to live is Christ and to die is gain.

PHILIPPIANS 1:21

◆

In the 1997 movie *The Shawshank Redemption*, Tim Robbins played Andy Dufresne, a quiet banker wrongfully accused of killing his wife. After 20 years in Shawshank Prison, Dufresne had enough. In one of the most dramatic scenes of the movie, he turns to his friend Red and in exasperation says, "I guess it comes down to a simple choice, really—get busy living or get busy dying."

Those words often echo in my head and heart as I teach weekly Bible studies in our local nursing homes. Sadly, when many people move into the nursing home, they get busy dying. They give up. They feel like they have nothing left to contribute. So they sit sadly in their wheelchairs and rooms waiting to die.

Again and again I find myself taking them back to one particular verse from the Bible: "For to me, to live is Christ and to die is gain."

The apostle Paul wrote those words as he sat in the city of Rome, chained to a Roman soldier, awaiting his trial before the Roman emperor. At the time, Paul didn't know if he would be set free or put to death.

Yet Paul didn't whine or fret or complain. It was actually a win-win situation for him. If he was set free, he would be able to share the good news of God's love with more people. If they put him to death, even better: He would get to go to the heaven Jesus had won for him.

For Paul, to live was Christ and to die was gain. He couldn't lose.

Usually as a preacher, I focus on the second part of that verse—to die is gain. That sounds crazy for many people in our world. How could death be a good thing? Those of us who believe in Jesus know that when we die, God will give us a home in heaven way better than anything we could ever experience here on earth.

Many of the people I speak to at the nursing home already know that. In fact, they tell me they don't want to be here anymore. They want to go to heaven, but God just won't take them.

That's when I have to remind them of the first part of the verse—that to live is Christ. In other words, if we are here, it means God still has things for us to do. It means there are people in our lives who still need us.

YOUR LIFE HERE ON EARTH IS YOUR OPPORTUNITY TO LIVE FOR CHRIST.

Your life here on earth is your opportunity to live for Christ who lived and died for you. Every life has a purpose. Every life has meaning. The problem is that when we can't do the things we used to be able to do—when we can't do the things we want to do—the devil tries to convince us that we can't do anything, or at least anything worthwhile.

The truth is that even when you can't do what you used to be able to do—even when you are living in a nursing home or a wheelchair, even when you are bedridden—your life still has purpose and meaning. God still has things for you to do.

You can be an example of faith and love to those around you: You can tell other people of God's love. You can give an encouraging word or smile to the other residents at the home. And if you can do nothing else, you can pray.

That seems insignificant, yet prayer can move mountains, end wars, and heal disease. If you can do nothing else, you can pray for me. God knows I need it.

One day, you will die. Through faith in Jesus, you will receive a home in the happiness of heaven. That is far better than life on earth.

But you aren't dead yet, so get busy living.

Today I am thankful for/that _____

_____

Lord, thank you for taking away my fear of dying, but while I am here on earth, help me to get busy living. Amen.

DAY 156
COME, LORD JESUS

He who testifies to these things says, "Yes, I am coming soon." Amen. Come, Lord Jesus.
REVELATION 22:20

When I was a boy, my family would pray a simple prayer before every meal: "Come, Lord Jesus, be our guest and let these gifts to us be blessed. Amen."

Admittedly, my mind would often wander to how hungry I was, how good the food smelled, or how I needed to be quick to beat my six brothers and sisters to the best piece of chicken.

It wasn't until I got older that I truly appreciated those words. I was asking my Savior God to honor us with his presence—to be with us and to bless our food and our time together.

That simple prayer—"Come, Lord Jesus"—is fitting for much more than family dinners.

"Come, Lord Jesus, watch over me as I sleep."

"Come, Lord Jesus, give me peace as I attend my mom's funeral."

"Come, Lord Jesus, help me fix my marriage."

Every moment of every day, a Christian can and should pray, "Come, Lord Jesus." He is our help. He is our guide. He is our comfort and strength when the earth quakes and the mountains fall into the heart of the sea.

Invite your Savior to come and walk with you every step of your life with the confidence that he will always come. In fact, he never leaves. He promises, "Surely, I am with you always, to the very end of the age" (Matthew 28:20).

Ultimately that isn't really what the prayer, "Come, Lord Jesus," originally meant to say.

It wasn't until I got into college that I learned where that simple little prayer came from. "Come, Lord Jesus" is the last prayer found in the Bible.

At the end of the book of Revelation, Jesus promised the apostle John, "Yes. I am coming soon." Jesus is coming to judge all people, end this present age, and destroy this world with fire. Jesus is coming on judgment day.

Jesus told John, "I am coming soon," to which John joyfully responded, "Amen. Come, Lord Jesus!"

As Christians, we eagerly ask our Savior to come and bless us here on earth. We trustingly pray that he would come and help us in times of trouble. We joyfully invite him to be with us in good and bad times, but to ask him to come in final judgment seems a little scary.

WE ARE FORGIVEN FOREVER BECAUSE OF JESUS.

Yet we can pray that simple prayer even about judgment day because Jesus lived and died to wash away all the filth from our lives. We don't need to be afraid of judgment day, because God has already told us what the verdict will be. All those who believe in Jesus have been declared innocent of all charges. We are forgiven forever because of Jesus. We can pray, "Come, Lord Jesus," because we know that he is coming to take us to live with him forever in paradise.

So pray that simple prayer every day of your life. Pray it with confidence. Pray it with eager anticipation.

Today I am thankful for/that _____

_____

Come, Lord Jesus! Amen.

DAY 157
PRAYERS, THOUGHTS, AND GOOD VIBES

**The prayer of a righteous person is
powerful and effective.**

JAMES 5:16

◆

It's a trend I am seeing more and more frequently on Facebook. Somebody posts about their grandma in the hospital. A concerned family member responds, "Sending prayers, thoughts, and good vibes your way!"

A friend lets everybody know about an upcoming surgery she will undergo. "Asking for prayers and good vibes," she posts.

Though the requests are sincere and the thoughts heartfelt, I can't help but cringe every time I read those words—especially when they are written by a fellow Christian.

Their motivation is good. They want to help. They want to comfort. They want to say something encouraging, but there is a big difference between prayers, thoughts, and good vibes.

"Good vibes" is a phrase made popular by the Beach Boys' 1966 hit song, "Good Vibrations." It stems from New Age philosophy which espouses that we can send out positive and negative energy, which affects the world and people around us. When people say they are sending thoughts and good vibes to a person, they are thinking positive thoughts for them-which will hopefully in some way help their health or cause their situation to improve.Prayer is different.

First of all, please understand that if you are sending prayers their way, you are sending your prayers in the wrong direction. We don't send prayers to each other. Prayers aren't positive or hopeful thoughts. Prayers aren't words meant to encourage or comfort other people.

Prayers are the words we speak to the God and Creator of all things. Prayers are the requests we bring in faith to our heavenly Father, who promises to always listen and answer us for our good.

Prayer has power. The power of prayer, however, isn't in the person offering the prayer. The power of prayer isn't in the words being said. Prayer is not some magical incantation. Prayer has power because we are praying to the all-powerful King of the universe.

Prayer has power because the one to whom we are praying can do anything.

Now that doesn't mean God will give us everything we ask for in prayer. It doesn't mean that if we believe hard enough or think positively enough we will get the result we want. God promises to hear our prayers and answer them, but he will only give us what is truly good for us. Not everything we ask for fits God's plan of love for us and for others.

Sometimes God says no to our prayers.

But he often says yes. Prayer makes a difference in our lives and the lives of others. Prayer has healed the sick and saved the dying. Prayer has changed history. Prayer turns our hearts and minds to the one person who can truly help in any and every situation—our God and Savior.

So instead of sending thoughts and good vibes (or even prayers) to those who are struggling or sick, tell them that you are praying for them. Then do it. It has become so mechanical to tell a person you are praying for them that sometimes we say it, but don't do it.

"GOOD VIBES" . . . STEMS FROM NEW AGE PHILOSOPHY.

Tell them you are praying for them and then pray for them. Your prayers make a difference. God is listening and ready to act.

Unlike thoughts and good vibes, prayer has power.

Today I am thankful for/that _____

Heavenly Father, thank you for always hearing my prayers and answering them for my good. Amen.

DAY 158
THE GREAT EQUALIZER

There is neither Jew nor Gentile, neither slave nor free,
nor is there male and female, for you are
all one in Christ Jesus.

GALATIANS 3:28

On January 4, 1847, Captain Samuel Walker of the Texas Rangers walked into the gun shop of Samuel Colt and placed an order for 1,000 revolvers. He had one stipulation. Colt would have to improve the design of his pistol. Though Colt's groundbreaking revolver was able to fire five shots in the time it took a flintlock pistol to fire one shot and reload, it was unreliable and could only fire tiny balls.

Walker insisted that the gun needed to be sturdier and able to kill a man in just one shot. What eventually came out of that fateful day was the Colt Single Action Army Revolver—a six-shooter known in history by many names: the Colt .45, the Frontier, the Peacemaker, and the Great Equalizer.

Colt's six-shooter became the preferred pistol of the Union Army during the Civil War and is known as "the gun which won the West."

A common expression of the day was: "God created men. Samuel Colt made them equal." Colt's Great Equalizer, though, was simply a tool of the true Great Equalizer, which is death.

Death puts all humankind on a level playing field. It makes no distinction of race or gender. It doesn't matter if you're tall or short, black or white, rich or poor. It doesn't matter how healthy you try to live. You may postpone it for a while, but every single person on this planet is going to die unless Jesus comes first.

When we die, we will all find ourselves in the same situation—guilty sinners standing in the presence of a holy God. It doesn't matter whether you went to church every Sunday of your life or were a mass-murdering terrorist. "All have sinned and fall short of the glory of God" (Romans 3:23). We are all guilty.

Thankfully, we have another Great Equalizer who saved us from the death and hell we deserve. Jesus lowered himself to become just like us—to suffer our punishment and death in our place. And he didn't just do it for us. John tells us that "he is the atoning sacrifice . . . for the sins of the whole world" (1 John 2:2).

THANKFULLY, WE HAVE ANOTHER GREAT EQUALIZER.

God doesn't show favoritism. Jesus, the Great Equalizer, died for everyone. He offers forgiveness and heaven to everyone. That doesn't mean, however, that everyone goes to heaven. God offers forgiveness and heaven to everyone, but they are only received through faith in Jesus. If you reject Jesus, you reject the heaven he won for you.

One of the tools which Jesus uses to give that faith, forgiveness, and heaven is the Sacrament of Baptism.

Baptism is the Great Equalizer because it doesn't matter where you come from, how old you are, or how much money you have. The promise of Baptism is the same for all people. The promise is that God has washed away all your sins, because of Jesus. The promise is that God has adopted you as his child.

Baptism is the Great Equalizer because it raises all who are baptized to the status of royalty. We are sons and daughters of the King of the universe. Everyone who believes in Jesus is a prince or princess.

Remember that when you find yourself frustrated with your fellow believers. Remember that when the devil tempts you to think you are somehow better than that disgraced celebrity on TV, or those people from the other political party, or any of those other dirty sinners out there.

We are all dirty sinners who one day will have to face the Great Equalizer of death. But thanks to Jesus, the Great Equalizer, and through the faith given in Baptism, the other Great Equalizer, we have been saved from the death and hell we deserve.

So love everybody the same. Treat everybody the same. Welcome everyone into your church with arms wide open.

Because Jesus is the Great Equalizer.

Today I am thankful for/that _____

Dear Jesus, forgive me for my judgmental heart. Help me to love all people as you have loved me. Amen.

DAY 159
MYSTERY SOLVED

"Whoever believes and is baptized will be saved, but whoever does not believe will be condemned."

MARK 16:16

◆

On March 8, 2014, Malaysia Airlines Flight 370 disappeared en route to Beijing Capital International Airport in China. What happened to the flight is unknown. The wreckage has never been found. The fate of flight MH 370 and its 239 passengers is still a mystery.

Theories abound—a mechanical failure, human error, terrorists, political intrigue, even aliens. After so many years, who knows if we will ever discover what actually happened on Flight 370. It may end up getting filed as one of history's great unsolved mysteries.

History's greatest mystery has nothing to do with a crime or disappearance. It isn't Amelia Earhart's missing plane or whether Lee Harvey Oswald acted alone. The greatest mystery of all time, the great unknown for humans, is what will happen when we die.

Theories abound. Some say death is the end. Others say we are reincarnated. Some say everyone goes to heaven (or something like heaven). Others say we will enjoy paradise here on earth. Still others teach that we become gods ourselves. Theories abound, but many are left wondering and worrying about that fateful day when they breathe their last.

HE HAS REVEALED TO US THE GREATEST MYSTERY OF ALL TIME.

God doesn't want you wondering or worrying, so he has revealed to you the mystery. Like a friend who tells you how a movie ends before you've seen it, God tells us the end of our life's story. In his Word, he reveals the truth behind life's greatest mystery.

In Hebrews 9:27, God tells us that "people are destined to die once, and after that to face judgment." Death is not the end. You will not come back as a cow. No souls are left here on earth to wander. When you die, you will face your Maker to be judged. You will be put on trial.

That in and of itself can be a scary proposition, especially when God tells us that he has a book in which is written everything you have ever thought, said, or done. The evidence is clear. We have failed to be what God made us to be. We are guilty.

But that is why Jesus came. Jesus allowed himself to be declared guilty in our place. God the Father punished him for our crimes. Therefore, we are justified by faith (Romans 5:1).

To justify means "to declare innocent." All those who believe in Jesus have been declared innocent of all charges. You don't have to worry or wonder what the Judge will say to you on the day you die, because you have already been declared innocent. Heaven is yours.

There really is no mystery. Jesus himself tells us, "Whoever believes and is baptized will be saved, but whoever does not believe will be condemned." If you believe in Jesus as your Savior, God gives you the gift of eternal life in heaven. Those who reject him, however, will receive the guilty verdict we all deserve and be condemned to the horror of hell forever.

The disappearance of Flight MH370 may go down as one of history's great mysteries. We may never know what happened. Thankfully, God has revealed to us the greatest mystery of all time. You don't have to wonder or worry about what will happen to you when you die. Through faith in Jesus, you are going to heaven.

Mystery solved.

Today I am thankful for/that _____

_____

*Almighty God, thank you for freeing me from
the fear of not knowing what will happen
to me when I die. Amen.*

DAY 160
IT'S NOT WHAT YOU SAID

Instead, speaking the truth in love, we will grow
to become in every respect the mature body
of him who is the head, that is, Christ.

EPHESIANS 4:15

My heart (and head) hurt.

Everywhere I look in our country people seem to be angry with one other. Many Americans are mad at our president. Our president is mad at those who are mad at him. Republicans are mad at Democrats. Democrats are mad at Republicans. Race, human sexuality, gun control, immigration—everybody is mad about something.

And they will tell you all about it on Facebook.

In the end, it comes down to the fact that we disagree. We disagree on how best to protect our country. We disagree about how to deal with illegal immigrants. We disagree on how to handle racism in our society. We disagree about when a protest is appropriate and when it isn't.

Each of us seems to know what is best. Each of us thinks we know what is right. Therefore, it upsets, frustrates, and angers us to hear others disagree with the core beliefs we hold deeply.

The problems we presently face as a country, however, are not because we disagree. They exist because we have lost the ability to disagree respectfully. As my father used to tell us when we were kids, "It's not what you said. It's how you said it."

In other words, it's not enough to be right.

IT IS NOT ENOUGH TO BE RIGHT.

The apostle Paul once encouraged Christians to grow in their unity by "speaking the truth in love." The same could also be said for our society today. Especially as Christians, we should speak the truth. We should speak out about what the Bible says is right and wrong. We should speak out if we see injustice.

But we should speak the truth in love. It's not enough to be right. It's not just what you say. It's how you say it.

Our goal when we speak the truth is to help, heal, and build up. Yet so often, we speak out because we are angry. We speak out to prove others wrong. We speak out to defeat those who disagree with us.

What makes matters worse is that we now have the megaphone of social media. Social media enables the mass dissemination of half-truths and lies. Social media gives us the opportunity to immediately shout our opinions into a microphone without taking the time to measure our response or tone.

From our president down to our own grandmothers, Americans have become accustomed to being rude and disrespectful on social media. We aren't taking time to think about what we post. We are forgetting that wisdom is often shown in silence. We aren't measuring our tone or response.

It is not enough to be right. We don't speak the truth to show people how smart we are. We don't speak the truth to tear other people down. We don't speak the truth to destroy our enemies.

We speak the truth to help. We speak the truth to heal. We speak the truth to unite. Tone matters. It's not enough to be right.

So speak the truth in love.

Today I am thankful for/that _____

---

*Merciful God, forgive me all the times I used
being "right" as an excuse to speak unkindly
or arrogantly. Help me to love even those
I disagree with and to disagree
with them respectfully. Amen.*

◆

DAY 161
DEEP AND WIDE

I pray that you, being rooted and established in love,
may have power, together with all the Lord's
holy people, to grasp how wide and long and
high and deep is the love of Christ.

EPHESIANS 3:17,18

◆

NASA has announced it is going to Mars. Though the mission is most likely at least 20 years away, the preparations have already begun.

The other day, my 11-year-old daughter and I were watching a report on how difficult such a mission would be. My daughter looked at me and asked, "Why would it be so hard? We already went to the moon."

As a sixth grader, she still struggles with relative distances. The distance from the earth to the moon is roughly 250,000 miles and takes our astronauts a few days to traverse. At its farthest point from the earth, Mars is approximately 250,000,000 miles away and would take nearly seven months to reach.

Sometimes we forget how big the universe is. In 1990, NASA launched the Hubble Telescope into space. The Hubble Telescope has allowed us to see farther into space than any other telescope in history. So far, the farthest reaches of the universe it has been able to photograph are 13.2 billion light years from earth. A light year is roughly six trillion miles.

And that's not the end of the universe. It's simply how far we've been able to see. Our minds can't really fathom how big the universe is.

Understanding that helps us to appreciate verses like Psalm 103:11. David wrote, "As high as the heavens are above the earth, so great is his love for those who fear him." The heavens to which David is referring are the universe—the deepest reaches of space.

God doesn't just love you to the moon (250,000 miles away). He doesn't just love you to Mars (250,000,000 miles away). He doesn't even love you merely to the farthest we can see into space (13.2 billion light years away). God's love for you is as deep and wide as the universe itself.

And that's no exaggeration. God isn't using hyperbole. He loves you that much. He loves you so much, he didn't just die for you. He suffered the punishment of hell for you. Because he did—because he suffered God's anger for all your mistakes and failings—you are forever forgiven.

The prophet Micah tells us that God will hurl all our sins into the depths of the sea (Micah 7:19). The average depth of the ocean is a little over two miles. The deepest part, however, is a channel just off the island of Guam. It reaches nearly six miles down. That depth is greater than the height of the tallest mountain in the world. In fact, no human has been able to descend that deeply into the ocean.

That's what God does with our sins. He throws them where they will never be able to come back. David says that he has separated our sins from us as far as the east is from the west. That's a distance which cannot be measured. Because of Jesus, all the selfish words and thoughtless actions which weigh heavy on your heart and conscience have been thrown into the depths of the sea. They are gone forever.

GOD'S LOVE FOR ME WILL NEVER END. Understanding the height, depth, and width of God's love and remembering how far he has removed our sins from us gives us a confidence which the world doesn't understand. God's love for me will never end. Because of Jesus, I cannot commit a sin which God will not forgive.

Heaven is mine, not because of what I have done, but because of God's immeasurable love for me.

Today I am thankful for/that _____

Almighty God, your love for me is immeasurable. Thank you for sending my sins to the depths of the ocean so I will never have to see them again. Help me to always be amazed at how deep and wide your love is for me. Amen.

———◆———

DAY 162
COUNTERFEIT

"Watch out for false prophets. They come to you in sheep's clothing, but inwardly they are ferocious wolves."

MATTHEW 7:15

◆

What do you think of when you hear about the Secret Service? You probably picture menacing-looking men in sunglasses standing solemnly next to the President of the United States. You imagine earpieces dangling from their ears and microphones in their sleeves. Images of agents diving in front of the president and taking a bullet quickly come to mind.

Interestingly, that is not why the Secret Service was formed. In the days during and immediately after the Civil War, counterfeit currency was plaguing our nation. Experts estimate that nearly one-third of the money in circulation at the time was phony. The Secret Service was formed on July 5, 1865, to suppress the counterfeiting. Today, the Secret Service still acts as our nation's police force against counterfeiting and financial fraud.

A number of years ago, I read how the Secret Service trains its agents to recognize counterfeit currency. They don't train them in the latest counterfeiting techniques or have them study bogus bills. Rather, they have them study the true money so long and so thoroughly that they can spot a fake bill just by looking at it or holding it.

Oftentimes, they can't even tell you why. They just know it's a fake.

JESUS WARNED US TO WATCH OUT FOR COUNTERFEIT TEACHERS.

Jesus warned us to watch out for counterfeit teachers. He called them wolves in sheep's clothing. Though it is unpopular today to talk about "false teachers" or say that a church is teaching "false doctrine," the Bible often warns us of the presence of false teachers and the dangers of false teaching.

The problem most people have is this: How do you know who is telling the truth? Every church you visit says it is teaching the truth—it is saying what the Bible says. Yet each one is teaching something different.

Some would say that is because the Bible can be interpreted in different ways, that it is somehow vague or open to different people's points of view. If you read the Bible, however, you will find it is not vague. It is not ambiguous. It says what it says.

Just because a church or preacher talks about God, Jesus, love, or peace does not mean they are teaching what the Bible says.

So how can you know? How can you spot the counterfeit teachers and teachings? Simple. Just study the real currency. Open your Bible. Read, learn, and inwardly digest it. The more you know what the Bible says, the more easily you will be able to spot a fake.

The reason so many people today are confused by or follow false teachers is that they don't open their Bibles. They don't challenge or question what they are told. That would be too much work. If what the preacher says sounds good or jives with their way of thinking, they just accept it.

Don't blindly accept what you are told. That is dangerous to your faith. It can lead you away from your God and Savior. Don't trust your preacher just because what he says sounds good.

Don't trust me. I could be making this all up. I could be a wolf in sheep's clothing. I could be a counterfeiter. Open your Bible to Matthew 7:15 and start reading. Check if what I am saying is the real deal.

The better you know the Bible, the more easily you will spot a fake.

Today I am thankful for/that _____

Eternal God, keep my mind and heart focused on your Word so that I can recognize the false teachers who endanger my soul. Amen.

DAY 163
THE PURSUIT OF HAPPINESS

"Seek first his kingdom and his righteousness, and all these things will be given to you as well."

MATTHEW 6:33

◆

"We hold these truths to be self-evident, that all men are created equal, that they are endowed by their Creator with certain inalienable Rights, that among these are Life, Liberty and the pursuit of Happiness."

That is the second sentence of the Declaration of Independence. So succinct and striking are its words that few people even remember the first sentence. Thomas Jefferson's most famous statement was truly revolutionary.

It has become the creed of American democracy. It basically states that God has endowed every human life with value. Every person is inherently equal before God. No one person's rights and freedoms are greater than another's.

Sadly, many in our country today understand these words to also mean that God's purpose for our lives is that we pursue happiness or that it's the government's responsibility to make us happy. If you look closely, however, the Founding Fathers simply wanted to ensure that every person had an equal opportunity to pursue their own happiness.

I'll be honest. That last phrase has always made me a bit uncomfortable. Where does God say in the Bible that he has created all people with the inalienable right to pursue happiness?

Our society today zealously pursues happiness. Hoping to find a career which makes them happy, young adults often bounce between jobs. Looking for someone who will make us happy, we join multiple online dating sites. Hoping that a million dollars will bring them happiness, people flock to buy lottery tickets. Advertisers assure us that a new car, a flat-screen TV, and a George Foreman grill will truly make us happy. Some people in their desperation run to drinking, drugs, sex, or pornography, hoping to find at least a moment of fleeting happiness.

Even some churches encourage us to pursue happiness. Their message is basically this: "God wants you to be happy. This is how you should live to be happy. The Bible is your guidebook to true happiness."

Now don't get me wrong. One of the gifts of the Holy Spirit is joy. The good news of God's love and forgiveness gives true happiness. Jesus won for us a home forever in the happiness of heaven.

But God has not placed you in this world for you to pursue your own happiness. He wants you to pursue godliness. The life of a Christian is a life of self-denial and sacrifice. God wants us to pursue the happiness of others. As we do, he promises to bless us with joy, peace, and contentment.

GOD HAS PLACED YOU IN THIS WORLD FOR YOU TO PURSUE GODLINESS.

Jesus said, "Seek first [God's] kingdom and his righteousness, and all these things will be given to you as well." We don't need to pursue happiness. We can pursue godliness. We can give and sacrifice and even suffer in our service to him with the confidence that he has already won for us the happiness of heaven.

Sadly, the pursuit of happiness is the predominant driving force in our society today. But what about you? What drives you? Has the pursuit of happiness become your creed?

Pursue godliness. Serve. Sacrifice. Seek the happiness of others with the confidence that God has already ensured your happiness forever in heaven.

Today I am thankful for/that _____

_____

Lord, instead of pursuing happiness, help me to pursue godliness. Help me to serve and sacrifice for others with the confidence that you will bless me with true joy and peace. Amen.

DAY 164
GOD'S GUT-WRENCHING LOVE

When Jesus landed and saw a large crowd, he had compassion on them, because they were like sheep without a shepherd.

MARK 6:34

◆

A woman was hanging laundry one day when a dog wandered into her yard. She could tell from his collar and well-fed belly that he had a home. When she walked into her house, the dog followed her. He meandered down the hall, plopped himself in a corner and fell asleep. An hour later, he walked toward the door and the woman let him out.

The next day, the dog returned. Once again he walked into the house, plopped himself in the corner and took a nap.

This routine continued for a number of days. Finally, curiosity got the better of the woman and she pinned a note to the dog's collar which read: "Every afternoon, your dog comes to my house for a nap."

The next day, the dog arrived as usual, but this time with a different note pinned to his collar. The note simply read: "This dog lives in a home with ten children. He's just trying to get some rest."

There came a point in Jesus' ministry when he tried desperately to get some rest. Word about him had spread throughout Galilee. People flocked from miles around to hear him speak or see a miracle. The paparazzi hounded him. The people mobbed him. He became so busy he didn't even have time to eat.

So he decided to get away for a few days. He got into a boat with his disciples and sailed across the Sea of Galilee to a solitary place. The people, however, wouldn't let him rest. As he sailed, they ran around the giant lake; in every town along the way, the size of the mob grew.

By the time Jesus and his disciples arrived on the other side, a horde of thousands was waiting. When Jesus saw the massive crowd, he didn't get mad. He didn't yell. He didn't shout, "Leave me alone!" To the contrary, when Jesus saw them, "he had compassion on them."

In the original Greek, it literally says, "his intestines were moved." That sounds strange to our modern ears. Today we talk about compassion being felt in the heart. The Greeks felt it in their intestines.

We can understand that. You see a heartbreaking story on TV—a natural disaster, a brutal murder, or children starving in Africa. You feel it deep down in the bottom of your stomach.

It's gut-wrenching.

E WAS NEVER TOO BUSY OR TOO TIRED TO HELP ANYONE.

That's what Jesus felt for those people. He was never too busy or too tired to help anyone. No request was too big; no request was too small. Jesus cared that deeply for them.

And he cares that deeply for you. You are never bothering Jesus. Sometimes we don't want to bother God with problems we think are too insignificant. Our God, however, is never too tired or too busy to listen.

Sometimes it doesn't feel that way. Sometimes it feels like God isn't listening. Sometimes it feels like he doesn't care. But the truth is that when you hurt, he feels it deep down in the bottom of his belly.

God loves you with a gut-wrenching love.

The fact that he allows you to hurt for a while doesn't mean he doesn't care. It is precisely because he does care deeply for us that he allows us to go through pains and problems to make us stronger—to bring us closer to him.

God's love for you runs so deep he allowed nails to be driven into his hands and a crown of thorns to perforate his skull. His compassion for you is so profound he died your death. He suffered the hell you deserve.

Sometimes it feels like God doesn't care. Sometimes it seems like he is too tired or too busy to be concerned with our puny problems, but that's not the truth.

Your God loves you with a gut-wrenching love.

Today I am thankful for/that _____

_____

Merciful God, though I don't deserve it, you love me more deeply than I will ever be able to fully understand. Thank you for all you do for me in your great love. Amen.

DAY 165
SPOILER ALERT

"I am the living bread that came down from heaven. Whoever eats this bread will live forever."

JOHN 6:51

◆

It was opening night at the theater. A new play—a mystery—was premiering. A man who loved mysteries excitedly entered the theater only to find that his seat was in the very back row.

He called an usher and told him, "I just love a good mystery and I've been waiting a long time to see this play, but now look where I'm sitting! In order to be able to follow the clues and figure out the mystery, I need to be up closer. If you can get me a better seat, I'll give you a big tip."

The usher nodded and whispered, "I'll be right back." He hurried to the box office to see if there were any open seats up front. Sure enough, there was one available seat in the second row.

Excited about the "big tip" he was going to receive, the usher went back and led the man down to the second row. When they got there, the man whispered, "Thank you," and slipped the usher a single dollar bill.

The usher looked down at the dollar bill, leaned in, and quietly whispered in the man's ear, "The butler did it."

Most people don't like to know the end of a book, movie, or play before reading it. On the internet, if writers are going to reveal details about a movie or TV show, they always write in bold print: "Spoiler alert!"

Spoiler alert! I am about to tell you the end of another story.

In the end, Jesus dies. That's right. The main character of the Bible dies in the end. But that's not the end of the story. He comes back to life. On the third day he rises again.

BUT THAT'S NOT THE END OF THE STORY.

Honestly, that ending shouldn't be shocking. God gave clues the whole way. For centuries before Jesus was even born, the prophets foretold that he would suffer, die, and rise again.

That still isn't the end of the story, though. I know, I know. I'm giving it all away. Because Jesus rose from the dead, we can be sure that we who believe in him also will live forever with him. There is no doubt how our story is going to end.

Before he died on that Friday afternoon 2,000 years ago, Jesus declared to the world, "It is finished." But Jesus wasn't saying his story was finished. The payment for sin was.

All our sins of impatience and pride, selfishness and gossip, adultery and drunkenness have been paid in full—washed away forever. Our ticket to heaven is paid.

Then, on that first Easter Sunday morning, Jesus proved to us that this story truly has a happy ending. He didn't stay dead. Death had no power over him and now has no power over us.

That's why we can live with such confidence. We know how our story is going to end. We are going to live with Jesus in the glories of heaven forever.

Spoiler alert! Your story has no end.

Today I am thankful for/that _____

Dear Jesus, thank you for winning for me a happy ending that has no end. Amen.

DAY 166
EMOTIONS ON STEROIDS

I call on the LORD in my distress, and he answers me.
PSALM 120:1

◆

The late 1990s and early 2000s have become known as the "Steroid Era" of Major League Baseball. With millions of dollars at stake and little to no testing, home runs and players' bodies ballooned. Steroid use became rampant.

All of the modern home run records were broken during the Steroid Era. Eventually, however, it became clear that every single one of the record breakers was also a rule breaker—Sammy Sosa, Mark McGwire, Barry Bonds, and Alex Rodriguez, to name just a few.

Workout routines, which would normally bring slow and steady muscle growth, changed Bill Bixby-looking baseball players into Lou Ferrigno seemingly overnight. That's what steroids do. They make everything bigger.

What many of us often fail to see is how certain events in our lives act like steroids on our emotions. Stress at work, lack of sleep, hormonal issues, and the death of a loved one are just a handful of emotionally charged situations which easily put our emotions on steroids.

During those times, little problems suddenly become overwhelming burdens. Small annoyances become unbearable frustrations. Insignificant squabbles turn into World War III.

Unfortunately, we often don't even realize our emotions are on steroids. We truly believe that the problems are that big or that the people in our lives are just that uncaring, insensitive, or evil.

Do you find yourself more stressed, frustrated, or overwhelmed than usual? Take a moment to look at yourself honestly. Ask yourself: Are problems in one area of my life affecting how I react to other situations and people? Is my anger or stress with my family related to health or hormonal issues I am having?

Such questions are hard to answer. Talk to a friend or family member whom you trust. Are things how I perceive them or am I reacting through the filter of other issues in my life?

If your emotions are on steroids, be honest about it. Tell your friends and family what you are going through. Don't make excuses. Rather, let them know you may struggle to react well to certain situations. Ask for their forgiveness and patience.

And then take it to God in prayer. Ask your Savior to forgive the ugly things you said in moments of rage or despair. Ask him to forgive your worry and doubt. Ask the Holy Spirit to give you the peace he has promised.

Then feast on the promises of God's Word. Find in Jesus forgiveness. If you don't know where to look in your Bible, open up to the middle and start reading the book of Psalms. Eventually you will find a Psalm which speaks to your situation.

HE WILL HELP YOU SEE THINGS FOR HOW THEY REALLY ARE.

Through his Word, God will help you deal with your exaggerated emotions. Through his Word, he will help you see things for how they really are. Through his Word, he will give you the peace the world cannot give.

Today I am thankful for/that _____

_____

Dear God, you know me. You know how, at times
when I am stressed or tired, my emotions get
the best of me. When I feel overwhelmed by
anger, worry, or frustration, help me find
peace in your promises and love. Amen.

DAY 167
WON'T YOU BE MY NEIGHBOR

"Love your neighbor as yourself."

LUKE 10:27

◆

It's an indelible image from my childhood—Mr. Rogers putting on his sweater, changing his shoes, and singing, "Won't you be my neighbor?"

Sadly, for many in our world today, Mr. Rogers may seem a bit naïve and schmaltzy. Eddie Murphy's old character from Saturday Night Live, Mr. Robinson, seems more apropos to modern sensibilities.

Mr. Robinson was a parody of Mr. Rogers—an African-American man talking in the sweet Mr. Rogers voice, expressing the brutal reality of life in the projects. It was both shocking and funny.

There is nothing funny, however, about the situation in our country today. People are angry with each other—black and white, Republican and Democrat, Muslim and Christian, gay and straight. The violence and vitriol are boiling over.

We have forgotten what it means to be a neighbor. Our God tells us, "Love your neighbor as yourself." Yet in our world today, we find ourselves asking the same question a young lawyer once asked Jesus, "Who is my neighbor?" (Luke 10:29).

Jesus' answer was a parable—the Parable of the Good Samaritan. Jesus' answer was simple—everybody.

Your neighbor includes people who are different than you, who look and talk and act differently than you. Your neighbor includes those with whom you disagree. Your neighbor includes those who hurt you and treat you badly. Your neighbor includes even your enemies.

We have forgotten that. We tend to love those who are easy to love—those who agree with us, those who look like us and dress like us. On Facebook, we like and share the posts which express what we believe. We angrily and sarcastically criticize those with whom we disagree.

The answer for some is that we should tolerate everyone and everything. For them, to disagree or to call something bad is unneighborly, but that's not the answer either. God has called us to confront and call out that which goes against his will.

Yet he tells us to do so in love. We confront sin in order to help a person repent and find forgiveness in Jesus their Savior. We do so because we love them.

That's hard to do, especially in our world today. In fact, we haven't done it. We have let our anger and pride divide us. We have stopped listening and loving. We haven't been good neighbors.

THERE ISN'T A PERSON JESUS DOESN'T LOVE.

The only answer for us and for our country is to find forgiveness in our Savior Jesus. There isn't a person Jesus doesn't love. There isn't a person for whom he did not die. That means, by the way, that he loves and died for you. That means he forgives your anger and pride, your racism and sarcasm.

Now, as he has loved and forgiven you, he wants you to love and forgive your neighbors. That includes the African-Americans in our community and country who are hurting and angry, whether you think they are justified for feeling that way or not. That includes the police officers who patrol our streets, even those who are unfair or racist. It includes terrorists, criminals, drunks, druggies. They are your neighbors.

So love them. Speak out against the evils and sins you see, but do so respectfully and in love. Watch what you say and share on Facebook and social media. Pray for those who are hurting and angry. Pray for those with whom you disagree. Pray for our nation.

Above all else, be a good neighbor.

Today I am thankful for/that _____

_____

Holy God, forgive me for all the times I have not loved others as you have loved me. Please help me and others to be kind and forgiving, just as you have forgiven us in Christ. Amen.

DAY 168
THERE IS NO "I" IN GRACE

It is by grace you have been saved, through faith—and
this is not from yourselves, it is the gift of God—
not by works, so that no one can boast.

EPHESIANS 2:8,9

◆

I still don't know how it happened. A little over a year ago I offered to be an assistant coach on my son's soccer team. Then, without warning, I found myself the head coach. Suffice it to say, my first season of coaching was a whirlwind of trying to figure things out.

As I begin my second season, I find I am now able to focus on certain details of the game. One thing I am trying to teach the boys this season is to work together, to encourage one another—to be a team.

So there I stood the other day in practice with a whistle around my neck telling nine- and ten-year-old boys, "There is no 'I' in team."

"There is a 'me,' though," one of the boys quickly replied as the rest of the team chuckled.

As I said, I'm still trying to figure this coaching thing out.

I thought about that old coaching cliché this morning as I read a passage from the book of Ephesians. "It is by grace you have been saved, through faith—and this not from yourselves, it is the gift of God—not by works, so that no one can boast."

There is no "I" in grace.

Grace is God's love that we don't deserve—his love which doesn't depend on us or on what we do. In fact, God loves us despite who we are and what we do. In his love, he came to this earth to live and die as our Savior. In his love, he forgives us. In his love, he saves us from the hell we deserve.

It is by grace we have been saved. It doesn't depend on what we do. Heaven is a gift, and a gift by its very nature is free.

As a pastor, I often ask people this question: "Imagine you were to die tonight and you found yourself standing at the gates to heaven. God asks you, 'Why should I let you into heaven?' What would you say?"

The answers I hear most often are: "Because I try to live a good life." "Because I chose Jesus Christ as my personal Savior." "Because I go to church." "Because I haven't killed anybody." But there's a problem with all of those answers.

The word "I."

That is boasting. That is saying, "Look what I did."

EVERYTHING WE ARE AND HAVE IS A GIFT WE DON'T DESERVE.

Even the response: "Because I believe in Jesus" isn't really the best answer. Yes, faith in Jesus saves us, but faith in Jesus is not something I can do on my own. The reason I believe is because the Holy Spirit worked faith in my heart.

If you have an "I" in your answer, there is a problem. There is no "I" in grace. Everything we are and have is a gift we don't deserve.

The fact that I am going to heaven is not something I did. It's not even something that was a team effort. God did it all on his own. He deserves all the credit. If you are going to boast about anything, boast about him.

Because there is no "I" in grace.

Today I am thankful for/that _____

_____

Gracious God, help me to always remember that everything I have and everything I am is because of your amazing grace. Fill my heart with humble gratitude for your love and forgiveness. Amen.

DAY 169
STOP GIVING ANGER A MEGAPHONE

The tongue is a small part of the body, but it makes
great boasts. Consider what a great forest is
set on fire by a small spark.

JAMES 3:5

◆

My heart hurts. The violence of the past few weeks in our country and in our world grieves my soul. Men, women, and children are being massacred by madmen. People are angry and frightened. At the heart of much of the violence are the most polarizing issues in our society—race, religion, and human sexuality.

Many African-Americans distrust and are afraid of the police. Much of White America subconsciously fears and distrusts Black America. Religious fanatics consider themselves their deity's instrument of vengeance on a corrupt and immoral world.

Fueling the fear, distrust, and anger is social media.

Don't get me wrong. I'm not saying Facebook is to blame for the massacres in Orlando, Dallas, or Nice. Sin is to blame. Man's pride, anger, and selfishness are to blame.

Violence and hatred are nothing new. As wise old King Solomon used to say, "There is nothing new under the sun" (Ecclesiastes 1:9). Hatred and violence have existed since Cain and Abel. Wars have raged throughout history. Across the centuries, religious zealots have persecuted and killed those with whom they disagree.

The difference today is that anger has been given a megaphone. Technology not only allows us immediate access to breaking news around the world, but now also gives us a platform to comment publicly on those events.

Social media is so new that most of us haven't taken the time to evaluate how we use it. Each of us has suddenly been given a megaphone to tell the world what we think and feel. Today we can post something on social media which potentially could reach hundreds, thousands, or even millions of people. But as Uncle Ben once told young Peter Parker, "With great power comes great responsibility."

It's time to step back and objectively evaluate how we use social media. Why are we posting what we post? How is it being perceived? How does our use of social media affect us and others?

Posting our personal thoughts and opinions feels good, especially as the number of likes increases. It makes us feel better about ourselves and justified in our opinions. Are we sharing on social media to encourage and enlighten others or simply to fill a personal need for acceptance or approval?

POSTS, THREADS, AND DISCUSSIONS ON SOCIAL MEDIA RARELY CHANGE ANYONE'S OPINION.

Even if our motives are pure, will what we post really encourage or enlighten others? Here is a truth few seem to accept: posts, threads and discussions on social media rarely change anyone's opinion. Those who agree with you will like and share. Those who disagree will ignore or argue.

Those who fill their Facebook feeds with "Black Lives Matter" or "All Lives Matter," with Donald Trump or Hillary Clinton, with rants for or against the LGBTQ+ agenda, rarely add anything to the discussion or change anyone's mind. They just polarize people more. They muddy the waters with propaganda and misinformation.

Arguing and debating politics, religion, or morality on a Facebook thread is not productive or effective communication. It tends to polarize us more and fuel the fury of unstable people.

You may feel that if you don't speak up, nobody will. I understand that. God wants us to stand up for the truth, but he also wants us to do so clearly and in love. Social media doesn't usually lend itself to that. Certain issues are better discussed privately or in person.

So instead of engaging in a public debate which devolves quickly into sarcasm and name calling, send the person a private message. Engage in real communication with the people God has placed around you. Take a step back. Consider carefully what you share and post on social media.

Stop fueling the fury. Stop giving anger a megaphone.

Today I am thankful for/that _____

Heavenly Father, help me to speak the truth in love, not only with what I say with my mouth, but also with what I post on social media. Amen.

DAY 170
JESUS LOVES ME

This is love: not that we loved God, but that he loved us
and sent his Son as an atoning sacrifice for our sins.

1 JOHN 4:10

✦

The year was 1860. The nation was on the brink of Civil War. Two sisters, Anna and Susan Warner, lived with their father next door to the United States Military Academy at West Point. Everyone knew what was coming, but no one knew what would happen.

During those years of uncertainty, Anna and Susan made a name for themselves as writers of popular religious and children's novels. In 1860, they collaborated on a novel called *Say and Seal*. The book became a national bestseller, but as with many literary works which were popular at the time, it has been all but forgotten today.

The novel would have been completely forgotten if not for a poem hidden within its pages. At one point, the protagonist, Mr. Linden, stood beside the bed of a dying boy. No one could comfort the distraught child. Mr. Linden recited a poem which Anna had composed specifically for the book:

Jesus loves me—this I know, for the Bible tells me so.
    Little ones to him belong—They are weak but he is strong.
Jesus loves me—loves me still, though I'm very weak and ill;
    From his shining throne on high comes to watch me where I lie.
Jesus loves me—he will stay, close beside me all the way.
    Then his little child will take, up to heaven for his dear sake.

The poem comforted the dying boy. During the terrifying and violent years of the Civil War, Anna Warner's words gave comfort to countless other children and adults.

In 1862, William Batchelder Bradbury, who had previously composed the music to a number of other popular hymns, including "Just As I Am," put the poem to music, adding one verse and a refrain:

Jesus loves me—He who died, heaven's gates to open wide,
    He will wash away my sin, let his little child come in.
Yes, Jesus loves me; yes, Jesus loves me;
    Yes, Jesus loves me—the Bible tells me so.

For over 150 years, "Jesus Loves Me" has been the first-learned and most-beloved hymn for countless children throughout the world. In my work with the elderly at nursing homes, I've learned it is also a hymn they never forget. Even after they can no longer remember their children or their own name, they can still remember and sing, "Jesus loves me—this I know."

Too often as a pastor I forget the tremendous power and comfort of the simple gospel message: Jesus loves me—this I know, for the Bible tells me so. At times I fail to cling to the simple truth that Jesus loves me—he who died, heaven's gates to open wide.

HOW DO I KNOW? THE BIBLE TELLS ME SO.

In our complicated world torn apart by turmoil, may we never outgrow or stop singing the simple and powerful message that, yes, Jesus loves me. He will stay close beside me all the way. He has washed away my sin. Heaven's gate is open wide.

How do I know? The Bible tells me so.

Today I am thankful for/that _____

_____

Dear Jesus, thank you for loving me so much.
I know I don't deserve it. Amen.

325

DAY 171
THIS ISN'T ABOUT ME

Praise the LORD. Praise God in his sanctuary; . . . Praise
him for his acts of power; praise him for his surpassing
greatness. . . . Let everything that has breath
praise the LORD. Praise the LORD.

PSALM 150:1,2,6

❖

In church this last Sunday, a thought kept going through my mind. As I sat in God's house hearing his Word and singing his songs, I kept thinking, "This isn't about me."

The problem is that it can so easily become about *me*. Without realizing it, many churches fall into the subtle trap of making worship about me. They look for music to entertain and inspire. They pick hymns that talk about how God makes *me* feel. They preach sermons that focus almost entirely on *me* and my life.

Don't get me wrong. All of those things can be good in the proper perspective. There is no "I" in team, but there is definitely an "I" in worship. I do go to worship to be inspired and taught. It should affect how I feel. It should apply to my life.

But, really, worship isn't about me.

WORSHIP ISN'T ABOUT ME. Worship is first and foremost about my God and Savior. The music of our worship shouldn't focus so much on how *I* feel as much as on what *God* has done to save me.

Good preaching should first and foremost proclaim the forgiveness and freedom that Jesus won for all people on the cross. Worship is about our God and what he has done.

Worship is also about those sitting around me. The writer to the Hebrews encourages us, "Let us consider how we may spur one another on toward love and good deeds, not giving up meeting together, as some are in the habit of doing, but encouraging one another" (Hebrews 10:24,25). Worship is about engaging and encouraging each other. We don't only sing our hymns to God; we sing them to encourage one another. We lift our voices in prayer for one another. In the creeds, we proudly proclaim to each other what we believe.

In our church, we use a liturgy—a set order of worship that has its roots in the ancient church. Do you know what the word *liturgy* means? It comes from a Greek word which means "service" or "work." Many people today go to church, sit back, and say, "Okay. Entertain me. Inspire me. Make me feel good."

But liturgical worship—Lutheran worship—takes work. It takes work to really think about what we are saying and singing. It takes work to listen to and apply the Word being proclaimed. It takes work to worship.

Think about that the next time you park yourself in the pew. This isn't about me. This is about God who speaks to me in Word and sacrament. This is about praising and thanking God for the wondrous works he has done. This is about encouraging and building up those who are sitting around me.

And the amazing blessing is that through the gospel message proclaimed in worship, I too will be encouraged. I too will be built up. I too will be inspired.

Today I am thankful for/that _____

_____

Lord God Almighty, thank you for the privilege to worship you in church. May my worship always be about you. Use it as a blessing to me and others. Amen.

DAY 172
OUR GOD REIGNS

"I tell you, do not worry about your life, what you will
eat or drink; or about your body, what you will
wear. . . . But seek first his kingdom and his
righteousness, and all these things will
be given to you as well."

MATTHEW 6:25,33

◆

As I write this devotion, the field for the 2016 presidential elections has finally been narrowed down to two (kind of). After a dizzying primary season full of surreal debates, crazy comments, and canned soundbites, the Republican and Democratic parties have nominated their candidates and wrapped up their conventions.

At this point, many Christians are anxiously wringing their hands wondering who the next president will be. I'm here to tell you not to worry about it.

Don't get me wrong. As a Christian, you should be concerned about the upcoming election. God has called you to be a light to the world and to speak the truth in love. As Christians, we should participate in the political process. We should let our voices be heard. We should vote our consciences.

We should be concerned about who becomes the next president. It should sadden us when government officials don't live up to their high calling. Injustices should anger us and lead us to act.

We don't need to worry, however. Again and again, our God tells us in his Word not to worry about the future. He lovingly whispers, "Do not be afraid." Why? Because no matter who is running our country—no matter what is happening at home or abroad—our God reigns.

**NO MATTER WHAT
IS HAPPENING . . .
GOD IS IN CONTROL.**

God is in control. In a quiet moment today, read Psalm 2 in your Bible. See how God reacts when leaders and governments contend against his will.

He laughs.

They can't win. In the end, Jesus wins, and because he wins, we too will win. Kingdoms will rise and fall. Presidents will come and go, but our God reigns. He will control all of time and history for the good of his children. If he did not spare his only Son, but gave him up for us all, how will he not also make everything else work for our good?

Now, that doesn't mean it will be easy. Look at history. Tyrants can quickly steal our freedoms. The power and prosperity we enjoy can disappear in less than one generation. Our nation's future as a world power is by no means guaranteed.

In the end, though, we need not fear. God's Word will still be preached. No ruler or government throughout history has been able to silence it. God will still provide for and protect his children. No matter what happens here, we are citizens of God's heavenly kingdom because of Jesus.

Yet many Christians in our country worry. They fret and fuss about our government. Some think that if we could get the right candidate or party in power, all our problems would disappear. They fear that if the wrong people get elected, we are doomed. Truthfully, the government cannot solve our problems. Only God can.

So this November as the candidates vie for your vote, let your light shine. Participate in the process. Let your voice be heard.

In the end, though, even if your candidate is not elected—no matter who becomes the next President of the United States—don't worry.

Our God reigns.

Today I am thankful for/that _____

_____

Almighty God and Lord, the political situation in our country seems to constantly be getting worse. Many of us worry about the way our leaders govern our country. Give our leaders wisdom and help them do what is right, but also take away our fears and help us always remember that you are in charge. Amen.

DAY 173
PERSPECTIVE

I have learned the secret of being content in any and
every situation, whether well fed or hungry, whether
living in plenty or in want. I can do all this through
him who gives me strength.

PHILIPPIANS 4:12,13

◆

As I write this devotion, the Games of the XXXI Olympiad are officially
beginning in Rio de Janeiro, Brazil. Over the next two weeks, 11,000
athletes will compete for 306 sets of Olympic medals.

Dr. Vicki Medvec, a professor of social psychology at Northwestern
University, has dedicated her life to studying Olympic medalists; specifically,
how they feel about their achievements.

What Dr. Medvec has discovered may surprise you. It sounds counterintuitive, but according to Dr. Medvec's research, bronze medalists tend
to be happier than silver medalists.

Medvec's study claims that silver medalists have a tendency to focus on
how closely they came to winning gold. Their silver medal is a reminder of
how they failed to win. On the other hand, bronze medalists usually focus
on how closely they came to winning nothing at all. They are simply
grateful to have a medal.

Dr. Medvec's study reveals an interesting facet of human nature. How
we feel isn't determined so much by our external circumstances, but
by our internal attitudes. The happiness of the Olympic medal winners
didn't depend on which medal they won. If that were the case, the
silver medalists should have been happier than the bronze medalists.
Instead, their happiness depended on how they perceived the medal
they won.

The same is true in our lives. In order to find happiness, most people
look to change their outward circumstances. "I would be happier if I
made more money or if I had a different husband or if I lived in a bigger
house." If our happiness depends on those things, what happens if we
don't get them? Are we then going to live unhappy, bitter lives?

Even when people do get what they want, they often find that those things don't actually make them happy. True joy, true happiness, begins on the inside.

The apostle Paul wrote to the Christians in the Greek city of Philippi, "I have learned the secret of being content in any and every situation." Paul had learned the secret to being happy. Do you know what it is?

He tells us, "I can do all this through him who gives me strength." In other words, "I can handle any and every situation in life with a happy heart through my God who gives me strength."

God changes our perspective. Through his Word, he points our eyes to the cross and the gold medal of heaven Jesus won for each of us. Through his Word, he shows us that our lives have meaning and purpose. Through his Word, he helps us see that even the difficulties of this world are actually blessings in disguise.

GOD CHANGES OUR PERSPECTIVE.

God changes our perspective. Look at your life. Look at the blessings God has showered upon you. Look at his love and forgiveness. Understand that God will take even the pains you are suffering and use them for your good. See the glory and perfection and happiness which are waiting for you in heaven. When you have that perspective, it doesn't matter what medal you win. It doesn't matter what happens to you or around you.

You can truly be happy.

Today I am thankful for/that _____

_____

Lord, help me to keep the proper perspective in my life. Open my eyes to see all that you have given me. Grant me a thankful and content heart. Amen.

DAY 174
HOT AS HELL

"They will throw them into the blazing furnace, where
there will be weeping and gnashing of teeth."

MATTHEW 13:42

◆

This has been an extraordinarily hot summer. South-central Texas is known for its heat and humidity, but this year takes the cake.

I can't imagine how it's been for our oilfield workers, farmers, construction crews, and all those who have to work under the hot Texas sun every day. They must spend the entire day dripping in sweat, drinking gallons of water just to stay hydrated.

The other day I was in Walmart when a man walked in and exclaimed in exasperation, "It's hot as a hell out there!" Some people were startled by the outburst. Others simply nodded in agreement.

I thought about it.

Yes, the heat has been miserable over the last few weeks, but is it hot as hell? Jesus described hell as a place of "weeping and gnashing of teeth" where "the worm does not die and the fire is not quenched." Imagine burning in fire forever.

Hell is a place of pure punishment. The punishment of hell is complete separation from God and his love—being locked out of his presence forever. One of the horrific ironies of hell is that those condemned to its dungeons will be able to see the heaven they are missing. They will be watching the happiness of heaven through a window from the outside looking in.

Hell is horror. Hell is suffering beyond our darkest nightmares. Working under the hot Texas sun doesn't even come close. We really have no concept of how horrible hell is.

And, thanks to Jesus, we never will.

Honestly, we deserve to burn forever in the lake of fire. The apostle Paul tells us, "The wages of sin is death" (Romans 6:23). The punishment of just one sin is an eternity in the prison of hell, and each of us has a lot more than just one sin. Every little lie, every dirty thought, every ugly word deserves the flames of hell.

But Jesus suffered that hell for us. When he hung on the cross, he didn't just suffer the nails in his hands and thorns in his brow. He didn't just suffer the physical agony of slowly choking to death under the weight of his own body. On that cross, Jesus suffered the punishment of hell.

No, he didn't go to hell. Rather, he suffered the agony we deserve—complete separation from God and his love. Because of our sins, he suffered the fists of God's fury. He suffered a pain and horror we can't even imagine. He suffered the punishment of hell.

And because he suffered our punishment in our place, God forgives us. He promises us that whoever believes in him will not perish in hell, but have eternal life in the happiness of heaven. All those who believe in Jesus will never know what hell feels like. You and I will never be able to fully appreciate what Jesus suffered for us because we will never have to experience even the tiniest flame of hell.

That's why so often we take our Savior for granted. We joke about hell. We compare it to an uncomfortably hot day. We shrug our shoulders at the mention of Jesus and the cross. We fail to fathom how amazing grace really is.

NOBODY LIKES TO TALK ABOUT SIN NOWADAYS.

Nobody likes to talk about sin nowadays. Churches tend to shy away from talking about hell anymore. They don't want to bring people down. But maybe if we spent a little more time honestly talking about our failings and the fiery pit they deserve, we might appreciate all the more the love of a God who suffered that horror and pain in our place.

Today I am thankful for/that _____

_____

Merciful God, thank you for saving me from the fires of hell which I deserve. Help me to always appreciate your amazing love which rescued me from the horror of hell which I deserve. Amen.

DAY 175
THE SLIPPERY SLOPE OF SIN

I said, "I will confess my transgressions to the Lord."
And you forgave the guilt of my sin.

PSALM 32:5

◆

The 2016 Olympic Games in Brazil included many wonderful storylines. Michael Phelps, Katie Ledecky, Simone Biles, and Usain Bolt all cemented their places among the greatest Olympians of all time. New heroes emerged and heartwarming stories of courage and perseverance were shared.

Sadly, the story which dominated the headlines of the 2016 Summer Olympics was that of Ryan Lochte. Ryan Lochte is one of the most decorated Olympian swimmers of all time. He won another gold medal that year, bringing his career total to 12, second all-time behind Michael Phelps.

After the swimming events were over, however, Lochte and three other American swimmers went out for a night on the town to celebrate. They got drunk and ended up breaking down a bathroom door at a convenience store. When confronted, they paid the manager of the store so he would not report it.

The next day, however, Lochte tried to cover up their bad behavior by telling his mother they had been brutally mugged at gunpoint. Lochte's mom told reporters. Suddenly Lochte and his cohorts found themselves repeating their lie not only on TV but also to the police.

Though reports soon surfaced claiming the robbery had been made up, Lochte and the other swimmers initially stuck by their story. The truth eventually came out, though. Video evidence and eyewitness accounts forced the swimmers to admit their lie.

The incident cost Ryan Lochte millions of dollars in endorsements. While Brazil did not press charges, Lochte was handed a 10-month swimming suspension and excluded from Olympic activities and US swimming events. Not only is his family still suffering the effects of his behavior, but his legacy has forever been tarnished.

The sad story of Ryan Lochte is just another example of how each of us is only two or three bad choices away from losing everything. We can usually recover from one bad mistake if we admit it and face the consequences of our actions.

Sin, however, is a slippery slope. When we make mistakes, the initial reaction of our sinful nature is to cover it up, to lie, to hide what we have done. We compound our bad choice by making more bad choices.

That's what King David did. One night, he saw a beautiful woman bathing. Though he knew she was married to one of his army commanders, he invited her to his palace to have sex with her. She got pregnant, and David panicked. He brought her husband back from the war to sleep with her so nobody would find out, but that didn't work. So he sent the husband back to the battlefront and gave orders to have him killed.

Sin is a slippery slope. We panic and try to find the easy way out. We don't want people to know what we've done, so we lie. We cover it up. We make everything worse.

Thankfully, Jesus died not only for our initial sins, but also for all the stupid sins which follow. God forgave King David his lust, adultery, and murder. Jesus died for Ryan Lochte's foolish mistakes and he has died for yours as well. You cannot commit a sin which God will not forgive.

ADMIT YOUR MISTAKES RIGHT AWAY.

With God's phenomenal forgiving love in mind, understand the slippery slope of sin and learn from Ryan Lochte's mistake. When you mess up—and you are going to mess up—don't make it worse by lying or covering it up. I know it's painful, but admit what you've done. Ask God for forgiveness. Ask those you have wronged to forgive you.

Admit your mistakes right away and you will save yourself a lot of hurt and heartache.

Today I am thankful for/that _____

Father, forgive me. You know what I have done. Help me to trust in your amazing grace and to humbly face the consequences of what I have done. Amen.

DAY 176
MY MOTHER'S PRAYER

Start children off on the way they should go, and even
when they are old they will not turn from it.

PROVERBS 22:6

◆

A few years ago, I sat in a theater with my third-grade daughter watching
the Disney Pixar movie *Toy Story 3*. Over the years, we had watched the
other *Toy Story* movies together—following the adventures of young Andy
and his toys, Woody and Buzz Lightyear.

In *Toy Story 3,* Andy is now 17 years old and preparing to leave for college.
At the end of the movie, we find him in his empty room holding the last
box to be loaded in his car before he leaves for college. His mom stands by
his side crying. He doesn't understand why.

I looked down at my eight-year-old daughter and started crying myself.
She didn't understand either. She won't until she has kids of her own.

I was thinking of that moment this week as I saw all the pictures on
Facebook of friends and family dropping off their kids at college. Though
it is still a couple of years away, I am already preparing myself for
that moment.

A little over 25 years ago, my parents drove my older sister and me to
our respective colleges. Just before we got to my college, we stopped at
a gas station. My father got out to pump the gas and my mom turned
and looked at my sister and me.

"I know you both are going to do things you shouldn't while you are
away at college," she told us, "but I want you to know that every night I
pray that God keep you safe until you grow up and learn."

He did.

When our children move out—when they go away to school or get their
first apartment—it can be scary for us as parents. While they are young,
we have a certain amount of control. We can keep them safe. We can
keep an eye on them. We can curb (to a certain extent) the trouble they
get into and discipline them when they do.

When they grow up, when they move out, when they go away to college,
they are suddenly on their own. We can't control what they do or where

336

they go. For the most part, we don't even know what they are doing or who they are with.

That's when we pray my mother's prayer. That's when we remember that our children are not alone. God promises to never leave them or forsake them. He promises to send his angels to watch over them in all they do. He promises, "Start children off on the way they should go, and even when they are old they will not turn from it."

Does that mean our children will never waver or stray from the faith? Does that mean they won't fall into the foolish sins of youth? No. But the seeds of God's truth sown in our children's hearts when they are young are not easily uprooted. The truth of God's love and forgiveness in Christ will help them face their failings and find their way.

The idea of our children transitioning from childhood to adulthood—from dependence to independence—is scary for many parents. It's hard to let go.

CONTINUE TO ENCOURAGE YOUR ADULT CHILDREN IN THEIR FAITH.

So pray my mom's prayer. Continue to encourage your adult children in their faith. Continue to be an example for them of what it means to love God and be loved by him. And then leave them in God's powerful hands, trusting that he loves them even more than you do.

Today I am thankful for/that _____

_____

Lord, keep all the children in my life close to you. Watch over them and keep them safe as they grow up and become what you have made them to be. Use me and others to show them your love. Amen.

337

DAY 177
THE PANDEMIC OF PORN

"Anyone who looks at a woman lustfully has already
committed adultery with her in his heart."

MATTHEW 5:28

◆

This last week, the *Wall Street Journal* published an editorial entitled, "Take the Pledge: No More Indulging Porn." The article caused an uproar, not so much because of its content, but rather because of its coauthor.

The article was written by Pamela Anderson. Yes, that Pamela Anderson—former *Baywatch* star, *Playboy* cover girl, and soft porn actress. Just a little over a year ago, she herself posed for *Playboy*'s final issue.

But now she has had a change of heart.

"This is a public hazard of unprecedented seriousness," she writes, "given how freely available, anonymously accessible and easily disseminated pornography is nowadays. How many families will suffer? How many marriages will implode? How many talented men will scrap their most important relationships and careers for a brief onanistic thrill?"

She also warned that children raised in the current digital environment will "become adults inured to intimacy and in need of even greater graphic stimulation. They are crack babies of porn."

Since the release of the editorial, Anderson has been lauded by some, but also derided by many. Who is she to talk? She just posed for *Playboy*.

What does it say, however, when a person who has spent the majority of her adult life inundated in the world of porn comes out and says how dangerous it is?

Porn is a blight on our society. It used to be that a man had to publicly purchase pornography. He had to sneak around and hide it. Today it is everywhere. It is free. It is socially acceptable.

That doesn't change the fact that it is sin. Though our world treats porn as inoffensive and even helpful to relationships, it damages brains, bodies, and relationships.

God clearly forbids it in the Bible. Jesus said, "You have heard that it was said, 'Do not commit adultery.' But I tell you that anyone who looks at a woman lustfully has already committed adultery with her in his heart" (Matthew 5:27,28).

THANKFULLY, JESUS DIED FOR OUR LUST.

Thankfully, Jesus died for our lust, just as he did for every other sin our eyes and ears and hearts commit. If you have allowed porn to infiltrate your marriage, your computer, or your phone, know that Jesus' blood washes away even the ugliest of filth. You are forgiven and loved by God.

But now is the time to turn it off. If you struggle to do so, find a trustworthy person to help keep you accountable. Turn to God in prayer and to his Word for strength. Talk to your pastor or find a good Christian counselor.

Do not allow porn into your marriage. No matter what your spouse says, it is cheating. It is adultery.

Parents, monitor your children's phones, tablets, and TVs. Once the heroin of porn grabs hold, many people (especially men) struggle to fight it the rest of their lives.

Porn is not harmless. It is addictive. It destroys lives and relationships. It angers God. There is no disputing those facts.

Even Pamela Anderson knows it's bad.

Today I am thankful for/that _____

_____

Lord, forgive me for all the ways I have not treated your gifts of marriage and sex as I should. Watch over my family and the families of our country. Help them to stay away from the dangers of porn. Amen.

DAY 178
A HOT MESS

Here is a trustworthy saying that deserves full
acceptance: Christ Jesus came into the world
to save sinners—of whom I am the worst.

1 TIMOTHY 1:15

◆

"I'm a hot mess."

I keep hearing that phrase. The term itself is nothing new. It dates all the way back to the 19th century. Then, a hot mess was a warm meal served to soldiers.

In the last couple of years, however, the phrase has taken on a whole new meaning. According to the Urban Dictionary, a hot mess is "when one's thoughts or appearance are in a state of disarray, but they maintain an undeniable attractiveness or beauty."

Comedian Amy Schumer is the epitome of a hot mess, or at least that's the public persona she portrays. She makes jokes about her messed-up personal life. She parties too hard. She often dresses in disarray. She's a mess.

Yet she also comes across as likeable and attractive. She's a hot mess.

We all have people in our lives who are an obvious mess. They have problems with drinking or drugs. Their marriages are in shambles. They struggle to function in society. Their lives are messy.

When we see such obvious messes, we sometimes feel sorry for them. Other times we get frustrated. I mean, it's their own fault, right? They've made the mess with their bad choices. Sometimes we even avoid such people because we don't want their messes spilling over into our lives.

What we so often fail to realize is that we are all a mess. Some of us are just better at hiding it.

I MAINTAIN AN ATTRACTIVE VENEER. . . . YET I KNOW WHAT'S IN MY HEART.

I'm a hot mess. On the outside, I maintain an attractive veneer. I am a Christian father and husband. I am a pastor and author. People respect me.

Yet I know what's in my heart. I see the sins and failures and struggles in my life which no

340

one else can see. I'm a hot mess of weakness, doubt, and anxiety. I often feel like a hypocrite, a failure, a fraud.

Then I remember Paul. Paul was an apostle. Jesus himself appeared to him on the road to Damascus. Paul is the greatest missionary the world has ever known. He wrote more books of the Bible than any other writer. Paul was a saint, right?

He knew better. "Here is a trustworthy saying," Paul wrote to his young protégé, Timothy, "Christ Jesus came into the world to save sinners—of whom I am the worst."

I guess we can understand that. Before Jesus called him to be an apostle, Paul persecuted the church; he arrested Christians and then had them killed. He was the worst of sinners.

But that's not what Paul wrote. He said, "I *am* the worst." Even after being called to faith, the great apostle was still a mess. He could see all the sins and failures and weaknesses with which he still struggled. He knew he was a hot mess.

Paul's comfort—my comfort—is that Christ Jesus came to save dirty sinners like Paul and me. He suffered the punishment of all my secret sins—the messes I've made in my heart and life. I am forever forgiven because of Jesus.

So are you. Whether your life is in obvious disarray or, like me, you are a hot mess, God loves you, mess and all. You don't have to clean up your act for God to accept you. You don't have to pretend with him. He sees what a mess you are and loves you anyway. He meets you in your mess and washes you clean in Jesus' blood. You are a forgiven mess.

Or as the author Kimm Crandall likes to say, "You are his Beloved Mess."

Today I am thankful for/that _____

_____

Holy and merciful God, I come before you just as I am, a hot mess of sin and weakness. Thank you for washing away all my sins and making me your dear child. Amen.

DAY 179
BITTERSWEET

No one could distinguish the sound of the shouts of
joy from the sound of weeping, because
the people made so much noise.

EZRA 3:13

◆

I was giddy with anticipation. After two months of exile (the COVID virus shut-down in spring of 2020), we were finally going to gather again to worship in church. Initially, I had envisioned our first service back to be a welcome home celebration. The church would be full. The music would be glorious. People would be hugging each other. Not a few tears of joy would be shed.

Life at church would go back to the way it used to be.

The reality of our first service back, however, was quite different. The church was only a quarter full. We couldn't socialize before or after. No hugs or handshakes were shared. People were forced to sit apart. The music was muted by masks.

Don't get me wrong. The service was still a celebration. We thanked God for his grace. We talked about never again taking for granted the privilege of worshiping together. We said and sang the words of Psalm 122, "I rejoiced with those who said to me, 'Let us go to the house of the LORD.'"

Tears were shed.

As I gazed on the masked faces in worship and saw the tears swell, I wondered if they were tears of joy or tears of sorrow. We were happy to be back, but it just wasn't the same.

Two thousand six hundred years ago, the people of Israel found themselves in a markedly longer and less luxurious exile. They were conquered by the Babylonians. The temple and the city of Jerusalem were destroyed. They were carried off into exile for 70 years.

At the end of those 70 years, God brought his people back. They began to rebuild the city, their homes, and, most importantly, the temple. When the foundation of the temple was finished, the people came together to dedicate it.

They had been waiting for this day for 70 years. They were finally going to be able to worship God again in his temple. Ezra the priest tells us that the people cried out in joy as they sang their praises.

Mixed in the crowd were also those who as children had seen the original temple in all its glory. They wept aloud when they saw the foundation, knowing the new temple was going to be nothing compared to Solomon's original.

Ezra the priest tells us that "no one could distinguish the sound of the shouts of joy from the sound of weeping, because the people made so much noise."

Like our return to worship this last Sunday, the Jews return to Jerusalem was bittersweet. It was wonderful to be back and to be able to worship God again, but it just wasn't quite the same.

THROUGH IT ALL, GOD'S PROMISES HOLD TRUE.

If the experts are right, things will probably never be quite the same again. We will soon have to adjust to a new normal. Such is life in a sin-filled world. Though God gives us times of joy and celebration, there are also times of sorrow and sickness. Our lives are a bittersweet mix of emotions. Yet through it all, God's promises hold true.

God will be with us every step of the way. He will make everything work for our good. Most importantly, Jesus lived, died, and rose again so that one day we will be able to stand in God's house of heaven and sing our praises with unrestrained joy.

In heaven, there are no tears of sadness, no pandemics, and certainly no masks. In heaven, we won't worship with mixed emotions. Right now our return to worship at our churches may be bittersweet, but it's there where we find God's promise of heaven.

And that is just plain sweet.

Today I am thankful for/that _____

_____

Lord, help me appreciate the sweet joys of this life and give me courage and peace as I face the bitter sorrows. Through it all, keep my eyes focused on the happiness of heaven waiting for me because of Jesus. Amen.

DAY 180
PRAISE GOD FROM WHOM ALL BLESSINGS FLOW

When you have eaten and are satisfied, praise the LORD
your God for the good land he has given you.

DEUTERONOMY 8:10

◆

In 1965, Jimmy Stewart starred in the Civil War era film *Shenandoah*. In the movie, Stewart played widower Charlie Anderson, a poor farmer in the Commonwealth of Virginia left to raise his seven children alone.

The movie keenly portrays Anderson's love-hate relationship with God. At the family dinner table every evening, he prayed, "Lord, we cleared this land. We plowed it, sowed it, and harvested it. We cooked the harvest. It wouldn't be here and we wouldn't be eating it if we hadn't done it all ourselves. We worked dog-bone hard for every crumb and morsel, but we thank you just the same anyway, Lord, for the food we're about to eat. Amen."

Is that what your dinner prayers sound like? I'm guessing not. As Christians, we usually say the right things. We thank God for the food we eat. We sing at church, "Praise God from whom all blessings flow." We tell our neighbors and friends how good God has been to us.

But at the end of the day, we look at our homes, our trucks, our campers, and our fishing boats and think, "Look what I've accomplished. I've worked hard for everything I've got. I earned it."

As Americans we take pride in the good ol' American work ethic. We admire those who pull themselves up by their bootstraps.

NOBODY CAN PULL THEMSELVES UP BY THEIR BOOTSTRAPS.

But did you know that is a physical impossibility? Nobody can pull themselves up by their bootstraps. Try it sometime. Sit on the floor, put on your shoes, and then try to pull yourself up using only your shoestrings.

It's impossible.

In the room where I change on Sunday mornings, a prayer hangs on the wall. It begins with the words, "Lord God, you have appointed me as a bishop and pastor in your church, but you see how unsuited I am to meet such a great and difficult task. Without your help, I would have ruined it all long ago."

344

Who gave you your mind, hands, talents, and abilities? Who allowed you to be born in this land of opportunity? Do you really think the reason we have so much in this country is because we are somehow better, smarter, or more hard-working than the people in third-world countries?

Everything we have and everything we are is a gift of God's grace. If it were left up to us, we would have ruined it long ago. We don't deserve what we have. In fact, there is only one thing any of us deserves.

We deserve hell.

We deserve God's eternal anger for our pride and materialism, our lust and drunkenness, our selfishness and doubt.

Yet in his amazing grace God came to this earth as a man and that man suffered God's punishment for every mistake we've ever made. Jesus paid for our sins. Jesus won heaven for us. We say those words so easily as Christians, but then often we add a *but*.

But I chose him. But I invited him into my heart. But I did my part. But I still have to be a good person to go to heaven. But I have to give my offerings. But I have to make up for the bad I've done. But I have to earn it.

That's just another form of Jimmy Stewart's prayer. Everything we have and everything we are is a gift of God's grace which we haven't earned or deserve. Everything we do now is simply our response—our thank you—for the forgiveness and heaven Jesus won for us and for all the other blessings God generously showers on us every day.

Praise God from whom all blessings flow.

Today I am thankful for/that _____

_____

Oh give thanks to the Lord, for he is good and his mercy endures forever. Amen.

DAY 181
PRACTICE

Let us consider how we may spur one another
on toward love and good deeds, not giving up
meeting together, as some are in the habit of
doing, but encouraging one another—and all
the more as you see the Day approaching.

HEBREWS 10:24,25

◆

As I have waded into the waters of youth soccer coaching, one of the biggest and most frustrating challenges for me are the practices. I love working with the kids, but scheduling practices is difficult. Trying to find an open field and work around everybody's schedules is almost impossible.

Then you have the parents who don't bring their kids to practice because Johnny was too tired from playing Fortnite or because they really wanted to stay home and watch a movie.

Many people underestimate the importance of practice. Like Allen Iverson once famously quipped, "It's just practice!"

But practice is important. It gets you in shape for the games. It builds up your endurance and strength. Even more important, you go through the motions of what you will do in the games. You repeat the movements and actions again and again so that when the game comes, you don't have to think about it. You naturally react and do what you are supposed to do without hesitation.

Athletes who don't practice regularly rarely succeed in games.

In a very real way, our worship on Sunday mornings as Christians is soccer practice for our faith. First and foremost, as we hear God's Word, as we receive the sacrament, as we worship together, God feeds our faith and builds up our spiritual muscles.

But it's more than that. Traditional Christian worship services are intentionally designed as a microcosm of what God wants us doing during the week. God wants us to be in constant conversation with him—talking to him in prayer and listening to him speak to us through his Word. God wants us as Christians to spend time every single day in prayer and Bible study.

Our Sunday morning worship is where we practice that conversation with God. In our worship, we speak to God in our prayers and hymns. He speaks to us in his Word and sacraments. What we do on Sunday morning in church feeds our faith as it helps us practice what God wants us to do in our daily lives.

In fact, one other important thing many churches do on Sunday morning is to stand up and say together one of the three traditional Christian Creeds. We say, "I believe in God the Father Almighty . . . and in Jesus Christ, his only Son . . . and in the Holy Spirit, the Lord and Giver of life." We say as Christians, "This is what we believe about God and what he did for us."

We do that on Sunday, in part, so that when game time comes—when our faith is challenged, when we are asked to say what we believe—we can do so. If we grow up saying a creed every Sunday morning, then when somebody asks us what we believe about God, we have practiced our answer and know what to say.

So don't underestimate the importance of practice. We need to go to church every week to keep our faith in good shape and to prepare us to put our faith in practice in our everyday lives.

But also understand that going to church is only a part of being a Christian. Never think that simply going to church on Sunday is what it means to be a Christian. That's not the game. Going to church helps prepare us for the game—to live our lives of faith during the week. To go to church and then not live what we practiced there is like going to soccer practice, but never going to the games.

GOING TO CHURCH IS ONLY A PART OF BEING A CHRISTIAN.

Living our faith is the goal, but never underestimate the importance of practice.

Today I am thankful for/that _____

_____

Lord, forgive me for the many times I have skipped "practice" and not worshiped you as you deserve. Help me to make the most of every opportunity to worship you with my fellow believers and then live what I learn from you. Amen.

DAY 182
STAND UP, STAND UP FOR JESUS

Stand firm then, with the belt of truth
buckled around your waist.

EPHESIANS 6:14

◆

I announced the hymn and sat down. The organist began to play as I paged through my hymnal to find the number. When I looked up, it had started.

The first one to stand up didn't surprise me. He has always marched to the beat of his own drum. But then another and another. Soon I joined them.

By the end of the first stanza, the entire congregation was on its feet with smiles on their faces. In fact, that was the last time we ever began the hymn "Stand Up, Stand Up for Jesus" sitting down.

It's just not a sit-down hymn.

"Stand Up, Stand Up for Jesus" was written in 1858 by a Presbyterian pastor and abolitionist named George Duffield. The hymn was inspired by a fellow pastor and abolitionist named Dudley A. Tyng.

Tyng was a young, fiery Episcopalian preacher from Pennsylvania who had recently been removed from his parish due to his abolitionist rhetoric. After his dismissal, he set out to begin an evangelical revival in his home state.

In March of 1858, Tyng gave a rousing sermon to over 5,000 men at a YMCA gathering. Reportedly over 1,000 men came to faith in Jesus that very night. Duffield was in attendance.

Only days later, Tyng was working in the study of his country home when he decided to take a break. He walked out to the barn where a mule was at work running a horse-powered machine to shell corn. Tyng patted the mule on the neck, but the sleeve of his silk study gown got caught in the cogs of the wheel. His arm was torn from its socket.

The wound became mortal and Tyng died less than a week later.

At his funeral, the preacher shared with those in attendance—including George Duffield—Tyng's dying words. Speaking to his father, Tyng

348

reportedly said, "Stand up for Jesus, Father, stand up for Jesus, and tell my brethren wherever you meet them to stand up for Jesus."

Inspired by Tyng's last words, Duffield wrote a sermon the following Sunday based on Ephesians 6:14: "Stand firm then, with the belt of truth buckled around your waist." The sermon ended with an original poem, which became the hymn we now know as "Stand Up, Stand Up for Jesus."

> *Stand up, stand up for Jesus, Ye soldiers of the cross!*
> *Lift high his royal banner; It must not suffer loss.*
> *From vict'ry unto vict'ry His army shall he lead*
> *Till ev'ry foe is vanquished And Christ is Lord indeed.* (CW 474:1)

We are at war. The devil and his demons whisper in our ears. Our own sinful selfishness pulls and pushes against our hearts. Our world pressures us to timidly sit in silence as it mocks our God.

But how can we still sit down? He has won the victory for us. He forgives us when we fail. He gives us the crown of victory we do not deserve. Besides, he gives us the strength to stand and overcome any and every temptation.

STAND UP—NOT JUST IN THE COMFORTABLE CONFINES OF OUR CHURCH.

So let's stand up—not just in the comfortable confines of our church—but also out there in the trenches. Stand up and let your voice be heard. Stand up and live a life which stands out. Stand up to the devil and the world and all their lies.

Stand up, stand up for Jesus!

Today I am thankful for/that _____

Dear Jesus, take away my fears and give me the courage to stand up for you every day of my life. Amen.

DAY 183
THINGS AREN'T ALWAYS WHAT THEY SEEM

"The beggar died and the angels carried him to
Abraham's side. The rich man also died and was
buried. In Hades, . . . he was in torment."

LUKE 16:22,23

◆

On April 11, 2009, a frumpy-looking, middle-aged woman walked onto the stage of the TV show *Britain's Got Talent*. The audience—especially snarky judge Simon Cowell—was prepared for what most likely was going to be an awkward, off-key, goofy performance.

But then the woman began to sing. She sang "I Dreamed a Dream" from the musical *Les Misérables*. Her voice was powerful, beautiful, stirring. The crowd went nuts. The entire auditorium, including Simon Cowell, gave her a standing ovation.

The woman's name was Susan Boyle. Before her performance, she had only sung at her local church and in karaoke bars. Within nine days, her performance had garnered over 100 million views on YouTube. Her first CD became the best-selling debut album in the history of Great Britain. Things aren't always what they seem.

Jesus once told the story of a poor bum named Lazarus. He had nothing. He lived like an animal. He ate from other people's garbage. He was covered in painful sores which were licked by neighborhood dogs as he slept on the street.

He was a loser.

The other man in Jesus' story lived in a mansion. He was rich. He was successful. He was popular.

He was a winner.

Then both men died. Death is the great equalizer. Money and success mean nothing to death. You and I will leave this world with exactly as much money as Bill Gates.

Jesus tells us that poor Lazarus went to heaven—not because he was poor, but because he trusted in God his Savior. The rich man went to hell—not because he was rich, but because money and success had become his god.

The loser was actually a winner. The winner was actually a loser. Things aren't always what they seem.

DO YOU EVER FEEL LIKE A LOSER?

Do you ever feel like a loser? Maybe your life hasn't turned out the way you wanted it to. Maybe you have failed as a parent or in your marriage or career. Maybe people pick on you because you're different or weird. We all have moments in our lives when we feel like losers.

But things aren't always what they seem. Just look at Jesus. He was literally born in a barn. He lived a poor, humble life. He was beaten and spit upon. Soldiers whipped him. People jeered. He died the most painful and humiliating death the Romans could come up with. According to our world's standards, Jesus was a loser.

Yet he didn't lose. He didn't stay dead, did he? Jesus wasn't just the simple son of a poor carpenter. He was and is the all-powerful, eternal Son of God. He allowed himself to be treated like a loser in our place. He lost everything for us, including his life. But then he won the victory over sin and death by rising from the dead.

Because of Jesus you are forgiven. Because of Jesus you are rich. Because of Jesus you are going to live forever in the happiness of heaven.

No matter how hard your life gets, no matter how badly you mess up, no matter how people look at you or treat you, you are not nor will you ever be a loser. It's all because of Jesus.

Things aren't always what they seem.

Today I am thankful for/that _____

_____

Dear Jesus, thank you for proving that things aren't always what they seem. When I feel like a loser, remind me of the victory that is waiting for me because of your great love and sacrifice. Amen.

DAY 184
GOD'S LAST NAME

"You shall not misuse the name of the LORD your God."

EXODUS 20:7

◆

A fellow pastor recently told me about a little boy who goes to their church's preschool. Let's call him Pete. Pete's teachers have struggled with him because of the language he uses. Pete has grown up in an environment where f-bombs and cursing are a part of the everyday vernacular.

To their credit, Pete's teachers have taught him to not use God's name in vain—so much so that Pete began to think he could never say the word "God."

"No," one teacher told him. "There are lots of good ways to use God's name. You can use God's name to pray to him and to praise him."

"Oh," Pete replied, "so I just shouldn't use God's last name then?"

The teacher was confused. "What's God's last name, Pete?"

"Dammit."

Of all the commandments, the Second Commandment seems to be the most nitpicky. Chiseled on the stone tablets we find God's great moral standards. You shall not murder. You shall not commit adultery. You shall not steal.

Sins against such commandments hurt other people, destroy marriages, and tear apart the fabric of society. But what's the big deal about using God's name without thinking? How did OMG become equivalent to murder and adultery?

THE WAY WE USE GOD'S NAME REVEALS OUR INNER ATTITUDES TOWARD HIM.

What we often fail to see is that the way we use God's name reveals our inner attitudes toward him. When we mindlessly use his name to curse or swear—when we flippantly say, "Oh my God" throughout the day—we are revealing a lack of awe for God in our hearts.

We are forgetting that he is the all-powerful God who created every last atom of our universe. He is the eternal God who has always existed. He is the God who fills all things, who sees all things, who knows all things.

He is the God who could squash you like a bug.

When we use God's name vainly, disrespectfully, or flippantly, we are showing that in our hearts and minds he is a small God. Saying or typing OMG doesn't seem like a big deal compared to other sins, but it makes God angry. It deserves his eternal punishment in hell.

Thankfully, the eternal, all-powerful God who fills all things is also a God of love. In fact, he loved you so much he gave up the glories of heaven to be born in a barn. He loved you so much he suffered his own terrible fury for every time you treated him as small.

Jesus suffered God's punishment for you. God forgives you for every time you've broken the second and all the rest of his commandments. He saved you from the fires of hell. Who God is and what he has done for you demand and deserve your respect.

So speak God's name with deep reverence and holy joy. Show your children what it means to have a loving respect for God. Kick the habit of using God's name as filler in your everyday conversations.

And for Pete's sake, stop using God's last name.

Today I am thankful for/that _____

---

*Lord, thank you for revealing yourself to us
in your names. Forgive me for the times I
have used your name disrespectfully.
Help me to use your name the way
you want it to be used—
to pray, praise, and give
you thanks. Amen.*

DAY 185
COMFORTABLE PEWS

The time will come when people will not put up
with sound doctrine. Instead, to suit their own
desires, they will gather around them a great
number of teachers to say what their
itching ears want to hear.

2 TIMOTHY 4:3

❖

A while back I was talking with a member about the new campus we are hoping to have in a neighboring town. We were talking about what kind of seating our new church would have—whether pews, chairs, or stadium seating.

"If we have pews," he said, "just make sure they have cushions. Wooden pews aren't very comfortable."

"We don't want them too comfortable," I thought as visions of members snoozing during my sermon ran through my mind.

Are you comfortable in your church?

The stated goal of many churches is to make you as comfortable as possible by providing cushy seats, easy parking, friendly staff, and greeters at every door. Some have cafés offering specialty coffee and treats you can take with you into the sanctuary. Everything you need to know and do is found on the large, conveniently located screens. They even take your kids to separate rooms during the service so you can relax and listen.

Your comfort is their goal.

That raises the question: Does church exist to make you feel comfortable? If you look at Jesus' ministry, his goal definitely wasn't to make people feel comfortable. He would challenge their preconceived ideas. He would confront their sins. He would put people on the spot.

Jesus frequently had uncomfortable conversations with his enemies, with total strangers, and even with his own disciples.

When making people feel comfortable in church becomes our primary goal, we are tempted to avoid those uncomfortable conversations—to not talk about sin, to not challenge people's prejudices, to not mention the parts of the Bible which people today find offensive.

God's purpose for his church is not to make people feel comfortable. God's purpose for his church is that it preach the whole truth of his Word whether it makes people comfortable or not. God has called his church to convict us of our sins and comfort us with his promises of forgiveness and heaven through faith in Jesus.

THE CHURCH DOES NOT EXIST TO MAKE YOU FEEL COMFORTABLE.

The church does not exist to make you feel comfortable. To be clear, that does not mean it's a sin to have comfy cushions in your church. Every Christian congregation should try to make visitors feel welcome and comfortable. I honestly hope you feel comfortable in your home church.

Just not too comfortable.

If you never feel the uncomfortable sting of the law in your church—if your preacher never makes you squirm uncomfortably in your seat—that's a problem. Only by feeling the uncomfortable sting of the law are we able to appreciate the comforting salve of the gospel.

The purpose of church is not to make you feel comfortable, but to comfort you with God's promises. That's an important distinction we all need to remember.

Today I am thankful for/that _____

_____

Lord, help me always to remember that my church doesn't exist to make me feel comfortable. Thank you for confronting me with the uncomfortable truth of my sins and for the comforting message of your forgiveness in Christ. Amen.

DAY 186
YOUR FIRST-DITCH EFFORT

"Call on me in the day of trouble; I will deliver
you, and you will honor me."

PSALM 50:15

◆

"Well, I guess the only thing we can do now is pray." How many times haven't we heard or spoken those words? I heard them recently from a friend who was sitting with her dying mother.

As I sat with her and her mother, I thought about what she said. "Well, I guess the only thing we can do now is pray." As we say those words, it almost sounds like prayer is what you do when everything else has failed—the last-ditch effort.

Prayer should never be a last-ditch effort. Prayer is our first-ditch effort. As soon as trouble strikes, God wants us to pray to him. "Call on me in the day of trouble," he tells us, "I will deliver you and you will honor me."

Jesus himself invites us to pray with confidence, "Ask and it will be given to you; seek and you will find; knock and the door will be opened to you. For everyone who asks receives; the one who seeks finds; and to the one who knocks, the door will be opened" (Matthew 7:7,8). Jesus' half-brother James tells us, "Is anyone among you in trouble? Let them pray. . . . The prayer of a righteous person is powerful and effective" (James 5:13,16).

God hears our prayers. God answers our prayers. Prayer has power because the all-powerful God is on the other end of the line.

SADLY WE OFTEN SEE PRAYER AS A CRAPSHOOT.

Sadly we often see prayer as a crapshoot—maybe it will work and maybe it won't. The truth is that prayer always works. It just doesn't always work the way we want it to. When you ask God for something in prayer, he has three ways of answering: "Yes," "No," or "Wait."

Sometimes God says, "Yes." You get the raise you wanted. Your daughter's cancer goes away. Your boyfriend pops the question. Sometimes God gives us exactly what we are asking for.

But sometimes God says, "No." You may pray real hard or have faith that God is going to do something for you, but that doesn't mean he is going to do it. It's not because God doesn't love you. It's because he does love you that he says, "No."

My son loves Doritos. He calls them "red chips." He asks for them 24 hours a day, seven days a week. As loving parents, we often say, "No." It's not good for him to eat Doritos 24/7.

God can see the future. He knows what is good for us and what isn't. Our Father knows best, so trust him when he says, "No." What you asked for wasn't good for you. He's got something better waiting for you.

Understand, though, sometimes God isn't saying, "No." Sometimes he is saying, "Wait." Look back at Psalm 50:15. God invites us to call upon him in the day of trouble. He promises to deliver us, but he doesn't say *when* he will deliver us. You may have to suffer for a while. God may be teaching you patience. But he will deliver us from all our problems, if not here, then when he takes us to heaven.

So pray. Don't wait until everything else has failed. Talk to God every day and trust that he will answer you for your good.

Make prayer your first-ditch effort.

Today I am thankful for/that _____

_____

Heavenly Father, thank you for always listening
and always answering me for my good.
Help me to always turn to you first and
to trust you most. Amen.

DAY 187
GOD IS WATCHING

The eyes of the Lᴏʀᴅ are everywhere, keeping
watch on the wicked and the good.

PROVERBS 15:3

◆

On August 25, 2010, I signed up for Facebook. Over the years, my Facebook page has been a wonderful communication tool for our church and my ministry.

There is one problem, though. Sometimes people forget that they have invited their pastor to see what they are writing. Every so often, they write something they shouldn't or use bad language. When that happens, I usually send them a private message with a little reminder: "You know I am reading this, right?"

One young lady once wrote me back, "Sorry, pastor. I forgot you were watching."

So often in our lives, we forget that *God* is watching. God is watching when you are sitting in the backseat of your boyfriend's car. God is watching when you sit alone at your house drinking yourself unconscious. God is watching as you gaze at those images on the computer screen.

God is watching.

He sees all you do. You can't hide it or deny it. But, thankfully, you can repent of it. You can ask God to forgive your "secret sins" with the confidence that he has and will always forgive you because of Jesus.

If you ever saw the movie *The Passion of the Christ,* you probably grimaced at the violent torments which Jesus suffered on the day he died. What no human eye could see, however, was what our Savior suffered at the hand of God the Father. On that cross, God punished his Son for all sins of all people of all time, including all of your secret sins that no one else can see. God sees them. He knows what you have done, yet he forgives you because of Jesus.

God is watching. Remember that next time you are alone with your boyfriend. Remember that next time you sit down at your computer. Remember that as you crack open your first beer after work. God is watching. Hopefully that truth will serve as a helpful reminder as you struggle against your secret sins.

THE FACT THAT GOD IS WATCHING IS ALSO A GREAT COMFORT.

But the fact that God is watching is also a great comfort. God is watching over you.

When you feel alone or afraid, find peace in the fact that your heavenly Father is an ever-present help in times of trouble. When you are in danger or in doubt, be still and know that your Savior God is there. Wherever you go, whatever you do, the all-powerful Lord of the universe is watching over you. As the old gospel hymn joyfully confesses, "My constant friend is he: His eye is on the sparrow, and I know he watches me." What a wonderful comfort it is to know that God is watching!

My church maintains an active Facebook page. If you have a chance, find us on Facebook (Redeemer Lutheran Church, Edna, Texas). I would love to add you to our group of friends. But if you choose me as your friend on Facebook, don't forget I will be watching.

Even more importantly, never ever forget that God is watching!

Today I am thankful for/that _____

_____

Lord, help me to never forget that you are always watching me. Amen.

DAY 188
GOD LISTENS

**She named him Samuel, saying, "Because
I asked the LORD for him."**

1 SAMUEL 1:20

❖

I have some friends who are trying to come up with a name for their baby
boy. According to the website BabyCenter.com, the most popular boy
names in 2020 are Liam, Noah, and Ethan. One hundred years ago, the
most popular names were John, William, and James.

Times have changed.

Do you know anybody who is about to have a baby boy? Are you looking
at lists of baby names? If you are, allow me to make a suggestion: Samuel.

In the Old Testament centuries before Jesus was born, decades before any
kings ruled over Israel or the temple was built, a Jewish man took his
family to worship at the tabernacle in Shiloh. The tabernacle was the tent
they used as a temporary temple.

The man's name was Elkanah. He had two wives. Their names were
Hannah and Peninnah. Peninnah had numerous children, but Hannah had
none. She was barren. In those days, being barren was a great shame.
Peninnah mocked her. Hannah's heart ached.

One evening, Hannah ran to the courtyard just outside of the tabernacle.
She fell on her knees and poured out her heart to God. Tears flowed down
her face as she prayed for a son. Her emotions poured out so passionately
that the priest Eli thought she was drunk. He yelled at her for being drunk
in the tabernacle.

"I'm not drunk," Hannah told him. "I am a woman who is deeply troubled.
I was pouring out my soul to the Lord."

"Go in peace," Eli told her, "and may the God of Israel grant you what you
have asked of him."

Soon after, Hannah became pregnant. She gave birth to a son. She named
him Samuel. The name Samuel means, "God listens."

God listens. God heard Hannah's prayer. He gave her the son she so
passionately prayed for.

God listens to you. Twenty-four hours a day, seven days a week, God is on call. He always hears you. He's always listening. He always answers for your good.

Sometimes, though, it seems like he's not listening. Sometimes we pray to God just as passionately as Hannah did, but nothing happens. Where is God at those times? Why isn't he listening?

The truth is that he is listening. He hears you. Not only does he hear you, but he also answers you. He just doesn't always say, "Yes."

HE HEARS YOU. . . . HE JUST DOESN'T ALWAYS SAY, "YES."

God sometimes says, "No." God sometimes says, "Not yet." Though God always listens, he doesn't always give us what we ask for because what we ask for isn't always for our good.

Father knows best. What would happen to your children if you gave them everything they asked for? They would become spoiled. Some of the things they asked for would eventually hurt them. Like a loving dad, God sometimes says, "No."

But he is always listening.

When you feel alone, when you are frightened, when you don't know what to do or where to turn, you can talk to him. He will comfort you with his promises. He will answer you for your good.

He will always hear you, because God listens.

Today I am thankful for/that _____

Dear Lord, thank you for always listening to and answering my prayers for my good. Amen.

DAY 189
MASKS

"People look at the outward appearance,
but the LORD looks at the heart."

1 SAMUEL 16:7

❖

My children don't have Halloween costumes yet. I'm not worried. This isn't the first year we've waited until the eleventh hour. God has blessed me with a creative and resourceful wife who works well under pressure.

I'm confident that by Halloween they will have fun and imaginative costumes for trick-or-treating.

For over 500 years, people have disguised themselves on Halloween. Because the Christian church has traditionally celebrated November 1 as All Saints' Day (All Hallows' Day in Old English), the night before—All Hallows' Eve—was often considered a night when evil spirits roamed and ruled.

People would disguise themselves to fool the evil spirits. They would wear costumes and hide behind masks.

Whether you dress up for Halloween or not, we all wear masks. Our public persona is not always who we really are. When we are dating, we clean ourselves up. We try to be the person we think the other person wants us to be. When we are in school we try to be like everyone else. When we go to church, we try to appear to be good Christian people.

Behind our carefully constructed masks, however, we are a mess. Behind the masks lie the ugly parts of us we don't let others see. Behind the masks are hidden the dirty, secret sins nobody else knows about.

The masks we wear can fool other people. They can fool your friends. They can fool your family. They can even fool your wife. But they can't fool God.

God once told the prophet Samuel, "People look at the outward appearance, but the LORD looks at the heart."

God sees behind your masks. He understands who you really are. He knows every dirty secret and every hidden sin.

You can't hide who you are or what you've done from God. You can repent of it, though. You can take off your mask and stand before God just as you are—naked and ugly and stained—knowing he has and will always forgive you because of Jesus.

YOU DON'T HAVE TO PRETEND WITH GOD.

You don't have to pretend with God. He loves you so much he suffered the horror of the cross—the punishment of hell we deserve for all the dirty sins we try so hard to hide.

He loves you despite the ugliness you masterfully hide behind your masks. He loves you and accepts you just as you are because of Jesus.

So stop pretending. Take off your mask. Stand before God just as you are—naked and ugly and stained. Tell him your shame and hurt and regret. Tell him you're sorry.

Then trust in his all-encompassing forgiveness. Trust that he loves you just as you are. You don't have to be somebody else for God to love you.

You don't have to hide behind a mask.

Today I am thankful for/that _____

_____

Lord, you know me better than I know myself. Thank you for forgiving me all the bad that I am and have done. Thank you for accepting me and loving me just as I am. Amen.

363

DAY 190
THE TODDLER'S TOP TEN RULES FOR SHARING

**You will be enriched in every way so that you can
be generous on every occasion.**

2 CORINTHIANS 9:11

❖

A fellow pastor recently shared with me what he called "The Toddler's Top Ten Rules for Sharing."

1. If I like it, it's mine.

2. If it's in my hand, it's mine.

3. If I can take it from you, it's mine.

4. If I had it a little while ago, it's still mine.

5. If it's mine, it must never appear to be yours in any way.

6. If I'm doing or building something, all the pieces are mine.

7. If it looks just like mine, it's mine.

8. If I saw it first, it's mine.

9. If you are playing with something and put it down, it automatically becomes mine.

10. If it's broken, it's yours.

We laugh, but do we ever really outgrow our childish selfishness? We like to think we're generous people. We help the less fortunate. We give to Goodwill.

But what do we give to Goodwill? We give them the broken old stuff we don't want anymore. We give them the things which take up space in our closets and garages. Then we pat ourselves on the back for our prodigious generosity.

When was the last time you went to the store and bought new clothes or furniture to give to Goodwill? When was the last time you gave more than what was left over?

Last weekend I went to our local Relay for Life and bought a bunch of raffle tickets. I felt pretty good about myself as I carefully read through the list of prizes I could possibly win. Is that what it means to be generous?

Don't get me wrong. I hope you give your hand-me-downs to Goodwill. I hope you support charities like the Relay for Life by buying raffle tickets. But don't think that makes you Mother Teresa.

Living in this country, we are wealthier than over 90% of the world. Experts estimate that roughly 100 billion people have lived throughout the course of history. You are richer than just about every single one of them. Think about it. Even the wealthiest people who lived in past centuries didn't enjoy the comforts and luxuries modern technology affords us today.

God has blessed us by allowing us to be numbered among the richest people who have ever lived. With that wealth, however, comes a tremendous temptation. The more we have, the more we want. The more we have, the more tightly we hold on to it. The more we have, the less we tend to share.

If you think you don't struggle with selfishness or materialism, I will say to you what Jesus once said to a wealthy man who had deluded himself into thinking he had lived a perfect life of love: Sell everything you have and give it to the poor. Then come talk to me.

Yeah. That's what I thought.

THANKFULLY WE HAVE A GENEROUS GOD.

Thankfully we have a generous God who gave up the riches and opulence of heaven to be born in a barn. Jesus literally gave until it hurt. He sacrificed everything for us. He suffered God's anger for our selfishness, for our materialism—for all the times we held onto our toys and cried, "It's mine."

Because he did, we are forgiven forever. We have a home waiting for us in heaven where the streets are paved with gold and the gates are made of pearl.

Seeing God's overwhelming generosity to you, knowing you have the riches of heaven waiting for you, and understanding you can't take any of this with you when you die, be truly generous.

Give it all away. Give until it hurts. Give as God has given to you.

Today I am thankful for/that _____

_____

Oh Giver of all good things, give me a generous heart which wants to give for others as you have given to me. Amen.

DAY 191
KEEP CALM

"Be still, and know that I am God."

PSALM 46:10

◆

If you spend any time on social media, you've probably seen the bright red pictures with a white crown on top which say, "Keep Calm." For a while, the craze on social media was to make up your own "Keep Calm" memes. "Keep Calm and Fake a British Accent." "Keep Calm and Grow a Beard." "Keep Calm and Eat Bacon."

What you might not know is that the "Keep Calm" meme was around long before Instagram, Facebook, Twitter, or even the internet. In fact, it was around before computers were even invented. Before "Keep Calm" was a meme, it was a poster.

In the summer of 1939, Great Britain prepared for imminent war with Germany. Everyone knew what that meant. England would soon be bombed. One minute the sun could be shining; the next, your world could fall apart around you.

At a time of such uncertainty, the British Ministry of Information released a series of posters. The posters were bright red. A simple, white Tudor crown sat above bold letters which read, "Keep Calm and Carry On."

In the end, however, the "Keep Calm" posters were rarely used and did little to encourage a terrified nation.

Not unlike the days before and during World War II, we live in a time of uncertainty. Instead of the Nazis, for us it's terrorists. Instead of aerial bombs, it's suicide bombers on subways and massacres in nightclubs. Great Britain has left the European Union, sending financial markets into a tailspin. Mexico is a mess of corruption. The coming presidential election in this country has the world on edge.

If there is one thing 9/11 and the subsequent terrorist attacks have taught us, it's that one minute the sun can be shining and the next your world could fall apart around you.

Find a quiet moment today and read Psalm 46. It describes what many of us have felt at one time or another in our lives—the world crumbling

366

around us. At such times of chaos and uncertainty, our God gives us a simple message: "Be still, and know that I am God."

Unlike the "Keep Calm" posters of World War II, God's promises are able to give us strength and peace even as the world falls apart around us. You'll notice the "Keep Calm" posters gave no reason for encouragement or calm. They simply said, "Keep Calm and Carry On."

WE HAVE A REASON TO KEEP CALM.

We have a reason to keep calm—to be still. Our God is in control. God is our refuge and strength, an ever-present help in trouble. His powerful promises are a stream of water which refreshes our souls. Though evil men and women fight against him and us, they can't win.

In fact, if you look carefully at Psalm 46, the words, "Be still and know that I am God" are actually directed at his enemies. When he says, "Stop," they have to stop. He is in control.

For now, God allows his enemies to rage against him and us. At times, the world seems to be falling apart around us. But we don't have to be afraid. Jesus has won for us a home in heaven. God will be our mighty fortress forever.

So keep calm. Be still. Know that he is God.

Today I am thankful for/that _____

_____

Heavenly Father, as I see chaos in the world around me, help me to keep calm and trust that you are God and Lord of all. Amen.

DAY 192
AMERICA'S CRISIS OF CONTEMPT

Get rid of all bitterness, rage and anger, brawling and
slander, along with every form of malice. Be kind and
compassionate to one another, forgiving each
other, just as in Christ God forgave you.

EPHESIANS 4:31,32

✦

I had never witnessed a State of the Union address quite like it. The president
failed to shake the hand of the Speaker of the House. Whether you believe it
was on purpose or not depends on your particular political leanings.

There was no ambiguity to the Speaker's actions, however. As the President
of the United States finished his speech, she tore it up in front of Congress
and a flabbergasted nation.

The actions of our leaders on February 4, 2020, revealed more clearly the
state of our Union than any words spoken by the president that night. The
divide in our nation is more bitter and visceral than during just about any
other period in our history, save the Civil War.

The problem, however, is not that we disagree.

The problem is how we disagree.

**THE PROBLEM IS
HOW WE DISAGREE.**
They say there are two topics which you should always
avoid at parties: religion and politics. The reason is
simple. They generally end in arguments. Both topics
reveal our deepest-held values. When others disagree
with those values or challenge them, we feel our belief system being
attacked. We feel the need to defend what we consider to be absolute truth.

Disagreeing about politics and religion is nothing new. Arguing about
politics and religion is nothing new. But our country and culture have
taken them to a whole new level. In days gone by, politicians at least
attempted to show a semblance of statesmanship and decorum.

If the 2020 State of the Union was any indicator, decorum is now a thing
of the past.

I honestly have no platform or opportunity to change or even influence the
behavior of the leaders of our country, though I pray for them often.

I do, however, have this platform to speak to you, dear reader.

If we are going to fix America's crisis of contempt, it begins with individuals. Dare I say it begins with us as Christians. We have Jesus' command to love our enemies. God wants us to forgive as he has forgiven us. Jesus wants me to love even the worst of sinners as much as he has loved me (the worst of sinners).

Love does not mean we need to agree. Love does not mean we should remain silent. Love speaks, but it does so respectfully. It does so humbly. Love leads us to not respond in kind when someone refuses to shake our hand or rips up our speech. Love leads us to not judge other people's motives or hearts simply because they disagree with us politically.

The majority of liberals in our country are not stupid, weak Communists who are out to rob us of our freedoms. The majority of conservatives are not racist, gun-toting Nazis who have succumbed to the ravings of a lunatic.

We are Americans who disagree on how best to protect and provide for our nation. The differences are important. We should feel passionate about them. We should discuss them. But we must do so thoughtfully, carefully, lovingly.

Look into your heart. Have you let contempt and condescension sneak in? Read carefully what you post and share on Facebook. Remember it's not always what you say. It's how you say it.

Especially be aware of how you respond when others lash out against you. Consider how Jesus responded as they slapped him, spit on him, and nailed him to a piece of wood. He forgave them. He loved them. He died for them.

Contempt has no place in the heart of a Christian.

Today I am thankful for/that _____

_____

Merciful God, forgive me the anger and contempt hidden in my heart. Help me to love as you have loved me and forgive as you have forgiven me. Amen.

369

DAY 193
THE SAINT AND THE THUG

I do not do the good I want to do, but the evil I do not
want to do—this I keep on doing.

ROMANS 7:19

◆

A while back, *Sports Illustrated* ran an article about the shooting death of
NFL star Will Smith. Smith was a former defensive end for the New Orleans Saints, a key figure on their 2010 Super Bowl winning team. He was
beloved in New Orleans. He had a beautiful wife and three small children
and participated in a number of local charities.

On April 9, 2016, he was involved in a traffic accident which escalated into
violence. He was shot and killed by Cardell Hayes, a hulking African-American man from the other side of the tracks. Almost immediately Hayes
was labeled by the media as a "thug" who had ruthlessly killed one of New
Orleans' most dearly loved residents.

The *Sports Illustrated* article dug deeper, however. It turns out the Saint
was driving drunk that night with a blood-alcohol level nearly three times
the legal limit. He had a history of violence. According to some witnesses,
he was physically and verbally abusive to Hayes and threatened his life.

The thug, on the other hand, was described by many who knew him as a
gentle giant—a big teddy bear. He was quiet and unassuming. He coached
a local peewee football team. According to his friends and neighbors, he
was anything but a thug.

What happened on that New Orleans street on the night of April 9, 2016,
is difficult to ascertain. It depends on whose testimony you believe. What
we know for sure is that the truth is much more complicated than the story
the media originally reported.

It is an innate human tendency to pigeonhole people into two simple
categories: good guys and bad guys, saints and thugs. Your friends and
family are the good guys. The coworker who stole your promotion, your
gossipy ex-wife, and the presidential candidate you despise are the
bad guys.

Unfortunately, life isn't as black and white as Santa's naughty or nice
list. Most people don't fall neatly into one category or the other.

370

We're complicated.

If we're honest with ourselves, we are all thugs. We are all born completely sinful (Psalm 51:5). We are selfish. We are rude. We are blinded by anger and hate.

That is why Jesus came. He is the only true saint who ever lived. He came riding in on his white horse and gave his life for us, the bad guys. God came to this earth and suffered the punishment you deserve for your selfishness, anger, and hate.

WHEN GOD LOOKS AT YOU, HE NO LONGER SEES A DIRTY THUG.

Because he did, you are forgiven. When God looks at you, he no longer sees a dirty thug. He sees a saint washed forever in the blood of his Son and the waters of Holy Baptism. Martin Luther once famously quipped, "We are at the same time saints and sinners." Using *Sports Illustrated*'s terminology, we are at the same time saints and thugs. We are sinners who have messed everything up, but, because of the forgiveness Jesus won for us, God treats us as saints.

We are complicated. Now that we believe in Jesus, each of us has an inner struggle. Inside each of us lives a saint and a thug—our faith and our sinful nature. Though we are forgiven, we are not perfect. That's why we cling to our Savior and the promises of our baptisms.

In God's eyes, you are a saint, forever forgiven because of Jesus. Trust that. Fight against the thug living in your heart. Remember that struggle as you deal with other sinners. Forgive as God has forgiven you.

And don't be so quick to categorize people as all good or all bad—as either saints or thugs. Remember, we are complicated.

Today I am thankful for/that _____

_____

Merciful God, thank you for taking me—a dirty, sinful thug—and making me into your dear child. Help me to not be quick to judge others, but to remember that we are all sinners in need of your grace. Amen.

DAY 194
YOUR EXPIRATION DATE

"But God said to him, 'You fool! This very night
your life will be demanded from you.'"

LUKE 12:20

◆

I have never been as sick as I was that night. I got home from playing
basketball. I was hot and thirsty, so I opened up the fridge and grabbed
the jug of orange juice. I poured a big glass. It was ice cold. I downed the
whole glass without even tasting it.

That was a mistake.

Only after the cramps and vomiting started did I look at the expiration
date on the label. By then it was too late. I spent the night hugging the
toilet and at one point even prayed to die.

I learned an important lesson that night. Always be aware of the expiration date.

You have an expiration date. God has set a date and a time when you will
die. No matter how well you eat, no matter how much you exercise, no
matter how many steps you take on your Fitbit, you are going to die.

And you are not the only one with an expiration date. Unless Jesus
comes first, everybody you know is going to die. You will attend many
funerals in your life, the last of which will be your own.

One of the great lessons of life is to always be aware of our expiration
date. The problem is that God does not print our expiration dates on our
foreheads. He doesn't tell us how long we will live or when we will die.

Though he doesn't tell us what that day is, God assures us that each of
us has an expiration date. That truth changes how we live each day. It
reminds us of the importance of trusting in Jesus today. Tomorrow may
be too late.

Today—right now—ask God to forgive you and trust that he has
removed our sins because of Jesus. The prophet Isaiah encourages us to
seek the Lord while he may be found. After you die, it is too late. Trust
in him today.

Knowing you have an expiration date, don't put off until tomorrow what you can do today. Time is short. Tell your family you love them. Have the tough conversations. Tell everyone you can about Jesus today. Tomorrow may be too late. Tomorrow could be their expiration date. Tomorrow could be yours.

HELP ME TO LIVE EVERY DAY AS IF IT WERE MY LAST.

A wise pastor once told me, "Plan as if you were going to live one hundred years. Live each day as if it were your last."

Life on this earth is short. Never forget you have an expiration date.

Today I am thankful for/that _____

_____

Eternal God, my times are in your hands. Help me to live every day as if it were my last here on earth. Help me live every day with the confidence that I will live forever with you in heaven because of Jesus. Amen.

DAY 195
READY OR NOT

"Keep watch, because you do not know on what day your Lord will come."

MATTHEW 24:42

◆

The story is told about the principal of a private elementary school who had a problem. It seems her school was a mess. The classrooms were cluttered. The kids' desks were in disarray. So she decided to try something new.

She went into one of the classrooms at the beginning of the year and told the students she was going to come back sometime during the school year and give $100 to the child who had the cleanest desk on the day she came in.

The children squealed with excitement and quickly cleaned their desks. Every morning that first week, every student checked his or her desk to make sure it was in perfect condition.

The next week, however, a few of the boys got tired of cleaning their desks and returned to their old habits. By the third week, several students could be heard saying, "I don't think she's coming back. She just said that so we would keep our desks clean."

After two months, no one in the classroom bothered to keep their desks clean except for one little girl. Every day she quietly organized and straightened her desk. You can guess what happened. Toward the end of the school year, the principal suddenly showed up at the door.

The children quickly flung their desks open, frantically trying to clean them. But the principal told them to stop and stand next to their desks. It was too late. The little girl who always kept her desk clean won the $100. The rest of the children spent the remainder of the year complaining and making excuses about why they weren't ready.

Nearly two thousand years ago, Jesus said, "I am coming soon" (Revelation 22:20). He said he was coming to judge all people and to bring the end of the world. He said to be ready.

But that was two thousand years ago. Today the devil whispers in our ear, "He isn't really coming." Our world tells us, "It doesn't matter anyway. Everybody goes to heaven (except for maybe the really bad people)."

When Jesus comes, though, he will come bearing books. In those books is written everything we have ever thought, said, or done—everything. That is the evidence and the evidence is overwhelming. We are guilty. On judgment day, the guilty will be sent to hell.

But that is precisely why Jesus came the first time. That's why we find him on the Friday we call Good, bleeding, groaning, and dying on the cross. On that cross, God the Father punished his Son Jesus for our guilt. On that cross he suffered our hell—our guilty verdict.

Because Jesus did that, God now justifies us—literally, he declares us innocent through faith in Jesus. All those who believe in Jesus as their Savior will be declared innocent by God the Judge. All those who believe in Jesus are ready for judgment day.

WE STAY READY BY KEEPING OUR FAITH FED. The challenge is to stay ready—to stay alert like that little girl who kept her desk clean every day. We stay ready by keeping our faith fed. We stay ready by regularly going to church, reading our Bibles, and having family devotions. We stay ready by being in God's Word.

It doesn't matter whether you are 80 years old or 8, today could be your last day here on earth. Jesus is coming. Be ready.

Today I am thankful for/that _____

_____

Lord, thank you for giving me faith in your Son Jesus and preparing me for his coming. Help me to keep watch and stay ready. Amen.

DAY 196
WHEN GOD MAKES YOU WAIT

**"Call on me in the day of trouble; I will deliver
you, and you will honor me."**

PSALM 50:15

◆

"I'm done praying."

His words took me aback. As I stood with this lifelong member of our church, I couldn't believe what he was saying.

"I'm done praying," he repeated. "For 15 years, I've prayed that God would heal my wife of her terrible back problems and he hasn't answered. Doesn't he promise to hear our prayers? Doesn't he promise to answer and help us? I'm not praying anymore!"

The thing is, the man was right. God does promise to hear our prayers. He does promise to answer them. He does promise to free us from every hurt and heartache in our lives.

He just doesn't say when.

In Psalm 50, God promises, "Call on me in the day of trouble; I will deliver you, and you will honor me." Every day for 15 years, the man from my church called upon God to deliver his wife from her debilitating back pain, but nothing happened. In fact, it got worse.

Look more closely at the verse from Psalm 50. God invites us to call upon him—to pray to him—the very day, the very moment, we are in distress. He promises he will deliver us. But you'll notice he doesn't say when he will deliver us. He never promises to deliver us that very day.

Sometimes God makes us wait. At times he makes us wait to teach us patience. At times he makes us wait to test our trust in him. At times he makes us wait because he has plans and purposes for our suffering that we can't understand right now.

Sometimes God makes us wait a long time. Sometimes he makes us wait a lifetime. But you can be sure that one day he will deliver you.

You can be sure because Jesus came and suffered pain we can never imagine and which we will never know. He suffered the agony and punishment we deserve for all the times we were impatient or didn't trust God's plan for us—for all the times we doubted his love.

And because Jesus suffered our punishment, because he conquered sin and death for us, we have a home waiting for us in heaven where we will one day be free from every trial and tear. God will deliver you.

You just may have to wait until heaven.

I don't know if that sweet man from my church really understood what he was praying for. Yes, God could heal his wife of her pain here on earth, but it doesn't seem like he will do that.

Her deliverance from pain most likely won't come until she gets to heaven. If her husband wants her healed of her pain today, that may mean her going to heaven today. I don't know if he's ready for that. That may be why God hasn't delivered her yet.

YOU CAN BE SURE THAT ONE DAY HE WILL DELIVER YOU.

God knows what he is doing. He loves us and doesn't enjoy seeing us suffer, but he also knows what's best for us.

So trust him. Trust that he will keep his promises. Trust that he hears your prayers and will deliver you from every pain and problem.

Trust him, even when he makes you wait.

Today I am thankful for/that _____

_____

Lord, give me patience and give me peace as
I wait for you to keep your promises. Amen.

DAY 197
INSTRUCTIONS NOT INCLUDED

Fathers, do not exasperate your children; instead, bring
them up in the training and instruction of the Lord.

EPHESIANS 6:4

One of my favorite television shows as a boy was a short-lived series called, *The Greatest American Hero*. It was the story of a high school substitute teacher named Ralph Hinkley who had an encounter with aliens during a class field trip. The aliens gave Ralph a bright red suit which gave him superhuman powers to fight crime and protect the innocent. The suit even came with its own instruction manual.

The problem is Ralph lost the instructions. In every episode, he would somehow save the day as he clumsily tried to fly and accidentally discovered one of the suit's many powers.

As a father, I often feel like Ralph Hinkley. I seem to have misplaced my children's instruction manual. In fact, I'm not sure the hospital ever gave it to me.

Without the instruction manual, I have been forced to face numerous situations over the years for which I have felt totally unprepared.

It's three o'clock in the morning. The baby's crying with a fever. Do we take him to the emergency room? Do we wait until morning? How do we figure out what is wrong if he can't tell us?

Kids are picking on my daughter at school. She's crying. Do we talk to the teacher? Do we tell her to be tough and stand up for herself? How do we help her hurting heart?

At what age do we start talking with our kids about sex? What video games and TV shows are appropriate for them to watch? How long is too long to be on their electronics?

As a dad, I often find myself longing for an instruction manual—especially as my daughter now enters her teenage years. I don't understand adult women. Now I am going to have to face a teenage daughter with no instruction manual.

Some might say that the Bible is our instruction manual.

And there is some truth to that. God in his Word does give us divine direction in raising our children. He commands us to discipline our children. He tells us to be firm yet loving. He tells us to "bring them up in the training and instruction of the Lord."

Our job as parents first and foremost is to teach and show our children what it means to be loved by God and to set an example of loving him. Our primary job is to show them Jesus so they can believe in him and be saved.

The Bible helps us do just that.

THE BIBLE, HOWEVER, IS NOT AN INSTRUCTION MANUAL.

The Bible, however, is not an instruction manual. It does not give detailed instructions on every aspect of child rearing. Nowhere in the Bible does God tell you what to do when your baby runs a fever or a boy asks your daughter to the junior high dance. Rather, in his Word God gives us the help we need to love, forgive, and discipline our children.

As far as the other aspects of parenting, God hasn't left us alone. If, like me, you lost your instruction manual, don't try to be a superhero. Seek out mature Christian parents from your church or family. Talk to your pastor. You don't have to figure it all out yourself. Learn from the wisdom of those who have been there before.

And when you face the inevitable situations in which you feel overwhelmed and underprepared, take it to God in prayer. Trust in his amazing love for you and your children. He'll be with you. He forgives our mistakes as parents. He works through our imperfect parenting to give our children what they need.

That being said, if you happen to find my instruction manual, please send it to me as soon as possible. My daughter turns 13 in just a few months.

Today I am thankful for/that _____

_____

Heavenly Father, forgive me for my failings as a parent. Keep me in your Word and give me wisdom as I seek to guide my children and grandchildren toward you. Amen.

DAY 198
WHEN IT RAINS IT POURS

Consider it pure joy, my brothers and sisters, whenever you face trials of many kinds, because you know that the testing of your faith produces perseverance.

JAMES 1:2,3

Just as we were getting our home and lives in order after Hurricane Harvey in 2017, I saw the report on the news. Another tropical storm was forming in the Atlantic, headed for the Gulf.

The first thought that came to my mind was when it rains, it pours.

Often our lives sound like an old country song. Your wife leaves you. Your boss fires you. Your dog dies. How often do problems seem to pile up all at once? When it rains it pours.

And when it pours, we get frustrated. We throw up our arms and say, "What else can go wrong?" Then when something does go wrong, we mumble under our breath, "It figures." We look up at the dark, cloudy skies and say, "God, why are you doing this to me?"

Why do problems seem to pile up all at once in our lives? Honestly, sometimes it's because we put blinders on. When we are frustrated, when we are hurting, when things aren't working out the way we want them to, we tend to see only the problems in our lives. We start looking for the next thing to go wrong.

We fail to see the flood of blessings which God showers on us every day. We forget that we have air to breathe and food to eat. We look right past our homes and trucks and smartphones. We forget what life was like before air conditioning and flat screen TVs and John Deere riding lawn mowers.

Besides all that, God has blessed us with family and friends to stand by us in our joys and sorrows. We have churches and pastors to support us in good times and bad. Most importantly, we have God's Word—his promises of forgiveness and heaven in Jesus.

Problems often seem to pile up in our lives because we are only looking at the problems and we fail to see the tsunami of blessings God has poured on our lives.

At other times, though, when it rains, it really does pour. A number of people you love die in a short period of time. Your health deteriorates. You lose your home. From time to time, God does let the problems pour down, but he always does so for a reason.

Sometimes it's to test us and make us stronger. James, the brother of Jesus, once wrote, "Consider it pure joy, my brothers and sisters, whenever you face trials of many kinds, because you know that the testing of your faith produces perseverance." At other times God sows suffering in our lives because it will sprout wonderful blessings later on. The apostle Paul tells us, "In all things God works for the good of those who love him" (Romans 8:28). When God pours problems into our lives, it is always for our good.

EVERY DAY, IN GOOD TIMES AND BAD, GOD FLOODS OUR LIVES WITH BLESSINGS.

When it rains, it pours. Every day, in good times and bad, God floods our lives with blessings. Remember that truth the next time you're going through one of life's storms. Stop focusing on what's wrong in your life and recognize all that's right.

Then you'll be able to say with a smile on your face, "When it rains, it pours."

Today I am thankful for/that _____

_____

Lord, you know the storms that each of us face and the moments we feel overwhelmed. Help us to accept the storms, knowing that you have a good plan and purpose for them. Open our eyes to see that even in the middle of the storms you flood our lives with blessings. Amen.

DAY 199
ONE SIMPLE PHONE CALL

"You will be my witnesses in Jerusalem, and in all Judea and Samaria, and to the ends of the earth."

ACTS 1:8

We had been praying for him every Sunday for a number of weeks. His name was Cresencio. His family called him Don Chencho. Don Chencho was the grandfather of a member of our church. He lived in the tiny town of Acámbaro, Guanajuato, in Mexico.

Don Chencho had cancer. Every Sunday, his granddaughter would remind me to please say a prayer for him. And so we did.

But Don Chencho just kept getting sicker. Then one Sunday, the granddaughter pulled me aside before church and told me that, according to the doctors, it wouldn't be much longer. So we prayed for Don Chencho one last time.

The following Thursday night about 9:30 P.M, my phone rang. It was the granddaughter. She was in tears. I was expecting to hear that Don Chencho had passed away. Instead she asked me, "Pastor, would you call my grandfather?" I didn't know what to say. I had never met him or spoken with any of the family down in Mexico. I wondered how they would react to this gringo pastor they didn't know calling them all the way from Texas.

But the granddaughter told me that they lived in a small *rancho* and didn't have any pastor or priest that would go and visit them. The family was torn up. Don Chencho was restless. So at 10 P.M on a Thursday evening, the gringo pastor from Edna, Texas, called Don Chencho in Acámbaro, Mexico.

I spoke for a few minutes with his daughter, sharing with her the comfort that God gives in his Word. I said a prayer with her. Then she said, "Would you like to speak to my father? He won't be able to respond, but I'm sure he would appreciate it."

She put the phone to his ear. The cancer had so invaded his throat that he couldn't speak. So I spoke. I spoke about God's great love. I spoke about how God punished Jesus for our sins so that we could be forgiven. I told him how Jesus said, "I am the resurrection and the life, whoever believes in me will live, even though he dies." I told him he could trust Jesus' promise because God never lies. I told him that all those who believe in Jesus go to heaven. Then I said, "Goodbye." And that was it.

The next day, the granddaughter called me. "Pastor," she said, "I don't know what you told him, but last night my grandfather had the most peaceful night he has had in days. Oh, and pastor," she added, "before he went to sleep he told my mom, 'I can now go in peace. I know I am going to heaven because God has forgiven me.'"

The following Sunday evening at 9:30 P.M., my phone rang once again. God had called Don Chencho home to heaven. Don Chencho was already a Christian when I spoke with him over the phone. He believed in God, but he didn't seem to fully understand how God had forgiven him because of Jesus. One simple phone call changed all that.

Do you have anyone you could call? Do you have a grandpa or grandma, son or daughter, family member or friend who lives in another city or state or country? Do you know anyone who doesn't believe in Jesus or is struggling in their faith? You don't have to see them face to face to be able to share with them God's promises or tell them of the forgiveness we have in Jesus. All it takes is one simple phone call. So pick up the phone. Make that call.

SO PICK UP THE PHONE. MAKE THAT CALL.

One simple phone call can make all the difference.

Today I am thankful for/that _____

_____

Holy Spirit, give me the courage and love I need to talk about you with the people you have placed in my life. Amen.

DAY 200
FLIRTING WITH MOSES

For the law was given through Moses; grace and truth came through Jesus Christ.

JOHN 1:17

◆

I didn't realize I still had my nametag on. I had just finished a pastoral visit at the hospital. I had one more stop to make on the way home—the carwash.

When I got there, I started chatting with the guy who always checks me in. Suddenly he looked down.

"I didn't know you were a pastor," he said with a smirk.

"Yes, sir," I replied, not knowing what to expect next.

Dramatic pause.

"If you're flirting with Moses, you're cheating on Jesus," he declared with a nod as he got into my van and drove away.

I stood there for a moment like a deer caught in the headlights, surprised by his abruptness and the poignancy of his words.

If you're flirting with Moses, you're cheating on Jesus. Moses was the great law-giver. On Mount Sinai God gave him the laws which were to govern the lives and worship of the nation of Israel. God gave Moses a succinct summary of his moral law for all people—the Ten Commandments.

To flirt with Moses is to flirt with God's law. But what's so bad about that? God's law is good. In fact, it is perfect. God wants us to obey his law. He expects us to obey his law.

The problem is that in his law God expects and demands perfection. If you want to earn heaven by obeying the law, you have to obey every commandment every moment of every day. If you've broken just one little command, you've broken them all.

You can't and haven't obeyed God's law perfectly. You can't and haven't earned heaven or God's love.

Thankfully, God loved us anyway. Thankfully, he sent his Son Jesus to obey his law perfectly in our place. Thankfully, Jesus suffered the punishment of our disobedience for us on the cross.

In Jesus, we have forgiveness. In Jesus, we have heaven. He did it all for us in his amazing grace.

Though as Christians we love and believe in Jesus, we are often tempted to flirt with Moses. We flirt with Moses when we think that God loves us because we go to church. We flirt with Moses when we imply that Christianity is simply a set of rules to live by. We flirt with Moses when we depend even a little bit on ourselves and what we do instead of depending completely on Jesus for our salvation.

What we do as Christians is simply our thank you card to our God for his love and mercy. As Christians, we obey God's law not so we can go to heaven, but because we are going to heaven. In loving thanks for his forgiveness and all the blessings he showers on us day after day, we follow the moral guide God gave Moses on Mount Sinai.

WE DON'T MAKE HEAVEN DEPENDENT ON WHAT WE DO.

But we don't trust in that law to save us. We don't burden consciences by telling people that God will love them or forgive them only if they do certain things. We don't make heaven dependent on what we do. That's flirting with Moses.

And flirting with Moses is cheating on Jesus.

Today I am thankful for/that _____

_____

Dear Jesus, forgive me when in my pride I flirt with Moses. Help me to trust in you, and you alone, for my salvation. Amen.

DAY 201
A PRECIOUS LIFE

**You created my inmost being; you knit me together in
my mother's womb.**

PSALM 139:13

❖

Have you ever heard the name Norma McCorvey? She is known in the
history books by a different name: Jane Roe.

Jane Roe was the pseudonym given to her as the plaintiff in one of the most
controversial court decisions in the history of the United States: Roe v.
Wade. Her case against the State of Texas led to the legalization of abortion.

Norma McCorvey grew up in a broken home and nearly abject poverty in
Houston, Texas. Her first arrest was at the age of ten for robbery. She spent
her teenage years in and out of state institutions. She was sexually abused
by a family member. She had her first baby at the age of 16.

Soon afterward, Norma spiraled into alcoholism and began to identify as a
lesbian. Her mother ended up raising Norma's daughter. A couple of years
later, Norma again became pregnant but gave the baby up for adoption. In
1969, at the age of 21, she once more found herself pregnant.

Depressed and at the end of her rope, she decided she wanted to have an
abortion. Abortion, however, was illegal in Texas at the time. Her attempts
to get an illegal abortion failed because authorities had recently raided and
closed local clinics conducting illicit abortions.

Two lawyers, Linda Coffee and Sarah Weddington, heard about Norma's
dilemma and recruited her to be the plaintiff in their case contesting Texas'
anti-abortion laws. It took three years, but the case made it all the way to
the Supreme Court.

In 1973, the United States Supreme Court found in favor of Jane Roe and
made abortion legal in every state. In the 44 years since, over 50 million
babies have been killed by legal abortion in the United States. That's over
five times more lives taken than were killed by the Nazis in the Holocaust.

By 1992, after years of supporting the abortion cause, Norma McCorvey
found herself working at an abortion clinic. In 1995, a pro-life group moved
into the same building. Though at first resentful of their presence, Norma
soon became friends with a number of the Christians working there.

One friend in particular, a seven-year-old girl named Emily—the daughter of one of the pro-lifers—changed Norma forever. She began to see every life as precious. At Emily's urging, Norma began to attend church. She was soon baptized and found in Jesus the peace and forgiveness for which she so desperately yearned.

For the next 20 years, Norma McCorvey adamantly opposed abortion and fought to protect the lives of unborn children. Norma's struggle ended in 2017, when God called her home to heaven.

As a Christian, as a pastor, as a father, my hope and prayer is that one day Roe v. Wade will be overturned. I am heartbroken and appalled that we as a society abhor genocide in our world, yet legalize infanticide.

HELP THEM SEE THAT EVERY LIFE IS PRECIOUS.

Even if the law is never changed, each of us can still do what seven-year-old Emily did for Norma McCorvey. We can befriend those who disagree with us. We can share with them the good news of the forgiveness and heaven Jesus won for us.

We can help them see that every life is precious.

Today I am thankful for/that _____

_____

Almighty God, please lead our nation to see the preciousness of life and the importance of protecting it. Use me and others to share your love and forgiveness with a broken world. Amen.

DAY 202
MY IMPENDING MIDLIFE CRISIS

**This is the day the Lord has made; let us
rejoice and be glad in it.**

PSALM 118:24 ESV

◆

The countdown has begun—only 219 days until I turn 40. For some reason, though, I can't get anyone to feel sorry for me.

My kids look at me like, "What's the big deal? You've always been old to us." One young lady from church keeps telling me, "Well, I'm almost 30, pastor" (as if that would make me feel better). And everyone older than me just smiles and says, "Just wait; forty's nothing."

As I deal with my impending midlife crisis, it got me thinking about how we look at our lives. Very few people seem to be content with their age.

When we're three years old, we want to be four or five so we can go to school. When we're in grade school, we want to be in junior high. When we're in junior high, we want to be in high school. When we're in high school, we want to be in college. And when we're in college, we dream of the day we graduate, the day we get a job, the day we get married and have kids. As young people we're constantly looking and longing for tomorrow and next year.

Then as we get older, we're torn. We look back on our younger years and long for our glory days. We somehow forget how miserable we were and how much we wanted to get out of school and be adults. At the same time, we look ahead and can't wait until retirement when we can finally take a break and do all the things we don't have time to do right now.

When we finally retire, our bodies slow down and we wish we could go back to work and be as productive as we used to be.

Human nature never seems to be content with today. It always wants to look back with nostalgia on yesterday or ahead with yearning to tomorrow. The psalmist, however, reminds us to celebrate today. "This is the day the Lord has made;" he wrote, "let us rejoice and be glad in it" (ESV).

Every day—every stage of life—has its struggles and every day has its blessings. Instead of constantly being miserable, longing for a better day or a better age, look at the good things God has given you today.

LOOK AT THE GOOD THINGS GOD HAS GIVEN YOU TODAY.

So, kids, enjoy watching cartoons, wearing *Minecraft* pajamas, playing with dolls, and getting dirty. Once those days are over, you'll never get them back.

Young people, enjoy the fact that you aren't an adult yet. Sure, you don't always get to do what you want, but you also don't have to worry about how your food or clothes or home are going to be paid for. Sure, you have to go to school, but you also get to hang out with your friends and lie around on your phones all day.

Adults, enjoy the fact that you can work and drive and clean your homes. The day will come when you won't be able to do that anymore. If you're in your twilight years, enjoy the fact that God has given you years of blessings, friends, and family. Enjoy the fact that you can now give other people the opportunity to help you as you helped others for so many years.

Be content with the age God has given you. Yesterday is gone and can never be brought back. Tomorrow may never come. Forever is waiting for you in the joys of heaven because of Jesus and his love.

Today is God's gift to you. Celebrate it—even if you are about to turn 40.

Today I am thankful for/that _____

_____

Dear God, thank you for today. Help me to appreciate and make the most of every day you give me. Amen.

DAY 203
INTO THE STORM

Jesus immediately said to them: "Take courage!
It is I. Do not be afraid."

MATTHEW 14:27

❖

As I write this, Hurricane Harvey is on his way to my house. I did not invite him. He is not welcome, yet here he comes.

By the time you read this, the rain and wind will have subsided. The storm, however, doesn't always end when the rains stop. As I sit here right now, I can only imagine the days, weeks, and months to come as we seek to recover and rebuild.

Storms don't always end when the rain stops.

Before Hurricane Harvey decided to make his unsolicited visit, I was preparing to preach this Sunday. My sermon was going to be about Jesus walking on water and calming the storm in Matthew chapter 14.

God knew Harvey was coming.

In fact, one of the things which strikes me most about the account of Jesus walking on water is that Jesus sent his disciples into the storm.

It was dark. It had been a long day. The last few people who had experienced the feeding of the five thousand finally said their goodbyes and headed home.

Jesus told his disciples he was going to stay behind and he sent them into the storm. He knew what was coming and he sent them straight into it.

This wasn't just any storm. The disciples were experienced fishermen. They had spent many a night on the Sea of Galilee and survived many storms. Yet this storm was different. This storm was bigger. They were terrified.

GOD OFTEN SENDS US DIRECTLY INTO THE STORM.

Then they saw Jesus walking on the water to them. He invited Peter to trust him. He pulled him out of the water when Peter didn't. He stepped into the boat and the storm stopped.

God often sends us directly into the storm, be it hurricanes, cancer, divorce, or whatever problems pound you with rain, hail, and heartache. He sends us into the storm because he knows it will be for our good.

389

Jesus sent his disciples into the storm to teach them to trust in his power and love. Through the storms of life, God teaches us to trust in him and not in ourselves. He reminds us what is truly important. He reminds us that we are not in control and shows us that he is.

That doesn't mean it will be easy. Just as with Peter, our feet are going to get wet. It's going to be hard. But God doesn't send us into the storm alone. He comes to us in his Word and promises. Though we cannot see him, he stands beside us, watching over us, protecting us, and at times carrying us through the flood in his powerful arms.

He also promises us that the storm will end. Right now we are in the middle of it, but the pain and trauma caused by Harvey will end one day. That's God's promise. Even if we struggle through storms our whole lives here on earth, Jesus has won for us a home in heaven where there are no hurricanes, floods, or any other pain or problem.

As you stand in the middle of the storm, don't forget that. Good will come from this. Your Savior is standing by your side, and he will get you through.

The storm will end.

Today I am thankful for/that _____

_____

Lord, you know the storms I am facing in my life. Give me the courage and confidence that comes from knowing you are with me in this storm. Amen.

DAY 204
SOMEBODY TO LEAN ON

When Moses' hands grew tired, . . . Aaron and Hur held
his hands up—one on one side, one on the other—so
that his hands remained steady till sunset.

EXODUS 17:12

◆

In 1972, Bill Withers found himself a long way from his childhood home in
the coal mining town of Slab Fork, West Virginia. He was living in a
decrepit house in a rundown section of Los Angeles, trying to make it as a
singer/songwriter.

As he sat down at his piano one day, Withers was overwhelmed with
nostalgia, aching for the community of friends and family he had left
behind. As he tinkered with the keys and chords, a phrase kept repeating
in his mind—lean on me.

"Lean on me," Withers soulfully sang, "when you're not strong and I'll be
your friend, I'll help you carry on. . . . If there is a load you have to bear
that you can't carry, I'm right up the road. I'll share your load, if you just
call me."

"Lean on Me" raced to the top of the Billboard charts. It is listed among
Rolling Stone's 500 greatest songs of all time. In fact, it is one of only nine
songs to have reached number one with versions recorded by two different artists.

**WE ALL NEED
SOMEBODY
TO LEAN ON.**

One of the reasons the song resonates with so many people from
so many walks of life is that we all need somebody to lean on.

Even pastors.

One of the blessings of being a pastor is I get to be the person
other people lean on. As they wobble under the weight of
divorce and death, abuse and addiction, rebellious children
and overbearing bosses, they come to me for advice and support. I have
the privilege of listening and sharing with them God's rock solid promises
and guidance. I'm sure, at one point or another, many of you have leaned
on your pastor or priest.

That's what they're there for.

But whom do they lean on? Hopefully they lean first and foremost on their Savior God. As sinful human beings, though, even pastors waiver and worry. When they struggle, when they need help and encouragement, whom can they call? Whom can they lean on?

Just recently, I happened to read again the story of Joshua leading the Israelites in battle against their enemies, the Amalekites. On that day, God miraculously helped his people through the prophet Moses. Whenever Moses raised his hands, the Israelites began to win the battle, but whenever he lowered them, the Amalekites gained the upper hand.

After a couple of hours, Moses' shoulders ached. His hands felt like manhole covers. He couldn't do it anymore. So God sent two men—Aaron and Hur—to hold up his hands.

No minister can handle the stress and strain of the ministry on his own. We need the strength God gives through his Word and sacraments. We need the help of fellow Christians to hold up our hands. We need somebody to lean on.

Fellow pastors, don't try to do this on your own. Find another pastor, a friend, or a family member whom you trust to talk about the burdens you carry. We all need somebody to lean on.

And for everyone else out there, support your pastor. He may not be perfect, but he is the one God has sent for you and others to lean on.

Pray for him. Give him a call. Encourage him. As the hymn writer says, "You can be like faithful Aaron holding up the prophet's hands" (CW 573:3)

Because we all need somebody to lean on.

Today I am thankful for/that _____

_____

Lord, be with and strengthen my pastor. Give him the courage and wisdom to speak your Truth in love. Use me and others to support him in his ministry. Amen.

DAY 205
SQUIRREL!

Blessed is the one . . . whose delight is in the law of the
Lord, and who meditates on his law day and night.
PSALM 1:1,2

❖

Dogs are easily distracted. In the 2009 Disney animated movie *Up,* the
villain of the story, Charles Muntz, uses a pack of highly trained dogs to do
his bidding. Because it is a cartoon, the dogs are fitted with collars which
allow them to speak to their master and each other.

Though the dogs are highly trained and intelligent, they are still dogs. So as
they carry out their tasks throughout the movie, they suddenly snap their
heads up at the most inopportune times and say, "Squirrel!" Whatever task
they were sent to do is quickly forgotten.

Dogs are easily distracted.

So are we.

Every Sunday at church, we are faced with our own mortality. We are
reminded that we are going to die. We are warned that Jesus could come
back at any time. In fact, you could die tonight. Jesus could come back
tomorrow. When he does return, we will all face judgment.

In church we are confronted with our sins and the hell they deserve.
Thankfully, we are also comforted with the truth that Jesus suffered the
punishment of those sins in our place. All those who believe in him are
forgiven and have a home waiting for them in heaven.

In church, our hearts and minds are focused on what is really important. We
are reminded that our lives in this world are a reflection of our faith in Jesus.
Everything else pales in comparison. We walk out of church focused on our
Savior and intent on living our faith in him.

Yet, almost without fail, as soon as we step out the door, "Squirrel!"

**CHURCH IS NOT MEANT TO
BE AN ISOLATED EVENT
WE DO ON SUNDAY.**

Well, for us, maybe it isn't a squirrel. For us it's,
"Pizza Hut!" "Television!" "Football!" "Work!"
"School!" "My family!" "My problems!"

We get distracted. We suddenly forget what we
learned and how important it is until the next
Sunday or the next month when we finally make
it back to church to be reminded.

In Psalm 1 the psalmist tells us God blesses those who meditate on his Word day and night. In other words, church is not meant to be an isolated event we do on Sunday morning with no connection to the rest of our week or life.

Don't get distracted. Keep your eyes and hearts focused on God's Word—on Jesus and the forgiveness he won for us. Think about what God is teaching you on Sunday morning. Be like a cow—bring it back up during the week and chew on it again.

Read your Bibles during the week. When you're finished, think about what you've read. Pray about it. Think about it on your drive to and from work.

And whatever you do, don't stop going to church. As sinful human beings, we need to be constantly reminded of what is important, because in many ways we are like dogs—easily dis . . .

Oh look, a squirrel.

Today I am thankful for/that _____

_____

Holy Spirit, help me to keep my eyes fixed firmly on Jesus my Savior and to never stray or get distracted from him. Amen.

DAY 206
STUPID PEOPLE

Love is patient, love is kind. It does not envy,
it does not boast, it is not proud.
It does not dishonor others.

1 CORINTHIANS 13:4,5

◆

One evening when I was in college, one of my good friends heard a phrase on a TV show which he found amusing. While rescuing abandoned children from a fire, one of the firemen from the show angrily commented, "Stupid people shouldn't breathe."

Immediately, my buddy came across the hall to share with us his new favorite phrase. Then he went back to his room and made a sign which he proudly placed on his door. The sign read:

"Stupid people shouldn't breath."

The irony of his spelling mistake was not lost on us. As you might expect from a bunch of immature college guys, we mocked him incessantly for weeks.

All of us at some point find ourselves frustrated with stupid people. You know, the idiot who cut you off on the highway. Those people at McDonald's who can't keep your simple order straight. Your boss at work who has no clue what he's doing.

You know, stupid people.

We find ourselves mumbling to our spouses about the stupid people at work. We complain on Facebook about the stupid people out there in the world. You know, those "lazy millennials who are whining in their protests, but don't know really understand what they are protesting." Or those "racist Republicans who are blindly following a madman."

Stupid people. They anger us. They frustrate us. They drive us nuts.

When I feel tempted to rant against the stupid people in our world, I remember my buddy from college. And then I look in the mirror.

You see, we get angry with stupid people because it makes us feel superior. We're smart; they're idiots. We get it; they don't. We fancy ourselves unabashed "truth-sayers." We call it like we see it.

But calling other people stupid is just plain stupid.

I get mad at that idiot who cut me off, but then I have to remember the times when I have accidentally cut somebody else off. I didn't see them. I was in a hurry. Whatever my reason, the other driver was probably mumbling under his breath, "Stupid people."

WE ARE ALL STUPID PEOPLE. JUST ASK GOD.

We are all stupid people. Just ask God. We are all at times lazy, foolish, inconsiderate, ignorant, rude, and otherwise utterly inept. Yet our God loves us anyway. He forgives us our stupid sins because of Jesus, and he calls us to forgive other people's stupid sins as he has forgiven ours.

Does that mean we should never speak out when we see stupid and hurtful things being done around us? Of course not. Our God calls us to point out the sinfulness in our society and even in other people. We are called to be truth-sayers.

But as my dad always used to say, "Being right isn't enough." God has called us to speak the truth in love. As Christians, we point out the sins of our world, not to make ourselves feel superior, but to lovingly effect change—to lovingly help others see his love and forgiveness.

Remember that the next time somebody swerves and cuts you off. Think about that when you are tempted to write or share sarcastic posts on Facebook which mock or otherwise deride those with whom you disagree. Learn to disagree respectfully.

Because calling other people stupid is, well, stupid.

Today I am thankful for/that _____

_____

Dear God, in your great mercy, forgive me my pride and anger. Help me to be patient with others as you have been patient with me and to watch not only what I say, but also how I say it. Amen.

DAY 207
A CINDERELLA STORY

**Thanks be to God! He gives us the victory
through our Lord Jesus Christ!**

1 CORINTHIANS 15:57

◆

It never takes long. Usually after the first day of the NCAA men's basketball tournament, my bracket is busted. Every year, millions of fans and non-fans alike fill out their brackets, picking who they think will win every game of the tournament.

Part of the allure of the NCAA tournament is the possibility of upsets. Every year one or two small or obscure schools pull off the miracle of defeating the mighty Goliaths of college basketball. They become the media darlings. They are called Cinderella stories.

I love Cinderella stories. My favorite Cinderella story is a movie called *Hoosiers,* starring Gene Hackman. *Hoosiers* is about a tiny Indiana high school basketball team from a tiny town called Hickory. In the movie, they win the 1954 Indiana State Basketball Championship, defeating schools 10 to 20 times their size.

Though the story is inspiring and heartwarming, sometimes I wonder if we can really call it a Cinderella story. You see, they would have never made it to the state finals if Jimmy Chitwood, one of the greatest players ever to play high school basketball in Indiana, hadn't joined their team midway through the season.

It's difficult to consider a team the underdog when they have the best player.

Sometimes as Christians, we like to think of ours as a Cinderella story. We've worked hard for God. We've sacrificed much for our team. We've given it our all. We've earned that trophy.

But the truth is that on our own we would never be able to win. The truth is we are bad. In fact, we're so bad that we actually score for the other team. Every day we listen to the other team's coach (the devil) and players (the world) and do what they want us to do. We cave under peer pressure to act like they do. We often end up living and acting and playing like they do.

Incredibly, though, we are still on the winning team—not because of our own hard work, sacrifice, or gumption, but because we have been blessed with the greatest player to ever play the game. We have Jesus on our team.

Jesus won it all by himself. The truth is we never even get in the game. We never leave the bench. Jesus took on the other team alone. He made all the sacrifices and did all the hard work. He won the victory, yet he allows us to enjoy the trophy.

OURS IS NOT A CINDERELLA STORY. WE DIDN'T PULL OFF THE UPSET.

Ours is not a Cinderella story. We didn't pull off the upset. We didn't do anything. Jesus did it all. He gets all the credit.

But because we have him on our team, we never need to wonder. We never need to worry whether we have been good enough to win the trophy. He won it for us. All those who are on his team—all those who believe in him—receive the trophy he won for them.

So stick with Jesus. Your bracket will never be busted with him.

Today I am thankful for/that _____

_____

Jesus, thank you for the victory you won for me. Help me to always remember that without you I am lost. Amen.

DAY 208
REAL MEN SING

Sing to the LORD a new song; sing
to the LORD, all the earth.

PSALM 96:1

◆

I love Broadway musicals. I always have. From *Phantom of the Opera* to *The Fiddler on the Roof* to *The Sound of Music,* I can watch them again and again. I love to sing along.

In fact, I have often told my wife I wish life was a musical. Wouldn't that be awesome? You could just walk around singing your conversations and thoughts throughout the day.

My wife just rolls her eyes.

I love Broadway musicals and I love to sing, but that doesn't make me any less of a man. I feel I have to say that because in our world today it seems like men don't sing. Many guys today are like Robert from the Disney musical *Enchanted.* As everyone is singing and dancing around him, he says with a frown, "I don't sing . . . and I definitely don't dance."

That's just not something most guys feel comfortable doing.

King David was a man. In fact, he was a man's man. He was a warrior. With God's help, he defeated a giant and led armies into battle. Men admired him while women swooned.

Yet when David looked at all God had done for him, he couldn't help but sing. For example, when wicked King Saul was hunting him down, David found a cave in which to hide for the night. The next morning, he couldn't contain himself. He came out of the cave singing his praises to God (Psalm 57).

The other men must have wondered if David was delusional. David didn't care. He didn't worry what the other guys thought of him. He was thanking and praising God for his mercy and protection.

I have a good friend who is a retired officer from the United States Air Force. Years ago while still in the service, he found himself playing catcher in a softball game. Throughout the game he growled at the batters with the traditional, "Hey, batter, batter." One of the players finally had enough. He turned to him with a smirk and told him he had the voice of a gravel pit.

He does.

Yet, every Sunday, there he is in church joyfully singing his gravelly praises to God.

Men can sing.

It doesn't matter what your voice sounds like. It all sounds good to God. He wants to hear you. He wants to hear your joy and thankfulness. He wants you to show others how great he is and how you feel about him.

WHAT YOU DO IN WORSHIP SAYS SOMETHING TO THOSE AROUND YOU.

What you do in worship says something to those around you. When you mumble or mouth the words or simply sit in silence in worship, what does it tell those around you? It gives the impression that you don't want to be there or that worshiping God isn't important. It tells the boys who are watching you that real men don't sing.

When you sing in church, however, it says, "I love my God and am not ashamed to let others know it." When men sing in church, it tells the boys that it's okay to sing. It tells them it's important to sing.

So be a man. Sing out in church. It may feel strange at first. Your wife may look at you funny the first time. But don't worry what other people think. Don't worry what it sounds like. You are making God smile. You are being an example of faith to the future men sitting around you.

You are being a real man.

Today I am thankful for/that _____

_____

Lord, as I see your mercy, providence and protection in my life, give me a thankful heart which wants to sing out my praises to you with joy. Amen.

DAY 209
THE POWER OF WORDS

The tongue is a small part of the body, but it makes
great boasts. Consider what a great forest
is set on fire by a small spark.

JAMES 3:5

◆

In her book, *The Female Brain,* Dr. Louann Brizendine, a clinical professor of psychiatry from the University of California-San Francisco, claims the average woman speaks 20,000 words a day, while the average man speaks only 7,000.

When I shared those numbers with my wife, she didn't believe me. She is convinced I speak a whole lot more than 20,000 words a day. I had to remind her that those numbers were just an average. Some men tend to talk a little more; some women a little less.

How many words do you speak a day? Are you closer to 20,000 or to 7,000? Either way, that's a lot of words.

Really the important question isn't "How many words do you speak a day?" The question we should be asking is "What are we saying?"

Words have power. In the book of James, we are told that the human tongue is like a spark that can set a whole forest on fire. A few words can cause a lot of damage.

Words can hurt. Just ask the awkward teenage boy who is constantly told how weird or dumb or worthless he is. Just ask the girl whose reputation was forever ruined by some untrue gossip. Just ask the wife who will never look at her husband the same because of the hurtful words that came out of his mouth in a fit of rage.

Whoever said, "Sticks and stones may break my bones, but names will never hurt me" was wrong. Words have the power to hurt. Sadly, every one of us has spoken words of anger. We have all gossiped. We have all lied.

That's why we take such great comfort in the words of our Savior. As he was being nailed to the cross, he spoke a word of forgiveness: "Father, forgive them." As his enemies spewed venomous words at him, he told the repentant thief, "Today you will be with me in paradise." He speaks those same words to us.

Our Savior speaks to us words of forgiveness and promise. Because of Jesus, God forgives you for the venomous words you said to your husband, your mom, and your neighbor. Because of Jesus, God gives you a home forever in paradise.

SOMETIMES WE UNDERESTIMATE THE POWER OF OUR WORDS.

Words not only have the power to hurt and tear down, they also have the power to build up, comfort, and heal. Sometimes we underestimate the power of our words. A simple word of kindness, encouragement and forgiveness can literally change lives—especially the beautiful words of our Savior God.

So whether you say 20,000 or 7,000 words today, think about what you say. Remember the power of words. Use your words to build up and encourage. Share with others our God's powerful words of forgiveness and love.

Today I am thankful for/that _____

_____

Dear God, help me to always remember the power of my words. Use them to build up and encourage others. Amen.

DAY 210
CONTROL

The LORD reigns forever, your God, O Zion, for all generations.

PSALM 146:10

◆

A while back, my wife and I were talking with a friend who had recently given birth to twins to go along with her two-year-old daughter. Suffice it to say, she was not getting a lot of sleep.

In our conversation, she told me something that surprised me. "For the first time in my life," she said, "I realize I am not in control."

I thought to myself, "You just realized that now?"

How often don't we all fall into the delusion of control? You are the one who studied hard in school. You are the one who earned that promotion. You chose your husband. You planned your retirement. You are in control of your life. You control your own destiny.

By nature, we all want to be in control. Control is like a security blanket, making us feel safe and warm.

Control, however, is an illusion. The mirage of control disappears when the doctor utters those fateful words: "You have cancer." The mirage of control disappears when your best friend dies in a car accident, when you lose your job and then your home, when flood waters or fire destroy everything you own.

You are not in control of what happens to you or around you. That is one of the great realizations of life.

With that realization comes stress. With that realization come feelings of hopelessness and helplessness. No matter what you do, how hard you work, or how well you plan, disaster can strike at any moment.

HONESTLY, IT'S GOOD YOU AREN'T IN CONTROL.

Honestly, it's good you aren't in control. No offense, but you would just mess it up. So would I. As sinful human beings we tend to make a mess of our lives and our world. Thankfully, we are not in control.

God is.

And that, my friends, is the greatest realization of all: God is in control. Though at times it seems like he's not—though at times our eyes gaze upon a world seemingly out of control—our God reigns. He controls all things, he controls all of history, and he controls it for our good.

God controlled all of history to bring his Son, Jesus, into the world to be our Savior. On a dark Friday two thousand years ago, it seemed like God had lost control as his Son hung helplessly dying on a cross. But it was all part of God's plan to win for us forgiveness and heaven.

In the same way, when your life feels seemingly out of control, find comfort and peace in knowing that God is in control. He has plans for you, "plans to prosper you and not to harm you, plans to give you hope and a future" (Jeremiah 29:11). He is working all things for your good.

You are not in control of what happens to you or around you. Accept it. The only thing you can really control is how you react to what happens to you. You do have control of your own feelings and actions.

So stop stressing. Stop worrying. Stop trying to control things you can't control. Trust God. Trust that he is in control. He is your security blanket. Let go and let God.

Today I am thankful for/that _____

_____

Almighty and eternal God, help me to always see and trust that you are controlling all things for my good. Amen.

DAY 211
THE LOUDEST VERSE IN THE BIBLE

The Lord himself will come down from heaven, with a loud command, with the voice of the archangel and with the trumpet call of God, and the dead in Christ will rise first.

1 THESSALONIANS 4:16

◆

I used to live in Monterrey, a large industrial city nestled in the foothills of the Sierra Madre Mountains in northern Mexico.

One morning, the city awoke to a startling sight. The sky was blood red. It was eerie. People were afraid to go outside. Many in the neighborhood I lived in ran to the nearest church.

They thought the world might be ending.

It turns out there was a scientific explanation. Winds had lifted the reddish sand of the desert on the other side of the mountains into the atmosphere.

That, combined with the heavy pollution in Monterrey, created the creepy crimson sky.

Suffice it to say, the world did not end that day.

When Jesus comes at the end of the world, you'll know. Trust me. You won't be left wondering, "Could this be the end?"

In the book of Revelation, John tells us that when Jesus comes, "every eye will see him" (Revelation 1:7). Think about that for a moment. The world is round. How can everyone see him all at once? Yet they will.

My favorite verse about Jesus' coming is in 1 Thessalonians chapter 4 where the apostle Paul talks about how Jesus will come and rapture believers up to the sky to be with him.

This rapture isn't some unseen, unnoticed disappearance of believers from the earth. Paul tells us, "The Lord himself will come down from heaven, with a loud command, with the voice of the archangel and with the trumpet call of God and the dead in Christ will rise first."

As one of my professors at the seminary used to say, "That's the loudest verse in the Bible."

WHEN JESUS COMES, YOU'LL KNOW IT. When Jesus comes, you'll know it. You won't miss it. You won't be standing there wondering, "Is this it?" It will be loud. It will be visible. It will be instantaneous.

The questions you need to ask yourself aren't "Will I know when it is happening?" or "Will I somehow miss it?" The question is "Are you ready?"

Ready or not, here he comes. In fact, he could come today. All the signs Jesus gave marking the end times are happening right now and have been happening for a long time: wars and rumors of wars, famines, earthquakes, false Messiahs, and societal unrest. Jesus could come back at any moment.

When he comes, he will judge you. He will open a book in which is written everything you have ever thought, said, and done in your life. That is the evidence by which you will be judged. The standard is perfection. The punishment is hell.

Yet God promises that all those who believe in Jesus—all those who trust in the forgiveness he won for them on the cross—will be declared innocent on that awesome and awful day. All those who believe in Jesus will be taken up to be with him forever.

Those who don't believe in him, however, will be declared guilty and condemned to hell. When Jesus comes, you won't have time to run to church. You won't be able to say, "No, wait, Jesus, I change my mind. I believe in you." It will be too late.

So don't worry and wonder whether you will know if the end of time is happening. You'll know. You won't miss it.

Just be ready.

Today I am thankful for/that _____

_____

Lord, take away my fears or worries about the end of the world. Help me to trust that you are coming to take me to be with you in heaven. Help me to say with confidence, "Come, Lord Jesus." Amen.

DAY 212
METAL DETECTORS

**"Then you will be handed over to be persecuted
and put to death, and you will be hated
by all nations because of me."**

MATTHEW 24:9

"Our church doesn't have metal detectors," I thought as I watched CNN report on the 2017 Palm Sunday ISIS attacks on Christian churches in Egypt. The second explosion occurred outside a Coptic church in the city of Alexandria. The bomb would have exploded inside the building, but the bomber couldn't make it past the security guards and metal detectors at the entrance of the church.

There are no security guards or metal detectors at the entrance of our church. We don't need them to keep our people safe—yet, but that's not the case everywhere. At least 45 people were killed in the Palm Sunday bombings with over 100 injured. The strike was just one of a string of attacks on the Christian population in Egypt.

Church historian David Barrett estimates that, since the time of the apostles, around 70,000,000 Christians have been martyred—killed for their faith in Jesus. What may surprise you is that the last one hundred years have been the bloodiest.

Roughly 17,000,000 Christians were killed or died in prison camps in Communist Russia. It is common knowledge that 6,000,000 Jews died during the Holocaust. What many don't know is that 1,000,000 *Christians* died in those same Nazi concentration camps.

In the last 100 years, millions of Christians have died in mass persecutions in China, Ethiopia, Uganda, North Korea, and throughout the Middle East.

Though the persecution and murder of Christians continue in many parts of the world today, it rarely makes the highlights on CNN. Most Americans are unaware or indifferent.

Persecution shouldn't surprise us. Jesus told us it would be this way. "No servant is greater than his master," he said. Just as he was persecuted and killed, Christians should expect and be willing to suffer the same.

PERSECUTION OF CHRISTIANS SHOULDN'T SURPRISE US.

Persecution of Christians shouldn't surprise us. It should sadden us, though. It should lead us to pray for our brothers and sisters in the faith. It should embolden us to stand up and speak out. Men, women, and children around the world—Christians like you and me—are suffering horrible atrocities rather than deny their Savior. They are trusting firmly in God's promise of heaven as they stare down the barrel of a rifle or are held at knifepoint.

In our country, persecution is more subtle. Most American churches don't need metal detectors at the door. We sit on cushy pews in comfortable churches. We are free to believe what we want as long as we don't speak up too loudly or openly oppose sin.

If we do speak out too loudly, however, we are crucified in the media. We are criticized, mocked, and called intolerant.

That's hard to handle sometimes. We are tempted to back down and keep quiet. Maybe it would help to remember that right now there are Christians who are literally being crucified for their faith. How can we back down just because some people may not like us?

Until Christ comes again, Christians will be persecuted in our world. So pray for your fellow believers whose lives and livelihoods are threatened. Follow their example of courage.

Stand up and let your voice be heard.

Today I am thankful for/that _____

Dear Jesus, give comfort and courage to my brothers and sisters in the faith who face persecution, imprisonment and even death for their faith in you. Help me to never be ashamed to call you my Lord and Savior. Amen.

◆

DAY 213
YOUR TRUE IDENTITY

You are a chosen people, a royal priesthood, a holy nation, God's special possession, that you may declare the praises of him who called you out of darkness into his wonderful light.

1 PETER 2:9

◆

"I'm Batman." You may remember that famous line from the Batman movies, but unless you are a comic book fan, you may not understand the depth of what Batman was really saying.

I know. My inner nerd is showing, but bear with me.

Batman is the secret identity of playboy, millionaire Bruce Wayne. If you read the comics or watch the movies, however, you will notice a tension between his two diametrically different personas.

For decades, fans have debated who really is the one wearing a mask: Batman or Bruce Wayne. Is his true identity the carefree, millionaire playboy or the cold, detached crime fighter?

Most experts agree that dark, brooding Batman is his true identity and that Bruce Wayne is just a mask he wears to keep his enemies at bay.

Like many comic book superheroes, you and I have two identities as Christians.

You are a sinner. That is who you are. You were born that way. Some in our society might find such a statement offensive, judgmental, or even a bit intolerant, but it's true.

Contrary to popular opinion, people are not by nature essentially good: The Bible says so. King David confessed, "Surely, I was sinful at birth, sinful from the time my mother conceived me" (Psalm 51:5). From the time we are tiny, we fight over toys, throw tantrums, and lie to get our way. As we grow older, our fights, tantrums, and lies simply grow more complex.

You are a sinner. That is who you are. At the same time, however, you are also a redeemed child of God. Your sins have been washed away in Jesus' blood and the waters of Holy Baptism. You are forever forgiven. You are a son or daughter of the King of the universe and an heir to the happiness of heaven.

The reformer Martin Luther once quipped that we are at the same time "saints and sinners." You have two identities, but only one is your true identity.

When you look into the mirror, who do you see? The devil whispers in your ear: "You are an addict." "You are a pervert." "You are an adulterer, liar, gossip, and cheat." He is right, of course, but that is not your true identity in Christ.

BECAUSE OF JESUS, YOUR SINS DON'T DEFINE YOU.

Because of Jesus, your sins don't define you. You don't have to live life with a scarlet letter sewn onto your clothes. When God looks at you, he doesn't see filth and ugliness. He doesn't see an addict or adulterer or liar. He sees his dear child. He sees a saint.

That is who you are. That is your true identity.

Today I am thankful for/that _____

_____

Heavenly Father, I am a sinner. I have messed up so many times and in so many ways, I can't even count them. Yet because of your Son Jesus, you don't see me as a screw-up. Thank you for your amazing forgiveness and for making me who I am—your dearly loved child. Amen.

DAY 214
EXCLUSIVELY INCLUSIVE

Jesus answered, "I am the way and the truth
and the life. No one comes to the
Father except through me."

JOHN 14:6

◆

Early in my ministry, I lived in the city of Miami. Whenever any friends or family came to visit, the first thing most of them wanted to do was go down to South Beach. So we would load up the car, drive them across the bridge, and walk them up and down the busy sidewalks packed with overpriced restaurants, overflowing bars, and tourists as far as the eye could see.

There comes a point on the strip where the crowds begin to thin. The hotels become more exclusive. The beaches have "no trespassing" signs. The clubs have bouncers at the door. The restaurants are by reservation only.

The message is clear: Not everyone is welcome. Only certain people are allowed.

The Christian church today struggles with the concept of exclusivity. The Bible itself seems to speak in contradictory terms. On the whole, the message of the Bible is extraordinarily inclusive. Jesus died for the sins of the whole world (1 John 2:2). God wants all people to be saved (1 Timothy 2:4). He loves everyone the same (Galatians 3:28).

It doesn't matter what gender you are, what color your skin is, or what language you speak. It doesn't matter how much money you make or how big your house is. Not even your sexual preference, your life choices, or the mistakes of your past matter. God loves everybody. He welcomes all people with open arms.

For many modern Christians, that means the church should open its arms to everyone, regardless of what they believe or do. Many think the Christian church should embrace the LGBTQ+ movements. We should accept non-Christian religions like Islam and Hinduism as equally valid.

God loves people in those movements and religions too. He welcomes everyone. So should we.

FAITH IN JESUS IS THE ONLY WAY TO HEAVEN.

On closer examination, the Bible also says that God hates sin and punishes it with eternal damnation in hell. The Bible calls homosexuality an abomination. It calls heterosexual sex outside of marriage a damnable sin. It calls a lot of things sin. The Bible clearly states that faith in Jesus is the only way to heaven (John 14:6; Acts 4:12). Whoever does not believe in him will be condemned to the horrors of hell (Mark 16:16).

Christianity in many ways is an exclusive religion. It says that sin separates you from God. It teaches that no other god or religion can save you.

So which is it? Is Christianity exclusive or inclusive? The answer to this seeming paradox is found in the cross. God hates sin and excludes all sinners from heaven, but he loves all people and therefore sent his Son Jesus to suffer their punishment in their place. Because of Jesus, God forgives all sins and welcomes all sinners—including you and me.

But only those who believe in him—only those who believe in Jesus—receive that forgiveness and heaven. God wants all people to be saved. He wants all people to recognize their sins and trust in him for salvation. If you reject him, though, you reject the forgiveness he won for you.

Jesus welcomed sinners. He dined with prostitutes and corrupt tax collectors. Yet he also confronted their sinful behavior and called them to repent.

As Christians, we should welcome everyone as Jesus did. Often we give the impression that the Christian church is exclusive—that certain people are not welcome. May God help us to warmly welcome everyone into our churches with open arms, no matter what they look like, what they sound like, or how they dress.

But that doesn't mean we should embrace their sins. That doesn't mean we accept every belief or opinion as equally valid.

Is Christianity inclusive or exclusive? It's both. It's exclusively inclusive.

Today I am thankful for/that _____

_____

Lord Jesus, you are the only God and the only way to heaven. Help me to trust in you with all my heart and to share you with everyone I can. Amen.

DAY 215
A SIMPLE INVITATION

"[The king] said to his servants, 'The wedding banquet is ready. . . . So go to the street corners and invite to the banquet anyone you find.'"

MATTHEW 22:8,9

◆

It all started with a simple invitation. In late November, Don Chencho Ibarra from a tiny little *rancho* in Mexico posted a video on Facebook inviting everyone from his rural community to the *quinceañera* of his daughter Ruby. (A *quinceañera* is an elaborate version of our American sweet sixteen parties.)

Don Chencho wanted only the best for his daughter. He promised that three local bands would play. Horse races would be held with a prize of $500. He vowed to feed everyone who came.

Don Chencho didn't know what he was getting himself into. The video went viral. People found his open invitation both funny and endearing. Within two weeks, 1.2 million people confirmed on Facebook they would attend the event.

Chencho and Ruby became national and international darlings. A major Mexican airline offered a 30% discount on fares to the nearest airport. Celebrities and millionaires offered to help pay for the event. The gifts began to pour in, including a new car.

As the day approached, no one knew what to expect. How many people would actually show up? The governor brought in a special security detail. On December 26, 2016, over 20,000 people attended Ruby's quinceañera in the tiny rural community of La Joya, San Luis Potosi, Mexico. Media from around the world were in attendance.

And it all started with a simple invitation.

"Come, follow me," Jesus said to four fishermen on the shores of the Sea of Galilee—a simple invitation, which also went viral.

In its essence, the gospel is an invitation. Come and see. Come and find in Jesus forgiveness. Come and find in him rest for your souls. Come and receive the inheritance he won for you.

You are cordially invited to the wedding banquet of heaven. If you are a Christian, you already know that. But God's invitation is an open invitation. All are invited. There is room for everyone. The invitation is meant to be shared.

In our age of social media, many Christians share that invitation over the internet. They share and like Christian videos and articles on Facebook which can be seen by millions of people.

I often wonder how much difference such posts and threads on Facebook really make. They easily get lost in the white noise. People see them one minute and forget them the next. Such is the fickle nature of social media.

Over one million people said they would attend Ruby's *quinceañera*. Only 20,000 actually showed up. In a few months, hardly anyone will remember Don Chencho and his charming invitation.

THE BEST INVITATIONS CONTINUE TO BE PERSONAL INVITATIONS.

In the end, the best invitations continue to be personal invitations—one beggar taking another beggar by the hand and leading him to the soup kitchen, one sinner telling another where to find forgiveness.

Don't be content simply sharing or liking Christian messages on social media. According to most polls, over 80% of those who don't regularly go to church say they would attend if a friend or acquaintance personally invited them.

So call up your friend, your cousin, your hunting buddy and invite them to go to church with you. Tell them you'll pick them up. Tell them you'll sit with them. Obviously, that's not as easy as sharing a post on Facebook, but in the end it may make all the difference.

It all starts with a simple invitation.

Today I am thankful for/that _____

_____

Dear God, thank you for sending people into my life who shared with me the good news of your love. Use me to invite many more people to the wedding feast of heaven. Amen.

———◆———

DAY 216
IN DEFENSE OF THE QUIET CHRISTIAN

In fact God has placed the parts in the body, every one of them, just as he wanted them to be. If they were all one part, where would the body be? As it is, there are many parts, but one body.

1 CORINTHIANS 12:18-20

◆

Nobody has ever accused me of being quiet. In fact, I am the quintessential extrovert. I am talkative. I am loud. I am Tigger on steroids.

Quiet people are a mystery to me. I am amazed at how they can just sit there and listen. Unlike me, they don't seem to feel that overwhelming need to participate in the discussion, to share, to be heard.

I have often wondered what it would be like to be quiet and shy. I know I would save myself more than a little grief. A wise man once said, "You can be quiet and let people think you are stupid or open your mouth and prove it."

I have generally chosen the latter.

But being an extrovert does have its upside. As a pastor, I get to know people quickly. I am not easily embarrassed and am willing to take chances. I feel comfortable speaking in front of groups and taking the lead on projects.

Being an extrovert opens many doors for me as a pastor and allows me to share the gospel with a large number of people.

You can always tell the extroverts in a church. They are the ones raising their hands in Bible class. They are the ones taking the lead in meetings. They are the ones who greet new people at the door and take charge when there is a crisis.

People look up to them. They are charismatic and aggressive. They are the ones who seem to be doing more in service to God and others. In fact, they sometimes get frustrated with quiet Christians whom they often perceive as lazy, unengaged, or apathetic.

Please allow me, quiet Christian, to speak in your defense. In 1 Corinthians chapter 12, the apostle Paul compares the Christian church to a body. We are all different parts of that body. Not all of us are mouths.

And that is a good thing.

Sadly, the service of quiet Christians often goes unnoticed. When I serve at church, everybody knows it because they can hear me a mile away.

Most people, however, don't notice the woman who picks up the rags from the church kitchen every week to wash them. You don't hear the silent prayers offered for you and others by the little old lady at the end of the pew. We easily fail to see the unassuming plumber who sits in the back of church—the one who always makes sure the toilets at the church and parsonage are in working order.

The mom who quietly cleans her home, raises her children, and loves her husband. The father who stoically and faithfully provides for his family. The young, single woman who visits her grandmother every day at the nursing home.

HELP ME TO SERVE YOU FAITHFULLY.

Now, don't get me wrong, quiet Christian. The devil is going to tempt you to use your quietness as an excuse to not serve, to not participate, or to not speak when words need to be said. Sometimes quiet Christians need to speak up, just like sometimes us loud Christians need to close our mouths and listen.

But please don't ever feel like your service to God is any less meaningful or important because nobody seems to notice.

God notices.

Today I am thankful for/that _____

_____

Dear Lord, thank you for making me who I am. Forgive me the times I have sinfully wanted to be something you didn't make me to be. Help me to serve you faithfully with the gifts and personality you have given me. Help me to appreciate those who have different gifts and personalities. Amen.

DAY 217
RANSOMWARE

"The Son of Man did not come to be served, but to serve, and to give his life as a ransom for many."

MARK 10:45

◆

I learned a new word recently: ransomware. Ransomware is a type of computer virus which hijacks the data on your computer and won't let you access it unless you pay a ransom.

On May 12, 2017, hackers unleashed a ransomware called "WannaCry" on the world. It targeted a weakness in the Microsoft Windows operating system and wreaked havoc around the globe.

In the end, over 230,000 computers in more than 150 countries were infected by the virus, which demanded a $300 ransom (paid in the internet currency Bitcoin) to allow you to access the information on your computer.

Businesses, government agencies, and even hospitals around the world were forced to shut down temporarily because of the virus. It literally made thousands of people want to cry.

Thankfully, experts and authorities quickly discovered methods to protect computers from the virus, and the number of infections soon slowed to a trickle.

You are infected with a virus. It has hijacked your life in every way. From the moment you were conceived, you were infected with a ransomware called "sin."

Sin is sadly now a part of your operating system. No matter what you do, no matter how hard you try, you cannot get rid of that virus yourself. It is a part of who you are. Sin manifests itself in our mistakes and failures. Sin colors our words and dirties our thoughts. Sin hijacks our lives and families and marriages.

It holds us ransom. We are its slaves. It often makes us want to cry.

The irony is that, because we are infected, we often willingly submit to its control. A part of us loves the virus. A part of us wants to sin. We suffer from Stockholm syndrome. We form an alliance with our captor.

Thankfully God loved us so much he paid the ransom. He paid the price of our freedom, not with gold or silver (or Bitcoin), but with his holy precious blood and innocent suffering and death.

Death and hell are the payment for sin. But God loved you so much he sent his Son Jesus to suffer that death and hell in your place. Jesus paid the ransom. All those who believe in him have a home waiting for them in heaven where they will be forever free from sin, death, and the devil.

While you are here on this earth, however, you will still be infected with the virus. It is still a part of your operating system. But God has given you the tools to fight against the ransomware of sin. His Word and sacraments give us the trust and strength we need to fight against the allures and entrapments of sin.

So keep going to church. Keep reading your Bible. Keep taking Holy Communion every chance you get. That is our antivirus which helps us in our struggle against sin.

TRUST THAT HE HAS PAID THE RANSOM.

And when the sin virus rears its ugly head in your life, turn to your Savior Jesus and trust that he has paid the ransom. You are forgiven. One day you will be free from the virus of sin.

417

That truth should truly make us want to cry—for joy.

Today I am thankful for/that _____

Dear Jesus, thank you for paying the ransom to set me free from my stupid sins. Help me to now live for you who lived and died for me. Amen.

DAY 218
DISCIPLINE AND ABUSE

Fathers, do not exasperate your children; instead, bring them up in the training and instruction of the Lord.

EPHESIANS 6:4

◆

On September 11, 2014, a Montgomery County grand jury indicted NFL star running back Adrian Peterson on charges of reckless or negligent injury to a child.

Peterson admitted that on May 18th of that year, he repeatedly hit his four-year-old son with a "switch" he made out of a tree branch. He said he was disciplining his son.

Much was made of the incident on the news and social media. It brought to light an important question: What is the difference between discipline and abuse?

The book of Proverbs frequently talks about discipline. For example, wise old King Solomon warns parents: "Whoever spares the rod hates their children, but the one who loves their children is careful to discipline them" (Proverbs 13:24).

We see two truths about discipline in that verse. First of all, discipline is done in love. The purpose of discipline is to teach and train—to help a child learn right from wrong. Discipline is good for children. Discipline is love.

The second thing we notice is that, like many other verses in Proverbs, this verse mentions the "rod." In the Bible, God not only condones physical discipline. He encourages it.

Physical discipline is not abuse. Used properly, a spanking, a slap on the hand, or even a switch can help teach a child right from wrong.

Then what is abuse? Where is the line? What is the difference between discipline and abuse?

Discipline is done in love and abuse is done in anger. Discipline is done to help a child learn. Abuse is done to vent or punish. Abuse can take place even if you didn't hit your child hard or even if you didn't touch them at all. Any angry response to a child's misbehavior is a form of abuse. In that sense, every parent, including me, is guilty of abuse.

When your child is driving you nuts in the store and you yank him by the arm and yell, "Knock it off; you're driving me crazy," you aren't lovingly and firmly trying to help your child learn. You are angrily venting your frustration.

So when your child pushes your buttons—and he or she will push your buttons at times—take a time out. Send them to their room and tell them you'll talk about their punishment later. Take time to calm down. Never forget that discipline is done in love, but abuse is done in anger.

DISCIPLINE HURTS, BUT IT DOES NOT HARM. There is another difference as well. Discipline hurts, but it does not harm. Discipline needs to sting, but it shouldn't do any lasting harm. That's why spankings are often a good form of physical discipline. Most of us have a nice cushion back there. It hurts for a moment, but it does no lasting harm. Again, the purpose of the discipline is not to make them pay for what they did, but rather to help them learn and see there are consequences for improper behavior.

So was Adrian Peterson guilty of abuse? I can't say if he acted in anger or love because I can't look into his heart. The pictures of the scars on his child, however, are telling. Harm seems to have been done.

Before we point a condemning finger, though, remember all the times you were too harsh or lashed out at your kids in anger. All of us as parents need to run to the forgiving arms of our heavenly Father. We are not perfect parents, but we are forgiven parents. In response to God's great love and forgiveness, let's do our best to discipline our children in love.

Today I am thankful for/that _____

Heavenly Father, forgive me for any and all of my failings as a parent. Help parents to lovingly discipline their children and to raise them in the instruction of the Lord. Amen.

DAY 219
SCHADENFREUDE

**"Watch and pray so that you will
not fall into temptation."**
MATTHEW 26:41

Do you know what *schadenfreude* is? Merriam-Webster defines schadenfreude as "enjoyment obtained from the troubles of others."

At 3 A.M. on May 29, 2017, police in Jupiter, Florida, pulled up to a running car stopped in the middle of the road. The driver was asleep at the wheel. When the police woke him, he was disoriented and slurring his speech. Though he passed the breathalyzer test, he failed every other field sobriety test. He was arrested for driving under the influence.

As you probably know, the driver was Tiger Woods. Woods claimed he had not been drinking; he insisted that he had taken pain killers from a recent back surgery and did not realize how they would affect him.

Tiger's disheveled, unshaven mugshot went viral. It was everywhere—TV, magazines, newspapers, and especially social media. Twitter and Facebook exploded with memes and mockery.

The man who at one time was the most famous and well-paid athlete in the world was now a drugged-out, balding, unshaven, middle-aged mugshot on Facebook.

People couldn't resist. They shared the memes. They made snide remarks. We just can't seem to get enough of celebrities who fall from grace (see also Brian Williams, Mel Gibson, Bill Cosby, and others).

Why do we derive such interest and, dare I say, enjoyment from the misfortunes of the rich and famous? It seems to stem from two unseemly corners of our own hearts: pride and jealousy.

The apostle Paul encourages us to "rejoice with those who rejoice" and to "mourn with those who mourn" (Romans 12:15). We tend to do the opposite. We stew in jealousy when we see others succeed where we have failed. And when they fall, we secretly (and sometimes not-so-secretly) revel in their misfortunes.

When we see the high and mighty fall, we feel better about ourselves. We're not like them—arrogant, corrupt, morally bankrupt. We are good, decent, hard-working people. They are getting what they deserve.

WE ARE ALL TWO OR THREE BAD CHOICES AWAY FROM LOSING EVERYTHING.

There is an old Spanish proverb which says, "Don't ever say, 'From that water I will never drink.'" It means, "Watch out! Don't think it couldn't happen to you." We are all two or three bad choices away from losing everything.

Imbibe in one too many drinks or accidentally mix pain medications, and you could find yourself in a jail cell or worse. One moment it's harmless flirting, the next your wife is filing for divorce. Your friend loans you a pill to take the edge off and help you sleep, and the next thing you know, you're strung out.

Don't ever say, "From that water I will never drink."

Then how should we react when we see celebrities like Tiger Woods fail and fall? Turn the channel. Scroll past it on Facebook. Pray for them.

Take a look at your own reflection in the mirror, your own sins, your own weaknesses. Then pray again. Pray that God would forgive your jealousy and pride. Pray that God would help you not to fall.

Today I am thankful for/that _____

Holy Lord, I have to admit that at times I derive pleasure from other people's failures. Forgive my pride and help me to fight against temptation. Amen.

DAY 220
CHANGE

"Be strong and courageous. Do not be afraid or terrified
. . . for the Lord your God goes with you; he
will never leave you nor forsake you."

DEUTERONOMY 31:6

❖

My whole life is about to change. No, I'm not moving. No, I am not getting married. No, my wife is not having a baby.

Today I meet my new partner. After 14 years of serving as the only pastor of our church, we are now going to have two. God has blessed our congregation. We have grown and are beginning a second campus.

But that means change and change can be scary.

The people of Israel understood that. Three thousand five hundred years ago, they stood at the edge of the Jordan River. On the other side was the Promised Land.

For 40 years they had wandered in the wilderness. For 40 years they had followed their strong, steady leader, Moses. For 40 years they had lived in tents. But now everything was going to change.

They were about to enter the Promised Land, a land flowing with milk and honey. But it was also a land filled with fortified cities and powerful armies.

Then God told them the news: Moses wasn't going with them.

Moses was the only leader they had known. He had led them out of Egypt. He had led them to Mount Sinai. He had led them for 40 years in the wilderness.

Yet when they crossed the Jordan, he wouldn't be with them. Everything was going to change. They were scared.

So when Moses introduced their new leader, Joshua, he reminded the people they wouldn't be alone. "Be strong and courageous," Moses told them. "Do not be afraid or terrified . . . for the Lord your God goes with you; he will never leave you nor forsake you."

They did not need to be afraid, because in this ever-changing world their never-changing God would be with them. He would guide and protect and comfort them.

My life is about to change. Though the changes I will face pale in comparison to what the Israelites faced, it is still daunting. How I've conducted my ministry for 14 years is going to drastically change. How will we get along? Will my new partner be able to handle my unique idiosyncrasies (i.e., my annoying habits)? What will my ministry be like from now on?

I don't know. What I do know is that the Lord my God will be with me. In this ever-changing world, he never changes. He will continue to keep his promises. He will continue to be with me. He will continue to forgive me, guide me, and comfort me.

THANKFULLY, MY GOD AND HIS PROMISES NEVER DO.

As soon as I finish this devotional, I am going to meet up with my new partner for the first time.

Deep breath. Pray. Trust.

My life is about to change. Thankfully, my God and his promises never do.

Today I am thankful for/that _____

_____

Almighty God, in this ever-changing world, help me to cling to your never-changing promises. Amen.

DAY 221
TOUGH LOVE

"If your brother or sister sins, go and point out their fault, just between the two of you."

MATTHEW 18:15

◆

Primum non nocere. First do no harm.

The origins of that phrase are unknown. Many people mistakenly believe it to be part of the Hippocratic Oath, which doctors take upon graduation from medical school. Though the phrase is not specifically found in the oath, it is a cornerstone of modern bioethics.

"First do no harm." Sometimes I feel like my dentist didn't take that oath. As I sit in the chair, tears running down my face, my jaw aching, and my mouth bleeding, it seems like my dentist is out to do me harm.

Yet when I leave, I tell him, "Thank you."

I tell him, "Thank you," because he isn't out to harm me, but to help me. What he did to my mouth hurt me, but it did not harm me.

To quote the 1970s band Nazareth, "Love hurts."

Sometimes love causes pain. Love, in its essence, does what is best for another person even when it is painful to them. We call that tough love.

Our world today has lost the concept of tough love. In fact, our society's definition of love in general is somewhat skewed.

Love is selflessness. God the Father loved us so much he gave up his one and only Son to save us. Jesus loved us so much he gave up everything for us. Love gives and forgives. Love sacrifices. Love does everything for the other person.

For many in our world today, however, love is defined by another word—*tolerance*. Now don't get me wrong. Tolerance is an aspect of love. Love accepts. Love receives. Love makes no distinction of persons. Jesus invited all people to come to him and find forgiveness.

LOVE DOES NOT TOLERATE EVERYTHING.

Yet love does not tolerate everything. In love Jesus rebuked people. He told them they were wrong. He told them their sins deserved the horrors of hell where there is weeping and gnashing of teeth.

Jesus powerfully and poignantly pointed out people's sins because he loved them. They needed to see their sin to be able to see their need for his forgiveness. Love sometimes hurts.

Many Christians today are being condemned for standing up and speaking out about sin. They are being called unloving for saying that homosexuality is a sin or abortion is murder.

To be fair, some Christians are not speaking those truths in love. They allow anger or biting words to cloud their confession.

Yet to speak those unpopular truths is love. We may be accused of being hateful or judgmental, but in the end it is love.

If my brother is asleep in a burning building, it is my business. It is love to wake him up. It is love to humbly tell others they are sinners in need of a

Savior. It is love to show them their sins so they can find forgiveness in Jesus and change their behavior.

Tough love is tough, though. Not everybody thanks the dentist. Speaking the truth will not win you any popularity contests. The truth sometimes hurts.

But it is love.

Today I am thankful for/that _____

_____

Holy Spirit, give me the courage to speak the truth in love even when others don't want to hear it. Amen.

DAY 222
MOCKING MILLENNIALS

Don't let anyone look down on you because you are young, but set an example for the believers. . . . Do not rebuke an older man harshly, but exhort him as if he were your father. Treat younger men as brothers, older women as mothers, and younger women as sisters, with absolute purity.

1 TIMOTHY 4:12; 5:1,2

Man buns and skinny jeans. Shaggy beards and yoga pants. Starbucks and selfies. That's how other generations tend to see millennials.

They live in their parents' basements. They march in protests. They are constantly on their phones. They are lazy. They are dreamers. They can't handle criticism.

That's how many of us from other generations tend to view millennials, so we mock them on Facebook. We make sarcastic remarks about how they were all given trophies in Little League. We share posts about how they are scared to eat at Chick-fil-A and how they don't even know what they are protesting. We call them lazy. We call them crybabies. We call them narcissists.

We wring our hands and worry about a future with them in control.

Like any generalization, some truth can be found in the stereotypes. Millennials are a product of the world in which they were raised—a world where truth is relative and all opinions are given the megaphone of social media. In the end, they are sinners, just like you and me.

In general, because millennials tend to view truth as relative, they treat all opinions as equally valid. They value tolerance above all else. From their perspective, the greatest sin of all is bullying.

GENERALIZATIONS AND STEREOTYPES ARE NEVER THE WHOLE STORY.

Generalizations and stereotypes are never the whole story. Stereotypes can warp how we treat and view millennials. Not all millennials wear skinny jeans and yoga pants. Not all millennials march in protests and live in their parents' basement. Not all millennials are selfie-taking crybabies.

Even when they are, mocking them doesn't help. One of the age-old responses toward those we consider weak or thin-skinned is to tear them down. We think we need to toughen them up, so we make fun of them. We mock them. They need to learn to not be so sensitive.

Though that is an age-old response, it is not God's response. In his letter to the Ephesians, the apostle Paul encourages us to build each other by "speaking the truth in love" (Ephesians 4:15).

Should we confront the weaknesses and sins of the millennial generation? Of course. But we should do so in love. We should do so remembering that not all millennials are the same. We should do so with grace and forgiveness flavoring our words and attitudes.

We should do so, understanding that many millennials consider bullying the worst of all evils. If you mock them or tear them down, they won't hear what you are saying. They will simply dismiss you as another intolerant bully.

As a pastor, I am constantly being bombarded by articles and posts on social media all saying the same thing: millennials are leaving Christian churches in droves. The reasons for this seeming mass exodus are diverse. Sometimes it is because of their sinful attitudes which flow from a warped worldview. Other times it is because they view Christian churches as intolerant and unloving.

So what should we do? How should we respond to this generation which sees the world differently than we do? Love them as our Savior God loves them. Speak to them honestly and openly about the dangers of moral relativism. Confront the sins and failings of this generation which have permeated their thoughts and attitudes. Let God's love and forgiveness shine in what you say and do.

Be firm. Be real. Be loving.

But more than anything else, please stop mocking millennials. That's definitely not helping.

Today I am thankful for/that _____

Dear Lord, you know the struggles I have to understand and communicate well with people from other generations and cultures. Help me to speak your truth with patience and love. Amen.

DAY 223
LETTERS TO GOD

Wait for the LORD; be strong and take heart and wait for the LORD.

PSALM 27:14

As often happens in book club, we weren't talking about the book.

We were talking about prayer. We were talking about how hard it is to trust God when we pray for something again and again and he doesn't seem to answer.

One of the ladies offered a solution. "I sometimes write my prayers down and put them in an envelope," she said. "Then I go back six months or a year later and read them. As I do so, I can see the prayers God has answered and the ones he hasn't yet."

I love that. For days, I haven't been able to stop thinking about her letters to God.

No one writes letters anymore. In days gone by, we wrote letters and often waited days, weeks, and even months for a response. Today, we want instant gratification.

We live in an age of lightning fast communication. If you want to communicate with somebody, you can call them, Skype them, or Facetime with them. You can text, message, or email them.

We get impatient if a person doesn't immediately answer our calls or respond to our texts. We expect instantaneous responses.

God doesn't work that way. For him a thousand years is like a day and a day is like a thousand years. He answers our prayers in his own time and his own way.

In Psalm 50, God invites us to call upon him in the day of trouble and he promises, "I will deliver you." But you'll notice he doesn't say when. He doesn't say, "I will deliver you that very day."

When we ask for something from God, there are really only three possible answers he can give: "yes," "no," and "wait." Sometimes God gives us what we want right when we ask for it. Sometimes God doesn't give us exactly what we ask for because it's not what is good for us or because he has something better.

And sometimes God makes us wait. He wants to teach us patience. He wants to teach us persistence. It's simply not the right time yet.

That's why I love the idea of writing letters to God. It teaches us patience. It gives us perspective.

LORD, GIVE ME PATIENCE AND PERSPECTIVE WHEN I PRAY.

Try it sometime. Take a week or month and every day write down your prayers. Write letters to God. Stick them in an envelope and put them away. Then go back in six months, a year, even five years and re-read your letters to God.

As you do, you will see the prayers God answered. You will see his every *yes* and *no*. You will see how, though he didn't give you exactly what you wanted when you wanted it, he made things work out the way they were supposed to.

And yes, even after all that time, you may still have a few unanswered prayers, but you will also have something you didn't have when you first prayed.

Perspective.

Today I am thankful for/that _____

_____

Lord, give me patience and perspective when I pray to you. Help me to trust that you will always deliver me and answer my prayers for my good, but in your own time and way. Amen.

DAY 224
GAZTELUGATXE

"Be holy because I, the LORD your God, am holy."

LEVITICUS 19:2

On the Bay of Biscay in northern Spain, there is a tiny island connected to the mainland by a man-made bridge. The island's name is *Gaztelugatxe*, which in the Basque language means "the difficult or rocky fort."

The island lives up to its name. As soon as you cross the bridge, you face over 230 oblong, rocky, blister-inducing steps winding up toward a small medieval church at the top of the island. The climb demands persistence and patience.

The church has a bell which you are allowed to ring upon finishing the long, arduous trek. That's not the only reward you receive for your tenacity. They say the view is breathtaking.

The name *Gaztelugatxe* has come to mean something that is difficult but worth the effort.

The stairway to heaven is a long and arduous climb. It demands persistence and patience. It demands perfection.

That's right. God demands perfection. He says, "Be holy because I, the LORD your God, am holy." He says, "Be perfect, therefore, as your heavenly Father is perfect" (Matthew 5:48). The stairway to heaven doesn't have 230 arduous steps. It has millions of blister-inducing steps—each more demanding than the previous.

Climbing the stairway to heaven means responding lovingly to your spouses every single time they fly off the handle. It means not only watching your actions, but also your words. It means controlling every thought and feeling which passes through your hearts and minds. It means giving everything and expecting nothing in return. It means never slipping or missing even one step.

THE STAIRWAY TO HEAVEN ISN'T SIMPLY DIFFICULT OR CHALLENGING.

The stairway to heaven isn't simply difficult or challenging. It is impossible for us to climb. You have already stumbled and fallen more times than you can count. You will never be able to get to the summit and ring the bell thinking, "Look what I have done."

Our lives are a never ending game of Chutes and Ladders. Sure we climb some ladders. We do some good, but we are endlessly sliding back down into sin.

Thankfully God loved us so much he sent his Son to do the hard work for us. Jesus walked that road for us. He perfectly climbed every step of the way, and he did so carrying a cross. He did so carrying the guilt of every one of our missteps. He climbed that hill and at the top he gave his life for us.

Jesus did all the hard work in your place. He promises that you and all who believe in him will get to ring the bell. All those who believe in Jesus will enjoy the breathtaking view of heaven forever.

But you can't say, "Look what I did." Jesus did it for you. He is the stairway, the escalator, the elevator which takes us to heaven. He did all the hard work and we get to reap the reward.

Today I am thankful for/that _____

_____

*Holy Lord, I have failed to be the person you
want me to be. Forgive me for all the times I
have slid into sin. Thank you for being
my stairway to heaven. Amen.*

DAY 225
DEHYDRATION

Blessed is the one . . . whose delight is in the law of the
Lord, and who meditates on his law day and night.
That person is like a tree planted by streams
of water, which yields its fruit in season
and whose leaf does not wither.

PSALM 1:1-3

◆

My backyard is a plant graveyard. Empty flower pots line the back wall of
my home. Plants come to my house to die.

It's not on purpose, mind you. We always have the best of intentions. We
love the idea of having live plants in our home. Green foliage, vibrant
flowers, even sweet smelling herbs have been welcomed joyously into our
house, only to suffer an ignominious death.

The cause of death for every single victim in our plant graveyard is the
same—dehydration. We simply forget to water them. We get busy. We
figure somebody else is doing it. And before you know it, another pot is
placed in the graveyard.

The Bible often compares our faith to different kinds of plants—trees, wheat, even mustard plants. What is true about all of those plants is also true of our faith. It needs to be watered regularly.

Faith is trust in God's promises. Faith is trusting God's promises even when we can't see or understand how.

Faith is hard.

That's why faith needs to be watered regularly. We need to hear and be reminded of God's promises often. That's why we go to church.

We don't go to church to show off. We don't go to church simply to do our duty. We don't go to church in order to earn God's love or heaven.

We go to church because that is where God waters our faith. As we hear his Word and receive his sacrament, God showers us with his promises: "You are forgiven." "I am with you always." "I will bless and keep you."

Through his promises God feeds our roots. He refreshes us. He strengthens our faith.

The problem is that we too often forget to water our faith. We get busy. We get out of the habit of going to church regularly because of work and summer vacations. Sunday is the only day we have to mow the yard, do the laundry, or sleep in.

We tell ourselves our faith can handle a few weeks without watering. We tell ourselves we'll water it later. We'll get back to church eventually.

We often don't even notice as our roots grow weak and our leaves wither for lack of hydration. Then, when the hot Texas sun of troubles, trials, and temptations beats down on us, we struggle to stay strong.

PLANTS NEED TO BE WATERED. . . . FAITH NEEDS TO BE WATERED TOO.

Plants need to be watered. That is a lesson I am still trying to remember in my home.

Faith needs to be watered too. That's a lesson we all need to remember. If you've gotten out of the habit of going to church, if you've forgotten about it for a while, if you only go every so often, get back. Find a church if you don't already have one. Go to church every Sunday you can. Open up your Bible and read it during the week.

Water your faith regularly.

Today I am thankful for/that _____

_____

Lord, forgive me for the times I have strayed from the life-giving water of your Word. Help me to drink deeply from it every day. Amen.

---•---

DAY 226
THE SOFTEST PILLOW

**In peace I will lie down and sleep, for you alone,
Lord, make me dwell in safety.**

PSALM 4:8

◆

The French have a saying, "There is no pillow so soft as a clear conscience." Do you want to avoid lying awake at night staring into the dark abyss? Do you want to fall fast asleep as soon as your head hits the pillow? Live right. Be honest. Treat others fairly.

You'll sleep like a baby.

Sadly, we've all experienced the opposite. The tossing and turning. The regret. The worry. The fear. Your wife just caught you looking at something you shouldn't on your phone. You both end up lying on opposite sides of the bed facing away from each other, eyes wide open. A no man's land stretches between you. Her heart is full of hurt and anger. Yours is full of embarrassment, regret, and frustration.

"That was so dumb," you tell yourself as you stare into the darkness. "Why did I do that?"

The never-ending stress of living a lie. The fear of facing the consequences of what we've done. Feeling like a failure. We relive the moment again and again in our minds, hoping that somehow we could just go back in time and make it right. But that's impossible. You can't go back. You can't undo what's been done.

So you lie there, your heart hurting, your stomach turning, unable to relax, unable to sleep.

And if that keeps you up at night, think about this: God hates what you did. Your failure, your sin, your mistake separates you from him. You deserve his punishment. You deserve to die. You deserve to rot forever in hell for what you did, no matter how relatively big or small your mistake.

That thought alone should keep you up at night.

If your failures give you insomnia—if regret and guilt keep you up at night—there is something you can do to help you sleep. And it's not counting sheep or popping a pill.

Repent. Talk to God about what you have done. Tell him you're sorry. Then trust that he has and will always forgive you. Because Jesus suffered your punishment in your place on the cross, God will never punish you. Every mistake, every failure, every mess up is gone forever. God is not angry with you. You will not die because of your sin. You will not go to hell.

Just because God forgives you, though, doesn't mean you won't have to face the consequences of your actions here on earth. You will still have to face your angry wife. You will still have to face the judge, the principal, or your boss. That can be scary. It can be painful. The thought of it can keep you up at night.

Yet even then God lovingly promises to be with you as you deal with the consequences. He promises to make everything work out for your good. Though it may be hard, he will bring you out on the other end stronger and with a peace only he can give.

The Psalm writer once wrote, "In peace I will lie down and sleep, for you alone, Lord, make me dwell in safety."

We can lie down with a clear conscience knowing the forgiveness Jesus won for us. We can sleep in peace because God promises to be with us and make all things work together for our good. We can close our eyes without fear because God promises us a home with him forever in heaven.

"WASH AWAY ALL THAT HAS BEEN WRONG TODAY."

God's promises are the softest pillow there is.

Today I am thankful for/that _____

"Jesus, Savior, wash away All that has been wrong today. Help me ev'ry day to be Good and gentle, more like Thee." Amen. (The Lutheran Hymnal 653:2)

DAY 227
THE HEART OF HATRED

Surely I was sinful at birth, sinful from the time my mother conceived me.

PSALM 51:5

It has become the most-liked tweet of all time. Reacting to the attack in Charlottesville, Virginia, on August 12, 2017, and the subsequent racial tensions around the country, former President Barack Obama posted on Twitter: "No one is born hating another person because of the color of his skin or his background or his religion."

President Obama was quoting Nelson Mandela's 1994 autobiography, *Long Walk to Freedom*. His point is that hatred and racism are learned behaviors.

They often are.

When children see and hear prejudice from their parents or grandparents, from their society, or from their culture, they often accept it and make it their own. Much of the vitriol and violence in our world today has been passed down from generation to generation—from father to son.

That being said, I feel I must respectfully disagree with President Obama and Nelson Mandela. Statements like theirs reflect a mistaken philosophy prevalent in our world today, namely, that people are inherently good and only act badly because of their upbringing or negative influences in their lives.

Our children are inundated by that philosophy on television, in the movies, and even at school. In the Disney movie *Frozen,* the trolls sang to our children, "People make bad choices if they're mad or scared or stressed, but throw a little love their way and you'll bring out their best!"

In other words, people do bad things because of the bad influences or problems in their lives. Deep down people are good. Sin is simply a learned behavior.

Unfortunately, you don't have to teach a child to sin. You don't have to teach a person to be selfish. You don't have to teach people to hate. We do it quite naturally on our own.

King David admitted in Psalm 51, "Surely I was sinful at birth, sinful from the time my mother conceived me." From the moment of conception we are stained with selfishness. We are sinful down to our very genes. Your infant daughter can figure out on her own how to get angry without ever having seen you get angry.

WE DO, HOWEVER, NEED TO BE TAUGHT HOW TO TRULY LOVE.

We don't need to be taught how to sin. We do, however, need to be taught how to truly love. To understand love we need to simply see Jesus who loved us, the unlovable. In fact, he loved us so much, he sacrificed everything, including his life, for us. He suffered the punishment of all our selfishness, anger, and hate on the cross.

Seeing his love and forgiveness shows us what true love is. His love and forgiveness are our motivation and strength to love everyone—even those who are different than us—even those who seem to be unlovable.

The attack in Charlottesville, Virginia, is a reminder that hatred and prejudice are alive and well in our world today. Much of the racism and tension in our country has been learned and passed from generation to generation. We need to do everything we can to stop that cycle.

But the roots of that hatred and prejudice go much deeper. They are ensconced in the heart of every human being on this planet.

The only cure for that is Jesus.

Today I am thankful for/that _____

_____

Lord, you know my heart. You know what I have
done. I have been sinful from the time my
mother conceived me. Forgive me my sins
and cure the anger and ugliness
in my heart. Amen.

DAY 228
MEETING GOD

"Where two or three gather in my name,
there am I with them."

MATTHEW 18:20

On November 2, 1512, the Renaissance master, Michelangelo, finished what would become his most famous painting. He painted the entire ceiling of the Sistine Chapel in Rome. The giant fresco took four painstaking years to complete.

The ceiling is divided between different episodes in biblical history. The most famous is the Creation. In the painting, God reaches down his finger and touches Adam's outstretched hand.

At the point of two fingers, God and man met.

Where can you meet God? You don't have to travel the world to find him. You don't have to leave your home. God is everywhere. Yet our God is a hidden God. You can't see him. You can't find him in a tree, visit him in his office, or watch him on TV.

You can't know God unless he reveals himself to you.

Our God has chosen to reveal himself to us in his Word—the Bible. Through his Word, we see God. Through his Word, we know God. Through his Word, we come to trust God.

IN HIS WORD, WE MEET JESUS, GOD MADE MAN.

In his Word, we meet Jesus, God made man. In Jesus, we meet God face to face. In Jesus, we see how much God loved us. In Jesus, we see how God saved us from an eternity of loneliness in the heartbreak of hell. On the cross, God's fist came down and punished Jesus for all our misspoken words and hurtful actions.

Because of Jesus, God forgives us. Because of Jesus, all those who believe in him will one day see God face to face in the happiness of heaven. Jesus is the point where God and man meet.

Do you want to meet God here on earth? Do you want to touch his finger and see his face? Every Sunday at church as we hear his Word proclaimed, God comes to meet us. Though we can't see him with our physical eyes, he reaches out to us through his Word and touches our hearts.

There in his house, God comes to meet his people in a very real and visible way. Holy Communion is one of those points where God and man meet. When you receive the bread and wine in the Lord's Supper, God is there. His body and blood are there. As you taste the bread and drink the wine, God's finger comes down and graciously touches you, assuring you that you are his and that heaven is yours.

At the Sistine Chapel, you can see God and man meet at the point of two fingers. You have the opportunity every Sunday to experience that through God's Word and sacraments.

That is where God and man meet.

Today I am thankful for/that _____

Lord, thank you for coming to meet me in your Word and sacraments. Amen.

DAY 229
IT'S THE END OF THE WORLD AS WE KNOW IT

"When you see these things happening, you know
that it is near, right at the door."

MARK 13:29

❖

The fall of 2017 was pretty rough. Four major hurricanes made landfall in North America in a period of four weeks, killing over two hundred people. Two major earthquakes hit Mexico soon afterward, killing hundreds more. The city of Houston was inundated. The tiny island of Barbuda was completely destroyed. The entire island of Puerto Rico was left without power. Huge buildings collapsed with people inside them. Thousands were left homeless. Billions of dollars were lost.

Oh, and North Korea was getting an itchy trigger finger with its nukes. The Middle East was still a hot mess. Our country was (and continues to be) so diametrically divided that calm conversations did not exist.

Our world was such a mess that an REM song kept playing like a broken record in my head: "It's the end of the world as we know it."

Little did I know at the time what was waiting for us in 2020.

During the last week of his life, Jesus' disciples asked him, "What will be the sign of your coming and of the end of the age?"

Jesus gave them a number of signs: "You will hear of wars and rumors of wars. . . . There will be famines and earthquakes in various places. . . . You will be handed over to be persecuted and put to death. . . . Many will turn away from the faith. . . . Many false prophets will appear. . . . Because of the increase in wickedness, the love of most will grow cold. . . ." (Matthew 24:6,7,9-12).

Sound familiar?

Now to be fair, all of those "signs" have been happening since Jesus' day. The world could honestly end tomorrow, or it may take another two thousand years. When the Bible points us to signs marking the end of the world, it isn't to help us build a timeline and countdown to the end.

It is to show us the imminence of Jesus' coming.

When we see hurricanes and pandemics, wars and terrorists, false teachers and hate, it should remind us that the world could end at any time. It

439

should remind us that this life is short and fleeting. It should remind us to be ready.

Don't worry, though. If you believe in Jesus, you are ready. When Jesus comes to judge on the Last Day, he will declare all those who believe in him to be innocent because he already suffered their punishment in their place. Whoever believes in Jesus will be saved. Whoever does not believe in Jesus, however, will be condemned to the eternal death sentence of hell.

THE WORLD COULD END TODAY.

God doesn't want that. He wants all people to be ready. That's why he points us to the signs—so that we are ready and so that we see the urgency of helping others be ready.

Don't wait to talk about your faith. Don't put off having the important conversations about God with your family. Tomorrow may be too late. The world could end today.

Just look at the signs.

Today I am thankful for/that _____

_____

Lord, as we look at the signs all around us, we know you could come back at any time. Keep us alert and ready. Take away our fears. Give us the faith to say, "Come, Lord Jesus." Amen.

DAY 230
YOU WILL SURVIVE

**I will not die but live, and will proclaim
what the LORD has done.**

PSALM 118:17

❖

Gloria Gaynor's disco hit "I Will Survive" blasted over the arena's loudspeakers as a large group clad in purple triumphantly marched around the oval. I was at our local Relay for Life, an event which raises money every year for the American Cancer Society. The group dressed in purple were the survivors.

They had survived. They were in remission. They were cancer-free. The crowd cheered. The survivors danced. Everyone celebrated because they had survived.

The question which haunted me was: Why? Every year, millions of people around the world die from cancer. Why did these people survive? Did they have a stronger will to live? Did they fight harder?

Though I don't doubt their fight and will to live, wouldn't many of those who died have fought just as hard?

In the end, the reason anyone survives cancer is because of God's grace. In his wisdom and love, God healed them. He kept them here, and he kept them here for a reason.

The apostle Paul once wrote to the Philippians, "For to me, to live is Christ." In other words, if God has me here—if I'm alive—then my life has a purpose. I am here to live for my Savior who lived and died for me. He still has things for me to do. He has people for me to love and help.

The reason anyone survives is because God still has plans for them here on earth.

But what about all those people who don't survive? On the same day we danced and cheered at the Relay for Life, the father of one of the boys from my soccer team died after a long battle with leukemia.

Why didn't he survive?

The thing is that he did survive. We need to remember the second part of what Paul said in his letter to the Philippians: "For to me, to live is Christ and to die is gain." Because Jesus suffered the punishment of all the ugly and hurtful things we have said and done, because Jesus died our death, because death couldn't stop him, we will survive.

To die is gain. Heaven is better than anything here on earth. Heaven is pure happiness. Heaven means being reunited with family and friends. Heaven means basking in God's glory forever.

I know it's hard to fathom, but the father of the boy from my soccer team did survive. He trusted in Jesus his Savior and is now enjoying the peace and perfection of heaven. One day his wife and children will see him again.

CANCER CAN'T WIN. DEATH CAN'T BEAT YOU. JESUS ALREADY DEFEATED THEM.

You see, cancer can't win. Death can't beat you. Jesus already defeated them.

So, don't be afraid. Don't be petrified. Trust in your Savior; he is by your side. Because of him you've got all your life to live. You've got all your love to give.

No matter what happens, you will survive.

Today I am thankful for/that _____

_____

Almighty God, be with those who suffer from cancer and their families. Give them the peace of knowing that no matter what happens, they will survive. Amen.

DAY 231
THE GIFT THAT KEEPS ON GIVING

"Every teacher of the law who has become a disciple in
the kingdom of heaven is like the owner of a house
who brings out of his storeroom new
treasures as well as old."

MATTHEW 13:52

◆

In 1925, the phonograph company RCA Victrola trademarked a slogan which adorned their advertisements for years to come. According to their ads, Victrola record players were "a gift that keeps on giving."

The gift of music was given every time a record was played.

God has given us a gift that keeps on giving—his Word. Through his Word, the Bible, we come to know our Savior Jesus. We see and learn how he suffered God's punishment for our sins and won for us a place in heaven. In his Word we find peace and comfort and guidance. God's Word reminds us of timeless truths and teaches us new lessons every time we read it.

In God's Word, we discover treasures old and new.

You will never graduate from God's Word. Even after a lifetime of study of Scripture, you will never stop learning or growing. We can open our Bibles every day and find a gift which keeps on giving.

I once heard the story of a missionary in Africa who gifted a Bible to a recently converted Christian from a tiny village. When the man received it, he hugged it close and expressed great appreciation for the precious gift the missionary had given him.

When the missionary saw him a few days later, however, he noticed, much to his dismay, that the Bible was all torn up and numerous pages were missing. The frustrated missionary asked him, "What happened? What did you do to your Bible? You said it was your most treasured possession."

The man replied, "Indeed, it is my most treasured possession. It is the finest gift I have ever received. It is so precious that when I returned to my village, I very carefully chose a page, tore it out and gave it to my mother. Then I tore out another page and gave it to my father. I then tore out another page and gave it to my wife. In fact, I gave a page of God's Word to every person in my village."

GOD'S GIFTS ARE MEANT TO BE SHARED.

We may be amused by that man's actions, but he truly understood. God's gifts are meant to be shared—to be given away as freely as God has given them to us.

Treasure the gift of God's Word. Open and read your Bible every day. Discover those treasures old and new. Then share that gift with everyone you can.

God's Word is truly the gift that keeps on giving.

Today I am thankful for/that _____

_____

Almighty God, thank you for your Word. Thank you for reminding me of the timeless truths I need to believe to be saved. Thank you for opening my eyes to learn and see new truths from your Word. Help me to share this amazing gift you have given me with others. Amen.

DAY 232
THE HEART OF THE ISSUE

"People look at the outward appearance,
but the Lord looks at the heart."

1 SAMUEL 16:7

For nearly three years now, I have had the privilege of serving on the ethics board of our local newspaper. The board consists of various personnel from the newspaper, including the publisher, editors, and three at-large members of our community. We meet monthly to discuss controversial articles, concerns readers have voiced, and the overall ethics of journalism.

Recently the newspaper published an exposé on a local politician who is now embroiled in controversy. Almost immediately people began accusing the newspaper of having a political agenda. The complaints were that the editors were getting revenge for previous wrongs or just didn't like the politician.

Having been allowed to peek behind the curtain and listen to the discussions beforehand, I am fascinated by how painstakingly the editors seek to be objective and evaluate the ethical ramifications of what they print.

Are they always perfectly objective? No. Do personal feelings at times affect decisions? I'm sure they do. But overall they truly do seek to be honest and objective.

The comments regarding the controversial piece remind me of something God once said to the prophet Samuel. "People look at the outward appearance, but the LORD looks at the heart."

Only God knows what thoughts and feelings fill our hearts and minds.

OFTEN WE FALL INTO THE DELUSION THAT WE ARE GOD.

Yet often we fall into the delusion that we are God. We fancy ourselves mind readers. We presume to know other people's reasons and motivations.

When your husband suddenly doesn't answer you, he must be mad at you because of what you said to him in the morning. When your coworker doesn't respond right away to your text, she must be ignoring you because she is a jerk. When the newspaper runs an article which says something negative about a politician, the writer/editor must have a political agenda.

That could be true. Or maybe your husband simply didn't hear you. Maybe he was distracted. Maybe your coworker's phone died. Maybe the newspaper is simply trying to report the facts a journalist has uncovered in his or her investigations.

One of my favorite phrases from Martin Luther is found in his explanation to the Eighth Commandment. As he expounds what it means to not give false testimony against our neighbor, Luther encourages us to "take [their] words and actions in the kindest possible way."

In other words, don't assume the worst. You cannot read minds. Only God can do that. You don't know why they did what they did or said what they said.

445

Remember that, especially when you and your spouse are having an argument. You can't say, "You said this or did that because. . . ." You can't see into the heart. Don't assume you know why. Talk about the behavior. Ask for an explanation. Discuss the impression it gives you, but don't assume you know the motive. Only God can see into people's hearts.

Are people, politicians, and news organizations at times driven by selfish and nefarious motives? Of course. In this sinful world, all of us at times are moved by misguided motivations. But be careful. As sinful human beings, we tend to assume the worst about people—especially those who have hurt us or with whom we disagree, particularly in our politically charged world.

May God forgive us our sinful assumptions and give us generous hearts which take other people's words and actions in the kindest possible way.

Today I am thankful for/that _____

_____

Heavenly Father, forgive me for judging other people's hearts. Help me to take their words and actions in the kindest possible way. Amen.

DAY 233
HOW GREAT THOU ART

Great is the LORD and most worthy of praise;
his greatness no one can fathom.

PSALM 145:3

Late one afternoon in 1885, an unknown 26-year-old Swedish writer named Carl Gustav Boberg was walking home with friends from his church in the town of Kronobäck to the nearby seaside village of Mönsterås, Sweden. Suddenly the sky grew dark. Lightning flashed across the sky. A violent wind swept across the grain covered fields. Boberg and his friends ran for shelter as the rain poured down, but then, just as quickly as it began, the storm subsided and a rainbow appeared.

When he arrived home, Boberg opened a window to his house and gazed in awe at the now calm Mönsterås Bay reflecting the clear blue sky like a mirror. Church bells chimed in the distance. Overwhelmed by the power and wonder of God's creation, Boberg sat down and wrote a poem, *O Store Gud,* literally, "Oh Great God."

The nine stanza poem was first published on March 13, 1886, in a local newspaper. Two years later, Boberg visited a neighboring church in Sweden and was surprised to hear the poem sung to the melody of an old Swedish Folk Tune. In 1891, Boberg once again published the poem, but this time with piano and guitar instrumentation.

In 1907, the hymn was translated into German and quickly spread throughout Germany. By 1912, it was translated into Russian as well. In 1931, the British missionary Stuart K. Hine heard the hymn in Russian as he shared the gospel in the remote villages in the Carpathian Mountains of the Ukraine.

Hine wrote an English paraphrase of the first two verses, the birth of the hymn we now know as "How Great Thou Art."

But the story doesn't end there. As Hine and his wife shared the good news of God's love in Jesus in the tiny Ukranian villages, they stopped outside a house where a local woman was reading and teaching God's Word to other villagers. As they sat outside, listening to people inside voicing their repentance and faith, they wrote down the phrases they heard. Hine later incorporated those phrases into a third verse of the English version of the hymn:

> *And when I think that God, his Son not sparing,*
> *Sent him to die, I scarce can take it in,*
> *That on the cross my burden gladly bearing,*
> *He bled and died to take away my sin. (CW 256:3)*

In 1933, Hine and his wife were forced to flee the Ukraine due to Joseph Stalin's Famine Genocide. Years later during World War II, Hine met a Russian refugee in England who told him about his wife who was left behind. He didn't know if he would ever see her again. The Russian Christian, however, expressed his confidence that he would see his wife again in heaven.

Moved by the conversation, Hine wrote the final verse of "How Great Thou Art."

When Christ shall come with shout of acclamation
And take me home, what joy shall fill my heart!
Then I shall bow in humble adoration
And there proclaim: "My God, how great thou art!"
(CW 256:4)

MAY WE NEVER STOP MARVELING AT GOD'S ASTONISHING LOVE.

May we never stop gazing in awe-filled wonder at God's created order. May we never stop marveling at God's astonishing love that he bled and died to take away our sins. May we never stop looking ahead to the day when we will see God face to face and there proclaim, "My God, how great thou art!"

Today I am thankful for/that _____

_____

O Lord, my God, how great thou art! Amen.

DAY 234
IMMORAL INDIGNATION

"The Pharisee stood by himself and prayed: 'God, I thank you that I am not like other people—robbers, evildoers, adulterers—or even like this tax collector.' . . . But the tax collector stood at a distance, . . . beat his breast and said, 'God, have mercy on me, a sinner.'"

LUKE 18:11,13

Moral indignation. We all feel it at times. Often we show it. When we see somebody do something which offends our sense of morality, we express our outrage.

A couple years ago, while discussing players kneeling during "The Star-Spangled Banner," Bob McNair, owner of the Houston Texans, said, "We can't have the inmates running the prison." In his defense, it is a common idiom. He wasn't literally calling the players "inmates." But in today's charged environment, his words were at best insensitive and unwise.

The reaction was over the top. Texans players talked about boycotting the next game. NBA star Draymond Green was morally indignant and angrily called the statement unacceptable. Then a few hours later he got into a Greco-Roman wrestling match with another NBA player during a game, was ejected, and left the game shouting expletives.

During Game Three of the 2017 World Series, Astros first baseman Yuriel Gurriel made a racially derogatory gesture about Japanese pitcher Yu Darvish. The gesture was immature, wrong, and uncalled for. The response, however, was overwhelming. Fellow players were outraged. Ironically, many of those same players could be seen during seemingly every close-up of the World Series shouting the F-word, yet relatively few seemed outraged about that.

MORAL INDIGNATION IS A WONDERFUL TRICK OF THE DEVIL.

Moral indignation is a wonderful trick of the devil. Every day we are tempted to pick and choose the sins which offend us, just like we pick and choose our food at Golden Corral. We are offended by the rudeness of our president, the lack of respect by NFL players, and the thoughtless woman who always leaves her cart in the middle of the Walmart parking lot.

"People are so stupid!" We shout to the four winds (or post on Facebook). "Politicians are so corrupt!" "Professional athletes are such spoiled crybabies!" And as we lament the offensive sins of the world around us, we turn a blind eye to our own thoughtlessness and disrespect. Somehow our own sins don't seem as offensive to us.

Yet every sin offends God. Every sin angers him. Moral indignation is immoral. It is pride. It is pharisaical. It is foolish. We are all rotten sinners who deserve God's eternal wrath.

Still, God loved us so much that he sent his Son Jesus to suffer the punishment for all of our sins—and not only for ours, but also for the sins of Bob McNair, Draymond Green, Yuri Gurriel, and that lady who leaves the carts in the middle of the Walmart parking lot.

Remember that the next time you feel like spouting off about the rude drivers on the road, the evil politicians in Washington, and the spoiled professional athletes.

We are all in the same boat. We are all sinners who desperately need a Savior—sinners loved and forgiven by a merciful God.

May that truth permeate and pervade the way we deal with and talk about all the other offensive sinners out there in the world.

Today I am thankful for/that _____

_____

Lord, when I am tempted to become morally indignant about the sins of others, help me to look in the mirror and remember that I too desperately need your forgiveness. Amen.

DAY 235
A JOYFUL NOISE

Make a joyful noise unto the Lord, all the earth: make a loud noise, and rejoice, and sing praise.

PSALM 98:4 KJV

◆

I have a friend who went to Game Five of the 2017 World Series. If you're not a sports fan, you might not know what that means. Game Five of the 2017 World Series was arguably the most exciting World Series game ever played. The Houston Astros won the game 13–12 in 10 innings on their way to capturing their first World Series title.

They say the crowd was electric. My friend said that it was deafening at times. He told me the sound of the 41,000 screaming fans is still echoing in his ears. It was an experience he will never forget.

The apostle John had a similar experience nearly 2,000 years ago. God allowed him to glimpse the glory of heaven. There he saw millions of people praising God in a loud voice. He said it sounded like "the roar of a great multitude . . . like the roar of rushing waters and like loud peals of thunder" (Revelation 19:1,6).

Forty-one thousand screaming fans gave my friend goose bumps. Imagine millions of believers celebrating the victory of heaven. Because of Jesus and the forgiveness he won for you, one day you won't have to imagine it. You will see it with your own eyes.

But you don't have to wait until heaven to join the celebration. Every time we worship in church, we blend our voices with the roaring crowds of heaven celebrating the victory Jesus won for us.

The problem is that sometimes we don't join in. We don't open our mouths. We don't sing. Can you imagine an Astros fan stubbornly sitting in silence with his arms crossed at Game Five while the other 41,000 fans celebrated? Yet that is exactly what we do at times in church, especially us men.

Somewhere, someone gave us the impression that real men don't sing. We feel embarrassed and self-conscious about opening our mouths in church. Yet we can scream wildly with 41,000 other fans at an Astros game. We can celebrate with our friends as we watch the game on TV. That's all we are really doing when we praise God in church.

"Yeah, but I don't know how to sing. I don't have a very good voice." To God it doesn't matter. In the Psalms, he doesn't tell us, "Sing a beautiful song." He says, "Make a joyful noise." It doesn't matter if you have the voice of an angel or the voice of a frog. To God it all sounds good.

THE MUSIC ISN'T THE PROBLEM. "Yeah, but the music in my church is boring. I wish we had better songs or better musicians." The music isn't the problem. The joy of worship doesn't come from the melodies or musicians, but from a thankful heart. The joy of worship comes when we think about the words we are saying and singing—when we truly grasp how unworthy we are and how amazing God's grace really is.

One day, you will hear the roar of the crowds in heaven. You will cheer and celebrate and praise God forever. But don't wait until heaven. Open your mouth now. Sing your praises to God.

Make a joyful noise.

Today I am thankful for/that _____

_____

*Lord, give me a joyful heart which wants to
sing out your praises and tell everyone
what you have done for me. Amen.*

DAY 236
A LOOK BEHIND THE CURTAIN

**"There is nothing concealed that will not be disclosed,
or hidden that will not be made known."**

LUKE 12:2

◆

I remember watching the movie *The Wizard of Oz* for the first time as a boy. Like the Cowardly Lion, I was terrified when the great Wizard of Oz made his first appearance in the movie. Only later when Toto pulled back the curtain did I realize the great and mighty Oz was really a stammering carnival conman from Kansas.

That day I learned an important lesson: when you pull back the curtain, things aren't always what they seem.

Jane hadn't been to a church in years. A friend invited her to visit the church down the street. Jane was overwhelmed with how wonderful it was. The people were friendly. The music was inspiring. Even more importantly, she learned so much from the pastor's sermons. She grew closer to her God and Savior. She loved her new church home.

Jane decided to become a member and get involved. That's when things started to change. She offered to help with a church picnic, but was soon saddened by the way the other ladies talked to and about each other.

Then she began attending the monthly congregational meeting. The meeting wasn't like going to worship. The discussion revolved around money. The business was slow and the topics mundane. At the second meeting she attended, two men from the congregation got into a heated debate about whether or not the church should buy a new riding lawn mower. The pastor made a snide remark to one of them and the other stormed out.

Jane became disillusioned with her new church. Worship was never the same. The curtain had been pulled back. She could never look at her pastor and fellow members the same again.

Sadly such stories are all too common in Christian churches today. Initially visitors are enamored with friendly people and wonderful worship, but then the truth comes out about struggles behind the scenes. Weaknesses or sins of the pastor become public. The curtain is pulled back and people become disillusioned.

As pastors and churches, what can we do about this sad phenomenon? First of all, we need to remember that we have a big sticker on our foreheads which reads, "Property of Christ."

HOW WE LIVE AND ACT DIRECTLY AFFECTS HOW PEOPLE SEE JESUS.

How we live and act directly affects how people see Jesus. Whether fair or not, many in our world judge Christianity by the behavior of Christians. So reflect Christ's love, not just as you worship on Sunday morning, but also in congregational meetings on Sunday night and at work on Monday morning.

As sinful human beings, however, we are not always going to be a positive reflection of our Savior's love. No matter how wonderful the church, the stain of sin still seeps through its walls. No matter how pious the pastor, sin still rushes through his veins. No matter how hard we try, every church has its warts and scars.

So how do we keep people from becoming disillusioned when they look behind the curtain? Simple. Get rid of the curtain.

No, I am not suggesting you hang your dirty laundry out for all to see. I am not encouraging you to publicize your failings and weaknesses. But as pastors and churches you can openly admit you aren't perfect. You can talk honestly about your struggles and confess your sins. You can show the world what it means to be sinners who appreciate God's amazing gift of forgiveness.

When new people express interest in joining our church, I always tell them, "Our church is wonderful, but it is not heaven on earth. Our church is not a museum of saints. It's a hospital for sinners."

They can't become disillusioned if there is no illusion.

Today I am thankful for/that _____

Dear God, help my church and me personally to shine the light of your love to the world. Give us humility and honesty to admit that we are a group of sinners who cling desperately to your amazing forgiveness. Amen.

———————◆———————

DAY 237
WORTHY OF MERCY

[God our Savior] saved us, not because of righteous things we had done, but because of his mercy.

TITUS 3:5

◆

"He doesn't deserve mercy." Those words caught my attention as I watched a recent documentary about O. J. Simpson on ESPN. They were spoken by an angry protestor demanding justice for the murders of Nicole Brown Simpson and Ron Goldman.

If we're honest with ourselves, such words often simmer in our hearts and even erupt from our lips. Some people just don't deserve mercy. Some people aren't worthy of forgiveness.

The man who massacred 26 men, women, and children at the church in Sutherland Springs, Texas. The sexual predators in Hollywood and Washington. Your abusive father. Your cheating husband. Your backstabbing best friend.

I know we have a forgiving God. I know he wants me to forgive others, but some people just aren't worthy of mercy. Some people just don't deserve forgiveness.

Actually, nobody does.

Mercy is not for the worthy. Forgiveness is not for the deserving.

FORGIVENESS IS NOT FOR THE DESERVING.

God doesn't have mercy on you because deep down you are a good person. He doesn't forgive you because you go to church and try to make amends. Mercy by definition is unearned and undeserved.

And that's a good thing because we definitely don't deserve it. We like to think we are more deserving because our sins aren't as bad. Our mistakes aren't broadcast on the ten o'clock news. Sure we're not perfect, but we deserve mercy because we try to be good, upstanding Christians.

That, however, is a delusion of the devil. In his Sermon on the Mount (Matthew chapters 5–7), Jesus delivers us from such delusions. You say you haven't killed anybody. Jesus tells us that in God's eyes anger and hatred are tantamount to murder. You say you haven't cheated. If you have looked at a woman lustfully, if you have peeked at porn, if you have longed for someone other than your spouse, you are just as bad as the perverted sex offenders in Hollywood and Washington.

If you keep the whole law and fail in just one minor detail, you are guilty of breaking it all. And we have failed miserably in more than just one minor detail.

O. J. Simpson does not deserve God's mercy, but neither do you. Neither do I. Yet that is exactly what we have received. Every day, God's mercies are new. Every day, God forgives us because Jesus suffered our punishment and died our death on the cross. Every day, God gives us new opportunities and blessings we definitely do not deserve.

When we truly begin to grasp God's undeserved, unearned, unfathomable mercy toward us, it changes how we view the other lousy sinners around us. How can you forgive your abusive father? How can you let go of what your husband did to you? How can you avoid looking at fallen celebrities and politicians as unworthy of mercy? By remembering God's mercy toward you.

Mercy is not for the worthy.

Today I am thankful for/that _____

Merciful God, thank you for not treating us as
we deserve. As you have had mercy on me,
help me to show mercy to others. Amen.

◆

DAY 238
OUR FAMILY TREE

This is the genealogy of Jesus the Messiah
the son of David, the son of Abraham . . .

MATTHEW 1:1

◆

Every family seems to have a family historian—that one person who is fascinated by the family tree. They are the protectors of the past, the guardians of family documents, photographs, and heirlooms. They are the ones who can tell you the name of your great-aunt on your mother's side and what town in Germany your great-great-grandfather was born in.

A whole industry has been built to assist family historians in finding their roots. You can research census records and test your DNA on Ancestry.com. You can join community genealogy support groups at your local library. Just google "genealogy help" and you will find a myriad of resources.

Many believe learning about previous generations will help them understand who they are today. Others find it a complete waste of time.

The Bible is full of family trees—long lists of names of fathers and sons, births and deaths. When most people come to those lists in their Bible reading, they skip right over them. It seems like such a waste of time reading lists of strange Semitic names. Why does God even include them in the Bible?

Those family trees are a reminder to us that the Bible isn't simply stories. It's history. These are real people who lived real lives, just like you and me. They are people who struggled with their own sin and selfishness. They are believers who trusted in the promise of a Savior.

Their story is our story. Reading and learning about them helps us understand who we are. Even more importantly, it helps us understand who our Savior is.

A thin red thread is woven into the tapestry of the Old Testament. It is a line, starting with Adam and ending with Jesus. If you have a chance today, read Matthew 1:1-17—Jesus' family tree through his mother Mary. Or read Luke 3:23-38—Jesus' legal genealogy through his stepfather Joseph.

Jesus is God himself, conceived by the Holy Spirit. Yet in the miracle of the incarnation, he can also trace his ancestry back to Adam and Eve. Jesus was born as a human being, the descendant of sinful people like you and me— Noah the drunk, Abraham the liar, Rahab the prostitute, David the murderer. Their story is our story—a story of sin and redemption, a story of God's amazing patience and love.

THOSE LISTS OF NAMES TELL US . . . WHO JESUS IS.

Those lists of names tell us who we are and, more importantly, who Jesus is. God loved you so much his story was woven into ours. The divine became human. The infinite God became an infant.

God became a part of humankind's family tree in order to take our place, to die our death, to free us from the punishment we deserve.

Whether you are fascinated by family trees or could care less about your familial roots, don't be too quick to pass over those lists of names in the Bible.

They help us understand who we are. They are history. They are *his* story.

In them we find God woven into our family tree.

Today I am thankful for/that _____

_____

Dear Jesus, thank you for becoming our Brother in humanity—for weaving your story into ours—in order to save us from the punishment we deserve. Amen.

DAY 239
TOUCHING THE UNTOUCHABLE

He reached out his hand and touched the man.

MARK 1:41

❖

In India, there is a group of people known as the Dalit. Dalit is the lowest level of India's strict caste system. If you are born a Dalit, there is little to nothing you can do about it. You are doomed to a life of menial labor, poverty, and persecution. *Dalit* in Hindi means "broken" or "scattered." In English they are simply called "Untouchables."

Though much has been done to overcome the racism and persecution of the Dalit in India, in rural areas they are still not allowed to eat or associate with people of other castes. They are not allowed to enter temples or even walk the same village paths as everybody else. They are untouchable.

Ancient Israel had its own group of untouchables. They were called "lepers." Strictly speaking, a leper is someone who suffers from the highly contagious and painful disease of leprosy. In biblical times, however, the term was used for a wide range of contagious skin conditions.

In ancient Israel, if a person was found to have leprosy, he or she would be forced to live away from the rest of society, not only due to the contagiousness of the disease, but also because they were looked at as "unclean." They were considered the scum of society. Most people thought they must have done something terrible to deserve such a terrible disease.

Few people would go near a leper. Nobody would ever dare to touch one. That's what makes what Jesus did so shocking.

One day, a leper ran up to Jesus. He fell to his knees. "If you are willing," he pleaded, "you can make me clean." Filled with compassion, Jesus reached out his hand and touched him. "I am willing," he said. "Be clean!" Immediately the man was healed.

It is difficult for us today to understand how shocking Jesus' simple act of compassion would have been. It was scandalous. It was unthinkable. In my mind's eye, I can picture the people around Jesus reaching out to him in slow motion, trying to stop him from touching the man, yelling, "Nooooo!"

Jesus touched an untouchable. In his love and compassion, he wasn't ashamed to meet a dirty, disgusting sinner where he was.

Jesus' love is shocking and scandalous. God, the Creator and Lord of the universe, the God who fills all things, reached down and met us dirty sinners where we were. He ate with us. He walked the same paths as us. He touched us.

He lived and died for us and among us.

JESUS' LOVE IS SHOCKING AND SCANDALOUS.

God is not some impersonal, distant deity who condescendingly looks down on us from above. He descends to us and meets us where we are.

In fact, that is what he does every time we receive the Sacrament of Holy Communion. Sometimes we fail to appreciate how shocking the Lord's Supper really is. In a very real way—in a way we can't see or fully understand—God reaches down and physically touches us.

The perfect God of the universe communes with sinners. He meets us where we are and heals us of the dirty and disgusting disease of our sins. He washes us clean. He forgives us.

Think about it. The Lord and King of all things reaches down and touches untouchables like you and me.

It's simply shocking.

Today I am thankful for/that _____

_____

Dear Jesus, thank you for your shocking, outrageous, scandalous love which reaches out to touch sinners like me. Amen.

DAY 240
BLESSED ASSURANCE

Now faith is confidence in what we hope for and
assurance about what we do not see.

HEBREWS 11:1

◆

Fanny Crosby (1820–1915) was blind. She blamed her blindness on a controversial treatment she was given for swelling in her eyes when she was just six weeks old. Modern physicians believe she was born blind due to a congenital condition. Either way, Fanny lived her life in darkness.

That didn't stop Fanny from becoming one of the most influential writers of her generation. She composed poems for Congress. She recited her poetry to presidents. She regularly contributed to the *Saturday Evening Post*.

She also wrote the words to over 8,000 hymns.

Among her many influential friends and collaborators was Phoebe Knapp, daughter of a notable Methodist preacher of the day and an accomplished organist.

One day Fanny was visiting Phoebe at her apartment in New York City. "Oh Fanny," her friend told her. "I have had a new melody racing through my mind for some time now, and I just can't think of anything else. Let me play it for you and perhaps you can help me with the words."

Upon hearing the melody, Fanny Crosby burst out, "Why, that music says, 'Blessed assurance, Jesus is mine!'"

So began the collaboration which produced one of the most beloved hymns of all time.

Blessed assurance, Jesus is mine!
Oh what a foretaste of glory divine!
Heir of salvation, purchase of God,
Born of his Spirit, washed in his blood.
(Let All the People Praise You, *p. 26*)

Fanny Crosby was sure. She was certain she was going to heaven. Are you?

For years, as I visited our local nursing home, a wonderful man named T. J. attended my Bible studies. Among other things, T. J. was one of the best domino players I have ever met. In the course of our Bible studies, I would often ask the residents if they were going to heaven.

"I hope so," was always T. J.'s response.

"Do you believe in Jesus?" I would ask him. "Do you believe that Jesus died for your sins on the cross?"

"Yes, sir," T. J. would always respond.

"Then you are going to heaven for sure," I would tell him.

T. J. is now with his Savior in heaven. So is Fanny Crosby. I can be sure of that, not because of anything they did or who they were, but because of who Jesus is and what he did. I can be sure because the Holy Spirit worked faith in their hearts—faith which they publicly confessed.

IT IS NOT ARROGANT OR PRESUMPTIVE TO BE CERTAIN YOU ARE GOING TO HEAVEN.

It is not arrogant or presumptive to be certain you are going to heaven. It doesn't depend on you. You have messed everything up. One sin condemns—you have thousands. You have said what God said not to say. You have touched what God said not to touch. You have gone where God said not to go.

You deserve hell, but you can be sure you are going to heaven, because it doesn't depend on you. You can be sure because Jesus said, "It is finished." You can be sure because the minister poured water on you and said, "I baptize you in the name of the Father and of the Son and of the Holy Spirit." You can be sure because God promises it to you and God does not lie.

Fanny Crosby was blind, but through faith she could see. Through faith she could be sure. So can you. May God grant you that blessed assurance.

Today I am thankful for/that _____

_____

*Thank you, Lord, for the blessed assurance
you have placed in my heart. Help me to
trust in you and your love every
day of my life. Amen.*

DAY 241
YOU NEVER RETIRE FROM BEING A CHRISTIAN

"As long as it is day, we must do the works of him who sent me. Night is coming, when no one can work."

JOHN 9:4

◆

According to recent reports, Baby Boomers are retiring at a rate of about 10,000 per day. Many, if not most, working Americans dream of retirement. They can't wait to finally be able to rest—to do the things they always wanted to do. Retirement, however, isn't always what it's cracked up to be. Many struggle in retirement because of financial constraints and failing health.

Some, however, live the dream. They travel when they want. They rest when they want. They do what they want because they are retired.

As Christians enters their golden years, there is a temptation to see themselves as "retired." They've put in their time at church. They've worked hard. They've earned the right to rest.

Others feel like there is nothing more they can do. They can't serve in the ways they did when they were younger. They can't mow the church yard. They can't teach Sunday school. They can't sing in choir anymore. Therefore, they are finished. They are retired.

What we often forget is that you never retire from being a Christian.

"As long as it is day," Jesus said, "we must do the work of him who sent me. Night is coming when no one can work." As long as we have breath in our lungs, God has work for us to do.

As the hymn writer once wrote, "Let none hear you idly saying, 'There is nothing I can do'" (CW 573:4). Even if you are in a nursing home or bedridden, you can still serve. You can pray for your families, for our country, for our world. If you have nobody else to pray for, please pray for me.

You can write letters and send care packages to missionaries. You can read Bible stories to your grandchildren. You can encourage younger generations in their faith. You can be an example of trust in God even as pain and time ravage your body.

The story is often told of a missionary who spent his entire ministry—over 45 years—in the deep bush of Africa. He sacrificed most modern comforts and was separated from family and friends for years at a time.

When he finally retired, he boarded a plane with his wife to return to the United States. When the plane landed, he looked out the window. A large crowd had gathered with "Welcome Home" signs. A band was playing.

The missionary was touched and overwhelmed by the reception. But as he was about to leave the plane, a federal marshal asked him to step aside. A famous senator was returning on the same flight from a peace-keeping mission in Africa. The band and well-wishers were for him.

By the time the missionary deplaned, no one was left to greet him. He angrily whined to his wife, "I served and sacrificed for 45 years, and now, when I finally retire, there isn't even one person here to welcome me home."

That's when he heard a voice whisper in his ear, "My son, you aren't home yet."

YOU AREN'T HOME YET.

My friend, you aren't home yet. Your work here isn't finished. Jesus has earned for you a pension beyond your wildest dreams. One day, you will celebrate your retirement party with the angels of heaven and with all the saints who labored before you.

One day you will rest from all your labors, but for now God still has work for you to do.

Today I am thankful for/that _____

_____

Lord, open my eyes every day to see the opportunities you give me to live and work for you who lived and died for me. Amen.

DAY 242
THE GREAT AND POWERFUL ME

All of you, clothe yourselves with humility toward
one another, because, "God opposes the proud,
but shows favor to the humble." Humble
yourselves, therefore, under God's
mighty hand, that he may lift
you up in due time.

1 PETER 5:5,6

◆

In Greek mythology, Narcissus was a hunter. His father was a god. His mother was a nymph. Due to his supernatural pedigree, Narcissus was strikingly handsome. Men wanted to be like him. Women swooned in his presence.

Yet for all his outward beauty, inside Narcissus was a rotting corpse of pride and vanity. He only cared about himself. He hurt others. Eventually Nemesis, the Greek god of revenge, lured Narcissus to a pool where he became so enamored of his own reflection he couldn't look away.

In time, Narcissus realized his reflection would never requite his love. He despaired and took his own life.

Narcissism is defined as "extremely self-centered with intense feelings of self-importance." Narcissism manifests itself in pride, vanity, and selfishness.

In a world dominated by selfie sticks and photobombs, narcissism reigns. Young people post selfies on Facebook and Instagram, judging their self-worth by how many likes and comments they get. Bloggers post articles and podcasts hoping to hear how smart or insightful they are.

Voters vote for politicians who tell them what they want to hear, who agree with their point of view, who tell them that they are not the problem. The problem is those who disagree with them. The other party is the cause of all the evils in our society today.

Church shoppers look for churches that fit them. The music needs to be apropos to their tastes. The preaching has to apply to their lives. They want churches who teach what they believe. In a narcissistic world, Salad Bar Christianity is the ideal. You can pick and choose what you want to believe.

DEEP DOWN, EVERY ONE OF US IS A NARCISSIST.

As we decry the narcissism of our world, however, we need to look more closely at our own reflection in the pool. Deep down, every one of us is a narcissist. All sin is essentially narcissism, because all sin is selfishness.

All sin is the idolatry of self, worshiping the great and powerful me. Sin is all about me and what I want instead of what God wants. And just as Narcissus' love of self led him to disillusionment and despair, our vain worship of self is a lie. It ends in the pit of hell.

Yet our God did something amazing. He didn't leave us to vainly waste away while staring at our own reflection. He selflessly sacrificed everything, suffering our pain and our punishment, so we could live with him forever in Paradise.

He lovingly and firmly turns our eyes from our own warped view of self so we can see his cross and sacrifice and love. He turns our thoughts away from ourselves and to him.

He helps us to see that church is about him and not about the great and powerful me. He leads us to temper our political zeal with love and respect for others. He uses us to build up and serve our neighbor.

But watch out. Until the day you die, the devil will try to lure you to the pool. Our world will encourage you to make everything about you. A part of you will always yearn to stare at your own reflection.

So keep your eyes on the cross. See your Savior's sacrifice. Follow his example of selflessness.

Today I am thankful for/that _____

_____

Holy God, forgive me my pride and narcissism.
Help me to turn my eyes from me and what I
want so that I can see you and what you
have done for me. Give me a humble
heart which wants to serve you
and others. Amen.

465

DAY 243
IMMUTABLE

Every good and perfect gift is from above, coming down from the Father of the heavenly lights, who does not change like shifting shadows.

JAMES 1:17

◆

"The only thing that is constant is change." The ancient Greek philosopher, Heraclitus, witnessed a world in constant flux. He recognized that things never stay the same. "No man ever steps in the same river twice," he famously observed.

What Heraclitus perceived 2,500 years ago we still witness in our world today. Fifteen years ago, who would have ever dreamed of a world dominated by smartphones and tablets? Thirty years ago, who would have foreseen President Donald Trump or Caitlyn Jenner? Few people today can truly grasp how much our world has changed in the last 100 years.

On a more personal level, not one of us has the same life we had 20, 10, or even 5 years ago. Children grow. Jobs evolve. Cars break down. Marriages begin and end. People die.

Even the weather is capricious. As the old saying goes, "If you don't like the weather here in Texas, just wait a minute. It will change."

In a world of constant change, only one thing always remains the same: God.

As James once wrote, our God "doesn't change like the shifting shadows." God's immutability—his changelessness—is rock to which we can anchor ourselves as the winds of change beat against us.

Our God never changes; that means how he feels about you will never change. God won't wake up 20 years from now and decide he doesn't love you anymore. If he loves you today, he will love you forever. If he forgives you today, he will forgive you forever.

YOU CAN COUNT ON GOD'S PROTECTION AND PRESENCE.

God's power and wisdom and control of all things are a constant. He has never and will never leave your side. In a world full of flip-flopping politicians and fickle people, he is the only one we can truly rely on.

Our God never changes; that means if he says he will do something, it will always be done. God's immutability means he always keeps his promises. You can count on God's protection and presence, his forgiveness and faithfulness, his help and heaven. Why? Because God promises you those things and God never changes. He always keeps his promises.

So as the winds and waves of our ever-changing world beat against you, cling to your never-changing God. He is our rock. He is our anchor.

He is immutable.

Today I am thankful for/that _____

_____

Immutable Lord, in a topsy-turvy, ever-changing world you are my rock and anchor. Help me to trust that you will always keep your promises. Amen.

DAY 244
THE ENDS DON'T JUSTIFY THE MEMES

The words of the reckless pierce like swords, but the tongue of the wise brings healing. Truthful lips endure forever, but a lying tongue lasts only a moment.

PROVERBS 12:18,19

I was skeptical. Since the Parkland school shootings in 2018, my Facebook wall had been bombarded with memes making statistical claims to support people's political opinions in favor of or against gun control. I wondered: Could they all be true?

Were there really 18 school shootings in just the first three months of 2018? Does Switzerland really mandate that every citizen own a gun, yet the nation has the lowest amount of gun violence in the world? Do 4,400 teens really commit suicide every year due to bullying?

Over the next few days I tried to investigate the validity of every political meme which found its way onto my Facebook page. Now, understand that the sample size is small, but do you know how many memes turned out to be true?

None. Zero. Not one.

Many contained elements of truth, but not one was completely factual. Yet people continue to proudly paste them on their walls to support their personal beliefs, opinions, and political positions.

Over the last couple of years, the term "fake news" has become a part of the American vernacular. We regularly complain about the media and politicians who twist the truth or flat out promote lies.

But when you share a meme or link which is not completely accurate, you are doing the same thing. You are propagating fake news. You are lying. Even if you believe your point or position to be just, using false or manipulative statistics is wrong. The ends do not justify the means.

God wants us to speak the truth in love. Blindly sharing untruths breaks the Eighth Commandment. It's giving false testimony. Just because friends or family members share it on their pages doesn't make it true.

Especially in the politically charged environment in which we live, we as Christians have a responsibility to verify what we share on Facebook and other social media. Otherwise we are just spreading gossip and hearsay. We become propagators of fake news. We become a part of the problem.

So when you find a meme or link which shows clearly why your position on gun control, immigration, abortion, LGBTQ+ rights, or any other political issue is correct, don't just click "like" or "share." Google it. Go to reputable news sources to verify it. Check it out on Snopes.com.

GOD WANTS US TO SPEAK THE TRUTH IN LOVE.

If you can't verify it, you shouldn't share it—even if it seems to perfectly prove how right your position is. Stopping the propagation of fake news doesn't begin with politicians and the media. It begins on your phone. It begins on your computer. It begins on your Facebook page.

To summarize, allow me to share a quote by the great Mark Twain which a friend recently shared with me on Facebook:

"Eighty-two percent of all statistics on Facebook are untrue."

Mark Twain was truly a man ahead of his time. The ends don't justify the memes.

Today I am thankful for/that _____

Lord of Truth, help me to speak the truth in love,
not only in what I say with my mouth,
but also in what I share and post
on social media. Amen.

DAY 245
FOOLS

For the message of the cross is foolishness
to those who are perishing.

1 CORINTHIANS 1:18

◆

It all began with an edict by Pope Gregory XIII in 1582. The Julian calendar used by most of the Western world failed to accurately mark the days and years. A new calendar, called the Gregorian calendar, established a more accurate number of leap years as well as other innovations.

Among other things, it officially set January 1 as the first day of the year.

Up to that point, many Western European countries celebrated New Year's on different days. In some countries, New Year's was celebrated at the end of March and beginning of April.

When Pope Gregory published his new calendar, Facebook did not exist, nor did CNN or even the telephone. Many continued to celebrate New Year's on their traditional dates, decades and even centuries later.

Those who continued to celebrate the new year at the end of March and beginning of April, either due to ignorance or just plain obstinacy, were soon mocked by their fellow countrymen. They were called fools and practical jokes were played on them.

According to some historians, thus began the celebration of April Fools' Day.

For those who don't believe in Jesus, our faith seems foolish. We believe that 2,000 years ago, the all-powerful God who fills every last corner of the universe was born as a baby to a virgin and laid in a feeding trough. We believe that he later was brutally tortured and killed by order of a Roman governor for no legitimate reason, but that, after a couple of days, he came alive again.

He then appeared to a few hundred people before disappearing into the clouds, never to be seen again. We believe that, because God was born as a man—was nailed to a piece of wood, died, and came back to life—we are now free from any guilt or punishment for every bad thing we do. We believe we will live forever with him one day in a perfect place of happiness called heaven somewhere beyond our existence here on earth.

Honestly, it does sound a bit far-fetched. Many of the greatest scientists and scholars of our age mock us and call us dumb for believing the Bible. Even the apostle Paul was laughed off by the educated elite of his day (Acts 17:32). As Christians we are fools.

The word *sophomore* literally means "a wise fool." By their second year of high school, teenagers are wiser, but they still have a lot to learn. They are "wise fools."

As Christians, we are sophomores in a different sense. Even though the world considers us foolish, we have true wisdom. In 1 Corinthians chapter 1, Paul acknowledges that, according to the world, what we believe as Christians is weak and foolish. Only through faith can a person see its true wisdom and power.

Through Jesus' humble death and glorious resurrection, we have become heirs of heaven. We are now sons and daughters of the King of all creation. Through faith, we have true understanding.

ONE DAY, GOD WILL REVEAL WHO THE TRUE FOOLS REALLY ARE.

Now I can't prove any of this, mind you. We accept it by faith. To some, that seems foolish. It seems ridiculous.

But instead of getting upset when the world calls us fools, instead of getting embarrassed, instead of feeling like you have to defend or prove what you believe, embrace the foolishness of the cross. Accept the fact that the world does not and will never understand. Jesus told us it would be that way. Some will mock us. Some will point and call us fools.

Don't worry about it. Don't be ashamed. Don't back down. One day, God will reveal who the true fools really are.

Today I am thankful for/that _____

_____

Lord God, as our society becomes more hostile toward Christianity, our crosses become heavier to bear. It is hard when people look at me as foolish for believing in you. Give me the courage and peace I need to not back down or be ashamed of you. Amen.

DAY 246
SWEET SORROW

After that, we who are still alive and are left will be caught up together with them in the clouds to meet the Lord in the air.

1 THESSALONIANS 4:17

◆

"Parting is such sweet sorrow."

As Juliet bid farewell to Romeo in their famous balcony scene, she was sad. To be separated from her true love was torturous. But the sorrow she felt in his absence would be "sweet" as she anticipated their next rendezvous. The anticipation of seeing Romeo again overwhelmed her with joy.

Recently I have had the privilege of conducting a number of funerals. For me, funerals are full of mixed emotions. On the one hand, they are sad.

Parting is sorrow. I have sat with families as they watched their loved ones gasp their final breaths. I have seen and shared in their tears.

Death hurts. Death separates. Family and friends ache with the realization that they will never again see their loved one in this life. In a sense, funerals are the final goodbye. They are often our last opportunity to see our loved one before the casket is closed.

PARTING IS SORROW, BUT A CHRISTIAN FUNERAL IS TRULY SWEET SORROW.

Parting is sorrow, but a Christian funeral is truly sweet sorrow. In a Christian funeral, I have the privilege of sharing God's powerful promises of forgiveness, heaven, and family reunions.

Because Jesus lived and died as our substitute, all those who believe in him are forgiven forever for every failure and falling. Because Jesus defeated death with his resurrection, those who die in faith will live with him forever in heaven. On the Last Day, they too will rise physically from the grave.

Those promises are true for all who trust in Jesus. They are true for your loved ones who died. They are true for you. That means one day, you will be reunited. One day you will see your mother again. One day you will hug your grandfather again. One day you will laugh and celebrate with your best friend.

At a Christian funeral we talk about that day—the day when we will be reunited. The anticipation of that day fills us with joy and excitement. Even as our hearts ache in their absence, we know we have an eternity with them waiting for us in a place where there will be no more tears, no more pain, no more regrets.

Many, if not most, pastors will tell you they would much rather conduct a funeral than a wedding, not because they delight in the sorrow of others, but rather because it is pure joy to point hurting hearts to God's powerful promises.

Tomorrow I have the privilege of conducting yet another funeral. I am sad. She was a friend whom I will miss dearly. But I know I will see her again.

And that is truly sweet.

Today I am thankful for/that _____

Blessed Lord, though it is hard for me to say,
thank you for taking my loved ones who have
died in the faith. I trust that they are with you
enjoying the happiness and perfection of heaven.
I know that by your grace I will see them again.
Give me patience and peace while I wait. Amen.

◆

DAY 247
PINTEREST-PERFECT

"His master replied, 'Well done,
good and faithful servant!'"

MATTHEW 25:21

◆

I recently returned from a pastors' conference. We had dynamic and inspiring speakers. The workshops gave us tons of useful ideas we could incorporate into our ministries. I was surrounded by talented pastors who shared the wonderful ministries their churches are doing.

And I came home feeling beaten up.

I was reminded of all the things we should be doing as a church and aren't. I was so overwhelmed by the sheer number of new ideas we could try, it's been hard to know where to even begin. As I admired the gifts and successes of other pastors, I found myself struggling with feelings of inadequacy and jealousy.

I think I now understand the pressure some moms feel in our Pinterest-perfect world. For example, you see your daughter's friend arrive at school with her intricately braided hair and perfectly pressed dress. You, however, got up late and your daughter's hair looks like a cross between a Chia Pet and Oscar Gamble.

You could walk through your neighbor's house with a white glove and never find a speck of dust. Their children's rooms have all the latest and greatest decoration ideas from Pinterest. Your youngest son is still sleeping in his sister's old room with pink walls and posters of Justin Timberlake glued to the closet door.

You go to your daughter's Valentine's Day party at school and one mom brings strawberries which look like perfectly shaped hearts. You forgot about the party and quickly grabbed a box of Pop Tarts on your way out the door.

Just like I at times feel the pressure to be the perfect pastor, many moms feel the pressure to be perfect Pinterest moms—able to incorporate every new and innovative idea pinned to the picture-perfect pages of Pinterest.

Sometimes I wonder if some moms don't feel like I do at a pastors' conference when they go browsing on Pinterest.

In the end, however, the problem isn't Pinterest or even my pastors' conferences. The problem is that we base our self-worth on how we measure up to others.

Our worth, however, has nothing to do with who we are or how well we measure up. It doesn't depend on how cool of a pastor I am or how well-braided your daughter's hair is.

OUR WORTH COMES FROM OUR GOD.

Our worth comes from our God who loved us in spite of the fact we haven't measured up. Though you are far from perfect, you are priceless to God. Jesus gave up everything for you. He sacrificed everything for you. He died for you so you could live with him forever in heaven.

You are forgiven. You are accepted. You are loved by God no matter what treat you take to your daughter's Valentine's Day party at school.

God doesn't demand that you be the best mom or that I be the best pastor in the world. He simply wants you to thank him for his love by being the best you. What God wants is faithfulness. He wants you to do the best you can with the gifts and opportunities he has given you.

You don't have to be what others are. So stop pressuring yourself to have picture-perfect Pinterest homes or families. That's impossible. That's pride.

Simply do your best to be the mom, the wife, and the person God made you to be. God doesn't want Pinterest-perfect. He wants faithfulness.

Today I am thankful for/that _____

Father, forgive me for the many times I have based my self-worth on how I measure up to others. Thank you for your amazing forgiveness and for accepting me as I am. Help me to be the best at what you made me to be. Amen.

DAY 248
THE CENTER OF THE UNIVERSE

When I consider your heavens, the work of your
fingers, the moon and the stars, which you have
set in place, what is mankind that you are mindful
of them, human beings that you care for them?

PSALM 8:3,4

In his book, *The Hitchhiker's Guide to the Galaxy,* Douglas Adams states the obvious: "Space is big." But have you ever wondered how big space really is? A friend of mine recently shared with me the following analogy.

If the ballpoint of the pen on my desk was the earth, the sun would be the size of a ping pong ball about 15 feet away. The next nearest star to our solar system, *Proxima Centauri,* would then be another ping pong ball located in the city of Toronto, Canada.

I live in Texas, by the way.

That's how relatively far *Proxima Centauri* is from the earth. And that is the closest star to our solar system. There are over 100 billion stars in our galaxy,

475

all of which are trillions of miles farther away. And that's just our galaxy. Scientists estimate that there are over 200 billion galaxies in the known universe, each containing between 100 billion and one trillion stars.

Douglas Adams was right. Space is big.

From the perspective of the moon, the earth appears to be the size of a marble. From the perspective of other galaxies, the earth is unperceivable. It is invisible. It is nothing.

So what does that make us? We are insignificant microscopic specks in God's universe. Yet God doesn't treat us that way. In his great love, he made tiny, insignificant human beings the crown of his creation.

If you have a chance yet today, read Psalm 8. It gives us a proper perspective of our relative size and place in God's universe. We are insignificant microscopic specks, yet God knows and loves each of us personally.

We need that perspective because often our perception is skewed. Like the warped images in a funhouse mirror, our sinful mind distorts how we look at ourselves. We see ourselves as bigger than we really are. We make ourselves the center of our own universe. My life, my goals, and my happiness become the purpose of my existence here on earth.

God made us tiny specks to be the crown of his creation. And what do we do? We treat him as small. We treat him as insignificant. Instead of our lives revolving around him, he becomes a satellite which enters our orbit only when we think we need him.

The amazing thing is that God loved us rebellious specks so much that he didn't want us to suffer the punishment we deserve for our distorted view of ourselves and our place in his universe. The God who created and fills the vastness of the universe became an insignificant microscopic speck just like you and me to take our place and die our death.

And because he did, we are forgiven for all the times we have made ourselves the center of our own universe. We are forgiven for all the times we have relegated God to being simply a small satellite which only enters our orbit occasionally.

DON'T RELEGATE HIM TO BEING JUST A PART OF YOUR LIFE.

The God who created and fills the vastness of space does not treat us as we deserve. He loves us. He forgives us. He gives us heaven.

Keep that perspective. Remember your place in God's universe. Remember who you are and what he has done for you. Don't make him simply a satellite which enters the orbit of your life every so often. Don't relegate him to being just a part of your life. He is your whole life. Everything you have and everything you are is because of him.

May God always be the center of your universe.

Today I am thankful for/that _____

_____

Almighty God, you created the vastness of space.
You fill the universe with your presence. Help
us to always remember our relative size
and place in your universe. May our
lives always revolve around you. Amen.

DAY 249
THERE IS NO TRY

Do not merely listen to the word, and so deceive
yourselves. Do what it says.

JAMES 1:22

In the movie *The Empire Strikes Back* young Luke Skywalker learned the ways of the force from a wise old Jedi Master named Yoda. When Yoda gave him the task of raising his spaceship from its swampy grave, Luke whined that it was impossible. When Yoda insisted that it wasn't, Luke shrugged his shoulders and said, "I guess I'll give it a try."

"No," Yoda snapped. "Try not. Do or do not. There is no try."

To try meant he would accept defeat. To try meant not being fully committed. To try meant failure.

If you search the Bible from cover to cover, never once will you hear God encourage us to try. He says, "Do and do not." The Ten Commandments are not ten suggestions. God says, "Do and do not. There is no try."

Yet, as Christians, we often lower our expectations of ourselves. We give ourselves a way out when we say, "God wants us to try to be good people, to try to control our anger, or to try to not drink too much." We make it sound like it doesn't matter to God whether we succeed or fail as long as we give it the old college try.

God doesn't speak that way in his Word. His law is clear. Honor your father and mother. Do not steal. Do not covet. Do not murder. Do not lust. Do not hate. Love your enemies.

GOD DOESN'T GIVE AN *A* FOR EFFORT.

If you fail to obey any one of God's commands, you deserve his anger and eternal punishment in the horrors of hell. It doesn't matter how hard you try. God doesn't give an *A* for effort.

His law simply says do or do not. There is no try.

Thankfully, God didn't simply try to save us. His love led him to do. Jesus obeyed every one of God's commands perfectly in our place. He paid the price. He died our death. He did it all.

Therefore, God forgives our failures. He forgives us for all the times we've lowered our expectations and were satisfied to just try instead of do his will. We are forever forgiven because Jesus did it all in our place.

But forgiveness doesn't mean God somehow lowers his standards. Forgiveness doesn't mean trying is good enough. God still says, "Do and do not. There is no try."

God's love does not negate his law. God still demands perfection. To water down his law is to cheapen his grace. Where we have failed, Jesus succeeded.

Because he did, you are forgiven. You are going to heaven through faith in him.

Now, out of love and thanks for what he has done for you, don't just try. Do. Live for him who lived and died for you.

Love your enemies. Control your anger. Stop gossiping. Stop lying. Stop cursing. Pray. Worship. Give.

Do and do not. There is no try.

Today I am thankful for/that _____

_____

Holy God and Lord, help me to perfectly obey
you in thought, word, and deed. Forgive me
for the times I fail, but help me to never use
that forgiveness as an excuse to be less
than what you expect of me. Amen.

DAY 250
WOW!

The fear of the LORD is the beginning of knowledge.
PROVERBS 1:7

As a boy, I was confused by that verse. For years, I struggled with fear. I knew the bad things I had done. In Sunday school, I was often reminded how God punishes sin—with floods and plagues and death.

God can be scary.

Yet I was also taught in Sunday school to be unafraid of God. He was my Savior and Friend. I could talk to him as a dear child talks to his loving father. I was forever forgiven because of Jesus.

So was I supposed to be afraid of God or not?

SO WAS I SUPPOSED TO BE AFRAID OF GOD OR NOT?

The fear of the LORD of which wise old King Solomon speaks is really what we call "awe." Awe is what you feel when something amazes you, astounds you, makes you say "Wow!"

In English, we have two words which have "awe" as their root: awesome and awful. Both actually mean the same thing—something which fills you with awe. Yet they are complete opposites.

For example, the Grand Canyon is awesome. When you stand in its presence, you can't help but say, "Wow! That is amazing!"

Cancer, on the other hand, is awful. When you see how it ravages the body and life of someone you love, you can't help but say, "Wow! That is horrible!"

Our God is both an awesome and awful God.

God is awful. The writer to the Hebrews wrote, "It is a dreadful thing to fall into the hands of the living God" (Hebrews 10:31). The God who created all things, who fills all things, whose hand controls time and eternity, is a holy God. He hates sin. He punishes it with the horrors of hell.

You and I are sinners. To face God means facing what we deserve. Just look how people reacted in the Bible when God appeared to them in his glory. As God descended on Mount Sinai in fire and smoke and lightning, the people trembled and cried out in fear.

It is an awful thing to stand as a sinner in the presence of a holy God.

That holy God, however, is also a God of mercy. The God who fills all things loved you and me so much that he was born in a barn. He lived as the poor son of a simple carpenter. He died a criminal's death.

Because he did, you and I are forgiven for every bad and ugly thing we have ever thought, said, or done. The all-powerful God who fills all things promises to always forgive, always protect, always watch over us. He promises that one day all those who believe in him will be freed from sin completely and will bask in his awesome glory forever.

The fear of the Lord is simply a healthy respect for who God is. The fear of the Lord means understanding that without the forgiveness Jesus won for us—if we turn our backs on him—we will face his awful judgment and the terror of his righteous anger.

Sadly, many in our world today have lost such fear of God. Without a proper respect for God's awful anger, however, they will never truly appreciate his awesome mercy.

Fear God. Appreciate his awesome mercy for you. Because of Jesus, you don't have to be afraid of God. You will never have to know his awful anger because Jesus suffered it in your place.

Because of Jesus, one day you will stand in the presence of the holy, all-powerful God and with a smile say, "Wow!"

Today I am thankful for/that _____

Almighty and merciful God, you are amazing.
I am in awe of your power and holiness, but
even more, I am grateful for your
awesome mercy. Amen.

DAY 251
THE TGIF CHALLENGE

Every good and perfect gift is from above, coming down
from the Father of the heavenly lights.

JAMES 1:17

◆

Thank God it's Friday. I'm sure a number of children in Edna, Texas, said those words yesterday. Friday was their last day of school.

TGIF. Thank God it's Friday.

Thank God summer's finally here. Thank God for vacations. Thank God for the weekend. Just think about how often in our lives we say, "Thank God this" and "Thank God that." Those words have become a part of the American vernacular.

Even people who don't believe in God joyfully celebrate TGIF.

But you'll notice we aren't actually thanking God when we say that phrase. We don't say, "TYGTIF" ("Thank you, God, that it's Friday"). We say, "Thank God it's Friday." In other words, we are telling other people they should thank God. We are inferring that we should thank God, but we aren't actually thanking him with those words.

If we are honest with ourselves, most of the time we aren't even thinking about God. We are just celebrating our good fortune.

That's why this Friday, I challenge you to actually thank God it's Friday. This Friday, as you leave your work or school, don't say, "Thank God it's Friday." Say, "Thank you, God, that it's Friday. Thank you, God, because you've gotten me through another week. Thank you, God, for this weekend when I can rest and worship you." Think about it. Mean it.

BY THANKING GOD, YOU ARE RECOGNIZING WHERE EVERY GOOD AND PERFECT GIFT COMES FROM.

I call that the TGIF Challenge. Every time you are tempted to say, "Thank God this" and "Thank God that," actually take the time to thank him.

By thanking God, you are recognizing where every good and perfect gift comes from. You are recognizing that everything we have and everything we are is because of our God's goodness which we don't deserve.

McDonald's was lying to me. I don't deserve a break today. I haven't earned the weekend with my hard work. The only thing I have earned or deserve in my life is God's punishment for all the good things I could have done which I have left undone. I deserve his punishment for all the times I took credit for the blessings in my life. I deserve his punishment for every time I failed to thank him for his goodness.

Thank God for his forgiveness. Thank God for his mercy. Thank God for Jesus.

Seriously. Take the time to say those words, "Thank you, God, for forgiving me. Thank you, God, for loving me after all I have done and failed to do. Thank you, Jesus, for suffering the horror and hell I deserve in my place."

Consider it practice. You see, when you get to heaven, you are going to be so happy—you are going to be so appreciative—you won't be able to stop saying, "Thank you, God!" Those words are definitely a part of the heavenly vernacular.

For now, though, go ahead and start small. Take the TGIF Challenge.

Thank God it's Friday.

Today I am thankful for/that _____

_____

Thank you, God, for today. Thank you for giving me so many good things I do not deserve. Thank you for not giving me what I do deserve because of my sins. Everything good in my life comes from you. Thank you. Amen.

DAY 252
I HAVE SINNED

I said, "I will confess my transgressions to the LORD."
And you forgave the guilt of my sin.

PSALM 32:5

❖

It's one of those indelible images from my youth—televangelist Jimmy Swaggart's now infamous, "I have sinned" speech. He had been caught with a prostitute. His multi-million-dollar media ministry was in jeopardy.

On national television, he apologized to his wife, his family, and his congregation. And then he cried out as tears poured down his face, "I have sinned against you, my Lord!"

Those tears proved to be crocodile tears as three years later he was once again caught with a prostitute. This time he abruptly told his congregation, "The Lord told me it's flat none of your business."

I have a confession to make. I have sinned.

That shouldn't come as a surprise to you. I know it doesn't come as a surprise to those who know me well. Every day I sin against God in my thoughts. Every day I sin against God with the words I say. Every day I sin against God with the bad things I do and the good things I leave undone.

The world doesn't consider some of my sins that bad. Many would laugh if I confessed them out loud. Some of my other sins would make you feel uncomfortable, disgusted, and horrified.

I have sinned against God and so have you.

Every single day of our lives, more often than we could ever count, we have disobeyed and disappointed our God. We deserve his anger and punishment. We deserve to rot forever in the Alcatraz of hell.

So we confess our sins to God. We ask the Holy Judge for mercy. But we don't beg God for mercy like the victim of a crazed gunman begging him not to shoot as the gun barrel presses against the back of our heads.

We don't ask for forgiveness hoping that maybe, just maybe, God might feel sorry for us and forgive us. We don't have to put on a show hoping that our tears might change his mind.

483

We can ask for forgiveness with the confidence that God has and always will forgive us because of Jesus. As Jesus hung on the cross 2,000 years ago on a dark Friday afternoon, God the Judge pounded him with our guilty verdict. Jesus suffered the punishment of every dumb and hurtful thing you and I would ever do.

There is now no punishment for those who are in Christ Jesus. You can trust that God has already forgiven you because of Jesus. When you confess your sins to God, you can do so with confidence. You can do so knowing that he loves you, that he forgives you, that he has removed your sin "as far as the east is from the west."

I have a confession to make. Sometimes I confess my sins to God with a smile on my face.

No, I'm not being blasphemous. I'm not being a hypocrite. It's just that I know God has already forgiven me. I don't have to stand in his presence shaking in my boots. I know that he loves me. I can bask in his warm embrace as a child in the powerful arms of his loving father.

Don't get me wrong. More times than I care to admit, I've been torn up over what I've done, the shame turning my stomach in knots, the tears rolling down my cheeks, and I have fallen on my knees before God. Sin hurts. Confession is hard.

DON'T EVER FEEL LIKE GOD DEMANDS A CERTAIN LEVEL OF SADNESS.

But don't ever feel like God demands a certain level of sadness. You don't have to put on a show. You don't have to beat your breast. You don't have to shed a requisite number of tears for him to forgive you.

You have been and always will be forgiven because of Jesus. Trust that truth. Believe it.

Confess your sins to God with confidence.

Today I am thankful for/that _____

_____

God, have mercy on me, a sinner. Amen.

DAY 253
FOR YOU

"This is my body given for you."

LUKE 22:19

◆

For you. Those are two tremendously powerful words. Every time I stand before God's altar to taste the bread and drink the wine, those words echo in my ears.

Though I stand in a church full of people, shoulder to shoulder with other Christians, sharing this meal with them, they all seem to fade away.

I stand alone with my Savior.

I stand before him, just as I am, full of warts and wickedness—a poor beggar in need of a forgiveness I definitely don't deserve. He comes to me and shows me what he has done for me.

"Here is my body which was bruised and beaten." "Here is the blood which gushed and sprayed from my back, from my head, from my hands, from my feet, and from my side."

As I stand there, how can I forget what he did? How can I forget what he suffered? And then he reminds me why.

"I did this . . . for you."

As Jesus died on the cross—as he suffered the punishment for the sins of every one of the hundreds of billions of people in human history—he was thinking about me personally. He was thinking about you personally.

He did it all for you. He did it so that God would never punish you for the crimes you have committed against him. He did it so that you could be forgiven. He did it so that you could live with him forever in heaven.

On the cross Jesus gave up everything for you. He bled for you. He died for you.

IT'S JESUS' LAST WILL AND TESTAMENT.

Holy Communion is a vivid, living, breathing reminder of what your Savior God has done for you. But it's more than a simple reminder.

It's also a covenant.

A covenant is a contract. In this case, it's Jesus' last will and testament—a legally binding guarantee.

485

Your name is printed in bold letters on the contract. Jesus has signed his own name in blood. It promises you—it guarantees you—that you are forgiven forever. You are washed clean. Jesus himself now lives in you.

How long has it been since you stood before your Savior—full of warts and wickedness—to be reminded of what he did for you? How long has it been since you last received that contract signed in his blood guaranteeing you the forgiveness of sins? When was the last time those two simple words, "for you," echoed in your ears?

Don't wait. You need that reminder. You need that forgiveness. You need that personal moment standing before your Savior. Holy Communion isn't something for other Christians or other churches to do.

Jesus gave it for you.

Today I am thankful for/that _____

_____

Dear Jesus, thank you. When I see all that you gave, all that you sacrificed, all that you suffered, I can't help but be amazed that you did it all for me. Amen.

DAY 254
IN THE SPHERE OF CHRIST

There is now no condemnation for those who are in Christ Jesus.

ROMANS 8:1

◆

I have a confession to make: I love Venn diagrams.

I know. My inner nerd is showing.

Invented by the 19th-century mathematician John Venn, Venn diagrams are graphs which help us visualize how things are related. Usually a Venn diagram will have two or more circles representing different groups or ideas. The areas where those circles overlap show what those groups or ideas have in common.

Venn diagrams are tremendous teaching tools. They also can be quite amusing. If you have a spare moment, google "funny Venn diagrams" and click on a few. Your inner nerd will thank me.

I was thinking of Venn diagrams this week as I was studying my Greek New Testament. (I know, my inner nerd is really showing.) In the Greek language, the preposition we usually translate as "in" has a unique connotation.

It literally means: "in the sphere of."

One of the most common descriptions of believers in the New Testament is to say that he or she is "in Christ," literally, "in the sphere of Christ." The expressions: "in Christ," "in the Lord," and "in him" occur 164 times in Paul's letters alone.

To believe in Jesus is to be in the sphere of Jesus. God promises wonderful blessings to those who find themselves in his sphere.

"There is now no condemnation for those who are in Christ Jesus," Paul tells us. In Christ, we are a "new creation" (2 Corinthians 5:17). God has reconciled us to himself in Christ (2 Corinthians 5:19). In Christ, we are saints (1 Corinthians 1:2) and temples of the Holy Spirit (Ephesians 2:22). In Christ, we have redemption and the forgiveness of sins (Ephesians 1:7). In Christ, we are given the strength to face any challenge (Philippians 4:13).

Through faith in Jesus, we are encircled by his grace. In the sphere of Jesus, we are safe and saved. In the sphere of Jesus, we find heaven.

Honestly, though, if you look at the Venn diagram of my life, my circle isn't always completely inside of Christ's circle. There is plenty of space where our circles overlap, but in my sin and selfishness I sometimes keep a part of me outside of the sphere of Jesus.

That part tends to overlap with the sphere of the world.

As Christians, we struggle at times to give ourselves completely over to God. We don't want people to think we are weird. We don't want to be different. We still want to have some "fun."

So we keep one foot in Christ and one foot in the world. We go to church and sing our hymns, but then cuss and tell dirty jokes with our buddies at work. We pray to God in times of trouble and find comfort in his forgiveness, but then use that forgiveness as an excuse to drink too much, sleep around, or wallow in our anger.

HE DOESN'T WANT OUR CIRCLE MERELY OVERLAPPING HIS.

As Christians, we love to talk about how God is a "part of our lives" or even "an important part of our lives." God doesn't want to be only a part of our lives. He doesn't want our circle merely overlapping his. To be a Christian means to live inside Christ's circle.

Through faith in Jesus, you are now surrounded by his grace and covered by his forgiveness. Out of love and thanks for all that he has done for you and trusting in him, make every effort to live completely in his circle. Don't worry what other people think of you. Don't listen to the lies of the world.

In the sphere of Christ, you have everything.

Today I am thankful for/that _____

_____

Dear Jesus, thank you for all that I am and have in you. Help me to live completely in you every day. Amen.

DAY 255
THE BLACK HOLE

Make the most of your time, because the days are evil.

EPHESIANS 5:16 EHV

◆

Black holes are the giant vacuum cleaners of the universe. They bend space and create a tremendous gravitational pull. Anything near them gets sucked in.

Time is a black hole. Have you ever noticed that? Many people long for the day when they can retire and finally have time to relax. Then when they finally retire, they take on tasks they never had time to do before. Their days fill up. All of a sudden they realize they have less time now than when they were working full-time.

IF YOU HAVE FREE TIME, IT WILL ALWAYS GET FILLED WITH SOMETHING.

If you have free time, it will always get filled with something. Whether it's cutting the lawn or cleaning your workshop, lounging in front of the TV or taking a nap, fishing or browsing Facebook, something will get sucked into that time.

So often I hear people tell me, "Pastor, we are extremely busy right now. We don't have time to go to church, but we'll get back when things lighten up." Sometimes they do. More often than not, however, they never come back. Why? Because once they have some free time, something else gets sucked into the black hole.

If you are waiting for your schedule to lighten up to get back to church or to have daily devotions in God's Word, it will never happen. Time is a black hole. Something else will always get sucked in.

The only way you are going to have time for God and his Word is if you make the time. Don't wait for a slot to free up in your calendar. Make time for God.

Remember he is the God who made time for you. He worked all of history to bring your Savior into the world. Jesus, your Savior, gave every second of his life for you. Because he did, you are forgiven for your poor use of time and poor priorities. Because of Jesus, you have an eternity waiting for you in the happiness of heaven.

God gives you an eternity in heaven. You can give him an hour or two on Sunday morning. You can give him 10, 20, 30 minutes a day to pray and read a little from your Bible. Try it. See if it doesn't end up being the most productive time you spend each week. The comfort, encouragement, and guidance we receive from God's Word are worth the investment of time. God is worth it.

So if you've been away from church and Bibles, get back. Take the time. Make the time. Don't wait for your calendar to free up, because it will never happen. Time is a black hole.

Make time for God.

Today I am thankful for/that _____

_____

Dear Lord, please forgive me for not always
making you and your Word the top priority
in my life. Thank you for forgiving me. Please
help me to give you the time you deserve. Amen.

---◆---

DAY 256
CHOOSE HAPPINESS

I have learned the secret to being content
in any and every situation.

PHILIPPIANS 4:12

◆

I found a mistake in the Declaration of Independence. No, I didn't discover
a typo, nor am I criticizing Thomas Jefferson's orthography. (Though I have
to say he does include some questionable semicolons and capitalizations.
Oh, and he did spell "British" with two t's at one point.)

The mistake I found is located in the Declaration's most iconic passage: "We
hold these truths to be self-evident, that all men are created equal, that they
are endowed by their Creator with certain inalienable Rights, that among
these are Life, Liberty and the pursuit of Happiness."

Did you catch the mistake? Nowhere in the Bible does God promise human
beings the inalienable right to pursue happiness.

He doesn't. Look it up. Search your Bible. God never guarantees you the
right to seek your own happiness, yet we as Americans cling to that right
with fervor. We passionately pursue happiness. For a large portion of our
population, happiness is life's primary pursuit.

Did you know that the word *happy* comes from the same root as our English word "happen"? For many people in our world today, happiness is the result of what happens to you. Simply put, when good things happen to you, it makes you happy.

Our pursuit of happiness, therefore, is a pursuit of the things we think will make us happy. "If only I win the lottery or get this new job or find the woman of my dreams, then I will be truly happy."

The truth, however, is that none of those things can make you happy. Actually, nothing can make you happy. Nobody can make you happy. For that matter, nobody can make you sad or angry either. You are the one who controls what you feel and how you respond to what happens to you.

When the Bible speaks about the joy of a Christian, it does so with disregard to a person's outward circumstances. The apostle Paul wrote that he had learned "the secret of being content in any and every situation, whether well fed or hungry, whether living in plenty or in want" (Philippians 4:12).

THE SECRET TO TRUE HAPPINESS ISN'T GETTING WHAT YOU WANT.

The secret to true happiness isn't getting what you want. It's recognizing what you have in Jesus. Because Jesus lived and died for you, you are forgiven for every lousy thing you've ever done. Because God forgives you, you are going to live one day in heaven where you will be happier than you could ever imagine here on earth.

In heaven, the only problem you will have is your cheeks hurting from smiling so much.

And if that's not enough, God also promises to be by your side every moment of every day during your time on earth. He promises to provide everything you need for your body and soul. He promises to make everything, even the pains and problems of this world, work out for your good.

Knowing that, you can smile even as the tears of pain roll down your cheeks. Knowing that, you can choose happiness even when tragedy surrounds you.

I know it's not easy. God doesn't expect you to jump up and down for joy when you are in the middle of pain or loss. But, knowing and trusting in God's promises, you can be at peace. You can be content regardless of what happens to you or around you.

In the end, the pursuit of happiness is a fool's errand. Pursuing the things which you think will make you happy can never bring lasting happiness.

So don't pursue happiness. Pursue godliness. Trust in God's promises and choose happiness.

Today I am thankful for/that _____

Lord, turn my eyes away from what I don't
have and help me see what I do have because
of your amazing grace. Help me to pursue
godliness and choose happiness. Amen.

◆

DAY 257
IN THE SAME BOAT

"Who is this? Even the wind and the waves obey him!"

MARK 4:41

◆

"We're all in the same boat." Some say the origin of that phrase can be traced back to the sinking of the *Titanic*. When the RMS *Titanic* sank on April 15, 1912, it made no distinction of persons. People from all walks of life and levels of society found themselves in the same situation.

They were all in the same boat.

I thought about that phrase this morning as I heard a friend preach about Jesus calming the storm. If you remember, he and his disciples had boarded a small boat to head to the other side of the Sea of Galilee, which is basically a glorified lake. To sail to the other side wasn't even a three-hour tour.

But just like with Gilligan and the Skipper, the weather started getting rough. Due to its unique location, the Sea of Galilee is prone to sudden, hurricane-like storms.

The tiny ship was tossed. It began to take on water. Though they were experienced fishermen, the disciples were far from a fearless crew. They were terrified. They thought they were going to die.

And where was Jesus as the storm raged and the waves walloped the despairing disciples? He was fast asleep at the stern of the boat.

The disciples shook him as water sprayed in their faces.

"Teacher, don't you care if we drown?"

"Be quiet!" Jesus said sternly—not to the disciples, but to the storm.

Silence. No more wind. No more waves. No more storm.

"Who is this?" the soaked disciples asked as they shivered in the cool night air. "Even the wind and the waves obey him" (Mark 4:35-41).

The disciples forgot who was in the boat with them. Sometimes we do as well.

When the storms rage, when chemotherapy ravages your body, when your marriage crumbles, when the world seems to be falling apart around you, do not forget who is in the boat with you.

Jesus is God himself. He is the one who can walk on water, heal the sick, and raise the dead. Even the wind and the waves obey him. He can and will help you in any and every trouble.

He will help you because he cares for you. In fact, he cares for you so much that he came to this world to be one of us. He got into the boat with us. Because of our sins, our ship was sinking faster than the Titanic, yet Jesus came. He rescued us by sacrificing himself, by suffering our punishment, by dying our death.

The God who rules over the wind and the waves—the God who literally loves you to death—that God is with you in the boat in the middle of the storm.

SOMETIMES IT SEEMS LIKE GOD ISN'T THERE.

I know. Sometimes it seems like God isn't there. Sometimes it seems like he is taking a nap. Sometimes it seems like he doesn't care.

Yet he will rescue you. He will save you from every storm and struggle . . . in his own time and his own way. He may test you like he tested his disciples. You may have to wait for a while. You may have to feel the wind and waves beating against your face. You may feel at times like the boat is sinking and all is lost, but don't be afraid. Don't ever give up.

Remember who's in the boat with you.

Today I am thankful for/that _____

Lord, sometimes it seems like you are not there. I can't see you and I feel very alone. Open the eyes of my heart to see you are here in the boat with me. Help me always remember who you are and what you can and will do for me. Amen.

◆

DAY 258
WHEN PRAYING THE LORD'S PRAYER IS A SIN

"When you pray, do not keep on babbling like pagans, for they think they will be heard because of their many words."

MATTHEW 6:7

◆

More Christians sin while praying the Lord's Prayer than while doing just about any other activity in life.

I know that is a provocative statement. I know it may offend some, but I stand by it. Here's why.

First of all, a little background: Jesus taught the Lord's Prayer on at least two different occasions (Matthew 6:9-13; Luke 11:2-4). Each time it was to show his disciples how to pray.

In its essence, the Lord's Prayer is a sample prayer—an example of how Christians should pray.

494

Though the Lord's Prayer is a perfect prayer, it is not more powerful than any prayer which comes from the heart of a believer. God doesn't listen to the Lord's Prayer more attentively than he does to my quiet pleas for mercy or my simple prayers of thanksgiving.

The Lord's Prayer is not a magical incantation. It does not protect you from demons or vampires. Repeating it over and over again will not bring you special blessings from God.

The Lord's Prayer is simply a sample prayer. It shows you how you can talk to God with confidence. It teaches you good things for which to pray. As Christians, we can and should pray the Lord's Prayer, but we can and should also pray our own heartfelt prayers based on its example.

The reason why more Christians sin while praying the Lord's Prayer than while doing just about any other activity is that so often we mindlessly repeat the words without thinking.

As a guy, I cannot do two things at once. Sometimes my wife will walk into the room while I am watching TV. She will talk to me. I will nod my head and maybe even respond without really paying attention to her or what I am saying.

How do you think that makes her feel?

How do you think it makes God feel when you are mindlessly repeating the words of the Lord's Prayer while you are thinking about how you want pizza for lunch, or how the pastor's sermon was too long, or how the lady in front of you is wearing too much perfume?

You are speaking to the almighty Lord of the universe who gave up everything to win heaven for you, and you aren't even thinking about what you are saying to him. That offends God. It angers him.

Yet he forgives you because of Jesus. He does forgive us our trespasses. Our feeble and poor prayers are purified in Jesus' blood. You are forgiven for all the times you have disrespected God by mindlessly going through the motions of prayer instead of speaking to him from your heart.

DON'T STOP SAYING THE LORD'S PRAYER.

But now, in loving thanks, think about what you are saying when you talk to God in prayer. Don't stop saying the Lord's Prayer; just think about it.

Today I am thankful for/that _____

---

*Our Father in heaven, hallowed be your name,
your kingdom come, your will be done on earth
as in heaven. Give us today our daily bread.
Forgive us our sins, as we forgive those who sin
against us. Lead us not into temptation, but
deliver us from evil. For the kingdom, the power
and the glory are yours, now and forever. Amen.*

DAY 259
WE WILL SURVIVE

My God will meet all your needs according
to the riches of his glory in Christ Jesus.
PHILIPPIANS 4:19

◆

The Walmart store in Edna, Texas, (population 5,499) will permanently
close its doors on July 20 of this year (2018). In the ever-changing world
of business and finance, such an announcement is neither shocking nor
appalling. It's a financial decision. It's just business.

For those of us who live in Edna, Texas, however, the announcement was
devastating. The closing of Walmart will dramatically affect the lives of
dozens of our friends and neighbors who work there. Hundreds of people
depend on the Walmart pharmacy for their medications. It could cripple
our local economy. Some communities never recover from such a closing.

The response from the public on the day of the announcement was one of
both shock and disbelief. Posts and threads began to appear on Facebook.

Some citizens were angry. Others were worried and wondered what this would mean for our tiny town.

Still others channeled their inner Gloria Gaynor and defiantly proclaimed, "We will survive." We are Texans after all. We are strong. We are resilient.

I agree with that sentiment. We don't have to worry. We will survive, but not because we are strong and resilient. We will survive because God promises that we will survive.

The word *survive* comes from a Latin word which literally means "to live through" or "to live beyond." We will live through this. That's God's promise. He promises to always provide everything we need for our bodies and lives.

Just look back on your life. Look back at the lives of your parents or grandparents. They survived the Great Depression. They survived the booms and busts of the oil fields. Sure, they may have survived by eating squirrel and rabbit, but they survived. They lived through it, not because they were strong, hardworking, or resilient, but because God in his grace got them through.

God promises to provide everything you need for your body and life. In fact, often he provides much more than we need. We don't have to worry about what will happen to Edna, Texas, or to our own families. God will provide as he always has. We will survive.

In fact, we will survive every pain and pandemic of this world, even death. We will live beyond death because the eternal Lord of the universe came to this earth and lived and died in our place. Jesus suffered the punishment we deserve for all the times we have doubted God and needlessly fretted and fussed. Jesus suffered the punishment for all the times we have whined and complained about the manner in which God has provided for us.

BECAUSE OF JESUS, WE WILL SURVIVE.

Because of Jesus, we are forgiven completely. Because of Jesus, we are going to heaven. Because of Jesus, we will survive. We will live beyond this world. We will live beyond death.

So what do we have to worry about? Absolutely nothing. While we are here on earth, God will provide everything we need to survive. When we die, we will receive the glory and happiness of the heaven Jesus won for us.

So don't worry when the local Walmart closes. Don't worry when the oil fields slow down. Don't worry when your husband loses his job or the doctor tells you it's cancer. God will find a way to provide what you need. You will live through it. You will live beyond it.

You will survive.

Today I am thankful for/that _____

_____

Dear God, thank you for providing all that I need for body and soul. Forgive me my doubt and help me to trust that because of Jesus I will always survive. Amen.

DAY 260
GREAT EXPECTATIONS

"Be perfect, therefore, as your heavenly Father is perfect."

MATTHEW 5:48

◆

"Give it your best shot." "Try as hard as you can." "I'm proud of you no matter how you do."

As a parent, I have found myself lately spouting such platitudes to my children before soccer games, piano recitals, and tests at school. None of us wants to be that pressuring parent who has unhealthy and unreasonable expectations of their children.

I want my children to excel in everything they do, but I don't want to give the impression that my love for them is dependent on their achievements. I try to challenge them to be the best they can be, but without crushing their spirits or creating an unhealthy need to win.

It's interesting to note how our heavenly Father deals with us, his children. God has great expectations of us. When it comes to his Commandments, God doesn't tell us to try as hard as we can. He doesn't say, "Give it your best shot." God is not proud of you no matter how well you obey his commandments.

GOOD IS NOT GOOD ENOUGH. God says, "Be perfect." Good is not good enough. Your best effort simply doesn't cut it. God expects his children to live perfect lives of love. Jesus often spoke about what it means to be his follower. It means sacrifice. It means commitment. It means giving up everything for him.

God expects a lot from us.

Thankfully, God's love for us does not depend on our achievements. He loves us despite our failures. Jesus, our brother in humanity, lived up to his Father's expectations in our place and suffered the humiliation of our failures. Because of Jesus, we are forgiven. Because of Jesus, God regards us as perfect in his sight. Because of Jesus, God no longer sees our failures.

But forgiveness doesn't mean God lowers his expectations. God doesn't tell us, "I forgive you, so it doesn't matter what you do." He still says, "Be perfect." Being a child of God is not a part-time job we do on the weekends.

Yet I believe we Christians in our country today have lowered our standards. We expect less from ourselves, from our children, and from others. Regular church attendance used to mean being in church every Sunday unless you were sick or had to work. Today regular church attendance means trying to get to church once or twice a month.

Often we put our leftover change in the offering plate instead of setting aside a weekly offering to God. Many Christian parents no longer make their kids go to Sunday school or memorize Bible passages. They no longer pray daily with their children or have family devotions.

And then they wonder why their children stop going to church when they get older.

We claim we don't want to turn our kids off to God by pushing too hard. The answer, however, is not to lower our expectations. The solution is not to water down our faith.

The remedy is the gospel. We need to show our children why we live for God. We need to remind them often why we go to church and Sunday school. We need to help them see God's amazing grace that loves and forgives sinners like you and me. That is what motivates us to commit, sacrifice, and give our all to the God who gave his all for us.

As Christians, as churches, and as parents, it's time we start expecting more from ourselves and from our children.

God certainly does.

Today I am thankful for/that _____

Lord, forgive me for the many times I lower my standards in my life of service to you. Thank you for your forgiveness, but help me to not use that forgiveness as an excuse to aim for less than what you expect of me. Amen.

DAY 261
A BAD PLACE

Out of the depths I cry to you, Lord; Lord, hear my voice. Let your ears be attentive to my cry for mercy.

PSALM 130:1,2

◆

I was in a bad place. It literally was the perfect storm. We had just gotten our second pastor. We were trying to get him settled and our new campus started. A seminary intern and his pregnant wife had just arrived the week before. A young man from our congregation had suffered a tragic accident and was having complications in the hospital.

And then came Hurricane Harvey.

We evacuated to Dallas. I frantically tried to connect with all the members of our church to make sure they were okay. Then came more complications for the young man. Then came the clean-up. The weeks that followed were a blur of activity and stress, much of which I brought on myself.

That's what often happens when you are in a bad place. You dig yourself deeper into the hole. You feel sorry for yourself. It's hard to see anything good in your life. You see only the problems and the stress.

Thankfully, we have a Savior who reaches out his hand when we are sinking in the middle of the storm and pulls us out of the water. Because of God's patience and love, I am much better now.

For a while, though, I was not in a good place.

ARE YOU IN A BAD PLACE RIGHT NOW?

Are you in a bad place right now? Are you so stressed you can't sleep? Is there tension in your marriage? Is your job unbearable? Does the guilt of knowing what you've done and the fear of people finding out keep you up at night?

Sadly, there is no secret formula for getting out of a bad place. Every person is different. Every situation is different, but let me share with you a few things which helped me.

Prayer. Even if nobody else on this planet understands, God does. He knows exactly what you're feeling. He loves you and he forgives you. He is always listening, so tell him what you are feeling. Be blunt. Be honest. He can handle it. He wants to hear it. It will help.

Go to church. I know you probably don't feel like it. You may feel alone and out of place there, but go. Listen closely to what is being said. God will speak to you through his Word.

Talk to a pastor. They may not be perfect and they may not have all the answers, but they are a good place to start. Sure, you may have had a bad experience in the past, but the overwhelming majority of pastors and priests really do care and want to help. If you don't have someone you can talk to, give me a call or send me a message. I would love to help.

Finally, read the Psalms. They are easy to find right in the middle of the Bible. Just open up anywhere in the Psalms and start reading. The first one you read may not deal with what you are going through, but if you keep reading, you will soon find one which does.

My personal favorite is Psalm 46 (especially verse 10). It got me out of my dark place.

May God help you get out of yours.

Today I am thankful for/that _____

Lord, you know all things. You know when I spiral into a bad place. You alone know how I feel. Open my eyes and my heart to see the truth of your promises. Help me to be still and trust that you are God. Amen.

DAY 262
TRADITION

Then John's disciples came and asked him, "How
is it that we and the Pharisees fast often,
but your disciples do not fast?"

MATTHEW 9:14

❖

I recently read that the standard U.S. railroad is 4 feet, 8.5 inches wide.
That's a rather random measurement, don't you think? I recently learned
that immigrants from England designed our railroads and that's the width
they used in England.

It turns out the people who built the railroads in England were also the
ones who earlier had built the tramways. That's the width they used. The
people who built the tramways were the ones who had also built wagons,
and that was the width they had used.

WHY ARE WE DOING WHAT WE ARE DOING?

Why did the wagon builders use that width? Because
that was the width of the wagon ruts already worn
into the roadways of England—ruts first made by
Roman chariots when Rome ruled England over
1500 years ago. The distance between wheels on an
ancient Roman chariot was exactly 4 feet, 8.5 inches.

So why are our railroad tracks 4 feet, 8.5 inches wide? Blame it on
the Romans.

Why do you do what you do at your church? Why do you worship the way
you worship? Why is your church decorated the way it is decorated or
managed the way it is managed?

In his Word, God gives us many directives on how to live and act as a
church, but, honestly, much of how we worship and run our churches is
simply based on tradition. Like when determining the width of railroad
tracks, we often don't even know why we do what we do in our churches.
We've just always done it that way.

Tradition can be a good thing. It ties us to Christians of the past. Often it is
based on centuries of wisdom and experience. Traditions have stood the
test of time for a reason.

As Christians, however, we sometimes treat traditions as divine directives from above. We cling to them. We cherish them. We get angry when anyone suggests we change them.

Change can be scary, but sometimes it's necessary. "We've always done it that way" is never a good argument to keep doing something. The way you've always done things may not be the best or wisest way.

As time passes, the opportunities, gifts, and challenges God gives each church change. Though the manner your church operates today was the best and wisest way to serve God 50 years ago, it may not be today.

Churches often get stuck in ruts exactly 4 feet, 8.5 inches wide when they don't take the time to periodically ask a few questions: Why are we doing what we are doing? Is this the best and wisest way? Should we be doing something else or adjust what we are doing to better and more efficiently serve God and others?

The answers to those questions aren't always easy. Wisdom and love dictate that we don't fall into the ditch on either side of the road. On one side of the road is the pitfall of despising tradition, of changing things simply for the sake of change. We shouldn't quickly cast aside the wisdom of time-tested traditions and the feelings of those who cherish them. The ditch on the other side of the road is just as dangerous—blindly clinging to traditions as sacred cows, refusing to honestly evaluate what we are doing or to consider new ideas.

It is healthy for Christians to periodically evaluate the ministry of their churches so they can serve God and others to the best of their abilities and to his glory. Every Christian congregation needs voices who lovingly and humbly ask, "Why are we doing what we are doing?"

Could you be that voice in your church?

Today I am thankful for/that _____

_____

*Almighty God, thank you for the traditions
passed down to us from our forefathers.
Help us to wisely and lovingly evaluate
how we carry out our ministries so that
we can serve you and others well.
Give us patience and understanding
as we deal with traditions and
change in our church. Amen.*

DAY 263
ONE LITTLE SPARK

The tongue is a small part of the body, but it makes
great boasts. Consider what a great forest
is set on fire by a small spark.

JAMES 3:5

◆

As I write this, the fires continue to rage. In Northern California, the Mendocino Complex Fire has already destroyed over 330,000 acres. It is now the largest wildfire in the history of the state of California and is still only 67% contained. Thousands have been evacuated and 258 homes destroyed.

At the same time, the Carr Fire rages to the north. It has wiped out more than 160,000 acres and is the sixth largest wildfire in the history of California. Due to the fact that it is in a more populated area, over 1,000 homes have been destroyed and eight people have died. As I write, only 59% of the fire has been contained.

Though the origins of the Mendocino Complex fire are currently unknown, the Carr Fire can be traced to a tire rim scraping against the road creating sparks. Tens of thousands of people have been displaced, 1,500 buildings have been destroyed, and eight lives have been snuffed out due to a few sparks on the road.

Jesus' half-brother James once compared the human tongue to a small spark which sets a forest on fire. Words have power. A few thoughtless words of anger can cause a lifetime of hurt. One little lie or juicy bit of gossip can leave a trail of scorched earth. Incendiary words sent in a text or posted on social media can spark a raging inferno.

Part of the problem in Northern California is that the conditions are ideal for large wildfires. The weather is often dry and hot in the summer. Strong winds called Diablo winds sweep down from the mountains, fanning the flames and pushing the fire into new areas.

In the same way, modern technology has created ideal conditions for fires to rage uncontrollably on the internet. Texting and social media create an environment in which people are often careless or thoughtless with their words. Statements are frequently misconstrued or misunderstood.

The winds of social media quickly spread misinformation, gossip, and incendiary words. Fuel is poured on the fire as people respond to, share, and like those words. Tempers flare. Fires rage. People are hurt. Lives are destroyed.

And it all starts with one little spark.

So often we underestimate the power of words and the damage they can cause. We say things like, "Sticks and stones may break my bones, but words will never hurt me."

That's simply not true. Words have power. Like a spark, they can start a fire you cannot put out.

SO DON'T TEXT WHEN YOU'RE ANGRY.

So don't text when you're angry. Talk to the person on the phone or face to face. Watch what you post, share, or like on social media. Don't share anything unless you can confirm it is true.

And even if it is true, ask yourself, "Will my words build up and encourage or will they tear down and add fuel to the fire of people's rage?" Just because something is true does not mean you should share it on the internet.

As Christians who understand how our Savior has rescued us from the raging inferno of hell, let's reflect his love with our words. Be careful not to spark or add fuel to online anger. Avoid gossip. Don't share incendiary words. Use your words to build up and encourage. Use your words to calm the fires and douse the flames.

Today I am thankful for/that _____

Merciful God, forgive me the many times I have not controlled my tongue. Thank you for your amazing grace in Jesus, and give me the wisdom to be slow to speak and quick to listen. Amen.

DAY 264
I DON'T CARE WHAT PEOPLE SAY ABOUT ME!

Though my father and mother forsake me,
the LORD will receive me.

PSALM 27:10

◆

"I don't care what people say about me!"

Every day, thousands of people post those or similar words on Facebook or share them on social media. Somebody uploaded a compromising photo of them on Instagram. Somebody spread an ugly rumor about them on Twitter. Somebody posted private information about them on Facebook.

In frustration, they announce to the cyber-world: "I don't care what people say about me!" "I don't care what people write about me!" "I don't care what people think about me!"

The problem is, whether they like to admit it or not, they do care. If they didn't care, they wouldn't write those words for others to see.

We all, to some degree, care what other people say, write, and think about us. According to the psychologist Abraham Maslow, all humans have a deep visceral need for belonging and acceptance. That is one of humankind's most basic emotional needs.

The question is *should* we care what other people say, write, or think about us? In one sense, no. As Christians, the only opinion which really matters to us is God's.

God knows you better than you know yourself. He knows all the garbage in your heart and your head. He knows all of your private, personal problems. God says, writes, and thinks that you are a terrible sinner who deserves his punishment in hell.

Yet, because he loved you, God became a man. That God-man suffered your punishment in your place. Because God the Father punished his Son Jesus for your sins, you are forgiven. God loves you. God accepts you just as you are. That is what God says, writes and thinks about you in his Word. You should care about that.

If God loves you—if he accepts you just as you are—who cares what other people think?

Sadly, you do. Sadly, I do. But we don't have to. Even if everyone here on earth hated you, God never would. King David once wrote, "Though my father and mother forsake me, the LORD will receive me."

That being said, our Savior does encourage us to be aware of what other people think about us. He tells us, "Let your light shine before others, that they may see your good deeds and glorify your Father in heaven" (Matthew 5:16). You can't control what other people say, write, or think about you, but you can control how you live your life.

YOUR LIFE IS A REFLECTION OF YOUR GOD.
Your life is a reflection of your God. As a Christian, you have Jesus' name tattooed across your forehead. The way you live can positively affect what other people think about Jesus, or it can be a stumbling block to their faith. In that sense you should care what other people say, write, and think about you.

In the end, though, you cannot control what other people do. You cannot control what another person thinks about you. You can only control how you live your life.

Don't live your life worrying and fretting about what other people say, write, or think of you. Live your life remembering what God says, writes, and thinks about you.

Live your life reflecting his love to the world.

Today I am thankful for/that _____

_____

Heavenly Father, thank you for loving me and accepting me just as I am. Thank you for forgiving all the bad I do. Help me not to worry what other people think about me. Amen.

DAY 265
WHEN YOU'RE STUCK SPINNING YOUR WHEELS

"We must go through many hardships
to enter the kingdom of God."

ACTS 14:22

❖

I am a Yankee living in Texas. I was raised in the great state of Michigan. Though I love and miss my home state dearly, there is one thing I definitely don't miss.

The cold.

I don't miss shoveling snow. I don't miss scraping the ice off my windshield. I don't miss having to bundle up in boots and gloves and a stocking cap just to go outside.

I don't miss driving on icy roads. One thing most Texans will never have to experience is getting your car stuck in a snowdrift. Once your car is stuck in the snow, it is really hard to get it out. Once your wheels start spinning, you aren't going anywhere.

Oftentimes in our lives, we feel like we are spinning our wheels. We're stuck in a snowdrift of problems or pain. No matter what we do, it feels like it's always going to be this way. The pain is constant. The problems keep piling up. The same bad thing keeps happening over and over again.

We feel like we're spinning our wheels.

Two thousand years ago, the apostle Paul visited some Christians who probably felt that way. They were being persecuted. People were making fun of them. Their families had disowned them. Some were getting beaten up and arrested for being Christians.

So Paul and his buddy Barnabas visited them to encourage them. "We must go through many hardships to enter the kingdom of God," they said.

I don't know about you, but that doesn't sound very encouraging to me.

If you look closely at that verse, though, there is one very important word—the word *through*. We are going through our hardships. When we are in the middle of the storm, it feels like we are stuck spinning our wheels. It feels like it will always be this way, but eventually every pain and problem we have will end.

GOD WILL GET YOU THROUGH THE HARDSHIPS.

Just look back on your life. Every one of us has had hard times. We have all had pains. But in one way or another, God has gotten us through them. In the same way, God will get you through the hardships you have right now. They are temporary.

They may last a while. Some pains and problems last for months or even years, but they will end one day, if not here on earth, then when you enter heaven. Because Jesus lived and died as your Savior, you are on your way to heaven. You are just passing through this world. You are just passing through your pains and problems.

What are a few days, a few months, or even a few years of pain compared to forever in the happiness and perfection of heaven? That is the perspective the apostle Paul wants to give us. Your pain will end one day. Your problems won't last. You are on your way to heaven where there will be no more "'death' or mourning or crying or pain" (Revelation 21:4).

And while you wait in the middle of the storm, your Savior God promises to be by your side. He will give you the strength you need. He will give you proper perspective on your problems through his Word and promises.

I know it feels like you are stuck spinning your wheels, but God will get you through.

Today I am thankful for/that _____

_____

Merciful Lord, you know the pain and problems I am going through. When I begin to despair, help me to remember that this is only temporary and to trust that you will get me through. Amen.

DAY 266
MEMORY WORK

When he takes the throne of his kingdom, he is to write
for himself on a scroll a copy of this law, taken from
that of the Levitical priests. It is to be with him,
and he is to read it all the days of his life so
that he may learn to revere the Lord his
God and follow carefully all the words
of this law and these decrees.

DEUTERONOMY 17:18,19

◆

I used to hate memory work. In Sunday school and Catechism class, my teacher assigned memory verses from the Bible. For some students memory work is fun and easy, but for most of us it is hard and monotonous.

When I assign memory work to the kids of my church today, I get groans and eye rolls.

So why do it? As a pastor, am I simply rubbing my hands together with an evil laugh as I torture the poor young people of our church? Why memorize verses from the Bible?

When God gave his law to the people of Israel on Mount Sinai, he told them that one day they would have a king. He told them what the king was to be and do. And one of the things he commanded the king to do was to take a copy of the book of the law (that is, the Bible) and copy it down by hand, word for word. God then commanded him to read and re-read his own personal copy all the days of his life.

Imagine the groans and eye rolls that command would elicit from the kings. God's purpose wasn't to torture them. By copying Scripture, reading it, and re-reading it, they would remember it. They would make it their own. They would find in it the strength, the help, and the guidance they would need as they took on the tremendous task of leading God's people.

Why do memory work? Simply put: because then you remember it. Then you make it your own. Then you have God's Word when you need it. Is it easy? No. But it's worth it.

It's worth it as you sit next to a friend in the hospital, searching for words of comfort, and you remember the words, "Surely I am with you always, to the very end of the age" (Matthew 28:20).

It's worth it as you face the hard truth that you messed up your marriage big time and you remember the words, "The blood of Jesus, his Son, purifies us from all sin" (1 John 1:7).

It's worth it as an unbelieving friend asks you why you believe what you do and you remember the words, "For God so loved the world that he gave his one and only Son, that whoever believes in him shall not perish but have eternal life" (John 3:16).

It will be worth it as you sit in the nursing home, confused and tired. You can't remember why you are there or the names of your children, but tears stream down your face as your pastor reads to you the comforting words, "The LORD is my Shepherd I shall not want . . ." and you find the words rolling off your lips as well.

WHY DO MEMORY WORK? BECAUSE THEN GOD'S WORD IS YOURS.

Why do memory work? Because then God's Word is yours. Nobody can take it from you. Could you memorize four verses in a month? Try it this month. Pick four verses and memorize one a week. You can pick any. Here are a few I would suggest if you don't already know them by heart: John 3:16; Romans 6:23; Romans 8:28; Philippians 1:21; Philippians 4:13. If you want a wonderful challenge, memorize a psalm. Psalm 23 is a good one.

Read it. Re-read it. Make it your own. It's worth the work.

Today I am thankful for/that _____

_____

Lord, thank you for your wonderful Word.
Help me to always read, learn, and
inwardly digest it. Amen.

DAY 267
DEATH AND PULLING TEETH

[Jesus] too shared in their humanity so that by his
death he might break the power of him who holds
the power of death—that is, the devil—and
free those who all their lives were held
in slavery by their fear of death.

HEBREWS 2:14,15

◆

I'll never forget the day my daughter lost her first tooth. It had been loose for weeks. It was hanging on by a thread. She didn't want me to touch it. She didn't want anyone to touch it.

But it had gone on long enough. I told her I was going to pull it out. She screamed and cried. She was convinced it was going to hurt. I promised her it wouldn't. It would be quick and painless.

I held her tightly in my arms, grabbed the tooth and told her I was going to count to three. "One," I said, as she shook and screamed, "No, no, no!"

"Two," I said, as I quickly and gently pulled the tooth from her mouth. She kept shaking and yelling, "No, no, no," not realizing the tooth was already out. When she finally saw the tooth in my hand, her face lit up with joy. She grabbed the tooth and ran through the house squealing in excitement.

I once had a friend who was dying of cancer. Though she believed in Jesus and trusted that he had won for her a place in heaven, she still struggled with the idea of death. Whenever I tried to talk to her about it, she would get mad.

"Pastor! I don't want to talk about it."

The last few months of her life, she acted kind of like my daughter, kicking and screaming. Though she struggled with the idea of dying, she did have true faith in Jesus. She knew he died for her sins and won heaven for her. She just had a hard time facing death.

The day she died, I immediately thought of the day my daughter lost her first tooth. Though she went kicking and screaming, I can imagine my friend opening her eyes in heaven and squealing for joy.

Death can be scary. For many, it's the fear of the unknown. For others, it's the fear of judgment, the fear of punishment, the fear of hell.

The writer to the Hebrews tells us that Jesus died "so that he might destroy him who holds the power of death—that is, the devil—and free those who all their lives were held in slavery by their fear of death."

Because Jesus died for you—because he suffered the punishment you deserve—you don't have to be afraid of hell. You aren't going there. You are forgiven. You don't have to be afraid of dying. You are going to live even though you die.

You don't have to be afraid of the unknown, because you now know. We don't know exactly what heaven will be like, but we do know it will be amazing. We know it will be perfect. We know there won't be any more pain or fear or sorrow. We know we will be reunited with our loved ones who have died in Christ. We know we will see God face to face.

We know it will be much better than here.

DEATH DOESN'T HAVE TO SCARE YOU.

Death doesn't have to scare you. Death is simply a door you walk through on your way to the happiness of heaven. As Christians, we have that sure hope and confidence.

But as sinful human beings, we still struggle with the idea of death. We worry and wonder what it will be like. Find peace in knowing that, though you may waver and wobble when faced with death, God's promises stand firm. Because of Jesus, the day you close your eyes in death you will open them and squeal for joy.

You will be happier than a four-year-old who lost her first tooth.

Today I am thankful for/that _____

Almighty and merciful Lord, you know my fears.
Death is scary. Take away my fears and
turn my eyes to the life you have
prepared for me in heaven. Amen.

DAY 268
ADONAI JIREH

So Abraham called that place The LORD Will Provide.
And to this day it is said, "On the mountain
of the LORD it will be provided."

GENESIS 22:14

◆

God had asked a lot of Abraham. He asked for his only son. "Take your son," God told him, "your only son, whom you love—Isaac—and go to the region of Moriah. Sacrifice him there as a burnt offering on a mountain I will show you" (Genesis 22:2).

The very next morning, Abraham got up, took Isaac, and went to the mountain God had shown him. As they walked up the mountain, Isaac noticed they had all the materials for the sacrifice—the fire and wood—but they didn't have the sacrifice.

"God will provide," was Abraham's answer.

You know the rest of the story. Abraham built the altar. He placed Isaac on it. He raised the knife. But God stopped him.

God never intended for Abraham to kill his son. He was testing him. He was teaching him. The lesson is clear. God wants us to love him even more than we love our own children.

But there's more. Abraham turned around and there in a thicket he saw a ram caught by its horn. He killed it and offered it as a sacrifice in place of his son.

Just as Abraham had said, God provided the sacrifice. So Abraham named the mountain *Adonai Jireh*—literally the LORD will provide.

The LORD will provide. The Bible overflows with examples of God's providence for his people: 40 years of manna in the wilderness, ravens feeding a famished prophet, 5,000 people fed with five small loaves and two small fish. Again and again we see the hand of God providing for and protecting his children.

In fact, he provided for his people the thing they needed most. Just as he provided a substitute sacrifice for Abraham's son, he provided a substitute for all people. The LORD allowed himself to be sacrificed in our place. Jesus took our place, suffering our punishment, dying our death.

God provided what we needed most—a Savior, forgiveness, and heaven.

The LORD provides. Look at your life. Have you ever gone a day when you didn't have any food to eat, clothes to wear, or a place to sleep? Probably not. Even when times were tough, even when you didn't know how you were going to make it, somehow God always provided.

The LORD will provide. He won't always provide everything we want. He won't always provide everything we ask for. But he will always provide everything we need for body and soul. If you have any doubt, just look at all the examples of his providence in the Bible. Look at all the examples in your own life. Look at the cross and your Savior.

If he did that for you, how will he not also provide everything else you need?

REMEMBER THAT THE NEXT TIME MONEY GETS TIGHT.

Adonai Jireh—the name says it all. The LORD will provide. Remember that the next time money gets tight. Remember that the next time an unexpected bill comes. Remember that the next time you are stressed or worried or afraid.

Adonai Jireh. The LORD will provide.

Today I am thankful for/that _____

_____

Lord God, thank you for always providing everything I need for my body and life. Forgive me my worry and fear. Help me to trust in you every day. Amen.

DAY 269
BACK TO SCHOOL

Grow in the grace and knowledge of
our Lord and Savior Jesus Christ.

2 PETER 3:18

❖

Every year as children go back to school, their mothers let out a collective sigh of relief. No more screaming kids. No more hearing "I'm bored" every five minutes. The house will once again be quiet from 8 A.M. to 3 P.M. When school starts, we get back to the routines, football practices, and homework.

As my daughter gets older, I have noticed something about her homework. It's actually a little embarrassing to admit, but here goes: her homework is hard.

I consider myself a pretty educated guy, but there are times when I look at her math homework and it looks like a foreign language. I never realized how much I had forgotten from my school days—or how much I had never really learned.

The same dilemma often rears its ugly head in our spiritual lives. Our parents take us to church as kids. We go to Sunday school. We learn about Abraham and Moses, Mary and Martha, Peter and Paul. We memorize the Commandments. We learn to sing "Jesus loves me this I know" and to trust that he is our Savior from sin.

And so we graduate. We take our first Communion. We get confirmed. We get into high school and college and stop going to church. We know what we need to know. We believe in God. We believe that Jesus is our Savior, so why go to church?

WHAT WE OFTEN DON'T REALIZE IS HOW EASILY WE FORGET.

What we often don't realize is how easily we forget. What we often don't realize is how much we still have to learn. The devil loves to lull us into complacency or overconfidence—thinking we know more than we really do.

The apostle Paul warned the Corinthian Christians, "If you think you are standing firm, be careful that you don't fall" (1 Corinthians 10:12). The apostle Peter encouraged believers everywhere, "Grow in the grace and knowledge of our Lord Jesus Christ."

We all need to hear, read, and study God's Word. Why? Because if we don't, we quickly forget what we learned. God gets pushed to the back burner in our lives. We start to think that we are good enough on our own—that we are going to heaven because of what we do. The devil whispers in our ears, "You're okay. You're a spiritual person. You think about God. In fact, you are probably more spiritual than all those hypocrites going to church. You don't need some preacher telling you what to believe. You've got it all figured out."

But it's a lie. We need to hear God's Word because we easily forget and because there is so much that we still have to learn. I started attending Sunday school when I was four years old. My parents took me to church every Sunday. I went to a Christian grade school, high school, college, and seminary. I have been a pastor for over 20 years. And I am still learning new things from God's Word.

As I write this, a new school year is about to begin. It's time to get back to school, time to get back into the routine, time to help our kids with their homework.

If you have been away from God's Word, it's also time for you to get back to school. Get back to church. Open up your Bible.

Learn and grow and find the peace which only God can give.

Today I am thankful for/that _____

_____

Merciful God, forgive me for all the times I have become complacent in my faith. Help me to always learn and grow in my faith and love for you. Amen.

DAY 270
SMILE

"The LORD make his face shine on you."

NUMBERS 6:25

◆

Lately my wife and I have been binge-watching a show on Netflix called *Lie to Me*. It's about an expert in facial expressions, Dr. Cal Lightman, who—according to the show—can tell if people are lying by their body language and the "micro-expressions" on their faces.

The show has opened my eyes to all the different faces we make to express our emotions and thoughts: happiness, sadness, resentment, fear. Your face says a lot about what's in your head and heart.

As Israel camped at the foot of Mount Sinai, God commanded Moses' brother, Aaron the high priest, to speak this blessing over God's people every time they gathered together: "The LORD bless you and keep you; the LORD make his face shine on you and be gracious to you; the LORD turn his face toward you and give you peace" (Numbers 6:24-26).

One phrase of that blessing has always stood out for me: "The LORD make his face shine on you." What does it mean that God's face shines on you?

Simply put, when God looks at you, he smiles.

But that's not the facial expression we deserve from God. So often we look at our own sins as if they were no big deal. "Sure, I drink a little too much sometimes, I maybe cuss a little at work, I maybe tell a little white lie every so often or join in some harmless gossip, but at least I haven't killed anybody."

God hates every sin. Every sin infuriates him. Just look at the anger on God's face as he punished Jesus on the cross for those sins that you say are no big deal. They cost Jesus his life. Because of them, he suffered complete separation from God—pure punishment—to the point that he cried out: "My God, my God, why have you forsaken me?" God the Father scowled at Jesus. He rejected him because of all those sins you consider no big deal.

We don't deserve God's smile. We deserve his scowl. We deserve to see his face burn with anger. But as Aaron's blessing says, he has been gracious to us. Because of Jesus, God forgives us. Since Jesus suffered God's

WHEN GOD LOOKS AT US THERE IS NO SCOWL.

anger for our sins in our place, when God looks at us there is no scowl. There is only an enormous, accepting smile.

That truth changes the look on our faces. We don't have to come into God's presence with fear in our eyes as if he were a judge who was going to punish us. He forgives us because of Jesus.

We don't have to go through life with bitterness or worry on our faces. God's face is always turned toward us. He is always watching over us with love and concern in his eyes.

So smile. Smile as you see the blessings God showers on you day after day. Smile, remembering his amazing grace which forgives all the foolish, hurtful things you do. Smile, especially every time you hear Aaron's blessing at the end of worship. Smile with the confidence that God is smiling down on you.

Today I am thankful for/that _____

_____

Lord, thank you for smiling on me in your great mercy and love. Help me to trust in your amazing forgiveness and to know that you will always look on me with favor because of Jesus. Amen.

DAY 271
LABOR PAINS

I consider that our present sufferings are not worth comparing with the glory that will be revealed in us.

ROMANS 8:18

◆

Years ago, I spent a week at a lake house with my brothers and sisters, their wives and children.

We all had a great time except for maybe my sister-in-law Maggie. Our family purposely rented a lake house near Maggie's home because, you see, Maggie was 39 weeks pregnant.

She was a trooper, though. Despite the fact that her legs, feet, and back hurt, there she was walking up and down stairs, playing with her three-year-old daughter by the dock, laughing and joking with my crazy family.

You could see she was tired. She was tired of being tired. She was tired of the pain and discomfort. She was tired of being pregnant.

I honestly don't know what it is like to be pregnant. I don't know what contractions feel like. I don't know the pain of childbirth.

I don't want to know.

Yet we all have groaned in pain, haven't we? I remember years ago, I got home from playing basketball one evening and quickly downed two large glasses of cold orange juice from the fridge. I was so thirsty I didn't even taste it as it went down. That was a mistake. The orange juice had gone bad.

That night I felt pain I had never felt before. I still remember lying on the floor next to the toilet groaning in pain, praying to God to just take me. Have you ever felt that kind of pain? Have you ever laid there at two o'clock in the morning, groaning in pain?

Or maybe your groans come from a different kind of pain. Maybe your groans come from a hurting heart. The love of your life cheated on you, lied to you, or left you. Maybe your heart aches for a friend or a loved one who has died.

In Romans chapter 8, the apostle Paul compares the pains we feel with the pains of childbirth. Because we are sinners living in a sinful world, we will have pains and problems in this world. Those pains may last months and maybe even years, but, just like labor pains, they are only temporary.

Because Jesus came and suffered the pain and punishment you deserve on the cross, the day is coming when God will set you free from every pain in your life. Not only will you be free from all the struggles and agony of this world, you will experience a joy and glory which words cannot even begin to describe.

On Friday, August 2, 2014, at 8:25 P.M., the doctors laid Everett James Schroer in my sister-in-law's arms. As she held her new son, all the pains of the pregnancy disappeared. They were replaced by pure joy.

When you get to heaven, the worst pains of this world will seem like an insignificant mosquito bite compared to the glory and happiness you will enjoy. On that day, your pains will disappear and be replaced by pure joy.

NEVER FORGET THAT YOUR PAINS ARE ONLY TEMPORARY.

Are you in pain right now? Does your heart ache? Never forget that your pains are only temporary. It may take a while, but one day you will be free. Wait for the Lord. Be patient.

Pure joy is coming.

Today I am thankful for/that _____

_____

*Lord, you know the struggles and pains I am
dealing with. Give me strength and patience
as I wait for the day when my pain will
be replaced with pure joy. Amen.*

DAY 272
NEVER EARNED

It is by grace you have been saved, through faith—and this is not from yourselves, it is the gift of God—not by works, so that no one can boast.

EPHESIANS 2:8,9

❖

When young men and women enter Marine Corps boot camp, they are not called "Marines." They are simply called "recruits." The title "Marine" can only be earned by going through the 13 weeks of basic training, culminating in a grueling 54-hour survival test called the Crucible.

Only upon completion of the Crucible have you earned the right to be called a United States Marine. Marines take great pride in that distinction.

They will be quick to tell you the title is earned, never given.

I am a Christian. I am a child of God. I am an heir of the glories of heaven.

I bear those titles with great pride and joy, but I have to admit I have not earned them. I do not deserve them. They were given to me as a gift.

Those titles were earned for me by Jesus, who endured 33 years here on earth, culminating in six grueling hours on the cross. I was given those distinctions by the Holy Spirit, who worked faith in my heart through the waters of Holy Baptism and the promises of God's Word.

The title of Christian is given, never earned.

Yet we each have a little pocket of pride in our hearts which likes to think that we earned it—at least in part. Deep down we think, "I have sacrificed so much for God. I go to church. I give my offerings. I am a good person. God loves me because of what I have done for him."

To earn the distinction of Christian, however, requires more than simply being a good person who goes to church and gives offerings. That title is earned only by living a perfect life of love, always sacrificing, always giving, always doing what is right.

I can't make it through even one day—one morning, one hour—without failing or falling in one way or another. The only thing I have earned in my life is God's disappointment and anger. The only thing I deserve is hell.

522

Yet I am Christian. I am a child of God. I am an heir to the glories of heaven because Jesus earned it for me.

I can't even take credit for accepting the gift. As Christians, we can say Jesus did it all, but if we take credit for even the simple act of faith, we are saying we did something to earn it.

The truth is I didn't find God. He found me. I didn't choose God. He chose me. I didn't accept God. He accepted me. The only way I can believe in him is because the Holy Spirit worked faith in my heart through his promises.

THE TITLE OF CHRISTIAN IS ALSO EARNED, BUT I DIDN'T EARN IT.

Marines rightly take great pride in the distinction of being called a United States Marine. They work hard for it. They sacrifice to deserve it. They have earned it.

The title of Christian is also earned, but I didn't earn it. Jesus earned it for me with his sacrifice and hard work. The Holy Spirit gave it to me through Baptism and the Word.

The title is given, never earned.

Today I am thankful for/that _____

_____

Father, thank you for the privilege of being able to call myself a Christian. Forgive me for the many times I have felt like I have earned or deserved that distinction. It is only because of your amazing grace, Jesus' tremendous sacrifice, and the working of the Holy Spirit that I can be called your child. Amen.

DAY 273
MY HOPE IS BUILT ON NOTHING LESS

No one can lay any foundation other than the
one already laid, which is Jesus Christ.

1 CORINTHIANS 3:11

◆

The year was 1834. A 37-year-old cabinet maker named Edward Mote was making his way to work through the busy streets of London. As he walked, his mind wandered. He contemplated what he called "the gracious experience of a Christian."

In his heart he began to compose a hymn. By the time he reached his workshop, the chorus played repeatedly in his head: "On Christ the solid rock I stand, all other ground is sinking sand." By the end of the day he had composed four verses.

The following Sunday, a friend from church informed Mote that his wife was gravely ill. Mote agreed to visit them that afternoon. During the visit, Mote's friend told him how it was his custom to read a portion of Scripture to his wife and sing a hymn to her before attending evening services. The husband, however, could not find his hymnal.

It just so happened that Mote had a copy of his new hymn in his pocket. "I have some verses in my pocket," he told his friend. "If you like, we could sing them." The man's wife enjoyed the hymn so much, Mote's friend asked for a personal copy.

That night, Mote returned home and composed two final verses to the hymn which he promptly took to his friend's home. Mote sang them to the dying woman. Her reaction to his hymn had a profound impact on Mote. He later studied for the ministry and became pastor of Rehoboth Baptist Church in Horsham, West Sussex, at the age of 55.

This last week, I had the privilege of standing by the hospital bed of a young man who was dying. As he coughed up blood and moaned in pain, we didn't talk about his job or sports or the weather. Death has a way of turning our thoughts and conversations away from the mundane.

Like Edward Mote, I had the privilege of reminding this young man of Jesus' love and sacrifice for him. At that moment, nothing else mattered.

So often we build our lives on our hopes and dreams. We want a family, a big home, a good job. We work hard so we can play hard. We spend our time and money on such seemingly important things.

DEATH HAS A WAY OF REMINDING US WHAT IS IMPORTANT.

Then we stand next to the deathbed of a son or brother or father. Then we find ourselves on the bed where we ourselves will breathe our last. Death has a way of reminding us what is important.

I am unrighteous. I am a sinner. I deserve to die and rot in hell. Yet Jesus came and did what was right in my place. His blood stained the ground below the cross to pay for my poor priorities and foolish ambitions. In him I have forgiveness. In him I have a home in heaven. He is my only hope—the only thing that matters.

Don't wait until your deathbed to remember that.

My hope is built on nothing less Than Jesus' blood and righteousness;
I dare to make no other claim But wholly lean on Jesus' name.
On Christ, the solid rock, I stand; All other ground is sinking sand.

When darkness veils his lovely face, I rest on his unchanging grace;
In ev'ry high and stormy gale My anchor holds within the veil.
On Christ, the solid rock, I stand; All other ground is sinking sand.
(CW 382:1,2)

Today I am thankful for/that _____

_____

Dear Jesus, help me to build my life,
my faith, my all on you. Amen.

DAY 274
JOHN 3:16

For God so loved the world that he gave his one
and only Son, that whoever believes in him
shall not perish but have eternal life.

JOHN 3:16

◆

When I was a kid, it was a staple at just about every NFL game. As the TV camera scanned the crowd, there would always be the one guy holding up a John 3:16 sign.

You don't see that much anymore.

John 3:16 is arguably the most well-known verse in the entire Bible. Children memorize it in Sunday school. Pastors quote it in their sermons. The elderly I visit at the nursing homes can recite it even when they can't remember their own children's names.

THE GOSPEL IN A NUTSHELL.

Simply put, John 3:16 is the gospel in a nutshell.

The problem is that many of us have seen and heard and repeated those words so often that we at times fail to appreciate what they are saying.

Imagine a crazy gunman walks into your church on Sunday morning. Sadly, in our world today, that is not difficult to imagine. He lines up all of our children against the wall. He tells us he is only going to shoot one of the children and then leave.

But we have to choose which child he will kill.

Could you say, "Kill my son—kill my daughter"? Could you say, "Shoot my grandson," to save all the other children? As a father, I tremble at the thought. I don't think I could do it. Can you imagine how hard that would be to sacrifice your own child to save all the others?

That is what God did. That is what John 3:16 is all about. When God reveals himself as Father and Son, he is, at least in part, trying to help us understand what he gave up for us. He sacrificed everything to save us. His love for us drove him to do what would be unthinkable for just about any parent here on earth.

God sacrificed his Son to save you. Why? Because he so loved the world. Martin Luther once said that the phrase "For God so loved the world" was even more comforting to him than if God had said, "For God so loved Martin Luther."

According to Luther's thinking, what if there was another Martin Luther in the world? Then how would he know those words applied to him? But when it says, "For God so loved the world," that had to include him. That has to include you.

God so loved you that he said, "Shoot my son" to save you. God so loved you that he gave up everything so that you could be forgiven, so that you would not perish, but have eternal life.

Believe that. Trust in him. It's that simple. You don't have to earn it. You don't have to be good enough to deserve it. He did it all. He gave it all. It is a gift. Whoever believes in Jesus will not perish in hell, but have eternal life in heaven.

My hope and prayer is that even when you are old and grey—even when you cannot remember your own child's name—you never forget the simple truth of John 3:16.

It is truly the gospel in a nutshell.

Today I am thankful for/that _____

_____

Heavenly Father, thank you for your amazing grace that saved a wretch like me. Help me to never stop being amazed at what you sacrificed to save me. Amen.

DAY 275
BATTING A THOUSAND

"Be holy because I, the LORD your God, am holy."

LEVITICUS 19:2

◆

I love October. There is nothing quite like October baseball. During the playoffs, every inning, every out, every pitch is significant. Every game is exciting.

Especially when the Astros are playing.

Baseball has always fascinated me. As a boy, I would spend hours watching games and devouring the information on the back of my baseball cards.

One thing about baseball distinguishes it from just about every other sport on the planet. The best athletes—the best hitters in baseball—fail more often than they succeed.

If a batter fails 75% of the time, he still would start for most Major League teams. If he fails only 70% of the time, he is an all-star. If he fails at 65% of his at-bats, he ends up in the Hall of Fame.

If you are a baseball player, you have to get used to failure. Every player will get out more times than he will get on base. That is just part of the game. The best players are simply those who figure out how to fail less often.

As human beings we tend to get used to failure. We have failed morally so many times, we lower our expectations of ourselves. Nobody's perfect, right?

"Sure, I may look at porn, but I don't actually cheat on my wife." "I may gossip and bend the truth a little, but I haven't killed anybody." "I may cut a few corners at work, fudge a few numbers on my taxes, or text while I'm driving, but that doesn't make me a bad person."

WE TEND TO GET USED TO FAILURE.

As long as we are good most of the time, or at least some of the time, we are good people. Good enough is good enough.

But good enough is not good enough for God. In baseball terms, God expects us to hit 1.000. In fact, for God, just one strike is failure. God expects perfection. He demands perfection. "Be holy, as I the LORD, your God, am holy," he commands.

528

The punishment for just one failure, the wage of just one sin, is death in hell. You may think that is unfair. You may find that unreasonable. But he is God. He made us to be perfect, but we have failed.

Thankfully God loved us so much, he sent a designated hitter. Yes, God plays for the American League. God himself came to this world and lived up to his own high expectations. Jesus took our place. He batted 1.000. He lived the perfect life we have failed so miserably to live. And then he died the death we deserve for our many errors and strike-outs.

Because Jesus took our place, we are forgiven. We have received the gift of heaven. "The wages of sin is death, but the gift of God is eternal life in Christ Jesus our Lord" (Romans 6:23).

Forgiveness, however, does not mean God lowers his standards. He doesn't say, "I forgive you anyway, so it's okay if you fail 70, 60, or even 50% of the time." God still expects perfection from us. We should still expect perfection from ourselves.

When we fail, when we fall, when we strike out, we have the comfort and assurance that we are forgiven. God's great forgiving love and free gift of heaven lead us to want to give our best for him and to expect the best from ourselves.

So don't lower your expectations of yourself. Don't settle for good enough. Set perfection as your goal. Live for your God who lived and died for you.

Today I am thankful for/that _____

Holy Lord, when I look into the mirror of your law, I see how miserably I have failed. I cling desperately to your promise of forgiveness. Help me, however, to never use that forgiveness as an excuse to lower what I expect of myself in my life of faith. Amen.

DAY 276
NOT KNOWING

Nothing in all creation is hidden from God's sight.

HEBREWS 4:13

◆

Not knowing stinks. Over the last couple of months, my daughter has been dealing with stomach pain. At times it is simply a tummy ache. Other times, the pain is debilitating.

We have tried changing her diet. We have gone to the doctor. They have run tests, but no one can tell us definitively what is causing her pain.

When you don't know, it's hard not to let your mind drift to the worst possible scenario. When you don't know, worry and fear easily overwhelm. When you don't know, the devil has a field day with your emotions.

Not knowing stinks.

They find a lump. The doctor tells you he has to run a biopsy and it will take a few days before they have the results. You're pregnant. The doctor tells you something is not quite right and they have to run a few tests. Your company may be letting a few people go, but nobody knows for sure.

Not knowing is excruciating. We tell ourselves it would be better to know one way or another. Then we can do something about it. Then we can deal with it.

The solution to not knowing, however, is not knowing. In other words, the way to get rid of the fear and worry isn't by finding out exactly what is causing my daughter's pain.

The solution to not knowing is knowing that God knows. God knows exactly what is happening in my daughter's stomach and what lies in her future. God knows whether the lump on your breast is cancer, whether your baby is okay, and whether you will have a job next week.

Truthfully, though, knowing that God knows is still not enough. If God knows, yet he is unwilling or unable to help us, what good does that do? Thankfully, God not only knows everything; he also can do anything. The all-knowing God is also all-powerful. He can heal our ills. He can raise the dead. He can provide everything we need for body and soul.

God not only can help us, he wants to. God loves my daughter more than I ever will. God loves you more than you will ever be able to fully understand. He loved us so much, he worked all of time and history to bring Jesus into the world. He loved us so much, he took our place and died our death. He loved us so much, he suffered the punishment of hell we deserve.

KNOWING THAT CHANGES EVERYTHING.

Knowing that changes everything. Though it is hard, in the end I don't need to know what is causing my daughter's pain. God knows. Her future is in his powerful and loving hands. He has won for her and for me a home in heaven. He promises that he will be with us. He promises to help and heal. He promises that he will make all things work together for our good.

Knowing that is enough.

Today I am thankful for/that _____

God, you know all things. You see all things. You can do all things. When I can't see or understand, help me to trust in your power, wisdom, and love. Amen.

DAY 277
DROWNING IN A SEA OF BAD NEWS

When [Peter] saw the wind, he was afraid and, beginning to sink, cried out, "Lord, save me!"

MATTHEW 14:30

❖

The news can be overwhelming. It doesn't matter whether you watch CNN, FOX, or MSNBC—whether you catch the local news on TV, glean it off the internet, or read the newspaper. The sheer volume of news can be overwhelming.

Especially when it's bad news.

Terrorists. Hurricanes. Earthquakes. Politics. Pandemic.

The more time we spend watching the news, the more it feels like the world is falling apart around us. The more we watch the news, the more helpless we feel.

We have no control over most of the events we read about and see on the news. I have little influence over what the president does. I can't stop hurricanes or earthquakes. I couldn't even stop our local Walmart from closing. The more informed I become, the more painfully obvious it is that I can do little about the chaotic events happening in the world around me.

Thankfully, God can.

Just look at the history behind the Bible. Great empires—the Egyptians, the Babylonians, the Persians, the Greeks, and the Romans—rose and fell as God's hand worked all of history to bring his Son Jesus into the world. Floods, earthquakes, and famines raged as God's loving plans and purposes came about through them.

Sometimes we are like Peter when he was walking on the water toward Jesus in the middle of the storm. He was doing fine until he started staring at the storm raging around him. He saw the whitecaps and waves. He looked down at his feet and thought, "I can't do this."

And he was right.

On his own, Peter couldn't walk on water. He couldn't stand in the middle of the storm. He began to sink. Thankfully Jesus lovingly and powerfully reached down his hand and pulled Peter up.

When we focus all our attention on the bad news cycling across the screen, we can easily become overwhelmed. We are forced to face our own impotence. We begin to feel like we are drowning in a sea of chaos.

There comes a point when we need to turn it off.

Don't get me wrong. I am not saying you should completely stop watching the news. A Christian should be well-informed of what is happening in our world. We need to know what is going on so we can do our best to influence, help, and heal the ills of our world.

But there comes a point when we need to turn the news off. If you find yourself obsessing and stressing about the state of affairs in our country or the world—if you are constantly worried about our president or the border or the Middle East or any of the countless other news stories flashing across the screen—it's probably time to take a break.

OPEN UP YOUR BIBLE AND READ THE GOOD NEWS.

Take your eyes off the storm for a while and take a long look at your Savior God. Open up your Bible and read the good news of his promises. He is in control. He is working all of time and history for our good. Even if this world goes to hell in a handbasket, you are going to heaven because Jesus lived and died as your Savior.

When you feel like you are drowning in a sea of bad news, the good news of God's promises will keep you afloat.

Today I am thankful for/that _____

_____

Lord, when I feel overwhelmed by the bad news around me, turn my eyes to the good news of your promises. Pull me up and help me remember that with you by my side I never need to worry or be afraid. Amen.

DAY 278
THE ILLUSION OF GRADUATION

Grow in the grace and knowledge of our Lord and Savior Jesus Christ.

2 PETER 3:18

◆

Every year at this time, hundreds of young people from our community walk up to a podium in cap and gown. Some dance. Some cry. A few do things which make their mothers cringe in embarrassment. All of them shake their principal's hand. Then they receive a piece of paper—a diploma.

According to that piece of paper, they have met the requirements of a high school education. They have taken the classes and learned what they need to learn.

For some, their high school diploma is a stepping stone to higher education. They will go on to college and eventually receive another diploma or two. Others will never set foot in a classroom again.

All of them at some point will end their formal education. They will get on with their lives. They will get jobs, get married, have kids and grandkids. They will be done with school.

Carol Burnett once quipped, "We don't stop going to school when we graduate."

The impression that your learning days are over is the illusion of graduation. Graduation simply means you have received the tools you need to continue to learn the rest of your life. Those who fail to learn that lesson have failed school, no matter what their diploma says.

Many of the young people in our community have received another kind of education. Their parents have taken them to church and Sunday school. They have attended vacation Bible school. They have gone to youth group outings and youth camps. As Christians, we highly value the importance of instructing our children in God's Word.

Some of our churches even have ceremonies to mark milestones in Christian education—First Communion and Confirmation. Sadly, when many of our young people get confirmed, they think they are graduating from God's Word. When they finish Sunday school, they feel they know everything they need to know.

The truth is that a Christian never graduates from God's Word. As sinful human beings, we have a constant need to continually study the Bible.

We have that need because we easily forget. A while back, a young woman I know returned to church and Sunday school after taking a couple of years off. Not too long after she came back, she made the comment, "I can't believe how much of this I had forgotten. I thought I knew what the Bible said. Or maybe I never really learned some of this in the first place."

WE ALL HAVE ROOM TO GROW.

That's the second reason we never graduate from God's Word: there is always more to learn. Most Christians tend to overestimate their Bible knowledge and the strength of their faith. The devil loves to keep us content right where we are. We know what we need to know. Our faith is good

534

just as it is. The truth, however, is that we all have room to grow. A faith the size of a mustard seed can move mountains. Have you moved any mountains lately?

As we watch our young people happily receive their high school and college diplomas, remember that we don't stop going to school when we graduate—especially as Christians. A Christian never graduates from God's Word.

Today I am thankful for/that _____

Dear God, thank you for the education I have received—both secular and religious. Help me to never stop learning and growing in my understanding of your amazing grace. Amen.

DAY 279
THE SUN IS COMING

"The sun of righteousness will rise with healing in its rays."

MALACHI 4:2

◆

Have you ever been to Alaska? I have. A number of years ago, I was sent to an Alaskan church to help for a week in December. The thing about Alaska in December is that the sun never comes out—ever.

My week in Alaska was one long, dark, cold, and depressing night.

That's how this world often feels. You are in pain. Your marriage is falling apart. You feel alone and unloved. Sometimes life feels like one long, dark, cold, and depressing night which will never end.

But God tells us in the book of the prophet Malachi that on judgment day, for those who revere his name, "the sun of righteousness will rise with healing in its rays."

The sun is coming. The night is almost over. God is coming to make everything right. Two thousand years ago, the Son of Righteousness— Jesus—came to make everything right between us and God. He lived the life of love we have failed to live. He died our death. He won for us forgiveness and peace with God.

He made us righteous—right before God.

Because he did, we can be sure that when he comes again he is going to take us to be with him in the happiness of heaven. On that day, the sun will finally rise. The long, cold night will finally be over.

In fact, the sun will come with "healing in its rays." We will finally be free from the cold darkness. We will finally be free from the depressing nights. We will finally be free from the sadness and struggles of this world.

ON THAT DAY, WE WILL SEE GOD FACE TO FACE.

On that day, we will see people we haven't seen in a long time. On that day, we will see God face to face. On that day, we will jump up and down and celebrate like a seven-year-old on Christmas morning.

Most people picture judgment day as something scary. Have you noticed that Hollywood movies about judgment day are always horror flicks?

For those who don't believe in Jesus (and therefore have rejected the forgiveness he won for them), judgment day will be a scary day. On that day, they will realize who God really is, but it will be too late. They will be forced to face the consequences of their poor choices forever in the horror movie of hell.

But God doesn't want that. That's why he sent his Son of Righteousness. That's why he sends us to tell others about him—so that they too can believe and celebrate on that day.

You don't have to be afraid of judgment day. The Son of Righteousness has made you right with God. When he comes, the long, dark night of this world will finally be over.

The sun is coming.

Today I am thankful for/that _____

_____

Lord, when I find myself in the dark, cold nights of this world, turn my eyes to the dawn. Help me remember that the dawn is coming when I will be free of every sadness and difficulty. Amen.

DAY 280
LIVE WITH THE END IN MIND

Even though you do not see him now, you believe in him and are filled with an inexpressible and glorious joy, for you are receiving the end result of your faith, the salvation of your souls.

1 PETER 1:8,9

◆

In his book *The 7 Habits of Highly Effective People,* author Stephen Covey asks the reader to imagine his or her own funeral.

Have you ever thought about your funeral? Have you ever wondered what your eulogist will say about you? What do you want them to say? Covey's point is that we should live our lives with the end in mind. If you can picture what you want to be and achieve, then you can map out a way to get there.

I was thinking about Covey's book as I watched President George H. W. Bush's funeral. I was awestruck by the emotional and eloquent eulogies. Again and again, friends and family beautifully encapsulated the life of a great man who achieved success in business, politics, and especially family—a man driven by faith and character.

As I watched, I wondered what the living presidents sitting in the front row were thinking. Were they imagining their own funerals? Were they wondering what people will say about them?

What will people say about you at your funeral?

Such mental exercises serve a purpose. It is good to live your life with the end in mind. It is beneficial to plan and set goals—to take the time to consider the bigger picture, the greater themes of life.

YOUR FUNERAL IS NOT THE END.

The problem with living your life based upon what you want people to say at your funeral is that such thinking often leads to vanity and pride. The problem is that your funeral is not the end.

I can tell you with utter certainty that on the day of his funeral, President George H. W. Bush didn't care what people were saying about him. We worry and fret about such things here on earth, but once we leave this earth we realize that they are what wise old King Solomon called "vanity—a chasing after the wind."

The successes and victories of President Bush's life were products of God's grace, not his own self-determination. From what I can tell, President Bush would have agreed with that statement. President Bush is now in heaven, not because of his great and public life of service, but because of his Savior's great and public death and resurrection.

I guess if I have one complaint about President Bush's funeral, it would be that. Though his faith and God's grace were mentioned, the impression was given that he is now in heaven because of his great life of service.

President Bush is in heaven because Jesus lived and died to pay the price for all of his failures. Though he was a good man—a great man by history's standards—he still failed and fell often in life. Like us all, he still deserved God's punishment in hell.

President Bush is in heaven because his God loved and saved him. President Bush is in heaven because he trusted and believed in God's amazing grace.

Live your life with the end in mind—not worrying what people will say about you at your funeral, but rather considering what will happen to you after you die. After you die, it won't matter to you how many people attend your funeral or what they say about you.

The only thing that matters is where you spend eternity. The only thing that matters is knowing and believing in Jesus.

Live your life with that in mind.

Today I am thankful for/that _____

_____

Lord, help me to live every day of my life with the end in mind. Amen

DAY 281
THE BEST MEDICINE

"This is my blood of the covenant, which is poured out for many for the forgiveness of sins."
MATTHEW 26:28

I recently visited a young lady from our congregation who was in the hospital. As I often do when visiting members in the hospital, we had a brief devotion and then I offered to give her Holy Communion.

She accepted with a smile, but when I opened my portable Communion kit, I realized I had forgotten to include the tiny clear plastic cups in which we put the wine.

Embarrassed, I slipped out and asked a nurse if they might have anything I could use. She went into their supply room and came out with a small clear cup used for medicine. It was just the right size.

When I came back into the room, I proudly showed the young lady the medicine cup I found.

"That's perfect," she said with a smile. "Communion is always the best medicine."

Two thousand years ago, Jesus sat with his disciples in an upper room, eating his last supper. Less than 24 hours later, he would be dead. As they ate, Jesus took the thin, cracker-like bread, broke it in pieces and gave it to his disciples saying, "Take and eat. This is my body which is given for you.

Do this in remembrance of me." Then he took the cup of wine and passed it among them. "Take and drink," he said, "this is the blood of the new covenant, shed for you, for the forgiveness of sins. Do this whenever you drink it in remembrance of me."

On the night before he died, Jesus gave us a meal to remember him by. As we receive his body and blood in Holy Communion, we can't help but remember what he did to save us. We can't help but think about what he sacrificed, what he gave, what he suffered to save us.

COMMUNION IS MORE THAN JUST A MEMORIAL MEAL.

But Holy Communion is more than just a memorial meal. Jesus gave it to us as a "covenant." A covenant is a contract. Communion is a contract, signed in Jesus' blood, guaranteeing us the forgiveness of sins.

When we receive Holy Communion, we stand in God's presence; we are stained with all the filth of our lives—the lies we tell, the bad words we say, our pride, our worry, our anger—and God shows us the contract, signed in Jesus' blood, which says, "All is forgiven."

The word *communion* means "to be joined together with." In Communion, we commune with Christ himself, receiving with our mouths Jesus' true body and blood. Through faith in him, we are united to God. In Communion, God reaches down and personally "touches" us, telling us we are pardoned.

That truth—that confidence—heals our hearts from the pangs of guilt and regret. It gives us strength to face every obstacle and misery of this world.

So take Holy Communion regularly and often. It really is the best medicine.

Today I am thankful for/that _____

_____

Dear Jesus, thank you for the peace and comfort you give in Holy Communion. As you now live in me, help me to live for you. Amen.

540

DAY 282
PERSISTENCE

**"If you, then, though you are evil, know how to give
good gifts to your children, how much more
will your Father in heaven give good
gifts to those who ask him!"**

MATTHEW 7:11

❖

"Papá,"—(that's what my kids call me)—"can I get the new skin for Minecraft? It only costs $4."

"I don't know. We'll see."

Two minutes later . . . "Papá, can I get the new skin for Minecraft? It only costs $4."

"No. We've spent a lot on your video games lately. Maybe later, but don't ask for a while."

Two minutes later . . . "Papá, when you say later, how long do I have to wait? I'm just asking."

"Stop asking or you won't get it at all."

Two minutes later . . ."Papá, I'm not asking about the Minecraft skin, but when can I ask you again?"

One minute later . . . "Papá, why is your face turning red? Why aren't you answering me? Did you hear me? I'm just asking. I've wanted this my whole life. I won't ask for anything ever again. Please, it's only $4."

One thing my son does not lack is persistence. I'm sure many parents can relate.

I have to confess that at times I have lost patience with my son's persistence. On more than one occasion, I have reached my tipping point. I get frustrated. I get annoyed.

Thankfully, we have a heavenly Father who never loses patience when we are persistent. Over the years I have heard people say things like, "I don't want to bother God with such little things" or "I'm giving up on praying because I've asked God to help and he just won't."

You can be sure you are never bothering God in your prayers. Take a moment today to read Matthew 7:7-11. God loves to hear from you. Unlike

541

easily frustrated human fathers, our heavenly Father never grows weary of hearing your persistent petitions.

In fact, sometimes he doesn't give us what we ask for right away precisely because he wants to see how persistent we will be. He wants us to turn to him and expect him to do what he has promised. Jacob literally and physically wrestled with God an entire night until God blessed him (Genesis 32:22-32).

So pray to God persistently. You are never bothering him. You will never annoy him.

PRAY TO GOD PERSISTENTLY. YOU ARE NEVER BOTHERING HIM.

But also understand that God has three ways of answering our requests. Sometimes he says, "Yes," and gives us what we ask. Sometimes he says, "Wait," and tests our patience and persistence.

Sometimes God says, "No."

The apostle Paul prayed persistently that God take away a physical burden he was suffering. God flatly told him, "My grace is sufficient for you" (2 Corinthians 12:9).

God does not promise to give us everything we ask for, because everything we ask for is not always what is best for us. It doesn't matter how persistent you are. God isn't a father like me. You can't wear him down or tire him out until he finally gives in and says, "Yes."

God wants you to be persistent, but he also wants you to trust him. Sometimes he will say, "No," because he loves you. If God gave you everything you wanted, your life would be a horrible mess.

So be persistent in your prayers, but then end each prayer with the words, "Thy will be done." Be patient, but then accept it when God says, "No." Trust that everything he does is for your good.

Your heavenly Father truly knows best.

Today I am thankful for/that _____

_____

Father, give me the persistence to ask for whatever is in my heart. Give me the faith to accept when you say no. Amen.

DAY 283
LET YOUR LIGHT SHINE

**"Let your light shine before others, that they may see
your good deeds and glorify your Father in heaven."**

MATTHEW 5:16

❖

My kids loved it. Not too long ago, we had the perfect conditions to see a total lunar eclipse. It was a crisp, clear night. No clouds got in the way. We had a perfect vantage point.

A lunar eclipse occurs when the earth moves between the sun and the moon causing the earth's shadow to cover the moon. The lunar eclipse we witnessed was extra-special because it also featured a blood moon in which dust in the earth's atmosphere caused the moon to turn a reddish-orange color.

In the end, however, nothing of what we witnessed that night actually happened to the moon. The bright light we see shining through our windows every night is not technically moonlight. The moon is just a dark rock floating around the earth.

The spectacle we witnessed wasn't caused by the moon, but rather the sun. The moon reflects the light of the sun.

In a very real sense, you and I are moons. In his Sermon on the Mount, Jesus calls us "the light of the world" (Matthew 5:14). Like the moon, however, we give no light. In fact, by nature our hearts are black holes of sin.

But the light of God's love has shone in our hearts and we can now see Jesus, the Light of the world. We can see the forgiveness and heaven he won for us on the cross. We can see the way to heaven through faith in him.

And now our Savior has called us to be lights illuminating the dark night of this world. Like the moon, we are not the source of the light. Rather, we reflect the light of the Son. Our words and actions as Christians reflect upon our Savior. They show people how wonderful he is and what he can do in the lives of simple, sinful human beings like you and me.

Sadly, however, the dark shadow of our sinful nature at times eclipses that light. When we as Christians act like saints on Sunday and then go out and cuss and argue and drink too much the rest of the week, it keeps people from seeing the light of Jesus' love. It leads people to think that being a Christian means just going through the motions. It makes it seem like Jesus isn't important enough to affect the way we live.

Whether you like it or not, Christ's name is tattooed across the forehead of every Christian. When we claim to love him and then are ugly to other people in person or even on Facebook, it leads them to say, "Why would I want to be a Christian?"

But the opposite is also true. When we show love and kindness—when in the middle of pain and sorrow we have the peace and confidence which only Jesus can give—people notice.

It's like when you're in a restaurant and you see someone eating a delicious-looking meal. You can tell by their body language and facial expressions they are really enjoying the food. What do you find yourself saying to the waiter?

"I want what they're having."

BEING A MOON IS A BIG RESPONSIBILITY.

Being the light of the world means living your life in such a way that people say, "I want what they're having." Being a moon is a big responsibility. You are the opportunity for the people in your life—your family, your coworkers, your friends—to see the light of Jesus' love.

Don't let anything eclipse that light.

Today I am thankful for/that _____

_____

Dear Jesus, Light of the world, thank you for opening my eyes and allowing me to see your amazing grace. Help me to reflect the light of your love in everything I say and do. Amen.

DAY 284
MAY I SUGGEST A NAME?

Joseph, a Levite from Cyprus, whom the apostles called
Barnabas (which means "son of encouragement").

ACTS 4:36

❖

The most popular names in 2020 for baby boys are Liam, Noah, and Ethan. Those names didn't even make the charts 100 years ago when the most common boy names were John, William, and James. Times have changed.

Do you know anybody who is about to have a baby boy? Allow me to make a name suggestion.

Barnabas.

I know. It doesn't really roll off the tongue. It sounds a bit old-fashioned, but let me tell you why I like the name Barnabas.

The name Barnabas means "son of encouragement." We first meet Barnabas in the book of Acts. He was a Jewish Christian who sold a field and gave the proceeds to the work of the church. Barnabas was an encourager. His love and thanks to his Savior showed itself in his support for the work of the gospel.

When early Christians began to be persecuted in Jerusalem, a large number moved north to a city called Antioch. There they shared the good news about Jesus with everyone they could.

The church in Antioch grew exponentially. They needed help, so what did the apostles in Jerusalem do? They sent Barnabas, the encourager. When Barnabas saw all the work that needed to be done in Antioch, he left to find Paul.

Paul had been a persecutor of the church. He had arrested and murdered Christians. Jesus, however, appeared to him on the road to Damascus and called him to be an apostle—to be his messenger.

Up to this point, nobody had really given Paul a chance, but Barnabas saw something in him. He convinced Paul to go to Antioch where together they worked for over a year, teaching and encouraging the Christians there. Barnabas later accompanied and encouraged Paul on his first missionary journey.

So what do you think? Would you be willing to name your son, Barnabas? It's okay if you don't.

But you can still teach him to be a Barnabas.

Raise your children to be encouragers. Show them what it means to support the work of the church and God's ministers.

BEING AN ENCOURAGER IS NOT ALWAYS EASY.

Being an encourager is not always easy. The fruitcake of God's church is made up of all kinds of nuts. Sometimes your pastor will not be your cup of tea. Sometimes his personality may rub you the wrong way or his style might get on your nerves. Don't let that stop you from encouraging him. God has placed him in your life for a purpose.

Too many Christians spend their days criticizing their churches, their pastors, and their fellow members. Show your children something different. Teach them to be sons and daughters of encouragement.

Even if you don't name them Barnabas.

Today I am thankful for/that _____

_____

Lord, forgive me for the many times I have criticized and complained about my church or pastor. Help me to give constructive criticism and always be an encourager. Amen.

DAY 285
THE DANGER OF ASSUMPTIONS

Everyone should be quick to listen, slow to speak
and slow to become angry.

JAMES 1:19

❖

I'll never forget the lesson. I was a junior in high school. My teacher asked the class, "Do you know what the danger of assumptions is?" He then wrote a word on the board separated by hyphens: ASS—U—ME.

"That is what we are when we assume," he said definitively.

I was thinking about that lesson a while back. On January 18, 2019, protesters clashed at the Lincoln Memorial in Washington, D. C. Just feet from the inscribed words, "With malice toward none; charity for all," three groups collided.

A protest of Indigenous rights activists was met by a large group of Catholic teenage boys in town for the upcoming March for Life. Both groups were taunted and insulted by a group of African-American protesters called the Hebrew Israelites.

One Native American protester, a veteran, began playing his drum in the middle of the scene. He walked up to the boys and soon was face to face with a young man wearing a MAGA baseball cap. The young man and the Native American elder stood inches from each other in a stare down as the elder beat his drum. A few of the young men acted immaturely and began to dance and chant to the beat of the drum.

A clip of the confrontation went viral. The video painted the boys as racist and taunting the Native American protester. Social media went nuts. Many mainline media outlets ran the story. The boys were condemned as racists.

Only later did the full picture become clear. The truth was much more complicated. Though some acted immaturely, the majority responded calmly and peacefully to vicious verbal attacks by some protesters. No evidence has been brought forth to back many of the claims of racist chants by the teens. The video clip wasn't the whole story.

Jesus' brother James once wrote, "Everyone should be quick to listen, slow to speak, and slow to become angry." Recent advances in technology now allow news to travel at the speed of light. You and I have a power to spread and amplify information which no other generation in history has ever enjoyed.

With great power, however, comes great responsibility. Many blame the media for prematurely condemning the Covington Catholic boys. Though countless questionable media sources and even a number of mainline media outlets quickly shared the clip and reported the story, in the end they only hold a part of the blame.

Remember what assuming does. There is no "they" in assume. You and I are the ones who quickly share videos, blogs, and memes reflecting our political and social views without ever checking their validity. We are the ones who angrily spout off our opinions without having all the facts. We are the ones who assume that those who disagree with us are malicious or evil.

In the end, the media—especially the less-reputable members of the media—report the information they know will be consumed and shared by the public. They are consumer-driven. We, the American public, are that consumer. We are the ones who are fueling this madness.

GIVE ME A KIND HEART. Be quick to listen and slow to speak. Make sure you have all the facts. Don't assume that everything you see on the internet or TV is the whole truth. Don't assume that those who disagree with you are evil or stupid or racist.

Remember what we are when we assume.

Today I am thankful for/that _____

_____

Merciful Lord, forgive me for all the times I assume the worst about people. Help me to be quick to listen and slow to speak. Give me a kind heart which takes other people's words and actions in the kindest possible way. Amen.

DAY 286
JUDGEMENT FREE ZONE

We must all appear before the judgment seat of Christ,
so that each of us may receive what is due us for the
things done while in the body, whether good or bad.

2 CORINTHIANS 5:10

◆

On July 22, 2018, a 34-year-old man named Eric Stagno walked into a Planet Fitness Gym in the state of New Hampshire. He stopped at the front counter, took off all his clothes and then proceeded to do yoga in the buff. Those exercising at the time were both shocked and disgusted. The police were called immediately.

Upon his arrest, Stagno claimed he thought he was in a "Judgement Free Zone," referencing the company's longtime slogan.

With 1,500 locations and over 10 million members, Planet Fitness is one of the most successful gym franchises in the world. Their claim to be a "Judgement Free Zone" resonates with many people. Embarrassment over their own bodies, coupled with the pressure of exercising beside sculpted body builders, often keeps people from going to the gym.

They feel like they are being judged.

Planet Fitness has found a way to create a comfortable and welcoming environment for the casual gym user. But, as Eric Stagno found out, there is no such place as a completely Judgement Free Zone.

One of the things our world today fails to distinguish is the difference between judging and being judgmental. Being judgmental means being quick to judge or harsh in your judgment. It means setting yourself above other people or thinking you are better than them.

God doesn't want us to be judgmental. We have no right to set ourselves up as judge and jury. In his Sermon on the Mount, Jesus speaks strong words about those who pridefully judge others (Matthew 7:1-5).

God, however, does judge. He is the Supreme Court of all creation. In the Bible, he has given humankind a moral code—a right and wrong—by which we will all be judged one day. There is no such thing as a "Judgement Free Zone" here on earth. Every single person will be judged by God for what they do in this life.

When we as Christians lovingly and humbly share God's moral code with the world—when we call sin "sin"—we aren't being judgmental. We are simply sharing the decrees of the Judge of all creation.

Our world, however, calls that judgmental. It doesn't want you or me to say that certain actions or attitudes are sinful. That is considered unloving and intolerant. For our world, love is living judgment free, letting people be and express themselves however they choose.

But when a guy gets naked in a gym or a pedophile molests a young boy or a terrorist massacres the innocent, then they suddenly see the importance of judges and juries. Then they suddenly recognize the existence of a higher moral code by which people should be judged.

Deep down we all know there is a higher moral code. Deep down we know we haven't lived up to that moral code. We have failed and fallen numerous times. We deserve to be declared guilty by God the Judge.

Yet because Jesus lived and died in our place—because he suffered our guilty verdict—God declares all those who believe in him to be innocent of all charges. Through faith in Jesus, we have been washed clean of our sins. Through faith in Jesus, we don't have to be afraid of judgment day.

THERE ARE NO JUDGMENT FREE ZONES HERE ON EARTH.

But that doesn't change the fact that judgment day is coming. There are no Judgement Free Zones here on earth. Don't fall into the trap of thinking that all judging is judgmental. God wants us to boldly and lovingly proclaim his moral code and his judgments even when people don't want to hear it. Only then will they be able to see how desperately they need Jesus as their Savior.

There is no such thing as a Judgement Free Zone.

Today I am thankful for/that _____

_____

O Holy God, you know everything I have ever thought, said, and done. I know one day I will stand before your judgment throne. Forgive me all my sins for Jesus' sake and help me to not be afraid of your judgment. Amen.

DAY 287
ROCK OF AGES

**It is by grace you have been saved, through faith—and
this is not from yourselves, it is the gift of God—not by
works, so that no one can boast.**

EPHESIANS 2:8,9

❖

Why are you going to heaven? Out of curiosity, I have asked that question
to a countless number of Christian friends and acquaintances over the
years. The most common answer I hear sounds something like this:
"Because I go to church and try to be a good person." The second most
common answer is, "Because I chose Jesus Christ as my Lord and Savior."

Why are you going to heaven? That is a question with which Augustus
Toplady wrestled.

Augustus Toplady was an Anglican priest who lived during the mid-18th
century. His father was an officer in the Royal Marines who died when
Augustus was just a baby. When he was 15 years old, he and his mother
moved to Ireland where young Augustus studied at Trinity College in Dublin.

In 1764, Toplady was ordained as an Anglican priest. Highly intelligent and
strong-willed, Toplady soon became embroiled in the great debate which
raged in England at the time: Calvinism versus Arminianism.

John Wesley (1703–1791), the founder of the growing Methodist
movement, was an Arminian. Toplady was a staunch Calvinist. One of the
issues in the debate was how a person becomes a Christian. John Wesley
taught that God has given all people the free will to choose to follow him
or not.

John Wesley wholeheartedly believed that Jesus is the source of salvation.
He believed Jesus lived and died to pay the price for all our sins. He
believed Jesus did it all. According to Wesley, the only thing you have to do
is choose to believe in him. You have to accept him into your heart. God
did 99.9%; you just have to do the 0.1% of choosing Jesus as your Lord
and Savior.

Augustus Toplady said that was impossible. All people are born dead in sin
(Ephesians 2:1). A dead person can't do anything. If I choose to believe in
Jesus, I can only do so because the Holy Spirit has already worked faith in

my heart through the good news of the gospel. According to Augustus Toplady, God effected 100% of my salvation. I contribute nothing.

In 1776, Toplady published an essay in which he compared the sins of an individual to the national debt of England—a debt which he said could never be paid by one person. Only Jesus could pay the debt we owe. He concluded the essay with a poem which later became a hymn:

Rock of Ages, cleft for me, Let me hide myself in thee;
Let the water and the blood From thy riven side which flowed
Be of sin the double cure: Cleanse me from its guilt and pow'r.

Not the labors of my hands Can fulfill thy law's demands.
Could my zeal no respite know, Could my tears forever flow,
All for sin could not atone; Thou must save and thou alone.

Nothing in my hand I bring, Simply to thy cross I cling;
Naked, come to thee for dress, Helpless, look to thee for grace.
Foul, I to the fountain fly—Wash me Savior, or I die! (CW 389:1-3)

WHY ARE YOU GOING TO HEAVEN?

Why are you going to heaven? There can be no "I" in that answer. You are not going to heaven because you go to church or are a good person. You are not going to heaven because you chose Jesus. You bring nothing to the table. You contribute nothing to your salvation. You are a born beggar.

The only reason you are going to heaven is because the Rock of Ages lovingly lived and died in your place. You are going to heaven because he chose you and gave you faith through water and his Word. He did it all. Everything you now do as a Christian is your response, your "thank you" to him who died that you might live.

Why am I going to heaven? Jesus is the answer.

Today I am thankful for/that _____

_____

"While I draw this fleeting breath, When mine eyelids close in death, When I soar to worlds unknown, See thee on thy judgment throne, Rock of Ages, cleft for me, Let me hide myself in thee." Amen. (CW 389:4)

DAY 288
BETTER DAYS AHEAD

**"See, I will create new heavens and a new earth.
The former things will not be remembered,
nor will they come to mind."**

ISAIAH 65:17

◆

I had a funeral today. Presiding over funerals is one of the great privileges I enjoy as a pastor. After the funeral meal, everyone sat around telling stories.

That's what happens when somebody dies. We become nostalgic. We reminisce and tell stories about the good ol' days.

As we talk about the good ol' days, we tend to view them through rose-colored glasses. We find ourselves wishing we could go back.

Things were better then. Life was simpler. The world was a kinder, gentler place.

Truth be told, the good ol' days weren't always so good. When we go to a funeral, we remember the wonderful times we had with the person—the laughter, the love, the fun. But, honestly, the good ol' days were not all good.

There were hard times too. There were problems. There were frustrations. The good ol' days were never as good as we remember them.

Don't get me wrong. At a funeral, it's good to talk about the good ol' days—to remember and give thanks to God for the blessing of having such wonderful memories.

But God doesn't want us living in or longing for the past. In Isaiah chapter 65, he says, "See, I will create new heavens and a new earth. The former things will not be remembered, nor will they come to mind."

Heaven is going to be so good, so perfect, so awesome, and so fun that even the best of times here on earth will seem like nothing in comparison. Heaven is going to be so wonderful that even the worst and most painful of times here on earth will seem like nothing.

In his letter to the Romans, the apostle Paul compares it to a woman having a baby. Being pregnant isn't easy. First there's the morning sickness. By the end, the baby is pushing against your bladder and kicking your ribs. You can't get comfortable. You can't sleep. And then there's the pain of labor. My wife often reminds my daughter of the 36 hours of labor she went through with her.

Interestingly, when they finally hand you your baby—when they lay your precious child in your exhausted, waiting arms—all the pain, all the frustrations, and all the struggles of the past nine months melt away. They are replaced by pure joy and excitement.

That's what it will be like going to heaven. God promises that when we die, all the pains and problems, all the regrets and guilt of the past, will melt away. They will be replaced by pure joy.

He promises the joy of heaven to everyone who believes in him. All those who trust in Jesus as their Savior are forgiven for all the mistakes and failures of their past. You can't commit a sin which God will not forgive. The happiness of heaven is God's gift to you.

TURN MY EYES TO THE HEAVEN THAT IS WAITING FOR ME.

Honestly, it was a joy today sitting and listening to the stories about the good ol' days. The danger for all of us, though, is getting stuck living in or longing for the good ol' days of the past.

Actually, my greatest joy today was how God turned our eyes to the new and better days our friend is now enjoying in heaven. Our peace and comfort is his promise that we will be reunited with him one day. We don't have to tearfully long for the good ol' days of the past. We can joyfully look forward to the new and better days waiting for us in heaven.

Today I am thankful for/that _____

_____

Heavenly Father, as I deal with the struggles of today, help me to turn my eyes to the heaven that is waiting for me and the better days ahead. Amen.

DAY 289
SWEATING THE SMALL STUFF

**He who did not spare his own Son, but gave him up
for us all—how will he not also, along with
him, graciously give us all things?**

ROMANS 8:32

❖

I grew up in the arctic tundra, also known as the great state of Michigan. During the summer months, there is no more beautiful place on God's green earth.

Winter, on the other hand, is long and cold.

Having lived in the south my entire adult life, I don't miss the cold. I don't miss bundling up to go outside. I don't miss scraping off the windshield or having to warm up the car for 15 minutes before going anywhere. I don't miss shoveling snow off the driveway.

A number of years ago, my dad was shoveling his driveway when he slipped on a patch of ice and banged his head on the pavement. He walked away from the experience embarrassed, with a huge knot on the back of his head and a pounding headache.

After a day or two, the knot went down and the headache went away. A week later, though, he began to lose feeling in his hand and then his whole arm. Concerned, he went to the doctor.

After describing his symptoms to his family physician, the doctor immediately sent my dad to the hospital where they drilled a hole in the back of his skull. Unbeknownst to my dad, blood had been accumulating between his brain and skull. The doctors rushed to drain the blood and ease the pressure on his brain.

The doctor told my father that if he had waited any longer, he could have died. This was serious. His life was on the line.

My dad told me afterward that the experience gave him a unique perspective on faith. Though the ordeal was difficult and scary, my dad's faith didn't waver. He knew God was with him. He trusted that no matter what happened he had a home waiting for him in heaven.

My dad was at peace no matter what happened.

"IT'S THE LITTLE THINGS THE DEVIL GETS US ON."

"As Christians, we tend to do well on the big stuff," my dad told me later. "It's the little things the devil gets us on."

An unexpected bill comes in. Your hours get cut at work. A pandemic happens and you don't have enough toilet paper, your kids can't finish the school year, your income or retirement takes a big hit.

Immediately your stomach turns. Anxiety sets in. You can't sleep. You worry. You stress.

When we Christians face the big stuff, we tend to run to God's arms and find comfort in his promises. When faced with death, we take a deep breath and trust that the God who controls all of time and history loved us enough to live and die as our Savior. We trust that he is with us and that we have a home in heaven.

But then we sweat the small stuff—money, relationships, work, and school.

In the end, stress, worry, and fear are all simply different forms of doubt. We forget that God's got this. We forget the blood, sweat, and tears Jesus shed to save us. If he loves us that much, how is he not also going to make everything else work out for our good?

So whatever you're facing right now—whether big or small—don't sweat it. God's got this.

Today I am thankful for/that _____

_____

Lord, forgive me my doubt. Help me to trust in you as I face every obstacle—both big and small. Amen.

DAY 290
BE A FRIEND

**The pleasantness of a friend springs
from their heartfelt advice.**

PROVERBS 27:9

❖

When I was in the seminary, I had three roommates. I have never been closer to any other men here on earth. We were like brothers.

Have you ever had anybody like that in your life? They might not be related to you, but they are family.

Family has your back. Family sticks by you when no one else will. Family will take your side when others come at you, no matter what.

It's wonderful to have family like that, but we all need at least one friend.

A friend is different than family. Like family, a friend will love you and stand by your side. A friend, however, will also tell you what you don't want to hear. A friend will tell you when you're wrong. A friend will push you to be a better person.

It's wonderful to have family who support you, but a true friend is a gift of God.

A friend doesn't enable you to do bad things. A friend doesn't silently sit by and watch you hurt yourself or others. A friend doesn't encourage you to get drunk. A friend doesn't help you get away with things at work or school or in your marriage.

A friend tells you when you've had too much. A friend takes away your keys. A friend encourages you to work things out with your wife.

A FRIEND WILL RISK YOUR FRIENDSHIP IF IT MEANS HELPING YOU.

A friend will risk your friendship if it means helping you.

A true friend will always take you back to Jesus. If you don't believe in God or are slowly sliding away from your faith, a friend won't stand idly by. Though you may not want to hear it—though it may mean losing your friendship—a friend will always try to help you see Jesus and what he did to save you.

557

A friend won't let you blindly wander down the road to hell without saying anything.

That's what we so often forget. If we truly believe what the Bible says—if faith in Jesus is the only way to be saved from the hell we all deserve—how can we not say anything? No friend would knowingly let their friend go to hell.

So that means having the tough conversations. It means inviting them to church. It means praying for them and being an example of faith and love in their lives.

At our church we have an annual Bring-a-Friend Sunday in which we encourage our members to invite a friend, a family member, or an acquaintance to go to church with them.

In reality, you don't need a special Sunday to invite a friend to church. If they don't know or believe in Jesus, if they have gotten away from God or church, what are you waiting for? You never know when it will be too late.

So have that conversation. Invite them to church.

That's what a friend does.

Today I am thankful for/that _____

_____

Heavenly Father, thank you for the good friends you have given me. Help me to be a true friend to others, even when it is hard. Amen.

DAY 291
STAND FIRM

Stand firm. Let nothing move you.

1 CORINTHIANS 15:58

◆

It is the classic superhero pose—fists placed proudly on the hips, feet firmly planted on the ground, eyes fixed confidently on the horizon.

When I read 1 Corinthians 15:58, I picture that pose.

Known as the resurrection chapter of the Bible, 1 Corinthians chapter 15 contains assurance from Paul that Jesus really did rise from the dead. And if Jesus rose from the dead, that means all those who believe in him will also rise.

Death is not the end. It cannot defeat us. It has forever been swallowed up in victory because of Jesus.

"Therefore," Paul tells us, "stand firm. Let nothing move you. Always give yourselves fully to the work of the Lord because you know that your labor in the Lord is not in vain."

Stand firm. There are times when I am in church hearing God's promises or at home reading them in my Bible, and I feel like Superman standing in his superhero pose, my cape fluttering in the wind.

I trust in God. Nothing can harm me. The victory is won. I am going to heaven.

I feel like nothing can move me.

Then the credit card bill comes in the mail. Then my mom finds a lump on her breast. Then my teenage daughter tells me, "I'm pregnant." Then my boss says, "You're fired."

Suddenly my knees begin to wobble. My hands begin to shake. I fall to one knee.

An interesting story arc which is common in comic books is when a superhero begins to doubt or deny his own powers. Suddenly the unmovable force becomes movable. He stumbles and falls. He forgets who he is.

THE TRUTH IS I AM NO SUPERHERO.

The truth is I am no superhero. On my own, I cannot stand firm. On my own, I stumble and fall. The reason I can stand firm—the reason I can stand with my head

559

held high and my eyes fixed confidently on the horizon—is because Superman is standing behind me.

The all-powerful God, my Savior from sin, is holding me up in his powerful hands. He has already defeated our archenemies: sin, death, and the devil. No matter what the devil and the world throw at me, they cannot win. Through faith in Jesus, I am going to heaven.

I can serve God with my head held high, knowing that my labor in the Lord is not in vain. At times it may look like it is in vain. It may look like the devil is winning or the world has won. As we stand over the graves of those we love, it looks like life has been swallowed up in defeat.

That's when we need to go back to 1 Corinthians chapter 15. As the hymn-writer wrote, "The strife is o'er, the battle done; now is the victor's triumph won."

Jesus rose. He won. Death has been swallowed up in victory. Now your all-powerful Savior stands behind you every moment of every day.

So strike the pose. Plant your feet firmly in the ground. Put your fists on your hips. Stick out your chest. Fix your eyes confidently on the horizon.

Stand firm. You are going to heaven.

Today I am thankful for/that _____

_____

Almighty God, take away my fears. Give me courage. Help me to stand firm in your promises. Amen.

DAY 292
RENOVATIONS

Do not conform to the pattern of this world, but be transformed by the renewing of your mind.

ROMANS 12:2

◆

Renovations are hard. This week we begin a major renovation on our home. When it is all done, we will have new floors, paneling will be replaced by drywall, and the kitchen and bathrooms will have new cabinets and counters.

The entire process is honestly a bit overwhelming.

You see, we are going to try to live at home while the renovations are being done. We've already begun to pack everything that was once contained in cabinets. We are preparing ourselves for the dust and discomfort because we know there will be hiccups and speed bumps along the way.

We know this is going to be a challenge. Renovations always are. But in the end it will be worth it. Our 50-year-old home will have a new beginning.

As I prepare myself for the challenges which lie ahead, I can't help but think about other renovations which need to be done. I am not, however, talking about showers or closets or the garage.

I am talking about my heart.

Because I am a Christian, God himself lives in me. The Holy Spirit dwells in my heart. Yet there are rooms deep in my heart which I have locked off to him. I have closets with dusty skeletons. I have dark cellars which a part of me likes to keep dirty and ugly.

I am at the same time sinner and saint. Because of Jesus, I am washed clean of my sins, forever forgiven. The faith worked in my heart by the Holy Spirit loves God and lives for him. God himself lives in me. But as long as I live here on earth, sin also resides in certain rooms of my heart and mind.

RENOVATING THE ROOMS OF THE HEART IS DIFFICULT.

As long as we live and breathe here on earth, we are in constant need of renovation. The old habits of our sinful nature die hard. New sins are constantly trying to find a place to grow like mildew in the walls.

Renovating the rooms of the heart is difficult. Anyone who struggles with addictions knows that. It's easier to just close the door of those rooms so others can't see them—to secretly live with the mess.

But when we remember what God has done for us—all that he has forgiven us—we take a deep breath and do the hard work of renovating. We talk about our sins and weaknesses with trusted Christian brothers and sisters or with a pastor or counselor. We face the pain and heartache of struggling against our sinful impulses and cleaning up our hearts.

Renovation is hard. You will have hiccups and speed bumps along the way. But it is worth it. As we, with the help of the Holy Spirit, open the doors of those dark rooms and do the hard work of renovation, it gives us new beginnings. It frees us to live for God and help others.

So pray for me as my renovations begin. I will pray for you. Turn to God in prayer. Turn to his Word for strength and guidance. Talk to a Christian friend or pastor whom you trust.

It will be hard. Renovations always are. But in the end, it will be worth it.

Today I am thankful for/that _____

_____

Lord, thank you for your all-encompassing forgiveness. Help me now to do the hard work of cleaning up and fixing the dirty and broken places in my heart. Amen.

DAY 293
ITCHING EARS

**The time will come when people will not put up with
sound doctrine. Instead, to suit their own desires, they
will gather around them a great number of teachers to
say what their itching ears want to hear.**

2 TIMOTHY 4:3

◆

"Stop touching your face," my wife scolds me. I know I'm not supposed to.
I know it increases the chances I could get sick. I know it is socially taboo,
but I can't help it.

My face itches. I have a beard. I have dry skin. I have allergies.

When you have an itch, it's hard not to scratch it.

My face isn't the only thing that itches, though. My ears do. My eyes do.
My heart does too.

> **WE ALL HAVE AN ITCH
> TO HEAR WHAT WE
> WANT TO HEAR.**

We all have an itch to hear what we want to hear.
Just look at social media. We like, love, and share
posts which tell us what we want to hear or agree
with our personal opinions and values. We tend to
hide, block, and scroll past those which don't.

Complicated algorithms on search engines and social
media platforms analyze our search patterns and
scroll history so that advertisers can give us the images and messages we
want to see and hear.

Our phones and Facebook feed our natural narcissism.

The temptation for us as Christians is to look for churches and preachers
who do the same. Two thousand years ago, the apostle Paul warned
young Pastor Timothy, "The time will come when people will not put up
with sound doctrine. Instead, to suit their own desires, they will gather
around them a great number of teachers to say what their itching ears
want to hear."

By nature, we all want to hear the affirmation that who we are and what we
think is good and right. None of us enjoys having our failures and
weaknesses pointed out to us. None of us likes being told we are wrong.

We want to hear we are good enough just as we are. We want positive, uplifting messages which reaffirm our personal opinions and values.

We want churches that teach what we believe.

Some Christian churches will do just that. They will cater to your personal whims. They will tell you what you want to hear or at least try to avoid what you don't want to hear. They scratch the narcissistic itch we all have in our hearts and minds.

And just like my itching beard, that's hard to resist.

Watch out for those who are willing to scratch the itch of your natural narcissism. Don't look for a church that teaches what you believe. Look for a church which tells you what God says in his Word even when you don't want to hear it. Seek preachers who openly proclaim the truths of God's Word even when they are not what our world deems politically correct. Church should make you feel uncomfortable at times. The preacher should make you squirm.

We are sinners who need to see our own weaknesses and failures. Only then can we appreciate God's amazing grace that saves sinners like us. Only then can we make any meaningful change in our lives.

Sometimes it's hard to hear what God wants to tell us in his Word. The temptation is to find a church that makes you feel good all the time. The temptation is to look for preachers who never make you squirm. We all have that itch.

But some itches just shouldn't be scratched.

Today I am thankful for/that _____

_____

Heavenly Father, thank you for giving me your life-giving Word. Help me to humbly listen to it, believe it, and follow it, even when it is hard for me to hear. Amen.

DAY 294
GOD'S TATTOO

"See, I have engraved you on the palms of my hands."

ISAIAH 49:16

❖

They say two things happen to you as you get older. One is that you start forgetting things.

I can't seem to remember the other thing.

I don't know if it is age or busyness or both, but I'm starting to forget things. I sometimes walk into my office and forget what I was going to get. My wife sends me to the store and I inevitably forget something. I forget names. I forget appointments. I would forget my head if it wasn't attached to my body.

To help me remember, I've started to write things down. Naturally, I often forget where I put the paper on which I wrote down what I needed to remember. For a while I tried writing reminders on my hand. That way, every time I looked down at my hand I would remember. The problem is that my hands would get sweaty and the ink would rub off. Besides, people look at you funny when you have a bunch of writing on your hand.

GOD'S PEOPLE . . . FELT LIKE HE HAD FORGOTTEN ABOUT THEM.

There was a time when God's people of the Old Testament felt like God had forgotten about them. They felt like he didn't care about them anymore.

Have you ever felt like that?

Your life is falling apart. You lose your home. Your husband dies. Your doctor tells you there's no cure. Where is God? Doesn't he care? Has he forgotten about you?

Listen to how God answered his people of the Old Testament: "Can a mother forget the baby at her breast and have no compassion on the child she has borne? Though she may forget, I will not forget you! See, I have engraved you on the palms of my hands" (Isaiah 49:15,16).

God can't and won't ever forget about you. Your name is written on the palm of his hands, and it is not written in pen. It is engraved there.

Your name is tattooed on the palm of God's hands.

You are important to him. He knows you perfectly. He thinks about you constantly. You are and will always be his dear child.

Sometimes it feels like God has forgotten about us at times because he allows heartache and misery in our lives. Sometimes it feels like God has forgotten about us because we pray to him and nothing seems to happen.

But God promises us in his Word that he does hear our prayers. He promises to answer them for our good, but in his own time and in his own way. Just because God doesn't do what you want doesn't mean he's forgotten about you. It may not be the right time; he may have different plans for you.

But that doesn't mean he doesn't care. He cared for you so much it hurt. He cared for you so much that God's Son suffered your pain and punishment on the cross. That's right. When he died on the cross, God remembered you before you were even born. He did it all for you.

As I get older, I am probably going to get more and more forgetful. There may come a point in my life when I don't remember anybody's name, including my own. Thankfully, I can know that no matter what happens my God will never forget about me.

Today I am thankful for/that _____

_____

Heavenly Father, thank you for the comfort of knowing you will never forget about me. Help me to always remember you. Amen.

DAY 295
AN INCONVENIENT TRUTH

**The time will come when people . . . will gather around
them a great number of teachers to say what
their itching ears want to hear.**

2 TIMOTHY 4:3

◆

In 2006, former Vice-President Al Gore produced a documentary about global warming called *An Inconvenient Truth*. The film won two Academy Awards and led to Al Gore receiving the Nobel Peace Prize in 2007.

The point of the documentary is that some people reject or ignore the idea of global warming because it would be too inconvenient for them to do something about it. I'm not saying I agree or disagree with the film. I honestly don't know enough about the issue to have an educated opinion. I do find the title to be interesting, though—*An Inconvenient Truth*.

God gave the prophet Jeremiah a difficult task. He sent him to tell the Israelite people what they didn't want to hear. Because of their sin, God was going to send the Babylonians to take them into captivity and destroy the city of Jerusalem. Nobody wanted to hear that. Everybody hated poor Jeremiah because of it.

What made matters worse is that a number of false prophets were telling the people that God would never do that. They were his people. He would never let the city of Jerusalem or the temple be destroyed.

Jeremiah was persecuted, beat up, thrown into a pit, and eventually led off in chains. The Babylonians did come, however, and they did exactly what Jeremiah said they would do.

Every time I feel sorry for myself as a pastor—every time I want to complain about how difficult my ministry is—I remember poor Jeremiah. God sent him to proclaim a truth nobody wanted to hear.

God has given 21st-century Christians in America the same task he gave Jeremiah: share an unpopular truth nobody really wants to hear. In our world today, the only thing not tolerated is intolerance. The only true sin is to say that what somebody else is doing is wrong. That's unloving. That's racist. That's being a Christian Nazi.

WHAT THE BIBLE SAYS ABOUT SIN . . . ANGERS MANY PEOPLE.

But God commands us to preach his law anyway—to call a sin a sin—to talk about guilt and God's punishment. Nobody likes to talk about those things. It's not fun when people point out our faults to us. What the Bible says about sin—especially about things like human sexuality—angers many people.

Many in our world would rather not talk about it. Many don't consider it sin. In the end, however, we don't get to decide what is or is not a sin. God does. He tells us clearly in his Word.

But that is an inconvenient truth. People don't want to hear it. Just look at the uproar caused by the United Methodist Church recently when they affirmed what the Bible says about homosexuality. People in our country, even many Christians, were infuriated.

That shouldn't surprise us. God said it would be that way. The apostle Paul wrote to young Pastor Timothy, "The time will come when people will not put up with sound doctrine. Instead, to suit their own desires, they will gather around them a great number of teachers to say what their itching ears want to hear."

All of us need to hear the truth of God's law. Sin is sin. We are guilty. We deserve to go to hell. If we fail to realize that, then the good news of the gospel will seem like an unnecessary truth.

The prophet Jeremiah told the people that God in his great love would forgive them if they repented. Because of Jesus' sacrifice on the cross, there isn't a sin that God won't forgive. But when you think you're okay just how you are, God's promises of love and forgiveness seem unnecessary.

God's Word is an inconvenient truth. God grant us the courage to lovingly and firmly share the truth of his law and the truth of his love, even if people don't want to hear it.

Because, in the end, whether you want to hear it or not, it's the truth.

Today I am thankful for/that _____

_____

Almighty God, help me to stand firm and speak your truth in love, even when people don't want to hear it. Amen.

DAY 296
IN THE EAR OF THE BEHOLDER

Praise the LORD . . . with the sounding of the trumpet,
praise him with the harp and lyre, praise him with
timbrel and dancing, praise him with the strings
and pipe, praise him with the clash of cymbals,
praise him with resounding cymbals. Let
everything that has breath praise the LORD.

PSALM 150:1,3-6

◆

I have eclectic taste in music. I like rock bands like Pearl Jam, Aerosmith, and Nirvana. I also like U2, Queen, and Elvis. I'm always in the mood for Bing Crosby, Sinatra, and Johnny Cash. I know all the Backstreet Boys hits by heart. I sing Garth Brooks on karaoke. I've even seen Whitney Houston and Sha Na Na in concert. Mozart and *The Phantom of the Opera* relax me.

You don't have to surf the radio stations to find something I like. I'll listen to just about anything. I even like old school rap.

But I know I am the exception. Most people have specific genres of music which they enjoy and others they don't. They love country and hate rap. They dig Metallica but despise Ariana Grande. Everybody has their own taste in music. Everybody has their own opinion about what classifies as "good music."

The same is true in church. Some Christians are old school. "Amazing Grace," "How Great Thou Art," and "It is Well with My Soul" make their hearts swell. Others are even more old school. "A Mighty Fortress," "Silent Night," and "Oh, Come, Oh, Come, Emmanuel" are their cup of tea. If you like the "Agnus Dei" and the "O Antiphons," I don't think they had schools back then.

Some love the organ. Others hate it. Some enjoy piano and acoustic guitar. Others want electric guitar, bass, and drums. I have heard classic hymns sung with country, gospel, and pop flavor.

We all have different tastes in music, and that's okay. God in his great wisdom made each of us different. God in his Word gives us freedom in the style of music and forms of worship we use. He does, however, want us to worship him. He does want us to worship him with music (Psalm 150). He does want us to do all things in a fitting and orderly way (1 Corinthians 14:40).

Despite all the wonderful Christian music out there, one of the complaints I hear most often is that people don't like the music in their church. Please allow me to share with you a couple of thoughts about music in church.

THE *MUSIC* ISN'T WHAT IS MOST IMPORTANT.

First of all, the *music* isn't what is most important. The *words* we say and sing in worship are. The music is meant to adorn the words, to highlight the emotions expressed in the words. If you find yourself coming home after church inspired by the beautiful music but can't remember the message the songs were conveying, there's a problem.

Some people blame the music in their church for the lack of attendance. "If only we had better music, more people would come." One thing I have found in my ministry is that the style of music doesn't impact others in worship as much as the joy with which the Christians in the church sing. When Christians are thinking about and joyfully singing and saying the words of worship, it makes an impression on others no matter what style the music is.

So think about what you are saying and singing. Don't sit there like a bump on a log, somberly mouthing the words. Sing out. Worship with joy.

Finally, be flexible. Understand that you probably have different tastes in music than the person sitting next to you or behind you in church. As pastors and music leaders, we try to pick hymns and music which can appeal to a wide range of personalities and generations. In the end, some hymns you will love; others, not so much.

Whatever the music, you can still appreciate the words. You can still praise your Savior God. You can still worship with joy.

Today I am thankful for/that _____

Lord of the church, thank you for the gift of music. Give me a heart which wants to sing out my praises to you, but also help me to appreciate and accept those whose style and tastes are different from my own. Amen.

DAY 297
GOOD FOR HIM

For to me, to live is Christ and to die is gain.

PHILIPPIANS 1:21

❖

A number of years ago, an elderly gentleman from our congregation passed away at three o'clock on a Sunday morning. I arrived at church later that morning to find another member setting out Bibles for Sunday school.

In a tired, somber voice I told him, "Just so you know, Marvin passed away this morning."

Without looking up, the member cheerily responded, "Good for him!"

Suffice it to say, that wasn't the response I was expecting. It was, however, the correct response.

Usually we think of death as tragic. Death is scary. Death is the enemy against which we rage with every fiber of our being.

We fear death—we fight death—because deep down we know death means judgment. Death means facing the consequences of what we've done in this life. Death means standing as a sinner before a holy God.

JESUS CHANGES OUR PERSPECTIVE ON DEATH.

But Jesus changes our perspective on death. The writer to the Hebrews tells us that Jesus shared in our humanity, "so that by his death he might break the power of him who holds the power of death—that is, the devil—and free those who all their lives were held in slavery by their fear of death" (Hebrews 2:14,15).

God became one of us so that he could live in our place and die the death we deserve. On the cross, Jesus faced the consequences of what we've done. He suffered our judgment. He died our death.

Because he did, we have been set free—free from sin, free from guilt, free from punishment. Jesus paid our ticket to heaven. Then, early on Easter Sunday, he rose from the dead, conquering death once and for all.

Now he promises that all those who believe in him will live even though they die. Death for a Christian is never the end. Death for a Christian is not a tragedy. Death for a Christian is simply a door through which we pass on our way to heaven.

I love the small town of Edna, Texas, in which I live. It fits my family well. But, if given the choice between Edna or heaven, there is no comparison. Edna is great, but heaven is pure, unadulterated happiness. Heaven is the best family reunion ever. Heaven is home.

So if a Christian friend or family member dies, why would we ever be sad about that? Even if they die young, there is nothing in this life which could ever compare to the joy they experience in heaven.

Though it is cliché, they are truly in a better place.

Yes, we may mourn because we will miss them, but because of Jesus, we know we will see them again. So even as the tears of sorrow roll down your cheeks, be happy for those who have gone before us. Celebrate God's amazing grace which saved them. Thank God for the happiness they are now enjoying.

This last Saturday, a lifelong member of my congregation suddenly passed away. On Wednesday, we will gather as family and friends for her funeral. We will gather to lay her body to rest.

We will gather to say, "Good for her!"

Today I am thankful for/that _____

Lord of life, thank you for changing my perspective on death. Take away my fears. Give me the faith to rejoice for those who die in the faith. Amen.

DAY 298
GROWTH

Like newborn babies, crave pure spiritual milk, so
that by it you may grow up in your salvation.

1 PETER 2:2

❖

The story is told of an American who decided to travel on foot through the small towns of northern England. As he traveled through the countryside, it seemed that every town or village had been the birthplace of someone famous—a writer, a politician, a famous athlete.

One day he entered a small village and asked the first person he met, "Excuse me, sir. Were any great men born in this village?" The man from the village reflected on the question and then replied, "No sir, only babies."

Great men and women are not born great men and women. They are born babies. The same can be said of the great men and women of faith. We aren't born with great faith. In fact, we aren't born with faith at all. We are born lost, sinful human beings.

Then through God's Word and the waters of Holy Baptism, we are born again. God gives us faith. When we receive faith, we receive the gift of heaven Jesus won for us. We are saved in an instant.

At that point, however, our faith is still a newborn faith.

Just as a baby needs his mother's milk, so faith needs to be fed to grow. As we grow in our knowledge of who God is and what he has done for us, our faith grows stronger. The more we listen to God speak to us in his Word, the more we will be able to trust in him and do what he wants us to do.

Growing and living our faith is a process. We need to remember that truth, especially as we deal with fellow Christians. People may not be living the life of faith they should, but that doesn't necessarily mean they don't have faith. It doesn't mean they are hypocrites. It merely means that their faith needs to grow. And the way faith grows is by being in God's Word.

INSTEAD, LET'S SAY, "I'M SO GLAD SHE'S IN CHURCH!"

So let's stop saying, "What a hypocrite!" or "Can you believe that she has the nerve to come to church after what she did this week?" Instead, let's say, "I'm so glad she's in church!"

After all, being in church is what we need when our faith is weak.

Faith is a process. We need to remember that truth every time we look at ourselves in the mirror. Sometimes we beat ourselves up because we aren't the great person of faith we feel we should be. The answer isn't to beat ourselves up. The answer is to get into God's Word and to bask in his forgiveness. That's what grows faith.

Also remember that the process of faith never ends here on earth. Sometimes we feel like we made it. We think our faith is fully grown. We think we are now great men and women of faith. That's when we need to be reminded how much room we still have to grow.

God wants you and me to be great men and women of faith. Never forget, though, that faith is a process. So keep feasting on God's Word and sacrament every chance you get.

That's what grows faith.

Today I am thankful for/that _____

_____

Holy Spirit, thank you for the faith planted in my heart in my baptism. Help me to always see the importance of regularly feeding that faith with Word and sacrament. Amen.

DAY 299
YOUR LIFE IS A MEXICAN SOAP OPERA

You are no longer a slave, but God's child; and since you are his child, God has made you also an heir.

GALATIANS 4:7

One of the unintended consequences of marrying a woman from Mexico is my now intimate understanding of Mexican soap operas. I didn't mean for it to happen, but I can now intelligently converse with any Mexican housewife about her favorite *telenovelas*.

While American soap operas can last for decades, Mexican soap operas last only a few months. They are simply serial novels brought to the small screen. With so many being produced, plotlines tend to repeat.

One common theme in Mexican soap operas is the Cinderella story. A young servant girl or street urchin falls in love with the handsome son of a multimillionaire or finds out she is the long-lost daughter of a wealthy tycoon.

She literally goes from rags to riches. The dirt is washed off her face. Her scraggly hair is styled. Suddenly, she is a new person enjoying a new life and living happily ever after.

My life is a Mexican soap opera. Your life is a Mexican soap opera. We were all born poor, dirty slaves—slaves to sin, slaves to guilt, slaves to death.

If you doubt that, just look at your life even now. Look at how you keep falling into the same stupid sins over and over again. Look at the things which enslave you: alcohol, drugs, or cigarettes. You keep losing your temper. You keep worrying. You keep gossiping even though you know it is wrong. We are all addicted to sin. We are slaves.

The apostle Paul tells us, "When the set time had fully come, God sent his Son . . . to redeem those under the law" (Galatians 4:4,5). Jesus redeemed us.

To redeem is to pay the price of freedom. To redeem is to pay the ransom of a kidnapped loved one. To redeem is to pay the fine to get your son out of jail. To redeem is to pay the price to set a slave free.

Jesus redeemed you. He paid the price of your freedom, not with gold or silver, but with his holy precious blood and innocent suffering and death. Jesus suffered the punishment you deserve for your slavish devotion to sin. He died to set you free. His blood, his life, was the price of your freedom.

Because he paid that price in full, you are now free. You are forgiven. The chains of hell will never tighten around your wrists or ankles. You are free from sin and free from guilt.

Not only did he set you free from your slavery to sin and death, he also adopted you as his son or daughter. As the waters of Holy Baptism poured over your head, as the Holy Spirit entered your heart and gave you faith, God adopted you as his child. Paul tells us, "You are no longer a slave, but God's child; and since you are his child, God has made you also an heir."

YOURS IS A RAGS TO RICHES STORY.

Think about that. Yours is a rags to riches story. You didn't earn it. You don't deserve it. You didn't pull yourself up by your bootstraps.

Yet you, who were a dirty slave, are now a son or daughter of the King. You are an heir to the fortune of heaven, all because of Jesus and what he did for you.

Because of Jesus, one day you will live happily ever after in heaven. As I said, your life is a Mexican soap opera.

Today I am thankful for/that _____

_____

Heavenly Father, thank you for adopting me, a dirty slave to sin, and making me your dear child. Help me to live a life worthy of the calling you have given me. Amen.

DAY 300
WORKING FOR THE WEEKEND

Diligent hands will rule, but laziness ends in forced labor.

PROVERBS 12:24

In 1982, the Canadian rock band Loverboy shot to the top of the charts with their single "Working for the Weekend." The song—and especially the title—resonated with many people. That's how they felt. That's how they lived their lives.

Work was a necessary evil through which they had to pass in order to get to the fun of the weekend.

That's how many people in our world today still look at work. Work is a necessary evil. We do it as long as we have to until we can finally clock out and go have some fun. We do it as long as we have to until we can finally retire and live the good life.

Not having to work is the goal. Then you can do what you want. Then you can have fun. Then you can relax.

Work, necessary or otherwise, is not evil. Some people point to what God said to Adam after the fall into sin to show that work is simply a sad consequence of sin. God said to Adam, "Because you listened to your wife . . . cursed is the ground because of you; through painful toil you will eat food from it all the days of your life. . . . By the sweat of your brow you will eat your food" (Genesis 3:17,19).

God wasn't saying that work was now one of the consequences of man's sin. What he was saying is that, because of sin, work would now be difficult, tiring, and stressful.

In this sinful world, work takes work. Oftentimes it is exhausting. You may have to work with people who are a challenge. You may have a boss who is unfair or lazy. Because of sin, work is not always fun.

Work, though, existed before sin. In fact, God designed human beings to work. He put Adam and Eve in the Garden of Eden with the express purpose of taking care of it and tending it.

Paradise does not mean lazily lying around, enjoying never-ending rest and relaxation. Adam and Eve worked in paradise.

God has wired all of us to work. Though rest and relaxation are also important components of life, being idle is not good for us physically, psychologically, or even spiritually. Work is healthy. It keeps our brains and bodies active. It gives us a sense of purpose. It provides opportunities to grow and learn and become better people.

God wants you to work. He wants you to work hard. He wants you to faithfully use the gifts and opportunities he has given you. As Paul wrote to the Thessalonians, "The one who is unwilling to work shall not eat" (2 Thessalonians 3:10).

WE NEED TO MAKE A DISTINCTION BETWEEN WORKING AND HAVING A JOB.

Now to be clear, we need to make a distinction between working and having a job. Some people are unable to be gainfully employed due to circumstances, age, or health. Even if you are on disability or retirement, God still wants you to work; that is, to use your time and abilities actively and productively.

Both rest and work are good for you.

So don't merely work for the weekend. Don't view work simply as a necessary evil you must endure for a while until you don't have to work anymore. Blessings can come from even the most challenging or menial jobs.

Work hard. Don't spend your days idly scrolling through Facebook or playing Fortnite. Don't waste the time God has given you here on earth. Use your gifts and abilities productively.

I know it's not always fun. It definitely isn't easy, but work is good for you. It is a gift of God.

Today I am thankful for/that _____

Lord, thank you for the opportunity and ability to work. Help me to stay busy living and working to your glory. Amen.

DAY 301
YOU AIN'T SEEN NOTHING YET

"See, I am doing a new thing!"

ISAIAH 43:19

On October 6, 1927, at the Warner Theater on Broadway, the motion picture industry was forever changed. On that night, the first talkie—the first feature-length movie with spoken dialogue—premiered. It was called *The Jazz Singer* starring Al Jolson.

In the opening of the movie, Jolson famously tells his orchestra and the audience, "Wait a minute, wait a minute, I tell ya. You ain't heard nothing yet."

Movies never sounded the same again.

Overnight, every Hollywood studio scrapped its silent movie projects to make talkies. Charlie Chaplin and other great silent movie stars quickly found themselves out of a job.

Yet knowing what we know now and having the technology we have today, if we could go back to that day in October of 1927, we could have said to Al Jolson, "No. You wait a minute. You ain't seen nothing yet."

Just think about how technology is constantly changing and improving. I remember when I thought VCRs were the most incredible thing ever. We could actually watch movies in our living room anytime we wanted. I remember my first cell phone which I bought in 1999. It was a big block I carried around on my belt. At the time I thought I was so cool. And then smartphones and tablets came out.

Just imagine what's coming next. I'm sure we ain't seen nothing yet.

In Isaiah chapter 43, God tells the Israelites how one day he will rescue them from the hand of the Babylonians. He reminds them of past deliverance—how centuries earlier he saved them from slavery in Egypt, how he divided the Red Sea, how he wiped Pharaoh and his army off the face of the earth.

God reminded the Israelites of his powerful deliverance in the past and then he told them, "Forget the former things; do not dwell on the past. See, I am doing a new thing!" (Isaiah 43:18,19). In other words, "You think it was pretty amazing how I saved you from the Egyptians—just wait. You ain't seen nothing yet."

In his great power and love, God would deliver them from the Babylonians. He would amazingly and miraculously protect and provide for them. He would work all of time and history to keep his promises and bring our Savior Jesus into the world.

When troubles come and life gets hard, don't throw up your arms in despair. Don't wring your hands in worry. Just remember. Remember what God did to the Egyptians. Remember what he did to the Babylonians. Remember what he did to save you.

Look back on your life. He has always provided. He has always gotten you through, even in the hard times. Remember how God amazingly and miraculously worked all of time and history to save you.

ALL THE BLESSINGS GOD SHOWERS ON US HERE ARE NOTHING COMPARED TO WHAT'S COMING.

Then don't think about it anymore. Seriously. Don't dwell on the past. Why? Because you ain't seen nothing yet. God's mercies are new every morning. He is going to get you through the problems you face today. He is going to comfort and strengthen and guide you through his Word. He is going to bless you in ways you can't even fathom right now—just like I couldn't have imagined smartphones and flat screen TVs when I was a kid.

Here is the most amazing part: all the blessings God showers on us here are nothing compared to what's coming. Just wait. You ain't seen nothing yet.

Because God worked all of time and history to bring Jesus into this world to live and die for you, you—a believer in Christ—are going to heaven where everything is always new, where there is no more death or mourning or crying or pain, where you will be reunited with your loved ones who died in Christ.

If you think God has been good to you so far, just wait. You ain't seen nothing yet.

Today I am thankful for/that _____

_____

Dear Lord, help me to not live in the past, but to live for you today, knowing you have great blessings for me tomorrow. Amen.

DAY 302
BELLY BUTTONS AND BAPTISM

Let us consider how we may spur one another on toward love and good deeds, not giving up meeting together, as some are in the habit of doing, but encouraging one another—and all the more as you see the Day approaching.

HEBREWS 10:24,25

Riddle: Who were the only two people to never have a belly button?
Answer: Adam and Eve.

You know why, right? Your belly button is actually a scar. It's what is left over from the umbilical cord which connected you to your mother. Adam and Eve were created by God. They didn't have a mother; therefore they didn't have the scar we call a "belly button."

When you look down at your belly button, it should serve as a reminder. We are all connected to someone. In fact, as human beings we are all connected to each other. God didn't make us able to survive, to live, to thrive on our own.

Sadly, our world today is disconnected. The rise of machines has led to our spending the majority of our time on electronics. When families get home from work and school, each person immediately goes to their individual screens. We don't talk. We don't communicate. We don't connect like we used to.

The only connections many people make today are the superficial connections we make through social media. Real personal connections are more difficult to make in our modern world. Younger generations often struggle to communicate and connect with other people on a deeper level.

Even though we are all connected by our belly buttons—by our common humanity—we are disconnected. Our world, our country, and even our own families are fragmented.

So what is the answer? The answer is found in our God who creates connections. In your baptism, God not only washed you of your sins, but also connected you to him. He adopted you as his son or daughter. You are a baptized child of God. Through faith in Jesus, God himself now lives in you and you in him.

IN YOUR BAPTISM, GOD . . . ALSO CONNECTED YOU TO HIM.

Your baptism is an umbilical cord which connects you to God. Every time you go to church and hear his Word, every time you receive his true body and blood in Holy Communion, God is feeding your faith. He is strengthening that connection to him—like a baby being fed by the umbilical cord.

You are connected to God through his Word and sacraments. You are sons and daughters of the King of the universe. That means you are also brothers and sisters with your fellow Christians. Our connection with Jesus is our connection to each other.

We are connected by belly buttons and Baptism.

That changes how we treat one another. It means we do more than merely nod and smile at our fellow believers at church. It means more than a quick "hello." It means we take the time to make real connections. It means not running out of church to be the first in line at Whataburger.

We are connected. We are brothers and sisters in the faith. We are family. Let's live like it. When the service is over on Sunday, don't run out of church like someone has just pulled the fire alarm. Get to know your brothers and sisters in the faith. Love them. Forgive them. Take the time to help and encourage them.

As a family, take time every day to turn off the electronics. Go outside and play with your kids. Play a board game with them. Talk to them, especially about God. Pray with them.

In your baptism, God washed you of all your faults and offenses. He adopted you as his child. You are connected to him and all those who believe in him.

Live that connection.

Today I am thankful for/that _____

_____

Lord, thank you for the family of believers you have given me. Help me to live my connection with them and with you. Amen.

———◆———

DAY 303
THE HIDDEN MESSAGE IN PSALM 23

The LORD is my shepherd, I lack nothing.

PSALM 23:1

◆

I see commercials for them every so often on TV. "The Hidden Codes of the Old Testament." "The Secret Message of Revelation." "Decoding the Bible."

The truth is that the Bible contains no hidden messages. No secret codes are concealed within. It says what it means and means what it says.

I should apologize. The title of this article was a bit of click bait. There are no hidden messages or codes in Psalm 23. There is, however, an implied lesson which many people fail to see.

Psalm 23 is arguably the most famous chapter of the Bible. The image of God as our Good Shepherd is just as poignant now as it was 3,000 years ago when King David first penned it.

The message of Psalm 23 is clear: God will always provide everything we need for our bodies and souls. He will protect, comfort, and guide us. Then, when our earthly journey is over, we will celebrate with him at the luxurious feast of heaven.

One salient detail, however, often eludes modern ears as they listen to the words of Psalm 23. If our God is our Good Shepherd, that makes us his sheep. In today's world, we find that image flattering. Sheep are cute and cuddly. We sing with pride and joy, "I am Jesus' little lamb."

When the Bible calls us sheep, however, it is not calling us cute and cuddly.

Like many pastors, for years I have bluntly told anyone who will listen, "Sheep are dumb." Recently I learned that is not completely fair. It's not that sheep are necessarily dumb animals. They are simply dependent. They struggle to survive on their own. They get lost. They get hurt. They go hungry without a shepherd to guide and protect them.

As 21st-century Americans, we fancy ourselves independent. We take pride in our do-it-yourself projects. We are masters of our own fates and captains of our own souls.

This last week, I sat with a friend who is dying of cancer. She is unable to do the simple things she always used to do: cook meals, clean her home, drive her car. She hates having to depend on other people to do what she could always do herself. It is frustrating and somewhat depressing for her.

The loss of independence as we age or succumb to sickness is difficult for many people to accept. We don't want to depend on anybody else. We want to do it ourselves. We want to be independent like we were when we were younger and healthier.

INDEPENDENCE, HOWEVER, IS A MYTH.

Independence, however, is a myth.

What we come to see clearly when we are old or infirm is the truth of who we are from birth. We are helpless. We are defenseless. We are utterly dependent creatures.

We are sheep.

The only reason we are who we are and have what we have is because our Good Shepherd has provided us with the means and opportunity to acquire it. The only reason we achieve anything in life is because of the people God has placed around us who support, guide, and encourage us. The only reason we have a seat at the lavish feast of heaven is because our Good Shepherd gave his life to rescue his wandering sheep.

On our own, we are sinful. We are weak. Dare I say, we are dumb.

Don't wait until you are old or infirm to recognize your utter dependence on your Good Shepherd. Read again the verses of Psalm 23. Recognize what it is implying.

You can't do it on your own. You need God. That is the "hidden" message of Psalm 23.

Today I am thankful for/that _____

_____

Dear Good Shepherd, everything good I have and everything good I am is because of you. Thank you. Amen.

DAY 304
WHEN THE WELL RUNS DRY

"Every teacher of the law who has become a disciple
in the kingdom of heaven is like the owner of a
house who brings out of his storeroom new
treasures as well as old."

MATTHEW 13:52

I have a confession to make. Actually, I have been dreading this moment for a long time. I am embarrassed to say it: I don't know what to write about.

The well has run dry.

After five years of writing a syndicated weekly devotional column, I am struggling to come up with new ideas and fresh ways to express the wonderful truths of God's Word.

This is a problem not uncommon among pastors. Week after week, month after month, year after year, we find ourselves staring at the soft glow of a computer screen, trying to figure out what to say in next Sunday's sermon.

Writer's block can afflict even the most creative of minds.

My problem, however, is not that the well has run dry. My problem is that I fail to go to the well. It happens to all pastors at one time or another. We get busy with meetings, family, youth soccer, and ballet. We become lax in our personal Bible study and family devotions.

Sure, we can coast for a while. Soon, however, our stories become stale. Our writing becomes rote. The well runs dry.

The remedy is obvious. As Jesus sat on the edge of a deep well in the middle of the desert, he offered a stranger a well which would never run dry (John 4). He promises every believer that, as they dip their cup into his well, they will find "new treasures as well as old."

As I drink deep from the waters of God's Word, I discover new treasures and truths I failed to see before. I see new applications to my life and the lives of others. As I drink deep from the waters of God's Word, old truths are painted in new and vivid Technicolor.

Writer's block is not the only symptom of spiritual dehydration. Failing to drink deep from the waters of God's Word dims our focus and resolve as Christians. Sure, we can coast for a while, but it soon affects the way we treat others, the decisions we make, and our emotional well-being.

Like a lobster slowly dying in a pot as the water temperature rises, we are often blissfully unaware of the dehydrating of our faith. The devil convinces us that we are just fine, that we know the truth, and that it won't hurt us if we get away from church and his Word.

WE ALL NEED TO DRINK DEEP FROM THE WELL OF THE WORD.

We all need to drink deep from the well of the Word, the promises of our baptism and Christ's blood in the sacrament. There we will find the forgiveness, the strength, and the help we need to face the wind and waves of the years to come.

So go to the well often and drink deep.

Today I am thankful for/that _____

_____

Merciful Savior, forgive me for the many times I have failed to drink deep of the water of your Word. Help me to make the most of every opportunity to hear your Word and put it into practice. Amen.

NEW YEAR'S — DAY 305
20/20

"I make known the end from the beginning, from ancient times, what is still to come. I say, 'My purpose will stand, and I will do all that I please.'"

ISAIAH 46:10

◆

They say hindsight is 20/20.

It's always easier after the fact to see what a person should have said or done. Once we see how things played out, we can see more clearly the road we should have taken.

The future isn't so clear.

As we look ahead to a new year, we can see only a blur of choices and roads not yet taken. Will I be able to find a job? Whom will I date? Should we get married? What am I going to do with my aging mother? What is going to happen to our country? Who will be our next president? Is another recession around the corner?

As I write this, we cannot yet see what the new year will bring. That can be scary for many, especially those who find themselves at a crossroads with difficult decisions to make this year. We worry. We fret. We stress. What if we make the wrong choice?

What makes matters worse is that our vision of even the present and the past is clouded by the cataracts of sin. How we view the world and the choices we have to make is blurred by fear, pride, and guilt.

As we look ahead to a blurry and unknown new year, however, we don't need to be afraid.

God can see it clearly. He will control it in his power and love. In the book of Isaiah, he tells us, "I make known the end from the beginning, from ancient times, what is still to come. I say, 'My purpose will stand and I will do all that I please.'" God has plans for you in this new year, "plans," the prophet Jeremiah tells us, "to prosper you and not to harm you, plans to give you hope and a future" (Jeremiah 29:11).

If you worry or wonder about that, just look to the past. Hindsight is 20/20.

Look at how God worked all of time and history to bring his Son, Jesus, into the world. See how your Savior loved you so much, he suffered the punishment you deserve for all the poor choices you made in 2019. See how he has gotten you through every trial and tribulation in this life.

God has always forgiven you, always helped you, and always seen you through.

IN THIS NEW YEAR, KEEP YOUR EYES FIRMLY FIXED ON HIM.

And he won't stop this year. So in this new year, keep your eyes firmly fixed on him. Turn to him in prayer when you have difficult decisions to make. Go to church. Read your Bible. Find in his Word the direction and encouragement you need. Through his Word, he will open your eyes to see clearly his love and power at work in your life.

Through the eyes of faith, you will be able to see clearly that we have nothing to fear in this year.

Today I am thankful for/that _____

_____

Eternal Lord, as I look ahead to an unclear future, help me to trust that my future lies in your loving and powerful hands. Take away my fears and give me peace. Amen.

NEW YEAR'S – DAY 306
O GOD, OUR HELP IN AGES PAST

Lord, you have been our dwelling place
throughout all generations.

PSALM 90:1

❖

Isaac Watts was a nonconformist in every sense of the word. Watts was born in 1674, 12 years after the British Parliament issued the Act of Uniformity. The act required a person to adhere to the doctrines and rites of the Church of England's *Book of Common Prayer* to be able to hold public office in the government or the church.

Those who conscientiously dissented or belonged to any Protestant denomination besides the Church of England were called Nonconformists. Nonconformists were often persecuted, jailed, and even beaten.

Though academically gifted, Watts was not allowed to attend Oxford or Cambridge, which were reserved strictly for Anglicans. He still managed to study theology, however, and pastored an independent congregation in London.

Watts was a nonconformist in another sense of the word as well. As a young man he grew frustrated with the music sung in churches at the time. The only music allowed was the Psalms sung metrically (and painfully slowly). Singing anything other than the very words of Scripture was considered an insult to God.

As a young man, Watts expressed his low opinion of church music at the time. His father purportedly responded, "Why don't you give us something better?"

Isaac Watts did. He composed over 600 hymns, including "Joy to the World," "When I Survey the Wondrous Cross," and "O God, Our Help in Ages Past." Today Isaac Watts is rightfully known as the "Father of English Hymnody."

Many of his hymns, like "Joy to the World," were paraphrases of the psalms from a New Testament perspective. In other words, Watts read the Psalms in light of their fulfillment in Christ.

"O God, Our Help in Ages Past" is a paraphrase of Psalm 90. In the psalm, Moses speaks of God's eternal rule and control of all things compared to man's relatively short life here on earth. God controls all of time and history—including our time and history.

"STILL BE OUR GUARD WHILE TROUBLES LAST AND OUR ETERNAL HOME."

Isaac Watts looked at God's eternal rule of all things from the perspective of his forgiveness and love in Christ. God has and will continue to work all of time and history for the good of his people. God has and will continue to work all of time and history for your good.

Despite suffering persecution and poor health nearly his entire life, Watts could joyfully look back and see God's powerful and loving hand at work in his life. He could look ahead with confidence to the rest of his days here on earth and to his eternal home in heaven.

As we look back on another year gone by and ahead to a yet unseen future, may we sing with confidence:

O God, our help in ages past,
Our hope for years to come,
Our shelter from the stormy blast,
And our eternal home. (CW 441:1)

Today I am thankful for/that _____

_____

"O God, our help in ages past, Our hope for years to come, Still be our guard while Troubles last And our eternal home." Amen. (CW 441:6)

NEW YEAR'S DAY – DAY 307
THE #NEWYEARSDAYCHALLENGE

Let us consider how we may spur one another on
toward love and good deeds, not giving up meeting
together, as some are in the habit of doing,
but encouraging one another—and all the
more as you see the Day approaching.

HEBREWS 10:24,25

❧

The best I can surmise, it started with the #IceBucketChallenge of 2014. Millions of people, including many celebrities, took video of themselves having buckets of ice water poured over their heads to show their support for ALS research.

Since then, numerous other challenges have sprung up on social media. One of the latest to go viral is the #MannequinChallenge. Millions of videos have been posted on Facebook, Instagram, and Twitter of people standing perfectly still in odd poses for exactly one minute as another person walks around videotaping them.

Every day new videos pop up on YouTube of people taking or making new "challenges," hoping to be the next viral sensation.

I have a challenge to add to the list. I call it the #NewYearsDayChallenge.

Every so often, January 1 falls on a Sunday. As a pastor, I know that means one thing. I will be preaching to the crickets. Church attendance plummets when New Year's Day is a Sunday. People are tired. They were up late. Maybe they imbibed a bit too much. Besides, they probably went to church the week before on Christmas.

The #NewYearsDayChallenge is simple: Go to church this Sunday. I know it's New Year's Day. I know you will be tired. I know it will be a pain to get the kids up and ready. I didn't say it was going to be easy.

That's why it's called a challenge.

Too often in our lives, we let any and every excuse keep us from going to church. We tell ourselves we don't have to go to church to believe in God. We tell ourselves we'll go back eventually. We tell ourselves we don't have to go to church in order to go to heaven.

Of course, you're right. We don't go to church in order to go to heaven.

We go to church because we are going to heaven. We go to church to thank Jesus for accepting the challenge of the cross for us. We go to church because in his Word and sacraments our God comes to us to give us comfort, strength, and guidance. We go to church to encourage and be encouraged by fellow believers.

Maybe your church attendance has become sporadic. Maybe you don't have a church home right now. Maybe you've been telling yourself you need to get back.

Take the #NewYearsDayChallenge. Go to church this Sunday. Start the year off right. Don't wait for an easier time to go. Don't wait until things get less busy in your life. That will never happen. Challenge yourself.

GOING TO CHURCH IS NOT SOME MAGIC PILL.

Understand, though, that going to church is not some magic pill which will overwhelm you with peace and take away all your problems. Don't expect God to change your life in one church service. Going to church one Sunday and expecting God to immediately fix everything is like dieting or exercising for one day and expecting a sculpted body. Our spiritual health is an ongoing process of which going to church regularly is a key element.

In the end, I highly doubt my #NewYearsDayChallenge will go viral. It doesn't matter. You are reading this. That's enough. This is a chance for you to evaluate your spiritual life. Use this Sunday as a stepping stone to challenge yourself spiritually.

If you haven't been going to church, start attending regularly. If you attend regularly, start going to Sunday school or a weekly Bible class. If you attend Sunday school regularly, start reading your Bible every day.

A journey of a thousand miles begins with a single step. That first step is this Sunday.

Take the #NewYearsDayChallenge.

Today I am thankful for/that _____

_____

Lord, as this new year begins, help me to resolutely be in church every Sunday I can this year. Amen.

NEW YEAR'S – DAY 308
BIRTH AND DEATH

The wages of sin is death, but the gift of God is eternal life in Christ Jesus our Lord.

ROMANS 6:23

❖

January 3, 2019, was an eventful day for me.

While we were visiting my wife's family in Mexico, her sister gave birth to her firstborn, a little girl with beautiful brown eyes named Valentina. As my sister-in-law was having her baby, I received a message from a member of our church. Her sister (who happened to live in the same city we were visiting in Mexico) was called home to heaven that morning after a long battle with cancer.

Soon after Valentina was born, I received a message from another member. A kind and funny older gentleman named John, whom I had been visiting in the nursing home for a number of years, also passed away.

As 2018 breathed its last and 2019 rose from its ashes, God reminded me how birth and death stand in constant juxtaposition in this world. Benjamin Franklin once quipped that the only things for certain in this world are death and taxes.

Really the only certainties in this world are birth and death.

It is the circle of life. We are all born and we will all die. Life on this earth is a gift. It is also short and fragile. As we begin a new year, not one of us can say with any certainty if we will ever see another.

Unless Jesus comes to end the world first, you are going to die. Everyone you know is going to die. You will attend many funerals in your life, the last of which will be your own.

> **EVEN IN THE MIDDLE OF OUR SORROW, GOD GIVES US REASONS TO BE GLAD.**

Even as the sorrow of death periodically interrupts our lives, the joy of birth brings new love and laughter. It never ceases to amaze me how often God allows a baby to be born into a family soon after a loved one dies. It is a reminder for us that life continues. Even in the middle of our sorrow, God gives us reasons to be glad.

Birth and death are certainties in this world, but so also is the life Jesus won for us. God loved you so much he became one of us to live and die as our

Savior. Jesus was born just as you were. Jesus died, as will you. As he died, though, Jesus suffered God's punishment for all the bad things you would ever do. Then on the third day, he conquered death forever by walking out of his tomb.

Your Savior promises, "I am the resurrection and the life. The one who believes in me will live, even though they die" (John 11:25).

This last week, my friend's sister closed her eyes to the pain of cancer and opened them to the happiness of heaven. My friend John is now living a life free of pain and sorrow. Four days after her birth, my beautiful niece was born again as the seed of faith was planted in her heart through Holy Baptism.

I am certain this year will bring more births and deaths in my life as well as in yours. You can be sure that—in both birth and death—God will give life because of Jesus.

Today I am thankful for/that _____

_____

Lord of life, as I feel the hurt and sadness caused by death, remind me of the life you have given me here and in eternity. Amen.

NEW YEAR'S – DAY 309
WHAT'S NEW?

There is nothing new under the sun.

ECCLESIASTES 1:9

Another new year is upon us. For many, January 1st is a day of optimism. A new year means new hopes and new opportunities—a fresh start.

What begins with optimism often turns into disappointment. Our goal to get healthy ends after one day of exercise and two days of eating raw carrots. Quitting smoking doesn't work either. We had hoped family and marriage problems would improve, but they don't. Work is still work and school is still school.

Our world is constantly changing. Telephones become cell phones which become smartphones which become smart watches. Governments rise and fall. Presidents come and go. Brad Pitt turns 60. Yet as wise old King Solomon once wrote, "There is nothing new under the sun."

HUMAN NATURE DOESN'T CHANGE. What he meant is that things don't really change much here on earth. Human nature doesn't change. The names and places of the wars change, but the selfishness and greed which spark them do not. Throughout human history, the rich have exploited the poor, children have rebelled against parents, and marriages have crumbled.

Though this year may seem new and different, not much will change. Politicians will still let us down. Work will still be difficult and stressful. Society will still praise sin and call Christians intolerant. People you know and love will still get sick and die.

There is nothing new under the sun.

Thankfully, our God, who dwells beyond the sun, promises us something new. The prophet Jeremiah tells us, "Because of the LORD's great love we are not consumed, for his compassions never fail. They are new every morning" (Lamentations 3:22,23).

God's mercies are new every morning. Every day he forgives us anew for the same old dumb sins we continually do day after day. Every day he provides us with new and special blessings we don't deserve. Even as we struggle with the same old problems, God gives us new hope and new strength to face them through his Word.

Even more importantly, because of Jesus, he promises us a home in heaven where everything will always be new (Revelation 21:5).

This year may bring you wonderful new opportunities and blessings, but it will also be more of the same old problems and struggles. Even so, know that God's mercies for you are new every morning. He promises to forgive you every day. Though surrounded by problems, you will see new blessings from God each day if you open your eyes.

May God bless you richly this year as you deal with the same old sin of this world and as you see God's wonderful mercies which are new every morning.

Today I am thankful for/that _____

_____

Merciful God, help me not to despair this year as I see the troubles and problems around me. There really is nothing new under the sun. Help me also to recognize your mercies which are new every day. Amen.

ASH WEDNESDAY – DAY 310
ASHES, ASHES, WE ALL FALL DOWN

"I despise myself and repent in dust and ashes."

JOB 42:6

*Ring around the rosie,
Pocket full of posies,
Ashes! Ashes!
We all fall down!*

You probably have heard that popular nursery rhyme. For at least 150 years, children have been singing "Ring Around the Rosie," or a variant of it. What you may not know is there is a great debate about what it means.

The rhyme was first published in print in the year 1881. Even then, people weren't exactly sure what it meant. By the mid-20th century, some scholars proposed that it was a reference to the bubonic plague which swept through Europe in the Middle Ages and in England specifically in the late 1600s.

The bubonic plague presents with pink sores around one's mouth. Posies were sometimes used as a folk remedy. Ashes were the result of cremating the dead bodies.

No one, however, can say for sure what the strange words of the nursery rhyme actually mean—especially the odd inclusion of the word "ashes."

Today is Ash Wednesday. For centuries Christians have received ashes on their foreheads in the sign of a cross. Ashes remind us from where we came and what we will be: ashes to ashes, dust to dust.

In biblical times, ashes were a sign of sorrow and repentance. People would sit in sackcloth and ashes as they mourned or repented. Though we don't know why ashes were included in "Ring Around the Rosie," we can say for sure why ashes are used on Ash Wednesday.

Because we all fall down.

LORD, HAVE MERCY ON ME, A SINNER.

Every day we sin. We fail. We fall—in school, at our jobs, in our marriages. We are dirty, lousy sinners who deserve to die. We are dirty, lousy sinners who deserve to burn in the flames of hell.

That is what Ash Wednesday is all about. As we begin the season of Lent, we begin our journey following Jesus on his road to the cross. We do so mourning the fact that it is our fault. Those are our sins he bears. That is our punishment.

Yet we do so remembering he bore that punishment willingly. Lent begins with ashes on Ash Wednesday and ends at the cross on Good Friday. On that cross Jesus willingly suffered the pain of hell we deserve for all the times we fall down. At the cross we see our Savior's forgiving love.

On Ash Wednesday, we sorrowfully sit in sackcloth and ashes. We confess our failings and fallings to God. But then we receive the sign of the cross on our foreheads—the sign of forgiveness. All our failings and fallings are forever forgiven because of what Jesus did on that old rugged cross.

Ash Wednesday is a day of sorrow over sin, but it is also a day in which we remember the peace and joy of God's forgiving love. Though we fall, we are forgiven.

What better way to begin our Lenten journey?

Today I am thankful for/that _____

_____

Lord, have mercy on me, a sinner. Amen.

ASH WEDNESDAY – DAY 311
LOVE MEANS SAYING YOU'RE SORRY

If we confess our sins, he is faithful and just and will forgive us our sins and purify us from all unrighteousness.

1 JOHN 1:9

❖

"Love means never having to say you're sorry." In 2005, the American Film Institute voted those words the 13th most memorable movie quote of all-time. From the 1970 movie *Love Story,* the line has become a part of the English vernacular.

The band Sounds of Sunshine used it as the title of their 1971 hit song. Variations of the words have been spoken in numerous films and TV shows. They can even be heard on a 2004 episode of *The Simpsons,* to which Lisa angrily retorted, "No, it doesn't."

Lisa Simpson was right.

In 2018, two seemingly contrasting holidays fell on the same day: Valentine's Day and Ash Wednesday. Valentine's Day is all about love and romance. Ash Wednesday is all about humility and repentance. One is secular; the other sacred.

Yet the two are tied together by one thin thread: love means saying you're sorry.

In our relationships here on earth, love leads us to not let those words go unspoken. A wise old marriage counselor once told me that the two most important words spoken in any relationship are, "I'm sorry." He added that the three most important words are, "I forgive you."

The same is true in our relationship with God. Love means saying we are sorry.

OUR SINS NAILED HIM TO THAT CROSS. Ash Wednesday marks the beginning of the season of Lent. During the six weeks of Lent, we walk with Jesus as he takes his long, lonely journey to the cross.

We begin that journey on Ash Wednesday by recognizing that our sins nailed him to that cross. It is our fault he died. It is our guilt he carries.

597

Yet Ash Wednesday isn't about beating ourselves up. The point of Ash Wednesday isn't to punish us for causing him pain. The point of Ash Wednesday is that we are forgiven.

Ash Wednesday is about repentance. We tell our God we are sorry for our lying lips and wandering eyes. We tell him we are sorry for our hurtful words and lack of love. We kneel before God and simply say we are sorry.

We do so with love and confidence in our hearts. You see, Jesus walked that road to the cross willingly. His life wasn't taken from him. He gave it up freely. His love for us drove him to suffer our punishment and die our death.

His love leads us to openly admit what we've done. His love leads us to trust in his forgiveness. His love leads us to turn away from those sins and now live for him.

This Ash Wednesday, make the time to go to church. Quietly go and tell God you're sorry for what you've done.

Tell him you're sorry with the confidence that he has and always will forgive you because of Jesus. Tell him you're sorry while trusting in his love for you. Tell him you're sorry because you love him.

Love means saying you're sorry.

Today I am thankful for/that _____

_____

Lord, I'm sorry. Forgive me for Jesus' sake. Amen.

LENT – DAY 312
GIVE IT UP FOR LENT

"**When you fast, do not look somber
as the hypocrites do.**"

MATTHEW 6:16

❖

During the six weeks of Lent, the worship in many Christian churches will become more subdued as Christians watch their Savior sacrifice and suffer. While the joy of faith remains undiminished throughout the year, our rejoicing during Lent is muted and quiet.

Lent is a time of reflection. Lent is a time of repentance. Lent is a time to quietly watch and pray as we follow our Savior to his cross.

Traditionally, Christians often "give something up" for Lent. The centuries-old tradition harkens back to the ancient custom of fasting. To fast is to not eat food for a certain amount of time. Believers in both the Old and New Testaments fasted on different occasions as an expression of their sorrow over sin or to focus their minds and hearts on prayer and Bible study.

Fasting during Lent soon took many forms. Some Christians gave up eating meat during Lent, a tradition still common among Christians today, at least on the Fridays of Lent. Soon people began giving up other things during Lent: alcohol, sex, hobbies, and fun activities. Today people give up things like smoking, Dr. Pepper, and their favorite game on their smartphone.

Some Christians today do the exact opposite. Instead of giving something up for Lent, they think it is better to simply give something for Lent—to do something. During Lent they volunteer for charity work. They go visit people in the nursing home. They mow the lawns of their elderly neighbors.

In a way, they are still giving something up for Lent. They are giving up their time.

Giving something up for Lent can be a wonderful way to focus our hearts and minds on what Lent is all about. As we sacrifice, we are forced to think about Jesus' sacrifice for us—what he gave up to save us from the hell we deserve. Giving things up declutters our lives so we can focus our attention on what is really important and meditate on God's great love.

Fasting is a worthwhile spiritual exercise.

But be careful. If you decide to give something up, make sure it is something that is truly a sacrifice. I personally love fish. Giving up meat on Fridays to eat a fish fry is not really a sacrifice for me. It's a treat.

MAKE IT A PRIVATE MATTER BETWEEN YOU AND GOD.

Jesus said, "When you fast, do not look somber as the hypocrites do. . . . [P]ut oil on your head and wash your face, so that it will not be obvious to men that you are fasting" (Matthew 6:16-18). In other words, don't show off. In fact, I would encourage you not to tell anyone that you are giving something up for Lent unless they ask. Make it a private matter between you and God.

And watch out for pride. The devil loves to stroke our egos, whispering in our ears what great Christians we are for giving something up for Lent. Remember that the sacrifices we make during Lent or any other time of year cannot and will not earn you God's love. Giving things up for God will not make him love you any more than he already does.

We give things up to help us remember and appreciate what our Savior gave up for us. We give things up to focus our hearts and minds on his great love which led him to die so that we might live.

If you've never done it before, try giving something up this year. Use it as a way to turn your mind to your Savior's great sacrifice for you. It all starts with finding something that would be somewhat difficult to give up for six weeks. Pray about it.

Then give it up for Lent.

Today I am thankful for/that _____

_____

Dear Lord, thank you for the season of Lent when I can remember your great sacrifice for me. Help me to humbly appreciate all that you gave up for me. Amen.

LENT – DAY 313
LIFE LIVED IN MINOR KEY

[Jesus] took Peter, James and John along with him, and
he began to be deeply distressed and troubled.
"My soul is overwhelmed with sorrow to the
point of death," he said to them.

MARK 14:33,34

◈

Have you ever noticed that the feel of the music in many churches changes at this time of year? Right now we are in the season of the Church Year known as *Lent*. During Lent, the sounds and singing in many of our churches could best be described as sad or somber.

Do you know what gives the music that sad, somber sound? Oftentimes it is because it's written in a minor key. In the music of our Western culture, songs are generally written in either a major or minor key. If they are written in a major key, they tend to sound more cheerful or upbeat. If they are written in a minor key, they tend to sound somber, sad, or even scary.

Go to YouTube and listen to hymns like "O Sacred Head Now Wounded" and "Stricken, Smitten, and Afflicted." They sound sad and somber. They sound like a funeral. They are written in a minor key.

Lent is life lived in a minor key.

During the 40 days of Lent, we watch from a distance as our Savior takes his final steps to the cross. We see him suffer. We watch him die. We are reminded that it is our cross which pressed down on his shoulders. It is our dumb and dirty deeds which caused his pain. Lent is a time of repentance and sorrow over sin.

But is Lent really such a sad season? Jesus bore that cross willingly in love. Because he did, we are forever forgiven for every last one of those dumb and dirty sins. Look carefully at the words of those sad and somber sounding hymns that we sing during Lent. "If my sins give me alarm And my conscience grieve me, Let your cross my fear disarm; Peace of conscience give me" ("Jesus, I Will Ponder Now," CW 98:4). As we cling to the old rugged cross, we are reminded that we will exchange it one day for the crown of heaven.

Is that really something to be sad about?

Scientists call the coastal regions where freshwater and seawater mix an *estuary*. Lent is an estuary where the bitter tears of sorrow over sin are mixed with the sweet, joyful tears of sins forgiven.

MAKE SURE YOU LISTEN CAREFULLY TO THE WORDS.

So, as you live life in a minor key during this Lenten season—as you sing those sad, somber melodies—make sure you listen carefully to the words. Yes, it is your sins that caused his suffering and your punishment which he bore, but he did so willingly in love. Because he did, you are forgiven. You are going to heaven.

When we really listen to the words, we come to realize that the sad, somber songs of Lent are really the happy hymns of heaven.

Today I am thankful for/that _____

_____

Thank you, Jesus, for the sad, somber songs of Lent. Help me to see and appreciate that they are truly the happy hymns of heaven. Amen.

LENT – DAY 314
SPRING TRAINING FOR CHRISTIANS

Grow in the grace and knowledge of our Lord and Savior Jesus Christ.

2 PETER 3:18

Well, it's that time of year again—spring training. Major League Baseball players have descended once again on the warm weather of Florida and Arizona. They are getting back into shape. Every day they stretch and jog and run. Many have worked out all winter, but their bodies aren't quite ready. Their skills are a bit rusty. Spring training is necessary to prepare them for the grueling 162-game season to come.

Well, it's that time of year again—Lent is once again upon us. During Lent, we walk behind and alongside our Savior as he travels his trail of tears to the cross.

Lent is a somewhat hot-and-cold season of the Church Year. The hymns of Lent seem to be songs of sadness. Lenten services focus on sin and repentance and Jesus' suffering.

That being said, Lent is actually a joyful season. As we follow our Savior to the cross, we see his great love for us. We see the punishment of our sins lifted from our shoulders to his. We see our sins nailed to the cross so that we need bear them no more. Lent is all about God's love and sins forgiven.

Lent leads us to the joyful celebration of Easter, of the resurrection, of the life eternal that is waiting for us in heaven.

Do you know where the name *Lent* comes from? The word *Lent* comes from the Old English word for spring. Lent is spring training for Christians.

USE THIS JOURNEY TO STRENGTHEN AND STRETCH MY FAITH.

Lent stretches our faith. Lent conditions our faith. It hurts as we are forced to face our sins. It pains us to see what our sins deserve, but, as we do, we see our Savior who died so that we might live. During the sad and joyful days of Lent, we exercise our faith so that we can be ready for the long and grueling 162-game season of life.

The forgiveness and strength we find in Lent gets us through the long, dark days of cancer and Alzheimer's. The peace we find in the message of Lent gets us through the heartbreaks of divorce and the sorrow we feel at the death of a loved one.

So celebrate Lent. Sing those sad songs. See your Savior suffer and die. Face your sins and find forgiveness. Stretch your faith to get you ready for the long season of life.

May God continue to bless you through the spring training of Lent.

Today I am thankful for/that _____

_____

Dear Jesus, as we follow you on your road to the cross this Lenten season, use this journey to strengthen and stretch my faith so I may serve you my whole life through. Amen.

LENT – DAY 315
THE NON-APOLOGY APOLOGY

Then I acknowledged my sin to you and did not cover up my iniquity. I said, "I will confess my transgressions to the LORD." And you forgave the guilt of my sin.

PSALM 32:5

❖

The Astros broke my heart. The 2017 season was special. The World Series was epic. The unmitigated joy with which the young Astros played was contagious.

It was fun being an Astros fan.

Then came the reports of sign-stealing, the public reaction, and the fallout. The worst part for me came when owner Jim Crane went on national TV to apologize.

Only he didn't.

He claimed the cheating had no effect on the games. He showed no remorse. He never actually said he was sorry.

As sinful human beings, we struggle to say we're sorry. In our pride and stubbornness, we don't want to admit our failings, or at least we try to pass off part of the blame.

We say things like, "I'm sorry you feel that way." "I apologize. I didn't know you were so sensitive." "I'm sorry you took it the wrong way."

That's not being sorry. Those are non-apology apologies.

Or we say we're sorry, but add a "but." "I'm sorry I said what I said, but you said some things you shouldn't have too." "I'm sorry I cheated on the test, but I didn't have time to study." "I'm sorry I drank too much, but I've been under a lot of stress lately."

WHEN YOU MESS UP, DON'T MAKE EXCUSES. DON'T BLAME OTHERS. SAY YOU'RE SORRY.

All of those buts may be true, but they don't justify what you've done. We like to make excuses. We love to blame others. But, in the end, if you have the choice between doing what is right and doing what is wrong and you choose to do what is wrong, there is only one person to blame.

You.

We always have a choice. So when you mess up, don't make excuses. Don't blame others. Say you're sorry—no buts, no excuses. You did it. Admit it.

During the season of Lent, we remember all that Jesus suffered and sacrificed on the cross.

During Lent, we admit it's our fault he had to die. My sins nailed him to that wood. I did it.

But we also remember that he went willingly. Jesus went to that cross because he loves you so much. And because he did, God fully and freely forgives you forever. You can ask God for forgiveness with the confidence that he will always forgive you.

So go to God. Tell him you're sorry—no buts, no excuses, no non-apology apologies. Admit what you've done with the confidence that he has and will always forgive you because of Jesus.

Today I am thankful for/that _____

_____

Holy and merciful God, I have sinned in thought, word, and action. I am truly sorry. Thank you for forgiving me because of Jesus. Amen.

HOLY WEEK – DAY 316
HOLY WEEK IS COMING!

"Worthy is the Lamb, who was slain, to receive power and wealth and wisdom and strength and honor and glory and praise!"

REVELATION 5:12

My favorite Christmas movie of all-time is the movie *Elf*. In the movie, Will Ferrell plays a man who was raised as an elf in the North Pole. At one point, Will Ferrell's character is standing in the toy department at Gimbels Department Store when the manager suddenly announces that Santa will be there the next day to meet the children.

"Santa!" Will Ferrell shouts exuberantly, jumping up and down like a four-year-old. "Santa is coming!"

That is how I feel when Holy Week is coming.

Every year, Christians around the world celebrate Holy Week, following the events of Jesus' life during his last days and hours on earth. It begins with Palm Sunday when we lay our palm branches in Jesus' path as he enters Jerusalem as our Savior King. Then on Maundy Thursday, we follow Jesus to the Upper Room where he celebrates the Passover with his disciples for the last time and gives the Lord's Supper for the first time.

On the Friday we call Good, we sit in somber silence as we see our Savior die in the darkness, suffering our pain and our punishment in our place. Dressed in white, we return on Sunday to celebrate his miraculous resurrection with lilies and alleluias.

Every day of Holy Week is unique. Every service is special. The music, the symbolism, and the truths proclaimed lead us on a rollercoaster of emotions and self-examination.

I love Holy Week. I can't wait for Holy Week to get here every year. I feel like Will Ferrell when Santa Claus was coming.

Most people aren't like me. I mean, sure, Holy Week is nice. It's important, but they don't get excited about it. They don't spend weeks getting ready like they do for Christmas. Sure, people get excited about Easter, but the rest of the week is somewhat of a drag.

I compare it to weddings and funerals. Christmas is like a wedding. Holy Week is like a funeral. Christmas is a celebration. Holy Week is somber. Christmas is about birth. Jesus dies at the end of Holy Week.

This Sunday, ask your pastor which he would rather conduct—a wedding or a funeral. I am guessing he will say a funeral. Why? Because though weddings are nice, everybody gets distracted with all the preparations and decorations and dresses. God and his promises get lost somewhere in the shuffle of cakes and flowers and bridesmaids. In many ways, the same is true for Christmas. The true message of Christmas often gets lost in the hustle and bustle.

Funerals are different. At funerals, people are hurting. They yearn for the comfort God offers in his promises. Death has a way of laser-focusing our hearts and minds on what is really important. Holy Week does that. Holy

HOLY WEEK HELPS US REMEMBER WHAT IS REALLY IMPORTANT.

Week turns our thoughts away from the distractions of this world to the most basic and important truths of our faith.

Holy Week helps us remember what is really important. It helps us appreciate what our awesome God did for us in his amazing grace. Holy Week is what the Christian faith is all about.

So celebrate Holy Week. Make the most of every worship service available to you. Each service is unique. Each service is special. Take the time to quietly remember what Jesus did for you in his great love.

Isn't it exciting? Holy Week is coming!

Today I am thankful for/that _____

_____

Jesus, thank you for all that you did for me in your great love on that Holy Week 2,000 years ago. Amen.

HOLY WEEK – DAY 317
THE CURE FOR CANCER

By his wounds we are healed.

ISAIAH 53:5

◆

I hate cancer. My brother Adam has brain cancer. Though modern medicine can slow it down, his cancer still can't be cured. My wife's grandmother in Mexico has stomach cancer. It's terminal. The doctors don't give her much longer here on earth. Countless friends and neighbors are facing and fighting this scourge of our modern world.

Few people know this, but I'm afraid of cancer. As I pray for and encourage others who have the disease, I secretly wonder and worry how I will react if one day the doctor tells me those fateful words, "You have cancer." Cancer kills. Roughly eight million people in our world are dying of cancer right now. Though modern medicine has found ways to treat and even at times cure it, cancer continues to kill at alarming rates.

WE ARE INFECTED WITH THE CANCER OF SIN.

I am not going to sugarcoat this for you. You have cancer. I have cancer. We are infected, however, with something even more dangerous than a tumor or cyst. We are infected with the cancer of sin.

It's a genetic disorder we inherited from our parents who inherited it from their parents all the way back to Adam and Eve. It's an illness we have fed and exacerbated with a lifetime of poor, selfish, and unloving choices.

The worst part is our cancer is terminal. Sin is the cause of death. You will die one day because of it. And when you do, you will be forced to face the consequences of your lifetime of poor choices.

Thankfully, God has provided a cure for our cancer. This week we celebrate that cure. Two thousand years ago, on a dark Friday we call Good, God himself "took up our pain" (Isaiah 53:4). God transplanted our cancer onto himself. He suffered the consequences of our poor choices in our place and "by his wounds we are healed."

Jesus is the cure for the cancer of sin. Through faith in him, you are healed. You are forgiven. You are not going to die. That is what we celebrate every year on Good Friday and Easter.

On the first Easter Sunday, Jesus rose, body and soul, from the grave. His promise is that you too will one day rise. "I am the resurrection and the life," he tells us. "The one who believes in me will live, even though they die; and whoever lives by believing in me will never die" (John 11:25,26).

Cancer cannot kill you. Death cannot beat you. When you die, God will take your soul to live with him in heaven. On the Last Day, he will raise your body from the grave. You will then live, body and soul, forever with God where there will be no more sin or sickness, cancer or death.

Though the doctors may postpone it a while, it seems that my brother will one day die from his cancer. My wife's grandmother is going to die from her cancer. You and I are dying right now.

Don't be afraid, though. This week we celebrate the cure for cancer, the cure for death, the cure for sin. This week nearly 2,000 years ago, Jesus died so that you might live.

He is the cure.

Today I am thankful for/that _____

_____

Almighty God, be the strength and peace of all those who suffer from cancer. Give them the courage of knowing you are with them through it all. Give them the confidence that you are the cure for cancer. Amen.

GOOD FRIDAY – DAY 318
WHAT'S SO GOOD ABOUT GOOD FRIDAY?

**When he had received the drink,
Jesus said, "It is finished."**

JOHN 19:30

I love Easter. When you walk into our church on Easter morning, the smell of our flower cross fills the sanctuary. The bright white of the banners and lilies provides a brilliant contrast to the pastel-colored shirts and dresses. Everyone is smiling. Church is full. The music is glorious. The message is all about life and victory and heaven. What's not to like about Easter?

Good Friday, however, is another story. Good Friday seems so sad. In our church, we have what's called a *Tenebrae* Service. As the service progresses, the lights in the church are slowly extinguished. At the end, we walk out in darkness and silence.

What's so good about Good Friday? On Good Friday, we are forced to watch Jesus suffer brutality and gore which rival anything Hollywood could ever produce. We watch him bleed. We hear him cry out. On that day, God abandoned God. On that day, God died. Why would we call it good?

Especially when we remember that it's our fault. In the movie *The Passion of the Christ,* director Mel Gibson made a famous cameo. You never see his face, but his were the hands which drove the nails. He later said why he chose that scene: because it was his fault.

It was my fault. It was your fault Jesus died. Sometimes we fool ourselves into thinking our sins are no big deal. It's just a little lie. I only drink on weekends. Nobody waits until marriage anymore to have sex. Sure, I know it's bad, but at least I haven't killed anybody.

Yet you have killed someone. You killed the Son of God. It was your hands which nailed him to that tree. It was your sins he carried. It was your punishment he bore. On Good Friday we are forced to face the horror our sins have caused—the horror we deserve.

WE CALL IT GOOD FRIDAY BECAUSE JESUS WON FOR US FORGIVENESS WITH HIS DEATH.

So what's so good about Good Friday? We call it Good Friday because Jesus carried our load, bore our burden, and suffered our punishment willingly. He could have stopped it, but he didn't because he loved you and me so much. On Good Friday, we get to see the amazing, extraordinary, overflowing grace of our God.

We call it Good Friday because Jesus won for us forgiveness with his death. Our sins were nailed to that cross forever. God will never punish you because he punished Jesus in your place. No matter how badly you mess up, no matter how far you fall, God will always take you back. He will always forgive you because of Jesus.

We call it Good Friday because we know it's not the end of the story. We leave in silence on Friday, but return in joyful song on Easter Sunday. Jesus didn't stay dead. He lives and, because he lives, we too will live.

As I write these words, my wife is packing our suitcases. We found out only a few hours ago that her grandfather in Mexico died. In just a few days we will stand next to his grave with tears in our eyes. But we know. We know Jesus died his death. We know that, though he was not perfect, my wife's grandfather was forgiven. Three hours ago, he closed his eyes to this world and opened them to his home in heaven.

All because of what happened on that dark Friday 2,000 years ago. That's why we call it Good.

Today I am thankful for/that _____

_____

Dear Jesus, thank you for giving up everything
that was good and suffering all that was bad
to rescue me from the hell I deserve. Amen.

HOLY SATURDAY – DAY 319
BETWEEN THE CROSS AND THE RESURRECTION

Be patient, then, brothers and sisters, until the Lord's
coming. See how the farmer waits for the land to yield
its valuable crop, patiently waiting for the autumn
and spring rains. You too, be patient and stand
firm, because the Lord's coming is near.

JAMES 5:7,8

◆

This week, Christians around the world celebrate Holy Week. Though most Christians celebrate Good Friday and Easter, every day of Holy Week is special—each day is unique.

On Palm Sunday, Jesus entered Jerusalem as a humble king. The crowds received him as the promised Messiah with palms and psalms and hosannas.

On Holy Monday, Jesus cursed the fig tree and cleansed the temple. Holy Tuesday bustled with busyness. Jesus taught the people in parables and watched a widow give everything she had. He answered every challenging question and described a distant day of judgment.

In contrast, Holy Wednesday was seemingly uneventful. One very important event occurred on that day, though. Mary Magdalene anointed Jesus with expensive perfume, prompting Judas to sell out his Savior for 30 pieces of silver.

Maundy Thursday was the Passover, the Last Supper, Holy Communion, the Garden of Gethsemane and the trial before the High Priest. The night ended with Jesus standing meekly in chains, Peter weeping bitterly, and Judas hanging himself.

The Friday we call Good is history's defining moment. On that day, God took our place and suffered our pain and punishment. On Good Friday, God died so that we might live.

Saturday was different, though. The only thing we know about Holy Saturday is that the leaders of the Jews asked Pontius Pilate to seal the tomb and place a guard so that nobody could steal the body. They were afraid the disciples would take Jesus' lifeless cadaver and claim he had risen.

What then follows is a long, dark silence until Easter dawn.

What must that Saturday have been like for Jesus' disciples? The guilt of having deserted him. The fear they may be next. The confusion. The doubt. He had warned them about his death and promised to rise again, but could that really happen? Maybe it was all a lie.

On Holy Saturday, the disciples waited and wondered. They could not yet see the victory. They had the promise, but their eyes saw only doom and despair. Jesus was dead. All seemed to be lost.

Caught between the cross and the resurrection, the disciples anxiously sat in darkness and fear.

And so do we. Jesus' cross lies behind us, as do all our sins. They were nailed to that cross where they will forever stay. What lies ahead is the victory, the resurrection, the happiness of heaven.

Yet, like the disciples, here we wait. We wait in the dark silence of a world where all seems to be lost. We wait wondering, often confused, sometimes doubting. Yet we wait in faith, trusting that Easter dawn is coming. Like the disciples, we too will see the day when our faith is validated with an empty tomb and a resurrection.

My old college English professor, Brian Dose, said it best. "Holy Saturday is where we too live and worship, between the darkness and the dawn. In the moment between our crosses and our empty tombs. Between doubting and touching the glorified wounds that paid for the sins of the world. But tomorrow only heaven."

KNOW THAT THE DAWN IS COMING.

As you wait for Easter this Holy Saturday—as you wait in this world of sin and suffering, caught in the darkness between the cross and the resurrection—know that the dawn is coming.

Tomorrow is heaven.

Today I am thankful for/that _____

_____

Lord, as I struggle with the dark night of this world, help me never to forget the dawn is coming. Give me patience and peace while I wait for your deliverance. Amen.

EASTER – DAY 320
BECAUSE HE LIVES

"Because I live, you also will live."

JOHN 14:19

◆

On New Year's Eve 1970, Gloria Gaither sat alone in the dark quiet of her family living room in Alexandria, Indiana. It had been a difficult year.

Gloria's husband, Bill, was still recovering from a long and exhausting bout of mononucleosis. Problems in their church had led to divisions and personal attacks against them. It was the height of the Vietnam War. The drug culture was in full swing. Racial tensions divided the country.

And Gloria was pregnant.

Both she and her husband wondered openly about the wisdom of bringing a child into such a world. Gloria later wrote, "Who in their right mind would bring a child into a world like this? I thought, 'The world is so evil. Influences beyond our control are so strong. What will happen to this child?'"

As she sat alone in the dark, her thoughts soon turned to Jesus' resurrection. "Gradually, the fear left," Gloria recounts, "and the joy began to return. I knew I could have that baby and face the future with optimism and trust. It was the Resurrection affirming itself in our lives once again."

Gloria Gaither soon put her confidence to words and, together with her husband Bill, composed a hymn that became one of the most popular hymns of the 20th century: "Because He Lives."

"God sent his Son, they call him Jesus. He came to love, heal and forgive. He lived and died to buy my pardon. An empty grave is there to prove my Savior lives."

Jesus' resurrection is our confidence. Because he lives, we know that God the Father accepted his payment for our sins. Because he lives, we can be sure God forgives us. Because he lives, we can be sure we will live with him one day in heaven.

"And then one day, I'll cross the river. I'll fight life's final war with pain. And then as death gives way to victory, I'll see the lights of glory and I'll know he lives."

Because Jesus lives, we don't ever have to be afraid. He conquered sin and death for us. He rose and now rules over all things for our good. As sinful human beings, we worry and fret about many things. But we don't need to. Because Jesus lives, you and I can't lose.

On July 12, 1971, Gloria Gaither gave birth to her first son, Benjy. Gloria, however, no longer worried about her infant son's future.

"How sweet to hold a newborn baby and feel the pride and joy he gives, but greater still the calm assurance this child can face uncertain days because he lives."

You and I were born into the same uncertain world into which Benjy Gaither was born. Wars still rage. Our country is still divided. Illnesses plague our families and divisions plague our churches. But we don't have to be afraid. We don't have to worry about tomorrow.

OUR PEACE AND CONFIDENCE IN THE MIDDLE OF THE STORM IS THAT JESUS LIVES.

"Because he lives I can face tomorrow. Because he lives all fear is gone. Because I know he holds the future and life is worth the living just because he lives."

Our peace and confidence in the middle of the storm is that Jesus lives. He conquered sin and death. He now rules over all things for our good. One day he will take us out of the dark storm into the warm, comforting light of his presence. How do I know?

Because he lives.

Today I am thankful for/that _____

_____

*Risen Savior, give me the peace and confidence of
knowing your resurrection. Help me to trust
that because you live the victory is won.
I cannot lose. Heaven is mine. Amen.*

EASTER – DAY 321
HE IS RISEN INDEED!

"He is not here; he has risen!"

LUKE 24:6

Since the earliest days of the Christian church, there is a greeting Christians have used on Easter. It began in the Greek language. The first person would say, *"Christos anesti!"* Then the other person would respond, *"Alithos anesti!"*

Christ is risen! He is risen indeed!

Around the world on Easter morning, Christians from every tribe and language greet each other with those words. *"¡Cristo ha resucitado! ¡De veras ha resucitado!"* (Spanish) *"Christus ist auferstanden! Er ist warhaftig auferstanden!"* (German) *"Kristus vstal z mrtvých! Vpravdě vstal z mrtvých!"* (Czech) "基督復活了他確實復活了" (Chinese)

The story is told of a man named Nikolai Ivanovich Bukharin, one of the most powerful men in early Communist Russia. In 1930, he went to Kiev to address a huge crowd on Easter Sunday. The subject was atheism. He attacked Christianity as a fraud. He pointed out the foolishness of faith. His talk was both eloquent and powerful. By the end, he was confident he had convinced the crowd of the errors of Christianity.

When he finished, an old man walked onto the stage and congratulated Bukharin for his eloquence. Then he turned to the crowd and quietly said, *"Christos voskres"* (Christ is risen). To that, the crowd of thousands thundered, *"Voistinu voskres!"* (He is risen indeed!).

I can't prove that Jesus rose. Sure, over 500 people saw him alive after his resurrection, but they could have been making it up. His disciples could have stolen his body. There is no empirical proof Jesus rose from the dead. The only real historical evidence we have that he ever lived is the Bible. I cannot prove Jesus died on a cross and rose again.

Yet I believe it. I believe the testimony of the men and women who saw the nail marks in his hands and feet. I believe that the Bible is God's true and never-changing Word. I believe that because the Holy Spirit convinces me as I read and hear it.

THE TRUTH ABOUT JESUS . . . WILL BE SPOKEN UNTIL . . . THE END OF THE WORLD.

As Christians we sometimes feel we need to prove we are right. We need to prove that God is real and that what we believe is true. The truth is, however, that we can't prove it. We can't argue someone into believing it. The only way to accept it is by faith. Seeing isn't believing. Believing is seeing.

On the other hand, those who reject God's Word have not and will never be able to prove it to be false. They cannot win. God's Word cannot be silenced. The truth about Jesus, his cross, and his resurrection will be spoken until the day Jesus comes at the end of the world.

The atheist movement in our country is growing rapidly. Those who believe God to be a lie are gaining influence and want to silence Christianity. We don't need to worry, though. We don't need to get angry and argue with them. They can't win. Besides, you can't debate someone into faith. Just stand up and speak out. Speak the truth in love. Share the simple, powerful message.

"Christ is risen! He is risen indeed!"

Today I am thankful for/that _____

_____

Risen Savior, give me the faith and courage to tell the world that you are risen indeed. Amen.

EASTER – DAY 322
RESTORATION

**"Destroy this temple, and I will raise
it again in three days."**

JOHN 2:19

❖

The cornerstone was laid 856 years ago. The initial construction took 180 years, but over the centuries it has been under constant renovation and improvement. The French government was in the middle of its most recent multi-million-dollar renovation when the fire began on April 15, 2019.

Notre Dame Cathedral in Paris was nine centuries in the making when fire destroyed a large portion of it in a matter of only 15 hours. French President Emmanuel Macron vowed it would be rebuilt within five years.

Two thousand years ago, Jesus stood on the grounds of another massive religious edifice—the great temple of Jerusalem. In the year 19 B.C., King Herod had undertaken the task of not only building a new temple, but also constructing a massive temple complex around it. The complex would measure over one million square feet and cover the entire temple mount.

**BECAUSE JESUS ROSE,
HE PROMISES THAT
WE TOO WILL RISE.**

The temple itself was towering by the standards of the day, measuring nearly 15 stories tall. The white marble and golden doors of the temple glowed in the glare of the sun. As Jesus stood in the temple courts 46 years later, the temple itself had long been completed, but the temple complex was still under construction. It wouldn't be finished until just a couple of years before the Roman legions leveled it to the ground in the year A.D. 70.

The temple itself has never been rebuilt. A Muslim shrine called "The Dome of the Rock" now stands where the temple once towered.

Two thousand years ago, when the temple still stood in all its magnificent glory, Jesus made a whip and drove out the merchants who had set up market in the temple courts. Stunned, the people demanded that Jesus give them a sign to prove he had the authority to do such a thing.

"Destroy this temple," Jesus answered, "and I will raise it again in three days."

The people laughed. "It has taken forty-six years to build this temple and you are going to raise it in three days?" John tells us that the temple of which Jesus was speaking, however, was his body (John 2:12-22).

To rebuild Herod's temple in just three days was laughable. I mean, imagine if President Macron had vowed to rebuild Notre Dame Cathedral in three days. Many find it implausible that he will be able to rebuild it in five years.

Yet Jesus promised to do something even more extraordinary. His enemies would destroy the temple of his body. They would kill him. On that first Good Friday, Jesus' body hung limp and lifeless from the cross. People stood and stared just as they did the Monday Notre Dame burned. They wrung their hands and shook their heads. Jesus was dead.

On the third day after his death, though, Jesus did the impossible. He restored the temple of his body. His soul once again entered his lifeless body. It sprung to life. In fact, it came back more glorious than the original.

Jesus kept his promise, and in doing so, destroyed death forever. Because Jesus rose, he promises that we too will rise. At the sound of the trumpet on the Last Day, Jesus will raise up all those who have died in the faith. That's God's promise. That is the purpose and peace of Easter.

As I watched Notre Dame burn on April 15, 2019, it broke my heart. I truly hope they do rebuild and restore it to its former glory. This Easter, though, remember that a much more impressive restoration project will happen one day on the temple of our bodies.

Because he lives, we too will live.

Today I am thankful for/that _____

_____

Risen Lord, thank you for the joy of the resurrection. As my body slowly fades and the pains of age take their toll, turn my eyes to the day when my body will be made new and I will live with you forever. Amen.

EASTER – DAY 323
BY THE RIVERS OF BABYLON

**How can we sing the songs of the Lord
while in a foreign land?**

PSALM 137:4

◆

They were strangers living in a strange land—carried off into exile by a conquering nation. They watched as homes were burned and their temple destroyed. They felt isolated, alone, and rejected by God.

To add insult to injury, their captors asked that they entertain them with their famous songs of joy from their homeland—their "psalms." As they sat "by the rivers of Babylon," the Jewish exiles wept, remembering the temple and the way things used to be.

"How can we sing the songs of the Lord while in a foreign land?" They asked.

As I sat in my 2020 pandemically-imposed exile, I could relate. To be honest, our exile was exceedingly more luxurious than that of the Jewish people. We didn't sit by the rivers of Babylon. We sat in fully furnished homes with central heating and air conditioning, big-screen TVs, and smartphones. Our biggest struggle was not having enough toilet paper.

Yet we did feel the same isolation and loneliness. We longed for the way things used to be.

As Christians, we especially struggled with not being able to worship together. I, together with Christians around the world, lamented the fact that we couldn't physically worship together in our churches on Good Friday and Easter Sunday in 2020. Our hearts ached and yearned to sing the joyous songs of Easter together.

WE COULD SING FOR JOY TO THE LORD BECAUSE HIS PROMISES WERE STILL TRUE.

Watching it on a screen was just not the same.

Like the Israelites of old, we asked, "How can we sing the songs of the Lord while in exile?"

We could sing for joy to the Lord because his promises were still true. Even as they sat in exile, God promised to be with his people and bless them. He promised to bring them home one day. He promised that their Savior from sin would still be born.

God kept every one of his promises to the nation of Israel, and he will keep every promise he has made to you. He will be with us (Matthew 28:20). He will make everything in our lives—even a pandemic—work out for our eternal good (Romans 8:28).

Most importantly, he will give to you and all who believe in Jesus the gifts of forgiveness and heaven Jesus won for us. You can be sure of that because his tomb is empty. Death had no power over Jesus and therefore it has no power over those who follow him. With his death and resurrection, Jesus won the victory for us over sin, death, and the devil.

Because he lives, we can face tomorrow. Because he lives, all fear is gone. Because he lives, we can sing our songs of joy to the Lord, even as we sit in exile—even when our churches sit empty.

Like the exiled Jews, we achingly longed for the day when we could gather together again in God's house to worship him. That didn't stop us, however, from singing our songs of praise to our Savior God.

Even though our churches sat empty, so did the tomb.

Today I am thankful for/that _____

_____

Risen Savior, thank you for giving us reasons to sing for joy every moment of our lives. Amen.

EASTER – DAY 324
BEATING THE UCONN HUSKIES

The sting of death is sin, and the power of sin is the law. But thanks be to God! He gives us the victory through our Lord Jesus Christ.

1 CORINTHIANS 15:56,57

❧

For basketball fans, March Madness is an exciting time of year.

For years, though, the women's NCAA tournament had lost all of its excitement. For nearly a decade, the University of Connecticut Huskies dominated women's basketball more than any other team in history.

Over one three-year span, their record was 113–1. They consistently beat the nation's best teams by 50 points. The UConn Huskies were the Harlem Globetrotters of women's basketball and every other team was the Washington Generals.

They were, simply put, unbeatable. I am guessing that some teams during that period threw up their hands in despair when they realized they had to play UConn. I mean, what's the use of even playing? There's no way you can win.

Death is the UConn Huskies women's basketball team. In fact, death has an even better record. There's no way *you* can beat it. Despite all the marvels of modern medicine, exercise, diets, and plastic surgery, every one of us is going to die. Like a UConn Huskies national championship, death is inevitable.

It all started with a tree, a serpent, and a lie. It started when Adam and Eve doubted God's love for them and disobeyed. From the moment they ate the forbidden fruit, they began to die. On that day, death's winning streak began.

It's a streak which continues to this day. From the moment we are born, we begin to die. Our bodies are wearing out. We are growing old. We are dying. Death's winning streak isn't going to end with us.

That's why Easter is so important. On that first Easter Sunday, Jesus did the unthinkable, the unimaginable—the impossible. He defeated death. He beat the UConn Huskies.

Yes, Jesus died. He died our death. He suffered the punishment we deserve for all the lousy things we do. On the cross Jesus' heart stopped beating. The synapses of his brain ceased firing. His soul left his body. He died.

But he didn't stay dead. He came back to life. On that first Easter morning, his soul re-entered his body. His heart once again began to beat. The synapses in his brain began to fire. Jesus defeated death.

His victory is our victory. He promises us, "I am the resurrection and the life. The one who believes in me will live, even though they die" (John 11:25).

Don't get me wrong—unless the end of the world comes first, you will die one day. You will be lying in a hospital bed or at an accident scene or in a nursing home and your heart will suddenly stop beating. The synapses in your brain will cease firing. Your soul will leave your body.

Yet because Jesus died for your sins, because he worked faith in your heart through his Word and the waters of Holy Baptism, God will welcome your soul into heaven. Death is just a door we pass through on our way to heaven.

OUR VICTORY WILL BE COMPLETE— ALL BECAUSE OF JESUS.

Then on the Last Day when Jesus comes to judge, he will raise our decaying corpses and glorify them. The perishable will be made imperishable. Never again will we grow old. Never again will we die.

On that day, death will die. The UConn Huskies will be vanquished. Our victory will be complete—all because of Jesus.

With him on your team, you can't lose.

Today I am thankful for/that _____

_____

Resurrected Lord and Savior, thank you
for defeating death for us. Help us to
trust that with you on our
team, we cannot lose. Amen.

EASTER – DAY 325
THE EASTER HANGOVER

Praise be to the God and Father of our Lord Jesus Christ! In his great mercy he has given us new birth into a living hope through the resurrection of Jesus Christ from the dead.

1 PETER 1:3

◆

My five-year-old son could barely keep his eyes open on Monday morning as I spoon-fed him his Fruity Pebbles.

I am guessing it was a combination of things: two Easter worship services, Sunday school, three Easter egg hunts, a water balloon fight, and a birthday party with two piñatas. I honestly don't want to think of how much candy my children consumed on Easter Sunday.

I didn't blame my son. I was having a hard time staying awake myself. In fact, after I dropped my kids at school, I went home and crawled back into bed.

I call it the Easter Hangover. For many pastors, the days leading up to Easter are hectic. Our church has an added worship service each week during the season of Lent. The choir is busy practicing. The staff is busy planning the Holy Week and Easter celebrations. Then Holy Week finally arrives. Personally it is my favorite week of the entire year, but it also means numerous worship services to prepare.

Then comes Easter, the highest festival of the Christian church year. The church shines bright white, showered in Easter lilies. The music is glorious. The message is inspiring. The church is full. On Easter, pastors easily fall into delusions of grandeur as they imagine the church that full every Sunday.

Then you wake up on Monday morning. The adrenaline has worn off and reality begins to sink in. The desk and the calendar are piled high with the things you put off during the Holy Week rush. Phone calls need to be made. Members need to be visited. You are tired.

Then you go to church the next Sunday. The sanctuary is now only half full. The music isn't quite so glorious. You are still tired and now also frustrated. That is the Easter hangover.

SO WHAT IS THE CURE? HYDRATION.

So what is the cure? Hydration. Ironically, the most common cause of a normal hangover is dehydration. Though it sounds counterintuitive, drinking alcohol leads to dehydration. The cure, therefore, for a normal hangover is to hydrate—to drink plenty of water.

The cure for the Easter Hangover is to drink deeply from the water of salvation. The irony of Holy Week and Easter is that we as pastors get so busy with the planning, preparing, and preaching that we ourselves fail to drink from the life-giving water of God's Word.

We don't take the time to meditate on Jesus' words, "This is my body. . . . This is my blood, given for you for the forgiveness of sins." We forget to sit quietly at the foot of the cross and ponder his great love for us.

We don't listen as carefully as we should to the words of those victorious hymns. The joy of Easter is a victory which is ours now through faith in Jesus, but which won't be seen until heaven.

On Easter, we feel a little like Peter did on the Mount of Transfiguration. It's fun basking in God's glory. Life here on earth, however, is not all mountaintop experiences. Everyday life and the everyday work of a church aren't all Easter lilies and victorious music.

We have to wake up on Monday morning, go down the mountain, and get back to work. But we can do so with renewed joy and energy—we can overcome the Easter Hangover—if we take the time to stay hydrated with the water of God's refreshing Word.

So go back to the promises of Holy Week. Hear him say, "Given for you. . . . Shed for you." See his cross and how it won your forgiveness. See the empty tomb and celebrate the fact that you will live forever in heaven.

Drink deeply from the water of salvation.

Today I am thankful for/that _____

_____

Risen Savior, sometimes my joy on Easter is superficial. Forgive me for forgetting at times what Easter is all about. Thank you for the joy of knowing I am forgiven and heaven is mine. Thank you for the joy of the resurrection. Amen.

EASTER – DAY 326
EVERY SUNDAY IS EASTER

**Early on the first day of the week, while it was still
dark, Mary Magdalene went to the tomb and saw
that the stone had been removed from the entrance.**

JOHN 20:1

◆

Easter is now over. The empty plastic egg shells and confetti have been removed from the churchyard. The dishes from the Easter breakfast have been washed and put away in the church kitchen. All the loose bulletins have been picked up in the sanctuary. Most importantly, the pastor finally got his nap.

Pastors find the days leading up to Easter to be hectic. Our church worships every Wednesday during the season of Lent. The choir is busy practicing while the staff plans the multiple Holy Week and Easter celebrations.

Then Holy Week finally arrives. Personally it is my favorite week of the entire year, but it also means numerous worship services for which to prepare.

Finally, Easter comes. Easter is the highest festival of the Christian Church Year. The church shines in its robe of bright white Easter lilies. The music is victorious. The message is inspiring. The church is full of people.

But now Easter is over. The church doesn't shine quite so brightly. The music isn't quite as victorious. There definitely aren't as many people.

I read recently that ticket sales for the new *Batman vs. Superman* movie dropped 70% in its second week. That's what they get for opening on Easter weekend. If there is one thing I have learned as a pastor after 17 years, it's that attendance always drops dramatically the week after Easter.

Christians around the world recognize the importance of worshiping on Easter Sunday. Easter is our victory celebration. On Good Friday, Jesus conquered sin with his death. On Easter Sunday, he defeated death with his resurrection.

Easter is our ticker tape parade for Jesus. On Easter, we celebrate his victory. On Easter, we celebrate the forgiveness and heaven he won for us.

But now, for most people, Easter is over. Life has returned to normal.

Easter isn't actually over, though. Every Sunday is Easter.

In biblical times, believers generally worshiped on Saturday, the Sabbath Day. In the early church, however, many Christians gathered together every day for worship and Bible study. Jewish Christians continued to worship on the Sabbath, but then all the Christians made sure to get together every Sunday morning. They made sure to celebrate Holy Communion on Sunday. They began calling it "The Lord's Day."

HELP ME TO CELEBRATE EASTER EVERY SUNDAY— EVERY DAY— OF MY LIFE.

You see, Sunday morning was special. They had to celebrate Sunday. Sunday was when Jesus rose from the dead. Every Sunday was Easter.

I don't know if you've seen the posts on Facebook, but sometimes young newlyweds today don't just celebrate their one-year anniversary. They celebrate their six-month anniversary. They celebrate their one-month anniversary. They celebrate their three-week anniversary. They can't help but celebrate their deep love for one another every chance they get. Those of us who have been married for 17 years or more just roll our eyes.

Maybe there's something we can learn from those lovey-dovey newlyweds. What Jesus did for us, what he suffered for us, what he won for us with his resurrection deserves more than a once-a-year anniversary.

You are going to die one day. I am going to die one day. Nothing in this life is more important than Jesus' resurrection. Nothing is more important than the forgiveness and heaven he won for us.

So make sure to go to church this Sunday. Wear your pastel shirt or white dress. Take some eggs for the kids. And on the way out of church, smile at your pastor and wish him a happy Easter.

Because every Sunday is Easter.

Today I am thankful for/that _____

_____

Almighty God, thank you for the victory over death Jesus won for me with his resurrection. Help me to celebrate Easter every Sunday— every day—of my life. Amen.

ASCENSION – DAY 327
POOR ASCENSION DAY

**"This same Jesus, who has been taken from you
into heaven, will come back in the same way
you have seen him go into heaven."**

ACTS 1:11

❖

Poor Ascension Day. Of all the major festivals of the Christian church, the Festival of the Ascension is probably the most neglected. No one greeted me this morning at Walmart wishing me a happy Ascension Day. Hallmark doesn't make Ascension cards. There is no Ascension Bunny.

Most churches don't even have Ascension Day services any more. Can you blame them? I mean, what are we really celebrating on Ascension—that Jesus left?

Actually, there is much we can celebrate on this forgotten holiday.

Even though Jesus left, he didn't really leave. He left visibly, but he promised his disciples that he would be with them and us every moment of every day until the end of the world (Matthew 28:20). We just can't see him.

Jesus left, but he isn't gone. The all-powerful Son of God who walked on water and calmed storms and raised the dead—our Savior who loved us so much he suffered in our place the punishment of hell we deserve—is and will always be by our side. That's something to celebrate.

Jesus left to prepare a place for us in heaven. On the night before he died, Jesus told his disciples, "My Father's house has many rooms; if that were not so, would I have told you that I am going there to prepare a place for you?" (John 14:2). Our ascended Lord is preparing a mansion in heaven with your name on the mailbox. That's why he came to this earth and that's why he left on Ascension Day.

Right now, at this very moment, our ascended Savior is sitting at the right hand of God the Father, ruling over all things for our good (Ephesians 1:22,23). That's something to celebrate.

Jesus left, but he's coming back. That's the real lesson of Ascension. As the apostles stood staring at the sky, their mouths hanging open in astonishment, two men dressed in white appeared with them. "Men of Galilee," they said, "why do you stand here looking into the sky? This same Jesus, who has been taken from you into heaven, will come back in the same way you have seen him go."

Jesus is coming back visibly to judge the world. He is coming back to take us home to heaven. When he comes, we will finally see him. We will finally understand fully. We will finally be free from all the pains and worries of this world. That's something to celebrate.

In the balcony scene of William Shakespeare's great tragedy *Romeo and Juliet*, the star-crossed lovers were forced to say goodbye for the night. "Parting is such sweet sorrow," Juliet lamented. She was sad to say goodbye, but boy did she love those beautiful words Romeo whispered to her as they bid farewell. Parting was sweet sorrow.

ASCENSION DAY ISN'T SWEET SORROW. IT'S JUST SWEET.

Ascension Day isn't sweet sorrow. It's just sweet. Today we remember that our ascended Savior is with us wherever we go, that he is preparing a place for us in heaven, and that he will come again to take us to be with him in heaven.

Now, that's something to celebrate.

Today I am thankful for/that _____

_____

Ascended Lord and Savior, thank you for preparing a place for me in heaven and ruling over all things for my good. Help me to look forward with joy to the day you will come back visibly to take me to be with you forever. Amen.

PENTECOST – DAY 328
HOLY WIND!

**Suddenly a sound like the blowing of a violent wind
came from heaven and filled the whole house
where they were sitting.**

ACTS 2:2

◆

Wind can be a powerful force. On September 11, 1961, Hurricane Carla made landfall at Port O'Connor, Texas. It was one of the most intense hurricanes ever to hit the United States. Winds reached speeds of 175 mph. The older members of my congregation remember Hurricane Carla vividly. They say it sounded like a freight train passing through their living rooms.

On the day of Pentecost, 50 days after Jesus rose from the dead, just 10 days after his ascension into heaven, his disciples heard that same sound— the sound of a violent wind—the sound of a freight train passing through their living room.

With that sound came the Holy Spirit.

You see, in the original languages of the Bible, wind and spirit are the same word. The Holy Spirit is literally *the holy wind,* the very breath of God. Jesus told Nicodemus, "The wind blows wherever it pleases. You hear its sound, but you cannot tell where it comes from or where it is going. So it is with everyone born of the Spirit" (John 3:8).

You can't see the wind. The only thing you can see is what it moves: leaves blowing, snow drifting, waves crashing against the shore. You can feel the wind on your face. So it is with the Holy Spirit—you can't see the Holy Spirit working.

You can see the results, though. You can see people joyfully worshiping and serving God. You can see the tears dry on your friend's face as she is comforted by God's promises. You can see the joy of the Spirit and the peace he gives. You can feel it yourself.

The Holy Spirit is like the wind. The problem is that many Christians want and expect hurricane force winds. They want to feel the overwhelming emotions that the Holy Spirit at times elicits as we hear his Word and promises proclaimed to us.

Yes, sometimes you will feel a hurricane of emotions as the Holy Spirit drives you to tears of sorrow over your sins and tears of joy over his forgiveness. Sometimes you will feel God's overwhelming presence fill your hearts as you sing out your praises to him.

Usually, however, the Holy Spirit doesn't work with hurricane force. Usually he speaks to us in the gentle whisper of his Word. Like a gentle fan slowly turning in your house, you may not even feel the breeze as the Holy Spirit quietly works faith and peace and confidence in your heart.

> USUALLY, HOWEVER, THE HOLY SPIRIT DOESN'T WORK WITH HURRICANE FORCE.

As you sit in church hearing his Word proclaimed, as you receive Jesus' body and blood in Holy Communion, as you spend quiet time reading your Bible at home, the Holy Spirit is gently stoking the flame of faith in your heart. We often don't even notice the Spirit working through his Word and sacraments, just like we often don't notice a gentle breeze blowing against our faces.

Don't despise the gentle whisper of the gospel. Don't think that the Holy Spirit only works when you feel overwhelming emotions in worship and prayer. The Holy Spirit can and does at times work with hurricane force, but he also quietly works in the gentle whisper of a Sunday sermon or a simple family devotion.

His great power is behind that gentle breeze.

Today I am thankful for/that _____

_____

Holy Spirit, thank you for breathing into my heart the life of faith. Help me to continue to fan that flame of faith with your powerful Word. Amen.

PENTECOST – DAY 329
REPEATING PENTECOST

**Those who accepted [Peter's] message were
baptized, and about three thousand were
added to their number that day.**

ACTS 2:41

◆

Wouldn't it be awesome if we could repeat Pentecost? On the Day of Pentecost nearly 2,000 years ago, Jesus' disciples were gathered together behind locked doors. Suddenly the house shook and they heard what sounded like a violent wind. Tongues of fire came to rest on each of them and immediately they were able to speak in other languages.

Yet none of those things was the greatest miracle of Pentecost. On that day, the disciples, who were always running away, who were always cowering in fear, who were always worrying about which of them was the greatest, were filled with the Holy Spirit.

They weren't afraid any more. They stopped fighting among themselves. They boldly went out to tell everyone they could about Jesus.

On Pentecost, 3,000 people came to faith in Jesus and were baptized.

Wouldn't that be awesome if it happened today? Just imagine if this Sunday 3,000 new people showed up at your church. The parking lot would be full. The building would be overflowing with people. The crowd would flood the church yard.

A number of years ago, a fellow pastor in my hometown shared with me a statistic. It seems that on any given Sunday about 20% of our local community's population is in church. According to the last census, our small, rural county has nearly 15,000 residents. That means that if every person in our county who goes to church would invite just one person to go with them next Sunday, there would be 3,000 new people in church next Sunday.

Boom. Pentecost.

**ALL WE NEED
TO DO IS INVITE.**

We don't need earthquakes, violent winds, or flames of fire sitting on top of our heads. We don't need to suddenly be able to speak in other languages. God has already given us his Holy Spirit.

All we need to do is invite.

The blessings go way beyond simply filling up our churches. Lives will be changed. The weak will be strengthened. The straying will be brought back. Souls will be saved.

Don't get me wrong. Obviously not everyone we invite will accept the invitation. A recent survey by Lifeway stated that only 35% of Americans said they would attend a worship service if someone they knew invited them.

That means only about 1,000 new people in church next Sunday.

Wait. How can we say "only"? That is 1,000 souls. That's countless families. That's lives forever changed.

And it all starts with an invitation—one friend taking another friend by the hand and leading them to Jesus. That is what it means to be a Christian. That is the primary job Jesus has given us—to share his gifts of forgiveness and heaven with those around us.

But Pentecost can't be repeated if we don't invite. So call up your sister and tell her you'll pick her up this Sunday. Take a deep breath and invite your friend from work. Go visit that fellow member you haven't seen in church in months.

Pentecost is possible. It all starts with a simple invitation. Whom can you invite?

Today I am thankful for/that _____

_____

Holy Spirit, Light Divine, open my heart
and my mouth so that I invite everyone
I can to see and hear about what
Jesus did to save them. Amen.

MOTHER'S DAY – DAY 330
MY MOM SHOWED ME JESUS

Start children off on the way they should go, and even when they are old they will not turn from it.

PROVERBS 22:6

❖

I love my dad. My dad is a pastor. He taught me about Jesus. Every night after dinner, he read Bible stories to us as children. Every Sunday, he stood in front of church and told me about the wonders of God's love. He taught me catechism and helped me memorize Bible verses. My dad taught me about Jesus.

My mom showed me Jesus.

She showed me Jesus every Sunday as she got seven little kids ready for church all by herself. She showed me Jesus as she sat alone in the pew trying to listen as she simultaneously wiped our noses, kept us still, and helped us find our places in the hymnal. Keeping seven kids still in church is like herding cats.

My mom showed me Jesus by not letting me run amok in my sinful nature. She showed me his love as she spanked me with the paddle. (My mom didn't have much kick to her spankings, so she cut off the rubber string and ball from a paddleball racket and used that.) My mom showed me Jesus by giving me a hug after every spanking.

My mom showed me Jesus as she bandaged my wounds and kissed my booboos. She showed me Jesus as she prayed with me every night, "Jesus Savior wash away . . . Now I lay me down to sleep . . . God bless Mommy and Daddy . . ." She showed me Jesus as she hugged me when I was afraid and told me Jesus was with me.

Our modern world expects too much of mothers. They need to be supermoms who keep up with all the creative crafts and meals they see on Pinterest. They have to make sure their kids have gluten-free and organic diets. They have to be taxi drivers making sure their kids get to every soccer practice, ballet rehearsal, and spelling bee. They have to clean up messes and pick up shoes. And in our modern society, oftentimes, they have to work a part-time or full-time job as well.

When they struggle—when the gluten-free and organic diet gets replaced with McDonald's and Pizza Hut, when they have to say no to ballet or soccer because there is no time, when the house is a mess and they are too tired to move—guilt crushes their souls.

MOM, ALLOW ME TO SHOW YOU JESUS.

Mom, allow me to show you Jesus. He has forgiven all your shortcomings as a mother. He is with you. He is watching over your children. He works through even your imperfect efforts to raise your children. You don't have to be supermom.

Don't think you have to give your children the perfect childhood. Just show them Jesus. That is the greatest gift you could ever give them.

Today is Mother's Day. For one day a year, we gush about the importance of motherhood and praise the virtues of mothers. For one day a year, we push aside whatever issues we have with our moms and tearfully muse about how wonderful our mothers are.

Neither of my parents are perfect. I love them dearly, but like me they are severely flawed by sin. On this Mother's Day, I am not going to wax poetic about the virtues of motherhood. I am not going to elevate my mother to sainthood. Rather I am going to thank God for her, because she gave me what was most important.

She showed me Jesus.

Today I am thankful for/that _____

_____

Heavenly Father, thank you for my mother, for her love, and for the lessons she taught me. Please help her and all mothers to show their children Jesus. Amen.

MOTHER'S DAY – DAY 331
UNHAPPY MOTHER'S DAY

Rejoice with those who rejoice;
mourn with those who mourn.

ROMANS 12:15

◆

On May 10, 1908, a woman named Anna Jarvis held a memorial service for her mother at St. Andrew's Methodist Church in Grafton, West Virginia. It was the first celebration of a new holiday called Mother's Day.

Jarvis' campaign to make Mother's Day a national holiday began three years earlier at the death of her mother, Anna Reeves Jarvis. By 1911, every state in the Union was celebrating Mother's Day due in no small part to Jarvis' efforts. In 1914, President Woodrow Wilson declared it a national holiday.

By the 1920s, Hallmark began mass-producing Mother's Day cards. Floral companies began selling red carnations by the thousands. Jarvis quickly became disillusioned with the commercialization of her beloved holiday—the original emphasis of the day was being lost.

Soon she found herself protesting candy factories and the selling of carnations. In 1943 she began a petition to rescind Mother's Day.

Anna Jarvis, the founder of Mother's Day, grew to despise the holiday.

Don't get me wrong. Mother's Day can be a very good thing. As it always takes place on a Sunday, it allows us a wonderful opportunity to go to church and thank God for the gift of our mothers. It is a fitting occasion to thank our moms and let them know how much we love them.

Mother's Day offers us a unique opportunity to talk about the important role mothers play in the spiritual life of their children. The greatest lesson my mother ever taught me was what it means to love God and be loved by him.

Today, however, Mother's Day is all about buying your mom a card and taking her out to eat. Mother's Day has become a multi-million-dollar industry. Emotion-driven commercials manipulate us into thinking the sign of a good son or daughter is spending money on your mom one day a year so that she knows you love her.

In fact, many people don't even go to church anymore on Mother's Day because they need to take Mom out to eat and they want to beat the crowds.

For many in our world today, Mother's Day is one of the unhappiest days of the year. For mothers who have lost children, for children who have lost mothers, or for women who do not have or are unable to have children, the holiday is a painful reminder of what they have lost or can never have.

I hope I don't sound like the Ebenezer Scrooge of Mother's Day. I believe Mother's Day is a wonderful holiday which should be celebrated. Unlike Anna Jarvis, I don't think it should be rescinded.

THE GREATEST GIFT YOU CAN ACTUALLY GIVE YOUR MOM IS . . .

But this year, as you celebrate Mother's Day, watch out for the emotional manipulation of commercialism. Mother's Day isn't about cards and flowers and going out to eat. The greatest gift you can actually give your mom is to worship with her in church on Sunday morning.

This Sunday, make sure to thank your mom and let her know you love her, but don't just do it one day a year, and don't just tell her. Show her you love her by honoring her, forgiving her, and supporting her throughout the year.

And please be sensitive to those who are hurting this Mother's Day. Be aware of the women around you who haven't been given the joy of motherhood. Be understanding of those who feel the pain of loss more keenly on Mother's Day.

Mother's Day can be a very good thing. Just keep it in perspective.

Today I am thankful for/that _____

_____

Heavenly Father, help me to keep the proper perspective on Mother's Day. Thank you for my mother, for the love she gave and the lessons she taught me. Help me to be sensitive to those who are sad today. Amen.

MEMORIAL DAY – DAY 332
WE REMEMBER

"Do this in remembrance of me."

LUKE 22:19

❖

The Civil War was the deadliest war in American history. The blood of over 600,000 American soldiers stained the soil of nearly every state of the divided union. The South was in shambles. The North was reeling.

So began the long and still unfinished process of healing.

In the weeks and months following the war, grieving families and friends would often decorate the graves of the fallen with flowers. In 1868, the Grand Army of the Republic, an organization of Union veterans, declared May 30 to be Decoration Day, a day to adorn the tombs of fallen soldiers with the newly blossoming flowers of spring.

In 1882, the name Memorial Day was used for the first time, but did not become the official name for the holiday until 1967. In 1971, the date was changed to the last Monday of May to allow for a three-day weekend.

Sadly for many in our country today, that is all Memorial Day is—a three-day weekend to start the summer, an opportunity to camp and cook out.

Memorial Day, however, means much more than hot dogs and apple pie and sales at Walmart.

Memorial Day is literally a day to remember—a day to honor those who gave the ultimate sacrifice for our freedom. We honor their memory by decorating their graves. We honor their memory by holding fast to the freedoms for which they died. We honor their memory by remembering their sacrifice.

As I remember their tremendous sacrifice, I can't help but think of another sacrifice. Though I can never sufficiently thank those who fought and died for the freedoms I enjoy, I still struggle to call their sacrifice "the ultimate sacrifice."

For me that phrase is reserved for the sacrifice Jesus offered on the altar of the cross. Jesus didn't just suffer the horrors of war. He suffered the horrors of the hell I deserve. He didn't just die to give me the right to life, liberty, and the pursuit of happiness. He died to give me freedom from sin and to share with me the eternal happiness of heaven.

As Christians, we don't have just one Memorial Day a year to remember Jesus' ultimate sacrifice. We have a Memorial Meal he himself gave us so we would never forget his body which died and his blood which was spilled so we might live.

Sadly, for many of us, the Sacrament of Holy Communion can become as mundane as Memorial Day has become for many Americans—a simple ritual we outwardly observe on Sunday during church.

Never forget what Holy Communion means. In the sacrament, Jesus gives us his body and blood so we never forget the ultimate sacrifice he offered for our freedom. He gives us his body and blood so we always remember the gift of forgiveness and heaven he gives.

ALSO TAKE TIME TO REMEMBER THE ULTIMATE SACRIFICE JESUS MADE FOR YOU.

On this Memorial Day, I encourage you to remember—to honor the memory of the over 1.2 million soldiers who have died defending our freedoms and lives. But also take time to remember the ultimate sacrifice Jesus made for you. Honor his memory by celebrating his Memorial Meal every chance you get. Never forget how he died so you might live.

Today I am thankful for/that _____

_____

Lord, thank you for the men and women who have given their lives to protect me and my freedoms. Thank you especially for the ultimate sacrifice you made for me. Amen.

FATHER'S DAY – DAY 333
CONFESSIONS OF A FLAWED FATHER

"But while he was still a long way off, his father saw
him and was filled with compassion for him;
he ran to his son, threw his arms
around him and kissed him."

LUKE 15:20

◆

Today is Father's Day. Later today my kids and wife will shower me with gifts and hugs. They will tell me they love me and how much they appreciate me. They will tell me what a great dad I am.

But I know the truth.

Don't get me wrong. I love my family. In many ways, I am a good father. I provide for them. I take them to church. I talk to them about God their Savior. I love them, nurture them, and forgive them.

But I don't always do those things.

Sometimes I take the stress of my ministry out on them. I lash out. I snap at them. I have failed miserably in having daily devotions with my family. I lose patience with them while I am driving. I am at times careless and thoughtless with my wife.

I am a flawed father.

Please understand, this is not false modesty. I am not looking for reassurance or fishing for compliments. By the world's standards, I am not a bad father. In fact, many would consider me a very good father.

OUR WORLD . . . HAS UNDERESTIMATED THE IMPORTANCE AND INFLUENCE OF FATHERS.

But God's standards are much higher than our world's. Being a father is an enormous responsibility. God holds me responsible for the spiritual welfare of my family. The man my son will become and the way my daughter sees herself as a woman will depend a great deal on the example I give and the words I say.

What I do today as a father—both good and bad—will affect my children for the rest of their lives and even influence future generations. That may sound like an over-exaggeration, but that's because our world for far too long has underestimated the importance and influence of fathers.

The comfort and peace I have as a flawed father is that I have a forgiving Father—a Father who wraps his arms around his prodigal sons and never lets us go. Because of my brother Jesus, my heavenly Father does not hold my failings as a father against me. Because of Jesus, I can begin every day with a clean slate and don't have to beat myself up for my past mistakes.

My forgiving Father promises to help my children overcome my failures in raising them. The mistakes I have made may affect them the rest of their lives. Just as I have issues today due to my flawed father, I am sure my children will have theirs. Yet my forgiving Father promises to help and heal and guide them.

This Father's Day, I encourage all fathers to recognize the huge and awesome responsibility you have been given. God has placed in your care the hearts and souls of your children. What you do today as a father has eternal consequences.

If, like me, you feel the sting of your failings as a father, remember that you have a forgiving Father who doesn't hold our failures against us. Find peace in his loving arms which are always open to wayward sons like us. Trust that he will help you and your children heal and overcome your mistakes.

Know that God uses even flawed fathers like us.

Today I am thankful for/that _____

_____

Heavenly Father, thank you for the fathers you have given us and for forgiving our failures as parents and children. Amen.

SUMMER – DAY 334
A VACATION FROM GOD

**Blessed is the one . . . whose delight is in the law of the
Lord, and who meditates on his law day and night.**

PSALM 1:1,2

◆

Well, it's that time of year again—time for the family vacation. Here in
Texas, that means a quick trip to the Hill Country, a long weekend at the
Frio River, your dream vacation to Mexico or Las Vegas or Disney World.

Whatever your vacation plans for this summer, enjoy them. Vacations give
us a chance to spend quality time with our families. They help us recharge
our batteries. And sometimes they are even restful (though I usually return
home more tired than when I left).

But there is a danger with summer vacations. No, I'm not talking about the
danger of sunburn or pickpockets. I am not talking about car troubles or
smelly hotel rooms. I am talking about taking a vacation from God.

It happens so easily. At home we are in a routine. We say our prayers before
meals and before bed. We have family devotions. We get up on Sunday
morning to go to church. God is part of our life—part of our routine.

But then we go on vacation. Prayers stop being said. Bibles and devotional
books get left at home. Sunday morning comes and goes without even a
thought of God or church.

**GOD NEVER TAKES A
VACATION FROM YOU.**

God never takes a vacation. The Bible tells us that he
never slumbers nor sleeps (Psalm 121:4). Even while
we are on vacation, God isn't. He is there watching
over us, blessing us, and especially forgiving us. God
never takes a vacation from you, so don't take one
from him.

This year when you pack for your vacation, throw your Bible or a devotional
book in your suitcase. Ask your pastor before you go to give you the name
and address of a nearby church. What a joy to worship with Christian
brothers and sisters in another city, state, or even country!

If there isn't a church nearby, you can do what my dad did one summer
when I was 11 years old. We were camping in Montana in the middle of
nowhere. There were no churches nearby, so we did our own church.

We sang a couple of hymns we all knew by heart. My dad read from the Bible and we talked about it as a family. We said the Lord's Prayer and Apostles' Creed together. We prayed that God would bless our trip—and he did!

That Sunday morning in Montana my dad taught me to never take a vacation from God—a lesson I hope to pass on to my children.

Enjoy your vacations this summer. Get some fresh air. See new places. Recharge your batteries. But this year, don't take a vacation from God!

Today I am thankful for/that _____

_____

Lord, thank you for the gift of your Word.
Help me to never take a vacation
from it or from you. Amen.

SUMMER – DAY 335
YOU THINK IT'S HOT IN SOUTH TEXAS

"It is better to enter the kingdom of God with one eye than to have two eyes and be thrown into hell, where 'the worms that eat them do not die, and the fire is not quenched.'"

MARK 9:47,48

◆

Summer is here in South Texas. Last week, we hit triple digits for the first time this summer. I'm sure it won't be the last. As the temperatures rise, there is one thing I can always count on. I know I will see at least one church sign which reads: "You think it's hot in South Texas . . ."

The implication is clear. If you think it's hot here, hell is much worse.

The Bible again and again describes hell as an eternal fire, a place of excruciating pain, a place of regret and anger and sadness. Hell is where "the worms that eat them do not die, and the fire is not quenched." It is a place of weeping and gnashing of teeth. And it never ends.

A number of years ago, Gallup surveyed Americans about their belief in the afterlife. It showed that 81% believe in the existence of heaven. Surprisingly, 70% said they believed in the existence of hell. Ever the optimists, 77% of Americans rated their chances of going to heaven as "good" or "excellent," while less than one-half of 1% believed they would end up in hell.

Though most people in our country believe in the reality of hell, few believe there is actually a possibility they could end up there. And nobody wants to talk about it.

Nobody wants to go to a church where they preach fire and brimstone. Nobody wants to hear about sin. That's too negative. We want smiling preachers on TV telling us to think positively and all our dreams will come true.

As a pastor, I don't particularly enjoy talking about hell. It is not fun to confront people with their sins. It definitely doesn't win me any popularity contests.

The problem is that hell is a very real place. The problem is that we do sin every single day. The problem is that each and every one of our sins—both big and small—deserves an eternity in the agonizing fires of hell.

We need to hear about hell to recognize the danger we are in. We need to feel the flames nipping at our heels to appreciate what God has done for us. If there is no hell—or at least if there is no real chance we would ever end up there—what do we need God for? What do we need Jesus for?

But hell is real. You and I do deserve to burn there forever. Though nobody likes to hear that, it is important they do. Only then will they see and appreciate how much we need Jesus.

WE NEED TO HEAR ABOUT HELL, BUT THAT SHOULDN'T BE ALL WE HEAR ABOUT.

We need to hear about hell, but that shouldn't be all we hear about. When the message of a church is only fire and brimstone, we are missing the point. Church isn't about beating us down. It's about building us up. The purpose of the Bible isn't to doom us to hell, but to give us the gift of heaven.

God loved you and me so much, he became one of us and suffered the fire of his own anger for our sins as he hung on the cross. His promise is that all who believe in him—all who believe in Jesus—are forgiven forever.

The truth is that we will never fully be able to appreciate what Jesus did for us because we will never have to personally know what hell feels like. We will never have to feel the fire or the anger or the sadness of hell because Jesus suffered it in our place.

But we do need to hear about it and be reminded of it, so we remember how much we need Jesus—so we remember what is waiting for us if we leave Jesus behind.

As things heat up here in South Texas and you run and hide in the air-conditioned comfort of your homes, maybe it's not bad to take some time to think about the hell we deserve—the hell Jesus saved us from.

Because if you think it's hot in South Texas . . .

Today I am thankful for/that _____

_____

O Holy God, help me to always remember the horror my sins deserve, and don't ever let me forget your great mercy which forgives them all because of Jesus. Amen.

SUMMER – DAY 336
THE VACATION BIBLE SCHOOL BLUES

"Let the little children come to me, and do not hinder them, for the kingdom of heaven belongs to such as these."

MATTHEW 19:14

◆

I am tired. This year's vacation Bible school (VBS) at our church is officially over.

The week of VBS is a tough week for me as a pastor. After three hours of hanging out with energetic, exuberant children all morning, I need a nap in the afternoon. Then, with what's left of the day, I have to squeeze in my normal visits and sermon preparation.

VBS week is stressful. It used to be simple, but now we've got videos, music, scenery, and skits to prepare. Trying to find helpers and volunteers is a headache because everybody is busy. Schedules in the summer quickly get filled with vacations, camps, conferences, and work.

Kids, on the other hand, aren't so hard to find. Sometimes it seems like parents are just looking for free babysitting. Although the kids are usually well-behaved the first couple of days, by Friday they are restless and wild. Sadly, the teenage and pre-teen helpers are sometimes worse than the kids. By the end of the week, the adult helpers and teachers are tired and frazzled. Just about every year, someone ends up in tears.

Sometimes that person is me.

There are days when I wonder if VBS is worth it. But then we sing a song like we sang this week. The words were simple. Over and over again we sang, "Jesus loves me." One of our volunteers suggested that I walk around during the song and tell the children by name that Jesus loved them. So while they sang the refrain, I wandered around, telling the children one by one, "Jesus loves Thornton" and "Jesus loves Jaxon" and "Jesus loves Isabella."

I ended up being the one in tears this year.

Then I noticed the five-year-old boy who lost all his brothers and sisters in a fire a couple of years ago. I saw him smiling as he learned about Jesus and heaven.

Then I saw some of our teenage young men quietly helping and encouraging the smallest children. I saw the joy on the children's faces this week as they worshiped their Savior and heard the good news of his love. I heard one of them say, "I went home yesterday and told my dad Jesus loves him."

THANK GOD FOR VACATION BIBLE SCHOOL.

Then I remembered that VBS is the only connection some of these children have to God and his Word throughout the year. I remembered that VBS creates a positive memory and image of church which will stay with these children the rest of their lives.

This week, the seed of the gospel was planted and watered in the hearts of over 60 children at our tiny, little church in our tiny, little town. What effect will it have on their lives? Will there be children in heaven because of the Word they heard this week? Only God knows.

As I write these words, I am worn out and a little frazzled. After a long, hard week, I have just one thing to say: Thank God for vacation Bible school.

*Thank you, Lord, for vacation Bible school,
Sunday school, and all the ministries my
church offers to help little children
know you and your love. Amen.*

FOURTH OF JULY – DAY 337
THE GREAT EMANCIPATOR

To the Jews who had believed in him, Jesus said,
"If you hold to my teaching, you are really my
disciples. Then you will know the truth,
and the truth will set you free."

JOHN 8:31,32

◆

"That on the first day of January, A.D. 1863, all persons held as slaves within any State or designated part of a State, the people whereof shall then be in rebellion against the United States shall be then, thenceforward, and forever free. . . ."

With those words, Abraham Lincoln began what is today called the Emancipation Proclamation. Signed on September 22, 1862, the Emancipation Proclamation declared slaves in areas still in rebellion against the United States free. It was a historic and long-overdue event. Thomas Jefferson originally wanted to include a denunciation of slavery in the Declaration of Independence, but it was removed to appease two southern states.

Following the Civil War, the United States government faced a daunting task. Besides the difficulty of rebuilding a war-torn nation, they had to deal with hundreds of thousands of former slaves. These men and women were for the most part poor, mistreated, and uneducated. Now free from their former masters, many faced the cruel reality that they had no place to go. The task of bringing this large portion of the population up to speed economically and educationally has been a long and difficult journey for our country.

On the Fourth of July, we as Americans celebrate our freedom. We take great pride in the many freedoms we enjoy as citizens of this land: freedom of speech, freedom of the press, freedom of religion.

THE SAD TRUTH IS THAT ALL OF US BY NATURE ARE SLAVES.

Despite our freedom, the sad truth is that all of us by nature are slaves. We are slaves to sin. Although we may not want to, we daily sin against God in thought, word, and deed. We are slaves to death. Even with advances in medicine, exercise, and plastic surgery, we all will die one day. By nature we are all slaves.

But we have been set free. Our Lord and Savior Jesus Christ issued his own Emancipation Proclamation on a dark and lonely Friday afternoon some 2,000 years ago. Hanging limply on the cross, he cried out: "It is finished" (John 19:30). He had suffered the punishment of our sins. He was suffering the death that we deserve. All was now paid. Freedom was ours.

We are now free. Sin and death have no power over us. Our sins have been punished. For Christians, death is the door to eternal life.

God has given us our independence. On our own, however, we find ourselves in the same situation as many of those former slaves after the Civil War: poor, alone, and scared. But we are not alone. God has freed us in order that we might trust in him. He has given us our independence so that we might depend on him for all things. He has freed us from our slavery to sin, death, and the devil so that we might serve him with joyful and thankful hearts.

Jesus, your Great Emancipator, has set you free. Live in that freedom every day of your life.

Today I am thankful for/that _____

_____

Dear Jesus, thank you for setting me free. Help me to thank you by living for you every day of my life. Amen.

REFORMATION – DAY 338
HAPPY ANNIVERSARY

"All people are like grass . . . ; the grass withers and the flowers fall, but the word of our God endures forever."

1 PETER 1:24

◆

In 2017, we celebrated the 500th Anniversary of the Protestant Reformation. On All Hallows' Eve (October 31) 1517, a monk named Martin Luther nailed a document to the door of the Castle Church in Wittenberg, Germany. The document consisted of 95 theses he wished to publicly debate concerning abuses he saw in the Roman Catholic Church.

The nailing of the 95 Theses changed the world. Most historians include it in their top 10 list of history's defining moments. Just about every non-Roman Catholic Christian church which exists today can trace its roots back to the moment Luther's hammer struck that nail.

The 500th Anniversary of the Reformation was celebrated not only in Lutheran churches, but by numerous church bodies around the world. A major PBS documentary was released. Historians and scholars waxed poetic as they gave their unique insights as to who Martin Luther was and what the Reformation means.

This year there will be no PBS documentary. Few non-Lutheran churches will notice. Even our Lutheran celebrations will be much more subdued. Sure, we will celebrate the Festival of the Reformation in our churches. Some communities will have joint Reformation services. Even then, it will be nothing like the 500th anniversary celebrations.

But why? Why is the 500th anniversary so much more important than the 499th or the 505th? Why is our world so fascinated with round numbers? We celebrate our parents' 50th wedding anniversary with big parties, fabulous trips, and wonderful family reunions. But what about their 47th anniversary or their 52nd? Why don't we celebrate those with as much fanfare?

Why mark the 100th day in office for the president and not his 123rd? Why celebrate a baseball player's 500th home run and not his 484th? It's because we as a society consider round numbers implicitly better and more important. One author calls it "the mathematical tyranny of round numbers."

In the end, they're just numbers.

Now, don't get me wrong. I enjoyed celebrating the 500th anniversary of the Reformation. It allowed my church many opportunities to share the good news of the Gospel with a world which desperately needs it. Because of the media attention, we were given the opportunity to talk about what it means to be a Lutheran. The 500th anniversary of the Reformation was a special occasion.

THE FESTIVAL OF THE REFORMATION ISN'T ABOUT MARTIN LUTHER OR BEING LUTHERAN.

But don't forget to celebrate the Festival of the Reformation this year. It is just as important and meaningful this year as it was in 2017. In the end, the Festival of the Reformation isn't about Martin Luther or being Lutheran. It's about how God has preserved his gospel throughout history. It's about how he has used flawed human beings like Martin Luther, you, and me to stand up for and speak out the truth. It's about the free gift of heaven and forgiveness which Jesus won for us by grace alone, through faith alone, in Christ alone.

That's something to celebrate every year.

Today I am thankful for/that _____

_____

Eternal God and Lord, thank you for preserving your Word throughout all generations. Help us to teach your Word in Truth and purity to everyone we can. Amen.

HALLOWEEN – DAY 339
TO TRICK OR TREAT? THAT IS THE QUESTION

Whether you eat or drink or whatever you do, do it all for the glory of God.

1 CORINTHIANS 10:31

◆

As a Christian parent I find myself in a Shakespearean dilemma each October. To trick or treat? That is the question.

Some Christians point to the pagan roots and demonic overtones of Halloween and say we're sinning if we join in. Others point to the Christian roots of the holiday and say it's harmless fun. Every year, thousands of Christian churches across the country sponsor trunk-or-treat events in their church parking lots.

SO WHICH IS IT? DEMONIC FESTIVAL OR HARMLESS FUN? So which is it? Demonic festival or harmless fun? Do you personally feel uncomfortable about participating in Halloween but don't have the heart to keep your kids from trick or treating? That is our dilemma.

As a Christian parent, here are some thoughts to consider:

Halloween isn't all harmless fun. It's true that for most children Halloween is all about dressing in costumes and asking for candy. Yet they are still surrounded by superstition and supernatural images.

As Christians, we know ghosts aren't real. Vampires and zombies and werewolves aren't real. Demons, however, are. Witchcraft is.

The devil and his demons want to either frighten us into doubting God's love and protection or lure us into their lair with an unhealthy curiosity. Halloween presents them a microphone and platform from which to do so.

Another more subtle problem with Halloween is it teaches our children to be selfish. They go from house to house demanding candy. They hoard it and celebrate it. They often overindulge in it. Halloween feeds our children's greed.

If for those reasons, you as a Christian parent decide to keep your child from trick or treating, I don't blame you. But also understand that though you can keep them from trick or treating, you cannot shield

650

them completely from a society bombarding them with images and ideas about Halloween.

I recommend that as your child grows you explain your concerns and reasons for not participating. I suggest you offer healthy alternatives for fun on Halloween.

On the other hand, you are not sinning if you take your child trick or treating. Halloween can be healthy family fun. It presents a unique opportunity to talk with your children about God's protection and his holy angels who watch over them. It also gives us a chance to have important discussions with our children about the dangers of the occult and demons.

I would encourage you to do what you can to curb your child's selfishness. Teach them to say "Thank you" at each house. Show them the joy of sharing their candy with other children on the street, especially those whose bags or baskets aren't as full. Set limits on how much candy they can eat. Be firm about when enough is enough.

Halloween presents an opportunity to teach our children to curb their selfish appetites—to learn to accept when Mom and Dad say no more.

In the end, however, understand that Halloween falls firmly in the sphere of Christian freedom. If you choose not to allow your children to participate, be careful not to proudly judge those who do. If you choose to participate, be careful not to look down on those who refrain as if they were fanatical prudes.

To trick or treat? That is the question. Think about it. Pray about it. Talk to your children about it. Whatever you choose to do, follow the apostle Paul's encouragement. Do it all to the glory of God.

Today I am thankful for/that _____

_____

Holy Spirit, Light Divine, give me wisdom
to handle Halloween in a way that
brings glory to your name. Amen.

THANKSGIVING – DAY 340
HAVE YOU EATEN?

**When you have eaten and are satisfied, praise the LORD
your God for the good land he has given you.**

DEUTERONOMY 8:10

◆

A good friend recently returned from teaching English in China. Trying to impress him with one of the few Chinese phrases I know, I greeted him with the words *Ni hao,* which basically means "How are you?" in Mandarin.

Where he lived in China, however, that wasn't the way most people greeted each other. The most common greeting where he lived was *"Ni chi fan le ma?"*

"Have you eaten?"

Harkening back to the days when food was often scarce in China, "Have you eaten?" became a common greeting. If you wanted to know how someone was doing, that was the question to ask.

When you are starving, that is the only question which really matters.

This week, we Americans celebrate Thanksgiving. On Thanksgiving, someone may ask you, "Have you eaten?" The person asking, however, most likely isn't wondering whether you have eaten in the last couple of days. He or she is simply wondering if you have eaten in the last couple of hours.

As Americans, few of us have experienced true hunger. Few of us know the desperation hunger causes. Few of us have felt the fear of not knowing whether we will eat tomorrow or the next day.

God, in his amazing grace, has allowed us to be born and live in one of the richest countries in the world. True poverty is far beyond the realm of our experience.

Yet often we consider ourselves poor. Or maybe we don't consider ourselves poor, but we aren't rich. We see our neighbors' big homes and fancy phones, their new trucks and fishing boats. Then we look at our small apartments and old smartphones which won't charge unless you position the cord at just the right angle.

We feel like we are barely surviving. We feel sorry for ourselves. We feel poor.

The question you need to ask yourself is, "Have you eaten?"

If you look at our daily needs—food, clothing, and shelter—few of us have ever gone even one day without them. In fact, we have so much food, we regularly have to clean out our refrigerators and throw food away. We have closets full of clothes, beds and couches, TVs and tablets, air conditioners and heaters, fast food and Cheetos.

The secret to happiness isn't getting what you want. The secret to happiness is appreciating what you've got.

THE SECRET TO HAPPINESS IS APPRECIATING WHAT YOU'VE GOT.

The wealth with which God has blessed our country is a test we often fail. We take for granted all we have. We take the credit for what we have. We fail to appreciate what God has done for us.

If you have a chance yet today, read Deuteronomy chapter 8 in your Bible. There God warned the Children of Israel of the danger of prosperity—the danger of forgetting what he had done for them.

As you celebrate Thanksgiving this year, open your eyes. See how God has provided for your daily needs—food, clothing, and shelter. See how he gives you immeasurably more. Remember his great love and forgiveness which you don't deserve and the heaven which is waiting for you because of Jesus. Recognize how rich you really are.

Appreciate the fact that nobody ever has to ask you, "Have you eaten?"

Today I am thankful for/that _____

_____

Giver of all good things, thank you for providing all I need and so much more. Forgive me for the times I take for granted or fail to recognize all that you have given me. Amen.

THANKSGIVING – DAY 341
NOW THANK WE ALL OUR GOD

Give thanks to the LORD, for he is good; his love
endures forever.

PSALM 118:1

◆

Every time I hear the hymn, it elicits memories of my childhood—an organ booming its stately and steady tempo, the congregation dressed in their Sunday best, smiling faces singing joyfully, me dreaming of turkey and pie and football.

For many Christian churches, the hymn "Now Thank We All Our God" is as much a part of Thanksgiving as the Macy's Thanksgiving Day Parade, turkey, and pumpkin pie. For others it is an old, somewhat outdated hymn which is rarely sung.

To truly appreciate the beauty of "Now Thank We All Our God," we need to know its story. So, for a moment, let's leave behind the creature comforts of 21st-century America and travel back to the dark, dreary days of 17th-century Germany.

Germany in the 17th century was ravaged by war and disease. The Thirty Years' War (1618–1648), the deadliest religious war in the history of the world, left eight million people dead. German cities, towns, and villages were leveled. Farms were destroyed. Those who survived lived in abject poverty.

Martin Rinkart was a pastor who served in the walled town of Eilenburg, Germany, during the dark days of the Thirty Years' War. The town's population swelled during the conflict as people from the surrounding areas sought refuge behind its walls.

Famine and disease decimated Eilenburg. In 1637, the plague swept through the town like the angel of death. Four pastors began the year in Eilenburg. By the end of the year, however, one had abandoned his post and Pastor Rinkart had presided over the funerals of the other two.

During that year, Rinkart conducted the funerals for up to 50 people a day, including the funeral of his beloved wife. In that one year, nearly 4,500 residents of the town died of disease.

Yet, despite being surrounded by the stench of death and staring at mere scraps of food on his plate, Rinkart was able to write these words:

Now thank we all our God With hearts and hands and voices,
Who wondrous things has done, In whom his world rejoices,
Who from our mother's arms Has blessed us on our way,
With countless gifts of love And still is ours today. (CW 610:1)

Are you struggling to find a reason to give thanks this year? Maybe you are frustrated with the political polarization of our country. Maybe your marriage is a mess. Maybe your cancer has returned with a vengeance.

No matter what struggles or problems we face, we can still sing with joy, "Now thank we all our God." Even in the middle of the turmoil and tears of this world, our God has showered us with countless gifts of love. If you have a hard time seeing that, try to make a list of all the good things in your life of which Martin Rinkart could have only dreamed.

We can also sing, "Now thank we all our God," because we know that even the pains and hardships are a part of God's plan of love for us. We can sing, "Now thank we all our God," because, among his countless gifts of love, our God gives us the gift of forgiveness.

THIS THANKSGIVING, JOIN YOUR VOICE WITH MARTIN RINKART.

What a wondrous thing he has done! He died for us so that we could live with him in the happiness of heaven where we will one day be free from all the ills of this world.

This Thanksgiving, join your voice with Martin Rinkart and the billions of Christians who for nearly four centuries have been able to sing, in good times and in bad, "Now thank we all our God."

Today I am thankful for/that _____

_____

O Giver of all good things, give me a heart
which can thank you in all situations. Amen.

THANKSGIVING – DAY 342
YOU DESERVE A BREAK TODAY

For the wages of sin is death, but the gift of God
is eternal life in Christ Jesus our Lord.

ROMANS 6:23

When I was a boy, McDonald's struck advertising gold. They ran a series of commercials, some featuring crooner Barry Manilow singing the words, "You deserve a break today."

The jingle struck a chord with consumers. The commercials often showed people exercising, working hard, or frantically running errands. After all that hard work, they deserved a break. They deserved a Big Mac and fries.

Advertisers love to stroke our egos. "You deserve a new car," they tell us. "You deserve a vacation." "You deserve our product."

We like to hear that. We look at our lives and convince ourselves that we've earned what we have. We deserve it. In fact, we deserve much more. We work hard. We are good people. We deserve a break today.

The truth is that it's all a lie. It's all a product of Madison Avenue manipulation.

You and I deserve only one thing: God's punishment.

The only thing we have earned with our lives is an eternity in hell. We are terrible sinners who do terrible things. If it were left to us, our homes, our lives, and our families would be in ruins.

That truth is hard to hear and even harder to accept.

Everything I have and everything I am is due solely to God's amazing grace. As Christians, we easily let those words flow from our lips, but then we look at our homes, our closets, our cars, and our families and think to ourselves, "Look what I have done! Look what I have earned with all my sweat and sacrifice."

Yes, you did work hard, but who gave you the ability and opportunity to do that work? There are people in many parts of the world who work just as hard or even harder than you do, yet have far less. There are people much smarter, much more talented, and much kinder than you who enjoy only a small percentage of the blessings you do.

Why do you have so much more? How did you become the person, the father, the mother, the husband, or the wife that you are?

It is because God in his grace doesn't treat you as you deserve. You deserve to die. You deserve to rot in hell for all your pride and prejudice, for all your lies and lust.

Yet God loved you so much that he sent his Son to die your death and suffer your hell. God loves you so much he showers you with gifts you don't deserve.

This week we celebrate Thanksgiving. As Americans we like to talk a big game about how thankful we are. Yet deep down whom are we really thanking on Thanksgiving?

THE ONLY THING I DESERVE IS HELL.

Think about it. If I earned what I have with all my hard work, then the person I should thank is me. But I didn't earn it. I don't deserve it. The only thing I deserve is hell. The secret to true and overwhelming thankfulness is seeing all God has given me and recognizing I don't deserve any of it.

Today I am thankful for/that _____

_____

Merciful God, thank you for not giving me what I deserve and for giving me so many good things I have not earned. Everything I have and everything I am is a gift of your grace. Amen.

ADVENT – DAY 343
HAPPY ADVENT, YOU BROOD OF VIPERS

But when he saw many of the Pharisees and Sadducees
coming to where he was baptizing, [John] said to
them: "You brood of vipers! Who warned you
to flee from the coming wrath? Produce
fruit in keeping with repentance."

MATTHEW 3:7,8

◆

I've never been good at getting ready for Christmas. Our tree is up, but only the bottom half has lights on it. It's been that way now for over a week. I haven't bought one present yet. A few years ago I gave up writing an annual Christmas letter when I didn't get that year's letter sent until Valentine's Day.

I am not exaggerating. I am really that bad at getting ready for Christmas.

Thankfully, in my church I get a little help preparing for Christmas. In our church we celebrate what is called Advent. The season of Advent consists of the four weeks leading up to Christmas. It's a time when we prepare our hearts and minds for Jesus' coming.

One of the key figures during the season of Advent is a guy named John the Baptist. John was the man God sent to prepare the people for Jesus' coming.

John was a Grizzly Adams kind of guy. He was a Nazarite, which means he never got a haircut or shaved his beard. He lived in the wilderness. His clothes were made of scratchy camel skin held together by a leather belt. He ate grasshoppers and wild honey.

John was a fire-and-brimstone kind of preacher. The people came out to him in the wilderness around the Jordan River. His message to them was loud and in your face. "Repent and be baptized!" he told them.

When the Pharisees—the spiritual leaders of the people—came to see him, he called them a "brood of vipers" and "white-washed tombs" (clean on the outside, but dead on the inside).

That's how God prepared the people for Jesus' coming, by calling them to repent.

That is the best way for us to prepare for Christmas as well. Yet can you imagine going to church on Christmas and hearing the preacher shout at you, "Repent, you brood of vipers!"?

We are used to hearing sweet, joyful messages at Christmas. Christmas is about cute Baby Jesus, the beautiful angel choirs, and peaceful shepherds.

But that really isn't what Christmas is about. That baby born in Bethlehem came to do one thing—to die. He came to suffer the punishment of your sins in your place so you could be forgiven and go to heaven.

The best way to get ready for Christmas isn't to put up your Christmas tree or go shopping. The best way to get ready for Christmas isn't to set up a charming nativity scene or sing "Happy Birthday" to Jesus.

THE BEST WAY TO GET READY FOR CHRISTMAS IS TO REPENT.

The best way to get ready for Christmas is to repent—to recognize that Baby Jesus came to suffer in your place the horrors and hell you deserve.

But John's message wasn't just, "Repent!" He told the people, "Repent and be baptized!" In the original Greek of the Bible, the word "baptize" literally means "to wash."

Your baptism is God's promise that your sins are washed away forever because that baby born in Bethlehem died at Calvary for you. As we prepare for Christmas, we confess the dumb and ugly things we do, trusting that God has already forgiven them forever.

Jesus came. He died for you. You are his baptized son or daughter.

So take the time during these weeks before Christmas to quietly think about what you have done, what you deserve, and what Jesus came to do for you. Repent. Tell God you're sorry and trust in the promise of your baptism.

And have a happy Advent, you brood of vipers!

Today I am thankful for/that _____

_____

Merciful God, forgive me for all the ugly things I have thought, said, and done today. Thank you for sending your Son to save me from the hell I deserve. Amen.

ADVENT – DAY 344
CONSUMERISM AND THE CHURCH

**The time will come when people will not put up with
sound doctrine. Instead, to suit their own desires,
they will gather around them a great number of
teachers to say what their itching ears want to hear.**

2 TIMOTHY 4:3

❖

This time of year is all about you. Black Friday, Cyber Monday, and really every day between now and Christmas is about convincing you, the consumer, to buy certain products. Advertisers will use every tool in their tool box to persuade you to buy what they are selling.

Honestly, most advertising today is blatant manipulation. They convince you that you need their product. You deserve their product. Their product makes you happier, cooler, or sexier. You aren't a good parent if you don't give your kids their product. Advertisers tug at your heartstrings, stroke your ego, and guilt you into buying what they are selling.

Consumerism has invaded every aspect of our lives in this country. It drives our economy. It permeates politics. It has even entered the world of journalism. Cable news networks are no longer interested in being objective. They want to attract more viewers so they can sell more advertising. To do so, they don't tell us what we need to hear, but what they think we want to hear.

It's business. It's all about the bottom line. It's about getting you, the consumer, to buy what they are selling.

Sadly, consumerism has even infiltrated the church. When someone is looking for a new church nowadays, they call it "church shopping." People are looking for churches where they feel comfortable. They are looking for churches which fit their lifestyles and schedules. They are looking for churches with uplifting music, programs for their kids, and preaching which applies specifically to their lives.

CHURCH FOR MANY AMERICANS HAS BECOME CONSUMER-DRIVEN.

Church for many Americans has become consumer-driven. Advertisers tell me it's all about me. Cable news networks tell me what I want to hear. Many think church should be the same. If your church isn't giving

660

you what you feel you need or deserve, then you should shop around and find one that does.

Many churches then feel the pressure to cater to the consumer. People want to be entertained. Therefore we need to have catchy songs. We need to have the latest technology. We need to have hip pastors who are funny and can keep people's attention.

People want to be inspired. They don't want to be brought down by preachers talking about sin. They don't want to hear about God's anger or judgment. They don't want religion. They want a relationship. So churches stop talking about sin. They talk about poor choices. They stop talking about God the Judge and Savior. They talk about God your buddy, your mentor, and your life coach.

The apostle Paul once warned young Pastor Timothy about the dangers of consumerism. "The time will come," he said, "when people will not put up with sound doctrine. Instead, to suit their own desires, they will gather around them a great number of teachers to say what their itching ears want to hear."

Church is not a place you go to make you feel happy. Church is not a place you go to hear what you want to hear. Church is a place you go to hear what you need to hear—a place of brutal and loving honesty. Church is a place where we see our sins and our Savior Jesus who died for them.

Don't get sucked in by the consumerism of our society. Don't pick a church because it's selling what you want to buy. Find a church that tells you what you need to hear even when you don't want to hear it.

Because church isn't about you, the consumer. It's about the one and only true God and what he has done to save you.

Today I am thankful for/that _____

_____

Heavenly Father, as I prepare to celebrate the birth of your Son at Christmas, free me from the frenzy of commercialism. Help me also to remember why I go to church. May it always be about you and what you did to save me. Amen.

ADVENT – DAY 345
HOPE

For in this hope we were saved. But hope that is seen is
no hope at all. Who hopes for what they already
have? But if we hope for what we do not yet
have, we wait for it patiently.

ROMANS 8:24,25

◆

Friday Night Lights is alive and well in Edna, Texas. As I write this, our hometown football team is on a roll. The Edna High School Cowboys are now in the state quarterfinals. The biggest game of the year takes place this Friday night against the Yoakum Bulldogs. Just a few weeks ago, Yoakum handed Edna its only loss of the season. Edna and Yoakum are now ranked seventh and eighth in the state, respectively.

Everyone in Edna is hoping the Cowboys can pull out a win.

Hope. At this time of year, we hear that word a lot. Christmas is a time of hope. For our world, these weeks before Christmas are a time of positive thinking, a time of wishing, a time of dreaming.

People hope for peace. People hope for a better tomorrow. People hope to find hope.

WHAT PEOPLE CALL "HOPE" TODAY IS A FICKLE THING.

But what people call "hope" today is a fickle thing. Just because you hope for something doesn't mean it is going to happen. I hope with all my heart that Edna wins this Friday, but it may not happen. By the time you read this, the result of the football game will long have been decided. Right now, I can only hope.

Sometimes in life our hopes become reality, but other times our hopes are dashed. No matter how positively we think—no matter how much we want something—things don't always work out the way we hope they will.

The Bible often speaks of hope. In Psalm 130, the psalmist encourages us to put our hope in the Lord. As Christians, we talk about our hope of heaven. We speak of the hope God gives.

When the Bible speaks about hope, however, it doesn't mean it in the way our world uses it today. In the original languages of the Bible, the word for hope can also simply mean something you are waiting for.

When we hope in the Lord, we are not saying, "I hope maybe, just maybe, God might keep his promises." When we speak of our hope of heaven, we are not saying, "I hope maybe, just maybe, I will get to go to heaven." Our hope as Christians is a sure hope. It's a sure thing.

We just have to wait for it.

Our hope in the Lord is a sure thing because God always keeps his promises. Our hope of heaven is a sure thing because Jesus paid it all for us. He suffered the punishment for our sins on the cross and conquered death with his resurrection.

Like Joe Namath, God guaranteed victory, and, just like Joe Namath, he backs it up.

You don't have to wonder or worry whether God will do what he promises. You don't have to hope that maybe, just maybe, you might get to go to heaven. All those who believe in Jesus as their Savior from sin are going to heaven (Mark 16:16). That is God's promise, and God always keeps his promises.

I truly hope the Edna Cowboys can pull out a victory this Friday, but we will have to wait and see what happens.

I know God gives me the victory of heaven through faith in Jesus. That is our sure hope.

Today I am thankful for/that _____

_____

Heavenly Father, thank you for the sure hope of heaven you give. Take away my fears and give me patience as I wait to see the victory Jesus won for me. Amen.

ADVENT – DAY 346
I PROMISE

**"The virgin will conceive and give birth to a son,
and they will call him Immanuel."**

ISAIAH 7:14

◆

Every election cycle we hear the promises. The candidates make promise after promise about the economy, immigration, and the war on terror. Politicians, however, are notorious for making campaign promises they can't or don't keep.

In 1988, George Bush the elder repeatedly insisted, "Read my lips—no new taxes!" But a spiraling deficit and a Democratic Congress made that promise impossible to keep. In 1940, FDR made this campaign promise: "I have said it before, but I shall say it again and again and again. Your boys are not going to be sent into any foreign wars." Less than a year later, the Japanese bombed Pearl Harbor and the United States entered World War II. In 1964, LBJ campaigned with the promise: "No troops to Vietnam." Well, you know how that worked out.

My favorite, though, is Herbert Hoover, who in 1928 promised continued prosperity for every American. He promised "a chicken in every pot and a car in every garage." Nine months into his presidency, the stock market crashed, plunging the nation into the Great Depression.

There's a TV show I used to watch about the presidency called *The West Wing*. In one episode, the president was forced to break a campaign promise he had made, because in the end it was what was best for the country. After doing so, he said something which stuck with me. He said, "Our mistake wasn't breaking a promise. It was making a promise we couldn't keep."

GOD DOESN'T MAKE PROMISES HE CANNOT KEEP.

God doesn't make promises he cannot keep. At this time of year, children often count down the days until Christmas. They impatiently ask, "Is it Christmas yet?" I've often wondered if God's people of the Old Testament ever asked that question. At times it must have seemed that Christmas was never going to come.

God first made the promise of a Savior to Adam and Eve thousands of years before Jesus was born. He promised Abraham that the Savior would descend from his family, but that was 2,000 years before Jesus was born. God promised King David that one of his descendants would be the Messiah, but that was still 1,000 years before Jesus was born. The last book of the Old Testament once again promised that the Savior was coming, but that was 400 years before Jesus was born—roughly 146,000 days until Christmas.

Yet when the time was just right, God kept his promise. Christmas finally came. Jesus, the Savior of the world, the seed of Eve, the son of Abraham, the descendant of David, was born.

God always keeps his promises. Sometimes it doesn't seem that way. Sometimes it seems like everything is falling apart, like God has forgotten, like he doesn't care.

That's why Christmas is so important. It proves that God keeps his promises. God has promised to always love you, to always be with you, to make all things work for your eternal good. He promises you forgiveness and heaven through faith in Jesus.

Those are promises you can count on. How can I be sure? Just look in the stable. Look at the manger. There's the proof.

God always keeps his promises.

Today I am thankful for/that _____

_____

Merciful God and Lord, thank you for always doing what you say you will do. As we look ahead to Christmas, help us to see and trust that you will always keep your promises. Amen.

ADVENT – DAY 347
IT'S NOT QUITE CHRISTMAS YET!

"I will send my messenger ahead of you, who will prepare your way"—"a voice of one calling in the wilderness, 'Prepare the way for the Lord, make straight paths for him.'"

MARK 1:2,3

◆

"On the first day of Christmas, my true love gave to me a partridge in a pear tree."

Unless you live at the South Pole, you will probably hear that song at some point over the Christmas season. In fact, if you love Christmas music, this is probably your favorite time of the year. It's everywhere—on TV, on the radio, in the stores, at the doctor's office.

As soon as Thanksgiving is over, the Christmas season begins.

But technically it doesn't.

Do you know which day is the first day of Christmas? December 25.

That's right. Christmas Day is the first day of Christmas. The 12 days of Christmas go from Christmas Day until January 5th. Technically not even Christmas Eve is a part of the Christmas season.

Over the centuries, however, as people prepared for Christmas, they began celebrating it earlier and earlier. Christmas parties, Christmas caroling, even family Christmas dinners are often now celebrated days or weeks before Christmas.

In the Christian church, the weeks leading up to Christmas are traditionally not part of the Christmas season. The weeks before Christmas are called Advent. The word *advent* means "coming." Advent is about getting ready for Jesus' coming at Christmas.

Advent is a time of preparation marked by Advent wreaths with their purple and pink candles. Advent calendars help us count down the days to Christmas with daily Bible readings which point our eyes to the real reason for the season.

Please don't misunderstand me. I am no Ebenezer Scrooge. I love Christmas music and Christmas parties (even in December). We put up our Christmas tree as soon as Thanksgiving is over. You are in no way sinning by celebrating Christmas early.

But I think we are missing something when we as churches and individual Christians skip over Advent. The season of Advent is a time to quietly prepare our hearts and minds for the birth of our Savior. Advent is a time of repentance—a time to recognize that it is because of our stupid sins that God had to humble himself to be born in a barn in Bethlehem in order to die on a cross at Calvary.

Advent helps us to truly celebrate Christmas.

ADVENT HELPS US TO TRULY CELEBRATE CHRISTMAS.

When we skip Advent, we easily get lost in the lights and presents and Santa Claus. We get caught up in the stress and frenzy of deadlines. Or we fall into the trap of thinking Christmas is about a cute baby born in a cute manger surrounded by cute shepherds and cute angels.

Christmas isn't about cute. Christmas is about the cross. Christmas is about God loving sinners so much he came to this earth to suffer the horror we earned but will never see.

Advent helps us remember that. Advent helps us to prepare our hearts and minds. Advent is a wonderful time of the year.

Go ahead and play your Christmas music already in December. Put up your Christmas tree. Go to your Christmas parties. But don't skip over Advent.

This year, take the time to put up an Advent wreath in your home and light the candles. Get an Advent calendar and read the daily Bible reading with your children each evening. Take the time to prepare your hearts and minds.

Because it's not quite Christmas yet.

Today I am thankful for/that _____

_____

Dear Jesus, as I prepare to celebrate your birth, help me to prepare my heart and mind to receive you as my Lord and Savior. Amen.

ADVENT – DAY 348
JOY TO THE WORLD

He who testifies to these things says, "Yes, I am
coming soon." Amen. Come, Lord Jesus.

REVELATION 22:20

◆

I have a confession to make. This last Sunday, I did something pastors are
not supposed to do. I had our congregation sing "Joy to the World."

You see, even though we hear Christmas music being played everywhere
at this time of year, traditionally Christian churches don't sing Christmas
hymns before Christmas Eve. Don't get me wrong. The Bible doesn't forbid
the singing of Christmas songs before Christmas; it's just that we are still in
the season of Advent.

During the season of Advent, we prepare ourselves to celebrate Jesus' birth.
Advent is a time of repentance—a time to remember why Jesus came in the
first place. As we prepare our hearts to receive our King at Christmas, we
also prepare ourselves for his second coming at the end of the world.

Because such preparation is good for us, we try not to get ahead of ourselves.
We traditionally wait to sing Christmas hymns until Christmas Eve.

**THE IRONY IS THAT "JOY TO
THE WORLD" IS ACTUALLY
NOT A CHRISTMAS HYMN.**

"Joy to the World" is one of the most popular
Christmas hymns ever written. In fact, it is the
most-published Christmas hymn in North
America. The irony is that "Joy to the World" is
actually not a Christmas hymn.

It's not. Look at the words. It doesn't mention
Jesus' birth, Bethlehem, a manger, Mary, Joseph,
shepherds, or angels. "Joy to the World" was written nearly 300 years ago by
a man named Isaac Watts. In England at the time, the only music allowed in
the church was the psalms—the songs of the Old Testament. The psalms,
however, were always sung slowly and methodically.

Watts found the singing depressing. He thought the music should reflect
the beauty of the words. He thought the words of the hymns should
show how the psalms pointed ahead to Jesus.

So young Watts would often complain to his father, who was a deacon
in the church. His father finally told him one day, "If you think you can

668

do any better, go ahead." So he did. In fact, during one period of his life, Watts wrote a new hymn every Sunday for two years. Isaac Watts wrote hundreds of hymns in his life, including "Joy to the World," a hymn based on Psalm 98.

If you read Psalm 98, you will see that it doesn't talk about Christmas. It doesn't talk about the Messiah coming to live and die for our sins. It talks about the Messiah coming to judge. Underneath the title of "Joy to the World," Watts wrote the inscription: "The Messiah's Second Coming and Kingdom."

"Joy to the World" wasn't written about Jesus' first coming at Christmas. It's about his second coming on judgment day.

Joy to the world, the Lord is come!
Let earth receive her King;
Let ev'ry heart prepare him room
And heav'n and nature sing. (CW 62:1)

Jesus came and is coming again. Sadly, for many people that's not a reason to sing, "Joy to the World." Judgment day scares a lot of people. Have you ever noticed that Hollywood's portrayals of the end of the world are always horror movies? Yet we can sing, "Joy to the World" because we know he already came once. When Jesus was born in Bethlehem, he took his first steps to the cross of Calvary where he won forgiveness and heaven for all people.

All those who believe in Jesus don't have to be afraid of judgment day. Jesus is coming to take us to heaven. That's why he came 2,000 years ago. That's why he is coming again.

That's why we can sing "Joy to the World" even though it's not Christmas yet.

Today I am thankful for/that _____

_____

Lord, as we prepare to celebrate your coming at Christmas, keep my heart and mind ready for your second coming at the end of the world. Amen.

ADVENT – DAY 349
OH, COME, OH, COME, EMMANUEL

"The virgin will conceive and give birth to a son,
and they will call him Immanuel"
(which means "God with us").

MATTHEW 1:23

❖

John Mason Neale was born on January 24, 1818, in Bloomsbury, London. Neale's father was an Anglican minister. He received his name from a Puritan cleric, John Mason, one of the first hymn writers in the Anglican Church and also an ancestor of Neale's mother, Susanna.

Neale was a gifted student and writer who purportedly spoke 22 different languages. Despite his academic gifts, Neale was relegated to serving as warden of Sackville College, a home for indigent men. He spent nearly his entire ministry in that humble and low-paying position. In 1854, Neale founded the sisterhood of St. Margaret, a group of women dedicated to helping the poor, sick, and needy.

Although Neale was a humble, caring pastor, he suffered resistance to his ministry and was even attacked and mauled during the funeral procession of one of the sisters of St. Margaret.

Why was such a gifted, loving, and humble pastor so despised in his day? John Mason Neale was high church. That means he promoted the use of liturgical rites and symbols which had been a part of the Christian church for centuries.

At the time, many in the Anglican Church distrusted anyone who seemed too Roman Catholic. Some feared that Neale and others like him were agents of the Vatican trying to bring the Anglican Church back under the papacy.

John Mason Neale, however, was not a closet Roman Catholic. He simply treasured the wealth of words and symbols found throughout the history of the church. Neale was a scholar who enjoyed reading ancient Greek and Latin texts of the church.

One evening, as he read a book of old Latin hymns called *Psalteriolum Cantionum Catholicarum*, he discovered an Advent hymn based on a series of ancient Latin chants called the *O Antiphons*.

The *O Antiphons* dated back to the Middle Ages and were meant to be sung on the seven days before Christmas, as Christians prepared their hearts to celebrate Christ's birth.

Neale translated the hymn into English. You may have heard of it. It is arguably the most well-known Advent hymn sung by Christians today: "Oh, Come, Oh, Come, Emmanuel." The hymn is an invitation to the promised Savior to come and rescue his people from "Satan's tyranny" and the "depths of hell." The hymn is a call to Christians to rejoice because Emmanuel—literally, "God with us"—is coming.

Then again, you may not have heard of "Oh, Come, Oh, Come, Emmanuel." You may not even know what Advent is. Over the last few centuries, many churches, especially in the United States, have lost Advent.

Now, don't get me wrong. I love Christmas. Christmas carols, both Christian and secular, bring a smile to my face and joy to my heart. But it saddens me that in our rush to Christmas, Advent gets lost. In our rush to sing Christmas carols, we lose the joy of preparing our hearts and minds with hymns like "Oh, Come, Oh, Come Emmanuel."

I hope I don't get mauled on the way to a funeral, but like John Mason Neale, I think we need to be careful not to lose the treasure of hymns and symbols which have been passed down to us throughout the centuries. They express the beauty of the gospel and the depth of our doctrine. They tie us to Christians from every generation.

IN YOUR RUSH TO CHRISTMAS, DON'T FORGET ABOUT ADVENT.

So, in your rush to Christmas, don't forget about Advent. Don't forget to sing "Oh, Come, Oh, Come, Emmanuel."

Today I am thankful for/that _____

_____

"Oh, come, oh, come, Emmanuel, And ransom captive Israel That mourns in lonely exile here Until the Son of God appear. Rejoice! Rejoice! Emmanuel Shall come to you, O Israel!" Amen.
(CW 23:1)

ADVENT – DAY 350
THE BEST LAID PLANS

"I am the Lord's servant," Mary answered.
"May your word to me be fulfilled."

LUKE 1:38

Young people dream. They dream about whom they are going to marry one day. They painstakingly try to decide what they want to be when they grow up. Some map out their entire lives: where they will go to college, what they will study, whom they will marry—even how many children they will have.

Think back to when you were a teenager. Has your life turned out the way you planned it when you were 15 years old?

The Scottish poet Robert Burns once wrote: "The best laid plans of mice and men often go awry." In other words, things don't always work out the way we plan them.

Many years ago, a young Jewish girl had plans for her life. She was about 14 or 15 years old. She was in love. She dreamed of what her life would be like with her future husband. She wondered and maybe even planned how many children they would have together.

But then plans changed.

An angel appeared to her. He told her she was going to have a baby. But wait. That's good news, right?

Not in Mary's day. She was going to be a single teenage mother. Even today that is difficult. In Mary's day, however, if a young woman became pregnant out of wedlock, her family would shun her. Society would ostracize her. She could have been stoned to death.

Imagine how you would react if your teenage daughter came to you and said: "Mom, Dad, I'm pregnant. But don't worry—I didn't have sex with my boyfriend; an angel appeared to me and told me I was going to have a baby."

Nobody would believe her. What was Joseph supposed to think? The only logical explanation was that she had cheated on him.

The news that she was going to have a baby meant that Mary could lose everything. All the plans she had made for her life had gone awry.

So how did Mary react? Did she respond like a typical teenager, screaming "That's not fair!" and slamming her bedroom door?

No. She said to the angel, "I am the Lord's servant. May your word to me be fulfilled." Basically she was saying, "Lord, take my body and life and do with me as you see fit. I trust you."

Mary trusted God's plans, and so can you.

MARY TRUSTED GOD'S PLANS, AND SO CAN YOU.

God had plans for Mary. The baby in her belly was no ordinary baby. He was God himself. He was her Savior from sin.

God's plans for Mary wouldn't be easy. She wouldn't always understand her son or why God sent him. She would have to watch him be brutally crucified before her very eyes. Yet God's plans were for her good. By his death, her son would wash away all her sin and win for her a home in heaven.

God's plans are always good. Trust that truth, even when things don't work out how you planned them—even when you don't understand why God is doing what he is doing. His plans end up with you in heaven. The best laid plans of mice and men often go awry, but God's plans never do.

Today I am thankful for/that _____

_____

God, help me to trust your plans for my life,
especially when your plans are
not my plans. Amen.

CHRISTMAS – DAY 351
THE SOUND OF BEING RESCUED

"You are to give him the name Jesus, because
he will save his people from their sins."

MATTHEW 1:21

❖

In September of 2013, Adrian Knopp, a hunter from Grand Ledge, Michigan, was stranded in the Alaskan wilderness with no food, shelter, or warm clothes.

It was the third day of his trip with friend, Garrett Hagen. They had just bagged a 700-pound grizzly bear. The two men and the bear didn't fit in the seven-foot skiff they had taken down the river, so Adrian stayed behind while Garrett took the bear and the boat. He was only supposed to be gone an hour or two, but he never returned. Garrett drowned. Adrian was alone.

After seven days trapped on a grassy knoll between the river and an impenetrable mountain, Adrian found himself becoming sleep-deprived, hallucinating, and slipping into hypothermia. Despairing of any hope to be rescued, he said a prayer, carved a message in the butt of his rifle and closed his eyes, waiting to die.

Then he heard the sound—the sound of helicopter blades beating against the wind. "It was probably the most wonderful sound I have ever heard," he said. Fifteen minutes later, he was rescued.

When we hear stories like that of Adrian Knopp, we can only imagine the exhilaration he felt when he realized he was being rescued. We can only imagine the relief of hearing those helicopter blades.

GOD DIDN'T COME IN A HELICOPTER OR A FIRE TRUCK OR A COAST GUARD VESSEL.

We are all born helplessly and hopelessly stranded in a wilderness of sin. If you doubt that, just look at the bad and hurtful things you have done and keep doing in your life. No matter how hard we try, we keep messing up. On our own we are lost and condemned to an eternity in the fiery inferno of hell.

But that is what the Christmas season is all about. At Christmas we celebrate the fact that God came to rescue us. God didn't come in a helicopter or a fire truck or a Coast Guard vessel. He came in the form of a tiny baby. He came to take our place. He came to live and die as our substitute. God was born as a human being to suffer our punishment in our place.

That same little mouth which cried out in hunger from the manger cried out in pain from the cross. Those tiny feet and hands would one day be nailed to wood for you. Jesus was born in Bethlehem to die on Calvary. Because he came to die for you, you have been rescued from hell and given a home in heaven.

Listen. Do you hear the small cry of that newborn baby lying in a manger? That is the sound of helicopter blades beating against the wind. That is the sound of being rescued. That is the most wonderful sound we could ever hear.

Today I am thankful for/that _____

_____

Dear Jesus, thank you for coming to rescue me from the horrors of hell I deserve. Amen.

CHRISTMAS – DAY 352
A PICTURE-PERFECT CHRISTMAS

She gave birth to her firstborn, a son. She wrapped him in cloths and placed him in a manger, because there was no guest room available for them.

LUKE 2:7

Did you have a picture-perfect Christmas this year? You know, the kind of Christmas you could put on a Hallmark card. The tree was big and beautiful. The stockings were hung by the chimney with care. The whole family was together—laughing, smiling, and playing games. The ham or turkey was cooked to perfection. The table was impeccable. The kids quietly played with their new toys.

The truth is we rarely have picture-perfect Christmases. Maybe not everyone made it home this year. The baby was sick. The kids were glued to their electronics. You didn't get all your decorations up. You had to work on Christmas Eve. This was your first Christmas without Grandma.

Yet we still yearn for picture-perfect Christmases. We desperately want the Hallmark card. We want the peaceful, beautiful Christmas we imagine the first Christmas to be.

You know, Mary and Joseph smiling peacefully. Jesus quietly sleeping in the manger. Shepherds gently kneeling nearby. Cows lowing in the background as angels quietly sing, "Sleep in heavenly peace."

We yearn for that peace. We long for that picture-perfect Christmas. But that isn't what we get. That isn't real. That isn't even the reality of the first Christmas.

The reality of that first Christmas is a young woman, probably in her teens, a long way from home and very pregnant. She had been travelling for days, probably riding on a donkey.

Then they arrive and the tiny little village of Bethlehem is bursting at the seams. It isn't quiet. It's packed. There is no room, so they end up in a back room or stable where the animals are kept.

Having a baby is hard enough, but imagine having a baby in a barn. This isn't peaceful. There are screams and sweat and blood. The baby comes out as all babies do—wet and sloppy. They have no blankets; this is a stable after all. They wrap him in strips of cloth and lay him in a feeding trough in the prickly, uncomfortable hay.

That's not what we usually see on Hallmark cards, but that's the reality of Jesus' birth: loud, crowded, and uncomfortable.

God doesn't promise us picture-perfect Christmases or picture-perfect lives here on earth. What he promises us is a picture-perfect heaven. That's why God humbled himself to be born in a barn. That's why he came to this earth, to pay for all the ugliness that flows from our hearts, minds, and mouths.

The true joy and peace of Christmas is not having a living Hallmark card in your living room. The true joy and peace of Christmas is knowing that because of that baby born in Bethlehem, God forgives us our less than picture-perfect lives.

THE TRUE JOY AND PEACE OF CHRISTMAS IS KNOWING . . . GOD FORGIVES US.

The true joy and peace of Christmas is knowing that no matter how ugly our lives get or how badly our hearts ache, we have a home waiting for us in a picture-perfect heaven.

Today I am thankful for/that _____

_____

Lord, as I look at my imperfect life, help me remember who that baby born in Bethlehem is and what he came to do. Thank you for the picture-perfect place he won for me in heaven. Amen.

CHRISTMAS – DAY 353
CHRISTMAS ISN'T ABOUT FAMILY

When the set time had fully come, God sent his Son, born of a woman, born under the law, to redeem those under the law.

GALATIANS 4:4,5

◆

I once read an urban legend about a department store in Kyoto, Japan. According to the legend the store placed a rather unique display in its main window for Christmas many years ago.

In the middle of the Christmas presents and decorations was a life-sized Santa Claus hanging from a cross.

The display wasn't meant to offend anyone. It wasn't intended to be modern art or a commentary on society. It was just a bit of cultural confusion.

Christmas at the time was just becoming popular in Japan. Apparently those responsible for the window had a vague idea that Christmas had something to do with Santa Claus and someone who died on a cross. Fact got mixed with fiction. The secular and the sacred were confused and the whole meaning of Christmas was lost.

Sadly, what happened in that store window in Japan often happens in our country and lives today. Our Christmas celebrations in the United States have become somewhat confused. In our front yards, we have Santa Claus and Frosty the Snowman standing next to the manger. The secular gets mixed with the sacred. Fact and fiction get shuffled together. The meaning of Christmas gets lost.

For many people in our world today, the meaning of Christmas has been lost entirely. Even many Christians and churches today give mixed messages. They talk about how Christmas is about family. For many, the joy of Christmas is that we get to spend time with our loved ones. The peace of Christmas is when families put aside their differences and get along for at least one day.

But Christmas isn't about family.

I know that sounds harsh, but when Christmas is about family, what happens when you can't be with your family on Christmas? What happens when you are alone on Christmas?

A temporary truce in your family—people pretending to get along for one day—is not real peace. In fact, more often than not, family gatherings at Christmas are filled with stress and tension.

There is a reason more people commit suicide at Christmas than any other time of year.

Christmas isn't about family. The spirit of Christmas isn't patching things up with your estranged uncle. Christmas isn't about learning to be more tolerant or accepting. Christmas isn't even about learning to be generous or giving.

CHRISTMAS IS ABOUT . . .

Christmas is about the Christ. Christmas is about God who became a man to live the life you haven't and to die the death you deserve. Christmas is about God giving up everything to save you. It is about his love, his sacrifice, and the forgiveness and heaven he gives.

The peace of Christmas is peace with God. The joy of Christmas is the joy of knowing that all the cruel and foolish things you have said and done are forgiven forever because Jesus was born in Bethlehem to die at Calvary. The joy of Christmas is knowing that you have a home waiting for you in the peace and perfection of heaven.

When we start making Christmas about family—when the message of Christmas is about tolerance or world peace—it's like hanging Santa Claus on a cross. The real meaning gets lost.

Christmas isn't about family. Christmas is about the Christ.

Today I am thankful for/that _____

_____

Merciful God, forgive me for the many times I lose sight of what Christmas is all about. Free me from the frenzy of the season and help me to appreciate your great love that led you to become one of us to save us. Amen.

CHRISTMAS – DAY 354
YOU CAN'T HAVE CHRISTMAS WITHOUT DEATH

He too shared in their humanity so that by his death he might . . . free those who all their lives were held in slavery by their fear of death.

HEBREWS 2:14,15

Every year our church puts on a children's Christmas program on Christmas Eve. The kids dress up as shepherds and sheep, angels and wise men, Mary and Joseph. The little ones are adorable and often funny as they recite their lines and sing their songs.

A few years ago I got into a little trouble with the children's Christmas program. It wasn't cute.

The first act featured a family on their way to Christmas dinner with Grandpa and Grandma. The two teenage daughters whined and complained the entire way because all their friends were going to a Christmas party that night, but they couldn't go.

The second act took place in Grandpa and Grandma's living room. Grandpa was sitting on his rocking chair and Grandma on hers. All the little children sat on the floor as the two teenage granddaughters slouched on the couch, texting on their phones defiantly.

As she did every year, Grandma asked the children questions about the very first Christmas, allowing them to tell the story of Jesus' birth. The two teenage granddaughters never looked up from their phones.

The third act took place a year later, once again in Grandpa and Grandma's living room. The little children again sat on the floor, the two teenage granddaughters on the couch. Grandpa sat on his rocking chair, but Grandma's rocking chair was conspicuously empty. The mood was somber. The teenage granddaughters sobbed with guilt.

A few people weren't too happy about that children's Christmas program. It wasn't cute. It wasn't funny. I mean, who wants to talk about death on Christmas Eve?

Yet you can't have Christmas without death. Every year people die at Christmas. My grandmother died on December 23. Even when they don't die right at Christmas, their absence is still sharply felt this time of year. Many homes this Christmas will feature an empty rocking chair in the living room.

Death is a part of life in this world. It invades our Christmas celebrations. All of us at some point, will feel death's sting during the holidays. But that's not why I say you can't have Christmas without death.

You can't have Christmas without death because Jesus was born to die. He was born in a barn in Bethlehem to die on a cross at Calvary.

You already know Christmas isn't about Santa Claus or Rudolph the Red-Nosed Reindeer. What some Christians fail to grasp is that Christmas also isn't about a cute baby lying in a cute manger. Christmas is about God becoming one of us and taking his first steps to the cross.

Jesus was born to die. He was born to die for your sins. He was born to die so that you could live with him forever in heaven. You can't have Christmas without death.

Yet Christmas isn't about death. It's about the life in heaven Jesus came to win for you.

When we truly grasp that, it changes how we look at the empty rocking chair in the living room. I miss my grandma, but she is in heaven. I will see her again. Because Jesus was born to die, I am forgiven for every one of my thoughtless words and selfish actions. Because Jesus was born to die, I will live even though I die.

That is the true joy and peace of Christmas. Christmas isn't about a cute baby lying in a cute manger. Christmas definitely isn't about cute children's Christmas programs. Christmas is about God's sacrificial love and the never-ending life Jesus came to win for you.

But that means you can't have Christmas without death.

Today I am thankful for/that _____

_____

Dear Jesus, during this Christmas season, I miss my loved ones who have died. Give me the true peace of Christmas, knowing that you yourself were born in this world to die so that they and I might live. Amen.

CHRISTMAS – DAY 355
DON'T MAKE SANTA SLAP YOU

The Word became flesh and made his dwelling among us.

JOHN 1:14

Santa Claus isn't what he used to be. Our modern manifestation of Jolly Ol' St. Nick with his big belly, white beard, and red coat is largely based on the writings of Washington Irving and L. Frank Baum, as well as the illustrations of Thomas Nast and the Coca-Cola ads painted by Haddon Sundblom.

Our modern Santa bears little resemblance to the real St. Nicholas. Nicholas was a bishop in the early Christian church who lived just over two centuries after Jesus. He was known for his generosity and penchant for gift giving.

He was also a defender of the faith. He was imprisoned during the empire-wide persecution of Christians under the Roman Emperor Diocletian. When Emperor Constantine later legalized Christianity, Nicholas was one of the bishops invited by Constantine to the Council of Nicea to discuss problems within the church.

A preacher named Arius was teaching that Jesus wasn't really God. According to Arius, Jesus wasn't eternal like God the Father and wasn't equal to him in power and majesty. His teaching, known as Arianism, had spread throughout the empire causing confusion and division in the Christian church.

At the Council of Nicea, the bishops of the church discussed Arius' teaching God is really triune, that is, three persons in one God. In the end, the teaching of Arianism was found to not agree with the Bible.

The overwhelming majority of bishops, including Nicholas, later subscribed to a confession of faith which many Christians still recite in their worship today—the Nicene Creed. The Nicene Creed confesses what the Bible says about Jesus, namely that he is the eternal, all-powerful God through whom all things were created.

According to a pious legend, at one point Nicholas became so frustrated with Arius at the Council of Nicea that he walked up and slapped him in the face.

Not exactly the Jolly Ol' St. Nick we've come to know and love.

Every year at Christmas, Christians lament the fact that Christ has been removed from Christmas. Santa Claus, Rudolph, and shopping have taken over.

The truth is you can keep Christ in Christmas and still miss the whole point. When Christmas is simply about a cute baby in an idyllic stable, surrounded by smiling shepherds and pretty angels, the true meaning of Christmas is lost.

CHRISTMAS IS ABOUT WHO THAT BABY IS.

Christmas isn't simply about a baby in a manger. Christmas is about who that baby is. Jesus is God—the all-powerful God who created everything that exists, the God who fills the universe and rules over all things.

The meaning and miracle of Christmas is the incarnation—that God became a man. God became one of us to take our place, to die our death, so that we could live with him forever in heaven.

As you celebrate Christmas this week, as you sit and stare at that cute little baby in the manger, never forget who he is. That's what makes Christmas special.

Today I am thankful for/that _____

_____

Dear Jesus, as I celebrate your birth this Christmas, help me not to get distracted by Santa Claus and all the trappings of the season. Keep my eyes focused on you, the only True God who was born as a man to live and die for me. Amen.

CHRISTMAS – DAY 356
KEEP THE CROSS IN CHRISTMAS

She gave birth to her firstborn, a son. She wrapped him in cloths and placed him in a manger, because there was no guest room available for them.

LUKE 2:7

We've all heard the complaints. We've seen the posts on social media. We've read the forwarded emails. Christians throughout our country are concerned about the *secularization* of Christmas. For many, Christmas is no longer the celebration of the birth of our Savior God, but rather the celebration of Santa Claus and Rudolph the Red-Nosed Reindeer. We join our voices with theirs in saying, "Don't take the Christ out of Christmas!"

But there is another danger at Christmastime, a much more subtle temptation for Christians. I call it the *cute-ization* of Christmas. For many Christians today, Christmas is about cute children's Christmas programs, sweet sounding Christmas carols, and quaint nativity scenes. It is about pretty angels and adorable sheep. But is that really what Christmas is all about—a cute baby asleep in a quiet stable?

You can keep Christ in Christmas and still completely miss the point. So let's take a moment to look past Santa Claus and the presents and even the cute nativity scenes in store windows to face the reality of Christmas.

The reality of Christmas is a teenage girl, a long way from her home and family. See her sweat and tears. We can only imagine that she was scared. This was her first baby and he was being born in a dirty barn. Smell the manure. Hear the screams. Remember, there were no IVs or epidurals in those days.

Then the baby was born. If you've ever witnessed a baby being born, you know that they don't come out cute. They come out slimy. Then comes the blood and the afterbirth.

I'm sorry if that sounds gross, but that's the reality of Christmas. Then, after the baby was born, he wasn't laid in a cradle or a crib, wrapped in soft, fluffy blankets. He was laid in a feeding trough, wrapped in rags.

ON THAT DAY, GOD BECAME A HELPLESS BABY.

Christmas isn't about a cute baby being born. It is about Christ's utter humiliation. The King of the universe left behind the power and glory and comfort of heaven to become one of us. On that day 2,000 years ago, God cried for the first time. On that day, God felt pain and hunger and sorrow for the first time. On that day, God became a helpless baby.

That was just the beginning of a lifetime full of humiliations. He allowed himself to be mocked and ridiculed. He allowed himself to be beaten and spit upon. He allowed himself to suffer the most humiliating death known to humankind. A life which began in utter humiliation in Bethlehem ended in utter humiliation on Calvary.

But why? Why did he allow himself to suffer such humiliation? Because he loved you so much. He did it to pay for all of your messed-up priorities; to pay for your angry words and ugly thoughts; to pay for all your dark and dirty sins. That baby was born to suffer your hell in your place to win for you heaven.

That's what Christmas is all about. Christmas is about the cross. We worry and fret so much about people taking Christ out of Christmas that we haven't even noticed that the cross has been removed.

There's an old cowboy poem written by Gail T. Burton called "How Far is it to Bethlehem?" It's the story of two cowboys on the open range at Christmastime debating about how far away Bethlehem was. At the end of the poem, one cowboy comes to a realization. He turns to his partner and says, "How far is it to Bethlehem? It's just halfway to the cross."

That's what Christmas is all about: our God beginning his journey to the cross to save us. My friends, during this Christmas season, don't take the cross out of Christmas.

Today I am thankful for/that _____

_____

Dear Jesus, as we celebrate your birth, help us to understand and appreciate your great love which led you to be born in the most humble of circumstances to die in my place. Amen.

CHRISTMAS – DAY 357
JESUS' FIRST STEPS

The Word became flesh and made his dwelling among us.

JOHN 1:14

As I look back on raising my children, there are certain things I would no longer rush. With our first child, we wanted her to crawl and walk and talk as soon as possible.

What I soon realized is that once your children start moving and talking, they don't stop. At times I am nostalgic for the good ol' days when my children were babies.

That being said, there is nothing quite as exciting as watching your children take their first wobbly steps. I remember the squeals and the tears as our children stumbled toward us with their arms out yearning for an approving embrace.

The Bible doesn't share with us the details of those emotional moments from Jesus' childhood. It doesn't reveal to us Jesus' first words or describe in detail his first wobbly steps.

In a sense, though, it does. Jesus' birth at Bethlehem was really his first step.

Over the centuries, the focus of Christmas, even for Christians, has shifted. Originally, the focal point of Christmas was the *incarnation*—the miracle of God taking on human flesh. God became a man. Then Christmas became about a cute baby in a cute manger. Then the focus morphed into gifts and shopping and Santa Claus and family.

Let's refocus. Christmas is truly about God becoming a man so he could live and die as our substitute.

You and I deserve to die. We do. We deserve God's anger and punishment for our thoughtless words and needless worry. We deserve his punishment for our disheveled priorities and all those "little" sins we foolishly consider no big deal.

God, however, loved you and me so much that he became one of us. He left behind the comfort and glory of heaven to experience all the frailty and pain of our humanity. He became one of us to suffer our punishment and die in our place.

CHRISTMAS IS REALLY JESUS' FIRST STEPS TO THE CROSS.

Christmas is really Jesus' first steps to the cross.

It's hard to imagine that a helpless baby, born in the backwater town of Bethlehem and laid in an animal's feeding trough, is God. For Mary and Joseph it must have been hard. As he said, "Mommy" for the first time or tumbled toward her taking his first wobbly steps, Mary must have wondered, "How can he be God?"

Christmas is a time to marvel at the mystery of the incarnation. The eternal God who fills all of time and space became a tiny ball of cells in Mary's belly and was born in the most unpretentious of circumstances.

Christmas is a time to excitedly watch as our Savior takes his first wobbly steps toward the cross. Jesus loved you so much that he gave up everything. He loved you so much that he suffered the humiliation of becoming a helpless baby. He loved you so much that he wouldn't let anything keep him from going to the cross to suffer the horrors of hell so you will never have to.

This week, take some time away from your family dinners and the chaos of Christmas to quietly do what Mary did—ponder all these things in your heart. The most important part of Christmas isn't spending time with your family. Christmas isn't about presents or Santa or even cute nativity scenes.

Christmas is Jesus' first steps to the cross.

Today I am thankful for/that _____

_____

Lord, as I marvel at the mystery of the incarnation, I can't help but see your amazing love that led you to become a lowly human like me to save me. Thank you. Amen.

CHRISTMAS – DAY 358
MY FAVORITE CHRISTMAS MOVIE

"Glory to God in the highest heaven, and on earth peace to those on whom his favor rests."

LUKE 2:14

One of my favorite things about this time of year is Christmas movies. I personally favor the comedies. Every year on Christmas Eve, I watch *Elf* with my children. *Scrooged* and *Christmas Vacation* often get squeezed in as well.

I relish the classics, too. *Miracle on 34th Street* always makes me smile. I could honestly watch *It's a Wonderful Life* a thousand times.

In fact, I believe I have.

Oh, and who can forget about *Die Hard*? Contrary to what some Scrooges and Grinches will tell you, *Die Hard* is a Christmas movie.

The movie I consider the most important and poignant Christmas movie of all time was not a blockbuster in theaters. In fact, it almost didn't air. It was completed only ten days before its release date, and all those involved in the project, including its producers, considered it an unmitigated disaster.

Despite their misgivings, *A Charlie Brown Christmas* aired on CBS on December 9, 1965. It immediately became a classic. Critics raved. People loved it.

A Charlie Brown Christmas was different than any other Christmas movie or special created up to that point. The cast was composed completely of children. No laugh tracks were added. The soundtrack was entirely comprised of jazz music.

Most shockingly, the climax of the movie finds Charlie Brown shouting in exasperation, "Isn't there anyone who knows what Christmas is all about?" to which Linus responds by reciting Luke 2 from the King James Version of the Bible.

Of the myriad of Christmas movies available to us on Netflix and the Hallmark Channel, *A Charlie Brown Christmas* is the only one I have ever seen which actually tells the real story of Christmas.

Just about every other Christmas movie contains some moral to the story. Christmas is about generosity. Christmas is about the holiday spirit. Christmas is about family. Christmas is about good will toward your fellow man.

Though all those morals are good in and of themselves, none are the true meaning of Christmas. Christmas isn't about our good will toward our fellow man. Christmas is about God's good will toward men.

Christmas is about God loving us so much he became one of us. Christmas is about the utter humiliation God submitted himself to—being born in a lowly manger, only to later die on an old rugged cross.

Christmas is about God taking your place, living the perfect life you haven't and suffering the punishment of every bad thing you do so you could be forgiven and live with him in heaven.

Christmas is about God's good will toward men. Remarkably, that is also what *A Charlie Brown Christmas* is all about.

So go ahead and watch *Elf* and *It's a Wonderful Life* and *Die Hard*. Watch all the Hallmark Channel movies. But if you want to know what Christmas is really all about, the one you need to watch is *A Charlie Brown Christmas*.

DO WHAT LINUS DID. OPEN UP YOUR BIBLE.

Or even better, if you really want to know what Christmas is all about, do what Linus did. Open up your Bible.

There you will find Jesus, the true meaning of Christmas.

Today I am thankful for/that _____

_____

Almighty God, give me the peace that only you can give—the peace of knowing your good will toward me. Amen.

CHRISTMAS – DAY 359
SILENT NIGHT

She gave birth to her firstborn, a son. She wrapped him in cloths and placed him in a manger, because there was no guest room available for them.

LUKE 2:7

On a cold Christmas Eve in the year 1818, a young priest named Joseph Mohr quickly walked from his home in the small town of Oberndorf, Austria, to the neighboring village of Amsdorf. He was carrying a piece of paper—a poem he had written two years earlier.

He made his way to the schoolhouse, walked up the stairs, and knocked on the door of the second floor apartment. He was greeted by his friend, Franz Gruber, the schoolmaster in Amsdorf and also the church organist.

Father Mohr asked his friend to help him put his poem to music. He wanted a new Christmas hymn for the mass that evening. There was a catch, though. He wanted it played on guitar, not the organ.

Over the years, many have speculated why. Some say the organ was broken. Others say it was because of Father Mohr's love for the guitar. Whatever the reason, Gruber quickly wrote a melody and guitar chords for the new Christmas carol.

That evening at midnight Mass, Father Mohr and Franz Gruber, quietly backed by the choir and accompanied by a single guitar, sang the new hymn for the first time. It was called *"Stille Nacht."* You may know it as "Silent Night."

"Silent Night" has since been translated into over 140 languages and sung in every corner of the world. In 2011, the United Nations declared it an intangible cultural heritage. It is arguably the most famous Christmas carol of all time.

Its popularity contrasts sharply with its humble beginnings. "Silent Night" scholar Bill Eagan once wrote: "Perhaps this is part of the miracle of 'Silent Night.' The words flowed from the imagination of a modest curate. The music was composed by a musician who was not known outside his village. There was no celebrity to sing at its world premiere. Yet its powerful message of heavenly peace has crossed all borders and language barriers, conquering the hearts of people everywhere."

The quiet words, the soft melody, and the lonely guitar reflect the reality of the first Christmas. It was truly a silent night. In the streets of the tiny village of Bethlehem, you might have been able to hear Mary's muffled moans as she gave birth to Jesus. You might have heard the delicate cries of the newborn baby coming out of the stable. Few, however, would have noticed.

JESUS' BIRTH WAS NOT REPORTED ON CNN.

Jesus' birth was not reported on CNN. There were no TV cameras or paparazzi at the stable. Social media was not alerted. Jesus' birth didn't go viral until years later. It was a night like any other.

On that night the almighty God was born as a helpless baby, and nobody noticed except a handful of shepherds who were tending their flocks in the fields outside of Bethlehem.

Yet from those humble beginnings came our salvation. That baby was born to die. He came to take your place and suffer your punishment for the countless hurtful things you think, say, and do. He came to win for you a home in heaven. Through that baby, God won and offers eternal life to all people from every nation, tribe, and language.

As you sing "Silent Night" on Christmas Eve, remember its quiet beginnings. Listen to its beautiful words. Appreciate the love of your God who was humbly born to die for you.

Today I am thankful for/that _____

_____

Dear Jesus, thank you for the joy of beautiful hymns like "Silent Night." As I sing it, help me to remember your amazing love and humility that led you to sacrifice so much for me. Amen.

CHRISTMAS – DAY 360
DON'T LET THE DEVIL DISTRACT YOU

When the set time had fully come, God sent his Son, born of a woman, born under law, to redeem those under law, that we might receive adoption to sonship.

GALATIANS 4:4,5

It used to be Santa Claus. I personally have nothing against Jolly Ol' St. Nick, but, because I am a pastor, he was my proverbial target. He was the symbol of how our world had lost the true meaning of Christmas. Christmas for most people had become about Santa Claus, Rudolph, and stockings hung by the chimney with care.

Then my target was busyness. People got so busy around the holidays with Christmas parties, shopping, decorating, and school events that they didn't take the time to quietly contemplate what Christmas was all about.

In recent years, my struggle has been with the cuteness of Christmas—a much more subtle distraction. People still went to church and talked about Baby Jesus, but the focus of their Christmas celebrations was on a cute baby born in a cozy, inviting stable while adorable animals, shepherds, and angels looked on reverently. Though they kept Christ in Christmas, the true meaning was still lost.

In the end, my problem wasn't really with Santa Claus or Christmas parties or even cute nativity scenes. The problem was that the devil is always trying to keep us from seeing and talking about what Christmas is really all about.

Though all the distractions mentioned above are still tugging at our hearts today, the always-innovative devil has now come up with a new one: Christmas is about family.

For most of our world today, that is the point of Christmas. Just watch the Hallmark Channel. The joy of Christmas is being surrounded by the ones you love. The most important thing about Christmas is being with your family.

But Christmas isn't about family.

Christmas is about Christ. If the joy of Christmas is being surrounded by the ones you love, then that joy of Christmas is easily lost. No wonder so many people get depressed around the holidays. They miss those who have died: their grandparents or parents, their husband or wife. How can they be happy at Christmas without them? How can we be happy if we can't go home for Christmas?

We can be happy, because the joy of Christmas isn't being with your family. The joy of Christmas is the promise of heaven. The joy of Christmas is knowing we have the family reunion of heaven waiting for us because that baby born in Bethlehem lived and died for us.

I've noticed an alarming trend over the last few years. Church attendance during the month of December and especially on Christmas Eve and Christmas Day has dropped dramatically. The reason is that people are so busy getting ready for company to come over that they don't have time. Family get-togethers on Christmas Eve and Christmas Day now take precedence over church.

INVITE THEM ALL—EVERY SINGLE ONE OF THEM.

My encouragement and prayer for you is to not let the devil distract you with any of his clever diversions. This year don't schedule church around your family gatherings. Schedule your family gatherings around church. Even better, bring your entire family to church with you on Christmas Eve and Christmas Day. Invite them all—every single one of them.

Help them to see, to remember, and to celebrate what Christmas is really all about.

Today I am thankful for/that _____

_____

Dear Lord, thank you for this time of year when I can gather with family and friends. Please help me, however, to never forget what Christmas is all about. Thank you for giving up everything that was good in order to suffer all that was bad for me. Amen.

CHRISTMAS – DAY 361
STRIPS OF CLOTH

She brought forth her firstborn son, and wrapped him in swaddling clothes, and laid him in a manger.

LUKE 2:7 KJV

Swaddling clothes. As a boy those words confused me. What did it mean that Jesus was wrapped in swaddling clothes? After the birth of my daughter, I learned that to swaddle means to wrap your baby tightly in a blanket. Babies love that snug feeling.

Jesus, however, was not wrapped in an ultra-soft blanket or clothed in a cute onesie. Swaddling clothes weren't really clothes at all. Swaddling clothes were strips of cloth. Swaddling clothes were rags.

693

Jesus was wrapped in rags and laid in an animal's feeding trough.

The point of Christmas isn't that a cute baby was born in an idyllic stable, surrounded by cows softly lowing and visited by cute shepherds as angels quietly hummed in the background.

Christmas is about the all-powerful Lord and King of the universe leaving behind his glorious throne in heaven to be wrapped in rags and laid in an animal's feeding trough.

Why did God do that? Why did he come to earth? To understand that, we need to remember some other strips of cloth.

When Jesus was crucified, he was stripped of his clothes. He hung naked from the cross, covered in a simple loin cloth. His clothes were divided among the soldiers as a part of their pay.

When Joseph of Arimathea removed Jesus' body from the cross, he took Jesus to his new tomb and wrapped his body in strips of linen cloth as was the custom of the day. Jesus was wrapped in strips of cloth at his birth and his death.

Just two days later, when the disciples found the stone rolled away from the tomb, they looked in and what did they see? The strips of cloth were neatly folded where Jesus' body had been. Jesus is now clothed in glory.

STRIPS OF CLOTH TIE CHRISTMAS, GOOD FRIDAY, AND EASTER TOGETHER.

Strips of cloth tie Christmas, Good Friday, and Easter together.

Often we try to celebrate Christmas separately. When we do that, Christmas simply becomes the joy of a birth, a sweet baby, and cute children's programs.

Christmas has no meaning without Good Friday and Easter. Jesus was born in order to die. He died in order to rise. When we remember that, we find the true joy of Christmas.

Recently, a young teacher from our local grade school was suddenly killed in a car accident. I had the painful privilege of sitting with her third grade class as they were told. Their hearts broke. I can only imagine the hurt her husband, her parents, and her family felt, hurt that never fully healed.

If Christmas is just about a cute baby being born, then there can be no joy for that young teacher's family this year. Their baby girl died. How could they ever celebrate Christmas again?

But Christmas means more than that. Christmas means that God loved us so much he came to this earth to suffer the punishment we deserve for our inability to stop saying and doing the wrong things.

Jesus died your death, but he isn't dead. Those strips of cloth are folded neatly where his body lay. Jesus is alive and is clothed in glory.

And so is that young teacher who died. She believed in Jesus. She is in heaven. Her family, her friends, and her students will see her again because Jesus was born in Bethlehem to die on Calvary and rise from the grave for them as well. That is the true joy and peace of Christmas.

This year, don't celebrate Christmas without the cross. Don't celebrate Christmas without also celebrating Good Friday and Easter.

They are all tied together with strips of cloth.

Today I am thankful for/that _____

_____

Dear Jesus, as we celebrate your birth this year, help us to tie it together with Good Friday and Easter so we never forget why you came. Amen.

CHRISTMAS – DAY 362
THE TRUE PEACE OF CHRISTMAS

Glory to God in the highest and on earth peace, good will toward men.

LUKE 2:14 KJV

◆

It all began on Christmas Eve 1914 on the dreaded Western Front of World War I. According to the reports, one part of the German line managed to slip a chocolate cake to their British counterparts who were knee-deep in mud in the water-soaked trenches.

The cake included a note. The Germans asked for a cease-fire so they could celebrate Christmas and the birthday of one of their captains. The British agreed and sent back tobacco as a return present.

After the appointed hour, heads began to pop up from the German line, singing Christmas hymns, followed by applause from their British counterparts. The Germans then asked the British to join in. One British soldier shouted, "We'd rather die than sing in German!" To which a German soldier replied, "It would kill us if you did."

By Christmas morning, soldiers began to bravely venture out into no man's land, greeting each other with a smile and exchanging gifts. Impromptu games of soccer broke out. Grown men in combat boots, covered in mud, ran around giddily kicking a soccer ball. By 8:30 that night, however, the soldiers were back in their trenches. Two shots were fired in the air and the war resumed.

For many, if not most, people in our world today, that's what Christmas is all about. That is the Christmas spirit: "Peace on earth; good will to men." Christmas is a time to put away our differences, at least for a day.

That sounds good, doesn't it? The Christmas Truce of 1914 is a sweet and wonderful Christmas story. But in the end, it was just a blip in a brutal war that killed well over nine million people. The same soldiers who played soccer and exchanged gifts on Christmas Day 1914 ended up shooting at each other the very next day.

To have peace and harmony on Christmas Day, yet seek to kill each other the day before and the day after borders on insanity. To pretend to get along with your family on Christmas because it's Christmas after all, and then hate each other the rest of the year is sheer lunacy. To be nice to people on Christmas in order to make up for a year of selfishness is just plain insincere.

But that's the Christmas spirit, isn't it? Peace on earth. Good will to men.

Yes and no. The angels spoke those words to the shepherds on the night Jesus was born: "Glory to God in the highest and on earth peace, good will toward men."

Peace on earth; good will toward men. The thing is the angels weren't talking about peace *between* men. They weren't talking about a truce in a war or the healing of a broken family. They weren't talking about showing good will to the less fortunate and downtrodden. Those are all good things and God does want us to live in peace and show good will to everyone, but that's not what the angels were talking about.

THEY WERE TALKING ABOUT OUR RELATIONSHIP WITH GOD.

They weren't talking about our relationship with other people. They were talking about our relationship with God.

The peace the angels were proclaiming is peace with God—not a temporary truce on Christmas Day, but a lasting peace.

The Baby Jesus whom we celebrate at Christmas was born to die on your behalf in the war against sin. He was born to make you at peace with God.

That's why the angels sang, "Glory to God in the highest!" That's why we sing those words every Christmas. We have peace with God here on earth and forever in heaven. Our sins are forgiven. God has and will always show good will to us.

That's the good news of great joy which is for all people. Even when wars rage all around us, even when our families can't get along at Christmas, we have a true and lasting peace. That's what Christmas is all about: peace on earth; good will to men.

Today I am thankful for/that _____

_____

Dear Jesus, thank you for giving me the peace the world cannot give. Amen.

CHRISTMAS – DAY 363
WHAT IF GOD WAS ONE OF US?

**"The virgin will conceive and give birth to a son, and they will call him Immanuel"
(which means "God with us").**

MATTHEW 1:23

When I was in college, the singer Joan Osborne shot to the top of the charts with her hit single, "One of Us."

"What if God was one of us," Osborne sang, "just a slob like one of us, just a stranger on a bus, trying to make his way home?"

Can you imagine? What if God was the guy next to you on the bus?

The first Christmas was no exception. We all know about Bethlehem and the manger. We know about the shepherds and angels. We know about the visit of the wise men. But often we stop there and fail to finish the story. When the wise men didn't report back to him, King Herod became furious. Obsessed with protecting his throne, he ordered the murder of all the baby boys two years old and younger in Bethlehem and its vicinity.

When I was a boy, I would often imagine legions of Roman soldiers going from home to home, slaughtering hundreds of children. The truth, however, is that Bethlehem at the time was just a little village. Experts estimate that there would have probably been no more than a couple dozen little boys under the age of two living in Bethlehem at the time.

But still, imagine the horror of the parents. Imagine the mothers screaming in terror as the soldiers drove swords into their baby boys. Imagine the fathers futilely trying to protect their sons—parents weeping for their children and refusing to be comforted because they were no more.

The joy of the first Christmas was tainted by tragedy.

How often does that happen even today? Think of all the victims of violence from recent years: the shootings in South Carolina and Oregon and California, the bombings in Paris, the massacres in Syria. What must Christmas have been like for their families?

How do we respond when tragedy taints Christmas? What do we tell those who are hurting?

We remind them of what Christmas is all about.

Christmas isn't about family. The primary purpose of Christmas isn't to spend time with people we love. Christmas is about God controlling all of history to bring his Son, our Savior, into the world.

Remember, Herod tried to kill him, but failed. God thwarted Herod's plans to kill Baby Jesus, but later allowed Pontius Pilate to crucify him. Why? Because that was his plan from the very beginning—his plan to save you and me—his plan to get us to heaven.

GOD HAS PLANS FOR YOU, AND THOSE PLANS END UP WITH YOU IN HEAVEN.

God has plans for you, and those plans end up with you in heaven. He often uses the tragedies and sorrows of this sinful world to bring about his good and loving plans for us.

Now that I think about it, maybe the slaughter of the baby boys in Bethlehem is the most fitting way to end the Christmas story—because so often that is the reality of living in this sinful world. Our celebrations of Christmas, our lives, aren't picture-perfect. They are tainted by tragedy and sorrow.

But because of that baby born in Bethlehem, we know that God has plans for us, good plans, plans which end up with us in heaven. That's why we can celebrate, that's why we can smile, that's why we can have peace, even when Christmas is covered in sadness.

Today I am thankful for/that _____

_____

Heavenly Father, comfort all those who are sad or hurting at this time of year. Give them the true joy of Christmas—the joy of knowing their Savior Jesus and the heaven he came to win for them. Amen.

DAY 365

Well, you've made it. A year has passed since you began this journey of devotion and thanksgiving. I hope and pray that this book and journey have helped you see God's goodness and grace in your life.

On day 365, I encourage you to read through your journal entries for each day of the year. See what God did for you this last year. See his hand working in your life. See his grace.

Now doesn't it make you wonder how many more days you could have continued listing God's blessings without repeating? When would you run out of things for which to be thankful?

Try it. Start another year of thanksgiving. Live another year of devotion to God.

May your life be filled with overwhelming thanks and devotion to the Giver of all good things!

SCRIPTURE INDEX